AN INTRODUCTION TO
Crime Scene
Investigation

SECOND EDITION

Aric W. Dutelle, MFS

Associate Professor
Forensic Investigation Program Coordinator
Department of Criminal Justice
University of Wisconsin-Platteville

JONES & BARTLETT
LEARNING

World Headquarters
Jones & Bartlett Learning
5 Wall Street
Burlington, MA 01803
978-443-5000
info@jblearning.com
www.jblearning.com

Jones & Bartlett Learning books and products are available through most bookstores and online booksellers. To contact Jones & Bartlett Learning directly, call 800-832-0034, fax 978-443-8000, or visit our website, www.jblearning.com.

Substantial discounts on bulk quantities of Jones & Bartlett Learning publications are available to corporations, professional associations, and other qualified organizations. For details and specific discount information, contact the special sales department at Jones & Bartlett Learning via the above contact information or send an email to specialsales@jblearning.com.

Production Credits

Publisher: Cathleen Sether
Acquisitions Editor: Sean Connelly
Editorial Assistant: Caitlin Murphy
Editorial Assistant: Audrey Schwinn
Production Manager: Tracey McCrea
Marketing Manager: Lindsay White
Manufacturing and Inventory Control Supervisor: Amy Bacus

Composition: diacriTech
Cover Design: Scott Moden
Rights & Photo Research Assistant: Ashley Dos Santos
Cover Image: © Andy Piatt/ShutterStock, Inc.
Printing and Binding: Courier Companies
Cover Printing: Courier Companies

To order this product, use ISBN: 978-1-284-04817-9

Library of Congress Cataloging-in-Publication Data
Dutelle, Aric W.
  An introduction to crime scene investigation / Aric W. Dutelle. — 2nd ed.
    p. cm.
  Includes bibliographical references and index.
  ISBN 978-1-4496-4542-7 (pbk.)
1. Crime scenes. 2. Crime scene searches. 3. Criminal investigation. 4. Evidence, Criminal. I. Title.
  HV8073.D875 2014
  363.25—dc23
                        2012034919
6048

Printed in the United States of America
17 16 15 14 13   10 9 8 7 6 5 4 3 2

Dedication

This book is dedicated to my parents, Gary and Sherry Dutelle. It is with your guidance, and because of your love and support, that I have found my path.

Brief Contents

Contents

SECTION I   Crime Scene Investigation   3

Chapter 1

An Introduction to Crime Scene Investigation   5

Chapter 2

The CSI Effect   33

Chapter 3

Ethics in Crime Scene Investigation   53

Chapter 4

Duties of the First Responder to the Crime Scene   69

Chapter 5

Specialized Personnel and Safety Considerations   89

Chapter 6

Methodical Approach to Processing the Crime Scene 111

Chapter 7

The Forensic Laboratory 145

Chapter 10

Blood and Biological Evidence   233

Chapter 14

Drug Evidence   353

Chapter 15

Digital Evidence   401

Section III Specialized Investigations 425

Chapter 16

Death Investigation 427

Chapter 17

Arson and Explosive Investigation 459

Chapter 18

Special Scene Considerations 477

Appendix A

Crime Scene Investigation Historical Timeline   502

Appendix B

Forensic Databases   508

Appendix C

Crime Scene Equipment   514

Appendix D

Examples of Evidence Collection Kits   516

Appendix E

Processing the Scene of Mass Fatality Incidents   518

Appendix F

Professional Organizations Pertaining to Crime Scene Investigation   524

Glossary   526

Index   546

Preface

It is not the critic who counts, not the man who points out how the strong man stumbled, or where the doer of deeds could have done better. The credit belongs to the man who is actually in the arena, whose face is marred by the dust and sweat and blood, who strives valiantly, who errs and comes short again and again, who knows the great enthusiasms, the great devotions and spends himself in a worthy course, who at the best, knows in the end the triumph of high achievement, and who, at worst, if he fails, at least fails while daring greatly, so that his place shall never be with those cold and timid souls who know neither victory or defeat.

—Theodore Roosevelt
(Paris Sorbonne, 1910)

In assembling this second edition, I have attempted to keep, and update as necessary, what was reported as being of use and benefit within the confines of training and education. Of equal importance, I have also attempted to incorporate changes and to make additions in areas that were constructively criticized within the first edition.

In presenting their 13 recommendations, assembled within "Strengthening Forensic Science in the United States: A Path Forward," the National Academy of Sciences (NAS) recognized that forensic science and investigation must work hand in hand. They cannot be completely separate fields with no overlap. They must function as a cohesive unit. Investigators, crime scene personnel, and those tasked with analyzing the evidence documented, collected, and preserved from the scene of the crime, must all understand their roles and be properly trained and educated in order to properly execute and perform them. There must be standardized terminology, agreed upon best practices, and acceptance of a lack of certainty. There is no "us" and "them" anymore. If the system is to work it must function together, not separately.

Just as a person who studies the topic of criminal justice does not go out into the world and become employed as a criminal-justicer, simply because someone reads a text on, or studies the topic of criminal justice, crime scene investigation does not in any manner imply that he or she will become employed as a crime scene investigator. This text is not meant to be a policy and procedure manual for a specific career field or job. It is intended to be an overview of the investigatory process as it relates to the crime scene and the evidence collected therein. However, it is impossible to discuss crime scene–related evidence without also discussing the forensic potential of evidence. In order to determine the forensic potential of evidence, one must be educated on what information can be gleaned from performing analyses of the evidence. This necessitates discussion of basic forensic science applications and analytical techniques, pertaining to each area of physical evidence.

Pertaining to science, this text is not intended to be a forensic science/criminalistics text. There are several amazing texts on the market pertaining to the in-depth natural science foundation associated with the analysis of physical evidence. This text is intended to educate the reader about the methodologies employed at a crime scene associated with documentation, collection, and preservation of physical evidence, while also educating the reader on the forensic value of evidence. How else can personnel know what to collect as evidence if they are not aware of the potential forensic value? However, it is not a realistic possibility to include both in-depth science and processing methodologies within one text, or else it would be well over 800 pages in length. Therefore, this is intended to be a foundational text on the topic of crime scene investigation including the collection of physical evidence. Those carrying on within the field of study will eventually study areas presented within this text in greater depth. For instance, criminal investigation and criminalistics are courses of study in and of themselves.

Therefore, while not presented with enough science for some, and too much science for others, this edition was assembled to address the lack of a foundational, non-assuming text, which contains the information and pedagogical components necessary to reach the individuals who will be responsible for the transformation of the forensic field the NAS report brought to the world's attention.

It was my experience as a new patrol officer that a large chasm existed about the topic of how to properly process a crime scene. The police academy provided a thorough education on search and seizure law, arrest control techniques, firearms, use of force, and driving tactics. However, the block of time devoted to the processing and documentation of crime scenes was typically less than 1 day, 8 hours, in duration.

As the reader of this text will find, and as I discovered during my time in law enforcement, it is not simply crime scene technicians or crime scene investigators who must be educated about the methodologies and theories relating to crime scene investigation. It is also necessary for police officers, police administration, medical personnel, forensic scientists, and a great many others to understand such matters.

It is my hope that the reader will find this text appropriate as a reference and educational resource for the topic of crime scene investigation, assuming no prior knowledge of the topic, and assembled to be both easy to follow and easy to instruct from. As you will note upon reading through the text, I have attempted to assemble a cadre of very knowledgeable and extremely experienced individuals to contribute to and assist with ensuring that this text is both timely and accurate. I will leave it to the reader to determine if I have hit my mark.

Introduction

Several notable introductory texts on crime scene investigation exist; unfortunately, the majority are written for those who are involved in some capacity in the field, and thus contain a great deal of assumed knowledge. There are over 400 academic programs within the United States (in undergraduate, graduate, and secondary education) that have a need for a text presenting a foundation of crime scene investigation. This need inspired me to cease use of texts that assumed too much for the level of my students, and to instead write one that is more appropriate. This text is written with the assumption that the reader is new to the field of crime scene investigation and crime scene processing.

An Introduction to Crime Scene Investigation is written to be a foundational reference for the investigative process as it relates to crime scene processing methods and procedures. The reader will find that the focus is on the day-to-day aspects of crime scene processing. The text describes the methodologies employed by crime scene personnel, details the steps in the process, and explains how to decide on the order of the methods. My hope is that this text will help to eliminate the warped impressions of crime scene personnel's duties created by modern forensic television and movie dramas, and will help the reader to identify the various interrelated components of the investigative process. Such public misconceptions are addressed in Chapter 2, which deals with the so-called *CSI effect*.

This text also provides the reader with a historical perspective on crime scene investigation. By understanding how we got to where we are today, the reader will have a better appreciation of, and an understanding for, the complexities and difficulties relating to the topic. If one is to be educated and to understand what crime scene investigation is, it is necessary to cover more than the simple "how-to's" relating to such matters. Therefore, in addition to the methods, motives, and motions needed to secure the crime scene, the text also covers an overview of the investigative process as well as the ethical considerations applying to such matters. Also, because it is imperative that personnel understand the forensic potential associated with physical evidence in order to know what to document, collect, and preserve, fundamental forensic science discussions associated with physical evidence examination and analysis are also covered. Discussions about crime scene procedures, detailed figures, and real-life examples enhance the reader's understanding and demonstrate precisely how to apply the techniques and tools of the trade.

An Introduction to Crime Scene Investigation provides those in training and those attending community colleges, universities, and police academies with a true introductory text that is written for those with no assumed knowledge in the area and for those who are either not in or are new to the field. My hope is that this text will be considered an essential source of foundational development, proper protocols, and best practices used in a successful crime scene investigation.

This text was assembled using a pragmatic, critical, and multidisciplinary approach. This text recognizes that many of the concepts and methods relating to the field of crime scene investigation are likely to be unfamiliar. For this reason, special instructional devices and learning strategies are utilized throughout, including:

- **Learning Objectives.** The learning objectives are listed at the beginning of each chapter. Emphasis is placed on active learning rather than passive learning. The hope is that the reader gains knowledge of how to apply the concepts and material, and not simply retains the information temporarily with plans to regurgitate it on a test. The learning objectives concentrate on the acquisition of knowledge and foundations needed to understand, compare, contrast, define, explain, predict, estimate, evaluate, plan, and apply.

- **Key Terms.** If one is to study the field of crime scene investigation, it is necessary to become familiar with the terminology and vocabulary associated with it. Key terms are listed at the beginning of each chapter to alert readers to specific terms they should understand.

- **Review Questions.** Knowledge and skills must be reinforced. Review questions are provided for student self-study options and for use by instructors who are developing written assignments and examinations.

- **"Ripped from the Headlines" Current Event Examples.** In an effort to apply the theory and guidelines addressed within the text, examples of real-world incidents involving the content are discussed in the chapters. This application to real-world situations will enable the reader to better grasp the concepts presented.

- **"Case-in-Point" Examples.** In addition to current events, there are case scenarios and summations to assist the reader in further comprehension of the presented material.

- **"View from an Expert" Insights.** As a way to further the real-world information that the reader is exposed to within the text, chapters also include insights from a forensic expert in the field of study discussed in each chapter.

- **Case Studies.** At the conclusion of many of the chapters are case studies that challenge the reader to seek out additional information from outside sources to assist them with a more in-depth comprehension of the presented material.

- **References.** Each chapter is supplemented with references pertaining to the key areas addressed within the chapter.

A comprehensive student companion Website, hosting downloadable Word Searches, Flashcards, a Glossary, Crosswords, and Case Study Weblinks, is available online at go.jblearning.com/CrimeSceneInvestigation2. PowerPoint Lecture Outlines and a Test Bank have also been created for instructor use.

Acknowledgments

There are a number of people who I would like to thank for their selfless assistance with this text, without whose assistance this work would fall incredibly short of hitting the mark.

I wish to thank:

Those who contributed their knowledge and expertise to the various chapter inserts entitled "View from an Expert:" Carmine Artone, Ronald Becker, Thomas Blackwell, Diana Johnson, Dale Kapla, Brent Kohls, Mike Krapfl, Timothy Kupferschmid, Gary Lind, Herbert McDonell, Marie-Helen Maras, Brendan Nytes, Sarah Owen, Randy Taylor, and Sandy Weiss. Your insight and experiences added greatly to the depth of the chapters and will allow the reader to gain additional views into the subject matter.

The numerous students and alumni of the University of Wisconsin-Platteville who contributed to the text: Sarah Bedish, Ellie Bruchez, Dana Gevelinger, Erica Lawler, Angela Lonski, Joseph LeFevre, Gabbie Mears, Elizabeth A. Sedgwick, and Nicholas Vesper. Your contributions help the content of this text to leap off of the pages and give the readers visual insight into the world of crime scene investigation. You each have exciting careers ahead of you.

Stacie Byers, without whom I would likely have made more than a few embarrassing errors throughout this text. I greatly appreciated you fitting time into your hectic schedule to review and provide feedback on the entire text. Your experience and professionalism where editing and proofreading are concerned and your ability to look at the content from an "outsider's" standpoint were invaluable to me. I am fortunate to call you a friend.

I also wish to thank Caitlin Murphy, Sean Connelly, Cathleen Sether, Tracey McCrea, Ashley Dos Santos, Danielle Schaeffer, Audrey Schwinn, and the entire editorial, production, and marketing staff at Jones & Bartlett Learning. Thank you for giving me the opportunity, assisting me with the production, and helping to create what I hope will be a work that will fill a void in professional education.

Lastly, I wish to thank my family and friends for their love and support. My passion for writing often takes me away from those that I love and that love me. I appreciate your understanding and support with yet another endeavor.

Reviewers

Thank you to the following reviewers for their valuable input in the revision of this text:

M. George Eichenberg, Tarleton State University

Andra Lewis-Krick, University of North Texas

Jerry Loar, Walters State Community College, Retired Special Agent of the FBI

James F. Nardozzi, Post University

David F. Nicholson, Missouri Western State University

Terry L. Pippin, College of Southern Nevada

Robert Skowron, Virginia Commonwealth University, and Captain, Chesterfield County Police Department

Sally Welch, Marygrove College

About the Author

Aric Dutelle has been involved in law enforcement for over a decade. During this time, he has held positions as a police officer, deputy sheriff, crime scene technician, and reserve medico-legal investigator. He has a Master of Forensic Sciences (MFS) degree, and is a POST-certified law enforcement officer. Since 2004, he has taught crime scene-related courses at the University of Wisconsin–Platteville. He is currently an Associate Professor and the Forensic Investigation Program Coordinator within the Department of Criminal Justice.

In addition to his university obligations, since 2006, the author has been a forensic instructor for the U.S. Department of Justice's International Criminal Investigation Training Assistance Program (ICITAP), specializing in and providing training in crime scene processing methodologies and techniques around the globe. He continues to be actively involved in training, consulting, and assisting law enforcement agencies with criminal investigations and crime scene processing around the United States and internationally.

Crime Scene Investigation

LEARNING OBJECTIVES

- Understand the definition of crime scene investigation (CSI).
- Understand the objectives of CSI.
- Gain knowledge of the historical figures who have contributed to CSI.
- Understand the types of evidence associated with a criminal investigation.
- Understand the value of physical evidence.
- Define the scientific crime scene method.
- Know how to establish a proper chain of custody.

An Introduction to Crime Scene Investigation

At present I am, as you know, fairly busy, but I propose to devote my declining years to the composition of a textbook which shall focus the whole art of detection into one volume.

Sir Arthur Conan Doyle (1859–1930)
Sherlock Holmes, in *The Adventure of the Abbey Grange*

KEY TERMS

Chain of Custody
Circumstantial Evidence
Crime
Crime Scene
Crime Scene Investigation (CSI)
Criminalistics

Direct Evidence
Evidence
First Responder
Fruit of the Poisonous Tree Doctrine
Investigate
Iterative Process

Locard's Exchange Principle
Real or Physical Evidence
Scientific Method
Scientific Investigation Method
Testimonial Evidence
Trier of Fact

What Is Crime Scene Investigation?

The word **investigate** means to make a systematic examination or to conduct an official inquiry. In law enforcement terms, this is used with reference to the investigation of a crime. **Crime** is defined as an act or the commission of an act that is forbidden by a public law and that makes the offender liable to punishment by that law. **Evidence** is anything that can help to prove or disprove that a crime was or was not committed, and by whom. The varieties of evidence are endless and are discussed later in this chapter.

Crime scene investigation (CSI) is the often used term relating to the process associated with the investigation of a criminal event. More specifically, it is the systematic process of documenting, collecting, preserving, and interpreting physical evidence associated with an alleged crime scene, in an effort to determine the truth relating to the event in question. Note that this does not define the purpose of a criminal investigation and thus the process of CSI as the determination of guilt or innocence. Rather, it is to document the truth. In the United States, the determination of guilt or innocence is left up to the **trier of fact**, who would be a judge or magistrate in a trial by the court, or a jury of one's peers in a trial by jury. The study of crime scene investigation therefore concentrates on guidelines, concepts, and principles associated with aiding the trier of fact to determine the truth. To accomplish this task involves techniques associated with locating, documenting, collecting, and preserving physical evidence.

CSI is not necessarily the analysis of the physical evidence and does not pertain to the entire investigative process. CSI often is confused with **criminalistics**, the analysis of physical evidence. More specifically, CSI is the application of science within the enforcement of law. Criminalists (also called forensic scientists) use instrumentation and education within the natural sciences associated with the interpretive value of the physical evidence submitted. However, it is important to note at this point that CSI is associated with the on-scene techniques applied in an investigation, and typically does not involve analyzing the physical evidence. The foundation of CSI is in documentation.

Who Is Responsible for Crime Scene Investigation?

There are many components of a criminal investigation. All support one another and none can stand alone or is more important than any other. The first tier of the investigative process begins with the **first responder**. This is typically the police officer who is dispatched to the initial scene. Through the course of his or her response to and documentation of the event, if the officer believes that a crime was committed, then that officer must analyze the necessity to have that crime and associated crime scene further processed. Sometimes the crime and associated crime scene are of a minor nature and can be handled by the first responder. Other times they will necessitate the response of specialized personnel.

Most police departments use uniformed or patrol officers as well as detectives or crime scene investigators to process a crime scene. On smaller scenes, sometimes the initial officer on scene will be responsible for photographing, fingerprinting, and documenting the crime scene. On larger scenes, a detective or investigator may be called in to assist. Some agencies have specialists who can be called upon to process a scene. These specialists may be either uniformed or civilian personnel.

There are five basic personnel components of a criminal investigation: the first responder, detective/investigator, crime scene investigator/technician, criminalist/forensic scientist, and the courts.

First Responder

Typically, the first responder is the patrol officer who responds to the initial complaint. His or her duty is to secure the scene and not to touch anything. The officer begins the initial stages of documentation through the securing and preservation of the physical evidence.

Detective/Investigator

This is a specialized police officer who has significant experience in investigations. He or she is concerned with the entire criminal investigative process. This officer could be compared with a central processing unit (CPU) for a computer, where each part of a computer's peripheral devices has a specific function, but all of them rely on the CPU to interpret the information fed into it in order to output a product that is understood and applicable to the task at hand. The detective will process the information presented by the first responder and others, and decide whether or not additional investigative methods are warranted, if search/arrest warrants need be issued, and whether or not arrests can be made. This individual rarely collects physical evidence but rather is primarily responsible for the collection of testimonial evidence.

Crime Scene Investigator/Crime Scene Technician

This individual (who could be a civilian or a sworn police officer) has advanced training in the documentation, collection, and preservation of physical evidence. Additional skills might include technical or college training and education in photography, mapping, crime scene processing, search and seizure law, and criminal justice practices. While this person is responsible for processing the crime scene, he or she is rarely involved with the subsequent analysis of the collected evidence, and is not involved with interviewing or interrogating suspects or witnesses. The primary area of concern is the crime scene and associated physical evidence. This may include conducting examinations for fingerprints or performing presumptive tests for the presence of blood at crime scenes. After documenting, collecting, and properly preserving the evidence, the crime scene investigator/technician transports the evidence to the evidence booking location, where it is booked in (recorded) and held until such time that it is needed for analysis or checked out to be transported to court.

Criminalist/Forensic Scientist

This individual is responsible for the analysis of submitted items of evidence. A criminalist uses the latest in scientific instrumentation and knowledge to assist with interpreting the value of the evidence submitted. Typically he or she will have a four-year degree in chemistry, biology, or another applied science. It is not the duty of the criminalist to determine guilt or innocence, or to otherwise investigate the crime. His or her only obligation is the proper interpretation of the submitted evidence, and providing a report on such matters to the detective for final determination on the investigative value of the evidence.

The Courts

This step includes the prosecution, defense, judge/magistrate, and jury (if applicable). It is left up to this step to determine whether the previous components of the investigative process have resulted in evidence showing that a crime was committed or not and, if so, then it shows by whom as well as defines the warranted punishment. At this step, it is pointed out whether there has been a breakdown or fault within the investigative process that would warrant retraining, education, or implementation of policies or laws to reduce future problems.

Objectives of Crime Scene Investigation

Although different personnel may be involved in processing a crime scene, their objectives remain the same:

- Determine whether a crime has been committed. If it is determined that there is no crime involved, or if the issue is one for the civil courts, law enforcement personnel have no responsibility. If uncertain, contact the district attorney's office.
- If a crime has been committed, determine whether it was committed within the investigator's jurisdiction.
- Discovery and documentation of all facts pertaining to the complaint in question.
- Identify and eliminate suspects as a result of collected physical and testimonial evidence.
- Locate and apprehend the perpetrator. Sometimes this means issuing an arrest warrant if the suspect is unable to be located.
- Throughout the entire process, maintain a proper chain of custody to ensure that collected evidence is admissible in court.
- Effectively testify as a witness to the collected evidence within court.

While the aforementioned are objectives of CSI, at all phases of the process, the obligation of the individuals involved is to the truth. All personnel involved in processing and investigatory efforts must be conscious of not simply collecting evidence to prove what they believe happened. Also, investigators should approach the crime scene investigation as if it will be their only opportunity to preserve and recover these physical clues.

History of Crime Scene Investigation

When considering the history of CSI, it is important to define its parameters. As mentioned earlier, CSI is not truly the forensic laboratory analysis portion of the investigation, but pertains to the processing methodology related directly to the scene of a crime. As such, the history of CSI spans thousands of years. Suffice it to say that since mankind first walked upon the earth, there have been cases of foul play. The following investigators are but a few of the individuals who have furthered the process that has come to be known as CSI.

Song Ci (1186–1249)

The Chinese death investigator Song Ci wrote a book entitled *Xi Yuan Ji Lu* (translated as *Collected Cases of Injustice Rectified*, in 1247) in which he discussed a number of murders. One such case took place in a village in which the victim had been slashed repeatedly. The local magistrate suspected that a sickle had been used, but repeated questioning of witnesses proved fruitless. Finally, the magistrate ordered all of the local men to assemble, each with his own sickle. It was a hot summer day and flies, attracted by the smell of blood, eventually gathered on a single sickle. Confronted with such evidence, the sickle's owner confessed to the murder. The book also offered advice on how to distinguish between a drowning (water in the lungs) and strangulation (broken neck cartilage), along with other evidence from examining corpses to determining if a death was caused by murder, suicide, or an accident (Gernet, 1962).

Sir Robert Peel (1788–1850)

In 1829, Peel established and subsequently headed the Metropolitan Police Force for London, based at Scotland Yard. The 1,000-member force became known as "Bobbies." They proved to be very successful in reducing the crime rate. Peel also was responsible for defining ethical requirements of policing officers through what became known as "Peelian Principles." His most memorable principle is summarized by the concept that the police are themselves the public, and the public are themselves the police. This is the earliest recorded reference to the idea of community-oriented policing efforts (Becker, 2009).

Auguste Ambroise Tardieu (1818–1879)

The preeminent forensic medical scientist of the mid-19th century, Tardieu participated in 5,238 cases as a forensic expert during his 23-year career. He wrote over a dozen volumes of forensic analyses, covering such topics as abortion, drowning, hanging, insanity, poisoning, and suffocation (Labbé, 2005). Tardieu wrote what may be the first book on the sexual abuse of children, entitled *Medical-Legal Studies of Sexual Assault*, which was published in six editions from 1857 to 1878. To this day, battered child syndrome is also known as "Tardieu's Syndrome."

Allan Pinkerton (1819–1884)

In 1849, Allen Pinkerton was appointed as Chicago's first detective by Mayor Levi D. Boone. This is the first known functional separation of investigations from patrol. Pinkerton is also known for creating the Pinkerton Detective Agency, which provided private service to railroad properties and other business enterprises.

Sir Arthur Conan Doyle (1859–1930)

While it might seem odd to list an author as a contributor toward advancing the work of crime scene investigation, few would argue the impact that Doyle had on popularizing the work associated with such matters. Doyle's fictional character, Sherlock Holmes, brought science to the process of investigation. In Doyle's first Sherlock Holmes novel, *A Study in Scarlet* (1887), Holmes used forensic investigation methods that were undiscovered at the time, but later would revolutionize crime scene work. One of these areas was the concept of *serology*, the study of blood and other bodily fluids. This foresight led many readers to become intrigued by the possibilities of the field of criminology, and undoubtedly was an impetus for many future scientists to explore its realm.

Hans Gross (1847–1915)

In 1893, Gross was responsible for authoring the first dissertation concerning the practical application of scientific disciplines to the field of criminal investigation. Gross spent much of his life as a public servant, serving as both a public prosecutor and judge in Graz, Austria. As such, he spent a great deal of time studying and developing principles relating to criminal investigation. His compilation of information became a classic book, entitled *Handbuch für Untersuchungsrichter als System der Kriminalistik* (*Handbook for Examining Magistrates as a System of Criminology*), which was later published in English under the title *Criminal Investigation* in 1906. This is the first known text to propose that investigators could expect investigatory assistance from such scientific fields as microscopy, chemistry, zoology, botany, physics, fingerprinting, and anthropometry (Saferstein, 2004). Gross was a very strong advocate for the application of the scientific method within investigations, although he did not make any specific technical contributions regarding such work.

Edmond Locard (1877–1966)

Locard was instrumental in demonstrating how the principles articulated by Gross could be applied within the crime laboratory. His educational background was in medicine and law, and both were used extensively within his work. Locard is credited with starting the world's first crime laboratory, when in 1910 he persuaded the police department in Lyon, France to give him space to begin work on such matters. His work in criminalistics led him to develop what has come to be known as **Locard's Exchange Principle**. The essence of this theory is that whenever two objects come in contact with one another, there is a cross-transfer of evidence that occurs (Saferstein, 2004). Locard was specifically referring to dust particulates and trace materials, an area in which he performed significant research. According to the premise behind Locard's Principle, every crime scene could be connected to a criminal, witness, and victim, and every criminal, witness, and victim could be connected to a crime scene. In addition to this concept, the theory has come to be the foundation behind many of the guidelines and steps taken at a crime scene to limit contamination.

Paul Leland Kirk (1902–1970)

A chemist and forensic scientist, Kirk is most known for his work on blood spatter evidence. He applied this expertise on bloodstain pattern analysis to the Sam Sheppard homicide case (on which the 1960s television program and 1993 Hollywood movie, "The Fugitive," were based). As a result of Kirk's contributions to the fields of forensic science and investigations, the highest honor that one can receive in the criminalistics section of the American Academy of Forensic Sciences carries his name.

Training and Education/Professional Development

Those interested in crime scene investigation will need to do more than simply hunker down and log endless hours of watching primetime television. There are various levels of education that one can accumulate in the field of CSI. Some regional technical/vocational schools offer certificate programs and/or two-year degrees relating to crime scene investigations. An increasing number of four-year colleges and universities are beginning to offer more comprehensive education than simply the criminal justice system to include in-depth studies relating to the specific sections and functions of crime scene investigation. Typical program offerings include: Introduction to Forensic Science, Introduction to Crime Scene Investigation, Evidence Collection and Preservation, Crime Scene Processing Techniques, Criminalistics, Investigative Photography, Fingerprint Classification and Development, and Criminal Investigation.

Most departments today prefer—if not require—some type of college degree. It is advisable to contact the departments or agencies where one resides or will be residing to find out their particular requirements and duties. Regardless of whether one's major education is in general studies, criminal justice, or forensics, augmenting those studies with supplemental courses in basic computer training, drafting, and photography will increase one's value to future employers. Any curriculum designed for crime scene investigation in criminal justice classes at most colleges will cover more general studies and not involve specifics.

After being selected for employment, most departments will have a probationary period where the employee will go through a training period and be assigned to a field training officer. Most of the experience about how to do the job will be gained in this phase of employment. Most departments also offer their employees opportunities for post-employment or in-service training to further their employees' skills and development. Most of the continuing

ICITAP: The Global World of Crime Scene Investigation

According to the United States Department of Justice (n.d.) the International Criminal Investigative Training Assistance Program (ICITAP) "works with foreign governments to develop professional and transparent law enforcement institutions that protect human rights, combat corruption, and reduce the threat of transnational crime and terrorism." ICITAP is located within the Department of Justice's Criminal Division, and receives its primary funding from the State Department.

ICITAP was established in 1986 with the first mission being the training of Latin American police officers. Over the last two decades this mission has evolved into the ICITAP becoming a full-service criminal justice development agency that plays a vital role in international stability and rule of law, both of which are paramount to U.S. security in the post-9/11 world in which we live.

In 2008, ICITAP was involved in carrying out 1,117 training programs involving nearly 83,000 foreign participants.

ICITAP's Forensic Services program assists in development of crime laboratories that support criminal justice institutions, while also providing technical assistance and training related to:

- DNA/Serology
- Engineering sciences
- Expert witness development
- Odontology

educational classes for the crime scene investigator are specifically geared to crime scene response, evidence collection, forensic photography, fingerprint technology, and homicide and death scene investigation.

Visiting the morgue or a local trauma center is another way to gain experience. This is a custom-tailored job not suited for everyone. What a person can do to a fellow human is not always a pretty sight. If someone is not able to stomach a busy weekend night in the local trauma center or morgue, then he or she surely will be unable to stomach some of the mutilation and/or uncommon sights that are part of the job.

To be successful in the field of crime scene investigation, an individual must dedicate him or herself to a career of continuing education and professional development. There are a number of professional accreditations that crime scene investigators can pursue in order to meet basic and advanced standards within their field. Competent crime scene investigators will acquire continuing education and training through regular attendance at conferences and training seminars, as well as by seeking advanced education within their areas of interest and specialty.

- Pathology and biology
- Physical anthropology
- Psychiatry and behavioral science
- Questioned documents
- Toxicology
- Forensic nursing
- Crime scene processing
- Forensic photography and digital imaging
- Computer evidence
- Forensic accounting

ICITAP recently has supported forensic developments in the following countries:

- Bulgaria
- Columbia
- Indonesia
- Iraq
- Kosovo
- Mozambique
- Senegal
- Tajikistan
- Tanzania
- Thailand
- Turkmenistan
- Uganda
- Ukraine
- Usbekistan

Information from: U.S. Department of Justice, International Criminal Investigative Training Assistance Program (ICITAP). Retrieved January 26, 2012 from http://www.usdoj.gov/criminal/icitap/programs/forensics/.

The International Association for Identification (IAI) offers numerous programs and levels of certifications within those programs to encourage professionals to continue their training and education, while also ensuring common training and standards of investigative strategies. The standards for certification are high, and thus achievement of certification serves to underscore the competence of the individual to perform their job-related duties, which assists in reducing or eliminating scrutiny of their qualifications by the court. According to the organization website (http://www.theiai.org) the IAI offers professionals within the field of crime scene investigation certifications in the following areas:

- Bloodstain Pattern Examiner Certification
- Crime Scene Certification
  - Certified Crime Scene Analyst
  - Certified Crime Scene Investigator
  - Certified Crime Scene Reconstructionist
  - Certified Senior Crime Scene Analyst

- Footwear Certification
- Forensic Art Certification
- Forensic Photography Certification
- Forensic Video Certification
- Latent Print Certification
- Tenprint Fingerprint Certification

What Is a Crime Scene?

A working definition of a **crime scene** (both primary and secondary) is anywhere evidence may be located that will help explain the events (Ragle, 2002). The crime scene is thought of as the location at which the crime was committed. However, a single crime may have numerous associated locations. Crime scene personnel should consider the first scene where evidence is located as the primary scene, even if it is not the most significant, and any subsequent locations as secondary scenes (Ragle, 2002).

Every crime scene is unique and each is dynamic. Although a standardized set of procedures must be followed at every location by the crime scene investigator, experience and observation will assist in developing a strategic operational plan for processing the area.

Types of Evidence

To learn about the proper manner in which to document, collect, and preserve evidence, it is wise to recognize the two types of evidence associated with criminal investigations: testimonial evidence and real or physical evidence.

Testimonial Evidence

Testimonial evidence consists of vocal statements that most commonly are made by a person who is under oath, typically in response to questioning. However, this type of evidence also can be obtained from witnesses, victims, or suspects during the course of the investigation, while not under oath.

Eyewitness identification is a type of testimonial evidence and one which has been increasingly scrutinized and one which many courts have been reticent to place great value in. While eyewitnesses play a key role in criminal investigative processes, eyewitness evidence is far from perfect. In fact, eyewitness misidentification was the leading cause of wrongful conviction in more than 75 percent of the first 183 DNA exonerations in the United States (Schuster, 2007). There are a number of reasons for misidentifications, some of which include memory loss, stress, incorrectly assembled police lineups, and improperly prepared potential witnesses. As a result, many states have begun to enact eyewitness identification reform legislation to reduce the potential for this form of testimonial evidence to improperly convict. See **Figure 1–1**. This legislation typically requires that "law enforcement agencies adopt written policies for eyewitness identification, designed to reduce the possibility of wrongful conviction" (The Innocence Project, n.d.).

While there is a certain amount of testimonial evidence that may occur at the crime scene (witness statements, victim statements, and spontaneous utterances by suspects), typically this is not the subject of collection efforts associated with crime scene work. Therefore, such matters are not addressed within the confines of this text. However, it should be noted that, from an investigatory standpoint, all testimonial evidence is considered to be lies until corroborated by other physical evidence or testimonial evidence. That is to say, the easiest way to tell when a person is lying is if his or her lips are moving.

Real or Physical Evidence

Real or physical evidence includes any type of evidence with an objective existence, that is, anything with size, shape, and dimension. This type of evidence can take any form. Gases, fingerprints, glass, paint, hair, blood, soil, and drugs are all examples of physical evidence. The variety is infinite.

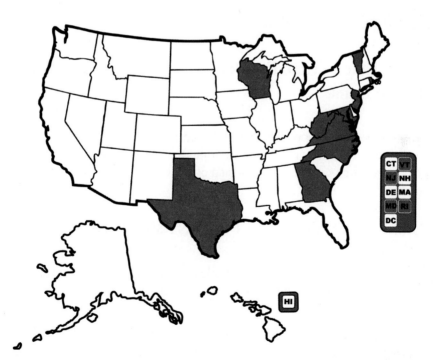

FIGURE 1–1   States that have enacted eyewitness identification reform legislation

Data from www.innocenceproject.org and compiled by Elizabeth Sedgwick, University of Wisconsin-Platteville.

The area of concern with respect to crime scene processing is with relation to physical evidence. Some texts break evidence into further categories of "direct" and "circumstantial" evidence, which simply sub-categorize the testimonial and physical evidence. This is because **direct evidence** is that which proves a fact without the necessity of an inference or a presumption. This can be true of either physical or testimonial evidence. **Circumstantial evidence**, on the other hand, involves a series of facts that through inference, prove a fact at issue. Again, at times this can be the case for either testimonial or physical evidence. Therefore, this book recognizes two chief categories of evidence: either testimonial (not emphasized herein) or real/physical evidence.

Some types of physical evidence may originate from a single source (such as fingerprints or DNA), however, most physical evidence is only associated with a single class or group (such as fibers, hairs, clothing, etc.). Although most physical evidence cannot definitively connect a suspect directly to having committed the crime should not diminish the usefulness of that evidence. Such evidence may serve the purpose of corroborating other evidence and information collected within the investigative process, may be capable of placing an individual at the scene, may give investigators added data to use in the interrogation of potential suspects, and many other purposes.

Value of Physical Evidence

It Can Prove That a Crime Has Been Committed or Establish Key Elements of a Crime

Example

An individual contacted on a traffic stop is found to have a large amount of ingredients commonly associated with the manufacture of methamphetamine. Based on this and other intelligence data, a search warrant is performed on the individual's home and an active methamphetamine laboratory is located.

It Can Establish the Identity of Persons Associated with the Crime

Example

Fingerprints and DNA are specific to individuals and, when located at a crime scene, help to associate the individual with having been at the scene of the crime.

It Can Place the Suspect in Contact with the Victim or with the Crime Scene

Example

Officers are dispatched to a series of burglar alarms at a retail outlet. When they arrive, they discover several businesses that have been broken into by gaining access through destruction of the windowed storefronts. An officer locates an individual walking in the area and, upon further investigation, the individual is found to have glass particles covering his clothing. Later analysis of the trace material would find that the glass was consistent with the glass windows that had been broken to gain access to the businesses.

It Can Exonerate the Innocent

Example

The Innocence Project was founded in 1992 by Barry C. Scheck and Peter J. Neufeld to assist prisoners who could be proven innocent through DNA testing. At this writing, 289 people in the United States have been exonerated by DNA testing, including 17 who served time on death row (The Innocence Project, n.d., Facts on post-conviction DNA exonerations). These individuals served an average of 13 years in prison before exoneration and release. According to the website for The Innocence Project, "In almost 40 percent of DNA exoneration cases, the actual perpetrator has been identified by DNA testing." Also, approximately 70 percent of individuals exonerated by DNA testing were members of minority groups. Exonerations have been won in 35 states and Washington, D.C. The leading causes of wrongful convictions in these cases were: mistaken eyewitness testimony, lab error, false confessions, and incriminating statements. The proper DNA analysis of the evidence resulted in the true story being told (The Innocence Project, n.d., Facts on post-conviction DNA exonerations).

It Can Corroborate the Victim's Testimony

Example

A victim of sexual assault claimed that she had been raped by her neighbor. There was no initial evidence of semen present during the medical examination, and the victim claimed that this was because the suspect had worn a condom. The victim also mentioned that the suspect had placed his mouth on her breast during the assault. The neighbor claimed to have never had intimate contact with the victim and said that he had never been inside her apartment. During a search of the victim's bedroom, hair was located that was consistent with the neighbor's. This evidence proved that the neighbor was being dishonest, but did not show that a sexual assault had occurred. Swabs collected from the victim's breasts were compared against saliva samples (called *buccal swabs*) taken from the suspect, and were found to be consistent in all respects with the biological profile of the suspect. Further forensic analysis of samples taken during the medical exam showed the presence of spermicidal lubricant commonly associated with condoms, located within the vagina of the victim. This information corroborated that what the victim had said was true.

A Suspect Confronted with Physical Evidence May Make Admissions or Even Confess

Example

A suspect in a series of construction site vandalisms was confronted with video surveillance tapes that had been set up to record the ongoing vandalisms. The suspect immediately admitted to the crimes and claimed to have been a disgruntled former employee.

Court Decisions Have Made Physical Evidence More Important

Example

Miranda v. Arizona, 384 U.S. 436 (1966), as well as a number of other high court decisions within the United States, have limited the authority of law enforcement to rely on statements and custodial confessions. This has resulted in a paradigm shift of attention being placed on physical evidence as fundamental to proving a case.

Juries Expect Physical Evidence

Due to the vast amount of influence on the jury pool portrayed in prime time forensic dramas, jurors expect litigation to involve physical evidence. Juries also expect the science associated with the analysis and testimony regarding such evidence to be infallible.

Negative Evidence (Absence of Physical Evidence) Also May Provide Useful Information (Such as Fraudulent Reporting)

Example

An owner of a local electronics store claimed that a burglary had occurred. Subsequent investigation revealed no sign of forced entry. There was no video surveillance evidence because the video system was not operating. The owner claimed that the video system had gone down from a power outage during the night and probably missed capturing the incident. A check of power records revealed no such outage, and when pressed on the inconsistencies the owner admitted to staging the incident due to financial difficulties. The lack of evidence prohibited the owner from committing the intended crime of insurance fraud.

Scientific Crime Scene Investigation

Most texts about crime scene investigation limit the investigator's responsibilities to the documentation of the crime scene and the subsequent collection of the associated physical evidence. While this is mostly true, and most responsibilities and actions are mechanical in nature, the reasoning behind this processing methodology is actually to ensure the admissibility of the evidence within a court of law. It must be remembered that the fundamental purpose behind a criminal investigation is the determination of the truth and successful investigation of a criminal episode. Because of this, the crime scene investigator has to take such mechanical steps a stage further.

A crime scene investigator must implement a scientific approach to CSI. This process includes the mechanical aspects of scene security, documentation of the crime scene, and the collection and preservation of the physical evidence, it also demands and expects more dynamic approaches, such as scene survey, scene definition, and analysis, development of the link between physical evidence and persons, and the reconstruction of the crime scene.

These more dynamic aspects of CSI play an extremely important role in the identification of the suspect(s) and the solution of the crime (Lee, 2003). The process of CSI is therefore scientific. This process adheres to the scientific method, which means that the investigation of the crime scene is a systematic and methodical approach.

The **scientific method** utilizes principles and procedures in the systematic pursuit of knowledge involving the recognition and formulation of a problem, the collection of data through observation and experiment, and the formulation and testing of a defined hypothesis. **Figure 1–2** shows the steps involved in the scientific method. If a crime scene investigator is to incorporate this methodology into CSI, the associated **scientific investigation method** could be used, as shown in **Figure 1–3**.

A process such as the scientific investigation method that involves backing up and repeating is referred to as an **iterative process**. This means that the investigator repeats the process throughout, and continually re-checks and analyzes that they have properly conducted the scene processing. Re-checks are continued until the results are negative, meaning that nothing

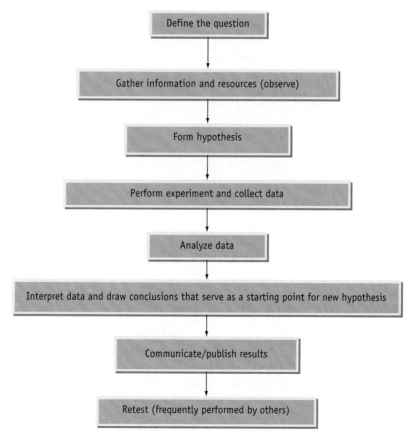

FIGURE 1–2   The Scientific Method

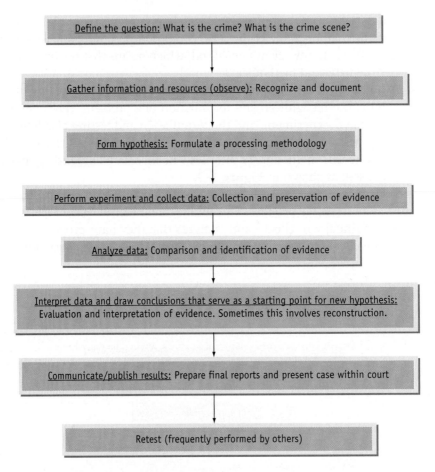

Define the question: What is the crime? What is the crime scene?

Gather information and resources (observe): Recognize and document

Form hypothesis: Formulate a processing methodology

Perform experiment and collect data: Collection and preservation of evidence

Analyze data: Comparison and identification of evidence

Interpret data and draw conclusions that serve as a starting point for new hypothesis: Evaluation and interpretation of evidence. Sometimes this involves reconstruction.

Communicate/publish results: Prepare final reports and present case within court

Retest (frequently performed by others)

FIGURE 1–3 The Scientific Investigation Method

further is required, and nothing has been overlooked. As with the scientific method, however, all steps within the scientific investigation method are subject to peer review.

Collection and Preservation of Physical Evidence

The need for proper recognition, collection, and preservation of physical evidence is apparent to all who are involved within the criminal justice system, and to those who regularly watch prime time TV dramas associated with such matters. Physical evidence can directly or indirectly lead to the solution of a crime. Charging and prosecutorial decisions are often affected by the quality of the physical evidence associated with the case, and the manner in which it was collected.

Because the laws and legal precedents concerning collection of physical evidence are subject to change, it is impossible to give specific, up-to-date information on acceptable procedures. It is, however, possible to provide guidelines. Foremost, it is of the utmost importance that extreme care be taken to use only approved and legal methods when collecting and packaging evidence (Wisconsin DOJ, 2009). If the individual involved in processing efforts is unsure of these procedures, close communication should be maintained between the prosecutor's office, the crime lab, and those persons responsible for the collection of physical evidence. This will ensure the evidence will not only be collected properly, but also be admissible within a court of law.

With regard to the admissibility and forensic usefulness of evidence, there are two main areas of concern relating to the collection and preservation of physical evidence. These include both legal and scientific considerations. Legally, before any evidence is seized, the investigator must decide if:

- Case law is pertinent. Has there been a case in which a decision was rendered relating to the case at hand?

- A search warrant is required. Is it necessary for the court to issue an order and permission for law enforcement to search an area for physical evidence?

- A court order is required. Is it necessary for the court to issue an order that requires a suspect/defendant to submit an evidence sample (DNA, handwriting, hair, etc.)?

If the investigator does not have legal grounds to be within the area at which the evidence is located, then the evidence cannot be collected. If evidence is found to be illegally collected (whether intentionally or unintentionally), then that evidence will be found to be inadmissible in court. This is commonly referred to as the **fruit of the poisonous tree doctrine** (Fisher, 2004). To avoid this and other pitfalls relating to the seizure of evidence, investigators should consult with the prosecutor's office and stay current with case law and court decisions.

With regard to scientific considerations in CSI, the "validity of information derived from examination of the physical evidence depends entirely upon the care with which the evidence has been protected from contamination" (Wisconsin DOJ, 2009, p. 16). More to the point, if the evidence is found to have been improperly collected, handled, or stored, its value may be destroyed and no amount of forensic laboratory work will be of assistance in restoring it. Therefore, it is imperative that items of evidence be collected, handled, and stored in a way that will ensure their integrity. In doing so, the likelihood is increased that useful information can be extracted by examination and that the item will be considered admissible within subsequent court proceedings (Wisconsin DOJ, 2009).

Scientific considerations include the following:

- Physical evidence should be handled as little as possible.

- Items should be packaged separately in individual containers.

- Known or control samples are needed for comparative laboratory analysis. (For example, if an item is submitted to the lab for DNA analysis, it would be necessary to also include a reference sample taken from the individual from whom the evidence is to be compared.)

- As a general guideline, paper is the preferred packaging material, because it allows the evidence to breathe and prevents mildew or degrade. It also prevents cross-transfer of evidence from occurring with nearby objects.

CASE IN POINT

The Scientific Method at Work

A homicide investigator has been called to the scene of an apparent suicide. In the kitchen of a small rural home, a body lies next to an overturned chair and a shotgun. The right foot of the deceased is bare, and a string tied in a bow around the big toe is also tied around the trigger of the shotgun. There is a large wound in the victim's chest and considerable tissue and blood residue on the barrel of the shotgun. Behind the victim is a waist-high hole in the wall about the size of a little finger.

These facts considered in their totality give some support to the hypothesis that this was a suicide. There appears to have been no struggle, and the weapon is in close proximity to the body. The hole in the wall is a bit troubling. The investigator's experience (inductive reasoning) tells him that shot shells do not leave such a hole unless they are chambered for a rifled round (shotguns have a cartridge that contains either numerous pellets or a single projectile). He examines the shotgun (analysis) and discovers that the two chambers of the double-barreled shotgun both contain a shell. One is spent. Upon removing it, he notes that the shell contains pellets. His hypothesis that a suicide occurred does not explain the hole in the wall (synthesis). If he is wedded to his hypothesis, he may choose to ignore this anomaly. Or he may begin to ask some additional questions:

- Who was present at the time of the shooting?
- Did the hole in the wall exist prior to the shooting?
- Are there other weapons on the premises?

Pursuing answers to these questions will provide information that can be used as a basis for further reasoning.

The investigator learns that only the victim's wife was present at the time of the incident, and she does not seem to be aware of any structural flaws in the kitchen wall. She tells the investigator that there is also a 30-caliber hunting rifle in the gun cabinet in the living room. Another hypothesis begins to take shape. Could the wife have murdered her husband? There are only two possibilities if the wife is telling the truth: suicide or homicide (with the wife as the primary suspect).

- Sealable, airtight containers are necessary for chemical evidence and evidence associated with accelerants (arson) to prohibit the gaseous evidence from escaping the container and thus becoming impossible to analyze.
- At all phases of collection, efforts should be made to avoid contamination of the evidence. This can include cross-contamination from incorrect collection and packaging

The investigator notices that the victim is wearing his wristwatch on his left wrist, which suggests he was right-handed. The investigator begins to gather information that he sees as consistent with right-handedness (classification):

- The wristwatch is on the victim's left wrist.
- The victim's wallet is in his right rear pants pocket.
- The victim's right front pants pocket is worn.
- There is a pocketknife in the right front pants pocket.
- There is a ballpoint pen in the left shirt pocket.

The wife confirms that her husband was right-handed.

The investigator begins to gather information that he sees as inconsistent with right-handedness (classification):

- The right foot has been bared.
- The string is tied to the right big toe.

The investigator's assumption, based on experience and reason, is that a right-handed person would have bared his left foot and tied the string to his left big toe (induction). That the facts conflict with this assumption suggests that someone else tied the string (deduction). The investigator suspects homicide (synthesis, theory), and he has the crime scene handled in a manner appropriate for an investigation of a homicide.

The medical examiner confirms that a hole consistent with the passage of a 30-caliber bullet through the body was made prior to the shotgun blast. The laboratory discloses that the bow tied to the victim's big toe was tied not from the victim's position but rather from a reversed position, by someone facing the sole of the foot. The prosecution's theory of the case, which it will attempt to prove by presenting forensic evidence, is that the wife shot her husband with the hunting rifle while they were both sitting at the kitchen table. She then took the shotgun and placed the barrel at her husband's chest and fired, thereby obscuring the original and fatal wound. Stripping his foot bare and tying the string to his toe was her final attempt at making the homicide look like a suicide.

Courtesy of Ronald Becker, JD, Professor, Chaminade Institute.

methods as well as contamination directly from the individual conducting the collecting and packaging.

Areas associated with the correct collection and preservation methods of physical evidence will be covered in more depth throughout the course of this book. This is simply an overview of the scientific considerations that one must consider when collecting and packaging evidence.

Legal Duty to Preserve Evidence

In addition to the obvious importance of collection and preservation of evidence from an investigative standpoint, crime scene personnel have a legal duty to collect and preserve physical evidence associated with a crime. In fact, courts across the country have enacted legislation imposing both civil and criminal penalties for failure to properly preserve evidence.

In addition to the District of Columbia, 31 states have created legislation that compels the preservation of evidence (**Figure 1–4**). To date, 19 states do not have statutes requiring the preservation of evidence (The Innocence Project, n.d., Preservation of Evidence). However, that certainly does not suggest that such preservation is not warranted or departmentally required within those jurisdictions lacking state legislation. Many departments have individual policies governing preservation and retention of evidence, along with strict sanctions for those failing to comply.

Requirements around the preservation of evidence are usually embedded in DNA testing access statutes. In 2004, Congress passed the Justice for All Act (H.R. 5107), which provides financial incentives for states to preserve evidence and withholds those same monies from states that do not adequately preserve evidence. Preserved evidence can help solve closed cases—and exonerate the innocent. Preserving biological evidence from crime scenes is critically

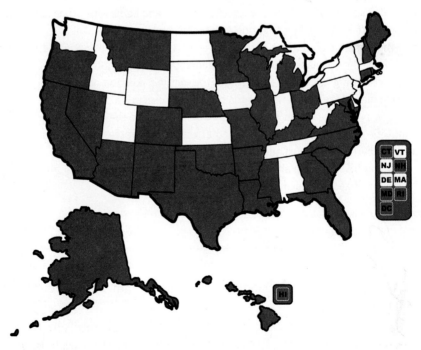

FIGURE 1–4 States that have created legislation that compels the preservation of evidence

Data from www.innocenceproject.org and compiled by Elizabeth Sedgwick, University of Wisconsin-Platteville.

Duty to Preserve Evidence

In 2009, a federal District Court sanctioned defense counsel and defendants for spoliation of electronic evidence. In *Swofford v. Eslinger*, deputies from the Seminole County Sheriff's Office (SCSO) encountered an armed man, Robert Swofford, and shot him. Through the course of the investigative process, Mr. Swofford's attorney served the sheriff's office with a letter that requested that any and all evidence related to the event be preserved. The request from Swofford's attorney specifically requested evidence "including firearms, clips and ammunition, training records, and electronic evidence" (671 F. Supp. 2d 1289; 2009 U.S. Dist). Despite the correspondence, which the SCSO's general counsel admitted to receiving, the guns that were used in the shooting were disassembled and one of the involved deputy's laptop computers was erased, thus deleting a relevant instant message thread (which was later recovered from another deputy's computer). As a result, District Court Judge Mary S. Scriven found that all of the defendants (both involved deputies, the sheriff) as well as the SCSO's general counsel acted in bad faith, and handed down sanctions against each of them.

Robin Lovitt, Virginia Death Row Inmate

Robin Lovitt was convicted of the capital murder and robbery of a pool hall employee in Arlington, Virginia and was sentenced to death in early 2000. When Lovitt sought to appeal the decision, it came to light that the evidence associated with his case had been destroyed. Despite being reminded that Virginia law required the preservation of evidence from the case, a court clerk nonetheless discarded the murder weapon: a blood-stained pair of scissors. The DNA testing available at the time of the trial could only conclusively tie the blood on the weapon to the victim and not to anyone else. More sophisticated DNA testing is now available, but the evidence—which could have proven guilt or innocence and/or informed the appropriateness of the death penalty—is not. The Supreme Court declined to address this issue, and Lovitt was ultimately scheduled to become the 1,000th person executed since capital punishment resumed in 1977. The wrongful destruction of the evidence that could have conclusively proven innocence or guilt denied a conclusive answer. Recognizing the ambiguity caused by the destruction of evidence, Virginia Governor Mark Warner commuted Lovitt's sentence to life in prison.

Source: The Innocence Project. (n.d.). Preservation of innocence. Retrieved from www.innocenceproject.org/Content/Preservation_Of_Evidence.php.

important because DNA can provide the best evidence of innocence—or guilt—upon review of a case. None of the nation's more than 200 DNA exonerations would have been possible had the biological evidence not been available to test. Had the evidence been destroyed, tainted, contaminated, mislabeled, or otherwise corrupted, the innocence of these individuals would never have come to light.

What and How Much to Collect

One question a crime scene investigator asks of him or herself is, "How much should I collect?" Because it is often impractical, and sometimes impossible, to return to a crime scene at a later time to collect additional evidence, it is suggested that the crime scene investigator ensure a thorough and systematic processing of the crime scene to be certain that all necessary evidence, in the correct quantity, has been collected. As a general rule, more is better than less. Judgment with regard to the amount of material to collect is largely a matter of experience.

One must remember that regardless of the amount that is collected, department policy and sometimes statutes will require that the items be preserved for a considerable amount of time, if not indefinitely. This can create significant storage issues within an evidence and property room setting. Therefore, crime scene personnel should consider the proper collection method that will ensure the proper amount of evidence has been collected that will result in the least amount of storage-related issues. For example, if a crime scene investigator is confronted with a bloody king-sized mattress at a homicide scene, would it be best to collect the entire mattress, or simply to photograph the complete mattress and then cut out a sufficient amount of the bloody mattress to submit as evidence? Due to the statute of limitations regarding homicide-related evidence, such evidence may be required to be kept indefinitely. Which takes up more room? The bloody mattress material, which could fit within a medium-sized paper bag, or the entire king-sized mattress? The evidence property room custodian will be much happier with the crime scene investigator who chooses to collect the sample rather than the entire mattress, because it will take up considerably less space and will have the same forensic analysis potential.

As illustrated in this example, it is imperative that the crime scene investigator recognize what is evidence and what is not. Also, it is important for the investigator to have a working knowledge of the forensic value of the evidence located and collected. If all of the natural and commercial objects located within the vicinity of a crime scene were collected and submitted as evidence, the deluge of evidence would quickly incapacitate any department's evidence and property facilities, in addition to further inundating the forensic laboratories charged with analyzing the material. Therefore, evidence can achieve its optimum value only when its collection is performed with a selectivity that is governed by the collector's knowledge of the crime laboratory's capabilities and limitations, and the forensic value of the evidence collected. Such matters will be the topic of discussion throughout this book.

Chain of Custody

The court will require proof that evidence collected during the course of an investigation and the evidence ultimately submitted to the court are one and the same. In order to accomplish this, those involved in the crime scene investigation must establish a secure **chain of custody**, sometimes referred to as a *chain of evidence*. This "chain" shows who had contact with the evidence, at what time, under what circumstances, and what changes, if any, were made to the evidence. What is needed to establish a chain of custody?

- Name or initials of the individual collecting the evidence and each person subsequently having custody of it.
- Dates the item was collected and transferred (as well as signatures of both parties, validating the item transfer).
- Agency, case number, and type of crime.
- Victim or suspect's name.
- A brief description of the item.

In addition to proper labeling and documentation, all collected evidence must be booked into, and subsequently stored, in a secured area prior to transportation to court. Any evidence reasonably assumed to have been tampered with by unauthorized persons because it was kept in an unsecured area may be inadmissible in court.

Teamwork

Successful CSI involves a team approach. A crime scene team is a group of professionals, each trained in specific disciplines. The common goal of the team is to locate and document all of the associated evidence at the scene. Of utmost importance, however, is that each member of the team is allowed to work the scene independent of the others' influence and to have the ability to challenge the others' findings. This system was purposefully designed so that no one person or entity can operate independently. No single element or person is more important than any other. Each has a vital role. There is no place within this process for those seeking fame or glory.

The team approach to CSI begins with planning. This includes a procedure that is agreed upon by all of the team members and agencies involved with the process. Training for each member is typically mandatory, but more important is the understanding of exactly what is expected of each individual at the scene and in the process.

Assemble any group of individuals and they will likely be able to investigate a crime scene, albeit not necessarily in a thorough and systematic manner. A successful investigation, and thus a methodical approach to CSI, is much more likely with a well-trained, experienced, and cohesive unit.

As it turns out, however, this is not necessarily the case in many jurisdictions. If a crime scene investigator does only what they are told to do, and collects only what the on-scene police investigator tells them to collect, then (this is by no means a systematic approach) it falls woefully short of the scientific method discussed previously.

Attributes of a Successful Crime Scene Investigator

While it is universally recognized that every person is unique and brings his or her own abilities and insights into any given situation, it has been found that there is a type of person who makes for a successful investigator. As with all information contained within this text, these are guidelines and by no means hard, fast rules. The following is offered as a framework for those taking a self-inventory, and those thinking about choosing individuals who would be successful at involvement within a crime scene investigation capacity.

Intuition

This attribute is not trainable. Someone either has this ability or does not. This component of intellect is what those in law enforcement term a "hunch" or a "gut feeling."

Eye for Detail

An individual's observation skills cannot be overlooked when discussing desirable attributes for a crime scene investigator. Someone who is detail oriented in both observation and notation will find him or herself to be very successful as a crime scene investigator.

Good Communication Skills

The ability to communicate is an extremely valued, and unfortunately rare, commodity. An individual who is interested in crime scene work should be adept at both oral and written forms of communication, as these are imperative for proper testimony and documentation regarding crime scene activities.

Knowledge of Methods for Locating and Preserving Evidence

If one is not familiar with the correct way to properly collect the various forms of evidence, or know where to locate the information that could aid in educating them on the correct manner, then the evidence risks being collected improperly and thus may be found inadmissible in court or unusable. This trait requires that the person be both scientific as well as process-minded, and have a working knowledge of pertinent case law.

Enjoyment of Continuing Education

Because crime scene work is dynamic, such things as technological innovations, case law, and human ingenuity changes it on an almost a daily basis. It is important for a crime scene investigator to have an affinity for continuing education. Without a drive to learn the latest strategies to achieve a successful gathering of appropriate evidence, the individual quickly will be collecting and processing materials in an archaic or perhaps even illegal manner.

Mistakes and Errors

Crime scene investigators are human. Mistakes will be made. The important thing is to limit these mistakes, learn from them, and not repeat them. Repetition of mistakes is seen as incompetence. Critics will always dissect and critique the actions and decisions taken at a crime scene. This is why it is extremely important to adopt a systematic approach to crime scene processing—to minimize the possibility for errors. Courtroom focus on forensic science is shifting from the lab to the crime scene. Defense attorneys are quick to learn that if they can show that the initial handling of the physical evidence at the crime scene was faulty, then the evidence may be kept out of the trial or at least be tarnished in the eyes of the jury.

Those entrusted with the investigation of criminal activity bear a heavy burden. Mistakes are often not forgiven; there are scores of examples where unintentional errors have been made that resulted in evidence being declared inadmissible by the courts. The best advice is to consider all of the ramifications before embarking on any action (Fisher, 2004).

WRAP UP

Chapter Summary

Successful CSI begins at the crime scene. If the investigator cannot recognize physical evidence or cannot properly preserve it, no amount of sophisticated laboratory instrumentation or technical expertise can rectify the situation. The crime scene investigator must implement a thorough and systematic methodology toward the documentation and processing of a crime scene in order to ensure a successful outcome to the investigation. While involved in this process, a crime scene investigator must remember that the underlying obligation is not to either the prosecution or the defense, but rather to the truth. Adherence to a scientific, legal, and systematic approach, in an unbiased manner, will ensure that the chain of custody for collected evidence will be intact, and will result in the subsequent admissibility of such evidence.

Review Questions

1. Define crime scene investigation.
2. What are the differences between criminalists and crime scene investigators?
3. What is meant by fruit of the poison tree?
4. Define Locard's Exchange Principle.
5. List the objectives of CSI.
6. What are the differences between real evidence and testimonial evidence?
7. List the steps of the scientific method.
8. List the steps of the scientific investigation method.
9. What was Hans Gross's contribution to CSI?
10. How did Sir Arthur Conan Doyle impact modern day CSI?

Case Studies

1. Look up the case of *Silverthorne Lumber Co., Inc. v. United States*, (251 U.S. 385; 40 S. Ct. 182; 64 L. Ed. 319; 1920) on the student companion Web site at go.jblearning.com/CrimeScene-Investigation2, and describe how the fruit of the poisonous tree doctrine was used.

2. After reviewing the case of Columbus County, on behalf of *Katie Brooks Plaintiff v. Marion A. Davis*, (163 N.C. App. 64; 592 S.E.2d 225; 2004 N.C. App.) on the student companion Web site at go.jblearning.com/CrimeSceneInvestigation2, discuss the importance of a complete chain of custody.

References

Becker, R. F. (2009). *Criminal investigation* (3rd ed.). Sudbury, MA: Jones and Bartlett Publishers.

Doyle, A. C. (1887). *A study in scarlet*. London, UK: Ward Lock & Co.

Fisher, B. A. J. (2004). *Techniques of crime scene investigation* (7th ed.). Boca Raton, FL: CRC Press.

Gernet, J. (1962). *Daily life in China on the eve of the Mongol invasion, 1250–1276* (p. 170). Stanford, CA: Stanford University Press.

The Innocence Project. (n.d.). Facts on post-conviction DNA exonerations. Retrieved from http://www.innocenceproject.org/Content/Facts_on_PostConviction_DNA_Exonerations.php

The Innocence Project. (n.d.). Preservation of innocence. Retrieved from www.innocenceproject.org/Content/Preservation_Of_Evidence.php

Labbé, J. (2005). Ambroise Tardieu: The man and his work on child maltreatment a century before Kempe. *Child Abuse & Neglect, 29*, 311–324.

Lee, H. (2003). *Henry Lee's crime scene handbook*. Burlington, MA: Academic Press.

Ragle, L. (2002). *Crime scene*. New York: HarperCollins.

Saferstein, R. (2004). *Criminalistics: An introduction to forensic science* (8th ed.). Upper Saddle River, NJ: Pearson Prentice Hall.

Schuster, B. (2007). Police Lineups: Making Eyewitness Identification More Reliable. *National Institute of Justice, 258*. Retrieved from at http://www.nij.gov/journals/258/police-lineups.html

U.S. Department of Justice. International Criminal Investigative Training Program. (n.d.). Retrieved July 14, 2009, from http://www.justice.gov/criminal/icitap/

U.S. Supreme Court Media OYEZ. *Miranda v. Arizona*. Retrieved August 26, 2012, from http://www.oyez.org/cases/1960-1969/1965/1965_759/

Wisconsin Department of Justice. (2009). *Physical evidence handbook*. (78th ed.). Madison, WI: Wisconsin Department of Administration.

LEARNING OBJECTIVES

- Understand the "CSI effect."
- Understand how Hollywood's portrayal of CSI-related work has impacted the various levels of the criminal justice system.
- Define and apply voir dire.
- Know how to overcome the CSI effect.

The CSI Effect

From 8 to 11 o'clock each night, television is one long lie …

David Rintels, Former President, Writers Guild of America

All television is educational. The only question is: what does it teach?

Nicholas Johnson, Commissioner, FCC

KEY TERMS

- American Academy of Forensic Sciences (AAFS)
- CSI Effect
- Forensic Science Educational Program Accreditation Committee (FEPAC)
- Voir Dire

Introduction

A look at news headlines and other media sources quickly reveals how the media is impacting the area of CSI. This impact has permeated nearly every aspect of society. Even religion is not devoid of its touch. An example of this is found in Ian Wilson's 2007 book, entitled *Murder at*

RIPPED FROM THE HEADLINES

Target Stores to Sponsor Forensics Lab in National Law Enforcement Museum

Due to the large number and popularity of television programs such as *CSI: Crime Scene Investigation*, Americans have become fascinated with forensic science. Through support from retail giant Target Stores, the public will now have the opportunity to experience the process associated with the forensic analysis of physical evidence in a realistic forensics lab setting within the National Law Enforcement Museum.

The National Law Enforcement Museum is scheduled to open in downtown Washington, D.C., in 2015. When it opens its doors, the Target Forensics Lab will help visitors better understand the science behind forensic investigation and gain appreciation for the dedication of the criminal justice professionals who are responsible for investigation of criminal events.

"To most Americans, television presents crime solving as a simple, almost routine process that takes 60 minutes, minus the commercials. But in reality, crime scene investigation is an intricate, scientifically grounded process," said Craig W. Floyd, chairman and CEO of the National Law Enforcement Officers Memorial Fund. "Thanks to generous support from Target, we will be able to show museum visitors what really goes into investigating crimes and how modern forensics labs are helping to bring criminals to justice and make our communities safer."

Exhibit features will include forensic stations that will give museum visitors hands-on experience with topics such as: fingerprinting, trace analysis, blood spatter analysis, DNA, toxicology, and impression evidence (firearms, toolmarks, footwear, etc.). It is also anticipated that visitors will have the ability to explore forensic accounting, entomology, and a realistic example of a medical examiner's office. Museum visitors will be given the chance to process evidence associated with one of four featured crimes within the exhibit. They will do this by collecting evidence and then analyzing it in the Target Forensics Lab before they identify a suspect.

For more information about the National Law Enforcement Museum, including a virtual tour, visit www.LawEnforcementMuseum.org.

Information from: "Target to Sponsor Forensics Lab in New National Law Enforcement Museum." (2008, June 3). National Law Enforcement Officers Memorial Fund. http://www.nleomf.org/newsroom/news-releases/Target-To-Sponsor-Forensics-Lab.html.

Golgotha: A scientific investigation into the last days of Jesus' life, His death, and His resurrection. But media influence prevails especially in the criminal justice system, particularly with respect to the areas of criminal investigation, the court system, and U.S. education.

Although many agree that there has been a significant impact, the theory is not without controversy. Some believe that television programs and movies about CSI concepts are simply more Hollywood extravagance, giving too much credit to a medium that could not possibly influence society to such a degree. While the concept of the so-called "CSI effect" is indeed controversial, it is ignorant to assume that it does not exist in any manner. The degree to which it exists is the topic of this chapter. It is now left up to the reader to determine through his or her experience, training, knowledge, and the information contained within this book whether or not the CSI effect is a reality.

Birth of a Problem

During the 1950s it was *Perry Mason.* The American public watched the fictional defense attorney on TV as Mason extracted last-minute confessions from the witness stand, thereby influencing public perceptions of the U.S. court system. From 1976 to 1983 television viewers were treated to the forensic wizardry of *Quincy M.E.* As a result of the show, the American public was led to believe that forensic pathology could be used infallibly to solve criminal mysteries. Today there is yet another primetime drama that is both educating and influencing television viewers and, thus, the potential jury pool.

CSI: Crime Scene Investigation is a CBS television series depicting physical evidence being gathered, processed, and used to solve crimes. The characters portrayed in the series use a number of costly and sophisticated techniques to produce unquestionable results through the scientific analysis of evidence. *CSI* first aired on CBS on October 6, 2000 and the show had aired 267 episodes as of this writing (IMDb, 2012). *CSI*'s television cousin, *Forensic Files,* first aired on Court TV in October 2001. The program was touted as the "real life/real case" version of *CSI.* It was the first in a long line of spin-off forensic shows that have exploded from the *CSI* craze. CBS eventually capitalized on its popularity by producing two additional shows, *CSI Miami* and *CSI New York.*

Highly publicized trials such as those of Casey Anthony, Conrad Murray, and O.J. Simpson have drawn many people into forensics. Basic-cable TV networks such as TruTV, Investigation Discovery, USA Network, and A&E also carry many programs depicting forensic investigations of actual criminal cases. These include: *48 Hours, Forensic Files, Cold Case Files, The First 48,* and *American Justice,* among others.

U.S. television viewing data show a drop in cinema audiences and a huge rise in TV viewing. Americans are now staying home to watch shows like *CSI,* which is currently one of the most influential and popular television shows in the world. With all of these viewers, there is no doubt that some sort of change in society will result. The portrayals presented within these episodes can best be described as "infotainment," a highly stylized, edited, and formatted form of entertainment that is disguised as informative or realistic, but in fact is not scientifically correct and in some cases not grounded at all in reality.

Any time a television show or movie reaches cult status, there are effects on society. Sometimes this is in regard to marketing or business. Other times it relates to morals, law, or politics. However, this infotainment may affect a person's view of reality. The *CSI* franchise is being pointed to as exerting an influence on all of these areas. This phenomenon has been coined as the "CSI effect."

Defining the CSI Effect

The CSI effect has been defined in a number of ways. In this text, the author chooses to combine the varying theories into one definition, although it might seem to contradict itself. The **CSI effect** is a phenomenon whereby forensic drama television has created unreasonable expectations, thereby increasing the prosecution's burden of proof, while presenting an air of infallibility with regard to forensic science, while also increasing overall interest and perceived understanding in the area of forensic science and crime scene work.

It is blamed for romanticizing forensic science as well as creating unreasonable expectations in the minds of jurors. Jurors have become conditioned to believe that every crime can be solved through forensic evidence, and that forensic evidence of guilt exists in every crime. Under this theory, jurors expect forensic evidence to be presented in every case, and require it before they will convict. Where forensic evidence does not exist, jurors may conclude that the evidence necessary to justify a guilty verdict does not exist, or interpret its absence as justifying acquittal. What many jurors do not understand is that even when available, forensic evidence is often contaminated and thus cannot be used or introduced at trial. In other instances, although powerful forensic tools such as DNA are available, they are neither the only nor the best method to prove guilt.

In a criminal case, the prosecution carries the burden of proving the defendant guilty "beyond a reasonable doubt." Courts have described "beyond a reasonable doubt" to mean that: (a) the evidence excludes to a moral certainty every hypothesis but guilt, (b) the inference of guilt is the only one that can be drawn from the facts, or (c) the evidence excludes every hypothesis of innocence. Where jurors refuse to convict without definitive forensic evidence, regardless of the strength of testimonial evidence, or unless the prosecution can exclude innocence via such scientific evidence, it increases the constitutional burden from "beyond a reasonable doubt" to "beyond any and all doubt" (Podlas, 2006).

On the *CSI* program, science leads to a singular, objective correct answer. Yet, in real life, forensic conclusions are only as good as the technicians who retrieve the evidence, test it, and draw conclusions from it. Television goes a step further through its character portrayals. *CSI* quashes concerns of human error while heightening the expert status of crime scene technicians. The *CSI* team never possesses a personal motivation to engage in wrongdoing or to violate the (nonexistent) standards of their profession. In the real world, however, forensic technicians often have come under scrutiny. Numerous forensic technicians, crime scene investigators, and crime reconstruction experts have lied under oath, faked their credentials, and fabricated evidence (Podlas, 2006).

Some view this supposed CSI effect as an aberration and say that there is not as large an effect on the public as we have been led to believe. However, when one considers the impact on education, on the court system, on crime labs, and on law enforcement, this impact is undeniable.

Impact of the CSI Effect

On television, forensic evidence is nearly always correct and the detective is never wrong. Unfortunately, in real life this is not quite true. Many cases are not solved. Many cases do not have physical evidence associated with them.

Popular television shows have resulted in a phenomenon that drives jury verdicts across America. People who end up on a jury know (or think that they know) a great deal about forensic science and the kind of science necessary to solve crimes. Criminal practitioners are being confronted by a population that believes TV shows are realistic.

Prosecutors say juries expect scientific evidence in every case, even though the majority of criminal cases do not call for such evidence. Resourceful defense attorneys are using this to suggest to the jury that fingerprints or DNA evidence should have been introduced, and that failure to do so shows incompetence or an incomplete investigation, and is thus enough to create reasonable doubt. Also, on television, forensic evidence is nearly always correct, and this assumption pervades the jury room. Unfortunately, it is not quite true. This is a growing area of concern for those in the law enforcement, legal, and scientific communities, as well as the public as a whole.

However, not all of the impact has been negative. *CSI* and its spawn of dramas about crime have increased the public's awareness of forensics and thereby increased funding resources for the profession of forensic sciences. It has created a profound interest in forensic science and crime scene work. People now look forward to jury duty. Jurors, now equipped with a better sense of what a crime scene technician does, are better able to understand and follow expert witness testimony.

Another positive aspect of the CSI effect is that the shows have made terms such as *DNA* and *gunshot residue* (GSR) household names. However, as a result, juries are calling for DNA and GSR every time. Juries have unrealistic expectations that simply cannot be met by existing technologies. While citizens or jurors might expect it, not every department or jurisdiction has the latest and greatest technology that is touted in the media.

Impact on the Courts

Since the advent of television, legal scholars and practitioners alike have contemplated the impact of law-oriented entertainment programming on the public. Even the Supreme Court and the American Bar Association have acknowledged that television impacts the public's perception of the legal system (Podlas, 2006).

Most people do not read statutory or scholarly legal resources; instead, they tend to learn about the law from secondary sources. Empirical evidence shows that most people learn about the law from media, and specifically from television. According to A.C. Nielsen, Co. (2008), 99% of Americans have at least one television set, and watch at least 28 hours of television programming per week. This results in television being, in essence, an institutionalized storyteller, explaining to the American populace how things work and what to do.

Over a decade ago, the forensic evidence used in the O.J. Simpson trial had most trial viewers perplexed. Today's viewers are a more educated lot, fueled by what they believe they have learned from television. Defense attorneys are seizing the opportunity to suggest to the jury that fingerprints or DNA evidence should have been introduced, and that failure to do so shows incompetence or an incomplete investigation, and thus is enough to create reasonable doubt. To combat this phenomenon, prosecutors have begun to use "negative witnesses" to explain to juries why forensic evidence might be absent or is not being introduced into court.

VIEW FROM AN EXPERT

Media Impact on CSI over the Past Three Decades

Thirty years ago, crime scene investigations were conducted to fool victims into believing that officers were exhausting all resources to solve their case as much as actual evidence was being gathered. It was common to spread fingerprint dust mostly to appease the victims because no viable central database existed for identifying suspects. Today law enforcement operates in a much different environment.

In the last 15 years advancements in the areas of fingerprint technology, impression evidence processing and recovery, voice recognition and analysis, trace evidence identification, and DNA have enhanced law enforcement's capability to competently investigate crimes and deliver conviction verdicts for prosecutors as well as exonerate the innocent. Partial prints three decades ago would have been trashed. No method existed to cast an impression in the snow. And a hair follicle might help to identify only a person's hair color.

In most cities, crime scene investigators were the officer that [*sic*] arrived on scene and took the original report. Gradually, investigators began to arrive at crime scenes and after a decade of increased success and technology, the concept of a specialized investigator emerged. This was the creation of the crime scene investigator.

After a decade of amplified successes, Hollywood leaped on board. The sensationalization of Hollywood is entertaining, yet few crime scene investigators can meet the expectations of make-believe. This can make the crime scene investigator's job difficult when dealing with real victims that [*sic*] live in make-believe dimensions. Even the most advanced technology cannot compete with the imaginations of Hollywood. It constantly sets a pace for us to endeavor. This

Influence on Jurors

Due to much of this false information pouring out of television infotainment, juries and potential jurors are being influenced inside and outside of the courtroom. The impact has been so dramatic on juries that the CSI effect tends to create unrealistic expectations. One example is that jurors believe that if there is a DNA link then a suspect must be guilty, when in fact there might be a completely plausible explanation for the suspect's DNA being present (such as being a roommate, etc.).

Before a person becomes a jury member, they must go through **voir dire** (the preliminary examination of a witness or juror to determine his or her competency to give or hear evidence), where both the prosecutor and the defense are provided with an opportunity to question each of the potential jurors. If any of the potential jurors have any biased opinions about the case, they are eliminated from the jury.

is not always a bad motivator. With the progressions of the last several years and the recent popularity of *CSI*-type shows, we are challenged to govern crime scene investigations like never before imagined.

The popularity of these shows has also helped in the education of victims. While many ideologies are ill-received, victims are still learning how to protect and preserve evidence. They've learned to leave crime scenes alone, contact law enforcement immediately, and maintain themselves as evidence when applicable by not bathing. They have even learned key elements to remember when witnessing a crime. These factors appear to be influential in the steady increase in the rate of criminal convictions over the past three decades.

Now is a great time to be involved in law enforcement. The public is holding us at a higher level of accountability and with a few exceptions we are able to meet these expectations. Technology and education has provided us with tools that give us a much greater chance at detecting and preserving evidence. While criminals are also becoming more educated, the public's education and enhanced self accountability is helping us narrow the gap of good versus evil. Just 10 years ago DNA was only a scientific term thought to be 30 years from providing evidentiary value. Today it is identifying suspects, victims, witnesses and innocent people daily.

What will tomorrow bring? It is rewarding to be a part of this profession that has grown from the flatfoot walking the beat to the crime scene professionals that Hollywood tries to replicate.

Randy S. Taylor, Chief of Police
Clarkdale Police Department, Clarkdale, Arizona

Courtesy of Randy Taylor, D.M., Chief of Police, Clarkdale, AZ.

Lawyers are now asking would-be jurors whether they watch any of these crime drama shows, and then changing their legal strategies depending on the answers. An example of this phenomenon is that prosecutors are now asking jurors whether any of them believe the state must produce scientific evidence in order to find the defendant guilty. Prosecutors may request certain scientific tests even if the jurors believe they are unnecessary. These prosecutors might even call experts to the stand to explain why evidence such as fingerprints or ballistics is not available (previously referred to as "negative witnesses").

People who overestimate the reality basis of shows such as *CSI* may develop unreasonable expectations of actual forensic practitioners. Although the technologies lauded on these fictional programs are found in real crime labs, they often require much more time and deliver answers more equivocal in real life than depicted in television crime dramas. Analysts worry that people will come to believe that real forensic science has become as swift and certain as we have always wished justice to be. DNA evidence in particular is expected more and more by jurors, no matter if it is relevant or not found in a given case. Some potential jurors feel startled during voir dire when they are asked whether they are viewers of shows such as *CSI*.

Prosecutors Feeling the Pressure

Along with the juries being influenced, prosecutors also are feeling the pressure of the CSI effect. Before, they rarely had to worry much about making a sophisticated presentation when explaining their case, or about presenting some sort of evidence in every case. Now, however, this is changing because juries have higher expectations after watching crime drama shows.

Prosecutors fear that trial juries who watch *CSI*-type programs are dazzled by the millions of pounds worth of equipment, huge forensic laboratories, and unlimited resources, and think a case can be solved conclusively within the hour. They say that these types of shows can make it more difficult for them to win convictions in the large majority of cases in which scientific evidence is irrelevant or absent (Willing, 2004). Prosecutors now have to supply more forensic evidence because jurors are expecting it, having seen it on television (Dowler, Fleming, & Muzzatti, 2006). Many prosecutors believe that this is unfair, because in many cases certain evidence was not found or was not applicable to the particular case. Some prosecutors now seem to be apologizing at trial for not having "reliable evidence." They believe that they must do this to have a chance to prove their case without the use of evidence. Other prosecutors do not go to the extent of apologizing, but have changed the way they present their case to the jury. Prosecutors in some areas are now telling the jury in their opening statements what type of evidence they can expect to see during the trial, and reminding them that this is real life and not a television crime drama like *CSI*. Some prosecutors believe defense attorneys are taking advantage of situations when physical evidence is lacking or minimal, as an opportunity to create holes within the prosecution's case (DiPasquale, 2006).

Defense Attorneys and the CSI Effect

Defense attorneys have both positive and negative opinions about the CSI effect. Some defense lawyers say that *CSI* and similar shows make jurors rely too heavily on scientific findings and are unwilling to accept that those findings can be compromised by human or technical errors (Willing, 2004). They fear that jurors may be overly influenced by the presence of DNA evidence due to their perception of it being "infallible" and the "authority" of its scientific exponents,

---

RIPPED FROM THE HEADLINES

The Casey Anthony Verdict: Undoing the Tech Effect

In the recent acquittal of Casey Anthony, many within the scientific and legal communities are pointing to the CSI effect as being responsible. The Oakland County Prosecutor's Office refers to the "tech effect," rather than the "CSI effect" as being responsible, but it would appear that it is a matter of semantics and titling. In the end it seems as though juror expectation, unrealistic or otherwise, was a contributing factor in the acquittal. There are many officials who point to a lack of evidence being the key in a Florida jury finding Casey Anthony not guilty of murdering her young child. Former Oakland County Prosecutor David Gorcyca said "the case lacked a tremendous amount of physical evidence. There was no DNA, there was no confession, there were no witnesses. So, that really hampered (the prosecution's) ability to convince the jury she was guilty beyond a reasonable doubt." The Oakland County Sheriff, Michael Bouchard, agreed, although he was not in agreement with the verdict. "I think that it was a miscarriage of justice. It's challenging to build a case purely on circumstantial evidence against a young mother, because people find it difficult to believe that someone could do that to their own child. Sadly, in the world we live in, that happens."

There is one thing that the former prosecutor and sheriff agree on: that juries can be tainted by television. "There's a predisposition that people expect that what they see on TV is reality. It's like watching Star Trek, seeing someone beam them somewhere and wondering why we can't do the same thing. DNA, fingerprints, hair fibers—today's juries expect it because they see it on TV. The public is constantly being bombarded by all kinds of physical and forensic evidence, some of which doesn't even exist. This places a much higher burden on the prosecution."

Whether it is referred to as the "tech effect" or the "CSI effect," there appears to be little disagreement that modern forensic drama television shows are creating unreasonable jury expectations, which are impacting legal decisions throughout the country, and possibly even around the world.

Information from: Phillips, D. (2011, July 7). "Local prosecutors on Anthony verdict: Undoing the 'Tech Effect.'" The Oakland Press. http://www.theoaklandpress.com/articles/2011/07/07/news/cops_and_courts/doc4e14faac67cff332457215.txt?viewmode=2.

even if, in the lawyers' view, the DNA evidence does not directly bear on their client's guilt (Goodman-Delahunty & Tait, 2006).

There are those defense attorneys who embrace the *CSI* effect phenomenon due to their clients being found "not guilty" as a result of insufficient evidence. This lack of evidence is often enough for juries to find "reasonable doubt," after having this seed of doubt planted by talented lawyers. Many of them do not see why all of the attention is being paid to such matters, and claim that they have not noticed any changes in patterns of jury verdicts. They argue that some forensic sciences, such as fingerprint science for example, have been around since the 1800s, so to say that forensic science is a new phenomenon that people were not aware of is very misleading. "Other defense lawyers say that jurors are not expecting anything different than in the past. Juries have always expected reliable evidence that corroborates eyewitness testimony" (DiPasquale, 2006, p. 2).

Impact on Law Enforcement

Police departments and crime laboratories have increased their efforts and spent much of their annual budgets to acquire modern technology and training to produce reliable results. Some departments are spending hundreds of thousands of dollars on DNA technology or trace evidence collection and analysis technology, while areas such as fingerprint or footwear evidence are being overlooked. This is financially burdensome for many departments. They find themselves in the position of believing they need to improve their forensic capabilities despite the fact that such areas as DNA and trace evidence are seldom—if ever—used in their jurisdiction.

Investigators, crime scene technicians, and officers are finding themselves collecting and booking more evidence than they did in the past. This is happening because they have found that failing to do so is pointed to as incompetence or inefficiency. However, the vast majority of these professionals know from their training and experience that the evidence they are collecting is not necessary to prove the elements of the crime—they are simply collecting it because of the results of the CSI effect.

Impact on Crime Labs

Crime labs also are feeling the overwhelming effects of this new phenomenon. Due to prosecutors' belief that if they present more evidence in more cases, then the courts will convict, the quantity of evidence that is being sent to these labs is increasing at an enormous rate. Investigating police are starting to put too much faith in the powers of forensic scientists, and sometimes expect miracles from their crime labs. They now "contain a scene" of murder for days, pouring over every inch while using a variety of chemicals to unveil evidence. They also take videos and hundreds of photos so they can be shown even years later to a jury, to help the jurors understand where and how someone died (Robertson, 2006). Police are now sending more samples to be analyzed because they think that forensic scientists can provide the answer to any case.

As the numbers of samples increase, so does the backlog of work for crime labs (Moscaritolo, 2005). These backlogs may be creating injustice in the criminal justice system by freeing the guilty and incarcerating the innocent. Crime labs now have to spend much more time analyzing different types of DNA. Files thick with evidence are required before justices of the peace will issue arrest or search warrants, plus transcripts of police interviews with witnesses and suspects often fill several cardboard cartons and accordion folders. In addition to unsolved cases, many of the brown cardboard boxes that fill endless shelves and rooms contain clues that can be revisited years later. It is also said that nothing is thrown out in a murder case (Robertson, 2006). A result of this is shown by the Department of Laboratories and Research in Westchester, New York, whose division of forensic sciences benefited from a $9 million overhaul in 2007. The renovation of its 17-year-old DNA lab aimed to address the steady increase in demand for its services. The lab, which has about 100 employees, handles nearly 1,000 DNA tests, up from 400 just five years ago. Nearly half of these cases stem from rape and murder-related investigations (Kelly, 2007).

The CSI Effect on Education

Since *CSI* first aired in the year 2000, America has seen approximately a 332% increase in the number of programs featuring forensic science as a course of study in colleges and universities. There also has been an impact on early education, with courses of study involving forensic science showing up within America's secondary education systems.

Some police departments were critical of these education programs, saying that in an effort to attract a larger student population, universities were offering unsuitable courses that left graduates unprepared for real-world forensic work. Traditionally, the academic route followed by a would-be forensic scientist had been to pursue a primary (bachelor's) degree in a general-science subject such as chemistry or biology, followed by a suitable post-graduate course or some type of in-service training.

In 2003, the **American Academy of Forensic Sciences (AAFS)** assembled an outline for accreditation standards relating to forensic science education through its **Forensic Science Educational Program Accreditation Commission (FEPAC)**. These suggestions were based on recommendations from the U.S. National Institute of Justice (NIJ). This was an important step and the information was seen as being professionally accurate due to the history of AAFS, which has served the forensic community for over 60 years. The outlining of educational standards fits precisely with the organization's mission statement:

> The American Academy of Forensic Sciences is a multi-disciplinary professional organization that provides leadership to advance science and its application to the legal system. The objectives of the Academy are to promote education, foster research, improve practice, and encourage collaboration in the forensic sciences (AAFS, 2012, About AAFS).

Conforming to the organization's mission, FEPAC was created with the stated mission:

to maintain and to enhance the quality of forensic science education through a formal evaluation and recognition of college-level academic programs. The primary function of the Commission is to develop and to maintain standards and to administer an accreditation program that recognizes and distinguishes high quality undergraduate and graduate forensic science programs (AAFS, 2012, FEPAC).

Statistics compiled by the AAFS show that in recent years, vocational and technical schools have begun adding forensic and practical investigations courses to their criminal justice programs. Colleges and universities are slowly beginning to follow suit. This trend is seen in **Table 2–1**. A number of programs at the university level dealt with forensic science prior to the *CSI* boom that has erupted since 2000. However, all of these programs were in the area of forensic science sometimes referred to as "criminalistics." This education was based on the analysis of physical evidence, typically from a chemistry, biology, and physics standpoint. It was heavily rooted in science and did not deal with actual investigative techniques. Such education was targeted toward the individual who desired to pursue employment in one of the over 300 forensic labs in the United States after graduation and become a forensic scientist or "criminalist." Prior to the year 2000, only 46 of these programs were available in the United States. Today there are well over 200 (AAFS, 2012). This list includes certificate, undergraduate, graduate, and doctoral programs with a primary or secondary emphasis on forensic science, forensic investigation, or an associated sub-discipline. However, although there is a plethora of degree programs to choose from, there are currently only approximately 13,000 forensic scientist laboratory positions that are available in publicly funded laboratories within the United States. However, some of the degree programs mentioned are more suited to crime scene investigation, law enforcement, and field work, where there are potentially over half a million jobs within the United

TABLE 2–1   Comparison of the Growth of Forensic Science–Related Programs in the United States and Other Countries

Type of Program	United States			Other Countries		
	2000	2005	2012	2000	2005	2012
Certificate Programs	0	5	34	0	0	0
Associate Degree Programs (A.A., A.S.)	0	6	19	0	0	0
Undergraduate Degree Programs (B.A., B.S.)	22	63	118	9	19	33
Graduate Degree Programs (M.S., M.F.S.)	9	36	49	9	14	22
Doctoral Degreem Programs	19	9	6	1	2	5
Total	65	119	226	19	35	60

Data From the American Academy of Forensic Sciences.

States in local, county, state and federal agencies. According to the AAFS, this same trend is evident worldwide (Table 2–1). The worldwide trend shows that program implementation and growth has doubled nearly every 6 years for the past 12 years, and shows no signs of slowing down.

Influence on the Criminal Mind

The CSI effect may be altering how crimes are committed. Many criminal experts have noticed an increase in criminal cases in which suspects burn or otherwise tamper with evidence (e.g., using bleach to destroy DNA evidence) in an attempt to carefully clean the crime scene of trace evidence such as hairs and clothing fibers.

Certain viewers watch these shows as a training ground to learn not only educational facts about forensic science, but also how to cover up their own tracks pertaining to crimes they have committed in the past or might commit in the future. It appears that these shows are educating potential offenders at an alarmingly quick rate, and may even encourage them when they see in the media how simple it is to get away with crimes.

A well-known example of this phenomenon comes from a man charged in a double homicide in Ohio. Jermaine "Maniac" McKinney, a 25-year-old *CSI* fan, allegedly broke into a house, killed a mother and daughter, and used bleach to remove their blood from his hands. He also allegedly covered the interior of a getaway car with blankets to avoid transferring blood. Prosecutors said McKinney burned the bodies, his clothing, and removed his cigarette butts, with his DNA, from the crime scene. His actions appeared to resemble many of the methods used and seen on episodes of *CSI*. Today, the use of bleach—which destroys DNA—is not unusual in a planned homicide. People seem to be getting more sophisticated with making sure they are not leaving trace evidence at crime scenes (Milicia, 2006). Many people fear the impact of these shows on crime, but are unable to decide on a way to eliminate this factor, aside from having the shows taken off the air.

In April 2008, the Associated Press reported a story about a group of third graders in Georgia who had an assault attempt on their teacher foiled. These students plotted to attack their teacher and had brought a broken steak knife, handcuffs, duct tape, and other items for their planned assault. The nine children involved in the plot had gone so far as to assign children various tasks, including covering the windows and cleaning up after the assault. When interviewed, several of the students reportedly commented that the ideas were hatched as a result of "television" (Bynum, 2008).

Overcoming the CSI Myths

Many viewers are watching forensic drama television and taking their implied messages too literally. Among the growing international viewing public, the guiding principle of *CSI*—that people lie but the crime labs do not—has been accepted as gospel truth when, in fact, it is quite far from the truth. Samples degrade, tests are inconclusive, and lab technicians make mistakes. Some of the science that is seen on *CSI* is state-of the-art but can only be performed by real lab technicians. However, many techniques used on these shows do not exist except conceptually; that is, they have yet to be invented. Too many people in the United States believe everything they see on television is true; unfortunately, however, many of the forensic sciences used on these crime dramas are pure fantasy. Because much of the technology that people see on fictional *CSI*-type programming does not exist, this fact is becoming a concern. One forensic scientist estimates that 40% of the so-called "science" on *CSI* does not exist, and most of the rest is performed in ways that crime lab personnel can only dream about (Schweitzer & Saks, 2007).

Some examples of fictional technology include the lightning speed with which cases are solved, the computer software that from a partial tire print can tell the analyst the model and year of a suspect's car, and fingerprints miraculously pieced together from a shattered glass; these are just a few among many examples of simple misinformation (Appleby, 2006). Real technicians do not pour caulk into knife wounds to make a cast of the weapon. Caulk does not work in soft tissue. There are machines on the show *CSI* that can identify cologne from other scents on clothing. In reality these machines are still in the experimental phase, though this is unknown to viewers who are watching.

Forensic drama television such as *CSI* is convincing the television viewing audience that forensic science and crime scene work is not only science, but super science. The irony of this myth is that it is a departure from the current reality of dealing with the law and science. Currently, both the courts and scientists are beginning to realize that there is surprisingly little science in some of the areas referred to as "forensic science." After such court rulings as *Daubert v. Merrell Dow Pharmaceuticals, Inc.* (505 U.S. 579, 1993) and *Kumho Tire Co. v. Carmichael* (526 U.S. 137, 1999), courts have begun to scrutinize such evidence with more skepticism and have been surprised to discover the degree of scientific weakness of some forensic fields.

An example of one weakness is the use of neuro-linguistic programming (NLP), a pseudo-scientific therapy developed in the 1970s that has since been largely scientifically unsupported. NLP touts that lies can be detected by the way a person's eyes shift when responding to a question, a strategy that has been used in primetime forensic dramas. In reality, evidence gained from an NLP session most likely would be dismissed by a judge due to its lack of credibility.

Lastly, on *CSI* the forensic scientist is a combination of a police officer, crime investigator, and forensic scientist, but in the real world, different professionals fulfill each role (Reville, 2006). *CSI* producers acknowledge that they take some liberties with facts and the capabilities of science, but they say it is necessary to keep their story lines moving (Willing, 2004). People are now asking whether crime drama shows should issue a type of warning at the beginning of episodes, stating that some of the technology used in the programs is fictional. They think that this might give viewers a better idea of what is real and what is not. Hopefully, doing so might help the current situation involving the influence of the CSI effect.

Overcoming the CSI Effect in Law Enforcement

To determine if a department or its personnel are being affected by the CSI effect consider the following questions. Are officers collecting more evidence at individual cases than they have in the past? Is this a result of additional training and experience or outside pressure and influence? Have citizen complaints regarding the manner in which criminal investigations are handled or processed increased since the year 2000? Has the department found itself spending more money on training and equipment relating to forensic investigations during the past four to five years? Have officers returned from court or the streets with stories or experiences where juries or citizens have expected or suggested that evidence should have been collected?

Some view this supposed CSI effect as an anomaly and say that there is not as large an effect as the public is being led to believe. However, when one considers the impact on education, the court system, crime labs, and on law enforcement as discussed in the previous sections, the impact is undeniable. So, how can this effect be countered?

Refresher Trainings

It has been suggested that departments conduct frequent refresher trainings to explain what is and is not needed with regard to preservation, documentation, and collection efforts. These trainings should cover the areas of evidence identification, documentation, collection, packaging, and preservation. They should concentrate on the procedures for processing a crime area and how to avoid its contamination. Educating personnel in the proper methodologies will ensure that the sworn officers, and not the citizenry whom they serve, are the experts.

Caseload

Departments should examine their current caseload. If the vast majority of their cases revolve around identity theft, fraud, and forgery, they might ask whether DNA technology is appropriate. For these jurisdictions, it would be wiser to train someone in handwriting analysis. Therefore, it is suggested that departments look at the demographic served and the caseload to determine the most appropriate training and technology necessary to efficiently and effectively work the cases presented.

Informing the Public

Departments would be well served to implement the area of forensic investigation into their Citizen Police Academies to help inform and educate the public as to the realities of forensic science available in their area. While there is often a fine line between educating the public and teaching criminals, it is important for the citizens served to feel safe and to know that law enforcement is capable of conducting a thorough investigation of a crime. Oftentimes this means informing the public about what the department is not able to do themselves but can depend upon other agencies or jurisdictions for assistance.

Educated Personnel

Perhaps the most important way in which departments can ensure that they are not caving into the CSI effect is to hire educated and trained personnel who have a background in forensic investigation.

Popular forensic television dramas have brought the science of forensic investigation into American's homes. When presented as such, the drama is not completely realistic. Law enforcement is left to react and respond to misconceptions relating to the bombardment of Hollywood myths about CSI. Departments should attempt through education and hiring to deal with the pressures to ensure that they continue to conduct their criminal investigations effectively and efficiently.

WRAP UP

Chapter Summary

The legal system within the United States demands proof beyond a reasonable doubt before the government is allowed to punish an alleged criminal. The criminal justice system must find ways to adapt to the increased expectations of those who are asked to determine guilt or innocence. For this to happen, it will take a major commitment to increasing law enforcement resources and will require equipping police and other investigating agencies with the most up-to-date forensic science equipment and technology. In addition, significant improvements will need to be made in the capacity of the nation's crime laboratories to reduce evidence backlogs and keep pace with increased demands for forensic analyses.

Courts must also find a way to address juror expectations. When scientific evidence is not relevant, prosecutors must find more convincing ways to explain the lack of relevance to jurors. Most importantly, prosecutors, defense lawyers, and judges should understand, anticipate, and address the fact that jurors enter the courtroom with potentially false preconceptions about the criminal justice system and the availability of scientific evidence (Shelton, 2007).

Successful CSI begins at the crime scene. If the investigator cannot recognize physical evidence or cannot properly preserve it, no amount of sophisticated laboratory instrumentation or technical expertise can rectify the situation. The crime scene investigator must implement a thorough and systematic methodology toward the documentation and processing of a crime scene in order to ensure a successful outcome to the investigation. While involved in this process, a crime scene investigator must remember that her or his underlying obligation is not to either the prosecution or the defense, but rather to the truth. Adherence to a scientific, legal, and systematic approach, in an unbiased manner, will ensure that the chain of custody for collected evidence will be intact, and will result in the subsequent admissibility of such evidence.

Review Questions

1. What is meant by the "CSI effect?"

2. How has modern forensic television drama affected the way in which police investigations are handled?

3. How has modern media impacted America's court system and processes?

4. What does voir dire mean?

5. What is the AAFS?

6. What is FEPAC and how does it relate to forensic education such as this text and perhaps even the course with which you are using this text?

Case Studies

1. Access the student companion Web site at go.learning.com/CrimeScene-Investigation2 and review the case of *King v. The State of New York*, #2007-009-171, Claim No. 88273; then consider that one result of the CSI effect is the belief that forensic investigators are infallible. Discuss the fiction of this belief.

2. Look up the case *Greer v. United States*, 697 A.2d 1207, 1210 (D.C. 1997) on the student companion Web site at go.jblearning.com/CrimeSceneInvestigation2 and investigate how the following statement supports the existence of the CSI effect: "In assessing whether the government has met its burden of proving guilt beyond a reasonable doubt, the jury may properly consider not only the evidence presented but also the lack of any evidence that the government, in the particular circumstances of the case, might reasonably be expected to present. For this reason, defense counsel may appropriately comment in closing argument on the failure of the government to present corroborative physical evidence."

References

American Academy of Forensic Sciences. (2012). Retrieved February 15, 2012, from http://www.aafs.org/colleges-universities

American Academy of Forensic Sciences. (2012). About AAFS. Retrieved from http://www.aafs.org/about-aafs

American Academy of Forensic Sciences. (2012). FEPAC. Retrieved from http://www.aafs.org/fepac

Appleby, T. (2006, November 22). When guilt or innocence depends on fact or fiction; CSI and similar shows are blurring the lines between television and reality. *The Globe and Mail* [Canada].

Bynum, R. (2008, April 2). Experts dubious of Georgia 3rd-grader plot. *USA Today*. Retrieved August 26, 2012, from http://www.usatoday.com/news/nation/2008-04-02-4018418455_x.htm

Daubert v. Merrell Dow Pharmaceuticals, Inc., (505 U.S. 579, 1993). Retrieved August 26, 2012, from http://caselaw.lp.findlaw.com/scripts/getcase.pl?court=us&vol=509&invol=579

DiPasquale, C. (2006). Beyond the smoking gun. *The Daily Record*, (September 8).

Dowler, K., Fleming, T., & Muzzatti, S. (2006). Constructing crime: Media, crime, and popular culture. *Canadian Journal of Criminology and Criminal Justice*, *48*(6).

Dutelle, A. (2006). The CSI effect and your department. *Law & Order*, *54*(5).

Greer v. United States, 697 A.2d 1207, 1210 (D.C. 1997).

Internet Movie Database (IMDb). (2012). CSI: Crime scene investigation. Retrieved February 15, 2012, from http://www.imdb.com/title/tt0247082/

Johnson, N. (1971, September 10). Federal Communications Commission. Life. Retrieved November 10,

2009, from http://worldcongress.org/wcfupdate/Archive02/wcf_update_228.htm

Kelly, C. (2007, September 16). Crime lab gets a shot in the arm. *The New York Times*. Retrieved July 19, 2009, from http://www.nytimes.com/2007/09/16/nyregion/nyregionspecial2/16mainwe.html?_r=0

King v. The State of New York, 2007-009-171, Claim No. 88273.

Kumho Tire Co. v. Carmichael, (526 U.S. 137, 1999). Retrieved July 19, 2009, from http://www.oyez.org/cases/1990-1999/1998/1998_97_1709

Milicia, J. (2006, February 4). CSI breeds killers who stick to script. *The Advertiser*.

Moscaritolo, M. (2005, September 28). TV sleuths put law under the microscope. *The Advertiser*.

Nielsen Co., A. C. (2008), Television statistics, compiled by TV-Free America. Retrieved August 1, 2009, from http://www.csun.edu/science/health/docs/tv&health.html

Podlas K. (2006, Winter) 'The *CSI* effect': Exposing the media myth. *Fordham Intellectual Property, Media, and Entertainment Law Journal*, (16)429–465.

Reville, W. (2006, November 22). 'CSI effect' tainting the real forensic evidence. *The Irish Times*.

Robertson, I. (2006, January 4). Courts feeling CSI effect; prosecutors say jurors want more forensic evidence than ever before because of hit television dramas. *The Toronto Sun*. Retrieved August 26, 2012, from http://www.thefreeradical.ca/television/courtsFeelCSIEffect.html

Schweitzer, N. J., & Saks, M. (2007, Spring). The CSI effect: Popular fiction about forensic science affects public expectations about real forensic science. *Jurimetrics*, (47)357.

Shelton, D. E. (2007, March). The 'CSI Effect': Does it really exist? *National Institute of Justice, 259*.

Willing, R. (2004, August 5). 'CSI effect' had juries wanting more evidence. *USA Today*. Retrieved July 19, 2009, from http://www.usatoday.com/news/nation/2004-08-05-csi-effect_x.htm

LEARNING OBJECTIVES

- Define and apply ethics in crime scene investigation.
- Understand a code of ethics and how it is incorporated into an agency.
- Understand the ethical concerns governing retention and disposition of crime scene artifacts.
- List and explain the history of important court decisions pertaining to expert witness testimony.
- Define and distinguish between an expert witness and a lay witness.
- Understand and research unethical practices involving crime scene work and forensic analysis, and provide arguments for why each is unethical.

Ethics in Crime Scene Investigation

> *I can discover facts, Watson, but I cannot change them.*
>
> Sir Arthur Conan Doyle (1859–1930)
> Sherlock Holmes, in *The Problem of Thor Bridge*

KEY TERMS

Code of Ethics
Credentials
Daubert Standard
Ethics

Expert Witness
Federal Rules of Evidence
  (FRE)
Frye Test

Hearsay
Morals
Perjury
Values

What Are Ethics?

Theodore Roosevelt said, "To educate a man in mind but not in morals is to create a menace to society" (Roosevelt, 1899). It is for precisely this reason that the topic of ethics is discussed within this text as a vital component of CSI. Public servants, of whom a crime scene investigator is one, must not only do technical things correctly, they must do ethically correct things. Everyone encounters ethical dilemmas. The question is when and whether we are ready for them.

Before the topic of how ethics plays a role in CSI can be discussed, there first must be an analysis of the meaning associated with the term. **Ethics** is the study of moral standards and how they affect conduct. The word stems from the Greek word *ethos*, which emphasizes the perfection of the individual and the community in which he or she is defined (Foster, 2003).

Often the term *ethics* is confused with the terms *values* and *morals*. These terms actually have quite different meanings, although all three terms are interrelated. **Values** are beliefs of an individual or group, for or against something in which there is some emotional investment. Typically, values are the rules by which an individual or group makes decisions as to what is right or wrong. **Morals**, on the other hand, can have a more widely reaching social acceptance than values. For example, a person is judged by societal standards of morality or immorality (right or wrong). Ethics are typically codified by a group of people or organization, and are not necessarily associated with societal norms. One can have professional ethics but seldom does one hear about having professional morals. Ethics are internally defined and self-imposed; morals relate to how individuals should behave but can be determined from personal conscience and/or common standards of justice so that the individual is encouraged to do good and be decent according to commonly accepted societal standards of justice. Despite the differences in meaning between these three terms, this text intertwines them and encourages the reader to incorporate values and morals into his or her personal ethical decisions.

Revisiting the Basics

Nearly all people acknowledge the importance of ethics. However, unfortunately few really understand ethics as well as they think that they do or as well as they should. Ethics can be meaningfully discussed and applied only when it is fully understood. This understanding requires a periodic revisiting of the basics. So, what then is ethics about?

Ethics is about right and wrong. John Stuart Mill addressed this in his work *Utilitarianism* (1863) when he wrote, "We do not call anything wrong, unless we mean to imply that a person ought to be punished in some way or other for doing it; if not by law, by the opinion of his fellow creatures; if not by opinion, by the reproaches of his own conscience" (Mills, 1863, p. 48).

Ethics is about virtue and vice. "Vice, the opposite of virtue, shows us more clearly what virtue is. Justice becomes more obvious when we have injustice to compare it to" (Quintilian, *Institutio Oratoria*).

Ethics is about benefit and harm. "The two essential ingredients in the sentiment of justice are the desire to punish a person who has done harm, and the knowledge or belief that there is some definite individual or individuals to whom harm has been done" (Mill, 1863).

While ethics encompasses all of these concepts, it is more simply about principle, "fixed, universal rules of right conduct that are contingent on neither time nor culture nor circumstance" (Foster, 2003, pp. 30–37). And yet, it is also about character, "the traits, qualities, and established reputation that define who one is and what one stands for in the eyes of others" (Foster, 2003). Lastly, it is about example, that is, "an established pattern of conduct worthy of emulation" (Foster, 2003, pp. 30–37).

Ethics Involves What?

There is more to ethics than simply knowing its definition. It is just as important to know what is involved in its makeup. Ethics is the way values are practiced. As such, it is both a process of inquiry (deciding how to decide) and a code of conduct (a set of standards governing behavior).

To think well is to think critically. Critical thinking, the conscious use of reason, stands clearly apart from other ways of grasping truth or confronting choice, such as impulse or habit. Impulse is nothing more than an unreflective spontaneity, a mind on autopilot. On the other hand, habit is programmed repetition. Similar to muscle memory, it applies to behavior that is repetitive without thinking about it.

Therefore, "the object of critical thinking is to achieve a measure of objectivity to counteract or diminish the subjective bias that experience and socialization bestow on us all" (Foster, 2003, pp. 30–37). This is imperative because, "when we are dealing with matters of ethical concern, the well-being of someone or something beyond ourselves is always at stake" (Foster, 2003, pp. 30–37).

The Road to Unethical Behavior

Scandals can be prevented. They result from an evolution of predictable and preventable circumstances (Trautman, 2006). When an individual makes a conscious decision to commit a tiny indiscretion, it becomes exponentially easier for that individual to then rationalize his or her behavior and decisions and continue down the road of unethical decisions. This is sometimes what is referred to as "traversing down the slippery slope."

The most effective solutions to corruption must be instilled with straightforwardness and honesty. The following suggestions may be implemented during a new employee's training in order to minimize the instances of corruption and unethical behavior within the scope of crime scene investigations:

1. Ensure thorough background investigations of all employees.
2. Ensure a high-quality field training program for new crime scene investigators.
3. Ensure consistent and fair accountability for employee actions.

4. Conduct effective ethics training.

5. Implement an effective employee intervention process.

Ethics in Crime Scene Investigation

The majority of forensic specialists realize that it is illegal to remove objects from a crime scene without proper authorization. It is, however, legal in the majority of jurisdictions to turn around and sell crime scene–related evidence (including photographs and mug shots) for a profit, but the integrity of the police force must be upheld at all times. Crime scene investigators and

VIEW FROM AN EXPERT

An officer's integrity is possibly the single most important asset they have as a keeper of the peace. Police deal with the worst society has to offer and over time they can become desensitized to unethical behavior. Further, temptations are a constant to police.

Since the mid 1980s law enforcement agencies across the country have been mired in a succession of publicized unethical behavior. These behaviors threaten law enforcement's effectiveness. Society's trust of police is needed to carry out the police mission of making society safe.

The methods commonly used to guide law enforcement behavior are codes of conduct and codes of ethics, but these are broad principles and provide only general guidelines. Without clearly written guidelines to guide the conduct of law enforcement personnel, ethical standards are left to personal interpretation. Police are given discretion to perform their duties because no set of laws and regulations can dictate how to act in every circumstance.

Without clear concise directions that dictate how every officer is to act in every situation, personnel are left to their own personal interpretations of how they are expected to behave given varying circumstances. The culture of an agency, personal beliefs, and feedback from peers all have an ability to guide a police officer's decision in making ethical choices.

Unethical behavior of law enforcement officers occurs throughout the United States. In 2009, Heinzmann reported misconduct complaints against the Chicago Police force were up 19%. The complaints jumped from about 2,300 complaints every three months to almost 2,800 or almost 1,000 a month. In October 1998, an eight-month investigation of the Washington, DC police department led officials to charge 65 officers with various acts of misconduct. Earlier that year 44 officers from Cleveland, Ohio were arrested and charged with conspiracy to distribute cocaine. In 1997 more than 300 cases were overturned in Philadelphia when police officers were charged with lying under oath. In 1998, 20 police officers were accused of protecting a brothel in exchange for sex. Officials believe this ongoing misconduct may have existed for 15 years (Police Corruption, 2004).

officers of the law thus must maintain the spirit of the law as well as the letter of the law. By preventing even the appearance of impropriety, the professional integrity of the police is maintained. Consider the damage a defense lawyer could do to an expert's reputation if it became known that the expert sold items obtained from former crime scenes.

While police and forensic specialists are ethically obliged to preserve the integrity of their investigation and their agency's reputations, the American Academy of Forensic Sciences (AAFS) provides no guidelines for crime scene ethics or the retention of items from former crime scenes. It is suggested that guidelines are "necessary to define acceptable behavior relating to removing, keeping or selling artifacts, souvenirs or teaching specimens from former crime scenes, where such activities are not illegal, to prevent potential conflicts of interest and appearance of impropriety" (Rogers, 2004, p 308). Once items have been legally obtained as part of a criminal

More recent examples of police corruption have been reported. Justnews.com (2010) gave an account of a veteran Florida Trooper who was arrested and plead guilty to writing fake traffic tickets. Prosecutors found 85 cases in which the state trooper wrote traffic tickets to drivers for offenses they did not commit. Drivers' licenses were suspended when the drivers that had been issued tickets by this trooper did not pay the tickets they did not know existed.

Wlwt.com (2010) reported that a Milford, Ohio police officer audiotaped himself having sex with the town's mayor while he was on duty. The investigation that followed the report of his unethical behavior revealed this was somewhat of a common occurrence. The officer only taped one of the occurrences.

More challenging issues of unethical behavior have also made the news. In July 2010, controversy resulted when the Detroit Chief of Police was fired for several issues with the city's mayor. One main issue was the Chief dating a lieutenant in his department. The University of Michigan ethicist, John Chamberlin, believes when an administrator dates a subordinate everyone between them in the chain of command is implicated. This is contrary to Jack Rinchich, president of the National Association of Chiefs of Police, who believes an officer should not be faulted for a personal matter that is not covered by policy (Goodman, 2010).

An officer from Stoughton, Massachusetts was honored for saving someone from a burning car and received additional recognition for his involvement in catching an accused killer. Shortly thereafter, the same officer resigned after fellow officers reported the officer had attended a strip club while on duty and in uniform. The officers that reported the recently honored officer attending the strip club were recognized by the administration for their work in attempting to change the reputation of the department.

Then there is the videotape that surfaced in 1991 of police officers beating Rodney King. This video was possibly one of the most damaging events regarding the public trust of police. Another highly publicized lack of officers' ethics was the brutal attack on 30-year-old Haitian immigrant, Abner Louima, in Brooklyn, New York, during 1997. Police officers reportedly beat Louima while transporting him to the police station and then ripped his bladder and punctured his lower intestine by sodomizing him with a night stick. They also broke his front teeth by shoving the night stick into his mouth. In 1999, a 22-year-old African Street vendor, Amaou Diallo was shot at 41 times by police as he stood in the entrance of his apartment.

Why do some police officers commit flagrant ethical violations and others with the same opportunities do not? Until recently, research on this subject centered on the learned behavior of the individuals who committed the unethical behavior. In the last 20 years, however, some research has targeted organizational behavior. In his 1996 book, Thomas Barker wrote that police culture is a major contributor to police misconduct. He stated a three-pronged approach is needed to control police corruption and misconduct. The prongs include decreasing the opportunity, undermining peer group support for unethical behavior, and increasing the risk of engaging in these types of behaviors. He further stated, "Police corruption exists only where it is tolerated by the police officers themselves" (p. 77).

In a recent study the author examined the influences and priority of influencing factors that exist in police administrators when making decisions to provide resources for training on ethical behavior. Identified by police administrators as influential factors when determining to expend resources were conduct, ethics, attitudes, and training. The most common factor

investigation, their disposition is generally guided by local agency policies. Some items, by law, must be returned to the owner, while other items may be deemed contraband or too dangerous for release. If the owner cannot be located, the item may be classified as "found" property and thus subject to disposition options ranging from destruction, to auction, to conversion for educational and training purposes.

When the law is explicit, ethical decisions are not always required to guide behavior, but the variety of crime scene types and circumstances facing forensic investigators produces many ambiguous situations. Because her or his skills and knowledge of the criminal investigation may establish the innocence or guilt of a defendant, professional ethics and integrity are essential to a crime scene investigator's effort. Their education, training, experience, skills, and opinions on technical matters often are of considerable importance during a criminal investigation. For this reason, all forensic practitioners owe a duty to the truth. They may never be biased for or against a suspect in an investigation. The forensic practitioner's sole obligation is to serve the aims of justice. What is important is that the forensic practitioner conducts an investigation in a thorough, competent, unbiased manner. Forensic personnel have an obligation not to overstate or understate scientific findings. As experts in the criminal justice system, they are placed in positions of authority and responsibility.

To ensure ethical behavior, veracity of testimony, and professionalism among individuals engaged within the field of crime scene investigations, some departments and organizations identified in this research, however, was the culture of the organization. Fifty-nine percent of all responses given by those interviewed referenced culture as the ultimate factor in determining the level, amount, and style of training they provided to their personnel regarding ethics.

In the synthesis process of all the data collected in the research project, culture emerged as the final meaning of the data. Culture was identified in the research as being more important to guiding the behavior of personnel than ethics-based training. All participants agreed that training is important to guiding their personnel, but overwhelmingly discussed the reinforcement of a strong organizational culture as the essence of guiding personnel behavior.

Culture is rapidly being identified as one of the most important elements of police behavior. Some participants in this research referenced training programs as a method to help guide their personnel in making appropriate decisions. Other participants described actions and attitudes to promote healthy and strong behavior. Still other participants relied on guidance from state regulations to determine the level, amount, and style of ethics-based training for their personnel. The key element, however, in the research project identified organizational culture as the primary factor administrators use in the guidance of their personnel's behavior.

Randy Taylor, D.M.
Chief of Police, Clarksdale, Arizona

Courtesy of Randy Taylor, D.M., Chief of Police, Clarkdale, AZ.

have implemented a **code of ethics** that an employee must sign and agree to function by as terms of their employment or membership. This code lists what the department or organization believes are acceptable behaviors, professional expectations, and values to which their employees should adhere. Failure to comply with the code can result in dismissal or removal of membership and certification. An example of one of these codes of ethics for CSI personnel is on the homepage of the International Association of Identification (IAI, 2009). Examples of codes of ethics for various crime scene professionals are on that Web site as well (http://theiai.org/).

Personnel involved with the processing of a crime scene have professional and moral obligations to work ethically and professionally. Legal, scientific, and ethical values can become tangled in the courtroom; however, the most important aspect of the trial is that the guilty are convicted and the innocent are exonerated (Fish, Miller, & Braswell, 2007). The obligation to the truth thus is paramount above all else.

The crime scene investigator must be professionally neutral to be effective. He or she must remain objective and all his or her actions must be unimpeachable as they follow the proscribed protocol at every crime scene. Acts of commission (intentional) and omission (unintentional) are not permitted and may in fact be criminal offenses in themselves.

No crime scene investigator wants to live with the possibility that a guilty person escapes prosecution or that an innocent person is punished based on his or her actions or inactions.

Therefore, the investigator should do everything possible to preserve the chain of custody, take all necessary precautions to prevent cross-contamination or deterioration of physical evidence, and leave the forensic analysis up to the criminalists and courts. It is up to the judicial system—not the crime scene personnel—to weigh the evidence and come to a determination of guilt or innocence (Fish et al., 2007).

Expert Witnesses

Specially trained personnel such as crime scene investigators, forensic scientists, criminalists, forensic technicians, and identification technicians collect and examine physical evidence from crime scenes. These individuals are often called upon to testify as expert witnesses. An **expert witness** is someone who is called to answer questions on the stand in a court of law in order to provide specialized information relevant to the case being tried. Because scientific principles relating to physical evidence are often beyond the knowledge of lay people, courts permit persons with specialized training and skills to appear in court to explain and interpret scientific evidence to juries. A person can be considered an "expert" when they have sufficient skills, knowledge, or experience in their field to help the "trier of fact" to determine the truth. It therefore is the duty of the expert witness to educate the jury and provide testimony using terminology that is easily explainable and will not be misunderstood (Fish et al., 2007). Clarity, simplicity, and honesty are essential elements of expert witness testimony. It is suggested that supervisors review reports and conclusions with an unbiased attention to detail to ensure that the paperwork submitted is clear, concise, and accurate. Witnesses cannot deliberately omit relevant facts or encourage incorrect conclusions; these are distortions of the facts. Overstatements of the facts or a suggestion that an individual is guilty will cost an expert witness their integrity.

History of Expert Testimony in U.S. Courts

But what exactly qualifies an individual as an expert? And when is such testimony admissible? There has been great debate and much litigation pertaining to what should be allowed as "expert testimony" and what should qualify an individual to be considered as an expert within court. To answer these questions, we must look back at a few historical rulings.

The Frye Test

In 1923, a D.C. circuit court offered a ruling pertaining to the admissibility of testimony associated with a systolic blood pressure deception test, an early precursor to the modern polygraph. In this case, a Federal Court of Appeals ruling [*Frye v. U.S.*, 293 F. 1013 (D.C. Cir. 1923)] held that evidence could be admitted in court only if "the thing from which the deduction is made" is "sufficiently established to have gained general acceptance in the particular field in which it belongs." Because in 1923 such a blood pressure test was not widely known about or even accepted among scientists, the court ruled that testimony associated with such a process could not be used. Therefore, according to this ruling, if an expert is to testify on a specific matter or area of science, that matter or area must be "generally accepted" by the relevant scientific community. This has come to be known as the **Frye test**.

Federal Rules of Evidence

On January 2, 1975, the **Federal Rules of Evidence (FRE)** became federal law. These rules were developed to govern the introduction of evidence within proceedings, both civil and criminal, in U.S. federal courts. While they did not specifically apply to suits brought within state courts, the rules of many states have been closely modeled upon the provisions found within the FRE. The FRE is continually updated and continues to be the governing rules for federal courts. Of specific interest is rule 702 of the FRE that states:

> If scientific, technical, or other specialized knowledge will assist the trier of fact to understand the evidence or to determine a fact in issue, a witness qualified as an expert by knowledge, skill, experience, training, or education, may testify thereto in the form of an opinion or otherwise, if (1) the testimony is based upon sufficient facts or data, (2) the testimony is the product of reliable principles and methods, and (3) the witness has applied the principles and methods reliably to the facts of the case (Expert Pages, 2008).

The underlying difference from the Frye standard, a ruling made over 50 years earlier, therefore was no incorporation of a "general acceptance standard." Instead, three provisions of the FRE governed admission of expert testimony in court:

- Scientific knowledge. Nothing is known with absolute certainty; however, the "knowledge" had to be arrived at by use of the scientific method.
- Assist the trier of fact. The scientific knowledge offered must be an aid in assisting either a jury or a judge in understanding the evidence or determining a fact in issue in the case.
- The judge makes the threshold determination. Such an assessment is meant to focus on methodology and principles, not the ultimate conclusions generated. It is left up to the judge to determine if the reasoning or methodology upon which the testimony is based is properly applied to the facts in issue.

The Daubert Standard

In 1993 the U.S. Supreme Court made another important ruling regarding the admissibility of expert witnesses' testimony during federal legal proceedings. The case was *Daubert v. Merrell Dow Pharmaceuticals*, 509 U.S. 579 (1993).

In the Daubert ruling, the court held that federal trial judges are the "gatekeepers" of scientific evidence. Under the **Daubert standard**, trial judges must evaluate whether testimony is both "relevant" and "reliable." This resulted in a two-pronged test of admissibility.

1. Relevancy: whether or not the expert's testimony is relevant to the facts of the case and directly pertains to the matter in question.

2. Reliability: The expert must have derived their conclusions from the scientific method.

With Daubert, the court supplanted the older Frye test's "general acceptance" standard. Because this applied to federal cases only and each state is permitted to create unique rules of evidence for use within its courts, the Frye test, or a variation thereof, may still be used in those states that have chosen not to adopt Daubert.

Kumho Tire Co. v. Carmichael

In July 1993, Patrick Carmichael was driving his minivan when the front tire blew out. This led to a vehicular accident resulting in one of the passengers in the vehicle dying and others being severely injured. The resulting lawsuit, filed by Carmichael, claimed that the tire was defective and the defect caused the accident. Carmichael's case rested largely on testimony from a tire failure expert. However, under Daubert, certain factors contribute to the reliability, and hence the admissibility, of expert testimony, one of which is the validity of the expert's methods. In the Carmichael case, the district court found the tire expert's methods not to adhere to the scientifically valid standard, and thus excluded the testimony.

In this ruling, the court looked at both the Daubert standard and the FRE for its ruling. The court noted that the line between "scientific" and "technical" knowledge is not always discernible. As such, the court held that the gatekeeping function set forth in the Daubert ruling applied to all expert testimony detailed in FRE 702, because there was no "convincing need" to draw a distinction between "scientific" and "technical" knowledge; both kinds of knowledge normally would be outside the grasp of the average juror.

Qualifying an Expert Witness

Usually when one talks about experience, the term **credentials** is used. Often this refers to a certificate, letter, experience, or anything that provides authentication for a claim or qualifies somebody to do something. However, as pertains to forensic and crime scene–related work, credentials as an expert will be established by the court through questioning pertaining to the witness's education, training, and experience. The ability and competence of the witness must be demonstrated through testimony relating to college degrees, continuing education, attendance at conferences, publications, ongoing research, and a variety of other possibilities that show rigor and knowledge within the area of expertise under consideration.

Unlike nonexpert witnesses, once credentialing as an expert has been established, an expert witness can provide opinions based on the outcomes of the examinations and the significance of their findings. Nonexperts who state opinions as part of their testimony will have such statements ruled as inadmissible due to them being classified as **hearsay**. Hearsay is unfounded information that is heard from other people. However, the court allows experts to state opinions due to their ability to assist the court in better comprehending the topic under consideration. In the case of an expert rendering an opinion on their findings, the opinion has a foundation in the expert's training and experience, and is not an arbitrary opinion with no factual relevance. It should be mentioned that simply because there is this ability to state an opinion, it does not mean that it is always a legal possibility. FRE Rule 703 provides for an explanation of the bases of opinion testimony relating to expert witnesses.

The facts or data in the particular case upon which an expert bases an opinion or inference may be those perceived by or made known to the expert at or before the hearing. If of a type reasonably relied upon by experts in the particular field in forming opinions or inferences upon the subject, the facts or data need not be admissible in evidence in order for the opinion or inference to be admitted. Facts or data that are otherwise inadmissible shall not be disclosed to the jury by the proponent of the opinion or inference unless the court determines that their probative value in assisting the jury to evaluate the expert's opinion substantially outweighs their prejudicial effect (Expert Pages, 2008).

Although it is not possible for an expert to render an opinion with absolute certainty, as an advocate of truth, the expert must base opinions on a reasonable scientific certainty. An expert must be confident in their statements made within a court of law. If they are found to be contradictory, or if it is pointed out that the witness intentionally lied or misrepresented the facts, they could be charged with perjury. **Perjury** is the telling of a lie within a court of law by somebody who has taken an oath to tell the truth.

As an expert witness, a crime scene investigator must remember that her or his integrity and professionalism are open for inspection. Each must be familiar with the scope of her or his actions and knowledge, and know where their level of expertise ends. When subpoenaed to testify as an expert witness, the way others perceive the expert is more important than the way experts perceive themselves. Once credibility as an expert witness is compromised, it is nearly impossible to recover in court (Rogers, 2004).

Issues with Ethics in Forensics and Crime Scene Work

A search of recent cases involving mismanagement, improper documentation, unethical testimony, and improper analysis of physical evidence is bound to bring the searcher a plethora of cases associated with such matters. Some of the most notorious names associated with these types of cases center upon those involved with the physical analysis and subsequent testimony about the physical evidence in a case. Names such as Joyce Gilcrest and Fred Zane, and locations such as the Washington state and Tucson, Arizona crime labs are infamous because they made media headlines. But for each person and laboratory that made a headline, there are dozens that did not. With only a cursory amount of research, one will find that ethical transgressions occur at all steps in the evidentiary process including: crime scene security, physical evidence collection and documentation, physical evidence processing and analysis, testimony regarding all aforementioned phases, and final evidence disposition. Ethics—or lack thereof—permeate all areas of the criminal investigative process. They are not isolated to particular geographic regions or departments. Instead, ethics are a product of training and personal values that are present in any setting.

As one can see, ethical issues by no means are isolated to only large or small agencies. Ethical issues transcend departmental size, demographic makeup, and job title. Examples of unethical behavior can be pulled from all areas of the criminal investigative process and from all levels of rank.

An examination of unethical issues relating to crime scene work also shows a variety of motivations for committing such transgressions. Sometimes the motivation is greed, and other times it is power, status, or promotion. But often it is simply a case of the individual forgetting that their obligation is to the truth and not to one side or the other. Many times individuals feel as though they are on the prosecutor's team, and so failing to present testimony or physical evidence and analysis of evidence that might assist the prosecutorial team would be tantamount to letting their team down. As addressed previously, such instances can be avoided by a thorough background investigation before hiring an employee, and proper ethical training, correct management practices, and frequent refresher trainings after they have been hired.

RIPPED FROM THE HEADLINES

Colorado Detective Indicted on Eight Counts of Perjury

The cries of "innocence" by an incarcerated individual and a six-year investigation determined that the murder case against Tim Masters, for the death of Peggy Hettrick, in Fort Collins, Colorado, was built on lies fabricated by a detective responsible for the case. Lt. Jim Broderick, then a detective assigned to the homicide case, was indicted on eight counts of perjury by a Colorado grand jury. Each perjury count carried a penalty of two to six years in prison and up to a $500,000 fine. One of the perjury counts related to an FBI profile that Broderick presented as evidence against Hettrick's killer. An investigation revealed that the profile had been manufactured by the detective himself and that the profile in no part originated from the FBI. Other counts of perjury related to allegations that the detective lied about the presence of physical evidence at or near the scene of the crime. The two lead prosecutors who presented the case against Masters to a jury in 1999 (Jolene Blair and Terry Gilmore) were formally reprimanded by an office of the Colorado Supreme Court in 2008 for their failure to ensure that Masters' original defense lawyers had all the information that police had gathered during their investigation. They were subsequently voted out of office in the fall of 2010. Masters' conviction was overturned by a visiting judge in 2008 and he was paid a $10 million settlement by the City of Fort Collins for his wrongful incarceration.

Information from: "A Look Back: Tim Masters Case: Peggy Hettrick's 1987 murder remains mystery." (2012, November 12). The Coloradoan. http://www.coloradoan.com/article/99999999/NEWS01/71107031/A-Look-Back-Tim-Masters-Case.

WRAP UP

Chapter Summary

Every time that a crime scene investigator responds to a crime scene, the potential for presenting the actions and observations documented at the scene within a courtroom exists. A crime scene investigator's reputation is based on the veracity of their work and the integrity of their actions. Their actions—or lack thereof—are the voice of the victim. While justice may be blind, investigators must present objective and unbiased testimony that clearly and accurately recreates the crime scene for the judge and jury. A crime scene investigator's actions should not detract from the credibility of the physical evidence. His or her behavior or testimony should not intentionally tarnish the voice of the evidence. As Paul Kirk (1953) said of a crime scene investigation,

> Wherever he steps, whatever he touches, whatever he leaves, even unconsciously, will serve as silent evidence against him. Not only his fingerprints or his footprints, but also his hair, the fibers from his clothes, the glass he breaks, the tool marks he leaves, the paint he scratches, the blood or semen that he deposits or collects—all of these and more bear mute witness against him. This is evidence that does not forget. It is not confused by the excitement of the moment. It is not absent because human witnesses are. It is factual evidence. Physical evidence cannot be wrong: it cannot perjure itself; it cannot be wholly absent. Only its interpretation can err. Only human failure to find it, study and understand it can diminish its value.
> (Kirk, P. L. (1953). *Crime investigation; physical evidence and the police laboratory.* New York: Interscience.)

Review Questions

1. Explain the term ethics.

2. What is a code of ethics?

3. What is meant by the term hearsay?

4. How is an expert witness different from a layperson within a court of law?

5. What does it take for a person to qualify as an expert witness?

6. Discuss the Frye test's direct impact on forensic testimony and evidence.

7. The Daubert standard is used by many courts today as a way to ensure the authenticity and veracity of testimony and forensic analysis. In this ruling, judges were given the role of _____.

8. The Daubert standard resulted in a two-pronged test of admissibility, which means that testimony must be both _____ and _____.

9. How did Rule 702 of the Federal Rules of Evidence (FRE) impact expert testimony? Does it apply to all courts?

10. _____ is the telling of a lie within a court of law by somebody who has taken an oath to tell the truth.

Case Studies

1. Look up the following case regarding missing drug-related evidence at an Arizona police crime lab on the student companion Web site at go.jblearning.com/CrimeSceneInvestigation2. Based upon the chapter reading, how did ethics play a part in this incident? Explain how this situation could have been avoided.

2. Access the following Web page regarding evidence-related issues on the student companion Web site at go.jblearning.com/CrimeSceneInvestigation2. Choose a headline and summarize the issues at hand and how they could have been avoided.

References

Barker, T. (1996). *Police ethics: Crisis in law enforcement.* Springfield, IL: Charles C. Thomas Publisher, Ltd.

Daubert v. Merrell Dow Pharmaceuticals, 509 U.S. 579 (1993).

Expert Pages. (2008). *The leading directory of expert witnesses* (homepage). Retrieved July 20, 2009, from http://www.expertpages.com.

Fish, J. T., Miller, L. S., & Braswell M. C. (2007). *Crime scene investigation: An introduction.* New York: LexisNexis Anderson Publishing.

Fisher, B. A. J. (2004). *Techniques of crime scene investigation* (7th ed.). Boca Raton, FL: CRC Press.

Foster, G. D. (2003). Ethics: Time to revisit the basics. In J. P. West & E. M. Berman (Eds.), *The ethics edge, Second edition.* Washington, DC: International City/County Management Association. Originally published in *The Humanist*, 63(2).

Frye v. U.S., 293 F. 1013 (D.C. Cir. 1923).

International Association for Identification. (2009). Code of ethics for certified crime scene personnel. Retrieved July 20, 2009, from http://theiai.org/certifications/crime_scene/ethics.php

Kirk, P. L. (1953). *Crime investigation; physical evidence and the police laboratory.* New York: Interscience.

Madura, D. (2012). A look back: Tim Masters case, *Fort Collins Coloradoan.* Retrieved April 28, 2012, from http://www.coloradoan.com/article/99999999/NEWS01/71107031/A-Look-Back-Tim-Masters-Case.

Mill, J. S. (1863). *Utilitarianism.* Retrieved August 26, 2012, from http://www.utilitarianism.com/mill1.htm

Quintilian, M. F. *Instituto oratorio.* (posted 2006). Retrieved July 20, 2009, from http://penelope.uchicago.edu/Thayer/E/Roman/Texts/Quintilian/Institutio_Oratoria/home.html

Rogers, T. (2004, March). Crime scene ethics: Souvenirs, teaching, materials, and artifacts. *Journal of Forensic Sciences*, 49(2), 307–311.

Roosevelt, T. (1899, April 10). Speech before the Hamilton Club, Chicago.

Trautman, N. (2006). The corruption continuum: How law enforcement organizations become corrupt (avoiding public scandal and corruption). In J. P. West & E. M. Berman (Eds.), *The ethics edge, Second edition.* Washington, DC: International City/County Management Association. Originally published in *Public Management Magazine* (June 1, 2000).

© McMac/ShutterStock, Inc.

LEARNING OBJECTIVES

- Understand the primary duties of a first responder to a crime scene.
- Identify the considerations involved with establishing a crime scene perimeter.
- Describe what is meant by transient evidence.
- Articulate when loss or destruction of evidence at a crime scene is acceptable.
- Explain multi-level containment.

CHAPTER

4

Duties of the First Responder to the Crime Scene

> *Crime is common. Logic is rare. Therefore it is upon the logic rather than upon the crime that you should dwell.*
>
> Sir Arthur Conan Doyle (1859–1930)
> Sherlock Holmes, *The Adventure of the Copper Beeches*

KEY TERMS

Command Post
In Situ
Mechanical Loss

Multi-level Containment
Perimeter
Primary Scene

Secondary Scene
Transient Evidence

The First Responder

Patrol officers, firefighters, and emergency medical personnel are usually first to arrive at the scene of a crime, and are thus referred to as *first responders*. Crime scenes are dynamic, rapidly evolving environments. Because of this, the initial actions—or inactions—of first responders can dictate the success or failure of investigative efforts.

First responders have two primary duties:

1. **Preservation of life**. The primary duty assigned to an officer responding to a crime scene is to render it safe and provide for emergency services for those in need.

2. **Secure and preserve the crime scene and associated evidence**. By effectively securing the crime scene, the first responder will prevent the destruction or diminished value of physical evidence.

Determining Jurisdiction

Prior to entering a crime scene, a first responder must ensure that he or she has the legal right to do so. As discussed earlier in this text, a search warrant or other legal right may be necessary in order for a crime scene to be properly entered and evidence obtained. Simply because an officer was dispatched to an area does not mean it was necessarily within the department's legal jurisdiction. An officer must be familiar with their assigned district, and if unsure of jurisdiction, such matters should be addressed before continuing with an investigation (Fish, Miller, & Braswell, 2007).

While city limits, county lines, or even nautical boundaries are invisible lines that do not impede an officer's ability to carry out his or her responsibilities, their legal significance is of paramount importance within the confines of a courtroom. There are numerous documented cases where jurisdictional issues or disagreements regarding which agency should be involved in conducting an investigation have lead to countless number of delays and the dismissal of charges because of technicalities not associated with the crime scene investigation itself. Such situations can be avoided by ensuring that the officer is within her or his jurisdictional domain and that any agencies that need to be notified have been before beginning a detailed crime scene investigation.

Approaching the Scene

A first responder must arrive at the scene safely if they are to have a chance to perform their necessary duties. It therefore is incumbent upon the officer to approach the scene in a controlled and safe manner. All movements should be prompt, deliberate, and calm. While it might appear to an outsider that police race with lights and sirens to each and every call, this is in fact a rare event. An emergency response (lights and sirens) is a very hazardous event that requires great skill and awareness. If an officer is injured, or injures another en route to a call, he or she defeats the purpose of the mission: to arrive safely to ensure the safety of whomever is calling for the police response.

Some police agencies have very specific policies for uniformed personnel concerning their duties and responsibilities at the crime scene. An officer should be familiar with these policies and execute their job to the best of their ability (Fisher, 2004). The duties of the first officer who appears at a crime scene are the same, regardless of his or her rank. The duties are also the same regardless of the type of crime scene.

Actions of the First Responder upon Arrival

Maximize the Safety of the Scene

The officer should be observant of any persons, vehicles, possible evidence, and overall conditions of the scene. The officer's approach to the scene should be in such a manner that it will reduce the risk of harm to her or himself, while maximizing the safety of potential victims, witnesses, and other persons in the area. If suspects or dangerous persons or situations are at the scene, those are the first priority.

Guide EMS to the Injured and Preserve the Scene

After controlling any suspects, persons, and/or any potential hazardous situations on scene, the officer's next responsibility is to ensure that emergency medical services (EMS) are provided to injured persons. Officers should make efforts to guide medical personnel to the victim by an indirect pathway established to reduce scene alteration and contamination. The indirect pathway established by the first responder should be used by both arriving medical personnel and investigative personnel to reduce potential contamination and destruction of evidence. It is suggested that such a pathway, as well as the entrance and exit to a crime scene, be established that is not consistent with the most likely path and entrance/exit of the suspect(s). This will ensure diminished evidence destruction.

If there is potential evidence in the proximity of a victim, officers should point out such evidence to medical personnel, and request that they minimize contact with such evidence. An example would be to cut around bullet holes or stab marks in clothing. Officers who are not actively involved in lifesaving efforts should concentrate on documenting the movement of persons or items during the lifesaving efforts. However, if through the efforts of saving a life, evidence is lost, this is what is referred to as **mechanical loss**. This is an accepted loss of physical evidence and is easily articulated within court. If a life is saved and evidence is lost, that is acceptable. It is far better to have saved a life and lost evidence than it is to save evidence

Physically Strong and Mentally Awake

A career in law enforcement is physically and mentally demanding on the human body. Working long shifts under stressful situations will wipe out the weak quickly. In the future, are your goals to be a detective with a local police or sheriff organization or do you prefer to travel and investigate larger scale crimes with a federal agency? Maybe you dream of becoming a commander or police chief, a homicide detective with a large city department, or a tactical operator on the FBI's elite Hostage Rescue Team. No matter what your goals are, a little preparation and planning can assist you in reaching them.

One of the most overlooked areas that contributes to a successful and safe career in law enforcement is fitness. The long hours of shift work, undercover operations, and surveillance will take their tolls. Give yourself the upper hand though and stay fit. Training on emotional survival and related topics all stress the same point: physical fitness is a necessary part of living a healthy, well-balanced career as a law enforcement officer.

If you want to do well at this job, you need to have a desire to delve into the specifics of any given situation and avoid accepting things at face value. Prepare yourself mentally by questioning how things appear to be and work hard to expose the truth. Oftentimes things will be intentionally constructed in order to distract you from reality. Only by strengthening your mind will you be prepared to outsmart those that hope to deceive you.

Another key component is composition. Being able to compose accurate and detail-orientated reports that flow well is critical. It will be necessary for you to tell stories of what

and lose a life. If a person dies, their visual and testimonial evidence dies with them. Gross incompetence or neglect are not acceptable reasons for losing or destroying evidence.

Protect the Integrity of the Crime Scene

Once these responsibilities have been fulfilled, concern is shifted toward the integrity of the scene. The scene must be protected until all physical evidence has been documented and collected. The first officer on the scene must attempt to "freeze" the scene as closely as possible to the condition in which it was found. This means that no one is allowed to needlessly move about or alter the scene. Persons present—victims or witnesses—must be isolated or removed from the scene so that they do not purposely or inadvertently alter or destroy evidence (Wisconsin DOJ, 2009). Suspects should be kept out of the scene in order to avoid scene contamination. If a suspect were to be brought back to a scene, and later DNA, fingerprints, hairs, and/or other evidence were collected in the course of the investigation, there would be an innocent explanation for their deposit.

you encounter and what happens at incidents you respond to daily. You will also be expected to explain why you made specific decisions. These reports are always read by people in higher pay grades than you. If they like what they read and see how well you can compose your reports, you will stand out and better your chances of getting to where you want to be in your law enforcement career!

The final key to becoming a well-rounded officer is your people skills. Police officers speak with all types of people in many different situations every single day. Having strong communication skills will only help further your goals, whether that is obtaining a confession from a suspect, mediating a neighborhood dispute, or consoling the victim of a crime. You will be expected to relate to those you come into contact with no matter what context or circumstances surround that contact. Remember, this job is servicing the community within very specific parameters. Having strong communication skills that are easily adapted to many different circumstances will benefit you in many ways.

If you work on organization, physical fitness, and written communication you will be better prepared and ready for a successful career in law enforcement. This job affects all areas of your life whether you want it to or not. These changes can be beneficial or detrimental based on how you've prepared yourself for the job. Take pride in doing things the right way, never compromise your values or integrity, and fight injustice wherever you find it. By holding yourself to a higher standard, you and your community will be rewarded for your efforts.

Officer Brent Kohls
Arvada Police Department, Arvada, Colorado

Courtesy of Officer Brent Kohls, Arvada Police Department, Arvada, CO.

Defining Crime Scene Scope and Establishing a Perimeter

Once emergency situations have been attended to, and witnesses and suspect(s) have been identified and removed from the scene, it is imperative that the first responder take actions to secure the identified crime scene to attempt to preserve the evidence present within. In order to do this, the officer must first identify the scope of the crime scene. Once the boundaries have been identified, a perimeter should be established. A **perimeter** is the outer confines of the crime scene. This involves some sort of delineation or physical boundary as to what area is considered inside of the supposed crime scene, and what is external to the area of investigation.

A perimeter can be established through utilizing a number of methods. The most common is stringing crime scene barrier tape around the defined area **Figure 4–1**. For some night scenes, flares or traffic cones may be used to identify a crime scene area (traffic accident). Sometimes, marked patrol cars or personnel are used in the absence of tape. In other situations, securing

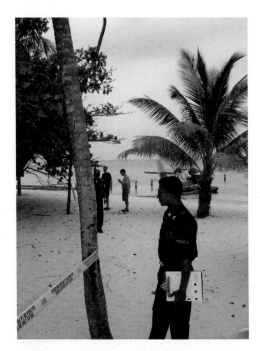

FIGURE 4–1   A first responder secures the perimeter of a crime scene

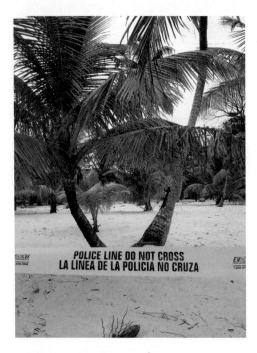

FIGURE 4–2   Multilingual barrier tape

a crime scene could be as simple as closing and locking a door. It is also possible to use existing structures such as walls, gates, or trees. Although a variety of options exist, a clearly defined physical perimeter will ensure that there is no mistaking what is and what is not the crime scene, which will allow police personnel to best enforce access to the scene, and thus ensure its integrity. However, it should be kept in mind that this barrier is by no means fixed. The area of the defined crime scene is always subject to modification dependent upon investigative progress and process.

Remember, it is better to overdefine an area rather than to underestimate and under identify an area. A crime scene can always be shrunk, but once a perimeter is established it is nearly impossible to increase the perimeter later and be certain that any evidence found within the expanded area has maintained its integrity. First responders will find that defining a perimeter (e.g., putting up barrier tape) is sometimes an invitation for onlookers to press forward to see what is going on. Interested parties will assemble as close to the barriers as possible to get their greatest vantage point. If the perimeter was incorrectly established, any evidence found outside the established perimeter most likely will be useless due to destruction and contamination (**Figure 4–2**).

In situations where it is feasible, the ideal procedure is to establish a perimeter that involves **multi-level containment**. This method utilizes several perimeters, and is the most effective for ensuring integrity while also allowing a workable scene structure (**Figure 4–3**).

Three levels of multi-level containment are:

1.   *The outer perimeter.* If there are media personnel present, a special area within this first level may be designated for their use. By providing the media with this area apart from the general public, a relationship of good will and cooperation is established between the reporters and law enforcement.

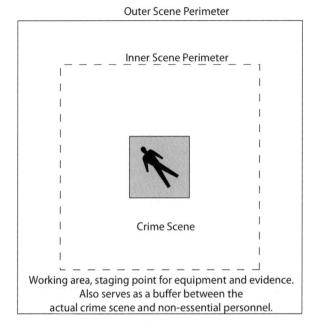

Outer Scene Perimeter

Inner Scene Perimeter

Crime Scene

Working area, staging point for equipment and evidence. Also serves as a buffer between the actual crime scene and non-essential personnel.

Area outside the controlled perimeters

FIGURE 4–3 An example of utilizing multi-level containment for securing a crime scene perimeter

Adapted from "Practical Crime Scene Processing and Investigation" by Ross M. Gardner (2004). Courtesy of Ellie Bruchez, University of Wisconsin-Platteville.

2. *Inside of the outer perimeter, adjacent to the actual crime scene itself.* This area is only to be accessed by police and emergency personnel. It is acceptable for emergency and crime scene vehicles to be within this area, as it will make investigative and processing efforts more streamlined. This area typically holds the **command post**, which is established to coordinate on-scene activities and efforts. Sometimes this is referred to as "incident command" under the incident command and control structure. Supervisory decisions are made and the scene is managed from this point. The incident commander is typically the first person on scene (first responder); however, this duty is passed along to higher ranking and specialized administrative personnel upon their arrival at the scene. The designated multi-level area allows higher ranking personnel access that is in closer proximity to the crime scene, without the chance of contaminating the actual scene. This area also is used by processing personnel to stage their equipment, as well as a place where they can take breaks.

3. *The perimeter that defines the specific crime scene target area.* This area should have the strictest level of access and control, and should only be entered by those actively involved in the processing and investigative efforts. Anyone not actively involved at the time should withdraw to area 2.

Exclusion of Official Visitors

One of the most difficult challenges is to prevent and/or prohibit so-called "official sightseers" such as other officers, superiors, or government officials who are not directly involved in the processing or investigatory efforts, yet demand to be admitted into the scene. Every attempt should be made to exclude these individuals, explaining the potential consequences of disturbing the scene, and stressing the importance of filing a narrative report noting observations and actions taken should they make entrance within the scene.

RIPPED FROM THE HEADLINES

Honoring First Responders

Corresponding with the 10th anniversary of the 9/11 attacks on the United States, communities around the United States held recognition ceremonies to honor their first responders. EMTs, firefighters, and police officers were recognized for their service and, in some cases, for their sacrifice. According to the National Law Enforcement Memorial, "On average, one law enforcement officer is killed in the line of duty somewhere in the United States every 53 hours. Since the first known line-of-duty death in 1791, more than 19,000 U.S. law enforcement officers have made the ultimate sacrifice" (NLEOMF, 2012). According to the U.S. Fire Administration, there have been an average of 100 on-duty firefighter deaths since 2001 (USFA, 2012).

Each of these individuals knew the risks inherent when they took their job, and yet they took the job and were willing to sacrifice personal lives, time, and in many cases their own lives in the service of others.

National Law Enforcement Officers Memorial Fund (NLEOMF). (2012). Fact & Figures. Retrieved on April 27, 2012, from http://www.nleomf.org/facts/ and U.S. Fire Administration (USFA). (2012). Retrieved April 27, 2012, from http://www.usfa.fema.gov/fireservice/fatalities/statistics/casualties.shtm.

Sometimes the exclusion of unauthorized personnel proves to be a more difficult task than expected. Crimes of violence are especially susceptible to the attention of higher-level officials and members of the press, in addition to the curiosity of neighbors and others. What must be remembered is that every individual who enters the crime scene is a potential destroyer of physical evidence, even if it is unintentional. One suggestion to aid with this difficult scenario is to establish multi-level containment quickly, as defined previously. This will allow such official sightseers minimal access to the scene without directly targeting the crime scene.

If proper control is to be exercised, the officer charged with the responsibility of securing and protecting the scene must have the authority to exclude anyone, including fellow police officers not directly involved with the investigatory process. Securing and isolating the scene is a critical step within an investigation, the accomplishment of which is a mark of a well-trained and professional CSI team.

Identification and Protection of Transient Evidence

Locard's Exchange Principle is important to remember when arriving at the crime scene and during the initial stages of crime scene efforts. There is trace evidence to be found at every crime scene and on every criminal. As time passes much of the trace matter and the ability to collect it is lost. It is crucial, therefore, to quickly identify, collect, and preserve trace and perishable evidence, both on the suspect and at the crime scene. Sometimes this evidence is referred to as transient. **<u>Transient evidence</u>** is physical evidence present at the crime scene that is either fragile or at great risk for loss, alteration, or destruction if not properly identified, documented, collected, and preserved as soon as possible.

Initial Scene Documentation

To ensure the integrity of a crime scene, once a scene is safe and is secured, a log should be established by the first responder to log all personnel who enter and leave the scene, including those present upon arrival. Most departments will have forms established for this task. This document is the initial documentation effort at the scene. It is important that the first responder record an accurate arrival time at the scene, and when the scene was secured. With modern technology and the advent of Computer-Aided Dispatch (CAD), often these times are noted by dispatch after an officer makes radio transmissions regarding arrival and scene situation updates. Because a first responder may be called away to respond to another call before the crime scene is properly processed, this initial documentation is important; it will set the foundation for later documentation efforts by other crime scene personnel.

It is also important that the first responder note any additional departments and personnel who were involved, the agency case number(s), and the contact person from each department who was involved in the efforts (**Figure 4–4**).

FIGURE 4–4   An example of a first responder's vehicle

A first responding officer should be cognizant of not becoming involved in lengthy interviews or interrogations with victims, suspects, or witnesses at a crime scene, as the officer cannot effectively protect the scene integrity when involved with such matters.

Processing Cases Involving Multiple Scenes

Sometimes a case will involve an expansive scene or multiple locations associated with the same criminal case. Typically, the **primary scene** is the first encountered location where evidence was located. This usually is the area where the officer was initially dispatched but can be the location of a witness who called in a complaint.

Other scenes may be identified later as being associated with the primary scene, however. These scenes are referred to as **secondary scenes**. An example would be a homicide where a victim is believed to have been killed within a residence, and then the body transported via an automobile and buried in a remote location, where it was discovered by a person walking a dog. In this case, the primary scene would be the location identified by the witness (i.e., the burial location), and the automobile and residence (when located) would be secondary scenes. In all three cases, each scene must be processed utilizing the same approach and guidelines discussed for dealing with responding to and properly processing a crime scene.

Sometimes, multiple scenes may mean the involvement of multiple jurisdictions in an investigation. This is not typically an issue, as most agencies have multi-jurisdictional or mutual aid agreements that predetermine areas of responsibilities in the event of a criminal event that encompasses more than one jurisdiction.

Scenes Involving Death

With regard to the initial response, however, if the first responder to the scene is able to establish through ocular (visible) signs of death (rigor mortis, odor, lividity, bug activity, decomposition, etc.) or by other means that a person is dead, then the body should not be touched or moved until a detailed examination has been conducted. While in most states a physician, coroner, or other medical personnel is the only person able to declare a person legally dead, an officer need not be a doctor to note if a body present at a scene exhibits characteristics inconsistent with sustaining life (i.e., missing major portions, insects protruding from orifices, positioning, catastrophic damage, etc.).

Once it has been established that a person is dead and a brief survey of the scene has been conducted, a first responder should notify his or her supervisor about the situation. It is suggested that such notifications be made via telephone, as media staff do monitor police radio frequencies.

Next, the medical examiner (ME) or coroner should be contacted. Whether it is the ME or coroner who is contacted is a matter of local custom. Many agencies wait to make such notifications until departmental investigative personnel arrive and begin their investigation, which can save the coroner's staff time by ensuring that they do not have to wait at a scene for the police to conclude their investigative efforts before they can enter and process the body. It is suggested that departments have policies in place to address such situations and the order of notification.

The ME or coroner's office typically has legal jurisdiction over the body at the scene, and many times, all associated evidence within the proximity of the body. In jurisdictions where this is true, the body may not be moved or searched without the notification and consent of the ME or coroner personnel.

In situations involving strangulation or hanging, where there is the presence of unmistakable signs of death, the officer should do nothing to the body. Again, no efforts should be made to cut down the body! If there appears the possibility that the hanging mechanism might break, the officer may attempt to support the corpse, but it should not be cut down. If, however, signs of life are present, the officer should make all efforts necessary to ensure that the victim lives. Knots and areas of articulation should be left intact, if possible. Knots can sometimes give investigators knowledge of a certain occupation or skill level. If a rope must eventually be cut, the loose ends should be appropriately labeled. Another option to labeling the ends is to tie the ends to one another with string. These are not actions typically conducted by first responding personnel, however.

Scenes Involving Firearms and Ammunition

As a general rule, any firearms and ammunition located at a crime scene should not be touched by first responders. Such items should remain **in situ** (as they are) until the arrival of investigative personnel who will make processing determinations. However, sometimes it becomes necessary, for safety and security reasons, to recover and secure weapons and ammunition. If the presence of the weapon and ammunition create an unsafe situation, if they may be inadvertently moved or compromised during the emergency care of an injured person, or if conditions exist such that the first responder cannot ensure the integrity and safety of the scene, which might lead to bystanders disturbing the weapon evidence, then the evidence may be collected and secured by the first responder.

If a weapon is to be collected, its collection should be made in such a way as to minimize the potential destruction of evidence, if at all possible. Nothing should be inserted within the bore of a firearm in order to lift the weapon. Doing so could dislodge trace evidence (e.g., gunshot residue, blood, particles of tissue, hair, etc.) that might be associated with the weapon's discharge. It is suggested that firearms be picked up by the gnarled pistol grip or other areas less likely to destroy fingerprint evidence, which would allow for print preservation and subsequent recovery. If there is the time to do so, the weapon and ammunition evidence should be photographed and their positioning sketched prior to removal. If there is not time, the officer should do their best to make a mental or written note. Information such as positioning often leads to a determination of whether the event was a suicide or it could explain the positioning of the assailant. The positions of the hammer and safety should be noted also (Fisher, 2004).

When weapons are collected the officer should keep in mind the evidentiary possibilities for the item of evidence. There may be reason to believe that fingerprints could be present. If so, keep in mind that excessive heat could destroy such useful evidence and, therefore, the firearm should not be removed to an excessively hot area.

Dealing with Media

Sometimes media personnel may arrive at a crime scene before the first responder. In these instances, the first responders should not—in any circumstance—provide the media with information concerning the case.

This duty falls to the police chief, sheriff, or public/press information officer (PIO). While an officer must not provide information, it is important that she or he behaves professionally with media personnel. The officer must remember that media personnel often provide invaluable assistance during the investigation of a crime. Reporters and staff are helpful in ensuring that a victim is identified or a suspect apprehended through distribution of photographs, videos, and other such evidence to the community. However, this information is never to be distributed by the first responder in the initial stages of the investigative efforts.

Crime Scene "Don'ts"

At no time during the process should a first responder or any individual present within the crime scene target perimeter do any of the following:

- Eat
- Drink
- Smoke
- Use landlines (telephone, computer) present within the crime scene
- Use a radio or cell phone (if it's a bomb scene, this could serve as a detonator)
- Use the bathroom, if present within a scene

It may be permissible for personnel to do the aforementioned (except use electronic or radio equipment if involved with the investigation of a bomb scene) while the personnel are present within the outermost perimeter, or the middle perimeter of a multi-level containment situation, but such actions must never occur within the target crime scene area. Doing so will place the evidence in serious danger of contamination or destruction.

First Response Overview

The following suggested process is to be followed by first responders, as given in the National Institute of Justice (2004) Special Report entitled, "Crime Scene Investigation: A Reference for Law Enforcement Training."

The First Response Process

1. Initial Response/Receipt of Information

Principle: One of the most important aspects of securing the crime scene is to preserve the scene with minimal contamination and disturbance of physical evidence. The initial response to an incident shall be expeditious and methodical. Upon arrival, the officer(s) shall assess the scene and treat the incident as a crime scene.

Policy: The initial responding officer(s) shall promptly, yet cautiously, approach and enter the crime scene, remaining observant of any persons, vehicles, events, potential evidence, and environmental conditions.

Procedure: The initial responding officer(s) should:

a. Note or log dispatch information (e.g., address/location, time, date, type of call, parties involved).

b. Be aware of any persons or vehicles leaving the crime scene.

c. Approach the scene cautiously, scan the entire area to thoroughly assess the scene, and note any possible secondary crime scenes. Be aware of any persons and vehicles in the vicinity that may be related to the crime.

d. Make initial observations (look, listen, smell) to assess the scene and ensure officer safety before proceeding.

e. Remain alert and attentive. Assume the crime is ongoing until determined to be otherwise.

f. Treat the location as a crime scene until assessed and determined to be otherwise.

Summary: It is important for the initial responding officer(s) to be observant when approaching, entering, and exiting a crime scene.

2. Safety Procedures

Principle: The safety and physical well-being of officers and other individuals, in and around the crime scene, are the initial responding officer(s)' first priority.

Policy: The initial responding officer(s) arriving at the scene shall identify and control any dangerous situations or persons.

Procedure: The initial responding officer(s) should:

a. Ensure that there is no immediate threat to other responders—scan area for sights, sounds, and smells that may present danger to personnel (e.g., hazardous materials such as gasoline, natural gas). If the situation involves a clandestine drug laboratory, biological weapons, or radiological or chemical threats, the appropriate personnel/agency should be contacted prior to entering the scene.

b. Approach the scene in a manner designed to reduce risk of harm to officer(s) while maximizing the safety of victims, witnesses, and others in the area.

c. Survey the scene for dangerous persons and control the situation.

d. Notify supervisory personnel and call for assistance/backup.

Summary: The control of physical threats will ensure the safety of officers and others present.

3. Emergency Care

Principle: After controlling any dangerous situations or persons, the initial responding officer(s') next responsibility is to ensure that medical attention is provided to injured persons while minimizing contamination of the scene.

Policy: The initial responding officer(s) shall ensure that medical attention is provided with minimal contamination of the scene.

Procedure: The initial responding officer(s) should:

a. Assess the victim(s) for signs of life and medical needs and provide immediate medical attention.

b. Call for medical personnel.

c. Guide medical personnel to the victim to minimize contamination/alteration of the crime scene.

d. Point out potential physical evidence to medical personnel, instruct them to minimize contact with such evidence (e.g., ensure that medical personnel preserve all clothing and personal effects without cutting through bullet holes, knife tears), and document movement of persons or items by medical personnel.

e. Instruct medical personnel not to "clean up" the scene and to avoid removal or alteration of items originating from the scene.

f. If medical personnel arrived first, obtain the name, unit, and telephone number of attending personnel, and the name and location of the medical facility where the victim is to be taken.

g. If there is a chance the victim may die, attempt to obtain "dying declaration."

h. Document any statements/comments made by victims, suspects, or witnesses at the scene.

i. If the victim or suspect is transported to a medical facility, send a law enforcement official with the victim or suspect to document any comments made and preserve evidence. (If no officers are available to accompany the victim/suspect, stay at the scene and request medical personnel to preserve evidence and document any comments made by the victim or suspect.)

Summary: Assisting, guiding, and instructing medical personnel during the care and removal of injured persons will diminish the risk of contamination and loss of evidence.

4. Secure and Control Persons at the Scene

Principle: Controlling, identifying, and removing persons at the crime scene and limiting the number of persons who enter the crime scene and the movement of such persons is an important function of the initial responding officer(s) in protecting the crime scene.

Policy: The initial responding officer(s) shall identify persons at the crime scene and control their movement.

Procedure: The initial responding officer(s) should:

a. Control all individuals at the scene—prevent individuals from altering/destroying physical evidence by restricting movement, location, and activity while ensuring and maintaining safety at the scene.

b. Identify all individuals at the scene, such as:

- Suspects: Secure and separate.
- Witnesses: Secure and separate.
- Bystanders: Determine whether a witness; if so treat as above, if not, remove from the scene.
- Victims/family/friends: Control while showing compassion.
- Medical and other assisting personnel.

c. Exclude unauthorized and nonessential personnel from the scene (e.g., law enforcement officials not working the case, politicians, media).

Summary: Controlling the movement of persons at the crime scene and limiting the number of persons who enter the crime scene is essential to maintaining scene integrity, safeguarding evidence, and minimizing contamination.

5. Boundaries: Identify, Establish, Protect, and Secure

Principle: Defining and controlling boundaries provide a means for protecting and securing the crime scene(s). The number of crime scenes and their boundaries are determined by their location(s) and the type of crime. Boundaries shall be established beyond the initial scope of the crime scene(s) with the understanding that the boundaries can be reduced in size if necessary but cannot be as easily expanded.

Policy: The initial responding officer(s) at the scene shall conduct an initial assessment to establish and control the crime scene(s) and its boundaries.

Procedure: The initial responding officer(s) should:

a. Establish boundaries of the scene(s), starting at the focal point and extending outward to include:

- Where the crime occurred.
- Potential points and paths of exit and entry of suspects and witnesses.
- Places where the victim/evidence may have been moved (be aware of trace and impression evidence while assessing the scene).

b. Set up physical barriers (e.g., ropes, cones, crime scene barrier tape, available vehicles, personnel, other equipment) or use existing boundaries (e.g., doors, walls, gates).

c. Document the entry/exit of all people entering and leaving the scene, once boundaries have been established.

d. Control the flow of personnel and animals entering and leaving the scene to maintain integrity of the scene.

e. Effect measures to preserve/protect evidence that may be lost or compromised (e.g., protect from the elements, such as rain, snow, wind, and from footsteps, tire tracks, sprinklers).

f. Document the original location of the victim or objects that you observe being moved.

g. Consider search and seizure issues to determine the necessity of obtaining consent to search and/or obtaining a search warrant.

Note: Persons should not smoke, chew tobacco, use the telephone or bathroom, eat or drink, move any items including weapons (unless necessary for the safety and well-being of persons at the scene), adjust the thermostat or open windows or doors (maintain scene as found), touch anything unnecessarily (note and document any items moved), reposition moved items, litter, or spit within the established boundaries of the scene.

Summary: Establishing boundaries is a critical aspect in controlling the integrity of evidentiary material.

6. Turn over the Scene and Brief Investigator(s) in Charge

Principle: Briefing the investigator(s) taking charge assists in controlling the crime scene and helps establish further investigative responsibilities.

Policy: The initial responding officer(s) at the scene shall provide a detailed crime scene briefing to the investigator(s) in charge of the scene.

Procedure: The initial responding officer(s) should:

a. Brief the investigator(s) taking charge.

b. Assist in controlling the scene.

c. Turn over responsibility for the documentation of entry/exit.

d. Remain at the scene until relieved of duty.

Summary: The scene briefing is the only opportunity for the next in command to obtain initial aspects of the crime scene prior to subsequent investigation.

7. Document Actions and Observations

Principle: All activities conducted and observations made at the crime scene must be documented as soon as possible after the event to preserve information.

Policy: Documentation must be maintained as a permanent record.

Procedure: The initial responding officer(s) should document:

a. Observations of the crime scene, including the location of persons and items within the crime scene and the appearance and condition of the scene upon arrival.

b. Conditions upon arrival (e.g., lights on/off; shades up/down, open/closed; doors, windows, open/closed; smells; ice, liquids; movable furniture; weather; temperature; and personal items).

c. Personal information from witnesses, victims, suspects, and any statements or comments made.

d. His/Her actions and the actions of others.

Summary: The initial responding officer(s) at the crime scene must produce clear, concise, documented information encompassing his or her observations and actions. This documentation is vital in providing information to substantiate investigative considerations.

National Institute of Justice. (2004). Crime scene investigation: A reference for law enforcement training, June 2004 Special Report, U.S. DOJ, Office of Justice Programs. NCJ200160. Retrieved August 31, 2012, from http://www.nij.gov/pubs-sum/200160.htm.

WRAP UP

Chapter Summary

While crime scenes are often complex and chaotic situations, the basic overview of duties for the first responder is as follows:

- Assist any victims.
- Search for, apprehend, and arrest suspects still on the scene or in the area of the crime scene.
- Detain and separate witnesses.
- Protect the integrity of the crime scene.
- Communicate with supervisors and appropriate agencies.
- Document all actions taken and observations made.

The first responder is responsible for ensuring that the initial response is accomplished quickly and competently. Once the scene is secure and the integrity of the scene is ensured, the investigatory process begins. This may require the use of specialized personnel, with additional training and experience pertinent to the scene or investigation at hand. It is important for those involved with crime scene processing efforts to admit when they are in over their head and to be able to ask for or seek out assistance in areas that they are not familiar with or have not had appropriate training.

Review Questions

1. What is meant by the term first responder?

2. Discuss instances when the loss or destruction of evidence at a crime scene is acceptable.

3. Explain what is meant by the term perimeter as it relates to crime scene investigation.

4. Utilizing multiple perimeter areas in order to segregate the crime scene, media, and crime scene processing personnel is referred to as _____.

5. What is transient evidence and how does it differ from other types of evidence in relation to how a first responder must deal with it?

6. Explain the difference between a primary and a secondary scene.

7. What are official visitors and how should they be treated in relation to other crime scene personnel at a crime scene?

8. _____ is the area from which the critical incident is managed and overseen.

References

Doyle, A. C. (1892). The adventure of the copper beeches. In: The adventures of Sherlock Holmes. *Strand Magazine*.

Fish, J. T., Miller, L. S., & Braswell M. C. (2007). *Crime scene investigation: An introduction*. New York: LexisNexis Anderson Publishing.

Fisher, B. A. J. (2004). *Techniques of crime scene investigation*, 7th ed. Boca Raton, FL: CRC Press.

National Institute of Justice. (2004). *Crime scene investigation: A reference for law enforcement training*, June 2004 Special Report, U.S. DOJ, Office of Justice Programs. NCJ200160. Retrieved August 31, 2012, from http://www.nij.gov/pubs-sum/200160.htm

National Law Enforcement Officers Memorial Fund (NLEOMF). (2012). Fact & Figures. Retrieved on April 27, 2012, from http://www.nleomf.org/facts/.

U.S. Fire Administration (USFA). (2012). Retrieved April 27, 2012 from http://www.usfa.fema.gov/fireservice/fatalities/statistics/casualties.shtm.

Wisconsin Department of Justice. (2009). *Physical evidence handbook*, 8th ed. Madison, WI: Wisconsin Department of Administration.

LEARNING OBJECTIVES

- Explain the purpose of a walk-thru.
- Identify the types of personnel involved in crime scene investigative efforts and list their job descriptions.
- Define and discuss the function of PPE.
- Understand the various levels of PPE.
- Name the pathogens and other most common health risks to CSI personnel.

Specialized Personnel and Safety Considerations

> *You see, but you do not observe.*
>
> Sir Arthur Conan Doyle (1859–1930)
> Sherlock Holmes, in *A Scandal in Bohemia*

KEY TERMS

- Barrier Protection
- Bloodborne Pathogen
- Cross-Contamination
- IDLH Environment
- Personal Protective Equipment (PPE)
- Universal Precautions
- Walk-Thru

Investigative Personnel

Once the first responder has secured the crime scene and all associated evidence, she or he will then contact their agency and request investigative personnel to respond to the incident. In some smaller agencies and in situations where the crime scene is of a minor nature, this investigative role may be handled by the first responder. If this is the case, efforts still are made to ensure the integrity of the crime scene while the officer is conducting their investigation.

If other investigative personnel are requested, this typically will be a detective or investigator, depending on the label given to such personnel within the department in question. Sometimes the first responder will speak with the investigator via phone and articulate to them the situation at hand. Often this will result in the investigator acquiring enough information to form an opinion about the manner in which the investigation should proceed, which can sometimes mean that the investigator will not respond to the scene, but rather will instruct the officer on what to do before reporting back on the findings.

If investigative personnel respond to the scene, this can be in a variety of degrees. Detectives/investigators are responsible for conducting the overall investigative efforts associated with the scene. These are the individuals who lay out the plan for the processing and investigative efforts. If the department in question has personnel who serve in a crime scene technician, evidence technician, or crime scene investigator capacity, such processing issues may be left up to them while the investigator concentrates on interviews, interrogations, and interagency cooperation efforts.

Once the scene is secure, investigative personnel should conduct a preliminary scene survey, which is also known as a **walk-thru**. The preliminary scene survey will have the greatest informational possibilities if the first responder is available to accompany the investigative personnel. This is because it is the first responder who has the most direct knowledge of what the scene originally looked like when law enforcement responded to the event. He or she also should know of any changes made to the scene since that initial response. It is very important that investigators are well briefed by first responders regarding the case before conducting their examination of the scene. This ensures that the preliminary scene survey will result in maximum information gathering, while minimizing scene contamination and evidence destruction. The primary purpose of the preliminary scene survey is to assess the scene for logistical and safety considerations. The following is the suggested process to be followed by investigative personnel in conducting a preliminary scene survey, as given in the National Institute of Justice (2004) Special Report entitled "Crime Scene Investigation: A Reference for Law Enforcement Training."

Until this point nothing should have been touched or moved by personnel unless there was cause to move an injured person, or conditions were present (e.g., foul weather) that necessitated the movement or collection of some evidence in order to best preserve it. With an unaltered (or minimally altered) scene as a continued goal, the survey is begun. The path should attempt to follow the indirect path that was cleared or identified by first responders to minimize evidence destruction and disturbance of the scene.

The following list contains 10 suggested matters to consider while conducting a walk-thru:

1. As with first responder efforts, make note of transient evidence present within the scene, and efforts needed to properly document, collect, and preserve such evidence. If steps have not already been taken to do so, it may be necessary at this point to document, collect, package, and preserve such evidence.

2. Make note of weather and climate conditions (both indoors and outdoors).

3. Note whether lights are turned on or off.

4. Document whether doors and windows are locked, unlocked, open, closed, or if there appears to be evidence of forced entry.

5. Note the presence of any particular odors that may be connected to an individual (perfume, cologne) or an event (gas, smoke, chemicals, etc.).

6. Look for signs of activity (meal preparation, house tidy or disheveled, etc.) or struggle.

7. If timing is of great concern, look for date and time indicators such as on food, newspapers, mail, etc.

8. Attempt to locate the most probable point of entry, point of exit, paths between them, and any other areas of apparent action within the scene. These areas should be noted to ensure that processing personnel will reduce their movements in such areas to allow for the optimum opportunity to discover and collect physical evidence within the scene.

9. Attempt to answer the questions of: Who? What? When? Where? How? and Why? as they pertain to the scene and the crime in question.

10. Assess the scene for personnel (How many? Specialized?), equipment (How much? What kind?), and logistical concerns (How long? Food needs for personnel? Bathroom needs? Media considerations? Budgetary issues?).

This walk-thru should be conducted in a cautious and aware manner. As with the first responders, nothing should be touched or moved. At this point, the scene should be secure and the evidence safe from harm as well. Typically, there is no need to touch or move evidence. The walk-thru is a minimally invasive information-gathering event, and not an evidence search or collection effort.

There are two schools of thought about whether investigative personnel should wear gloves while conducting this scene survey. One view is that if personnel wear protective gloves they will be more inclined to touch items and, therefore, they should not wear gloves and should adhere to the "hands in pockets" approach. The other view is that personnel should always wear gloves whenever they are inside of a crime scene. The author agrees with the latter line of thinking for several reasons. First, the purpose of gloves is to both protect the wearer from contamination and to protect any item touched from contamination by the wearer. While it is true that in the walk-thru there should be no touching of items, this is not to say that transient evidence will not be discovered that necessitates movement or collection. Having gloves on will ensure that such evidence is minimally damaged if such contact is necessary. Also, a "hands

Preliminary Scene Survey Process

Principle:
The scene "walk-thru" provides an overview of the entire scene, identifies any threats to scene integrity, and ensures protection of physical evidence. Written and photographic documentation provides a permanent record.

Policy:
The investigator(s) in charge shall conduct a walk-thru of the scene. The walk-thru shall be conducted with individuals responsible for processing the scene.

Procedure:
During the scene walk-thru, the investigator(s) in charge should:

   a. Avoid contaminating the scene by using the established path of entry.

   b. Prepare preliminary documentation of the scene as observed.

   c. Identify and protect fragile and/or perishable evidence (e.g., consider climatic conditions, crowds/hostile environment). Ensure that all evidence that may be compromised is immediately documented, photographed, and collected.

Summary:
Conducting a scene walk-thru provides the investigator(s) in charge with an overview of the entire scene. The walk-thru provides the first opportunity to identify valuable and/or fragile evidence and determine initial investigative procedures, providing for a systematic examination and documentation of the scene. Written and photographic documentation records the condition of the scene as first observed, providing a permanent record.

National Institute of Justice. (2004). Crime scene investigation: A reference for law enforcement training. June 2004 Special Report, U.S. DOJ, Office of Justice Programs. NCJ200160. Retrieved August 31, 2012, from http://www.nij.gov/pubs-sum/200160.htm.

in the pocket approach" is not realistic because the point of a walk-thru is to document conditions present throughout the scene. The investigator most certainly will have her or his hands outside of any pockets, and will be writing and pointing throughout the process. It is best to have personnel wear gloves with the thought in the forefront of her or his mind that nothing is to be touched unless it is absolutely imperative.

After the initial walk-thru has been conducted, investigative personnel should have the information they need to apprise supervisors of the situation and to lay out the crime scene processing strategy. At this stage there may be a call for more specialized personnel. Some of these personnel may be from within the ranks of law enforcement. Other specialists such as entomologists or engineers may be necessary to provide technical assistance that is outside of the training and education of those in law enforcement. Agencies are encouraged to think broadly and utilize sources such as local universities and other private, local, state, and federal agencies to maximize the investigatory potential. If an individual has not been trained to collect or document certain evidence, then they should not; instead, they should rely upon experts to do so.

A brief, and by no means all-inclusive, list of personnel who may be called upon to assist with the investigative effort is given in this section.

Crime Scene Investigator/Crime Scene Technician

These are police or civilian personnel who are specially trained to process a crime scene. Their purpose is twofold: to collect and preserve physical evidence.

Identification (ID) Officers

They are responsible for photographing the scene and searching for latent fingerprints, but they are not responsible for other types of physical evidence. Often these individuals are fingerprint experts who later will perform comparative analyses.

Forensic Surveyors

Often they are used to provide an accurate architectural rendition of the crime scene. They typically utilize Computer-Aided Drafting (CAD) to assist them with their documentation efforts.

Forensic Photographers

Specialized photography (low light, aerial, infrared, underwater, etc.) demands specific skills. These photographers have advanced training in photographic concepts and specialized situations.

Forensic Scientist/Criminalist

This person has gained specialized training and education in chemistry and biology as applied to the recognition, ID, collection, and preservation of physical evidence.

Medical Examiner/Coroner

Typically, a forensic pathologist is responsible for performing autopsies in criminal cases. This may include providing an ID of the deceased; determining cause, manner, and time of death; and taking custody of the remains.

Forensic Nurse

This licensed nurse has specialized training in proper evidence collection, and most often is utilized in sexual assault investigations. Such nurses usually are certified Sexual Assault Nurse Examiners (SANE).

District Attorney

When called upon, this person provides a search warrant or a court order to obtain known specimens from a defendant. A district attorney may operate in an advisory capacity when a case involves a police officer (e.g., a police-related shooting, in-custody death of suspect, etc.).

Hazardous Materials Specialists

These experts assist with recognition, collection, destruction, clean up, disposal, and preservation of hazardous materials at the crime scene.

Forensic Engineers

This type of engineer analyzes the structural integrity of a building or other structures in accident investigations.

Firearms Examiners

This expert assists in crime scene ballistic recovery and can assess the trajectory of fired weapons. He or she also may assist in determining whether a shooting was accidental or intentional.

K-9 Officers

This sworn officer and trained dog may be called upon to assist with searches and tracking of individuals; if the individual is believed to be dead or buried, cadaver dogs may be utilized. Cadaver dogs are specially trained to recognize the scent of decaying remains.

Federal Authorities

Numerous federal agencies can be called in to assist or take over a crime scene involving mass disasters, terrorist acts, bombings, major fires, and bank robberies. Some examples of these agencies include: the Federal Bureau of Investigation (FBI), the Drug Enforcement Administration (DEA), the Bureau of Alcohol Tobacco Firearms and Explosives (ATF), and the United States Secret Service (USSS) (**Figure 5–1**).

Crime Scene Investigation Processing Models

With regard to the utilization of specialized personnel, there are several different models for assembling a response to investigating and processing a crime scene. Each has its positive and negative attributes. The factors determining which model will be implemented include: available resources, manpower and training, type of crime investigated, and the degree of scientific and technological advancement of involved agencies.

Local or Traditional Model

Many agencies choose to employ a more traditional approach to crime scene processing efforts. In this case, patrol officers and sometimes investigators are utilized as the primary crime scene

FIGURE 5-1   An example of specialized personnel (federal)

personnel. This is seen as being beneficial to those agencies with limited budgets, minimal crime rates, and where the need for crime scene processing efforts is very low. This is also the default model in the absence of any other model. Negative attributes of this model include the fact that typically personnel are not highly trained in specific areas and are more generalists than specialists. Also, crime scene processing efforts may interfere with designated patrol duties.

Crime Scene Investigator/Crime Scene Technician Model

Some departments employ civilian or sworn personnel who are dedicated to crime scene documentation and physical evidence collection and preservation efforts. This allows such individuals to become specialized and have a better understanding of the procedures involved with such processes. Most times these individuals work the crime scene from a technical standpoint, but are not actively involved in the investigative process. Such matters are left up to the investigator or detective who typically has considerably more investigatory experience.

Crime Lab Model

Some crime labs, specifically state and federal labs, operate a crime scene response team that will respond to serious cases. These teams are comprised of forensic scientists/criminalists with specific job skills who are responsible for individual areas of crime scene documentation and processing efforts. These individuals are typically highly skilled but lack experience due to their limited use. Also, it must be remembered that these individuals are performing a scientific or technical function and usually lack investigative experience; therefore, the information

VIEW FROM AN EXPERT

Law Enforcement K-9s—A Useful Investigative Tool

Overview

Law enforcement has been training dogs for a variety of tasks, including narcotics detection, criminal apprehension, natural disasters, and war for over 400 years. Their usefulness as an investigative tool is well documented in law enforcement magazines, Hollywood productions, and academic publications. Numerous police agencies at all levels of government in the U.S. and abroad utilize K-9s. In the U.S., these include local municipal, township, county, state, and federal agencies. Interestingly, these agencies have separate K-9 training and deployment procedures based upon their needs. Conversely, in most other countries, such variety in types of agencies rarely exists, as their law enforcement structure is centralized and nationalized. This centralization results in consistency of training methods, as all dogs and officers train at one location using identical methods.

Regardless of the country, all agencies have different needs requiring different types of dogs. Predominately, K-9s fall into two categories: single use or dual-purpose. Dogs in the former group are trained to detect various accelerants and/or explosives, and are often referred to as bomb dogs. With some very rare exceptions, bomb dogs are not trained in other types of detection, such as narcotics our human tracking. The latter group is trained for several task areas such as narcotics detection, searching for evidence, tracking a fleeing suspect, and criminal apprehension (aggression), and is commonly referred to as patrol dogs or general-purpose dogs. Normally, larger metropolitan police departments and federal agencies employ several K-9s, each with their specific specialty. Conversely, smaller local police departments normally utilize one general-purpose dog and may, if needed, elicit the services of larger departments employing specially trained K-9s such as bomb dogs.

The following section is a brief discussion of some of the most important considerations concerning K-9 use in law enforcement. These include the breed of K-9s, selection of a K-9 handler, legal considerations, and the future of K-9 in law enforcement agencies and beyond.

Breeds of K-9s—Looks Are Important

Law enforcement agencies vary widely in their purpose, which means just as much variability in the breed of dog they utilize. Most have seen or heard of the Bloodhound and its use as a tracking dog. Bloodhounds gained notoriety for tracking prison escapees, and some state corrections departments still use them for that purpose. Many search and rescue organizations, both volunteer and government, also use the Bloodhound. Another category of breed commonly used throughout the world is the various hunting breeds. These include the Yellow, Chocolate, and Black Labradors, Beagles, and many varieties of Spaniels. Such dogs are not traditionally "aggressive" and therefore are not suited for general-purpose work. This means most are single-purpose dogs utilized for bomb or narcotics detection. These breeds are used mainly because their expression is "softer" and less threatening. This is an important consideration for agencies such as the Transportation Security Administration and Customs and Border Protection, where a less threatening presence is needed in crowded public areas. Undoubtedly, the most common K-9 breed is the German Shepherd Dog (GSD). Known for its intimidating look and athletic ability, most K-9 programs utilize at least one for dual purposes. However, gaining more popularity is a breed called the Belgium Malinois. Also normally trained as dual-purpose, and sometimes described as a GSD with shorter hair, many believe them to be more trainable and more agile. It is important for departments to determine which breed suits them best based on their needs.

Becoming a K-9 Officer—Myth vs. Reality

Working as a K-9 officer is both interesting and rewarding, and is a facet of law enforcement that not many officers experience. This is because even though the Bureau of Justice Statistics reports nearly 18,000 state and local law enforcement agencies in the U.S. (and about 80 federal agencies), not all of them employ a K-9. In fact, almost half of that number employs fewer than 10 officers, and most of those do not have the resources to support a K-9 program. This means that the opportunity for employment as a K-9 officer is somewhat small. However, opportunity does exist in larger departments, and should one aspire to do K-9 work, there are several issues to be aware of.

The obvious issue is that you must apply at departments that currently have a K-9 program. This is because starting a program is very difficult and rare. Also rare are departments who advertise for "new" K-9 officers with no experience. Most departments fill vacant K-9 officer positions internally, meaning they choose K-9 officers from their ranks. Because of this, aspiring K-9 officers must first hire in as an entry-level patrol officer and "work their way up" to K-9 officer. Normally, officers must work as a police officer for at least three, sometimes five or more years, to be eligible for special assignments like K-9. The key word is eligible, as there will quite likely be many of your fellow officers applying for the same assignment.

The application process usually includes a written and physical agility test and an oral panel interview. Some departments also require interested K-9 officers to attend regular department K-9 training to play the role of "bite decoy," in addition to acting as a fleeing criminal for tracking and apprehension training. This gives K-9 supervisors an opportunity to evaluate potential handlers and provides the applicant with first-hand experience with K-9 work so they too can determine if such an assignment is right for them.

If selected, you can expect monthly training sessions and long and extended working hours. Additionally, K-9 officers take possession of the dog for its working life. The dog belongs to the department, of course, but it becomes a new member of the officer's family, and officers are responsible for 24/7 care of the dog. Many departments provide K-9 officers with kennel facilities and pay for food and veterinary care. K-9 officers are also expected to be on 24-hour call, ready to respond quickly when needed, and are normally provided a take-home vehicle for this purpose. The working life of a K-9 varies, but normally lasts about 7–8 years. Officers are then given the option of purchasing the dog (most do), normally for the nominal sum of $1. Finally, depending upon department policy, K-9 officers with recently retired dogs rotate back into the patrol ranks and must wait a certain number of years to re-apply. This system allows other officers the opportunity to experience K-9 work.

Guiding Principles of K-9 Teams

Probably the most important consideration realized by any K-9 officer is the fact that their new canine partner is a tool. Similar to an officer's regular tools such as firearms, Tasers, and patrol cars, dogs are purchased (some cost in excess of $10,000) by departments to fulfill a law enforcement purpose. Whether single-use or dual-purpose, K-9 officers can expect to utilize their dog in extremely dangerous situations. Obviously, a single-purpose dog searching for a suspected bomb is one such situation. Similarly, a dual-purpose dog searching for a fleeing drug suspect in the middle of the night and not knowing whether they are armed or unarmed also ranks near the top. In either situation—and there are many others—the officer must be ready to deploy their dog as needed. Department policy almost always mandates it. Most situations end favorably for the K-9 team, but there are exceptions. All K-9 officers think about such situations daily and rehearse how they would respond if faced with certain scenarios. If you aspire to become a K-9 officer, ask yourself if you could deal with these scenarios.

Legal Considerations

Because K-9s are law enforcement tools, they must adhere to numerous, but very definitive, legal considerations. First, initial training of the K-9 team must be documented and ongoing proficiency training must be conducted and verified. Department policy should mandate this, as any legal challenge arising from a K-9 team's actions will most certainly include a thorough examination of all training records. Secondly, because the majority of K-9 deployments involve some use of force or the dog's superior sense of smell, it is important that K-9 officers become intimately familiar with the case law surrounding such uses.

There are literally hundreds of legal challenges concerned with the use of a K-9, but probably the most important to officers having to deploy their dogs in use of force situations is that of *Graham v. Connor* (1989). This decision placed the onus on the K-9 officer to determine the existence of one of three circumstances when deploying a dog in a use of force situation, which include the severity of the crime, whether the suspect(s) pose an immediate threat to officers or citizens, and whether the suspect(s) are resisting arrest or actively avoiding arrest by running away. If any of the three are not present, deployment of K-9s should not occur. Furthermore, and certainly less restrictive for K-9 officers, are the cases of *U.S. v. Place* (1983) and *Illinois v. Cabellas* (2005), which concern the use of a K-9's superior sense of smell and the Fourth Amendment. In both decisions, the court determined that a dog's "sniff" is not a search, and therefore, as long as the officer and dog are legally in a location, the Fourth Amendment does not apply. Although it is incumbent upon K-9 officers to be very familiar with such cases, individual departmental policies and procedures should assist in guiding how an officer and their K-9s are used.

The Future of K-9 Teams

Since September 11, 2001, the use of K-9s in law enforcement has accelerated. Numerous agencies at all levels of government now employ K-9s at numbers never before seen. This new demand for more trained dogs has necessitated the need for agencies needing dogs to contract with private, nongovernmental training centers to supply the dogs. Prior to this proliferation of K-9 teams, many agencies bred, raised, and trained their own dogs. In fact, if they did not breed the dogs, they at least trained them "in-house." Today, however, most agencies do not have the monetary resources or time to engage in in-house training, and have opted to obtain trained dogs from private vendors. Most of these vendors also train the officer in the use of the dog—yet another timesaving measure. However, the use of vendors does not come cheap. Departments can expect to pay between $5,000 and $10,000 for a trained dog and a week or two of training for the officer.

What does this mean for someone aspiring to become a K-9 officer? Even though there are limited K-9 teams, this increase means that law enforcement officers have much better opportunities to engage in K-9 work. This, coupled with continued judicial backing that is favorable to K-9s and their human partner, means man's best friend will continue to be a very useful investigative tool.

Dale Kapla, PhD
Department Chair, Criminal Justice
Northern Michigan University

Courtesy of Dale P. Kapla, PhD, Department of Criminal Justice, Northern Michigan University.

derived from their efforts must be passed along to the appropriate investigatory personnel for use within the case.

The Team Model

This is the most effective but also the most specialized model. It incorporates highly trained personnel at all levels of the investigation, and has its greatest effect when all levels are able to utilize personnel with experience and who are not mandatorily rotated out or lost due to promotion, retirement, or other reasons. In this model, the individual team members are assigned specific crime scene duties, dependent upon their specific training and experience. This results in the most efficient and successful crime scene investigation. Utilization of the team model requires cooperation and collaboration between agency departments as well as between agencies. Cooperation, coordination, and communication are the trident by which this model operates.

Crime Scene Safety Concerns

Certainly crime scenes always have been hazardous environments. While such a phenomenon is by no means new, the last decade has brought significant awareness and has seen crime scene personnel exposed to a far greater risk of infection by a pathogen while engaged in their job-related duties. HIV, AIDS, Hepatitis B and C, tuberculosis, and tetanus, as well as other bacterial- and virus-caused diseases are quite common in today's society. Such blood and airborne pathogens can be transmitted via minimal contact, such as by simply touching or breathing in confined spaces (Lee, Palmbach, & Miller, 2001). Although this might appear disconcerting to crime scene personnel, the chances of acquiring such diseases is dramatically reduced by adherence to some basic **universal precautions**. These are typical good hygiene habits: handwashing and use of barriers and aseptic techniques, and appropriate handling of cutting or puncturing objects like needles, syringes, and razor blades (called *sharps*).

At the scene of a crime, it is up to every individual to be aware of the safety issues and hazardous conditions that may be present and potentially create dangerous situations for emergency responders and investigative personnel. This information is included within Specialized Personnel and Safety Considerations chapter so that individuals will learn the importance of developing routine personal security measures that will reduce their potential exposure to situations that might be hazardous to health. Each department or agency has its own guidelines pertaining to employee safety considerations. Information is provided here as part of this text so that the safety of crime scene personnel will be enhanced, and the possibility of **cross-contamination** of physical evidence is minimized. Cross-contamination refers to the unintended movement or transfer of material between two objects, and should be avoided and/or minimized during processing efforts. While the primary objective is the protection of crime scene personnel, with the continued modernization and sensitivity of forensic equipment and analysis capabilities, the potential for contamination of physical evidence by investigators has dramatically increased. Through adhering to the use of barrier protection, the possibility of crime scene personnel depositing their own DNA or causing a secondary transfer of unrelated material between two or more objects is significantly reduced (Lee, Palmbach, & Miller, 2001).

Personal Protective Equipment

Crime scene personnel, who include the first responders, never should enter the crime scene without having the proper **personal protective equipment (PPE)**. Most likely, first responders will not know the appropriate level of protection when they arrive on the scene, and safety and security issues often do not allow for them to assemble the proper equipment prior to entry. However, once they have secured the scene and have made an initial assessment of the situation, those observations should be passed along to subsequent personnel so that those individuals can enter the scene properly protected.

PPE equipment typically consists of gloves, Tyvek suits, shoe covers, eye protection, and respiratory equipment. A crime scene is home to many hazards, both obvious and hidden, which demand that crime scene personnel remain vigilant and approach the scene from a contamination point of view. This means utilizing **barrier protection** when processing a crime scene. Barrier protection involves creating a barrier between the personnel and their surroundings to ensure they are not contaminated by the scene and they themselves do not contaminate the scene and evidence within. It is imperative that universal precautions be followed to minimize the risk to personnel of coming into contact with potentially infectious materials.

The role of the Occupational Safety and Health Administration (OSHA) mandates that all employers must train their employees about job-related safety strategies as well as supply them with appropriate levels of PPE for the specific job functions performed by their employees. Even with this measure, personnel must remember that the use of PPE does not guarantee total protection; rather, it is used to minimize the exposure contact possibility. Keeping up with immunizations is important medical prophylaxis. After an exposure, a medical checkup or monitoring might be necessary.

PPE Levels

The Environmental Protection Agency (EPA, 2009) has defined a tiered level of protection according to the severity of a hazardous materials response. These PPE levels are general guidelines, as some situations will necessitate other combinations of equipment. The four recommended PPE levels and examples are presented in this section.

Level A (Figure 5–2)

This event, termed an **immediately dangerous to life or health (IDLH) environment**, contains the greatest risk for exposure to potentially life-threatening biological hazards. It requires the

FIGURE 5–2   Level A PPE example
Courtesy of Joe LeFevere, Fox Valley Technical College.

maximum respiratory, eye, and skin protection. Equipment could include: a totally encapsulated chemical- and vapor-protective suit; inner and outer chemical-resistant gloves; positive-pressure, full face-piece self-contained breathing apparatus (SCBA) or positive pressure supplied air respirator (SAR) with escape SCBA; and disposable protective suit, gloves, and boots.

Level B (Figure 5–3)

This level of protection is required in circumstances where the responder needs the highest level of respiratory protection but a moderate level of skin protection. This level is the minimum required PPE for entering an unknown hazardous environment. The full-face SCBA or a positive-pressure SAR with escape SCBA should be used. All clothing should be chemical-resistant and include hooded coveralls, inner and outer gloves, boots, and a face shield.

Level C (Figure 5–4)

When the concentration and type of airborne substance(s) are known and the criteria for an air-purifying respirator (APR) are met, responders should wear Level C protection. Besides the APR, the same types of chemical-resistant clothing should be worn as those for Level B hazards. This is the highest level for using an APR.

FIGURE 5–3   Level B PPE example
Courtesy of Joe LeFevere, Fox Valley Technical College.

FIGURE 5–4   Level C PPE example
Courtesy of Joe LeFevere, Fox Valley Technical College.

Level D (Figure 5–5)

For situations where no contaminants are present or may involve splashes, immersion, or a potential for unexpected contact/inhalation of chemicals, only the minimum protection is required. Level D equipment might include gloves, coveralls, safety glasses, face shield, and chemical-resistant steel-toed boots.

Types of Respiratory Protection (Figures 5–6 and 5–7)

SCBA, SAR, and APR apparatus must be approved by the National Institute of Occupational Safety and Health (NIOSH) and certified according to PPE level. If the PPE is reusable, it must be decontaminated according to standard practices for the particular biological agent before taking it off. This may be as simple as a thorough scrubbing with soap and water and/or bleach, but depends upon the material, contact time with the hazard, and the specific contaminant. Disposable gear is worn only once and should be disposed of according to departmental regulations to preserve safety and security.

FIGURE 5–5 Level D PPE example
Courtesy of Joe LeFevere, Fox Valley Technical College.

FIGURE 5–6 Examples of various respiratory equipment
Courtesy of Joe LeFevere, Fox Valley Technical College.

FIGURE 5-7   Example of a self-contained breathing apparatus (SCBA)
Courtesy of Joe LeFevere, Fox Valley Technical College.

Common Crime Scene–Related Pathogens

Bloodborne pathogens are microorganisms found in the blood that can cause infection and disease, and may be transported in biological fluids. However, it bears mentioning that fluids other than blood may contain pathogens because they contain microscopic traces of blood within them. These include, but are not limited to: feces, urine, tears, sweat, saliva, semen, vaginal secretions, nasal secretions, breast milk, and vomitus. It also should be noted that feces, nasal secretions, sweat, tears, vomit, and urine (when not contaminated with blood) are not addressed under universal precautionary materials. However, they can transmit other infectious diseases, so caution should be used with anything produced by the human body. The most commonly encountered pathogens are human immunodeficiency virus (HIV)/acquired immunodeficiency deficiency virus (AIDS), Hepatitis, and tuberculosis (TB).

Human Immunodeficiency Virus and Acquired Immunodeficiency Deficiency Virus

This disease starts off as HIV, which is a retrovirus. Most people will not know that they are infected and highly contagious until seroconversion. This involves four clinical stages of illness

---

ServiceMASTER Provides Trauma and Crime Scene Clean-up Services

According to their website (http://www.smabsolute.com/trauma-crime-scene-clean-up/) ServiceMASTER now provides trauma and crime scene clean-up services at a number of their locations. In the event of a traumatic event, like a homicide, suicide, or other fatality, it is important that all affected areas of a building or property are professionally cleaned to eliminate any biohazardous waste. Failure to properly and safely remove all biological and chemical contaminants can pose serious health issues for occupants, employees, customers, and owners. ServiceMASTER Absolute offers specialized trauma and crime scene clean-up services that will decontaminate the area quickly and safely to restore the scene to its preincident state.

ServiceMASTER is certified to process for:

- Crime Scenes   - Industrial Accidents

- Homicides   - Tear Gas Cleaning

- Suicides   - Methamphetamine Laboratories

- Natural Deaths   - Uninhabitable Residences

- Traumatic Accidents   - Vehicle Mishap Cleaning

When contracted for a trauma or crime scene cleanup job, ServiceMASTER will:

- Clean up and dispose of dangerous material.

- Remove any sign of incident occurrence quickly.

- Safely transport any biohazards that result from such an incident.

- Restore the scene to its preincident state so families and businesses can get back to normal.

- Provide a paper trail for future buyers/sellers that substantiates a professional, CAL-OSHA-certified company restored the property.

---

beginning with a fever, joint pain, rash, and enlarged lymph nodes. Symptoms slowly (over 5–10 years) become more severe, and by stage 4 signals that the HIV has progressed to AIDS. By this time, the retrovirus has invaded the individual's DNA and thereafter depresses the immune system, causing an irreversible reduction in the body's ability to fight off infection and making the individual more susceptible to such opportunistic infections as pneumonia or HIV-related cancer. Exposure to any AIDS-contaminated blood or body fluids carries a risk of infection. There is no known cure for AIDS to date. Vaccines and medications can delay disease progression, but the outcome is death.

Hepatitis

Transmitted by way of blood and body fluids, this is an infectious disease of the liver. The three different forms of this virus are known as types A, B, and C. Of these, Hepatitis B and C are the most deadly. There are vaccinations for both Hepatitis A and B, but none for type C. Hepatitis B is sometimes known as *serum hepatitis* and can result in jaundice, cirrhosis, and in some cases cancer of the liver.

Tuberculosis

Unlike the aforementioned pathogens, TB is a bacteria (*Mycobacterium tuberculosis*) that it airborne. Infection occurs when sputnum is aerosolized by an infected person's cough, shouting, or spitting, and the individual breathes in the minute particles. This disease affects the lungs and most cases can be treated successfully via antibiotics. A small group of organisms known as atypical TB can live alongside the body's normal bacteria and not cause any damage, meaning that the infected individual is a carrier of TB but does not get sick. Because this strain is more resistant to antibiotics, it can take up to a year and a half of medication before being cured.

Crime Scene Precautionary Steps to Reduce Risk

There are several simple habits that will help allay or prevent infection at a crime scene.

- Consider all blood and body fluids, wet or dry, to be infectious. Current research indicates that the infectious activity of some organisms persists more than several days after drying.
- Protect eyes, nose, and mouth by using goggles and a mask. These provide a barrier to spraying, splashing, or aerosol transmission of infectious materials.
- Be extremely aware and cautious when handling sharp items. Never shear, break, or bend a contaminated sharp.
- Place all syringes, razor blades, needles, and other sharp instruments in a puncture-resistant sharps container.
- Latex or nitrile gloves should be worn when handling potentially contaminated items. Remove jewelry before putting on gloves. Most latex gloves have microscopic holes and openings, so double gloving (wearing two pairs of gloves at the same time) and changing gloves frequently aids in protection.
- Avoid hand-to-face contact (eating, smoking, drinking, rubbing eyes, rubbing nose, etc.) when processing a crime scene.
- Immediately wash hands, arms, face, and any exposed skin after removing and disposing of barrier equipment when crime scene processing efforts are completed. Frequent handwashing is a good safety practice.

- Any contaminated equipment should be decontaminated with a solution of one part household bleach to nine parts water. Afterward, the item can be wiped down with soap and water or isopropyl alcohol to remove the smell of bleach.

Steps to Take for Exposure to Blood/Body Fluids

Immediately following an exposure:
- Wash needle sticks and cuts with soap and water.
- Flush splashes/splatters to the nose, mouth, or skin with water.
- Irrigate eyes with clean water, saline, or sterile irrigates.
- Report the exposure to the department (e.g., occupational health, infection control) responsible for managing exposures. Prompt reporting is essential because, in some cases, postexposure treatment may be recommended and it should be started as soon as possible.

There is no scientific evidence to show that using antiseptics or squeezing the wound will reduce the risk of transmission of a bloodborne pathogen, and using a caustic agent such as bleach is not recommended.

WRAP UP

Chapter Summary

Each crime scene encountered by investigative personnel is unique to itself. Although it may appear similar to others, there is none exactly like it. Investigators must decide the most appropriate CSI model to utilize in the investigatory and processing efforts. This often involves the utilization of many different specialized personnel. Because many of these specialized personnel may not necessarily come from law enforcement backgrounds, it is imperative that all involved make use of strong interpersonal skills. Working together with the understanding that all concerned are working toward the same goal, and working in a spirit of mutual cooperation and respect, will ensure a professional and successful investigation.

However, it is not simply enough for such individuals to work together. They must work in a manner that ensures each of their safety and well-being. For this reason, all personnel must be cognizant of health and safety risks and put into practice universal precautions within their processing efforts. Doing so will ensure that all personnel will literally live to fight another day.

Review Questions

1. A preliminary scene survey is often referred to as a _____.

2. Explain the fundamental differences between the four CSI processing models.

3. PPE, as it relates to CSI, is an acronym for _____.

4. _____ refers to the unintended movement or transfer of material between two items.

5. Name three bloodborne pathogen risks to crime scene personnel that can be encountered during their processing efforts.

6. Explain what is meant by barrier protection as it relates to processing hazardous materials scenes.

7. List things for the investigator to consider and do during the walk-thru.

8. Explain why the team method is the most effective way to process a crime scene.

9. What is OSHA, and what is the organization's purpose with regard to CSI?

References

Doyle, A. C. (1892). A scandal in Bohemia. In: The adventures of Sherlock Holmes. *Strand Magazine*.

Environmental Protection Agency (EPA). (updated 2009). Personal protective equipment. Retrieved, from http://www.epa.gov/emergencies/content/hazsubs/equip.htm

Fish, J. T., Miller, L. S., & Braswell M. C. (2007). *Crime scene investigation: An introduction*. New York: LexisNexis Anderson Publishing.

Graham v. Connor, 490 U.S. 386 (1989).

Illinois v. Caballes, certiorari to the supreme court of Illinois, No. 03-923. Argued November 10, 2004—Decided January 24, 2005.

Lee, H. C., Palmbach, T., Miller M. T. (2001). *Henry Lee's crime scene handbook*. San Diego: Academic Press.

National Institute of Justice. (2004). *Crime scene investigation: A reference for law enforcement training*, June 2004 Special Report, U.S. DOJ, Office of Justice Programs. NCJ200160. Retrieved August 31, 2012, from http://www.nij.gov/pubs-sum/200160.htm

Occupational Safety and Health Administration (OSHA). Retrieved July 21, 2009, from http://www.osha.gov/

United States v. Place, 462 U.S. 696 (1983).

© McMac/ShutterStock, Inc.

- Understand the basic components of crime scene documentation.
- Identify the three photographic ranges in crime scene photography.
- Understand the concept of "fair and accurate" standard of evidence photography.
- Identify the various types of and perspectives on crime scene sketches.
- Differentiate between sketching and mapping.
- Identify the necessary components of a final sketch.
- Identify the various methods of crime scene mapping and know which is best for different crime scenes.
- List the crime scene search patterns and when/where they are most effective.

Methodical Approach to Processing the Crime Scene

> It is a capital mistake to theorize before one has data. Insensibly one begins to twist facts to suit theories, instead of theories to suit facts.
>
> Sherlock Holmes, in *A Scandal in Bohemia*
> Sir Arthur Conan Doyle (1859–1930)

KEY TERMS

Close-up Photographs
Crime Scene Sketch
Final Sketch
Legend

Mapping
Mid-range Photographs
Overall Photographs
Photo Log

Photo Placard
Rough Sketch
Swath

Methodical Approach to Crime Scene Processing

The first step in crime scene processing is to establish a plan. However, it is not always a simple task to establish a plan as to how to approach crime scene processing efforts. Crime scenes are complex and confusing creatures. In Shakespeare's 1600 play, *Hamlet*, Polonius says, "Though this be madness, yet there is method in it" (Act 2, Scene 2). All steps of crime scene response should be calculated and methodical to ensure the most positive result. It is for this reason that investigative personnel should take the information garnered from their walk-through and develop a systematic plan for proceeding with the processing efforts. A systematic plan will ensure that nothing is overlooked and no pertinent evidence is lost in the course of the subsequent investigation.

All crime scenes are different, but there are guidelines that exist in all cases that serve as a framework for the processing efforts. The general crime scene processing structure is as follows:

- Initial scene assessment
- Search for and recognition of physical evidence
- Documentation of physical evidence
- Collection of physical evidence
- Packaging and preservation of physical evidence
- Crime scene reconstruction

These are guidelines for the overview of efforts involved with the processing of a crime scene. However, often these tasks are not separate from one another but may overlap, as will be discussed. In any case, investigative and processing efforts should start in the least intrusive and destructive manners and progress to the most intrusive and destructive. Processing the scene in this way will ensure evidence integrity for as long as possible. This section concentrates on the processing activities following the initial assessment. The first phase is documentation.

Documenting the Crime Scene

Documentation efforts at the crime scene begin the moment that an officer gets a call and continue until the case is closed. This is often the most time-consuming but also the most important step in crime scene investigation. It is the purpose of crime scene documentation to record and preserve the location and relationship of discovered evidence, as well as the condition of the crime scene as it was when the documenter was observing it. For the purposes of this text, there are four primary methods of documentation that are involved in CSI. These are:

1. Reports and note-taking (sometimes audio)
2. Photography
3. Videography
4. Crime scene sketching and mapping

The end purpose of documentation should be the successful notation of all observations made within the scene of the crime, which will ensure the individual engaged in the documentation efforts will best be able to recall the events in the future. This is particularly important as this information may be presented in court. As Sherlock Holmes explains in *The Five Orange Pips*, "The observer who has thoroughly understood one link in a series of incidents should be able accurately to state all the other ones, both before and after" (Doyle, 1892, p. 81).

Each of these methods is an integral part of crime scene documentation. None is a substitute for another. While some of the methods might appear to be redundant, this serves to corroborate the other methods, ensuring that nothing is overlooked and that all areas are accounted for. Notes and reports are not sufficient by themselves because they do not accurately portray the scene in detail the way photographs can. However, photographs are not sufficient by themselves, as they often need more explanation, which is the purpose of reports and notes. Sometimes notes are dictated into a tape or digital recording device, yet at some point are transcribed into a written format for court purposes. Here, therefore, notes and reports are defined as being both audio and written. While photographs are a good tool for documenting the visual aspect of a scene, nothing brings the scene to life as much as videotaping. However, video cannot be used in the same manner as photographs from a forensic analysis standpoint when documenting physical evidence.

Because each type of record has its place in documentation efforts, all must be considered and utilized when available and appropriate.

Written Documentation/Reports

There is an old adage in police work that sums up the importance of documentation: "If it's not written down, it didn't happen." To a large extent, this is true. It is important that each step of the process and every action taken be documented extensively by using notes, photographs, sketches, and reports. The written notes begin with the first responder and continue throughout the investigative process. At each step, those individuals involved in the process are responsible for documenting all observations that they made and all actions they performed. This includes documentation of efforts that resulted in negative findings as well. An example of a negative finding is a search for latent fingerprints that yielded nothing.

Each department typically has its own format and requirements for various levels of documentation within the investigative process. At the very basic level, written documentation consists of:

- Notification information
- Arrival information
- Scene description
- Victim description
- Crime scene team

Essentially there are two types of written documentation. The first are notes. *Notes* are brief, often in a bulletpoint format, documentation of efforts, observations, and actions. Notes are taken at the time of the incident and are informal. The second type of written documentation is a report. *Reports* can be either fill-in-the-blank forms that are utilized to record pertinent information relating to a case or they can be of narratives. These are formal and are typically unique to a particular department and specific to a certain type of scene or case. Narrative reports are formally written, usually in the first person, active voice, and past tense. They document all actions taken by the report's author, and all observations he or she made.

Taking Notes

Field notes are typically the first step of written documentation, and are typically conducted while at the scene or during the initial stages of the investigation. Note takers should record field notes while they are still under the stimuli that made something seem noteworthy, not later. Field notes constitute the most readily available and reliable record of the crime scene. They do

Elements of Field Notes

The Five Ws and an H

Who

- committed the crime?
- had a motive to commit the crime?
- was the victim?
- saw what happened?
- reported the crime?
- might know something?
- were the first people on the scene?

What

- was the relationship between victim and perpetrator?
- crime was committed?
- was said and by whom?
- evidence might there be?
- evidence has been discovered?
- is missing?
- was left?

not necessarily form a logical flow of events but rather make up a hodgepodge of information gleaned from numerous perceptions, observations, interviews and efforts. In complex investigations, the task of note-taking can seem overwhelming, but the basic principles remain the same.

Field notes are the building blocks that are used to develop hypotheses and, later, a theory of the crime. Field notes can also help to stimulate memory if and when the case goes to court. They provide the basic information for the official report, which is the foundation for trial testimony. The official report will contain numerous entries. Crime scene personnel will produce the initial report early in the investigative process; as the investigation develops and new information is discovered, personnel will add supplemental reports to the original. The compilation of these reports, in conjunction with the field notes, allows personnel to recollect the investigation in detail and thus form the backbone of the prosecution and the defense efforts.

All courtroom testimony is balanced against the documentation that personnel have accumulated, including field notes. At the time of trial, personnel may use the field notes to refresh their memory, however, doing so allows the defense an opportunity to examine the notes and conduct a cross-examination of the witness pertaining to the notes. With that in mind, personnel

---

- was moved?
- was touched?

Where

- did the crime occur?
- was evidence located?
- are all the witnesses now?
- were all the witnesses?
- do the witnesses live?
- is the suspect?
- was entry made?
- was exit made?

When

- was the crime committed?
- was the crime reported?
- was evidence discovered?
- did the first responder arrive?
- was the scene secured?
- was the scene released?

Why

- was the crime committed?
- was the victim chosen?
- was the location chosen?
- were the criminal implements chosen?

How

- did the perpetrator gain entry?
- was the crime committed?
- did the perpetrator depart?

Important Information

Field notes should also contain the following:

- *Identification of date and time* (the date and time of assignment to the case; the date and time of arrival on the scene).

- *Description of the location* (description of the scene on arrival, including weather, lighting, approaches, and geographic location). Information regarding the location can be useful in establishing lines of sight and the distance of visibility.

- *Description of the crime scene* (broad overview that narrows to specific noticeable details, such as forced entry, disarranged furniture, bloodstains, blood spatter, and the condition of doors and windows).

- *Listing of absent items*. What should be at the crime scene but is missing often reveals something about the perpetrator and the nature of the crime. A serial killer might

should put nothing in their notes that they would not be willing to share with the defense, the judge, or the jury. Also, all notes are available to the defense upon request, and personnel testifying from a field notebook are not permitted to remove anything from their notebook. Therefore, each notebook should contain notes about one investigation only, so that sensitive material from another investigation is not publicized inadvertently.

In some states, there is a rule of procedure with the legal process that allows the defense to inquire of the witness whether there are any other writings or statements taken or made by the witness that are not included within the official report. An affirmative answer allows the defense to request a recess and an order directing the witness to obtain the documentation and return immediately with it to the courtroom. Even if the witness is not using the notes to refresh his or her memory, the defense may still obtain them if they exist.

take a souvenir or trophy that features prominently in fantasies associated with the killings. Such a souvenir or trophy may be helpful in establishing a profile of the killer and figuring out the killer's signature (the pattern associated with his or her killings).

- *Description of wounds on the victim.* The types and locations of wounds should be recorded. If discoloration is present, its location and color should be included.

- *Photograph log.* The photographer should keep a separate photo log; if the investigator takes the pictures, he or she should place an entry in the field notes for each entry. The entry should include a description of the content of the photo, the speed of the film, the shutter speed, the distance from the object photographed, the location and direction from which the photo was taken, and the date, time, and case number or name.

- *Video log.* If the investigator is taking the video, then the following information should be recorded: the type of recording device, the type of film (if not using digital), the type of lens or lenses, and whether artificial light was used.

- *Identification of the evidence recovered and its location.* All evidence must be geographically and temporally located. It is the investigator's job to record sufficient information to adequately place each piece of evidence. All measurements should be recorded, as well as the identity of the person who discovered the evidence. To identify evidence, the investigator should provide a description of the evidence and note its location, the time discovered, who discovered it, the type of container used to store it, the method of sealing the container, the markings used on tags and evidence, and where the evidence is being kept (maintenance log).

Courtesy of Ronald Becker, JD, Professor, Chaminade Institute.

Memory is always suspect and subject to extrapolation and interpolation, the grist of cross-examination. Memory corroborated by reports and notes takes on a believability not possessed by unaided memory.

Crime Scene Photography

Entire texts have been written solely on this topic. Photographers are urged to seek out books and courses that will help them to continually refine their skills. This introduction comprises a succinct but thorough overview of the purpose and skills involved in crime scene photography.

The purpose of crime scene photography is to capture adequate images for the best possible documentation and reproduction of the reality present at the moment in time when the scene was photographed. When attempting to shoot precisely, one must remember that photography is a mechanical means of retaining vision. When properly taken, a photograph is one of the only ways to capture an instant of time. However, the camera was never intended to replace vision, and it certainly cannot (Weiss, 2009). Crime scene photography is visual storytelling, and as such, the photographs should be a fair and accurate representation of the scene about which the story is being told.

Photographs are almost universally accepted by the courts and allowed into evidence irrespective of their image quality as long as the images contained within them are not

VIEW **FROM AN EXPERT**

Fair and Accurate

Photographic images of evidence have been presented in court for over a century. The admissibility of the images is decided by the judge. The judge may use the credibility and competency of the witness presenting the images, plus other important factors, as parameters for the decision. Opposition counsel has the right to challenge the images and to try to demonstrate that they are not, in fact, accurate representations of the evidence.

Photographs are usually allowed into court regardless of their quality. The actual photographer is rarely asked to testify about image accuracy, because the photographs are not considered as evidence but simply representations of the physical evidence.

Photographic images, whether captured on film or digital sensors, may be questioned regarding their degree of accuracy as representations of the imaged subject. In the courtroom, photographs must provide the best possible illustration of a very specific reality. In order to promote an industry-acceptable degree of quality and credibility in evidentiary photographs, professional organizations, including the Evidence Photographers International Council (EPIC), have published standards for evidence photographs.

A *standard* is an established norm or requirement. It is a formal, peer-accepted document that establishes uniform engineering or technical criteria, methods, processes, and practices. All standards for evidence photographs define *admissibility* essentially as a matter of a *fair and accurate representation of the subject portrayed*.

How are photographers and the court to interpret *fair and accurate*? *Fair* is a relative term. The judge is tasked with making the determination of what is fair, and often this call will be based on the credibility of the witness. Even poor photographic quality will not necessarily cause an image to be inadmissible if the judge believes the image is fair and relevant to the proceedings. It should be noted that there is not a standard definition or set of parameters for the term *"accurate"* Judge John Panos, a state court judge in DeKalb County, Georgia, stated, "I would like to see a standard definition of 'accurate' made and published. This can then be referred to as the standard of the industry." Why is this definition necessary? The broad definition of accurate includes some of the subtler and more technical aspects of photography, including, perspective, angle of view, and dimensionality. It is conceivable that any photographic image could be questioned.

inflammatory or prejudicial in nature (Weiss, 2009). Although it used to be necessary for a person to also be able to testify as to how a photo was developed or processed, today this is rarely the case, as the images themselves are not the evidence but rather what they represent.

Photographers often may attempt to create photographs of objects or scenes "as seen" by someone else. Undoubtedly this is an impossible undertaking, as no one can accurately document an item or moment as someone else saw it. Instead, it is an appropriate step to document the image or scene from the perspective of the viewer in approximately the same position, although not at the same moment in time (Weiss, 2009).

Terms such as color management, dynamic range, resolution, perspective, angle of view, or dimensionality may not be fully understood by the professional photographer or the attorney, let alone the juror. How many people can properly explain the difference between vision and perception, and articulate how this correlates to the accuracy of a photographic representation? It cannot be taken for granted that anyone in the courtroom understands photography on that level.

Photographers may attempt to create photographs of objects or scenes "as seen" by someone at the moment in question. Of all the purposes or goals that apply to photography, probably the most impossible is to create an image of anything exactly as another person would have seen it. It is, however, possible and much easier to take images and then use those images to help explain how it looked to you.

Thus in the real world, the definition of fair and accurate might be what the image is intended to show. In most cases, in order for an image to be a fair and accurate representation, it should show the questioned area or object in its most natural state. For example, if an attorney wishes to show the approximate physical or general area of involvement, then the judge may not be too strict in interpreting the term fair and accurate. In this case, a photograph of the scene would suffice for the purpose of identifying a location. On the other hand, if the primary purpose of the image is to illustrate exact details of a scene or object, such as the measured distance between two objects or the details of a latent print, then determining whether the image is fair and accurate will require much closer scrutiny.

If an attorney wants to show the exact distance between a crosswalk and a traffic signal, photographic experience and expertise becomes very important. If that photo, submitted as evidence was created by someone lacking a high level of experience and expertise, a judge may not allow a witness to testify that, based on the photograph, the distance between the crosswalk and the traffic signal is 25 feet.

Fair and accurate may amount to different things at different trials. It will always be a measure of the competence and credibility of the person presenting the photographs, rather than the sophistication of the camera and equipment used to create the images.

Sanford Weiss, EPIC Crime Scene Photographer
Author, *Forensic Photography: The Importance of Accuracy*

Photographic Ranges and Perspectives

In keeping with the storytelling theme, the first photos taken at a scene should not be of gore or an item of physical evidence. Instead, they should be of the overall crime scene. They should set the stage for the beginning of the story. As such, there are three important ranges of photographs that are taken at the scene of a crime: overall photographs, midrange/evidence-establishing photographs, and close-up/comparison/examination photographs.

Also, it is important to remember to take a photograph of a photo placard as the first photo taken at the crime scene. A **photo placard** is a handwritten or agency-developed sheet (**Figure 6–1**) that lists pertinent case information for the photographs to follow. Taking a photo of this as the first photo on a roll of film or as the first digital photo of a case will ensure that personnel are familiar with which photographs pertain to which case, and the name of the photographer. Only one case should be photographed on a roll of film; however, with today's digital media, often several (if not more) cases are photographed on a single digital media card prior to downloading onto a computer. Photographing a photo placard will serve as a separator between the cases, so that case photos will not become commingled.

Overall Photographs (**Figure 6–2**)

Overall photographs are exposed with a wide-angle lens or in such a fashion that allows the viewer to see a large area in the scene at eye level. Their function is to document the condition and layout of the scene as found. They help eliminate issues of subsequent contamination (e.g., tracked blood, movement of items). Typically, these are shot from the four corners of the crime scene. If indoors, usually they are taken from the corners of the room, shooting toward the center. If outdoors, they are often shot from the direction of a cardinal heading (North, South, East, and West). These four photographs most likely will capture the entire scene. If not, then additional photographs from an appropriate vantage point can be taken. These overall photographs set the scene and should include street signs and addresses if possible.

Also, it may be necessary to not only take overall photos facing the building or scene in question, but also overall photos facing away from the scene to show the surrounding area.

Mid-range/Evidence-Establishing Photographs (**Figure 6–3**)

The function of **mid-range photographs** is to frame the item of evidence with an easily recognized landmark. This visually establishes the position of the evidence in the scene, with its relationship to the item's surroundings. These types of photographs are

City-ville Police Department

Case #:

Date:

Location:

Photographer Name:

Photographer ID:

FIGURE 6–1   Example of a photo placard

FIGURE 6–2   Example of an overall photograph

FIGURE 6–3   Example of a mid-range photograph

the most overlooked in crime scene work. They are taken of the evidence prior to movement or manipulation and should never include a scale of reference in the photo. The evidence-establishing photograph is not intended to show details, but simply to frame the item with a known landmark in the scene. The close-up and the evidence-establishing photograph go hand-in-hand.

Close-up/Comparison/Examination Photographs (**Figure 6–4**)

The function of **close-up photographs** (also called *comparison*, *examination*, or *macro* photographs) is to allow the viewer to see all evident details on the item of evidence. This photo should be close and fill the frame with the evidence itself. They are taken with and without a scale. It is extremely important that photographs of this type are first taken without a scale of reference, and then with a scale of reference. The first photo shows the scene prior to contamination or manipulation by the photographer or crime scene personnel. The second includes a scale of reference with which the viewer is able to gauge the size of the item presented within the photograph. This scale will allow for a 1:1 ratio reproduction of the photograph (i.e., 1 inch equals 1 inch). Failure to photograph the close-up without a scale prior to incorporating a scale in the photo could result in the photo being inadmissible because of the allegation of scene tampering.

The preceding photographic ranges are used any time there is an item of evidence that is important and will have a bearing on the investigation. While there might be a variety of perspectives photographed, any photograph taken at a crime scene will fall under one of the preceding ranges. For instance, photographs taken from the reported position of a witness would fall into the overall range category. Those taken to show the address of a residence would fall into the mid-range category if they showed more than simply the numbers/letters and included the façade of the house or entry to the home. However, if it was only of the letters/numbers this photograph would fall into the close-up range.

Photo Logs

Regardless of the perspective or range taken, each photograph taken at a crime scene should be documented on a **photo log**. A photo log is a permanent record of all information pertaining

FIGURE 6–4   Example of a close-up/comparison/examination photograph

to documentation by photographs. Department policy often dictates what is found within a photo log; however, if no policy exists, the following suggestions are offered (**Figure 6–5**). Information that should be included in a photo log includes:

- Title and information block consisting of date/time/case number/agency name
- Photo equipment used
- Numerical ordering of each photo taken
- Brief description of each photo taken
- Direction facing for each photo taken
- Approximate distance from subject matter in each photo taken
- Shutter speed, aperture setting, and ISO for each photo. If photographed with conventional photography, then pertinent photographic information should be included for

Case Number:		Month	Day	Year	Page of
Location of Incident			City		Time
Victim's Name		DOB		CDL	
Photographer/ID #		Scribe/ID #			
Camera, Lenses, and Flash Used					

#	Description of Photo	Polarizing Filter (Y or N)	Tripod (Y or N)	Lens Used (if zoom, length set on)	Flash (yes/no & normal, bounce, or off camera)	Direction Facing	F-Stop	SS	Distance from subject
1									
2									
3									
4									
5									
6									
7									
8									
9									
10									
11									
12									
13									
14									
15									
16									
17									
18									
19									
20									

FIGURE 6–5 Example of a photo log

each. If photographs are taken in a digital format, documenting such information is not as imperative, because it will be digitally recorded when each photo is taken as part of the digital file for each photo.

The photo log should be a documentation of visual storytelling that flows from the general to the specific. The log itself is not always constructed at the crime scene, but rather the foregoing information will sometimes be included on a rough copy of a photo log or within the field notebook of the photographer and transferred onto a photo sheet at a later time, to include information pertaining to the digital properties of each photo, retrieved from the camera or computer at the time of download. Most agencies use pre-printed log sheets divided into categories for ease of recording efforts.

Order of Taking Photographs

While this manner of documentation is listed near the beginning, obviously taking overall photos is much less intrusive to a crime scene than taking close-up photos (due to movement of items and the addition of scales of reference). It therefore is important that you realize that although these are listed together, not all ranges of photographs are taken together or at the same time during a scene investigation. After the initial scene survey has been conducted, but before a detailed search or examination is undertaken, the crime scene should be photographed. However, usually this only includes the overall photographs, but if items of evidence have been located, then mid-ranges can be taken from a safe position. Close-ups are not typically taken until a thorough search of the scene has been conducted, unless the item is of a transient nature.

Guidelines for Crime Scene Photography

The following strategies have proven useful in crime scene investigations.

- Always use a photo placard on the first shot of each roll to demonstrate administrative data (see Figure 6–1).
- Always use a crime scene photo log (see Figure 6–5).
- Document the entire scene in situ as soon as possible using overall photographs.
- Photograph all fragile evidence as soon as possible.
- In the documentation stage, photograph all known evidence using close-up photos.
- As items are discovered in later stages, return and document them fully, including additional overall photographs if needed.
- Create photographs that fully demonstrate the results of additional examinations (e.g., latent prints, bloodstain pattern analysis, trajectory analysis).
- Try not to include the photographer or other people in the photographs, if possible.
- Shoot all close-up photographs with the use of a tripod.

- Close-up photos should be taken with and without a scale of reference.
- Be sure that the scale is on the same plane as the item of evidence being photographed.
- The subject matter should be parallel to the film plane/camera to eliminate distortion caused by skewed angle photographs (**Figure 6–6**).
- If in doubt, photograph it!

Crime Scene Videography

As a result of digital media gaining widespread acceptance within U.S. courts, in the last few years videography has become a routine method of documenting major crime scenes. While this is an obvious and useful method of providing visual documentation of the conditions and items encountered at the crime scene, it must be remembered that doing so is not a substitute for still photography. Each has its merits.

Video is taken to record the scene in as close to its original condition as possible, as this is an easy method to employ and is relatively quick in its application. Oftentimes, video is shot while conducting the initial walk-through as a way of recording the layout and conditions of the scene. This documentation is useful to supervisors and investigative personnel in determining logistic and equipment needs, as well as reducing official visitors by giving them the opportunity to look at the crime scene without actually entering into it themselves. It also

FIGURE 6–6 Example of correct camera angle for close-up photographs
Courtesy of Dana Gevelinger, University of Wisconsin-Platteville.

enables investigative personnel to later "enter" the scene as often as necessary through viewing the video without the need for a search warrant. This is especially useful if the crime scene is no longer available to personnel.

Videography is a useful method for documenting a crime scene. It can provide a perspective that is more easily understood and perceived by the viewer than those offered by notes, sketches, or still photographs. However, it must be remembered that this is a supplemental method and not a replacement for still photography or other documentation methods.

Guidelines for Videotaping a Crime Scene

While some of these points are similar to those for photography, a few key points are important to remember when shooting a moving data stream:

- Begin with an introductory placard that states case number, date, time, location, and other pertinent case and chain of custody information.

- This video should be a storytelling event. Start with a general view of the area surrounding the crime scene. Following this should be an overview of the crime scene itself. It is suggested to take overalls from the cardinal compass directions (North, South, East, West) for orientation purposes.

- Turn off the audio on the video recorder unless you intend to narrate.

- Do not move the camera too quickly by panning (moving side to side), or zooming (moving in for a close-up view) as this results in abrupt motion and bad focus.

- Unless in sunlight, always use a video strobe. Never use a flashlight to illuminate the scene.

- Do not use the zoom unless it is necessary because of an inability to get physically closer to the subject matter, or if it is unsafe to do so. The human eye cannot zoom. If the video is to be a fair and accurate representation of how the videographer observed the scene, no zoom should be used.

- Video never should be edited or altered in any manner following the initial taping. The original copy should be kept as evidence, and duplicate copies should be made for viewing purposes.

Sketching and Mapping the Scene

Sketching

A **crime scene sketch** is a permanent record of the size and distance relationship of the crime scene and the physical evidence within it. The sketch serves to clarify the special information present within the photographs and video documentation, because the other methods do not allow the viewer to easily gauge distances and dimensions. A sketch is the most simplistic manner in which to present crime scene layout and measurements. Often photographer/camera positions may be noted within a sketch also.

Why is a sketch important to crime scene documentation?

- It accurately portrays the physical facts.
- It relates to the sequence of events at the scene.
- It establishes the precise location and relationship of objects and evidence at the scene.
- It helps to create a mental picture of the scene for those not present.
- It is a permanent record of the scene.
- It usually is admissible in court.
- It assists in interviewing and interrogating.
- It assists in preparing the written investigative report.
- It assists in presenting the case in court. Well-prepared sketches and drawings help judges, juries, witnesses, and others to visualize the crime scene.

When should sketches be made?

- Sketch all serious crimes and accident scenes after photographs have been taken and before anything is moved.
- Sketch the entire scene, the objects, and the evidence.

Two types of sketches are produced with regard to crime scene documentation: rough sketches and final/finished sketches. **Rough sketches** (**Figure 6–7**) are developed while on-scene, typically during the crime scene assessment/preliminary scene evaluation phase to assist with development of a strategic plan for processing. The sketch is not done to scale, can be drawn with any implement (crayon, chalk, pencil, pen, etc.), and is very rough artistically. As work progresses at the crime scene, the sketch will include not only the crude crime scene layout, but also will be used to record measurements of items and structures and distances between items.

A **final sketch** (**Figures 6–8** and **6–9**) is a finished rendition of the rough sketch. They are usually prepared for courtroom presentation and often will not show all measurements and distances originally recorded on the rough sketch. Only significant items and structures are typically present within a final sketch. A final sketch is produced in either ink or on a computer, in a way that cannot be modified (i.e., not in pencil or erasable ink). The sketch should be clutter-free and should accurately depict all pertinent items of evidence, typically through the use of an accompanying legend. A **legend** is a note of explanation, outside of the sketch area, which relates to a specific item, symbol, or information contained within the graphical representation of a sketch. A final sketch should include:

- Title (What does the sketch represent? e.g., Sketch of Bank ABC Robbery)
- Legend (What do symbols within the sketch mean?)
- Case information. (i.e., date, time, place, case number)
- Initials/name (person who drew the sketch)
- Indication of direction (e.g., North)
- Scale (e.g., 1″ = 1′)

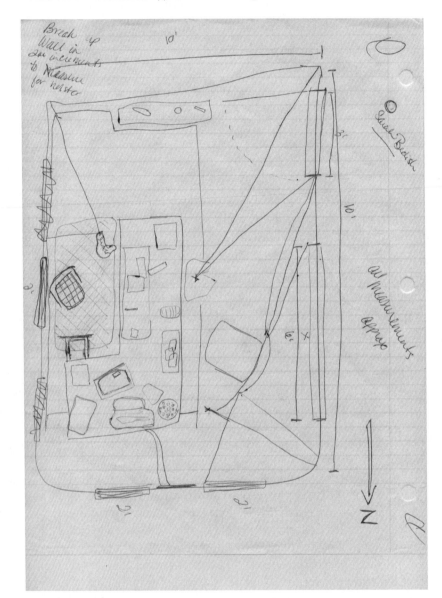

FIGURE 6–7   Example of a rough sketch
Courtesy of Sarah Bedish, University of Wisconsin-Platteville.

- Measurement table (If measurements are not represented within the confines of the sketch, an accompanying measurement table should be included to explain the distances and measurements associated with it.)

- There should also be a notation following the scale or measurement table stating: "All measurements are approximate." This will ensure that the sketch's author does not get into a credibility argument in court that a measurement is documented as the listed measurement, but could in fact be greater or lesser due to rounding errors or other factors.

Three different crime scene perspectives can be represented within a sketch: (a) the bird's eye or overhead view (**Figure 6–10**), (b) the elevation or side view (**Figure 6–11**), and (c) the three-dimensional (3D) view (**Figure 6–12**). Sometimes personnel choose to incorporate several perspectives within a sketch (e.g., using both elevation and overhead sketches to draw an exploded or cross-sectional view of a scene) (**Figure 6–13**).

An overhead or bird's eye view is the most common form of crime scene sketching. It is prepared with the perspective being as though the author was looking down upon the scene from above. This type shows the floor layout but cannot represent heights of items or show associated evidence on walls. In order to show such information, a person must sketch an elevation or side-view sketch

FIGURE 6–8   Example of a final hand-drawn sketch
Courtesy of Sarah Bedish, University of Wisconsin-Platteville.

to show evidence located on a building façade, interior wall, or any item of which height is an important aspect (e.g., death involving a hanging). A 3D crime scene perspective is created with the aid of computers, and has its primary function as being crime scene activity reconstruction to help explain what happened and in what order.

Crime Scene Mapping

Mapping is the term associated with crime scene measurements. Sometimes a person may sketch but not map, meaning that he or she draws a sketch of an area but does not apply measurements to the sketch produced and items represented. Rarely, however, will one map without sketching (i.e., record measurements with no graphical representation for what the measurements represent). Sometimes this step is referred to as *measuring*. There are a variety of methods for mapping a crime scene, depending upon whether the crime scene is an interior or exterior scene. As this is an introductory text, only the most basic and most often used methods are covered here. The basic types of mapping methods utilized for crime scene sketching and mapping are: (a) baseline, (b) rectangular coordinates, (c) triangulation, and (d) polar/grid coordinates.

FIGURE 6–9   Example of a final computer-generated sketch

Adapted from an original illustration by Alex Albright, University of Wisconsin-Platteville.

FIGURE 6–10   Example of an overhead/bird's-eye view sketch

Courtesy of Dana Gevelinger, University of Wisconsin-Platteville.

FIGURE 6–11   Example of an elevation/side-view sketch
Courtesy of Dana Gevelinger, University of Wisconsin-Platteville.

FIGURE 6–12   Example of a three-dimensional crime scene sketch

Baseline Mapping

This is the most basic—and least accurate—form of crime scene mapping. For this method, a baseline is developed or identified from which to conduct measurements. This can be an existing area, such as the edge of a roadway, a wall, fence, etc., or it can be developed by personnel, such as by placing a string or tape measure through the scene and conducting measurements from there. In the case of the latter, the line should be run between two known fixed points, such as trees or other identifiable points, so that the points can be found in the future and the scene reconstructed if necessary (**Figure 6–14**). Once the baseline is established, measurements are taken from the baseline at an approximate 90-degree angle from the baseline to a point on the identified item or area of the crime scene. Typically, most measurements are made

FIGURE 6–13   Example of a cross-sectional/exploded sketch
Courtesy of Dana Gevelinger, University of Wisconsin-Platteville.

FIGURE 6–14   Example of a baseline map
Courtesy of Dana Gevelinger, University of Wisconsin-Platteville.

either to the center mass of the item or to the nearest point of the item to the baseline. Because it is impossible to ensure that the measurement was taken at 90 degrees, the possibility exists that the measurement will be longer if the measurement was over 90 degrees from the baseline, or if it was less than 90 degrees from the baseline. For this reason, this method is not as accurate as some of the other methods; however, it is quick and extremely easy to use.

Rectangular Coordinate Mapping

The rectangular coordinate mapping method is a slightly more accurate variation of the baseline method because it utilizes two such baselines instead of one. Two measurements are taken to a point on an item or location at the scene, one from each identified baseline. Some personnel choose to measure to two or more points on an item, using multiple rectangular measurements as a way of increasing accuracy, while others simply choose to measure to an arbitrarily identified center mass of the object in question or point to which the measurements are being taken. As with the baseline method, it cannot be determined that such measurements are taken precisely at 90-degree angles from the baseline, so there exists a greater possibility of errors than with some of the other methods. However, due to this method having two measurements, it has much greater accuracy than with the single line baseline method. This method is especially useful in confined spaces and smaller interior scenes (**Figure 6–15**).

Triangulation Mapping

This is the most accurate method of mapping that does not make use of advanced technology. While it is quite a bit more laborious and time consuming, it is sufficiently more accurate than the aforementioned methods of mapping to be worth the effort. The accuracy of this method lies in its foundation: two fixed points. From these two fixed points, measurements are taken to specified points on an item or within the crime scene. There is no need to worry about whether or not measurements have been made at a right angle because the points derive from a known fixed point, such as the corner of a room, or edge of a door frame. From these fixed points, a minimum of two measurements are made to each identified point. If the object is of a fixed or constant shape (e.g., a firearm or item of furniture), then the object is measured to two points, from the two fixed points, for a total of four measurements. If the object is of a variable shape or size (e.g., a puddle of water, pool of blood, or pile of clothes), then the object is measured to an approximate center of mass (**Figure 6–16**).

FIGURE 6–15 Example of a rectangular coordinate map
Courtesy of Dana Gevelinger, University of Wisconsin-Platteville.

FIGURE 6–16 Example of a triangulation map
Courtesy of Dana Gevelinger, University of Wisconsin-Platteville.

Polar/Grid Coordinate Mapping

Utilizing polar coordinates is the third method of crime scene mapping used to document evidence location at a crime scene. Like those previously mentioned, this is a two-dimensional (2D) system that indicates the location of an object by providing the angle and distance from the fixed or known point. Obviously, in order to conduct measurements by this method a transit or compass is necessary to measure the angles and polar directions. This method is best utilized in large outdoor scenes with very few landmarks (e.g., a plane crash in forest or large field (**Figure 6–17**).

Advanced Mapping Techniques

Some departments may have the ability to better utilize modern technology, such as global positioning systems (GPS), Total Stations, and 3D crime scene mapping systems, which are mapping systems that can take measurements in polar coordinates and then convert the measurements into grid coordinates. The benefit of this technology is that it is able to provide precise electronic distance measurements and is extremely useful in mapping large-scale scenes and events.

GPS is a satellite-based navigation system comprising a network of 24 satellites that have been placed in the earth's orbit by the U.S. Department of Defense (Garmin, 2009). GPS was originally used by and intended for the military; however, in the 1980s the government made the technology available for civilian use. The benefit of GPS is that it works in any weather condition, anywhere in the world, 24 hours a day. There are no subscription fees or setup charges to utilize GPS. These satellites complete two very precise orbits of the earth a day, during which they transmit signal information. It is these signals that GPS receivers gather and then use triangulation to calculate a user's location. A GPS receiver must be locked on to the position signal of at least three satellites in order to calculate a 2D position (latitude and longitude) as well as track movements of an object. If the GPS receiver is able to lock on to four or more satellites, the receiver can determine the user's 3D location (latitude, longitude, and altitude), along with object movement. The more satellites that the GPS is locked onto, the greater the accuracy of the position. Once the user's position has been determined, an additional service is that calculation of movement can provide GPS users the ability to record information such as speed, bearing, track, trip distance, distance to destination, sunrise, sunset, time, and many more possibilities (Garmin, 2009).

FIGURE 6–17   Example of a polar/grid coordinate map
Courtesy of Dana Gevelinger, University of Wisconsin-Platteville.

How accurate is GPS? In most cases, commercially available GPS receivers are accurate to approximately 12 meters, with higher end units capable of accuracy in the 3- to 5-meter range. This is sufficiently accurate for large scenes that have no known/fixed landmarks. A GPS reading is typically used to "mark" a known point and then measurements are made from that location, thereby ensuring that any measurements taken will all be "off" by the same amount because they all originate from the same location.

A Total Station is an electronic surveying instrument that has an integrated computer and can measure angles in the horizontal and vertical planes, utilizing a laser rangefinder instead of the more archaic method of a manual tape measure. This is especially useful because changes in elevation are very difficult to both measure and depict on a crime scene sketch. The Total Station is capable of recording evidence positions in three dimensions, thus simplifying this otherwise complicated situation.

Within the past several years, several vendors (i.e., Panoscan and Leica) have developed 3D, panoramic crime scene photography and mapping systems. (**Figure 6–18**) "This results in a 3D representation of the scene from which any measurement can be made even after the scene has been released" (Leica, 2012). This enables such technology to be utilized for pre-event planning, crime scene documentation, and post-event analysis. Another benefit of this new technology is that it is capable of accurate crime scene documentation efforts in both bright sunshine or total darkness, often at a distance of up to 900 feet.

As with all other crime scene measurements, all measurements are approximate, and they are never documented as or testified to as being 100% accurate. Crime scene mapping is about doing the best possible documentation with the resources available, realizing that rounding and other factors inhibit the ability to be completely accurate.

Searching the Crime Scene

Searching the crime scene for related evidence is a potentially damaging event and should be undertaken only after overall photographs of the scene have been taken. As evidence is located, personnel should mark the location of the evidence and mid-range photos should then be taken.

FIGURE 6–18 A Leica ScanStation P20 3D laser scanner
Courtesy of Leica Geosystems.

Important things to remember when conducting a search are:

- Do not touch, handle, or move evidence.
- Mark or designate found items without altering them.
- Found evidence must be documented before any evidence can be moved or collected.

Factors Impacting Search Methods

A variety of factors can affect a search method and these will determine the best, most accurate way to approach the scene.

Environment

Environmental conditions such as wind, rain, snow, heat, cold, etc., will have an impact on the method chosen due to how they affect the scene and the personnel involved.

Object Being Searched For

Obviously, a larger item will not entail the same level of searching detail as a smaller item (e.g., a handgun versus a bullet).

Number of Available Personnel

Some search methods are designed to incorporate a greater number of searchers in order to be most effective. If such personnel are not available, a method that utilizes fewer personnel needs to be considered.

Terrain

Obstructions (trees, buildings), ground cover (asphalt, grass), and grade (steep, flat) will all impact the type of method employed, as they will have a bearing on the ability of searchers to perform the task, and the ability to properly locate the necessary items of evidence.

Exigency

In cases of lost children, search for a loaded handgun (public safety issue); in this and certain other events, often there is the need for exigency that trumps the more detailed search patterns that would be preferable. Therefore, a quick and efficient method should be chosen, making use of the maximum number of resources available in the quickest manner possible.

Swath Size

A **swath** is the effective area that a searcher can cover while conducting a search. Swath is affected by all of the aforementioned matters and is itself a consideration in the determination of a proper search method to employ. If looking for a firearm, a larger swath would be possible in a parking lot than in high grass for instance. Also, a search conducted at night or in low light would have an impacted swath due to the ability of a flashlight to illuminate the area of responsibility.

Types of Crime Scene Search Patterns

Depending on the aforementioned factors, a variety of crime scene search patterns exist that can be employed at a crime scene. Regardless of the search pattern chosen, the crime scene investigator must be sure that the search is conducted in a systematic and thorough manner. This will ensure that all evidence is properly located, documented, and collected.

Lane/Strip Search

This type of search pattern breaks the scene up into manageable lanes in which the searcher(s) proceed back and forth, in a slightly overlapping fashion. This is similar to mowing one's lawn. This method is typically conducted by only one person (**Figure 6–19**).

Line Search

This method is incorporated when there is a large number of personnel available, often volunteers. In this method, searchers assemble in a line that runs along a chosen edge of the crime scene. Searchers stand side by side and spread apart, incorporating a manageable swath distance between each person. A search coordinator should place her or himself in the middle of this line to make certain that everyone walks forward in as straight as possible a line. If one end begins to lag, then the other end is requested to slow down. At no point should anyone be encouraged to search faster! Keeping all searchers in a straight line reduces the possibility of missing an area and thus not discovering potential evidence. This method is the most commonly employed type during an exigent search for an item or person, especially when a large number of people are available (**Figure 6–20**).

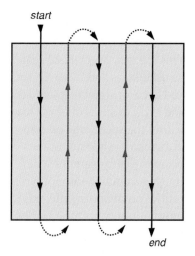

FIGURE 6–19 Example of a lane/strip search
Courtesy of Dana Gevelinger, University of Wisconsin-Platteville.

Grid Search

This sometimes is referred to as a *double strip* or *double lane* method. In this method, a lane is searched in one direction, similar to the line search method. However, as the lane terminates, a 90-degree direction change is made and another lane is searched. This can either occur through the use of two searchers (one responsible for one direction, and the other for the perpendicular direction), or else it can utilize a large number of searchers incorporating the line method as described earlier, and then turning 90 degrees and performing a second line search perpendicular to the original lane. While quite time consuming, this method

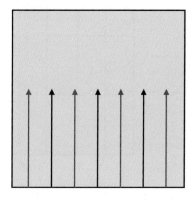

FIGURE 6–20 Example of a line search
Courtesy of Dana Gevelinger, University of Wisconsin-Platteville.

allows the same area to be searched two separate times, and at different angles. This redundancy will reduce searcher boredom, and will change the lighting and obstruction conditions present, thus increasing the ability of the searcher to locate evidence (**Figure 6–21**).

Zone Search

This method is typically utilized in an area that is already broken up into defined or manageable zones (e.g., a house or car). It is typically used indoors, but may be used outdoors if the areas are broken down into defined zones. Zones can be searched independently and later researched by different search personnel to ensure that no evidence has been overlooked. This method also can be used as a way to break up a larger crime scene, so the search coordinator then can choose from any of the search methods to cover a zone area (**Figure 6–22**).

Circle/Spiral Search

This is a very specialized search pattern method that is seldom utilized; however, it does have its usefulness and merit. In this method, searchers can either start at a defined outer boundary and circle or spiral in toward the defined critical point, or else they can begin at the critical point and circle or spiral outward toward the crime scene perimeter. Physical obstructions and barriers within the scene will present problems with this method. This method is typically employed in bomb or explosive scenes with a defined seat of explosion. It may be used in underwater or open water searches where there was a last known location for an item, vessel, or victim. If using a circling rather than a spiraling pattern, to ensure thoroughness it is suggested that a central point and an effective swath width be determined. Once this is done, searchers should move out in concentric circles, often through the use of a lanyard affixed to a point at the center of the scene (especially true for underwater searches). The searcher proceeds to search in a 360-degree manner, around the central point, and once they reach the end of their circuit, they

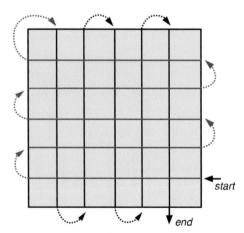

FIGURE 6–21   Example of a grid search
Courtesy of Dana Gevelinger, University of Wisconsin-Platteville.

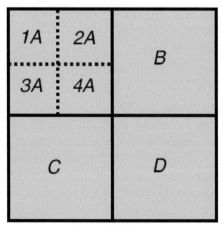

FIGURE 6–22   Example of a zone/quadrant search
Courtesy of Ellie Bruchez, University of Wisconsin-Platteville.

let out the lanyard a pre-determined amount, incorporating manageable swath width, and then proceed to conduct another 360-degree circuit of the scene. It is suggested that this new circuit be in the opposite direction of the previous circuit to both reduce the possibility of entanglement, and also to reduce the searcher's vertigo issues from walking in a continuous circle (**Figure 6–23**).

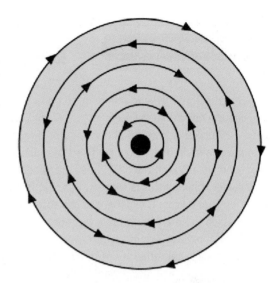

FIGURE 6–23   Example of a circle/spiral search
Courtesy of Dana Gevelinger, University of Wisconsin-Platteville.

The physical nature of a crime scene will suggest what type of search is best to employ, but the characteristics of the scene should have no effect on the quality of the search. Obviously, there will be exceptions. Large-area searches in mass-disaster investigations may have to sacrifice some quality for expedience, but in the average investigation, there is no excuse for haphazard searches. Proceed slowly, for evidence not only can be contaminated by being stepped on but can be destroyed easily or overlooked entirely by the unwary. An experienced investigator will have completed the walk-thru before beginning the search, and the walk-thru must be conducted with trace evidence foremost in the mind of crime scene personnel.

Collecting, Packaging, and Preserving Physical Evidence

After intensive crime scene search and documentation, collection and preservation of evidence should begin. The remainder of this text will be devoted to the different manners of collection and preservation specific to the type of evidence presented. At this point in the process, the following strategies should be done to ensure the most thorough and accurate investigation:

- Designate one person as the evidence collector/custodian (this ensures that nothing is missed).
- Document, collect, package, mark, seal, and preserve.
- Transient, fragile, or easily lost evidence should be collected first.
- Paper is the preferred packaging.
- Package items separately.
- Properly mark containers.
- Properly seal containers.
- Seals should be marked with initials and date/time.

Remember the Fundamentals

Success is neither magical nor mysterious. Success is the natural consequence of consistently applying the basic fundamentals. – Alice Glynn

Success as a criminal investigator is experienced at a time and location that most would have never anticipated. Recruit officers are initially trained in the academy to believe that success is synonymous with the clicking of the handcuffs on a suspect. And many officers go through their career thinking this is success. But that is only the illusion of success.

True success is experienced in a solitary moment in the back of a cavernous courtroom, sitting dressed in an uncomfortable business suit on a hard wooden bench, watching prosecutors show jurors boxes of exhibits you have provided for them...full of photographs, sketches, diagrams, interviews, and other items of evidence. Taken cumulatively, that evidence representing months of hard work and attention to detail, overwhelmingly proves the defendant's guilt beyond a reasonable doubt. At that moment in time, you realize that success does not happen by accident, it happens when you consistently apply basic crime scene fundamentals.

Searching, photographing, sketching, and collecting evidence at a crime scene are, at their essence, simple processes. Yet day after day, we read news reports of investigations gone awry because basic fundamentals were not applied or adhered to. Like a basketball team that needs all five players to properly execute the basic fundamentals for a play to be successful, so too do patrol officers and investigators need to perform the basic fundamentals at a crime scene in order to ensure success in the coming months, and sometimes years, down the road. Inattention to the fundamentals results in missed physical evidence, undocumented evidence, and worse, suppressed evidence.

First, master the fundamentals. – Larry Bird

Searching the crime scene. The most frequent fundamental mistake in searching the crime scene is the lack of a systematic search method. Due to the chaotic method in which witnesses, EMS personnel, and first responding officers discover and arrive at the crime scene, the crime scene is oftentimes searched in a haphazard fashion, thus contaminating the scene for a more systematic and thorough search of the scene utilizing a grid or sector search. Patrol officers must be cognizant that this is their primary responsibility and must think of the crime scene as a flowing river...once you put your foot in that river, you have forever altered that river and will never be able to put your foot in that same river again. Securing the crime scene and then organizing a grid or sector search where every officer knows his or her responsibility on every crime scene ensures that irrevocable mistakes are not made.

Also, consistently using the practice of secondary searches of the crime scene places an extra amount of due diligence on the officers performing the primary search. There is probably no better teaching lesson for a young patrol officer than to have another officer discover a critical piece of evidence during a secondary search. Consistently adhering to these basic crime scene search fundamentals makes it possible to enjoy that success in the back of the courtroom.

I discovered early on that the player who learned the fundamentals of basketball is going to have a much better chance of succeeding and rising through the levels of competition than the player who was content to do things his own way. – John Wooden

Photographing the crime scene. Common fundamental mistakes in crime scene photography include the failure to take overall, mid-range, and close-up photographs of every piece of evidence; failing to include a scale of reference in photographs; and failure to produce a photo log to accompany the photographs. Many times these are not fatal mistakes to the case, but hinder the prosecution by not consistently providing the information we are expected to provide. It may seem redundant to have to photograph a single piece of evidence four times, but it ensures that the jury will see the photograph that most accurately and fairly represents the facts of the case. Including a scale of reference is oftentimes overlooked or deemed not necessary at the crime scene, only to provide a moment of regret at trial preparation when we wish to document size or relationship. Photo logs are also an interesting dilemma, in that officers find it cumbersome to write down a description of every photograph as they take it. However, they prove absolutely critical six months later at trial as an officer or investigator tries to explain to the prosecutor the meaning or purpose of a particular photograph, especially if it is a close-up photograph of a critical piece of evidence.

Learn the fundamentals of the game and stick to them. Band-Aid remedies never last. – Jack Nicholas

Sketches. Sketches are specifically designed to supplement photographs by denoting size and dimension, yet many officers feel uncomfortable sketching a crime scene because of a perceived obligation to produce a highly technical final sketch for court purposes. At the minimum, completing a rough sketch at the scene ensures you have size and dimension information recorded that can later be transposed into a more technical final sketch, if needed. Officers and investigators alike must be well-versed in the use of both baseline and triangulation measurement techniques, depending on the location of the crime scene, to complete that rough sketch. Without that training, we find that officers routinely fail to use fixed points to reference their measurements, instead choosing points of reference that are not fixed. Today, officers have the benefit of having investigative units that can transform that initial rough sketch into a final sketch rather easily utilizing GPS technology and computer-aided software. However, those final sketches are only as good as the information that is collected at the scene.

Many criminal investigators have similar personal attributes to athletes and coaches... desire, will, competiveness, and a work ethic. Those attributes bring them success in both their personal and professional lives. But the truly successful investigators have something else, just like the truly successful athletes and coaches...an unrelenting will to learn, master, and apply the fundamentals.

Special Agent Mike Krapfl
Iowa Division of Criminal Investigation

Courtesy of Special Agent Mike Krapfl, Iowa Division of Criminal Investigation.

WRAP UP

Chapter Summary

Scientific crime scene investigation is the best methodology to ensure that an investigation is properly conducted and that justice is served. Use of this methodology will prevent the abrupt end of an incomplete investigation and allow for the best use of the physical evidence found at crime scenes. The general rule relating to crime scene documentation is "if it isn't written down, it didn't happen." This is important to remember when conducting the various steps of crime scene documentation. It reminds the individual to be as thorough and precise as possible to correctly retain and be able to recall the events, items, and locations involved with a crime scene.

Review Questions

1. _____ is a note of explanation, outside of the sketch area, that helps to relate or give information on a specific item or area within a sketch.

2. _____ is a drawing or graphical representation that forms a permanent record of the size and distance relationship of the crime scene.

3. _____ is the term associated with crime scene measurements.

4. In order to ensure all photographs, information contained within them, and equipment that was used to capture them are properly documented, an investigator should make use of a _____.

5. What factors can affect the choice of search method at a crime scene?

6. What is the difference between a strip/lane search pattern and a line search pattern?

7. When conducting a search of a crime scene, _____ refers to the effective area that a searcher can cover.

8. Regardless of the search pattern chosen, the crime scene investigator must be sure that the search is conducted in a _____ and _____ manner.

References

Doyle, A. C. (1892). The five orange pips. In: The adventures of Sherlock Holmes. *Strand Magazine*.

Doyle, A. C. (1892). A scandal in Bohemia. In: The adventures of Sherlock Holmes. *Strand Magazine*.

Garmin. (2009) What is GPS? Retrieved July 23, 2009, from http://www8.garmin.com/aboutGPS/

Leica. (2012). Leica Scanning Station C10. Retrieved May 27, 2012, from http://www.leica-geosystems. us/forensic/downloads/LeicaScanStationC10.pdf

Weiss, S. L. (2009). *Forensic photography: The importance of accuracy*. Upper Saddle River, NJ: Pearson Education Inc.

© McMac/ShutterStock, Inc.

The Forensic Laboratory

I am glad of all details, whether they seem to be relevant or not.

Sherlock Holmes, *The Adventure of the Copper Beeches*
Sir Arthur Conan Doyle (1859–1930)

KEY TERMS

Accreditation
Backlogged
Certification
Forensic Crime Laboratory

Known Evidence
Miranda Ruling
Proficiency Testing
Protocols

Quality Assurance (QA)
Quality Control
Questioned Evidence

History of the Forensic Laboratory

Before crime scene investigators or other police personnel can know what to collect and determine the forensic potential of the evidence, they must understand the abilities and inabilities of their local forensic laboratory. Edmond Locard was responsible for the development of what is considered to be the first forensic laboratory in the world. Locard's educational background was in medicine and law, the foundation of what would emerge as the science of criminal investigation. By 1910, he had persuaded the police department in Lyon, France to provide workspace to analyze trace materials associated with crime scenes and criminal investigations.

It should come as no surprise that a society as dependent on science as ours would turn to that discipline to solve crimes. Forensic laboratories were first introduced as reform efforts to provide a reliable alternative to the vagaries of eyewitness testimony and the "third degree" abuses used in eliciting confessions. Nevertheless, their history is checkered with periods of rapid growth followed by years of neglect. Moreover, their place in the police organizational structure remains questionable at times, and their function in the adversarial court system is often at issue.

Experts disagree about which group initiated the first crime laboratory in the United States. Some credit August Vollmer for helping to establish a crime laboratory within the Los Angeles Police Department (LAPD) in 1923 (Saferstein, 2010) and others identify the Chicago Police Department as initiating the oldest crime laboratory in 1929 (Federal Bureau of Investigation [FBI], 2012). Most of this controversy depends upon the definition of a "crime laboratory" at that time.

Vollmer, a police chief within the Los Angeles area, was assisted by Dr. Paul Kirk (who later established the forensics program at University of California, Berkeley) in developing the LAPD Crime Lab. However, during approximately the same time period, the Chicago police established their own laboratory. The Chicago lab owes its roots to the infamous 1929 St. Valentine's Day Massacre, when five gangsters and two of their acquaintances were gunned down by assailants dressed in police uniforms who fled the scene in a police squad car. The massacre attracted national attention. As part of the investigative efforts, Colonel Calvin Goddard, who maintained an independent firearms laboratory in New York, was asked to analyze the crime scene bullets and cartridge cases. Goddard's findings subsequently excluded all police-issued guns as the murder weapons and months later matched the bullets to two machine guns seized from the home of Fred Burke, a suspect in the killings. As a result of these efforts, a member of the coroner's jury was so impressed with Goddard's work that he funded what became The Scientific Crime Laboratory of Chicago. This laboratory, with Colonel Goddard as its first director, was housed at the Law School of Northwestern University during the winter of 1929–1930, and the city of Chicago took over its operations in 1938 (Muehlberger, 1955).

The oldest federal laboratory owes its beginnings to J. Edgar Hoover. Intrigued with the idea of creating a place to incorporate the latest scientific methods into criminal investigations, Hoover sent an FBI agent, Charles Appel, to attend a training course offered at Goddard's lab in 1931. The Criminological Laboratory opened in 1932 and by the next year it was known as the Technical Laboratory. Ten years later it was renamed the FBI Laboratory and this name remains today. At its inception, the FBI lab could provide firearms identification ("ballistics") and fingerprint examiners. "During its first month of service, the FBI Laboratory examiners handled 20 cases. In its first full year of operation, the volume increased to a total of 963 examinations. By the next year that figure had more than doubled" (FBI, 2012). Handwriting comparisons, the examination of various types of trace evidence (e.g., hairs, fibers, soils), and serological testing of blood and semen were added later (FBI, 2012).

Growth of the Modern Crime Laboratory

Currently, there are approximately 411 publicly funded crime laboratories within the United States (United States Department of Justice [USDOJ], 2012). According to the U.S. Department of Justice, a **forensic crime laboratory** is defined as a scientific laboratory (with at least one full-time natural scientist) that examines physical evidence in criminal matters and provides reports and opinion testimony with respect to such physical evidence in courts of law (USDOJ, 2012). These laboratories provide services for various levels of government: federal, state, county, and municipal. This number has dramatically increased since the mid-1960s, when there were approximately 100 operational U.S. labs (Girard, 2008) (**Figure 7–1**).

This tremendous growth can be attributed to three primary historical factors. One reason is a direct result of Supreme Court decisions, specifically the **Miranda ruling**. This ruling, coming out of the 1966 *Miranda v. Arizona* case, placed greater emphasis on the collection, preservation, and analysis of physical evidence. According to this decision, individuals now have two Constitutional rights: police must advise individuals that they may have an attorney present during questioning, and they have the right to remain silent. This all but eliminated suspects' confessions and placed the emphasis on physical evidence relating to the crime in question.

A second factor can be traced to the explosive increase in crime rates across the United States since the 1960s. The introduction and proliferation of illicit drugs have been directly linked to the onslaught of crimes against property and persons. Because the crime of possession of a drug or controlled substance is the physical possession of the item—not an action that is done—every item or substance must be tested before the possessor can be charged with the offense. The ever increasing numbers of drug samples to be tested are a burden for crime labs to handle efficiently and accurately. Only confirmatory testing of an illicit possession by the lab can be used as evidence in court.

The final reason for the dramatic growth in the number of crime labs is due to scientific advances and the CSI effect. As a result of public awareness and scientific as well as technological advances, there is renewed emphasis on the analysis of

FIGURE 7–1   Example of a modern forensic laboratory
Courtesy of the Massachusetts State Police.

physical evidence. This has led to monies being spent to train individuals associated with such matters and to design instrumentation and equipment to aid in such analysis.

Today, laboratories all over the United States struggle with the backlog of evidence due to the aforementioned reasons. A case is classified as **backlogged** if the analysis is not completed within 30 days of the item being submitted to the lab. As of the most recent USDOJ census, the nation's publicly funded crime labs completed approximately 3.9 million requests during 2009 and had an estimated backlog of 1,153,700 cases at yearend. Forensic biology accounted for nearly one-third of the approximately 4 million analyses requests, and approximately three-quarters of the total backlog for 2009 was related to these types of requests. More specifically, due to an increase in mandated DNA sample collection, approximately 60% of the estimated 887,000 requests for forensic biology services that were reported as backlogged in 2009 were reported by the FBI Laboratory (USDOJ, 2012).

In an effort to reduce backlog and improve the quality of forensic science services offered, crime labs have continued to hire and train personnel and have also begun to outsource some analyses. According to the most recent data, in 2009, publicly funded crime labs employed an estimated 13,100 full-time personnel. This is a significant increase from approximately 11,000 personnel in 2002. Also, approximately 30% of publicly funded crime labs outsourced some forensic work to private labs or other publicly funded facilities in 2009 (USDOJ, 2012).

Each forensic laboratory has its own organizational structure and each is responsible for its own jurisdictional region. Regardless of its structure or location, each lab has the underlying purpose of providing a fair and accurate analysis of the submitted item(s).

Types of Forensic Laboratories

Federal

While the FBI Laboratory in Quantico, Virginia is what most would consider the national forensic laboratory, in truth, the U.S. federal government does not have a single laboratory with unlimited jurisdiction (**Figure 7–2**). Instead, as evidence of continued advancement and emphasis on forensic matters, crime laboratories are located across the United States that are designed to process evidence from suspected federal violations. These include the following:

- *Department of the Treasury.* National laboratory located in Chicago, IL.
- *Bureau of Alcohol, Tobacco, Firearms, and Explosives* (ATF). National laboratory located in Ammendale, MD.
- *Regional Forensic Laboratories* (RFLs) are located in Atlanta, GA and San Francisco, CA.
- *U.S. Secret Service.* In 2003, the U.S. Secret Service was moved from the Treasury Department to the Department of Homeland Security (DHS), which has its national laboratory located in Washington, DC.
- *Federal Bureau of Investigation* (FBI). National laboratory (Forensic Science Research and Training Center is also located here) in Quantico, VA.

- Sixteen *Regional Digital Forensic Laboratories* (RDFLs) throughout the United States.

- *Drug Enforcement Administration* (DEA). National laboratory located in Washington, DC.

- Regional laboratories are located in New York City; Largo, MD; Miami, FL; Chicago, IL; Dallas, TX; San Francisco, CA; and San Diego, CA. The specialized laboratories are in Sterling and Lorton, VA, both part of the metropolitan Washington, DC area. Subregional laboratories are in Kansas City, MO and San Juan, PR, with the mobile laboratory currently stationed at El Paso, TX.

FIGURE 7–2   FBI Laboratory, Quantico, Virginia
Courtesy of the Federal Bureau of Investigation.

- *U.S. Postal Service* (USPS). National laboratory located in Dulles, VA.

- *Department of the Interior* (DOI). National laboratory in Ashland, OR, which provides forensic services in support of investigators who patrol the national parks.

State

Every state has developed its own crime laboratory system that serves both state and those local law enforcement agencies that lack such abilities within their locale. Some states have gone so far as to develop a specialized laboratory structure that minimizes duplication of services. These states include California, New York, Illinois, Michigan, Texas, Florida, and Virginia (Girard, 2008).

Local/Regional

Local laboratories are operated by municipal or county governments to serve primarily their locality. However, many have developed specialized sectors that can make such services available to outside agencies through interlaboratory and interagency cooperation agreements. While many may think of municipal laboratories as being small, some are significantly larger than their state lab counterparts (the New York Police Department's lab, for instance).

As costs of associated services have risen, some jurisdictions have seen fit to combine resources and create regional laboratories. In these instances, several counties or municipalities have pooled their personnel, budgets, and equipment to service the most common forensic needs. This reduces overall expenses for each while continuing to maintain regional forensic capabilities without relying upon a state system that typically has a considerable wait time for forensic analyses.

Private

At this time, the majority of forensic labs within the United States are public and are funded by taxes and operated by government agencies. However, the recent explosion in demand for DNA technology and analyses of everything from criminal investigations to paternity testing,

From Battlefield to Homefront: Mobile Laboratories Are Changing the Way We Respond to Crisis

"Mobile forensics laboratories are an innovative and efficient way to expand or replace forensic capabilities in combat areas or regions that have experienced a natural disaster or other crisis. They were developed by the National Forensic Science Technology Center in partnership with the Department of Defense, which used similar laboratories in Iraq and Afghanistan to study impro- vised explosive devices. In addition to helping agencies respond to natural disasters, the mobile forensics laboratories can be used for security training exercises."

Source: Cote, B. (November, 2009). From battlefield to homefront: Mobile laboratories are changing the way we respond to crisis. *National Institute of Justice Journal, 264*. Retrieved July 7, 2012, from http://www.nij.gov/journals/264/ battlefield.htm.

Nuts and Bolts

- Because they are created from a standard shipping container, mobile forensics labo- ratories can be delivered by truck, transport plane, train, ship, or helicopter, bringing laboratory support to even the most remote areas.

- Each laboratory measures 8' × 20' × 8.5' and rests on a standard transport trailer for ease of movement. Once folded out, the laboratory provides a maximum of 400 square feet of usable space, complete with lighting, wraparound power access, and open floor space. Multiple laboratories can be connected to allow for different disciplines, contamination prevention, administrative areas, or other uses.

- Each section is self-supporting and can be used separately for smaller projects. A diesel-powered generator offers a minimum of 33 hours of power on a single tank, providing air conditioning or heat, light satellite communications, and even condi- tioned power for sensitive forensic equipment. Interior separators can provide dust- and light-proof work areas within each unit.

- A small team can set up the laboratory in less than an hour, not including equipment startup. Each lab features full data sharing and an access-controlled entryway.

combined with the subsequent backlog at law enforcement forensic labs, has led to the creation of numerous private forensic labs throughout the United States. These private laboratories charge a fee for their services and anyone with the financial ability to pay can request the use of their services.

In fact, some corporations have developed their own forensic labs in an attempt to reduce inventory shrinkage and increase convictions of theft, fraud, and other retail crimes.

RIPPED **FROM THE HEADLINES**

Mobile Laboratory Helps Cedar Rapids Recover From Devastating Flood

In his 18 years on the force, Cedar Rapids Police Sergeant Joe Clark thought he had seen it all. However, nothing prepared him for the sight of the department's crime lab swamped in more than eight feet of water.

"It was unbelievable. Water was almost up to the ceiling," he said. "The crime lab was completely ruined."

Luckily, in what they thought was an abundance of caution, his investigative unit had moved its new Automated Fingerprint Identification System out of the crime lab that occupied the basement of its headquarters before the flood. However, no one had anticipated that more than 30 feet of water would engulf the city. The rest of the forensic equipment was destroyed.

For a few months, the officers conducted forensics analysis in a makeshift lab set up in an unventilated garage.

"You can imagine how difficult that was—with cross-contamination and security issues," said Clark. "Not to mention how cold it got in there as fall arrived."

Clark contacted Joe Polski, chief operating officer of the International Association for Identification, who put him in touch with the National Forensic Science Technology Center in Largo, FL, to discuss using one of its mobile labs. Within a few weeks, Clark had a 400-square-foot mobile forensics lab up and running in the parking lot.

Although the town of Cedar Rapids is still a long way from being back to normal after the historic flood, the police department's crime scene investigation unit is now running again. "I don't know what we would have done without this lab," said Clark. "Our evidence processing ability would have been next to nothing during the last several months. And we can't just quit investigating crimes because we get flooded."

Source: Cote, Bill. (October, 2009). Mobile Forensics Laboratory helps Cedar Rapids CSO Recover from Devestating Flood. *National Institute Justice Journal, 264.* Originally published by the National Institute of Justice, U.S. Department of Justice" Retrieved from http://www.nij.gov/journals/264/battlefield.htm.

Target is but one example of a corporation with forensic labs, with locations in Las Vegas and Minneapolis. There has been much debate about the jurisdiction, accreditation, and legal admissibility of evidence analyzed by private labs, as well as the training and certification of their employees. However, it should be pointed out that these are the same issues found in public labs.

Publicly funded forensic labs are also making use of the private sector in order to meet their demands for forensic services. In fact, according to the U.S. Department of Justice 2012 Bulletin

The Role of Private Forensic Laboratories

Having spent over half of my forensic science career with the government, then transitioning to the private sector nine years ago, I have had the privilege of working in both environments. In all senses, working for either the government or private companies in forensic science is a very rewarding career that promotes the Common Good for all of us. Today, I lead a private forensic DNA company located in Salt Lake City, Utah. There are many advantages of working in the private sector as well as a couple of disadvantages compared to our government colleagues. While private DNA laboratories are the most common private sector forensic science laboratories in the United States, they are not exclusive. A close second in number to private DNA laboratories are private forensic toxicology laboratories. The reason being is that both DNA and toxicology disciplines have the advantage of creating high-throughput laboratory environments with relative ease. To my knowledge, there is only one private laboratory that handles several other disciplines such as firearm analysis, latent finger print analysis, and the like. These latter disciplines are manual and very time consuming. There are dozens of smaller private operations, usually a one-person con-sultancy that processes criminal evidence. Typically, these consultancies are comprised of retired forensic scientists from the firearms, questioned document, or latent print units.

Private laboratories commonly contract directly with public laboratories, law enforcement departments, or medical examiner offices. Our primary role is to further the criminal justice system by assisting those public sector agencies in reducing their backlogs by handling older cases or, in some cases, working current cases. The vision of my laboratory is to act as a collaborative partner with our clients, the governmental bureaus. We act as an extension of the government laboratory by processing the evidence to their exacting specifications. The greater number of clients each private laboratory has, the greater the challenge of processing evidence to the highest quality standards, but by slightly different means.

Several private sector companies excel in areas of high throughput and high efficiency. Additionally, in many instances, we offer greater customer service and we also have the perception of being unbiased. This latter point became an important national issue after the National Academy of Sciences recommended, among many other things, that forensic laboratories become unaffili-ated with law enforcement or prosecutorial offices.

in the Bureau of Justice Statistics section, a recently completed census of publicly funded crime labs reported that approximately 28% utilized the services of private laboratories in order to aid with their backlog. This was a decline from the percentage of labs that outsourced forensic work in 2002 (42%) and 2005 (51%). Forensic biology (typically DNA analysis) accounted for approximately 80% of reported outsourcing during 2009 (USDOJ, 2012).

One of the things that I am most proud of is that our company pioneered the adaptation of Lean/Six Sigma quality and process improvement methods to forensic laboratories. We successfully implemented these principles in our own laboratory, but more importantly, we have taught these principles to public laboratories with astonishing success. (For further reading about this program, see [Richard & Kuperferschmidt, 2011].)

Another advantage of a private laboratory is that we are not restricted to working within a particular jurisdiction. My passion today is to bring modern forensic science technology to developing countries. We have successfully assisted two African countries with the establishment of forensic DNA laboratories and are working with several other countries in Africa, Asia, and the Americas.

As mentioned previously, there are also disadvantages of private forensic laboratories. First and foremost, there is a direct cost to agencies using the services of a private laboratory. In most jurisdictions, a law enforcement department can submit evidence to their crime laboratory and incur no direct costs. However, in actuality, if all costs of a government laboratory were compared to a private laboratory including salary, benefits, pensions, overhead, rent, etc., the private laboratory would be more cost effective. But because those costs are not enumerated, it is difficult to justify outsourcing with tight budgets. The cost of courtroom testimony is also higher for private laboratories because of the simple fact that private laboratories work cases from jurisdictions coast to coast. If all of the laboratory's cases were within the same city, or even the same state, traveling to court would be a relatively simple matter. Finally, because of privacy and security concerns of the federal government, private laboratories do not have access to national databases for fingerprints, shell casings, and DNA profiles. This is disadvantageous to the customers of a private laboratory because if a suspect is not known, then that information must be submitted to and reviewed by the state agency to input the case into the database.

Despite the few disadvantages, a career in a private laboratory is a gratifying experience. Private laboratories play an important role in the criminal justice system by addressing the case backlog crisis. We perform identical work as our government counterparts, but we have a host of opportunities generally not available in governmental agencies.

Timothy D. Kupferschmid, MBA, MFS
Executive Director, Sorenson Forensics, Salt Lake City, Utah

Courtesy of Timothy D. Kupferschmid, MBA, MFS, Executive Director, Sorenson Forensics.

Private laboratories have another vital function within the legal system. They are able to provide independent analyses of forensic evidence for those accused of crimes. Typically, public laboratories will not provide services for individuals, but rather only for government agencies or departments. However, most private laboratories are niche agencies, meaning that they specialize in one or two specific areas, such as DNA, digital technology, toxicology, drugs, or questioned documents, among other investigative technologies.

Role of Private Labs, as Seen from the Public Sector

Increasingly, private labs have developed and played an integral role in the analysis of forensic evidence. Many private labs have been instrumental in allowing some public laboratories to out-source their evidence in certain disciplines to aid in backlog reduction or allow for analysis of evidence for which the public lab does not have a forensic discipline. Conversely, some private labs have not properly sought out and undergone rigorous quality assurance inspections and accreditation by external bodies. Absent these critical steps, some products produced by these labs may be suspect.

The primary difference between public and private labs is one of economics. Public labs typically do not charge for their analysis and will testify in courts of law for free as part of the overall analysis. Private labs, however, will charge for all aspects of the analysis and direct court testimony can get quite costly for the client.

Defense counsel has long utilized private labs to challenge the work of the public lab. Typically, this has not been an issue because in most cases the same result is achieved. Conversely, some so-called "forensic experts," many of whom have never analyzed a piece of evidence, have begun to show up at defense counsel tables to make baseless claims regarding lab reports or offer opinions without any real experience in the scientific discipline being challenged. Historically, some public labs may have never been challenged, as many courts took experts, testimony as "gospel" and few analysts were challenged, on their testimony. However, the recently published National Academy of Sciences report (commonly referred to as the NAS report) called into

Services Offered

The experienced staff of a forensic laboratory typically examines and identifies materials such as suspected accelerants, drugs, explosive residues, fingerprints, glass, paints, fibers, metals, biological stains, toxins, and soils to extract as much information as possible (Wisconsin Department of Justice [WisDOJ], 2001). The laboratory examines **questioned evidence** and compares it with **known evidence** to determine whether or not the source is the same, and whether or not a relationship exists between them (WisDOJ, 2001). A *questioned* item refers to any type of evidence or material of an unknown, unacknowledged, or unaccounted for source (e.g., glass particles recovered from the body of a victim of a hit-and-run motor vehicle accident). *Known* items refer to any type of evidence that originates from a known, acknowledged, or accounted for source that is to be compared to an unknown or questioned material (e.g., glass pieces from a motor vehicle to be used to compare against glass particles found on a victim of a hit-and-run motor vehicle accident). This is done for many reasons; however, often it is to provide an question many forensic science disciplines as not being scientifically valid. Although this left DNA and chemical analysis somewhat untouched, it did call into question the use of "pattern recognition" disciplines such a toolmarks, tire impressions, etc. It even called into question long established identification disciplines such as latent prints. This is surprising given the fact that, say in the instance of identical twins, they have exactly the same DNA; however, they both would have different and unique fingerprints. If anything this has contributed to all laboratories, both public and private, becoming more transparent both in their testing as well as report writing. The issues have also required some laboratory accreditation bodies to require uncertainty calculations to allow for variances in weights and calculations. The transparency and accreditation of some public labs have also shown some oversight and training issues.

A few public labs have been shuttered due to allegations of misconduct by the scientific staff in states like Texas and New York. This has led to some private labs gaining a stronger hold on the analysis in certain areas or to even "come to the rescue" while the public lab retools itself to gain back public trust. The advantage of a private lab facing issues of misconduct allegations is that they may be able to simply fire the analyst, review and revise policies, and remain in business. Due to the scrutiny of public labs, this simplistic approach would be difficult. The downside for a private lab with misconduct allegations would be a lack of trust from clients, canceled contracts, and potentially bankruptcy. Yes, the almighty dollar does play a role in this.

Thomas Blackwell
Laboratory Director
DEA Northeast Laboratory

Courtesy of Thomas Blackwell, Forensic Chemist.

investigatory focus, which may lead investigators to follow an entirely different direction from that originally thought to be the most significant, prior to the analysis.

Organization of Forensic Laboratories

Regardless of the jurisdiction serviced or the agency that operates the laboratory, each offers different levels of service. For instance, in a statewide system a minimum of one laboratory will operate as a full-service forensic lab, whereas established regional labs typically only offer a limited number of forensic services. Wisconsin, for example, operates two full-service laboratories in Milwaukee and Madison. However, the North Central Laboratory in Wausau supports only sections for drug analysis, fingerprint/footwear analysis, imaging, audio-tape enhancement, and field response. This is significantly less than those services offered by the other two full-service laboratories. Regardless of size or location, crime labs are typically responsible for several types of analytical services. As of 2009, USDOJ statistics reported that on average, crime labs typically provide a median number of five functions of analysis. Identification of controlled substances was the type of analysis performed by the largest percentage of labs (82%), while examinations of printed or written documents (16%) and digital evidence (19%) were the functions reported by the fewest number of laboratories (USDOJ, 2012).

The following section addresses the services offered by a full-service forensic laboratory. It is worth mentioning that *full service* means different things to different agencies and states. Because there are an inordinate number of forensic specialties, it is unrealistic to have every state lab provide all services. However, there are a few recognized primary sections that are almost universally included within most forensic full-service labs.

Firearms/Ballistics

This unit is responsible for the examination of firearms and ballistic components, which can include: shells, cartridge casings, discharged bullets, and ammunition. Sometimes other objects are examined to determine the presence of discharge residues and to approximate muzzle to target distance at the time of the weapon being discharged. Often laboratories also will make use of the principles used within this section to analyze striation and compression marks made by tools. Approximately 55% of the publicly funded labs in the United States examine firearms-related evidence (USDOJ, 2012).

Toxicology/Chemistry/Drug Analysis

This unit is responsible for the examination of body fluids and organs in order to determine whether or not drugs or poisons are present or, in some cases, absent. This section also typically makes use of the intoxilyzer, a machine used to measure the intoxication level of individuals who have consumed alcohol. In some laboratories this section incorporates all other analyses that require chemical analysis. This can include drug identification, explosives analysis, and accelerant analysis from suspected arson scenes.

Trace

The trace unit has as its operational foundation Locard's Exchange Principle. This principle drives all efforts within the trace unit. *Trace evidence* is microscopic, but there may be infinite amounts of the material or substance. These may include paint, glass, fibers, hair, soil, and cosmetics, to name a few.

Biology/Serology/DNA

This section may be known by a number of different titles, but its basic mission remains the same: the identification of biological components, which are typically associated with blood. Conventional serology (i.e., blood typing) has largely been replaced by DNA analysis. The types of substances typically examined by this section include blood, saliva, semen, vaginal secretions, and hair (if not by the trace section). DNA testing is performed by over half of all publicly funded forensic laboratories (USDOJ, 2012).

Document

The document section analyzes handwriting, digital documents, and typewriting on questioned documents to determine authenticity, originality, and source. Some of the related responsibilities of this unit include ink and paper analysis and analysis of indented writings, erasures, obliterations, and burned documents.

Photography

The photography unit may be involved in both examination and documentation of evidence. While providing services to examine submitted photographic evidence, the unit often is responsible for photographically documenting other types of physical evidence in an effort to aid in its subsequent analysis. This unit makes use of highly specialized photographic techniques that may include digital imaging, ultraviolet photography, x-ray photography, infrared photography, aerial photography, and underwater photography.

Fingerprints

This unit is responsible for processing and examining submitted evidence (typically in conjunction with other lab examinations) for the presence of latent fingerprints. In the case of visible prints and processed latent prints, this unit is responsible for identification. More than 60% of crime laboratories perform fingerprint analyses (USDOJ, 2012.)

Tire Track/Footwear/Toolmark Impressions

If not incorporated within the firearms unit, the impressions section provides analysis and examination services to provide information about and aid in identifying the source of an impression.

Polygraph/Voice Stress Analysis Unit

While this area of forensic technology has increasingly found its way into the investigatory sector, it was originally housed, and in some cases continues to be housed, within the confines of the forensic laboratory.

It is this section that is responsible for utilizing the polygraph and voice stress analyzer (VSA) to determine the truthfulness of testimonial evidence. This is the only section within a forensic lab whose primary function does not relate to the analysis of physical evidence, but rather to the examination of testimonial evidence.

Crime Scene Field Response

Many laboratories have begun to incorporate crime scene response units within their structure as a way of ensuring that crime scenes are properly processed and the evidence properly collected and preserved to ensure the ability to subsequently analyze it. This unit typically will only respond in the cases of felonies and only when requested by an agency to do so, if the crime scene does not already fall within the jurisdiction of the lab in question.

Functions of a Criminalist

Today, the nation's crime labs employ over 13,000 full-time personnel whose responsibility is to analyze and examine the various forms of physical evidence that are submitted (USDOJ, 2012). The role of the criminalist in CSI efforts is to provide investigative leads through the scientific analysis and examination of physical evidence and reconstruction efforts. This role is supported by accompanying reports of actions taken, observations made, and results and conclusions noted. In addition to preparing and returning a written report relating to the scientific findings, laboratory staff may be required to appear in court as expert witnesses to give testimony explaining and supporting their analyses.

Investigator

While criminalists are typically involved in investigatory activities at the crime scene, they must make use of their own ability to be inquisitive and do their best to investigate the information available to them. Unlike the scenarios shown on television, criminalists are not responsible for the investigation efforts; however, if they are to know what to analyze and what types of analyses to perform on the submitted evidence, they do require some background information relating to the case. For this reason, communication between the investigating officer and the criminalist is imperative. Paul Kirk addressed this point in his 1974 book, *Crime Investigation*:

> The efficiency of the laboratory usually bears a direct relationship to the willingness of the police officer to keep the laboratory workers informed of all pertinent facts. Complete frankness and confidence between the two types of investigators is most desirable and profitable and unfortunately not so common as it might be. Only good understanding, by both, of their reciprocal functions can completely eliminate this barrier to the realization of the full benefits of a well managed crime laboratory (Kirk, P. L. [1974]. *Crime investigation* [2nd ed]. New York: John Wiley & Sons).

Educator

An often unrecognized and overlooked area of importance related to the criminalist is the role of educator. During his or her tenure as a criminalist, an individual will have many opportunities to educate law enforcement officers, attorneys, crime scene personnel, judges, and medical personnel. The training performed will vary depending upon the recipient but typically centers around the correct way to collect, package, and preserve evidence in order to ensure the most successful analysis. The criminalist also is responsible for educating with regard to the interpretation and meaning behind the scientific conclusions to ensure the correct probative value. As always, the results or conclusions of these analyses will be limited by the quality, quantity, and type of the submitted physical evidence (James & Nordby, 2009).

Student

The dynamic world of forensic science requires that the criminalist be a life-long student with a thirst for continuing education. Improved technology and new crime trends demand that the criminalist stay abreast of current literature; continue to perform experiments; conduct research; and attend professional seminars, conferences, and workshops. Of particular value is the *Journal of Forensic Sciences*, which is published by the American Academy of Forensic Sciences. It is also wise for a criminalist to be aware of historical forensic materials such as those produced by innovators like Edmund Locard, Paul Kirk, Hans Gross, Charles O'Hara, Calvin Goddard, James Osterburg, and Matthew Orfilia. In perusing the works by these contributors to forensic science, the criminalist will note that while technology may change and increase the efficiency of forensic analysis, the fundamental principles and approach to analysis remains the same.

For the most part, gone are the days of the criminalist being a generalist, where the individual knows a little bit about a lot of areas of forensic science. Today's criminalist is typically a specialist within a specific area and must remain adept at the latest instrumental and analytical techniques, technologies utilized, and the areas where further research must be conducted to close gaps within his or her area of specialty. If criminalists do not adhere to the concept of continuing education, the techniques and concepts they learned and used initially very quickly will become obsolete, as will their ability to provide effective analyses.

Requesting Aid

When a forensic laboratory's assistance is desired during the course of an investigation, it is suggested that the district attorney of the appropriate county be advised that an investigation is being undertaken and that the laboratory's services are necessary and are requested. It bears mentioning that most forensic labs reserve the right (as authorized by state statutes) to decline to provide services in any matter not involving a potential felony charge.

Regardless of whether or not a lab accepts a case, they are typically available for consultation relating to forensic matters. If questions arise during the course of investigative efforts that relate to the collection, preservation, or potential analysis of physical evidence, law enforcement officials should communicate with laboratory personnel for advice, counsel, and/or recommendations relevant to the challenges confronting them within their investigation (WisDOJ, 2001).

Submitting Evidence to the Laboratory

After evidence is collected at the crime scene, it is transported to and stored at an evidence facility, typically found at a police department or other governmental agency.

Evidence is submitted to the crime laboratory either by personal delivery or via mail. The U.S. Postal Service (USPS) and other parcel carriers have specific policies and procedures

CSI: Target

The $63 billion (revenue) retailer, Target Stores, has entered the world of forensics. In 2003, in an effort to investigate safety, as well as theft, fraud, and other crimes involving its more than 1,600 stores, Target developed its own forensic lab in Minneapolis, Minnesota. In 2005, another followed in Las Vegas, Nevada to help assist with the growing workload. Although the primary purpose of Target's forensic labs is to investigate occurrences within its stores, the investigators and analysts assigned to the labs typically spend only 70% of their time doing such. The remainder of their time is frequently spent assisting local, state, and federal law enforcement in investigating crimes unrelated to Target. In fact, since their inception, Target's labs have been instrumental in solving a number of felony criminal cases both in the United States and internationally.

Much of the equipment is similar to what would be found within a publicly funded crime lab. But, says Craig Thrane, a video analyst for the retailer, "Target investigators can work more quickly."

As with many other retail giants, Target installed cameras in most of its stores during the 1980s; however, they found that was not sufficient to significantly impact in-store thefts. "We had a volume of evidence from our cameras but no expertise," says Fredrick Lautenbach, the retailer's crime lab manager. Target did not want to burden already overloaded law enforcement with case after case of petty theft (which quickly adds up for the retailer and provides for numerous cases for law enforcement). In order to both combat the shrinkage of its inventory and not unduly burden law enforcement, Target created its first lab in Minnesota, hiring experts with prior law enforcement investigative and forensic experience to staff the lab. The labs are best known for their ability and technology associated with digital video analysis. Due to several successful analyses relating to law enforcement cases, Target has been overwhelmed with requests to restore or analyze tapes, track cell phones, and also to process and analyze fingerprints. Due to the tremendous amount of requests from outside agencies, Target decided to limit its volunteer work to cases that involve murder, sexual assault, or armed robbery. The work is considered voluntary, as part of Target Stores' partnership with law enforcement. It does not charge for its services, but instead asks law enforcement agencies to donate one of their agency patches when the work performed by Target assists them with an investigation. As of spring, 2008 Target had 136 patches on display in its corporate office, located in Brooklyn Park, Minnesota.

Source: Egan, M. S. (April 21, 2008). CSI: Target. *Forbes Magazine*. Retrieved August 1, 2009, from http://www.forbes.com/forbes/2008/0421/102.html.

that apply to the shipment of evidence from a police department or crime scene to a forensic laboratory. Investigators and evidence technicians should check with the carrier prior to shipping items of concern. For instance, postal regulations prohibit shipping live ammunition via the USPS, but both FedEx and UPS do permit live ammunition shipments.

Every item shipped to the laboratory for analysis should be packaged separately. Every shipment should include an evidence submission form (either an agency-specific form, or one prepared by the laboratory for that purpose). The submission form typically will list specific details about the item to be analyzed, the submitter's name and agency, an agency case number, a list of requested analyses to be performed, and a brief case synopsis. It should be noted, however, that often the submitting agency or individual is not always completely aware of the forensic capabilities of the crime laboratory. Therefore, although there is a list of requested analyses to be performed, the criminalist is not limited by those requests and is encouraged to use his or her training and experience to perform the most scientifically correct examinations. Sometimes this in fact may mean not performing an examination at all, if the criminalist determines that the sample size is too small, the sample is too degraded, or there simply is no way to garner any useful information from the submitted sample.

Accreditation of Crime Laboratories

In 2008, the USDOJ reported that 80% of publicly funded crime laboratories were accredited (USDOJ, 2012). The term **accreditation** refers to the endorsement of a forensic laboratory's policies and procedures. Accreditation is a sign of industry recognition and acceptance of the manner in which the laboratory performs its forensic analyses. This is a necessary component of establishing credibility within the court system. In order to qualify for accreditation, a crime laboratory must meet minimum requirements set forth by the certifying authority. A number of requirements must be met, but the following policies and programs are typical:

- Develop a quality control manual. **Quality control** measures within a laboratory ensure that analysis results meet a specified standard of quality.

- Develop a lab testing protocol. **Protocols** are the steps and processes undertaken by the laboratory to ensure that the correct tests are performed and that they are performed with accuracy.

- Develop a **quality assurance (QA)** manual. QA is a way of ensuring and verifying quality control, as well as providing for standardized methods of measurement. A laboratory's QA assessment measures are necessary to oversee, verify, and document the performance of the laboratory.

- Develop a program for proficiency examination. **Proficiency testing** is a measure for determining whether or not the individuals working in the lab and the laboratory as a whole are operating at an industry-established standard. For this testing process, a criminalist is given a sample for which the analytical results are already known, and if the results of the subsequent analysis do not match up, then there is an identified problem within the lab's analytical operation. Tests are given in one of two fashions, either blind (the criminalist is not aware that an examination is being issued) or known (the criminalist is cognizant of the examination and is free to consult any resources they deem necessary) (Girard, 2008).

The American Society of Crime Lab Directors/Laboratory Accreditation Board

The American Society of Crime Lab Directors/Laboratory Accreditation Board (ASCLD/LAB) is responsible for the accreditation of forensic laboratories within the United States. While not all crime laboratories are accredited, 388 crime laboratories were accredited by ASCLD/LAB as of April, 2012. "The list of accredited laboratories includes 192 state laboratories, 132 local agency laboratories, 23 federal laboratories, 17 international (outside the United States) laboratories and 24 private" (ASCLD/LAB, 2012).

Certification of Personnel

One of the steps that will assist with the accreditation process and lend professional credibility to a laboratory is the employment of certified criminalists. **Certification** is a voluntary process of peer review by which a practitioner is recognized as having attained the professional qualifications necessary to practice in one or more disciplines of criminalistics (American Board of Criminalistics [ABC], 2012). There are a number of organizations that are involved in certification processes and to which employees within a lab may be members of in order to receive continuing education within their respective fields.

American Board of Criminalistics

The ABC offers a certificate in comprehensive criminalistics as well as in the specialty disciplines of molecular biology, drug chemistry, fire debris analysis, trace evidence (e.g., hairs, fibers, paints, and polymers) (ABC, 2012). The ABC lists the following four "areas of testing" for certification of criminalists:

1. The philosophical, conceptual, and scientific basis of criminalistics.
2. Basic technical subjects of criminalistics, including:
    *   Drug analysis
    *   Crime scene reconstruction
    *   Firearms and toolmarks
    *   Molecular biology and DNA
    *   Fire debris and explosives
    *   Photography

- Trace evidence
- Safety

3. Ethics.

4. Appropriate areas of civil and criminal law.

International Association for Identification

The International Association for Identification (IAI) is one of the oldest professional organizations to certify crime scene–related personnel. For individuals employed in the field of crime scene processing, belonging to this outstanding organization will help them to maintain competency and professionalism. The IAI is responsible for publication of the monthly peer-reviewed *Journal of Forensic Identification*. Many states have IAI divisions and one may consider becoming a member to stay abreast of local forensic and crime scene–related advances and rulings. The IAI is responsible for numerous seminars and training opportunities around the globe each year where members are able to receive the latest information and training relating to their respective field of employment. With over 6,000 members from the United States and many other countries, the advancement of forensic discipline–related education and certification continues to be one of the IAI's top priorities (IAI, 2012). The IAI offers certification in the following fields:

- Bloodstain pattern examination
- Crime scene
- Footwear examination
- Forensic art
- Forensic photography
- Latent print examination
- Tenprint fingerprint examination

American Academy of Forensic Sciences

The American Academy of Forensic Sciences (AAFS) is a multidisciplinary professional organization that provides leadership with the goal of advancing science and its application within the legal system. The objectives of the organization are to promote education, foster research, improve practice, and to encourage collaboration within the forensic sciences (AAFS, 2012). One way that the AAFS meets its goals is through publication of the *Journal of Forensic Sciences*, produced six times a year. The organization's approximately 6,000 members are divided into 11 different sections of forensic specialty. While not intended to be a certifying agency, the AAFS serves its members and the greater field of forensic science by hosting various conferences and meetings that bring together professionals from around the globe to exchange research findings and initiate new research.

WRAP UP

Chapter Summary

The future of the forensic crime laboratory within the United States is secure. Whether privately or publicly funded, there will continue to be a need for crime labs and for an increasing number of criminalists to be employed within them in order to keep up with forensic analysis–related requests. Based on its most recent census of publicly funded crime labs, the USDOJ estimated that laboratories performing DNA analysis would need an estimated 73% more staff to complete requests for DNA analysis. Biological screening (typically a task performed in preparation for DNA analysis) represented the next highest need for an increase in full-time criminalists (57%), followed by firearm and toolmark analysis (46%) and examination of trace evidence such as hair and fibers (43%) (2008). There is increasing need for specialists within each of these fields in both the private and public sectors.

The forensic laboratory relies upon the knowledge and proficiency of those within the field to properly identify, document, collect, and preserve physical evidence. Without that quality of evidence, the laboratory is a useless commodity. As a result of courtroom decisions, social changes, and historical events, the crime lab industry and the number of submitted items of physical evidence continue to grow at a rapid pace. Such growth requires that crime laboratories maintain or improve upon their levels of proficiency and reliability. This is accomplished through accreditation of the laboratories and certification of its employees. Continuing to strive for technological efficiency and the proper forensic knowledge requires a dedication to employee continuing education and constant re examination of a laboratory's analysis techniques and processes.

Review Questions

1. _____was responsible for the development of what is considered the first forensic laboratory, which was located in _____.

2. The first crime laboratories in the United States began in which decade?

3. Who was Colonel Calvin Goddard, and what role did he play in the early forensic laboratory?

4. List and explain three reasons for the tremendous growth in the number of crime laboratories in the United States.

5. Which landmark case is partially responsible for the growth of the number of crime laboratories in the United States?

6. A case is classified as _____ if the analysis is not completed within 30 days of the item being submitted to the lab.

7. A _____ item refers to any type of evidence or material of an unknown or unacknowledged or unaccounted for source.

8. What is a VSA and how is it used in the crime laboratory?

9. Why have many crime laboratories incorporated crime scene field response teams within their structure?

10. What is the acronym ASCLD and what is its role in crime laboratories?

References

American Board of Criminalistics (ABC). (2012). What is the American Board of Criminalistics? Retrieved May 1, 2012, from http://www.criminalistics.com/

American Academy of Forensic Sciences (AAFS). (2012). Homepage. Retrieved May 1, 2012, from http://www.aafs.org/

American Society of Crime Laboratory Directors/Laboratory Accreditation Board (ASCLD/LAB). Retrieved May 26, 2012, from http://www.ascld-lab.org/lab-status/accreditedlabs.html

Cote, B. (2009). Mobile forensics laboratory helps Cedar Rapids CSI recover from devastating flood. *National Institute of Justice Journal*. (264). Retrieved July 7, 2012, from http://www.nij.gov/journals/264/battlefield-mobile.htm

Doyle, A. C. (1892). The adventure of the copper beeches. In: The adventures of Sherlock Holmes. *Strand Magazine*.

Egan, M. S. (April 21, 2008). CSI: Target. *Forbes Magazine*. Retrieved August 1, 2009, from http://www.forbes.com/forbes/2008/0421/102.html

Federal Bureau of Investigation (FBI). (2012). Birth of the FBI's technical laboratory 1924–1935. Retrieved September 6, 2012, from http://www.fbi.gov/about-us/history/highlights-of-history/articles/laboratory

Girard, J. E. (2008). *Principles of environmental chemistry*. Sudbury, MA: Jones and Bartlett Publishers.

International Association of Identification (IAI). (2012). Welcome to the IAI! Retrieved August 1, 2009, from http://www.theiai.org

James, S. H., & Nordby, J. J. (2009). *Forensic science: An introduction to scientific and investigative techniques* (3rd ed.). Boca Raton, FL: CRC Press.

Kirk, P. L. (1974). *Crime investigation* (2nd ed.). New York: John Wiley & Sons.

Miranda v. Arizona, 384 U.S. 436 (1966).

Muehlberger, C. W. (1955). Col. Calvin Hooker Goddard 1891–1955. *The Journal of Criminal Law, Criminology, and Police Science, 46,* 103–104.

National Academy of Sciences. (2009). "Strengthening Forensic Science in the United States: A Path Forward." U.S. Department of Justice. Retrieved December 6, 2012, from http://www.nap.edu

Saferstein, R. (2010). *Criminalistics: An introduction to forensic science* (10th ed.). Upper Saddle River, NJ: Pearson Prentice Hall.

Richard, M. & Kuperferschmidt, T. D. (2011). Increasing efficiency of forensic DNA casework using Lean Six Signma tools. *National Institute for Justice*. Retrieved from https://www.ncjrs.gov/pdffiles1/nij/grants/235190.pdf

U.S. Department of Justice (USDOJ). (2012). *Census of publicly funded forensic crime laboratories, 2009.* Bureau of Justice Statistics Bulletin, NCJ, 238–252.

Wisconsin Department of Justice (WisDOJ). (2009). *Physical evidence handbook* (8th ed.). Madison, WI: Wisconsin Department of Justice.

Physical Evidence

© McMac/ShutterStock, Inc.

- List the contributions of historical individuals who developed and refined fingerprint evidence.
- Describe the categorical methods for fingerprint processing.
- Explain ACE-V.
- Distinguish between the two primary methods of U.S. fingerprint classification.
- Define AFIS.
- Explain SWGFAST and how it relates to fingerprints.

Fingerprint Evidence

Every human being carries with him from his cradle to his grave certain physical marks which do not change their character, and by which he can always be identified …This autograph consists of the delicate lines or corrugations with which Nature marks the insides of the hands and the soles of the feet.

Mark Twain (1835–1910)
Pudd'nhead Wilson, 1894

KEY TERMS

ACE-V
Alternate Light Source (ALS)
Anthropometry
Automated Fingerprint
    Identification System
    (AFIS)
Classification
Cyanoacrylate Ester Fuming

FBI National Crime
    Information Center–
    Fingerprint Classification
    (NCIC-FPC)
Henry System
Latent Prints
Minutia
Ninhydrin

Patent Prints
Plastic Prints
Points of Comparison
Scientific Working Group on
    Friction Ridge Analysis,
    Study, and Technology
    (SWGFAST)
Small Particle Reagent (SPR)

History of Fingerprints

Since the beginning of humankind, there has been a desire and attempt to identify individuals. Fingerprints are among the oldest and most probative types of forensic evidence. There is evidence throughout history, from Neolithic cave carvings to Chinese artifacts over 5,000 years old, that humans have had some inclination of the individuality inherent in fingerprints.

But while artifacts upon which this historical premise is based are thousands of years of age, modern study and understanding of fingerprints has its foundation in 1684.

Nehemiah Grew (1641–1712)

British horticulturalist Nehemiah Grew is the first documented person to study and accurately describe the ridge patterns present on the surfaces of the hands and feet. In addition to writing on the topic, he also published detailed drawings of finger and palm patterns and descriptions of pore detail (Lee & Gaensslen, 2001).

Although Grew published these findings, more than 200 years would pass before the permanency, classification, and individualized identification of fingerprints were studied in depth and presented to the world. Those influential in such matters are given in the next sections.

Alphonse Bertillon (1853–1914)

Bertillon's system, entitled **anthropometry**, was a series of 11 body measurements of the bony parts of the body, and an in-depth description of marks (scars, moles, warts, tattoos, etc.) on the surface of the body. Anthropometric measurements could be taken from individuals who were over the age of 20, as it was assumed that such individuals had completed their vertical growth so their measurements would remain constant from that point onward. Bertillon's system of identification was the accepted method for policing agencies until 1903, when an incident at the federal penitentiary in Leavenworth, Kansas identified the shortcomings of the system.

Upon being incarcerated, Will West was photographed and his Bertillon measurements taken. The resulting photograph and measurements were nearly identical to those of another prisoner, William West, already on file. Will West denied having ever been incarcerated at Leavenworth, and a subsequent investigation led authorities to realize that they had two separate prisoners—Will and William West—both incarcerated within the walls of the penitentiary, who bore an almost identical resemblance both visually and in their anthropometric measurements. However, when authorities decided to collect fingerprints from the two men, they realized that each had unique fingerprints from the other. This event led authorities to realize that Bertillon anthropologic measurements were an unreliable method for personal identification, and that two people who have nearly identical facial features and measurements nevertheless have unique fingerprints.

Sir William J. Herschel (1833–1917)

As an Englishman stationed in India during the mid-1800s, Herschel was flummoxed with designing a method for having Indian workers sign legal documents for the British government in a way that was not subject to ease of forgery, such as signing with an "X" or other non-unique mark. He began experimenting with having the workers "sign" legal documents by applying their inked palm and, later, thumb impressions, to the documents. Through examination of hundreds of such document signatures and examination of his own fingerprints for over 50 years, he noted that the prints did not change over time. He attempted—unsuccessfully—to convince others within the government to implement his practices (James & Nordby, 2009).

Henry Faulds (1843–1930)

Faulds, a Scottish physician working in a hospital in Tokyo, Japan, became involved in local archeological digs. Noticing the fingerprints of artisans left on pottery shards, he began to study contemporary hand and fingerprints. In 1880 he is reported to have written a letter to the scientist Charles Darwin about his findings, suggesting that fingerprints could be classified and noting that their ridge details appeared to be unique between individuals. Faulds also mentioned that he had used these unique print details to apprehend criminals and to exonerate the innocent. Darwin forwarded Faulds' letter to his half-cousin, Sir Francis Galton, an English scientist.

Sir Francis Galton (1822–1911)

In 1892 Galton published the first recognized in-depth study of fingerprint science, entitled "Finger Prints." This text included the first classification system for fingerprints, wherein Galton identified the characteristics that enable fingerprints to be identified. These minute variances within fingerprints are termed **minutia**, but are often referred to as *Galton points* or *Galton details* in honor of his recognition of such characteristics. However, although Galton's work in fingerprints became the foundation for modern fingerprint science, his method of classification was much too awkward and involved to make it practical for use in criminal investigations.

Sir Edward Henry (1850–1931)

In 1897, a trainee of Galton's developed a more functional classification system independent of Galton, while working in India. In 1901, Scotland Yard appointed Edward Henry their Assistant Commissioner of Police. While working in this capacity, he introduced his fingerprint system, and within a decade, Henry's system had been adopted by police and prison forces in most English-speaking countries around the globe, and it remains in use to this day (Girard, 2008).

Another individual, however, is responsible for development of a classification system used in many non–English-speaking countries.

Juan Vucetich (1855–1925)

The Argentinean police official Vucetich came to understand the value of fingerprints as a method of criminal identification because of his correspondence with Galton. Through his growing interest in the matter, he developed his own system for classifying fingerprints. Vucetich, originally named his system *icnofalangometrica*, meaning "finger track measurement". In 1896, he renamed the system *dactiloscopia*, meaning "finger description" (Rodriguez, 2004). By 1896, Argentine police had implemented Vucetich's system of identification involving fingerprints and had abandoned anthropometry. Vucetich has the distinction of being involved with the first recorded case in which fingerprints were used to solve a crime. This case took place in 1892 and involved the homicide of illegitimate children. As a result of his experience with this case and his continued study of fingerprints, Vucetich wrote *Dactiloscopia Comparada* in 1904 (Caplan, 2001). The system of classification developed by Vucetich is still in use in many Spanish-speaking countries, particularly in South America.

What Are Fingerprints?

Structure of Fingerprints

Skin is the outer covering of the human body and is the largest and heaviest organ of the body. The majority of the skin on the human body is referred to as *smooth skin*. Smooth skin contains hair, sebaceous glands, and sweat glands. Volar skin, on the other hand, is found on the soles of the feet, palms of the hands, and on the underside of the fingers and toes. It is furrowed, hairless, lacks pigmentation, and only contains sweat glands. Volar skin does not secrete sebaceous oils, but sometimes bodily oils are found on volar skin (especially the hands) due to contact with other areas of the body's skin surface. The friction ridges present on volar skin are a textured surface, continuously corrugated with narrow ridges that run parallel to one another and form patterns that do not appear in the same place or sequence from one finger, hand, or toe to another. The purpose of friction ridges is to increase friction between the volar surfaces and any other surface they contact.

A close examination of the friction ridges reveals that all along their length the surface is broken in an irregular fashion by sweat pores. The pores are openings for the ducts leading from the sweat glands found in the subcutaneous tissue. The human body has three kinds of sweat glands:

- Eccrine glands are found on all parts of the body and are the only sweat glands found on the palms of the hands and the soles of the feet.
- Apocrine glands are located in the pubic, mammary, and anal areas.
- Sebaceous glands are located on the forehead, chest, back, and abdomen and produce an oily secretion called sebum.

All three kinds of glands secrete water as well as many different organic and inorganic substances. Water is excreted to help control body temperature. As the water moves to the surface, it evaporates and picks up waste products from other parts of the body. Only the sebaceous glands secrete oily substances; fingers touching those areas are likely to pick up oily residues and transfer them on contact, thus leaving fingerprints.

Composition of Fingerprints

You will observe that these dainty curving lines … form various clearly defined patterns, such as arches, circles, long curves, whorls, etc., and that these patterns differ on the different fingers. The patterns on the right hand are not the same as those on the left. Taken finger for finger, your patterns differ from your neighbor's. (p. 159)

Mark Twain
Pudd'nhead Wilson, 1894

The term *fingerprints* actually refers to oil, perspiration, and other residue left behind by a person's friction ridge skin after they have touched something. Friction ridge skin is characterized by hills called *ridges* and valleys called *furrows*. These ridges and furrows form three basic fingerprint patterns—arches, loops, and whorls—with each pattern type having several subtypes: ulnar and radial loops, plain and tented arches, plain whorls, central pocket loop whorls, double loop whorls, and accidental whorls (**Figure 8–1**).

In addition to the overall patterns, there are many tiny variations and irregularities within the ridges themselves, termed *minutia* or *ridge characteristics*. The ridges of the fingerprint form the minutiae by doing one of three things: ending abruptly (ending ridge), splitting into two ridges (bifurcation), or by forming ridge dots.

These ridge characteristics result in individuality not simply between individuals but between the fingers themselves. No two prints have been found to be the same. The FBI has over 70 million fingerprints on file and not one is the same as another. While it is impossible to physically observe each and every fingerprint in the world throughout history, the study of fingerprints within the past 200 years has failed to produce two prints with identical features. This has been known for over a century before the discovery of DNA. In fact, fingerprints are more unique than DNA, for while each person has his or her own DNA, monozygotic (identical) twins, triplets, and other multiples all have individual fingerprints. In in his book *Pudd'nhead Wilson* (1894), Mark Twain wrote about the individuality of fingerprints between twins:

> The patterns of a twin's right hand are not the same as those on his left. One twin's patterns are never the same as his fellow-twin's patterns. You have often heard of twins who were so exactly alike that when dressed alike their own parents could not tell them apart. Yet there was never a twin born into this world that did not carry from birth to death, a sure

A   **B**   **C**

FIGURE 8–1   Basic fingerprint patterns. (a) whorl pattern, (b) plain arch, and (c) loop pattern
Courtesy of the Federal Bureau of Investigation.

identifier in this mysterious and marvelous natal autograph. That once known to you, his fellow-twin could never personate him and deceive you. (p. 159)

Types of Fingerprints

Although personnel often use the term *latent* prints to describe all fingerprints found at a crime scene, many of the prints discovered are visible and should not be called latent. Any investigator, lawyer, or expert who inartfully uses "latent" to describe a visible print can expect to be challenged on competent cross-examination. Such a simple point is not lost on jurors, who generally are swayed by simple reasons to find one witness more believable than another. While there are three distinct categories of fingerprints (arches, loops, and whorls), the patterns can leave three different types of transfers. The three distinct types of prints found at a crime scene are **plastic**, **patent**, and **latent** impressions.

Plastic Fingerprints

If fingers come into contact with a soft material such as soap, wet putty, wet cement, wet paint, dust, or melted wax, a ridge impression may be left sufficient for performing a comparison. These impressions have a distinct three-dimensional appearance and often do not require further processing. They are documented using oblique photography (**Figure 8–2**).

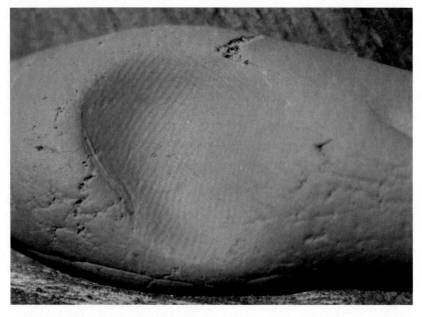

FIGURE 8–2   Example of a plastic fingerprint
Courtesy of Dana Gevelinger, University of Wisconsin-Platteville.

Patent Fingerprints

Patent prints are easily identifiable as fingerprints by the unassisted eye. Fingers that have been in contact with a colored material such as toner, ink, blood, paint, oil, or chocolate leave visible prints. Once the material has soiled the fingers, the material may be transferred to a surface with which the ridges come into contact. These prints require no processing to be recognizable as a fingerprint and are often suitable for comparison (**Figure 8–3**).

Latent Fingerprints

These are prints that require additional processing to be rendered visible and suitable for comparison. Body perspiration and oils might leave invisible residues on surfaces that, if visualized, would constitute a usable impression of the friction ridges. Processing of latent prints is accomplished through development, enhancement, or visualization appropriate for the type of surface upon which the prints repose (**Figure 8–4**).

FIGURE 8–3   Example of a patent fingerprint
Courtesy of Dana Gevelinger, University of Wisconsin-Platteville.

FIGURE 8–4   Close-up photo of a powder-dusted latent fingerprint

Searching for and Processing Latent Prints

Although one might think that due to the general knowledge that fingerprints are individualistic and that finding prints at a scene might implicate someone, many criminals continue to deposit their prints at crime scenes. Therefore, fingerprints should be sought at all types of crime scenes, especially at scenes of crimes committed by unknown perpetrators. Recognition of fingerprint evidence requires training and experience, however.

Persons processing a crime scene should keep in mind two seemingly paradoxical truths: (1) Latent prints can be found on almost any type of surface and (2) latent prints will not be developed on every attempt. Past studies have shown that many departments locate usable latent prints at 30% to 50% of the scenes visited, and in some of those cases the prints belong to persons with legitimate access. Investigators should not be discouraged by recovery rates as low as one in three crime scenes. The likelihood of the recovery of usable latent prints is increased by the resourcefulness and diligence of the person conducting the search.

Another important consideration is to initiate a search for latent prints as soon as possible after the discovery of the crime and to protect areas to be processed for prints from adverse weather conditions. Ordinarily, fingerprints are primarily composed of water and body fats and oils. These can evaporate if not processed in a timely manner or if exposed to sun, heat, or wind. Prints may be washed away by rain or dew if not protected.

Searches for latent prints should progress from the least invasive and destructive method to the most invasive and destructive method in hopes of minimizing potential evidence damage and maximizing the evidence potential. Suggested search and processing guidelines are in the box.

Once a print has been located, it must be documented with photography and then a processing methodology must be determined. How a print is developed, enhanced, or visualized is dependent upon a number of factors including substrate of the material on which the print is located, age of the print, color of the background on which the print is found, environment (wet/dry/humid), and other factors. While there are over 80 ways to process a fingerprint, they can be grouped into four methods: physical, chemical, special illumination, and a combination approach.

General Rule

Evidence should be collected intact and submitted to the lab for processing and examination. If impossible or impractical, apply latent development techniques at the scene, preferably by trained personnel.

Search and Processing Guidelines for Fingerprints

Visual Examination

- Sometimes all that is needed to visualize a print is to use oblique lighting.
- After a visual exam, use a laser/alternative light/ultraviolet (UV) light search.
- Photograph all patent prints and other evidence in the impressions prior to removal or tape lifting.

Processing with Physical or Chemical Methods

- Photograph latent prints after development or visualization.
- Draw sketches of the location and orientation of the latent impression on the lift card or in the investigator's notes. The documentation of the *location* and *orientation* of the latent impressions detected will provide details for any reconstruction efforts for testing statements by a suspect with regard to innocent placement of the latent impressions.
- As a rule, wet items or surfaces should be allowed to air dry without the use of heat or forced air before processing.
- Items in freezing weather should be allowed to warm to room temperature before dusting.
- When drying is not feasible, the item may be processed for latent prints by applying small particle reagent (SPR; discussed later in this chapter).

Casting Plastic Impressions

- Impressions should be photographed with oblique lighting and a cast prepared from silicone casting material in the case of indented patent impressions.

Remember at all times that crime scene fingerprints are perishable.

Physical Methods

Methods that do not involve chemicals or reactions are physical methods. These utilize the application of fine particles to the fingerprint residue, thereby creating a contrast between the ridges and background. The most common physical method is *powder dusting* with a brush and inorganic powders. Another variant is *magnetic powder dusting*, which has the advantage of being gentler and not as destructive as inorganic dusting because no bristles make contact with the print. A third common physical method is small particle reagent, which typically is used on evidence that has been wet.

Powder and Brush

Fingerprints on smooth, non porous surfaces such as glass, paint, glossy plastics, and other polished surfaces can usually be developed with inorganic (non–carbon-based) powders. The fingerprint brush should be clean and free from oils or other materials that may affect the efficiency of dusting with the brush. The brush should be swirled vigorously to remove excess powder, and then dipped lightly into the powder with a swirling action, lifted, swirled again, and finally applied lightly to the surface in a circular manner (**Figure 8–5**). Once the latent becomes visible, the print should be dusted lightly in the direction of the ridges until clearly visible. It is important to avoid over-dusting because the print may be wiped clean by too much dusting. The print is then lifted with fingerprint tape. The fingerprint tape should be applied by releasing an adequate length of tape from the roll, placing the leading edge to the side of and over the print, and then sliding the finger down the tape to cover the entire area of the print while holding the tape roll in the other hand so that it does not fall onto the surface of the print. The tape should be rubbed sufficiently to remove any bubbles present. If the tape cannot be removed without destroying the print, then the tape is left on the surface and the object collected. If the tape can be removed, it should be pulled up from the end away from the tape roll, and the tape should then be transferred to a latent card. The card should be labeled immediately and a sketch placed on the card illustrating the location and orientation of the print.

FIGURE 8–5   Inorganic powder and brush
Courtesy of Nick Vesper, University of Wisconsin-Platteville.

Magnetic Powder Dusting

Magnetic powder has been available since the early 1960s and adds a wide range of flexibility to fingerprint processing techniques. Typically, magnetic powder is used on nonmagnetic surfaces, and inorganic powder on iron-based surfaces. However, the crime scene investigator will find that inorganic powder is inappropriate for some surfaces, including many textured and plastic surfaces (e.g., vinyl imitation-leather, lightly textured automobile dashboards, automobile door panels), where magnetic powder performs quite well.

One of the primary advantages of magnetic powder over inorganic powder dusting is that with magnetic powder, there is no brush to touch and possibly damage the print. Nothing but the powder itself touches the print (**Figure 8–6**).

Small Particle Reagent

Small particle reagent (SPR) is a suspension of molybdenum sulfide grains in water and a detergent solution. The grains adhere to the fatty components of a latent print deposit and assist with visualizing latent fingerprints. The reagent is first shaken to disperse the molybdenum sulfide grains in the liquid and then sprayed onto the surface suspected of bearing latent deposits. The surface is next sprayed with clean distilled water to remove excess reagent. Developed impressions are then photographed or lifted with tape after drying. The SPR method has the advantage that it can be used on wet and/or dirty/greasy surfaces; however, it also can be used on dry surfaces. In any case, SPR must be used with the understanding that the possible benefit of latent recovery must outweigh the possibility of water damage to the object.

FIGURE 8–6 Magnetic powder and applicator

Courtesy of Nick Vesper, University of Wisconsin-Platteville.

Chemical Methods

Chemical methods of fingerprint processing are those that involve a chemical reaction taking place in order to enhance, develop, or visualize a latent fingerprint. The two most frequently utilized methods are ninhydrin and cyanoacrylate fuming.

Ninhydrin

The amino acid reagent **ninhydrin** has been available for crime scene use since 1910. This chemical is used to detect ammonia or amino acids within print residue, which reacts to form a bluish-purple color (**Figure 8–7**). It is most useful on porous surfaces (e.g., paper and raw wood) and is primarily used in document processing efforts. Ninhydrin may also be used as a preliminary treatment prior to the use of other chemicals or the use of laser or an alternate light source (ALS). Heat and humidity expedite the development process (**Figure 8–8**). Because ninhydrin reacts with amino acids, it should only be applied in well-ventilated areas to prevent serious health complications ensuing from its improper usage.

Cyanoacrylate Ester Fuming

Cyanaocrylate ester fuming (also called *super glue fuming*) is a technique that stabilizes latent prints. Super-glue fuming has been used since the early 1980s. In this method super glue is induced to fume and the fumes interact with latent fingerprint residue by polymerizing them, yielding a stable friction ridge impression that is off-white in color (**Figure 8–9**). This process can be accomplished by placing the items to be processed in a fuming chamber and then fuming with any of a number of commercially available kits or with kits prepared by the analyst. Of particular interest is the development of the super-glue fuming wand for cyanoacrylate fuming (**Figure 8–10**). This technique should allow for effortless fuming in the

FIGURE 8–7 Close-up of a latent print processed using Ninhydrin

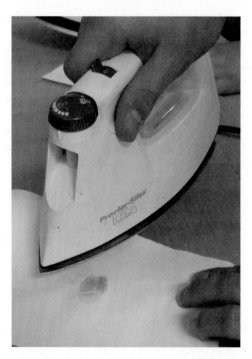

FIGURE 8–8 An evidence technician using heat and humidity to expedite ninhydrin processing

FIGURE 8–9 An example of a latent print processed using cyanoacrylate fuming

FIGURE 8–10 Cyanoacrylate fuming wand and cartridges

field by investigators. The cartridges can be ordered with dye added, which can be visualized with fluorescent lighting and thus eliminate the additional step of treating the fumed impressions with a fluorescent dye or powder. The process requires humidity (moisture source). It is primarily used on non porous surfaces and is an initial step in fingerprint processing. Due to the fact that cyanoacrylate ester encapsulates the latent print in an off-white polymer shroud, it does not necessarily lend itself to effective visualization for identification purposes. Prints often will need to be dusted or further processed to result in the best visualization or enhancement. This method is also used as a way of "fixing" a print prior to the object being transported. This method safely encapsulates and protects the print from any rubbing damage during transport and will allow the lab to continue visualization and enhancement methods.

Special Illumination

Sometimes all that is required to visualize a latent fingerprint is oblique lighting. Light is a basic tool for crime scene searches. Clean white light is necessary for basic observation; however, specialized lighting is often necessary. **Alternate light sources (ALSs)** are light-emitting devices supplied with colored filters that filter the source light so that the developed latent print can be viewed with light of a narrow wavelength range, rather than at the usual full spectrum ("white light") viewing range (**Figure 8–11**). The ALS produces additional light energy to visualize different types of evidence and can be used for more than simply visualizing latent prints.

An ALS will help visualize:

- Fluids and biological matter
- Fibers and some hairs
- Bruises or bite marks
- Nearly invisible bloodstains
- Alterations to documents

Combined Approach

While many fingerprint development techniques can be divided into either physical or chemical types, often a combined approach will yield the best enhancement of a latent print. An example

FIGURE 8–11   Alternate light sources and associated barrier filters

of a combined approach is utilizing the chemical method of cyanoacrylate ester fuming to locate and protect the print, and then following up this method with powder dusting to create the best contrast for visualization.

Advanced Lifting Techniques

For the majority of scenes, a simplified approach to latent processing, such as powder dusting, will be sufficient to properly locate and preserve latent fingerprint evidence. Sometimes, however, the crime scene investigator will encounter a surface believed to contain latent prints but that does not lend itself to processing in the typical manner (**Figure 8–12**). Irregular surfaces such as the dimpled surface of steering wheels and vehicle dashboards, or curved surfaces such as door handles or wood stairway spindles, may prove challenging for lifting prints.

A suggestion for dealing with these difficult surfaces is to utilize a combined approach of powder dusting along with lifting utilizing forensic casting material versus tape. The method is described below:

1. For rough or irregularly shaped objects.
   - Dust the location of the latent print with powder.
   - Apply a forensic casting material or silicon (e.g., Mikrosil™ casting putty) to the developed print area and lift the latent print (**Figure 8–13**).
2. Certain surfaces are textured which makes it difficult to lift powdered fingerprints in their entirety. Examples are Styrofoam and rough leather.

FIGURE 8–12 Using silicon casting material to process the remains of a human fingerprint

FIGURE 8–13   Using silicon casting material to obtain a fingerprint

- In these cases, white or black silicone rubber casting compound can be used. The casting compound is mixed and placed over the print developed with fingerprint powder. After the silicone rubber has cured, the fingerprint is lifted.

- Depending on the color of the fingerprint powder that was used, white or black silicone rubber is used for contrast.

Preserving and Packaging Latent Prints

When a crime scene investigator applies physical or chemical methods of processing to latent prints, they are developing and visualizing the actual fingerprint that was left behind by an individual; they are not creating and lifting a copy of the print. The chemicals or powders will interact with or adhere to the residues left behind by the finger that touched the surface. Therefore, the recovery efforts and documentation should be the same as with any other item of physical evidence. When the print is collected and later presented within court, it does not simply represent the print left at the crime scene, it *is* the print that was at the crime scene. This is important for a crime scene investigator to realize so that, regardless of whether or not they believe the print to be identifiable, the print should be properly processed, documented, and recovered so that the print can serve as future evidence.

As with plastic and visible prints, once an investigator has developed a latent print, he or she must prepare and preserve it for possible use in the laboratory and courtroom. First, it must be photographed with a scale of reference. Next, if possible, the print should be removed from the crime scene, either by preserving the item upon which the print lies or by lifting the print. Numerous manufacturers provide specialized adhesive lifters for this purpose (**Figure 8–14**).

A lifter is a transparent tape that is placed on the powdered print with the adhesive side down. When the tape is removed, the fingerprint powder is removed with it. The lifter is provided with a black or white card onto which the transparent tape and powdered print can then be placed, adhesive side down. The colored card provides contrast to the colored powder used, helping to visualize the print. Lift tape also comes in a variety of sizes and configurations so that the right type can be chosen for the size, number, and location of the prints to be lifted.

The majority of times the prints recovered from crime scenes are used from a visual identification standpoint, using the actual characteristics within the print to identify the person whose print is a match to such characteristics. Lifted prints can be packaged either as tape lifts adhered to print cards, or protected within an evidentiary envelope. An object bearing friction

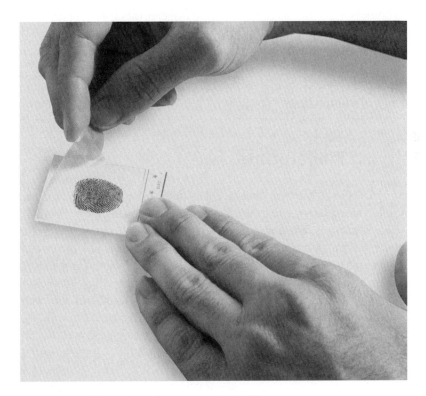

FIGURE 8–14   Lifting a fingerprint using an adhesive lifter
Courtesy of Sirchie Acquisition Company, LLC.

ridge prints must be properly handled and packaged to avoid destroying the prints while in transit. Do not place items in plastic bags or allow surfaces that contain latent prints to come in contact with or rub against the sides of the packaging materials. Mark these containers with the word "Fingerprints."

Recent advances have allowed for the use of DNA analysis with regard to latent print lifts. Some chemical methods of processing may prohibit the ability of this type of forensic analysis to be performed. If DNA analysis of print residue is expected to be used, the crime scene investigator is encouraged to contact their appropriate crime lab prior to utilizing chemical methods of processing so that any contamination or damage of DNA-related evidence can be avoided.

No two fingers have yet been found that have identical characteristics. Fingerprint individuality is not dependent upon age, size, gender, or race. Fingerprint individuality, and therefore fingerprint identification, rests on four premises:

1. Friction ridges develop in their definitive form when humans are still in the womb.
2. Friction ridges remain unchanged throughout life with the exception of permanent scars.
3. Friction ridge patterns and their details are unique.
4. Ridge patterns vary within certain boundaries that allow the patterns to be classified.

The entire point of recognizing and collecting fingerprints is to identify them in order to find a suspect or identify a person. However, most people have never given much thought to the process by which fingerprint identification is actually done. When prints are found, an expert compares them with samples known to have been made by a suspect. He/she first compares overall patterns and then looks for identical ridge characteristics. When these match, they are known as **points of comparison**. The general guideline in the United States is that prints

---

Identifying Fingerprints

Every human being carries with him from his cradle to his grave certain physical marks which do not change their character, and by which he can always be identified—and that without shade of doubt or question. These marks are his signature, his physiological autograph, so to speak, and this autograph cannot be counterfeited, nor can he disguise it or hide it away, nor can it become illegible by the wear and mutations of time. This signature is not his face—age can change that beyond recognition; it is not his hair, for that can fall out; it is not his height, for duplicates of that exist; it is not his form, for duplicates of that exist also, whereas this signature is each man's very own—there is no duplicate of it among the swarming populations of the globe! This autograph consists of the delicate lines or corrugations with which Nature marks the insides of the hands and the soles of the feet. (p. 159)

Mark Twain
Pudd'nhead Wilson, 1894

must match at 12 points of comparison before an identification (ID) is considered to be a positive match. However, there is no definitive rule on how to achieve this comparison. Current training in fingerprint comparison stresses that the quality of the print and the quality of the comparison are more important than a numerical match (**Figure 8–15**).

The examiner must decide if sufficient quality and quantity of the ridge detail is present. If not, it may be concluded that there was "insufficient ridge detail to form a conclusion." The print is analyzed to determine its proper orientation, decide suitability, and then proceed to the comparison. The overall pattern and ridge flow is examined. Next, the minutiae are compared, point by point, as to type and location. Finally, pore shape, locations, numbers, and relationships, and the shape and size of edge features are compared. Any unexplained differences between known and latent during this process results in the conclusion that the known is "excluded as a source." If every compared feature is consistent with the known, and enough features are sufficiently unique when considered as a whole, the examiner makes an ID. Therefore, in fingerprint identification, there are three possible conclusions that can be drawn from an analysis:

1. Insufficient ridge detail to form a conclusion
2. Print exclusion
3. Print identification

In law enforcement, IDs are always made by trained and often certified examiners. Sometimes inked prints may be compared with a set of inked prints on file. More commonly, the examiner compares a developed latent print to inked prints from a known person.

Fingerprint examiners are trained extensively and are required to accumulate significant experience before being entrusted with this responsibility. In addition to the general principles and approaches used, therefore, the knowledge, training, and experience are also considered. Most examiners are certified or have been declared an "expert" by a court of law.

FIGURE 8–15   Manual identification using a 10-print card

Classification of Fingerprints

A classification system is necessary if large sets of fingerprint files are to be useful for criminal identification. **Classification** is a formula given to a complete set of 10 fingers as they appear on a fingerprint card generally based on pattern type, ridge count, or ridge tracing. Today the **Henry System** and the **FBI National Crime Information Center–Fingerprint Classification (NCIC-FPC)** are used to classify prints.

Henry System

Developed by Sir Edward Henry, the Henry System of print classification has been used for well over a century and remains in use in many departments today. This system requires the complete classification of all 10 fingers of an individual in order to properly file the information. When this system was developed, it allowed for efficient searching and maintenance of large fingerprint files. However, it did not allow for manually searching for a single print. The system was built around whether or not an individual had whorl patterns present within his or her prints (primary classification) and then had a series of five extensions to the primary classification, dependent upon the type and size of the patterns present in the fingers. An example of utilizing the Henry System of classification is shown in the box.

Henry System of Classification

10	I	1	R	-	r	2
	S	17	U	2 a		

This Henry classification is representative of the following:

Primary: 1/17

Secondary: R/U

Subsecondary/small letter group: - r/2a

Major: I/S

Final: 2

Key: 10

When trained to understand the Henry System of classification, the examiner is able to determine that there is one whorl pattern present within the hand (in the right thumb), a radial loop with a ridge count of 10 is present in the right index finger, a radial loop is present in the right ring finger, ulnar loops are present in the right middle finger, the right little finger (with ridge count of 2), the left thumb, the left index finger, and the left little finger. There are also arches present in the middle and ring finger of the left hand.

CASE IN POINT

Can Fingerprints Lie?

Fingerprints do not themselves lie; however, their interpretation can certainly mislead. Brandon Mayfield, an immigration lawyer from Washington State, found this out in a very publicly humiliating and professionally damaging way in the summer of 2004. After a misidentification led to his subsequent incarceration, the FBI issued the following press release:

May 24, 2004

Statement on Brandon Mayfield Case

After the March terrorist attacks on commuter trains in Madrid, digital images of partial latent fingerprints, obtained from plastic bags that contained detonator caps, were submitted by Spanish authorities to the FBI for analysis. The submitted images were searched through the Integrated Automated Fingerprint Identification System (IAFIS). An IAFIS search compares an unknown print to a database of millions of known prints. The result of an IAFIS search produces a short list of potential matches. A trained fingerprint examiner then takes the short list of possible matches and performs an examination to determine whether the unknown print matches a known print in the database.

Using standard protocols and methodologies, FBI fingerprint examiners determined that the latent fingerprint was of value for identification purposes. This print was subsequently linked to Brandon Mayfield. That association was independently analyzed and the results were confirmed by an outside experienced fingerprint expert.

Soon after the submitted fingerprint was associated with Mr. Mayfield, Spanish authorities alerted the FBI to additional information that cast doubt on our findings. As a result, the FBI sent two fingerprint examiners to Madrid, who compared the image the FBI had been provided to the image the Spanish authorities had.

Upon review it was determined that the FBI identification was based on an image of substandard quality, which was particularly problematic because of the remarkable number of points of similarity between Mr. Mayfield's prints and the print details in the images submitted to the FBI.

The FBI's Latent Fingerprint Unit will be reviewing its current practices and will give consideration to adopting new guidelines for all examiners receiving latent print images when the original evidence is not included.

The FBI also plans to ask an international panel of fingerprint experts to review our examination in this case.

The FBI apologizes to Mr. Mayfield and his family for the hardships that this matter has caused.

Information retrieved from the Federal Bureau of Investigation (FBI). (2004). Press release. Statement on Brandon Mayfield Case. Retrieved August 3, 2009, from http://www.fbi.gov/pressrel/pressrel04/mayfield052404.

VIEW FROM AN EXPERT

A Life of Fingerprints

The first time I ever searched a fingerprint using a computer was in the mid-1960s. The computer was not a fingerprint computer at all; it was an IBM 083 card sorter. What I remember about it is it was a machine that sorted cards that had punch holes in them. As the cards passed through the machine at a very fast rate, they were sorted into various bins as the machine "read" the information provided by the punch holes on the cards. A system was devised whereby information about the fingerprint, such as loop, whorl, etc., type of loop or whorl, ridge count, tracing, and varied other information was "coded" onto the punch cards. When the "computer" made a hit, we would pull the latent from the file and make the manual comparison. A fingerprint examiner by the name of Alex Russak, who worked for the City of Miami Police Department, devised what I believe was the first such system (or at least one of the first) and the Dade County Sheriff's Office, now the Miami Dade Police Department, used a variation of that system. We had at best a database of a couple dozen, maybe a hundred, prints coded into the system. The coding process was cumbersome and tedious, but we did get a few "hits."

Automated fingerprint systems have come an astonishingly long way since then. Today these systems are searching multi-millions of fingerprints and palm prints with amazing speed and accuracy.

Live scan fingerprinting has been around for a number of years now. Live scan has replaced the ink and roller system in many police agencies; however, ink is still widely used. With live scan prints, the operator can watch the print being rolled on a monitor and check the quality of the prints before accepting them. That's only one small advantage of the new technology. With live scan, prints can be scanned directly into systems where they will be automatically searched through local, state, and federal databases.

Scanning technology is still evolving. There is technology available now that allows for the fingers to be scanned without the fingers ever touching the glass scanning plate.

From the earliest uses of fingerprints as a means of identification in criminal cases to today, the science has continually evolved.

Computers, as wonderful as they are, still require the competent comparison skills of a trained fingerprint examiner to make the final decision concerning the identification of a friction ridge print.

Training and continuing education are still extremely important factors. Unfortunately, with the budget problems realized by government at all levels over the past few years, many agencies are operating with very limited funds. Training of forensic personnel is all too often not a priority.

There are differing views concerning what training a novice fingerprint examiner should receive. There are those that say: "We don't need to know the Henry System of Fingerprint Classification anymore because no one uses it. What good is learning about the history of fingerprints?"

I am a firm believer in knowing the basics of your science/profession. You need a solid foundation from which to build if your goal is to become an expert in your profession.

All of the skills you acquire and put to use in your examination of evidence in a criminal case will be put to the test when you are called to testify in court regarding the results of your examination. The courtroom is where you will have to explain and defend everything you did to reach the decision in the case you have worked. All of your time and effort will prove fruitless if you cannot explain yourself to the court and jury. You never know what questions might be asked in court; they might be as simple as "what is a fingerprint" or complex such as "can you explain to the jury how the error rate for fingerprint identification is calculated."

Although fingerprint identification has been accepted in court for over 100 years as a reliable science, attacks on the examiner and the science are a common occurrence and a fingerprint examiner has to be able to defend his/her testimony as well as the science.

There are those who claim that fingerprint identification is not a proven science, or perhaps not scientific at all. Since the late 1990s there have been numerous attacks against the fingerprint community in the form of Daubert hearings in various courts across the United States. Simply put, Daubert is concerned with the admissibility of scientific evidence in court. A Daubert motion is a motion raised before or during trial to exclude the presentation of unqualified evidence to the jury. The Daubert rule requires the judge to be a "gatekeeper" in determining whether certain scientific evidence is admissible. It must past certain standards, such as:

1. Is the evidence based on a testable theory or technique?

2. Has the theory or technique been peer reviewed?

3. Is there a known error rate?

4. Is the underlying science generally accepted?

Fingerprint examiners today have to be better educated and have a solid understanding of what it is that leads one to form an opinion and reach a conclusion. I believe that the basics of fingerprint identification were and still are very important. These skills must now be coupled with a better understanding of the methodology that leads you to your conclusion.

Continued training and education, certification and laboratory accreditation have all been positive steps in the career of latent print examiners. To date, all of the challenges to the science have been successfully met; however, fingerprint examiners continue to face challenging cross-examination from attorneys who are keeping abreast of all of the latest information on fingerprint identification. The Internet is a wealth of information available to anyone, including defense attorneys, who want to learn about the science of fingerprints.

Recent published accounts of "mistakes" and outright wrongdoing by a small minority of fingerprint examiners have provided fodder not only for defense attorneys, but also for those who would like to see the demise of the fingerprint science. When all is said and done, I believe that fingerprint science is extremely sound and will continue to be an effective tool for law enforcement and civilian use for many years to come.

Each generation of fingerprint examiner has the advantage of learning from those who have preceded him/her, and today's examiners have the further advantage of being part of an age of

Although recognized the world over as an effective method for fingerprint filing, with the increased efficiency and affordability of computer systems, many departments are choosing to file and classify prints using a method developed by the FBI.

National Crime Information Center-Fingerprint Classification (NCIC-FPC)

This system of classification, developed by the FBI (2012), assigns a 20-character string of letters and numbers to a person's fingerprints. Every print entered into the FBI system is classified by this method, and it allows trained law enforcement personnel in the field to determine fingerprint compatibility with prints on record, along with providing an efficient and effective way for filing fingerprints. The following is an example of an NCIC-FPC.

POAA05TT19CISR58DIXX

PO: Right thumb is a plain whorl with an outer tracing.

AA: Right index finger is a plain arch.

05: Right middle finger is an ulnar loop with a ridge count of 5.

TT: Right ring finger is a tented arch.

19: Right little finger is an ulnar loop with a ridge count of 19.

CI: Left thumb is a central pocket loop whorl with an inner tracing.

SR: Left index finger is unclassifiable due to scarring.

exploding technology. Digital information is the norm for just about everything now, a far cry from the photo-phone of years ago used to send fingerprint images anywhere in the world in a matter of seconds. Many of the old tried and true methods are still very useful and productive, and they have a place alongside of today's lightning fast computers, scanners, and new chemical development methods. Fingerprint powder and a fingerprint brush can obtain amazing results in the hands of a knowledgeable latent print examiner.

Carmine Artone
Retired Branch Chief
Identification and Research Branch
Forensic Services Division
United States Secret Service

58: Left middle finger is a radial loop with a ridge count of 8.

DI: Left ring finger is a double loop whorl with an inner tracing.

XX: Left little finger is missing (possibly amputated, or missing since birth).

ACE-V

A systematic and thorough approach to crime scene processing means employing the scientific method within the efforts, referred to as scientific crime scene investigation. A similar methodology is utilized with reference to the comparison and identification process of latent fingerprints. David R. Ashbaugh, a scientist with the Royal Canadian Mounted Police, developed a formal method known as **ACE-V** for the scientific comparison of prints. The acronym stands for *a*nalysis, *c*omparison, *e*valuation, and verification. The purpose of this comparison methodology is to either identify a print, via individualization, as having originated from the same source, or exclude impressions as having no common origin (Coppock, 2007). There remains the possibility of the print ID process being determined as inconclusive.

Analysis

The first level of this process begins with the study of the questioned print to determine the overall print orientation, quality, shape, and ridge flow. The comparison (or known) print is analyzed in the same manner. If the information derived is found to be consistent, the analysis proceeds to the next level. If nonmatching characteristics are observed, the examination is terminated, which results in an exclusion.

Comparison

If the analysis portion of the process yields sufficient information to warrant a further investigation, the next level begins with orienting the questioned and known print in the same manner and identifying a common unique point in each print to utilize as a starting point. The examination will continue from this common starting point and progress along with recognition of other areas of commonalities between the prints, with regard to ridge characteristics, beginning with the most distinctive feature identified and continuing until all of the characteristics are accounted for and there are no unexplainable variances. Differences may exist due to print quality; however, it is the print characteristics present that are being compared, not necessarily their clarity.

Evaluation

In the event of a clear variance between the prints, following the comparison stage, an exclusion would be made. However, if the information appears consistent between the two prints, an ID can be made. Typically, this ID is based upon the degree of ridge detail. If the print is lacking in sufficient print detail, then pore distribution and ridge shapes and edges may be utilized instead or in combination.

Verification

Regardless of the conclusion reached, either exclusion or identification, another examiner reexamines the print for verification utilizing the aforementioned process. Under ideal conditions, the examiner making the identification or exclusion should be an analyst who is in no way associated with the case, or who had any significant knowledge of the case. This could impart bias to the decision process.

One important case of misidentification was the FBI's arrest of American citizen Brandon Mayfield in 2004 in connection with the Madrid bombings that killed 191 and injured over 2,000. It wasn't until the Spanish government identified a different man from the fingerprint evidence that Mayfield was released (see Case in Point).

Automated Fingerprint Identification System

Television, books, and movies often emphasize the value of fingerprints in solving serious crimes. Until the advent of computer technology, however, that value was mostly mythical. Fingerprints were used to inculpate or exculpate based on a suspect group. A search of fingerprint files for the match to a fingerprint found at the scene of a crime occurred mostly in fiction. The classification system used in categorizing stored fingerprints and the large number of fingerprints stored made it impossible to check through a fingerprint collection manually looking for a match. Computers turned fantasy into reality.

An **Automated Fingerprint Identification System (AFIS)** is an automatic pattern recognition system that consists of three fundamental stages:

1. *Data acquisition:* The fingerprint to be recognized is sensed.

2. *Feature extraction:* A machine representation (pattern) is extracted from the sensed image.

3. *Decision making:* The representations derived from the sensed image are compared with a representation stored in the system.

Different systems may use different numbers of available fingerprints (multiple impressions of a single finger or single impressions of multiple fingers) for person identification. The feature extraction stage may involve manual override and editing by experts. Image enhancement may be used for poor-quality images. Depending on whether the acquisition process is offline or online, a fingerprint may be one of three types: an inked fingerprint, a latent fingerprint, or a live-scan fingerprint.

Fingerprints no longer need to be manually matched to files. Time is often the critical factor in determining the success of a criminal investigation. The use of this computer technology not only saves time, but significantly increases the accuracy match rate compared to manual comparisons. Because of this, and due to the systems becoming more affordable, AFISs are rapidly being implemented throughout law enforcement agencies (see **Figure 8–16**).

Ten-print cards are scanned into the system. They are run against current latent prints within the system from "unknowns" The AFIS also can scan in latent prints and compare them against the 10-print cards on file. The computer assigns a percentage of probability on the matches generated. Searches can be conducted in seconds/minutes versus months for manual searches. It should be noted, however, that final determination is always left up to a professional print examiner and NOT the computer.

For the AFIS to pull up candidates for a "match," an examiner must first ensure that minutia points are properly identified; sometimes these must be added or edited manually, which can be very time consuming. However, if not performed, and minutia points are incorrectly identified, or unidentified altogether, then the chances of finding a proper match decrease dramatically.

This often tedious and problematic situation saw a dramatic improvement when in April 2009 the National Institute of Standards and Technology (NIST) released results of biometric research they had conducted with reference to Automatic Feature Extraction and Matching (AFEM). Utilizing automated fingerprint feature extraction, most of the tested print's identities were found within the top 10 prints listed as possible matches. This shows a dramatic increase in efficiency of automation and

© Kevin L Chesson/ShutterStock, Inc.

FIGURE 8–16　AFIS terminal

bodes well for accelerating fingerprint data input and identification (Indovina, Dvorychenko, Tabassi, et al., 2009).

Today, the FBI has an Integrated Automated Fingerprint Identification System in place (IAFIS). This system allows agencies to be linked together and compare/share evidence. However, not all systems are integrated. The majority of time when someone thinks of AFIS, they believe the system to be an IAFIS, but that is not necessarily the case. An AFIS accepts and stores input data within that system alone, and is not integrated with outside systems. Therefore, if a comparison to other prints outside of the agency's own system is to take place, the print must be e-mailed or otherwise sent digitally to an agency that has IAFIS capabilities. Agencies that are integrated, whether to the FBI IAFIS system or simply to a larger network such as several interstate crime laboratories, are able to run a print against all prints within the integrated system.

Palm Prints

The palms of the hands (as well as the soles of the feet) yield the same volar skin, and thus friction ridge skin, as that of the fingers (and toes). However, the large-scale classification of palm impressions relating to data entry or archiving is a relatively new concept. Until recently, the technology necessary to document and compare such information was not available on a large scale. Most AFIS computer databases would only allow searches of fingerprints. However, an increasing number of vendors are making modifications and updates to their systems that will allow for the input of and comparison of palm print impressions.

Although palm prints are relatively new for AFISs, latent print comparisons are not new. One of the earliest latent print identifications, possibly the first in a criminal case in this country, was a palm print identification. Palm print and footprint identifications have been part of the friction ridge identification process for many years. Palm print identifications at the Secret Service, for example, historically have been very high because of the large number of forged U.S. Treasury checks that were processed. This was especially true before forgery and general financial fraud became mostly electronic in nature. Quite often palm prints of the side of the palm are developed under the signature area. This area of the palm is sometimes referred to as the *writer's palm* because it contacts the document when a person is writing (Artone, personal communication, October 25, 2008).

Palm prints often are found during crime scene search efforts. The most commonly encountered areas of friction skin impressions typically correspond to the large padded areas of the palmer surface. As technology continues to improve, the comparison and identification efforts will also improve. A crime scene investigator should not let this deter him or her from the collection of the friction ridge evidence. To a crime scene investigator, all prints should be viewed as potentially identifiable. Such identification efforts are left up to the experience and technology of the forensic laboratory.

Preparing Fingerprint Cards

The 2009 Wisconsin Department of Justice (WisDOJ) *Physical Evidence Handbook* suggests the following with regard to collection of inked fingerprints:

> Law enforcement personnel should strive to develop the skills necessary to take legible record ("inked") finger and palm prints (**Figure 8–17**) [*sic*]. Absolute clarity of detail is paramount. Unless ridge detail is perfectly clear, it may be impossible to conduct comparisons against the latent prints. This can result in identifications not being made that would have been possible if the inked impression had been clearly recorded. Submissions made to the laboratory should record finger and palm prints of all persons known to have had or suspected of having had access to the item or scene. (It is especially important to secure finger and palm prints of the victim if he/she has died, since it will be nearly impossible to secure prints once the body has been interred) (Wisconsin Department of Justice (WisDOJ). (2009). *Physical evidence handbook* (8th ed.). Madison, WI:Wisconsin Department of Justice p. 103).

Taking Record Fingerprints

Preparing Inked Fingerprint Cards

Prepare the inking slab by placing several small dabs of ink on the surface and rolling it uniformly over the surface. Be careful not to use too much ink. The rolled out ink should be only thick enough so that when a digit is rolled across the surface, the areas where the ridges picked up the ink will appear clean. The print recorded should have good contrast with the

FIGURE 8–17 A 10-print fingerprint card

card. Practice will allow for proper inking on a consistent basis. It is suggested that a test ink impression be made on a scrap of paper to check for proper ink density. If possible, adjust the fingerprint cardholder so that it is at the height of the person's elbow.

The person to be printed should wash his/her hands if excessive grease, dirt, or perspiration is present. Inked impressions should not be taken of digits having open cuts. The person being fingerprinted should be instructed not to assist with the process, but to cooperate by relaxing his/her arm so it pivots more easily. With the person positioned to the right side of the person taking the prints and slightly to his or her rear, the right hand of the person to be printed should be grasped firmly. Then, holding the four fingers back and clear of the inking slab, the thumb is inked by rolling it toward the body. Then roll the inked thumb in the designated space on the card. Repeat the process for the fingers, except roll the fingers away from the person's body. This prevents possible drag and secures a more uniform impression. When the right hand is completed, have the person turn so he/she is standing at a right angle to the card stand, with his/her back to you. Grasp the left hand and repeat the process. Do not push down on the fingers while recording them; use only enough pressure to guide and to ensure the digit does not slip. Excessive pressure will blur the impression.

To record the simultaneous impressions, re-roll ink on the slab (add more ink if necessary) and have the person wipe excess ink from his/her fingers with lint-free toweling. Simultaneous prints are not rolled; the four fingers are extended and joined. Ink and print by pressing them straight down in the appropriate block. Use only a very slight amount of pressure on the back of the person's fingers when pressing them onto the card. Repeat with the thumbs. If the inked impressions are not properly inked or recorded, re-take them.

Recording Palm Prints

If palm prints are found at the crime scene then palm prints should be recorded from suspect(s) and victim(s) (**Figure 8–18** and **Figure 8–19**). To do this, remove excess ink from the person's hands and then re-ink the entire palm and fingers. Palm prints are more clearly recorded by the following method:

Secure an 8" × 8" plain card to a 3" to 4" diameter cylinder with rubber bands. Possible cylinders include a short section of plastic drain pipe or a section of the cardboard tubing on which carpet is shipped. Place the tube (with card attached) on a counter top so it can roll toward the front edge, placing it so it can make one complete revolution. After inking the palm, instruct the person to hold his/her hand perfectly flat, palm down and parallel to the counter top. Grasp the person's arm and guide the hand so the wrist is placed on the card at the bottom, ending with the tips of the fingers at the top edge of the card. As the palm draws across the card, apply very slight pressure to the back of the person's hand with the heel of your hand (this will ensure the hollow of the palm will be recorded). The impression will be more clear if only slight pressure is applied during the procedure (only enough pressure to ensure the hand does not slip across the surface of the card).

Source: Wisconsin Department of Justice (WisDOJ). (2009). *Physical evidence handbook* (8th ed.). Madison, WI: Wisconsin Department of Justice, p. 105.

FIGURE 8–18   Example of palm print card
Courtesy of Nick Vesper, University of Wisconsin-Platteville.

FIGURE 8–19   Example of palm print card
Courtesy of Nick Vesper, University of Wisconsin-Platteville.

All finger and palm print cards must be signed and dated by both the person and the officer. The fingerprinted person should fill out all information required on the card. This information should appear in the person's handwriting or printing.

Scientific Working Group on Friction Ridge Analysis, Study, and Technology

The **Scientific Working Group on Friction Ridge Analysis, Study, and Technology (SWGFAST)** was established in 1997 in response to a number of inconsistencies and controversies relating to fingerprint identification and technological advancement, and continues to operate through sponsorship from the FBI. Its mission is to assist the latent print community in providing the best service and product to the criminal justice system. Membership in SWGFAST comprises a diverse group of professionals within the fingerprint community. This includes not only latent print examiners from law enforcement agencies, but also defense experts, researchers, instructors, academics, managers, and others. This group's diversity provides an objective yet varied perspective to all matters of interest to the group. The group was formed to establish consensus guidelines and standards for the forensic examination of friction ridge impressions. To date, that has been limited to the concerns of the latent print community. Although it has been realized that there are areas of common interest to other fingerprint applications (e.g., criminal history and biometrics), the existing SWGFAST guidelines were not developed with the intention of being applied to non latent print-related matters.

WRAP UP

Chapter Summary

What is not looked for will not be found. What is not found cannot be identified. Fingerprints are one of the most probative types of evidence in crime scene investigation and as such, they should be searched for and gathered whenever possible. A crime scene investigator should consider all prints as being potentially identifiable and should call upon his or her training and experience to determine the best method for processing latent prints at a crime scene. If it is possible to collect the item and submit it to the lab for processing, it is always preferable to do so. Lacking that, processing and recovery efforts should be put to use at the crime scene.

Review Questions

1. _____ are a textured surface, continuously corrugated with narrow ridges and found on the surface of the volar skin.

2. Friction ridge skin is characterized by hills called _____ and valleys called _____.

3. What are the two paradoxical truths of processing a crime scene for latent fingerprints?

4. What is the primary advantage of magnetic powder over inorganic powder?

5. What is SPR and what is it made of? What types of evidence can an ALS be used to visualize?

6. List the four premises on which fingerprint individuality rests.

7. The two types of classification systems used today in the United States are _____ and _____.

8. Describe the issues regarding fingerprint analysis that arose during the Brandon Mayfield case.

9. What is ACE-V and how is it used in fingerprint analysis?

10. What is the SWGFAST and what is their purpose?

References

Artone, C. (October 25, 2008). Personal communication.

Caplan, J. (2001). *Documenting individual identity: The development of state practices in the modern world.* Princeton, NJ: Princeton University Press.

Coppock, C. A. (2007). *Contrast* (2nd ed.). Springfield, IL: Charles C. Thomas Publisher, Ltd.

Federal Bureau of Investigation (FBI). (2012). Birth of the FBI's technical laboratory 1924–1935. Retrieved September 6, 2012, from http://www.fbi.gov/about-us/history/highlights-of-history/articles/laboratory

Girard, J. E. (2008). *Principles of environmental chemistry.* Sudbury, MA: Jones and Bartlett Publishers.

Indovina, M., Dvorychenko, V., Tabassi, E., Quinn, G., Grother, P., et al. National Institute of Standards and Technology (NISTIR). (2009). *An evaluation of automated latent fingerprint identification technologies,* NISTIR 7577. Retrieved September 6, 2012, from http://www.nist.gov/customcf/get_pdf.cfm?pub_id=901870

James, S. H., & Nordby, J. J. (2009). *Forensic science: An introduction to scientific and investigative techniques* (3rd ed.). Boca Raton, FL: CRC Press.

Lee, H. C., & Gaensslen, R. E. (2001). *Advances in fingerprint technology* (2nd ed.). Boca Raton, FL: CRC Press.

Rodriguez, J. (2004). South Atlantic Crossing: Fingerprints, Science, and the State in Turn-of-the-Century Argentina. *The American Historical Review,* April 2004.

Twain, M. (1894). *Pudd'nhead Wilson.* Hartford, CT: American Publishing Company.

Wisconsin Department of Justice (WisDOJ). (2009). *Physical evidence handbook* (8th ed.). Madison, WI: Wisconsin Department of Justice.

LEARNING OBJECTIVES

- Understand the value of associative evidence and how it relates to trace evidence analysis.
- Apply probability and statistical significance as they relate to trace evidence.
- Describe the proper methods for collection and preservation of trace evidence.
- Describe the forensic significance of glass breakage analysis.
- Know the capabilities of the PDQ database and how it is used in the investigative process.
- Differentiate between hair and fiber analysis and the forensic information possibilities relevant to each.

Trace Evidence

Wherever he steps, whatever he touches, whatever he leaves even unconsciously, will serve as silent witness against him.

Paul L. Kirk, 1953

KEY TERMS

Associative Evidence
Bayesian Statistics
Concentric Fractures
Conchoidal Fractures
Cortex
Cuticle
Medulla

Primary Packaging
Primary Transfer
Probability
Product Rule
Radial Fractures
Secondary Packaging
Secondary Transfer

3R Rule
Trace Evidence
Transfer Evidence

Introduction to Trace Evidence

Connection of an object or person to a specific location or item is often paramount to establishing guilt or innocence. Locard's Exchange Principle states that, "whenever two objects come into contact with one another, there will be a cross-transfer of material which will occur" (Gale, 2005). This theory is the underlying premise behind the documentation, collection, preservation, and identification of trace evidence. While the types are limitless, the term **trace evidence** typically refers to any evidence that is small in size, such as hairs, fibers, paint, glass, and soil, which would require microscopic analysis in order to identify it. The purpose of microscopic analysis is to determine whether or not an association between persons, places, and things can be established, and the subsequent strength of such an association. This association would be as a result of **associative evidence**. However, sometimes enough uniqueness is present within the trace evidence to allow for an individualized association.

Probability/Product Rule

Another way to approach the level of individualization is through association with numerous levels of class characteristics. This association brings to light a mathematical concept known as **probability**. Probability is most simply defined as the frequency with which an event will occur, sometimes referred to as the *odds of occurrence*. For instance, if one were to flip a coin 10 times, the probability of the coin landing heads down will be 5 in 10. The concept of probability is important to comprehend from a forensic aspect because it is this frequency of occurrence that an examiner is depending upon to limit potential suspect items or individuals, and to explain the odds of such occurrences to the potential jury.

The concept of probability can be taken a step further when considering all aspects of probability associated with an event in an effort to determine a statistical probability for the event or item in question, using classical or frequentist statistics. For instance, if all eye witnesses agree that a white male suspect over the age of 30 committed a crime, then utilizing the **product rule** would lend statistical support to such matters and explain the frequency of such an event occurring. The product rule is when the frequencies of independently occurring variables are multiplied together to obtain an overall frequencies of occurrence for the event or item. **Table 9–1** shows the product rule applied to the case example given here.

Most evidence is not truly individualistic; instead, it is looked at as being individual in nature because the probability of a match between any other item is so remote (so large a number). However, the establishment of probabilities relating to evidence is typically the duty of the criminalist who analyzes or interprets the evidence, or of the attorneys or other forensic expert presenting the evidence within court, rather than of the crime scene investigator. Criminalists will determine probability and utilize the product rule during their analysis, interpretation, and eventually within their testimony. They will do this in order to attempt to explain the probability of a person's DNA matching that of the evidence presented (e.g., 1 in 1,476,565,780), or the frequency of another carpet fiber matching the one discovered at the

TABLE 9–1   Utilizing the Product Rule

Demographic	Statistic	Percentage	Equation
Number of people in the United States (est.)	295,734,134		
Population that is white	241,614,787	81.70%	(241,624,787 ÷ 295,734,134)
Population that is white male	118,705,344	49.13%	(118,705,344 ÷ 241,614,787)
Population of white males over age 30	42,401,549	35.72%	(42,401,549 ÷ 118,705,344)
Using the product rule, 0.817 × 0.4913 × 0.3572 = 0.1433, or 14.33%, or 1 in 7 persons could have been involved in the commission of the crime.			

Data from the Central Intelligence Agency. (2006). The World Factbook. Retrieved August 4, 2009, from http://www.cia.gov/library/publications/the-world-factbook/.

crime scene (e.g., 1 in 7,896). Their utilization of such statistical analysis does not by any means define an absolute but instead presents the trier of fact with an educated extrapolation of a number that a reasonable person would infer as being sufficient to believe that the probability of a more likely match being present is extremely remote.

Bayesian Statistics

Many analysts are making use of **Bayesian statistics** in interpreting and explaining the forensic potential of evidence. Bayesian techniques are an alternative to classical or frequentist methods, although frequentist statistical techniques are still more commonly used. Bayesian statistics is a subset of the field of statistics in which evidence is expressed in terms of degrees of belief or in Bayesian probabilities. These probabilities represent an individual's degree of belief that a particular event will occur. Thus, the Bayesian approach is based on personal or subjective probabilities (Tessella Technology and Consulting, 2009).

If the same coin in our earlier example was flipped 10 times and heads appeared 10 times, should it be concluded that the coin has two sides containing heads? A frequentist would calculate the probability value as 0.001 that the coin is normal and contains both a head and a tail side. However, this does not mean that there is a 99.9% certainty that there is a two-headed coin. It simply means that, given a normal coin, the occurrences are highly unlikely. This is an objective fact but is not an answer to the original question. It must now be ascertained how small the probability value must be in order to be convinced that the coin in question has two heads. This is where the frequentist analysis becomes subjective. The Bayesian approach requires a prior for how likely two-headed coins are. If it is believed that only one coin in a million has two heads then, despite seeing 10 heads in a row, the probability of this being a two-headed coin is still only 0.001. If, however, the coin is quite old and there is the assumption that two-headed coins were more common when it was minted, this changes prior belief factored into the Bayesian approach and thus would lead to a higher posterior probability of the coin having two heads. Using this method, the Bayesian approach has given a clear answer to the original question, but the answer is subjective and is dependent upon beliefs about the prevalence of two-headed coins (Tessella Technology and Consulting, 2009).

"In frequentist inference, tests of significance are performed by supposing that one particular hypothesis, the null hypothesis, is true, and then computing the probability of observing a statistic at least as extreme as the one actually observed during hypothetical future repeated trials (this is the probability value or P-value). In other words, frequentist statistics examine the probability of the data given a model (hypothesis). The Bayesian approach, on the other hand, allows one to examine the probability that a possible model is true, given the data available. It also allows for the comparison of different possible models and the ability to assess their relative probabilities of being true" (Tessella Technology and Consulting, 2009). However, it must be remembered, that regardless of the method chosen to explain and interpret the results, it is only one of a number of interpretations of probability.

Collection of Trace Evidence

Trace evidence is collected in a variety of ways, including with the use of a forceps, tweezers, by hand, tape lift, or even vacuuming. If possible, the entire item containing the suspected evidence should be collected and preserved for later analysis. If conditions do not allow for this, then on-scene steps must be taken to properly collect and preserve the trace evidence (**Figure 9–1**).

When collecting trace evidence, the crime scene investigator must document and collect not only the questioned samples but also collect known samples for comparison purposes. For example, if a suspect is located in a burglary case involving entry through a broken glass

FIGURE 9–1   Collection of trace evidence from crime scene evidence

CASE IN POINT

The Product Rule at Work

While investigating a cold hit-and-run accident, a crime scene investigator located a piece of plastic that appeared to be from a turn signal of a vehicle. The plastic did not match the struck vehicle and was believed to have belonged to the vehicle that fled the scene. The plastic piece had a number stamped on it, along with the Chrysler logo. This led the investigator to contact a local Chrysler dealer's parts department, which was able to give the investigator information that the plastic piece belonged to a 2003 Dodge Ram pickup truck. The dealership was confident in this because that part was only placed into that specific year and model. The crime scene investigator knew that the vehicle that fled the scene was a white-colored vehicle due to paint transfer found on the red Chevy S-10 that was struck.

The crime scene investigator contacted local body shops and asked that if they had anyone who showed up with a 2003 white Dodge Ram pickup truck with right front-end damage, that they call the investigating officer. Within one week a body shop called to report that an individual was requesting bodywork be done on the front of a damaged vehicle that had resulted from "accidentally striking their garage." The crime scene investigator responded to the body shop and noted red transfer paint on the damaged portion of the vehicle. Photographs were taken, and eventually hit-and-run charges were filed against the registered owner for the accident.

In court, the evidence was presented and the prosecution brought up the probability of a Dodge Ram pickup truck being the vehicle involved. It was determined through contact with Chrysler that there were 1,196, 2003 Dodge pickup trucks sold within 100 miles of the accident scene. Of those, 257 were white. This meant that the probability of the fleeing vehicle having been a 2003 white Dodge Ram pickup truck was 21.48%. The prosecution took this a step further and looked at the number of registered vehicles within a 100-mile radius through information derived from the Department of Motor Vehicles. It was determined that there were 175,765 validly registered vehicles within the defined area. Utilizing the product rule, the frequency of a 2003 white Dodge pickup being the vehicle involved in the incident was explained as follows:

2003 Dodge pickup (1,196 out of 120,125) 0.99%

2003 white-colored Dodge pickup (257 out of 1,196) 21.48%

Therefore, 0.0099 × 0.2148 = 0.0021, or 0.21%, or 1 in 500 vehicles on the road were 2003 white, Dodge Ram pickups.

This was a very large number and the jury took this as evidence of there being a very remote chance that another vehicle matching the description of the defendant's vehicle also sustained front-end damage consistent with the crash.

window, the crime scene investigator should document and collect trace glass evidence from the clothing, or submit the clothing to the lab for trace glass analysis. The crime scene investigator must also collect known samples of the glass from the broken window for comparative analysis. Failure to collect the known/comparison sample will almost always result in the forensic lab declining to conduct an analysis, although this is dependent upon the expertise of the laboratory and analysts within the lab. The possibility exists that, with proper experience, the possible sources for the glass may be narrowed down by the analyst. Ultimately, the crime scene investigator is attempting to show that Locard's Theory of Exchange is alive and well, and that the broken glass from the window can be used to show transfer and thus connectivity to the suspect, and vice versa.

It is important for crime scene investigators to understand the mechanisms of primary and secondary transfer. As trace evidence can be transferred during the commission of a crime, it can also be transferred during the search process. Not only can investigators inadvertently pick up hairs and fibers, they can also be inadvertently deposited at the crime scene. The following are important considerations to keep in mind at the crime scene:

- Elimination hair and/or fiber samples may need to be obtained from personnel conducting the search.
- Prioritize the order of evidence collection. Collect large items first and then proceed to the trace evidence. Use caution when walking the crime scene.
- Once the trace evidence is collected via vacuuming, taping, or tweezing, take blood samples, remove bullets, dust for fingerprints, and so on.
- Processing the crime scene for fingerprints prior to trace evidence collection is not recommended because it can inadvertently transfer trace evidence onto the clothing of the technicians, move trace evidence, and/or contaminate trace evidence with dusting powder.

When collecting most types of trace evidence, personnel typically make use of a druggist/pharmacist fold or bindle as a primary method of evidence preservation (**Figure 9–2**). The trace evidence is placed onto a clean sheet of paper and the paper is then folded into thirds and then into thirds again, with one end of the paper tucked back into itself so as to safely encapsulate the trace material. This is referred to as **primary packaging**. This is not sufficient in itself. The primary packaging should then be placed into **secondary packaging** such as a paper envelope or paper bag, or into a plastic bag if drug materials that will not be analyzed for biological material, and then sealed appropriately. The secondary packaging serves to protect the primary packaging from damage and ensures that no trace material will be added to nor lost from the initial evidence that was collected.

Glass Evidence

Because glass is so prevalent, breaks easily, and when fragmented has a tendency to adhere to clothing and body surfaces, it is frequently encountered within the context of crime scene investigation as **transfer evidence**.

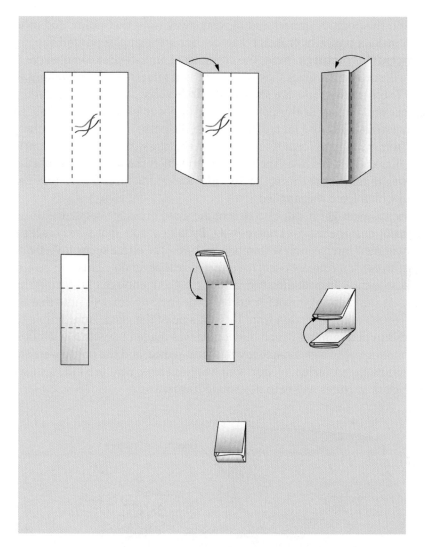

FIGURE 9–2   Example of how to fold and use a pharacist/druggist fold for primary packaging of trace evidence

Courtesy of Dana Gevelinger, University of Wisconsin-Platteville.

Fracture Analysis

Examination of glass that has been fractured can lead the crime scene investigator to determine from which direction the impact originated. This can be useful in determining whether or not a window was broken from the inside or outside (e.g., in attempting to identify whether or not a window was broken to cover up an employee theft and disguise it as a burglary). To make this determination, the crime scene investigator must understand what happens when glass fractures. First of all, a crime scene investigator can observe the **radial fractures**, those originating from the point of impact and moving away from that point, and other fractures that appear to make a typically broken series of concentric circles around the impact point, known as **concentric fractures**. Next, the crime scene investigator can observe the edges of the glass and will see that the glass shows characteristics referred to as **conchoidal fractures** (**Figure 9–3**). These stress marks are shaped like arches that are perpendicular to one side of the glass surface and curved nearly parallel to the opposite glass surface. This is telling to a crime scene investigator because for radial fractures, the perpendicular edge is always opposite the direction from which the force was applied to the glass surface. In concentric fractures, the perpendicular end always faces the direction to which the force was applied to the glass surface. One way to remember this is the **3R rule**: Radial fractures form a Right angle on the Reverse side to which force was applied.

A crime scene investigator can also determine glass breakage sequence through careful analysis of present characteristics (**Figure 9–4**). By taking note that some cracks reach a termination point at their intersection with other fractures, the crime scene investigator can conclude that fractures that terminate occurred after those that do not. This will give an idea as to the glass break sequence. Impact direction can be gauged if enough of the initial impact point is still present. At the point of impact, a crime scene investigator will note that there will be evidence of a cone-like core ejection from the exit side of the glass. An example of when this would be used is in determining which bullet hole was made first within a window pane. If a suspect was shooting out of a glass picture window at police, and the police were shooting into the picture window from outside, a court will want to know who fired the first shot. Careful analysis of the glass fractures will help determine this fact.

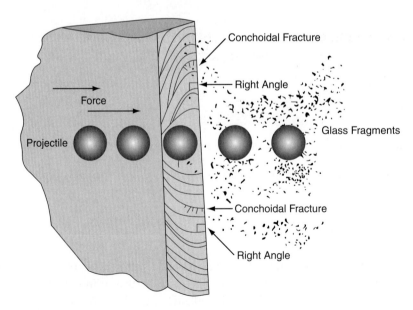

FIGURE 9–3   Determining glass break direction
Courtesy of Ellie Bruchez, University of Wisconsin-Platteville.

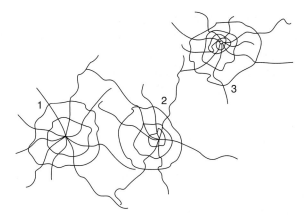

FIGURE 9–4   Determining glass break direction
Courtesy of Ellie Bruchez, University of Wisconsin-Platteville.

Collecting and Packaging Glass Evidence

In order for glass evidence to serve an evidentiary purpose, it must be properly collected and preserved. The gathering of glass evidence at the crime scene and from a suspect or victim must be thorough if the forensic lab is to have a chance to attempt analysis that would individualize the glass fragments as being from a common source. This requires that the crime scene investigator have a working knowledge as to what kinds of information can be derived from glass evidence.

Firstly, glass evidence is typically viewed as class evidence and is only rarely able to be individualized. This can result in both inclusions and exclusions of persons and glass surfaces, which although not unique, is certainly advantageous within the context of a criminal investigation.

Depending upon the crime, and the scene of the crime, it may be necessary for the crime scene investigator to attempt to collect all of the glass evidence located at the scene. In other cases it may only be necessary for the crime scene investigator to collect a known sample of the glass. For instance, in a vehicle versus pedestrian hit-and-run accident, a crime scene investigator may find it necessary to recover all related headlight and reflector lens glass so that if a vehicle is later identified, the pieces can be puzzled together to show the uniqueness and thus include the vehicle as a suspect vehicle. Simply collecting a known sample of the glass at the scene would only result in glass analysis being able to determine that the suspect vehicle had glass components consistent with the glass found at the scene, which would typically be the case for any such make and model vehicle having the same automotive parts. This would be enough to include the vehicle as a possible suspect vehicle but not sufficient to individualize it, as would be the puzzling together of all related glass and showing the corresponding match.

However, when an individual fit is not likely or necessary, the crime scene investigator should collect a reference sample of broken glass found at the scene of the crime, and then properly collect and package the suspect or victim's clothes for comparative analysis.

The reference sample should be collected as near the point of impact as possible. Approximately one square inch of material is all that will be required for forensic analysis relating to this comparison. Therefore, there is no need to collect an abundance of glass from the scene.

The fragment(s) should be packaged in solid containers, which will avoid further breaking the glass while in transit, and also not allow the glass to protrude from the packaging and injure personnel handling the evidence. If there are suspect or victim clothes that will be submitted to the lab for glass analysis, they should be wrapped individually in paper to ensure that the trace evidence is not lost in transport, and then packaged in a porous material such as paper bags or cardboard boxes. When the item is wrapped in the paper, the item should be folded within the paper in such a way that no surface of the clothing touches another surface of the same clothing, but instead has paper between them. This will ensure that there is no transfer or contamination of trace evidence and the trace evidence is properly contained. The crime scene investigator should not attempt to shake the clothes to dislodge and thus collect the glass particles but should instead leave the discovery, collection, and analysis of glass evidence to forensic lab personnel.

If direction of force analysis is to be determined by the forensic lab, the crime scene investigator should attempt to collect as much of the glass evidence at the scene as possible. Also, if possible, the crime scene investigator should note which side of the glass was interior and which was exterior. If unknown, dirt, residue, etc., may be used to assist with the determination.

Paint Evidence

Paint chips and fragments of other protective coatings such as varnishes, sealers, lacquers, enamels, and plastics are frequently recovered at scenes of burglaries, hit-and-run vehicles and scenes, forced entries, and other crime scenes. A determination of common origin is possible in cases where irregularly shaped adjoining edges of paint chips can be physically joined to form a fracture match. However, the value of a single-layered paint chip or paint smear should not be overlooked.

Paint Evidence Analysis

The International Forensic Automotive Paint Data Query (PDQ) is a searchable database of chemical and color information of original automotive paints. Developed by Forensic Laboratory Services (FLS), the database represents 30 years of accumulated information provided by automotive companies and samples of vehicles submitted by other forensic laboratories or police. The PDQ contains information about the make, model, year, and assembly plant for many vehicles.

The PDQ is used by forensic laboratories around the world to assist with criminal investigations requiring vehicle identification. FLS maintains the database so that forensic laboratories can provide timely and effective support to police investigations. Police agencies do not access the PDQ directly.

The PDQ is one of the most collaborative ventures to be found in forensic science. Accredited users are given a free copy of the PDQ in exchange for submitting 60 new automotive paint samples per year. The paint samples are collected from vehicles at body shops or junkyards as well as from automobile manufacturers. Contributors to the PDQ include the Royal Canadian Mounted Police (RCMP), provincial forensic laboratories in Ontario and Quebec, 40 American forensic laboratories, and police agencies in 21 other countries. According to the RCMP, as of July 2012, the PDQ contained information on more than 13,000 vehicles, with a library of over 50,000 layers of paint (RCMP, 2012).

Paint samples provided by automotive manufacturers are analyzed for their chemical composition. The chemical components and proportions are coded into the database. An automotive paint job usually consists of four layers. These known paint samples are then available for comparison against paint samples taken from a crime scene or from suspect vehicles.

The PDQ team samples each paint layer and the chemical composition of each layer is determined by an infrared micro-spectrometer, which outputs a spectrum containing the unique chemical information pertinent to each layer. Once unknown vehicles are potentially identified within the database, police can use the possible make, model, and year information to search for the vehicle involved in the criminal activity, most often a hit-and-run.

The PDQ serves to narrow the search for vehicles to enable further investigation. Once a suspected vehicle is located, the comparison of paint from the crime scene with paint of the suspected vehicle can be conducted to associate the vehicle more conclusively to the crime.

Soil Evidence

Soil is a generic term for any disintegrated surface material, natural or man-made, which lies on or near the earth's surface (Saferstein, 2010). This is important for a crime scene investigator to realize because forensic analysis of soil not only relates to such naturally occurring components as rocks, vegetation, pollen, minerals, and animal matter, but it also includes the identification and examination of such man-made components as paint particles, glass, asphalt, concrete, and other items present that may assist in characterizing the soil as being unique to a specific or definable location.

The evidentiary value of soil has its foundation in its prevalence at crime scenes and the ease with which it is transferred between the scene and the suspect. Thus, soil or the dried remains of mud found adhered to a suspect's clothing or footwear, when compared to soil samples collected from the crime scene, may provide an associative link between a suspect or an object and the crime scene. As with most physical evidence, soil analysis is comparative in nature. This means that soil that is located in the possession of a suspect must be carefully collected in order to be compared to soil samples from the crime scene and its surroundings. However, even if the scene of a crime has not been determined, the crime scene investigator should not overlook the evidentiary value of soil. For instance, a forensic geologist who is educated in the local geology may be capable of using her or his knowledge along with geological maps to

Collecting and Packaging Paint Evidence

The following procedures are recommended for recovery of paint samples (WisDOJ, 2009):

A. Recover, package, and seal all paint samples separately.

B. Recover known paint samples from areas immediately adjacent to the damaged area. The hoods, trunks, and fenders of vehicles may not be painted at the same location or with the same paint used on the body. Therefore, it is of utmost importance that a known paint sample be taken from the exact part of the vehicle upon which the damage occurred. In hit-and-run investigations, the known paint samples should be taken near the point of impact, but should not be taken from areas of corrosion, such as the rocker panels (**Figure 9–5**).

C. When tool marks exist on a damaged object, recover paint samples from areas immediately adjacent to tool marks without mutilating the tool mark.

Tape a clean sheet of paper (do not use envelopes) to the object, forming a pocket. Mark the paper for identification. Scrape the questioned paint into the pocket formed by the paper. It is important to use a new, disposable scalpel blade or razor blade for each sample to avoid contamination. Some razor blades are coated with oil to prevent rusting. Therefore, all razor blades should be thoroughly cleaned with a clean cloth or tissue just before they are used. Carefully remove the paper from the object and fold each edge toward the center so that the packet is completely closed. Insert each packet into a separate new, clean bottle, together with the scalpel blade or

direct law enforcement to the possible vicinity where the soil most likely originated from, and thus provide a possibility as to the area where the crime was committed.

Sand or soil is encountered in many types of investigations and should not be overlooked by the investigating officer. The following items frequently have soil related to the crime scene adhering to their surfaces: footwear, clothing, tool containers, vehicle operating pedals, under-carriages, or wheel wells. Soil found on the floor of a vehicle also may become valuable evidence. Most soil adhering to such objects is representative of the upper one-fourth inch of surface soil from which it originated and may be associated with its source if proper known samples are recovered.

Most times soil can be distinguished through a gross examination, primarily based upon coloration. It is estimated that there are approximately 1,100 different soil colors; thus, comparison of soil color is a logical first step in soil analysis. A crime scene investigator should note, however, that soil is darker when it is wet and, therefore, color comparisons should always be made when the samples are dry.

razor blade used in recovering the sample. Seal and label according to instructions previously recommended.

D. When areas of paint are missing from sheet metal parts of vehicles or doors and windows of residences and businesses, consideration should be given to bringing the entire part to the laboratory for possible fracture match analysis.

E. Avoid use of any container that would permit loss or contamination of contents, especially envelopes and plastic petri dishes, because the manufacturer's seal is not leak proof.

F. Use a new, clean scalpel blade or razor blade for each sample recovered; enclose in the bottle with the sample.

G. Do not use gummed tape to recover paint samples because it interferes with the chemical analysis.

1 = Paint transfer sample
(damage area)

2 = Paint standard sample
(undamaged area)

FIGURE 9–5 Example of how to collect paint evidence from a vehicle

Courtesy of Nick Vesper, University of Wisconsin-Platteville.

Source: Wisconsin Department of Justice (WisDOJ). (2009). *Physical evidence handbook* (8th ed.). Madison, WI: Wisconsin Department of Justice.

Collecting and Packaging Soil Evidence

Because soil variation is the fundamental consideration in soil analysis, establishing such variation must be considered when gathering soil specimens. It is suggested that standard/reference samples of soils are collected at various intervals within a 100-meter radius of the crime scene, in addition to collection at the site of the crime, for comparison to the questioned soil. All samples should be dried and then packaged as discussed in the box.

Hair Evidence

Hairs, which are composed primarily of the protein keratin, can be defined as slender outgrowths of the skin of mammals. Each species of animal possesses hair with characteristic

Collection of Soil Evidence

A. Photograph impressions (tire, footwear, etc.) that have patterns containing discernible class and/or individual characteristics.

B. Do not recover soil samples until proper photographs and casts have been made.

C. Obtain samples consisting of three (3) tablespoonfuls of soil from the top 1/4 of soil from within the impression. Collect a soil sample from each impression that has a different color or texture (dirt, clay, sand, etc.).

D. The tablespoon should be cleaned after each area has been sampled to avoid cross-contamination of samples.

E. The soil samples should be recovered using a systematic method.

F. Prepare a diagram of the area showing the point from which each sample was recovered and submit copy of diagram. On the diagram, show distance and direction of each sample recovered. The diagram should be oriented with fixed objects in the area such as buildings, utility pole, etc. (**Figure 9–6**).

G. If soil samples can be immediately transported to the Laboratory, put samples in individual clean glass containers and seal.

H. If samples cannot be transported to the Laboratory immediately, to prevent the growth of mold, spread the samples on separate sheets of clean paper to air dry for at least 24 hours. When dry, package and seal. Do not mix or contaminate samples. However, if a pollen analysis is to be completed on the sample, it is discouraged to leave the samples uncovered.

I. If suspect shoes have been recovered and soil is present on the shoes, recover soil sample from the area of the footwear impression that corresponds to the location of

length, color, shape, root appearance, and internal microscopic features that distinguish one animal from another (**Figure 9–7**). Considerable variability also exists in the types of hairs that are found on the body of an animal. In humans, hairs found on the head, pubic region, arms, legs, and other body areas have characteristics that can determine their origin. On animals, hair types include coarse outer hairs or guard hairs, the finer fur hairs, tactile hairs such as whiskers, and other hairs that originate from the tail and mane of an animal.

Because hairs can be transferred during physical contact, their presence can associate a suspect to a victim or a suspect/victim to a crime scene (**Figure 9–8**). The types of hair recovered and the condition and number of hairs found all impact on their value as evidence in a criminal investigation. Comparison of the microscopic characteristics of questioned hairs to known hair samples helps determine whether a transfer may have occurred.

the soil on recovered shoes. Example: clump of soil adhering to arch of shoe.

J. When excavating grave sites, remember soil could be adhering to the tools used by the suspects or their clothing. Therefore, a core sample should be taken from as close to the grave as possible and to a depth equal or greater than the grave itself. The core sample should be kept intact and packaged so the layer structure is not altered or damaged during drying, handling or shipping.

FIGURE 9–6   Diagram showing an example of how to collect and document soil evidence samples

Courtesy of Nick Vesper, University of Wisconsin-Platteville.

Source: Wisconsin Department of Justice (WisDOJ). (2009). *Physical evidence handbook* (8th ed.). Madison, WI: Wisconsin Department of Justice.

Hair is composed of three primary sections or layers. The outermost layer is known as the **cuticle**. The cuticle contains the scaly protective layer that covers the shaft of the hair. Each species has identifiable cuticle characteristics. The innermost region is known as the **medulla**. The medulla in humans is amorphous and lacks visible cellular material, whereas the medulla of other species is often seen as cellular in nature, some displaying characteristics similar to a bead of pearls. The region between the medulla and cuticle is known as the **cortex**. The cortex contains the pigment cells that are responsible for imparting hair color characteristics (**Figure 9–9**).

Hair is present on many different regions of the body. Each region, such as the head, pubic area, chest, axillae, and limbs, has hairs with microscopic characteristics attributable to that region. Although it is possible to identify a hair as originating from a particular body

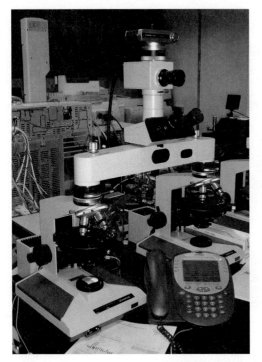

FIGURE 9–7   Hair and fiber comparison microscope

FIGURE 9–8   Photograph of hair/fur evidence at a crime scene

area, the regions of the body that are primarily used in forensic comparisons are the head and pubic areas. As hairs undergo a cyclical growth (anagen) and resting phase (telogen), the visible microscopic characteristics are sufficient to determine the phase of growth of the hair.

During the anagen phase, the hair is actively growing, and materials are deposited in the hair shaft by cells found in the follicle. Metabolically active and dividing cells above and around the dermal papilla of the follicle grow upward during this phase, to form the major components of the hair: the medulla, cortex, cuticle, and accompanying root sheath. In the telogen phase, the follicle is dormant or resting. The transition period between the anagen and telogen phases is referred to as the catagen phase.

Hairs are routinely lost during the telogen phase and often become a primary source of evidentiary material. An example of this natural shedding process can be seen when one combs through the hairs on the head. It is common for hairs of this type to be transferred to another individual or to an object during physical contact. Hairs also can become dislodged from the body while they are in an actively growing state, such as by pulling or by striking with an object. The microscopical appearance of the root area will allow for the determination of the growth phase.

The basic morphology of human hairs is shared by each individual in the population, but the arrangement, distribution, and appearance of individual microscopic characteristics within different regions of hair routinely allow a skilled hair examiner to differentiate hairs between individuals. An analogy would be the ability of an individual to recognize the face of a friend or relative in a crowd even though each person in the crowd possesses ears, eyes, a nose, and a mouth.

Animal Hairs

Animal hairs discovered on items of physical evidence can link a suspect or location to a crime of violence. A victim placed in a vehicle or held at a location where animals are routinely found often have animal hairs transferred to the victim's clothing. Cat or dog hairs can be found on the adhesive portions of ransom and extortion notes prepared by pet owners. The transfer of pet hairs to the victim or crime scene may also occur when the suspect is a pet owner and has animal hairs on his or her clothing when the contact occurs. This is referred to as a *secondary transfer* of trace material (discussed in the following paragraphs).

The Structure of Hair

FIGURE 9–9 The structure of hair
Courtesy of Erica Milks, University of Wisconsin-Platteville.

When an animal hair is found, it is identified to a particular type of animal and microscopically compared with a known hair sample from either an animal hair reference collection or a specific animal. If the questioned hair exhibits the same microscopic characteristics as the known hairs, it is concluded that the hair is consistent with originating from that animal. It is noted, however, that animal hairs do not possess enough individual microscopic characteristics to be associated with a particular animal to the exclusion of other similar animals.

The collection of a suitable known animal hair standard is necessary before a meaningful comparison can be conducted. Because hairs can vary widely in color and length on different areas of the body of an animal, hairs should be collected from each area. While a minimum number of hairs is difficult to determine, good judgment should be used in collecting enough hairs to represent the various types and colors of hairs found on the animal. The sample should contain full-length hairs and should include combings as well as pluckings. If the animal is not available for sample collection, a brush or comb used for the animal may be substituted. Sometimes hair samples collected from a dog or cat bed may be useful when actual samples from the animal cannot be obtained.

In crimes where personal contact has occurred, especially if there was physical force, hair and fibers are frequently found as evidence.

A cross-transfer of hair and/or fibers between a victim and an assailant can provide supportive evidence of an association. In addition, hair recovered from the scene may serve to associate an individual with the scene. Fibers recovered from the clothing of the victim, suspect, and crime scene can be compared to known textile materials to determine possible sources of origin.

If a hair is determined to be of human origin and is deemed probative to a case, DNA analyses may be performed on the root (if present) of the hair. If DNA is obtained from a questioned hair root, this DNA can be compared to DNA from a standard blood sample from an individual. Identification may be the result. Mitochondrial DNA (mtDNA) could possibly be extracted and analyzed on a hair that does not contain a root. However, the information obtained from mtNDA is much more limited.

Body Area Determination

The body area from which a hair originated can be determined by general morphology. Length, shape, size, color, stiffness, curliness, and microscopic appearance all contribute to the determination of body area. Pigmentation and medullar appearance also influence body area identification. Hairs that exhibit microscopic characteristics shared by different anatomical areas are often referred to as *body hairs*. These include hairs found on the upper legs, lower abdomen, and back. Because there is a wide range of interpersonal variation in head and pubic hairs, the majority of work in forensics has been on comparing and differentiating hairs from the head and pubic regions.

Racial Determination

The identification of race is most useful as an investigative tool, but it can also be an associative tool when an individual's hairs exhibit unusual racial characteristics.

A human hair can be associated with a particular racial group based on established models for each group. Forensic examiners differentiate between hairs of Caucasoid (European ancestry), Mongoloid (Asian ancestry), and Negroid (African ancestry) origin, all of which exhibit microscopic characteristics that distinguish one racial group from another. Head hairs are generally considered best for determining race, although hairs from other body areas can be useful. Racial determination from the microscopic examination of head hairs from infants, however, can be difficult, and hairs from individuals of mixed racial ancestry may possess microscopic characteristics attributed to more than one racial group.

Age and Sex

The age of an individual cannot be determined definitively by a microscopic examination; however, the microscopic appearance of certain human hairs, such as those of infants and elderly individuals, may provide a general indication of age. The hairs of infants, for example, are generally finer and less distinctive in microscopic appearance. As individuals age, hair can undergo pigment loss and changes in the configuration of the hair shaft to become much finer and more variable in diameter.

Sex of an individual is impossible to determine from microscopic examination. Sex can be determined from a forcibly removed hair (with tissue), but this is not routinely done. Definitive determination of sex can be accomplished through the staining of sex chromatin in the cells found in the follicular tissue, but nuclear DNA and mitochondrial DNA (mDNA) tests will provide more specific information regarding the possible origin of the hair.

Significance of Hair Evidence

The significance of hair examination results is dependent on the method of evidence collection used at the crime scene, the evidence processing techniques employed, the methodology of the hair examination process, and the experience of the hair examiner. Head hairs and pubic hairs are routinely held as more significant than hairs from other body areas.

Collection of Hair and Fiber Standards

It is necessary to obtain standard hair and fiber samples from all possible sources (suspect, victim, and scene) for comparison with questioned hairs and fibers. DNA analysis on hair roots has replaced microscopic hair comparisons. Pubic and head hair standards are still necessary for determining which foreign, questioned hairs may be subjected to DNA analysis. Due to the ease of head hair transfer and potential limited probative value, DNA analysis on hairs will be limited.

Collection of Questioned Hair and Fibers

Pubic Hair Combings

These are usually collected in sexual assault cases and from homicide victims.

Place a piece of paper under the pubic region of the individual and comb through the entire pubic area to dislodge any foreign hairs or other material that may be present. Place the used comb onto the paper and fold the paper around the comb, being careful not to lose any of the dislodged evidence. Place the wrapped comb in a clean, properly labeled envelope, and seal.

Other Recovered Questioned Hairs and Fibers

Separately package the hairs and fibers collected from different persons and different locations.

When the amount of evidence is very small, extreme care should be exercised so that the material is not contaminated or inadvertently lost. The hair or fiber should be placed on a piece of clean white paper and the paper should be tightly folded around the hair or fiber. Place the paper packet in a clean, properly labeled envelope or glass jar, and seal.

Collecting and Packaging Hair Evidence

Submit individual hairs and fibers in clean paper or in an envelope with sealed corners. The primary paper or envelope should be placed inside a secondary sealed envelope with all corners taped. Many times individual hairs identified on items of clothing are not removed or secured. These hairs may move or be lost, so it is recommended that they be removed and placed in an envelope (first noting where they were removed).

Suggestions for Collection of Hair and Fiber Standards

Head Hair Standards

Obtain at least fifty (50) head hairs by cutting them at the skin surface. These hairs should be collected from various areas of the head such as the crown, sides, front, and back to assure that all shades of color and texture have been adequately sampled. The quantity of hairs obtained from a deceased individual should be doubled and the hairs should be pulled. Place the hairs in a clean, properly labeled envelope, and seal.

Pubic Hair Standards

Obtain at least twenty (20) pubic hairs by cutting them at the skin surface. The hairs should be collected from various areas within the pubic region. If this is a deceased individual, double the number of hairs to be collected and pull them. Place the hairs in a clean, properly labeled envelope, and seal.

Known Fibers

Known fibers should be obtained from all possible sources (clothing, drapes, rugs, etc.). Submit the suspected source in total if possible. Place the source in a clean, properly labeled paper bag, and seal. If it is not feasible to submit the source in total, a sufficient quantity should be taken to ensure that each color and type of fiber involved has been sampled. Place the fibers in a clean, properly labeled envelope or glass jar, and seal.

Source: Wisconsin Department of Justice (WisDOJ). (2009). *Physical evidence handbook* (8th ed.). Madison, WI: Wisconsin Department of Justice.

If a floor surface is vacuumed, the debris should be placed on a white sheet of paper (8 × 11 inches) and folded at the corners. This paper should be placed in a heat-sealed or re-sealable plastic bag.

Hair Evidence Analysis

When evidence is received by the forensic laboratory, the case is assigned to an examiner. The examiner will read the incoming communication to determine the nature of the offense, the names of the suspects and victims, and the types of requested examinations. It is important to have an understanding of the offense to help determine the course of action in the laboratory. Contact between family members or friends would be treated differently, as the transfer of trace evidence would be more likely in these cases.

Typically, there are several processes by which debris is collected. This is conducted through a combination of picking, scraping, and sometimes taping. Whereas taping is considered by some laboratories to be a preferred technique, it can be time consuming and tedious, and may present a storage problem for the tape collections. Vacuuming is not recommended for clothing items. The clothing of a victim is processed in a room other than the room in which the suspect's clothing is processed. The collected debris is placed in pillboxes and examined with a stereo-binocular microscope. Hairs are then mounted on glass microscope slides for identification and comparison purposes.

When a questioned hair exhibits the same microscopic characteristics as the known hairs of an individual, the hair could have originated from that individual (see Figure 9–7). If the questioned hair is microscopically dissimilar to the known hair standard, it cannot be associated with the individual. Different people generally have different hair characteristics, but differences in microscopic characteristics also can be the result of time and alteration. Known hair samples should be collected from individuals as soon as possible to the date of the crime. As time passes, microscopic characteristics can change, and the individual may alter the color with dyes.

Certain case situations affect the significance of identifying hairs. When a family member may be involved in a crime, the location, number, and condition (forcibly pulled or burnt, for example) of recovered hairs may be important. The involvement of the victim's associates, including dates, coworkers, and other people who may have logical contact with or access to the victim and/or crime scene is an additional consideration in hair examinations. Situations involving strangers have greatest significance when hair associations have been made.

Fiber Evidence

A *fiber* is the smallest unit of a textile material that has a length many times greater than its diameter. Fibers can occur naturally as plant and animal fibers, but they can also be man-made. A fiber can be spun with other fibers to form a yarn that can be woven or knitted to form a fabric. The type and length of fiber used, the type of spinning method, and the type of fabric construction all affect the transfer of fibers and the significance of fiber associations. This becomes very important when there is a possibility of fiber transfer between a suspect and a victim during the commission of a crime.

As discussed previously, fibers are considered a form of trace evidence that can be transferred from the clothing of a suspect to the clothing of a victim during the commission of a crime. Fibers also can transfer from a fabric source such as a carpet, bed, or furniture at a crime scene. These transfers can either be direct (primary) or indirect (secondary). A **primary transfer** occurs when a fiber is transferred from a fabric directly onto a victim's clothing,

Trace Evidence: What You See Isn't Always What You Get

Trace evidence is a diverse, if not the most diverse, area of forensic science. It requires knowledge of many different types of evidence including but not limited to the types of evidence detailed in this text. It can also include substances that are received in the laboratory as unknowns.

The scientist cannot conduct a proper examination without the initial collection of evidence that is regularly performed by the crime scene investigator. This initial collection of evidence at a crime scene is crucial and may lead to an important investigative lead or even back to an individual. The investigator's knowledge of types of evidences and their possible significance can aid the scientist's analysis, and more importantly, the investigation as a whole.

The evidence that a trace scientist typically examines has comparison samples. However, sometimes the analyst is given evidence without a comparison sample. A knowledgeable and experienced scientist can not only analyze and identify the type of evidence present, but provide leads based on the evidence without a direct comparison sample. For example, at a crime scene fibers were found on a victim that did not belong to their clothing. A trace examiner could identify those fibers and possibly determine sources for the fibers (e.g., carpet, clothing, etc.). This comparison-less analysis can also apply to other types of trace evidence including glass, tape, paint, soil, etc.

Sourcing of trace evidence is dependent not only on its identification but on the uniqueness of it and hence its evidentiary value. For example, if many white cotton fibers were discovered on a victim and the suspect was wearing a white shirt, this may suggest a transfer of evidence.

whereas a **secondary transfer** occurs when already transferred fibers on the clothing of a suspect transfer to the clothing of a victim. An understanding of the mechanics of primary and secondary transfer is important when reconstructing the events of a crime.

When two people come in contact or when contact occurs with an item from the crime scene, the possibility exists that a fiber transfer will take place. This does not mean that a fiber transfer will always take place. Certain types of fabric do not shed well (donor garments), and some fabrics do not hold fibers well (recipient garments). The construction and fiber composition of the fabric, the duration and force of contact, and the condition of the garment with regard to damage are important considerations.

Another important consideration is the length of time between the actual physical contact and the collection of clothing items from the suspect or victim. If the victim is immobile, very little fiber loss will take place, whereas the suspect's clothing will lose transferred fibers quickly. The likelihood of finding transferred fibers on the clothing of the suspect a day after the alleged contact may be remote, depending on the subsequent use or handling of that clothing.

However, white cotton fibers have myriad different sources and it is highly unlikely that it could be ever associated back to a single garment (just think about how many white shirts you own, and most of these are likely cotton). Given this, white cotton fibers do not have much evidentiary value. However, a black-dyed synthetic fiber can be very unique. The rarity of a type of evidence can increase its evidentiary value. Evidence with significant value makes a stronger link between suspect and victim.

Knowledge and training are not the only two things needed to be able to identify unknown samples without a comparison. Reference collections are a necessary part of a laboratory that does unknown samples. Our laboratory has reference collects for most items you would encounter in trace evidence. We have soil/sand, glass, fibers, hairs, paint, and wood, to name a few. These reference samples can be used as a comparison to characterized unknowns received in our laboratory. Because the industries of some of these materials are ever changing, samples must be constantly added to a reference collection.

Trace evidence is a wide-reaching area of forensic science. With the wide breadth of materials trace experts have to examine, knowledge of these areas is necessary. Trace evidence requires continued learning throughout one's career. However, it does have many interesting and rewarding experiences along the way.

Brendan Nytes
Forensic Scientist
Microtrace LLC, Elgin, IL

Courtesy of Brendan Nytes, Microscopist, Microtrace, LLC.

Natural Fibers

Many different natural fibers originating from plants and animals are used in the production of fabric. Cotton fibers are the plant fibers most commonly used in textile materials, with the type of cotton, fiber length, and degree of twist contributing to the diversity of these fibers. Processing techniques and color applications also influence the value of cotton fiber identifications.

Other plant fibers used in the production of textile materials include flax (linen), ramie, sisal, jute, hemp, kapok, and coir. The identification of less common plant fibers at a crime scene or on the clothing of a suspect or victim would have increased significance.

The animal fiber most frequently used in the production of textile materials is wool, and the most common wool fibers originate from sheep. The end use of sheep's wool often dictates the fineness or coarseness of woolen fibers: Finer woolen fibers are used in the production of clothing, whereas coarser fibers are found in carpet. Fiber diameter and degree of scale protrusion of the fibers are other important characteristics. Although sheep's wool is most common, woolen fibers from other animals also may be found. These include camel, alpaca, cashmere, mohair, and others. The identification of less common animal fibers at a crime scene or on the clothing of a suspect or victim would have increased significance.

Man-Made Fibers

More than half of all fibers used in the production of textile materials are man-made. Some man-made fibers originate from natural materials such as cotton or wood; others originate from synthetic materials. Polyester and nylon fibers are the most commonly encountered man-made fibers, followed by acrylics, rayon, and acetates. There are also many other less common man-made fibers. The amount of production of a particular man-made fiber and its end use influence the degree of rarity of a given fiber.

The shape of a man-made fiber can determine the value placed on that fiber. The cross-section of a man-made fiber can be manufacturer-specific: Some cross-sections are more common than others, and some shapes may only be produced for a short period of time. Unusual cross-sections encountered through examination can add increased significance to a fiber association.

Fiber Color

Color influences the value given to a particular fiber identification. Often several dyes are used to give a fiber a desired color. Individual fibers can be colored prior to being spun into yarns. Yarns can be dyed, and fabrics made from them can be dyed. Color can also be applied to the surface of fabric, as found in printed fabrics. How color is applied and absorbed along the length of the fiber are important comparison characteristics. Color fading and discoloration also can lend increased value to a fiber association.

Fiber Evidence Analysis

Whenever a fiber found on the clothing of a victim matches the known fibers of a suspect's clothing, it can be a significant event. Matching dyed synthetic fibers or dyed natural fibers can be very meaningful, whereas the matching of common fibers such as white cotton or blue denim cotton would be less significant. In some situations, however, the presence of white cotton or blue denim cotton may still have some meaning in resolving the truth of an issue. The discovery of cross-transfers and multiple fiber transfers between the suspect's clothing and the victim's clothing dramatically increases the likelihood that these two individuals had physical contact.

It is argued that the large volume of fabric produced reduces the significance of any fiber association discovered in a criminal case. It can never be stated with certainty that a fiber originated from a particular garment because other garments were likely produced using the same fiber type and color. The inability to positively associate a fiber with a particular garment to the exclusion of all other garments, however, does not mean that the fiber association is without value.

Another important consideration is coincidence. When fibers that match the clothing fibers of the suspect are found on the clothing of a victim, two conclusions may be drawn: The fibers originated from the suspect, or the fibers originated from another fabric source that not only was composed of fibers of the exact type and color, but was also in a position to contribute those fibers through primary or secondary contact. The likelihood of encountering identical fibers from the environment of a homicide victim (e.g., from his or her residence or friends) is extremely remote (**Figure 9–10**).

Collecting and Packaging Fiber Evidence

Collection and preservation of fiber evidence is quite similar to the methodology for collection of hair evidence. Reference and elimination samples must be collected, and each must be properly documented and packaged, as mentioned previously in regard to hair evidence.

FIGURE 9–10   Scaled photo of fiber evidence
Courtesy of Brendan Nytes, Microscopist, Microtrace, LLC.

WRAP UP

Chapter Summary

Edmond Locard dedicated his life to the microscopic analysis of trace evidence in an effort to prove that one's actions could be traced back to a particular item or location. It is this study that the forensic value of trace evidence is based upon. Utilizing the product rule, one is able to determine the frequency for the occurrence of an event and the probability that the item of trace evidence in question is related to a particular location, item, or person. While most trace evidence is not individualistic in nature, this does not minimize its forensic importance. Such matters are up to the analyst who is performing the analysis of the evidence. What is imperative is that the crime scene investigator knows the proper method for documenting, collecting, and preserving the various types of trace evidence to ensure their ability to undergo proper forensic analysis.

Review Questions

1. _____ is the frequency of an event occurring.

2. The _____ is when the frequency of independently occurring variables is multiplied to obtain an overall frequency of occurrence for the event or item.

3. The 3R rule means: _____ _____ _____.

4. It is important for crime scene investigators to understand the mechanisms of primary and secondary transfer. As trace evidence can be transferred during _____, it also can be transferred during _____.

5. Which type of trace evidence samples need to be collected from personnel conducting the search and collection of trace evidence?

6. What is PDQ and how is it involved with CSI?

7. _____ is a generic term for any disintegrated surface material, natural or man-made, which lies on or near the earth's surface.

8. Most soil can be distinguished through a gross examination, primarily based upon _____.

9. Hairs are routinely lost during the _____ phase and often become a primary source of evidentiary material.

10. Polyester, nylon acrylics, rayons, and acetates are all examples of _____.

Case Studies

Research the case of Wayne Williams and determine how it relates to the topics presented in this chapter. Discuss how trace evidence was used within that case, and how statistical analysis assisted crime scene personnel with limiting the possible suspect pool.

References

Gale, T. (2005). Locard's Exchange Principle. *World of Forensic Science*. Retrieved September 6, 2012, from http://www.encyclopedia.com/doc/1G2-3448300354.html

Kirk, P. L. (1953). *Crime investigation* (p. 4). New York: Interscience.

Royal Canadian Mounted Police (2012). Retrieved July 4, 2012, from http://www.rcmp-grc.gc.ca/fs-fd/pdq-eng.htm

Saferstein, R. (2010). *Criminalistics: An introduction to forensic science* (9th ed.). Upper Saddle River, NJ: Pearson Prentice Hall.

Tessella Technology and Consulting. (2009). *Bayesian Statistics*, Newton, MA. Technical Supplement. Retrieved June 23, 2012, from http://www.tessella.com

Wisconsin Department of Justice (WisDOJ). (2009). *Physical evidence handbook* (8th ed.). Madison, WI: Wisconsin Department of Justice.

© McMac/ShutterStock, Inc.

- Identify the necessary steps to address universal precautions where biological fluids are concerned.
- Differentiate between nuclear and mitochondrial DNA and the types of evidence each can yield.
- Understand the types and differences between presumptive tests and confirmatory tests for biological fluids.
- Explain the purpose of CODIS and how it is used within the law enforcement community.

Blood and Biological Evidence

A man is suspected of a crime months perhaps after it has been committed. His linen or clothes are examined and brownish stains discovered upon them. Are they blood stains, or mud stains, or rust stains, or fruit stains, or what are they? That is a question which has puzzled many an expert, and why? Because there was no reliable test. Now we have the Sherlock Holmes test, and there will no longer be any difficulty.

Sherlock Holmes, in *Study in Scarlet*, 1887
Sir Arthur Conan Doyle (1859–1930)

KEY TERMS

Agglutination
Antibody
Antigens
Blood Type
Combined DNA Index System
  (CODIS)

Complimentary Base Pairing
Deoxyribonucleic Acid (DNA)
Luminol
Mitochondrial DNA (mtDNA)

Nucleotide
 Polymer
Sexual Assault Kit (SAK)

Biological Evidence

In addition to being dynamic and unique, crime scenes also present hazards to crime scene personnel. One of the greatest hazards to personnel comes in the form of biological fluids. Crime scenes frequently involve such biological evidence as blood, saliva, seminal fluid, vaginal secretions, urine, and feces. It is imperative that personnel take proper universal precautions in such instances for two reasons: to protect themselves from the hazards inherent with such evidence, and also to prevent the contamination of the evidence from the crime scene investigators themselves. Once precautions have been taken, then crime scene personnel must set about the task of attempting to identify, interpret, document, collect, and preserve the biological evidence. This chapter considers the recognition, collection, and preservation of some of these commonly encountered forms of biological evidence.

Blood Evidence

Is it blood? When a crime scene investigator encounters material at a crime scene that he or she believes may be blood, the following questions must be answered:

- Is it blood?
- Is it human blood?
- If the blood is of human origin, how closely can it be associated with a particular individual?

These questions are answered through a variety of methods. The first step is to test to see whether or not the item in question is in fact blood. In answering the first question, personnel can use a variety of chemical tests known as *presumptive determinants* (presumptive because some substances other than blood test positive as well). A good presumptive test for blood should be specific, simple, sensitive, rapid, and safe.

Presumptive Tests for Blood

Crime scenes may often contain minute quantities of blood that, because of their small size, may not be readily noticed. Presumptive blood tests are initial screening tools that indicate, but are not specific for, the identification of blood. A positive result can result from the presence of human or animal blood and a variety of plant materials that contain the chemical peroxidase (e.g., horseradish, potatoes, etc.).

In some cases, presumptive blood tests are used as a search method. They can also help to differentiate blood from the presence of rust, chocolate, tar, or other brownish-colored stains that are often incorrectly assumed to be blood. Utilizing a presumptive test can also assist the crime scene investigator in identifying priority areas or evidence that must be tended to prior to other crime scene processing activities. It is extremely important to collect and preserve biological evidence early in the investigative process in order to prevent its loss or deterioration. Common presumptive tests for the presence of blood are discussed in the following paragraphs.

Luminol

Luminol is an example of a presumptive search technique that results in chemiluminescence due to a chemical reaction occurring between the reagent and the biological stain. It is fast acting and must be documented in darkness, using photography in an expeditious manner. Most times the chemiluminescence will not be present for more than 30 or 40 seconds.

Luminol is dispensed as a spray upon the surface to be examined. The sprayed object or area must be viewed in the dark—the darker the surroundings, the greater the luminescence. The luminol test is very sensitive and allows application to large areas or to areas that may appear to be blood free but might still carry a residue of blood after a hasty cleaning. Luminol can be applied specifically to a small area using an ampoule applicator or to large areas by spraying (**Figure 10–1**). Luminol does not interfere with DNA testing, making it an appropriate choice for many investigators. The luminescence caused by luminol when contacting blood can only be viewed in the dark, making application difficult at best. Using a red light allows the eyes to adjust to the darkness and provides enough light to work by. When luminescence occurs, the eyes have adjusted to the dark, making even dim stains highly visible. Luminol may provide a reaction even after the scene has been cleaned.

Phenolphthalein

Phenolphtalein is considered one of the most reliable of the crime scene blood tests. When a blood specimen is mixed with phenol-phthalein and hydrogen peroxide, the hemoglobin in the blood will cause a deep pink color to form. This test is not conclusive, because some other substances will cause the same reaction, but the result is strongly suggestive. The reagent may be used from a bottle (which introduces shelf time into the equation) or ampoules (which are more expensive but have indefinite shelf lives). Reagent ampoules are contained inside a plastic applica-tor (**Figure 10–2**). To be used, the reagent ampoules must be crushed and then the plastic applicator shaken for 30 seconds. A piece of moistened contact paper is rubbed over the stain (a cotton swab can be used) and the phenolphthalein applicator rubbed lightly across the dampened transfer stain. A pink reac-tion indicates the stain is blood.

FIGURE 10–1   Luminol
Courtesy of Sirchie Acquisition Company, LLC.

Tetramethylbenzidine

Tetramethylbenzidine (TMB) is a presumptive test for blood that is based on the peroxidase-like activity of hemoglobin. It is also the most common lab presump-tive test performed on suspected blood. TMB testing is easily conducted in the field, making use of the chemi-cal TMB, distilled water, and 3% hydrogen peroxide. TMB also will yield false-positives on stains that visu-ally resemble blood, such as rust and iodine. This is

FIGURE 10–2   Phenolphtalein reagent ampoules
Courtesy of Sirchie Acquisition Company, LLC.

why it is only a presumptive test and the stain must be confirmed as being human blood in a forensic laboratory.

Leucomalachite Green

The leucomalachite green test uses a low-sensitivity reagent consisting of 1 g of leucomalachite green powder, 100 milliliters (ml) of glacial acetic acid, and 150 ml of distilled water, with the entire mixture diluted with hydrogen peroxide. The application of this reagent produces a characteristic green color in the presence of blood. Many investigators consider this the most sensitive of the reagents. A positive reaction produces a purple response. As far as sensitivity is concerned, research conducted in 2007 (based on a study conducted and published in the *Journal of Forensic Sciences* in January of 2007) revealed leucomalachite green to have a sensitivity of one part per ten thousand of blood (1:10,000). However, it has also been found to limit or eliminate the possibility of DNA recovery and amplification.

Lueco crystal violet (LCV)

Lueco crystal violet is a safe, rapid, and simple to use reagent for the enhancement and development of blood on virtually all types of surfaces. The oxidized reaction of LCV is a dark violet color, which is specific for blood, as opposed to protein stains. It is an efficient, one-step technique that is easy to prepare and apply and that does not stain the background. This method is very sensitive and will reveal trace blood that was not visible to the naked eye.

Hemastix

The product "Hemastix," manufactured by Bayer and widely used in clinical screening tests for detection of blood in urine, provides a safe and simple alternative to the other listed reagents. It contains o-Tolidine immobilized behind a membrane. The membrane acts as a barrier to contact by the user, but permits aqueous extracts to pass and react with the reagent. It is rapid, sensitive, and does not interfere with DNA recovery and amplification.

Hemident

Hemident was developed in 1981. It is a presumptive test for blood that is self-contained within a unit containing two ampoules of reagent. The reagents are sensitive and capable of identifying one part per million (1:1,000,000) of blood. However, items processed with Hemident have been found to eliminate the potential for DNA recovery and amplification.

Bluestar

Bluestar is a commercial product that is available to crime scene personnel for the presumptive testing of potential blood evidence. Bluestar is among the most sensitive presumptive field tests for blood. Unlike luminol, Bluestar luminescence lasts for several minutes and can be reapplied. Also Bluestar does not alter DNA and will allow for subsequent DNA testing.

Comparing the Options

Based on a study conducted and published in the *Journal of Forensic Sciences* in January of 2007, the "best overall presumptive blood test was luminol. It had the greatest sensitivity and specificity. It did not destroy DNA, and it could be reapplied." Its drawback was that application must occur in almost total darkness. Leuchomalachite green was found to be "as specific to blood as luminol, but its sensitivity was 10 times less, and it destroyed the DNA." Hemistix "were easy to transport and use, were sensitive, but not very specific." However, they did allow for recovery of DNA. Hemident was "specific and sensitive, but destroyed DNA and so should not be used where subsequent DNA analysis would be necessary. Bluestar had good sensitivity, but very poor specificity" (Tobe et al., 2007, pp. 107–108). Also, the need for complete darkness complicates usage.

Once the item or area has been identified as being presumptive-positive for blood, it is up to the forensic laboratory to conduct confirmatory testing that will identify whether or not it is truly blood, and if it is, whether or not it is of human origin. It is important to note that using two or more of the presumptive tests listed here to conduct confirmatory testing would not be appropriate. Because they are all presumptive tests, carrying out two or more tests does not substitute for or constitute a confirmatory test.

Confirmatory Tests

There have been a variety of tests developed to confirm whether or not a stain is or contains blood. According to research by the National Forensic Science Technology Center, "The oldest is chemical confirmation of the presence of hemoglobin or its derivatives by the formation of specific crystals. For example, the Takayama or hemochromogen test, in which ferrous iron from hemoglobin reacts with pyridine to produce red feathery crystals of pyridine ferroprotoporphyrin. Another confirmatory test uses the Teichman reagent, consisting of a solution of potassium bromide, potassium chloride and potassium iodide in glacial acetic acid, and is heated to react with hemoglobin. The reaction first converts the hemoglobin to hemin, and then the halides react with the hemin to form characteristic brownish-yellow rhomboid crystals" (National Forensic Science Technology Center [NFSTC], 2012).

Precipitin Test

Blood can be identified as being of human origin by precipitin reactions with antisera specific for components of human blood. Usually this is an antihuman serum serum—that is, an antiserum to human serum. Strictly speaking, this is a test for human origin not for human blood, as serum constituents such as albumin and some globulins are found in the extra-vascular space.

The original precipitin reaction was carried out by layering a solution of antibody on top of a solution of stain extract in a tube and left for a period of time to allow the development of a precipitin band at the interface. This is referred to as the tube method, and it is still used in a few laboratories today.

ABAcard®

Rather than utilize a precipitin test, the most common method used today is the ABAcard. The ABAcard HemaTrace test strips are manufactured by Abacus Diagnostics, Inc. When using these strips, a "stain extract is applied to the bottom of the test strip, where any human hemoglobin present in the extract will combine with a monoclonal antihuman hemoglobin antibody. The antibody is labeled with a dye. Any antibody-antigen formed then migrates through an absorbent membrane to the test area of the strip. The test area has an immobilized polyclonal antihuman hemoglobin that will capture the Ag-Ab complex to form an Ab-Ag-Ab sandwich. The pink dye becomes visible as a band in the test region at concentrations of human hemoglobin above about 0.05 µg/ml. An internal control consisting of human hemoglobin antibody–dye conjugate cannot bind to the antibody in the test area but is captured by an antibody in the control area. A correctly functioning positive test will therefore show two pink bands, one in the test area and one in the control area. A correctly functioning negative test will show only one pink band, in the control area. If there is any problem with the test there will be no visible bands. The ABAcard test has been extensively validated and shown to be sensitive, specific, and rapid" (NFSTC, 2012).

If the blood is of human origin, then it may become necessary to identify whether or not the blood can be sourced back to a particular individual. With regard to this, there are both class and individual characteristic options available to assist the investigator.

Blood Typing

Blood typing is not individualized but is considered to be class information. This can assist in either including or excluding individuals from consideration, but will not specifically identify them. **Antigens** are chemical structures residing on the surface of each red blood cell. **Blood types** are determined by the kind of antigen on the surface of these cells. Although numerous antigens exist on the surface of each red blood cell, the ones used for typing are the A, B, O, and Rh antigens.

Characteristics of Blood Types

Blood types are distinguished by the following antigens:

- Type A blood has A antigens on its surface.
- Type B blood has B antigens on its surface.
- Type AB blood has both A and B antigens on its surface.
- Type O blood does not have either A or B antigens on its surface.
- Rh-positive blood has D antigens on its surface.
- Rh-negative blood does not have D antigens on its surface.

Blood Type Antigens and Antibodies

For every antigen, there is an **antibody**. Each antibody name has the prefix anti- followed by the name of the corresponding antigen. An antibody will react with its specific antigen. If serum containing anti-B is added to red blood cells carrying the antigen B, the antibodies will attach themselves to the cells, creating a network of linked cells through a process called **agglutination**.

- Type A blood has A antigens and anti-B antibodies.
- Type B blood has B antigens and anti-A antibodies.

- Type AB blood has AB antigens and neither anti-A nor anti-B antibodies.
- Type O blood has neither A nor B antigens and both anti-A and anti-B antibodies.

The process of cell linking allows blood to be typed. In typing blood, only anti-A and anti-B serum are required. Blood of type A will be agglutinated by anti-A serum, and blood of type B will be agglutinated by anti-B serum, AB blood will be agglutinated by both anti-A and anti-B serum, and blood of type O will not be agglutinated by either anti-A or anti-B serum. Both anti-A serum and anti-B serum are available commercially.

Deoxyribonucleic Acid (DNA)

There was a time when the closest that one could get to identifying blood to a person was through blood type, which was class evidence and not at all individualistic. In 1901 Dr. Karl Lansteiner discovered that blood could be grouped into four different categories, called *types*: A, B, AB, and O blood types. This finding intrigued Dr. Leone Lattes and in 1915 he devised a procedure for determining the blood group of a dried bloodstain. This offered forensic significance for the analysis of crime scene–related blood. However, again, it only offered the ability of investigators to isolate the evidence to a particular group but not to an individual. It was not until 1984 when Sir Alec Jeffreys made the revolutionary discovery of *deoxyribonucleic acid (DNA) fingerprinting* that the ability to isolate a specific individual (or individuals in the case of identical twins) was possible.

DNA Structure

Deoxyribonucleic acid (DNA) is the genetic building block for all living organisms, including some viruses. **Figure 10–3** shows the double helix structure of DNA. Virtually every cell contains DNA. DNA does not change throughout a person's life. With the exception of red blood cells, nearly all of the cells in the human body contain nuclear DNA that is housed within the nuclei of each cell. In blood, however, only white blood cells have a nucleus. Red blood cells shed their nucleus during their early formation.

Nucleic acid is typically extracted as source material for most crime scene DNA. Each nucleated cell has a single nucleus, and each nucleus holds 23 pairs of chromosomes. At conception, each parent

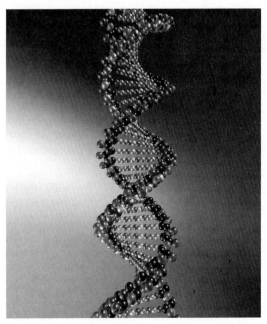

FIGURE 10–3   The double-helix structure of DNA

contributes one half of these 23 pairs, creating a completely distinct set of chromosomes in the offspring. A person therefore inherits half of his or her genetic material (DNA) from each parent. However, what is important to understand about heredity is that a person inherits the information required to produce his or her characteristics in the form of DNA, but they do not inherit the characteristics, only the information to produce them.

DNA is a **nucleotide polymer**, which means it is a molecule that is formed by linking together a series of repeating units known as **nucleotides**. A nucleotide is composed of a sugar

Understanding DNA Evidence

"DNA fingerprinting" or DNA typing (profiling) as it is now known, was first described in 1984 by the English geneticist, Alec Jeffreys. Dr. Jeffreys found that certain regions of DNA contained DNA sequences that were repeated over and over again next to each other. He also discovered that the number of repeated sections present in a sample could differ from individual to individual. By developing a technique to examine the length variation of these DNA repeat sequences, Dr. Jeffreys created the ability to perform human identity tests.

These DNA repeat regions became known as VNTRs, which stands for variable number of tandem repeats. The technique used by Dr. Jeffreys to examine the VNTRs was called restriction fragment length polymorphism (RFLP) because it involved the use of a restriction enzyme to cut the regions of DNA surrounding the VNTRs. This RFLP method was first used to help in an English immigration case and shortly thereafter to solve a double homicide case. Since that time, human identity testing using DNA typing methods has been widespread. The past 15 years have seen tremendous growth in the use of DNA evidence in crime scene investigations as well as paternity testing. Today, over 150 public forensic laboratories and several dozen private paternity testing laboratories conduct hundreds of thousands of DNA tests annually in the United States. In addition, most countries in Europe and Asia have forensic DNA programs. The number of laboratories around the world conducting DNA testing will continue to grow as the technique gains in popularity within the law enforcement community.

DNA evidence is playing a larger role than ever before in criminal cases throughout the country, both to convict the guilty and to exonerate those wrongly accused or convicted. This increased role places greater importance on the ability of victim service providers to understand the potential significance of DNA evidence in their clients' cases.

Information retrieved from National Institute of Justice and Office for Victims of Crime. (May 2001). *Understanding DNA Evidence: A Guide for Victim Service Providers*. Brochure.

molecule, a phosphorous-containing group, and a nitrogen-containing molecule called a *base*. There are only four types of bases associated with DNA: adenine (A), cytosine (C), guanine (G), and thymine (T). There is no specified length of the DNA strand; in fact, a DNA strand can be composed of a long chain having millions of bases.

The unique feature of a DNA molecule is that it is composed of two DNA strands coiled into a *double helix*. The only way the bases (A, C, G, T) on each strand can be properly aligned is in specific paired combinations. G always pairs with C, and A always pairs with T. This is known as **complimentary base pairing**. Although A-T and G-C pairs are always required, there are no restrictions on how the bases are to be sequenced on a DNA strand. Any base can follow another on a DNA strand. Therefore, the possibilities of sequencing are staggering. In fact, the average human chromosome has DNA containing 100 million base pairs. In the human body, all of the chromosomes taken together contain approximately 3 billion base pairs.

During Alec Jeffreys' process toward discovery of DNA fingerprinting, he found that portions of the DNA molecule contain sequences of letters that are repeated numerous times. What is important to understand is that all humans have the same type of repeats, but there is tremendous variation in the number of repeats in each individual. It is this variation that gives each person his or her biological equivalent of a fingerprint.

Mitochondrial DNA

Mitochondrial DNA (mtDNA) is found outside the nucleus of the cell and is inherited solely from the mother. Each cell contains only one nucleus but hundreds to thousands of mitochondria. Therefore, there are hundreds to thousands of mtDNA copies in a human cell compared to just one set of nuclear DNA in that same cell.

This is useful in situations where nuclear DNA is significantly degraded, such as in charred remains, or in cases where nuclear DNA may be present in small quantity (e.g., a hair shaft). In situations where authorities cannot obtain a reference sample from an individual who may be long deceased or missing, an mtDNA reference sample can be obtained from any maternally related relative. However, mtDNA is not as unique as nuclear DNA. All individuals of the same maternal lineage will be indistinguishable by mtDNA analysis.

Value of DNA Evidence

DNA is a powerful investigative tool because, with the exception of identical twins and other multiples, no two people have the same DNA. However, even with that being true, only one-tenth of a single percent of DNA (about 3 million bases) differs from one person to the next. Scientists can use these variable regions to generate a DNA profile of an individual, using samples from blood, bone, hair, and other body tissues and products.

In criminal cases, this generally involves obtaining samples from crime scene evidence and a suspect, extracting the DNA, and analyzing it for the presence of a set of specific DNA

CASE IN POINT

DNA Can Both Exonerate and Convict

In 1985, Steven Avery was convicted in the State of Wisconsin for sexual assault, attempted murder, and false imprisonment. On July 29, 1985, a woman was jogging on a Lake Michigan beach when a man attacked and sexually assaulted her. Three days later, the victim identified Avery from a police lineup. He was sentenced to 32 years. On September 11, 2003, Avery was exonerated as a result of efforts by the Innocence Project, due to reanalysis of DNA evidence that matched a hair found at the crime scene to Gregory Allen, a man already serving a 60-year sentence for a similar sexual assault. Contributing causes to Avery's original conviction were eyewitness misidentification and unreliable science at the time of analysis.

DNA had set Avery free, but it was also to put him away for life. In November of 2005, while in the midst of a civil case that he had filed regarding the false rape conviction, Avery was charged with the murder of Teresa Halbach. DNA evidence at the scene of the brutal murder tied Avery to the homicide event. He was found guilty of murder and of illegally possessing a firearm. Avery was sentenced to life in prison.

---

regions (markers). If the sample profiles do not match, then the person did not contribute the DNA at the crime scene. If the patterns match, the suspect may have contributed the evidence sample. DNA from crime scenes also can be compared to profiles stored in a database.

Since its introduction in the mid-1980s, DNA typing has revolutionized forensic science and the ability of law enforcement to match perpetrators with crime scenes. Thousands of cases have been closed and innocent suspects freed with guilty ones punished because of the power of a silent biological witness at the crime scene.

DNA evidence collected from a crime scene can be linked to a suspect or can eliminate a suspect from suspicion. During a sexual assault, for example, biological evidence such as hair, skin cells, semen, or blood can be left on the victim's body or other parts of the crime scene. Properly collected DNA can be compared with known samples to place a suspect at the scene of the crime.

The effective use of DNA as evidence also may require the collection and analysis of elimination samples to determine the exact source of the DNA. These elimination samples help determine if the evidence is from a suspect or another person. The types of elimination samples to be collected depend on the details of the crime, but they are generally samples of blood or saliva. For example, in a residential burglary where the suspect may have sipped from a glass of water, DNA samples should be obtained from every person who had access to the crime scene

RIPPED **FROM THE HEADLINES**

Using DNA to Hunt for Osama bin Laden

In May of 2011, U.S. Navy SEALS raided a compound in Abbottabad, Pakistan, killing Osama bin Laden in the process. The U.S. military became aware of bin Laden's presence within the compound as a result of a fraudulent vaccination program that was used to gather DNA evidence. A Pakistani doctor, Dr. Shakeel Afridi, assisted the CIA with development of the vaccination program. According to a CNN article, neighborhood residents reported two women appearing to be nurses who visited homes within the area and offered free vaccinations. The goal was to try to obtain DNA evidence from bin Laden family members. Any DNA obtained from people could then be compared against a sample from bin Laden's sister, who had died in the U.S. in 2010, as evidence that relations of bin Laden, or perhaps even bin Laden himself, were in the compound. In the end, the ruse worked and DNA helped provide a piece of the intelligence that was used to locate Osama bin Laden. There were many who pointed to the fraudulent use of medicine and of doctors engaged in malfeasance as gross negligence, but as one senior U.S. official told CNN, "If the United States hadn't shown this kind of creativity, people would be scratching their heads asking why it hadn't used all the tools at its disposal to find bin Laden."

Information from: CNN. (2011). Pakistani doctor faces treason charges after bin Laden raid. October 6, 2011. Retrieved July 7, 2012, from http://articles.cnn.com/2011-10-06/asia/world_asia_pakistan-bin-laden-investigation_1_senior-pakistani-security-official-bin-osama?_s=PM:ASIA.

both before and after the burglary. The laboratory will then compare these samples with the saliva found on the glass to determine if the saliva contains probative evidence. Elimination samples may be taken from anyone who had lawful access to the crime scene and may have left biological material. When investigating a rape case, for example, it may be necessary to obtain an elimination sample from everyone who had consensual intercourse with the victim within 72 hours of the alleged assault to account for all the DNA found on the victim or at the crime scene. Comparing DNA profiles from the evidence with elimination samples may help clarify the results.

If no suspect exists, a DNA profile from crime scene evidence can be entered into the FBI's Combined DNA Index System (CODIS) to identify a suspect anywhere in the United States or to link serial crimes to each other.

The study of DNA is often challenging. Read the President's DNA Initiative: Advancing Justice Through DNA Technology for more information (http://www.dna.gov).

RIPPED **FROM THE HEADLINES**

CODIS Not the Only Database for DNA

A recent article on CNN.com revealed that DNA databases and analysis of DNA and comparison to known databases is not simply limited to the FBI's CODIS database. According to the article, a New Hampshire apartment complex is requiring residents to submit mandatory mouth swabs from their pets as reference DNA samples in the hopes of maintaining a clean place to live. The apartment complex recently began using PooPrints (a subsidiary of BioPet Vet Lab in Knoxville, TN) to perform DNA comparisons between samples of unclaimed pet waste and resident pets. Identified violators "receive a warning if caught, paying a $60 fee to cover the DNA costs. However, if it happens again, it's a lease violation and the offender will be forced to live somewhere else."

Information from: Golgowski, N. (2011). DNA tests provide the poop on bad dog owners. Retrieved June 24, 2012, from http://articles.cnn.com/2011-06-27/us/new.hampshire.dog.dna_1_biopet-vet-lab-pooprints-dna-analysis?_s=PM:US.

CODIS

The **Combined DNA Index System (CODIS)** is an electronic database of DNA profiles administered through the Federal Bureau of Investigation (FBI). "CODIS began as a pilot software project in 1990 serving 14 state and local laboratories. The DNA Identification Act of 1994 formalized the FBI's authority to establish a National DNA Index System (NDIS) for law enforcement purposes. Today, over 180 public law enforcement laboratories participate in NDIS across the United States. Internationally, more than 60 law enforcement laboratories in over 30 countries use the CODIS software for their own database initiatives" (FBI, 2012). However, international laboratories that make use of the CODIS software do not have connectivity to the U.S. CODIS system. The system lets federal, state, and local crime labs share and compare DNA profiles. All 50 states have enacted legislation that requires offenders convicted of particular crimes to submit DNA samples for inclusion within the CODIS database.

According to the FBI CODIS website, there are several indexes that help to categorize the profiles entered into CODIS. These include:

1. Convicted Offender: contains DNA profiles of individuals convicted of crimes.
2. Arrestees: contains profiles of arrested persons (if state law permits the collection of arrestee samples).
3. Forensic: contains DNA profiles developed from crime scene evidence, such as semen stains or blood.

4. Missing Persons: contains DNA reference profiles from missing persons.

5. Unidentified Humans (Remains): contains DNA profiles developed from unidentified humans and remains.

6. Biological Relatives of Missing Persons: contains DNA profiles voluntarily contributed from relatives of missing persons.

The purpose of CODIS is to generate investigative leads in instances where biological evidence is recovered from crime scenes. Matches that are made among profiles within the Forensic Index of CODIS can potentially link crime scenes together. This has the added potential of possibly identifying serial offenders through DNA evidence. If there is a database match, law enforcement from multiple jurisdictions can coordinate their respective investigations and share the leads they developed independently. Matches made between the Forensic and Offender Indexes provide investigators with the identity of a suspected perpetrator(s). Because names and other personally identifiable information are not stored in NDIS, qualified DNA analysts in the laboratories that are found to have matching profiles must then contact each other to confirm the candidate match (FBI, 2012).

"The match of the forensic DNA record against the DNA record in the database may then be used to establish probable cause to obtain an evidentiary DNA sample from the developed suspect. The appropriate law enforcement agency can then use such documentation to obtain a court order authorizing the collection of a known biological reference sample from the suspect or offender. The laboratory will then perform a DNA analysis on the known sample for presentation as evidence within court" (FBI, 2012).

Collection of Blood Evidence

In crimes of violence, blood is usually found in the form of dried stains. Blood frequently can be identified and genetically compared to blood standards from individuals if a sufficient quantity is properly collected and submitted. In addition to identification and comparison

---

Measuring Success

"The National DNA Index (NDIS) contained over 10,718,700 offender profiles and 427,500 forensic profiles as of April 2012. Ultimately, the success of the CODIS program will be measured by the crimes it helps to solve. CODIS's primary metric, the "Investigative Aided," tracks the number of criminal investigations where CODIS has added value to the investigative process. As of April 2012, CODIS had produced over 178,300 hits, assisting in more than 171,000 investigations" (FBI, 2012).

Federal Bureau of Investigation (FBI). (2012). CODIS. Retrieved from http://www.fbi.gov/about-us/lab/biometric-analysis/codis/ndis-statistics.

testing, the shape and pattern of the bloodstaining may provide information concerning how the blood was deposited.

The following information should also be recorded:

- Physical state (fluid, moist, dry)
- Amount present (few drops, small pool, etc.)
- Shape (smear, round drops)
- Exact location in relation to fixed objects
- Pattern of stains (all in one spot, trail)
- Atmosphere conditions (temperature, humidity)
- Date and time of observation
- Scaled and unscaled photographs of stains

Liquid Blood

If wet blood or a blood pool of fluid blood is present, collection should be made in the following manner:

- Wear gloves, mask, and eye protection while soaking up samples.
- Using cotton swabs, soak the suspected blood onto the swabs (**Figure 10–4**).
- Continue collecting the stain until it is either completely collected or until five swabs have been saturated.
- Make sure to avoid contamination of swabs.
- It is recommended to change gloves frequently and to change them immediately if contamination of gloves occurs.
- Allow the swabs to dry in place or place them on a nonporous surface like a glass microscope slide and allow to thoroughly air dry.
- Package the dried swabs in a paper container (e.g., white slide box, envelope, paper bag, etc.). Use separate containers for each area recovered. Label the paper container with a "biohazard" sign (**Figure 10–5**).
- Properly label and seal each container.
- Select an unstained area adjacent to the suspected bloodstain and collect a sample from this area as before. This sample will serve as a control. Package, label, and seal this control separately from the stained material (**Figure 10–6**).

Remember

Dried or Moist Bloodstain Recovery

If the stained object is transportable, submit the item intact. If the suspected blood is still moist, allow it to thoroughly air dry in a well-ventilated but draft-free area prior to packaging. Label the area with "biohazard" signs. Package the item in a clean paper container and then seal and label it. If it is impractical to submit the bloodstained item to the laboratory or it is not possible

FIGURE 10-4 An example of using a cotton swab to collect wet blood evidence

Courtesy of Nick Vesper, University of Wisconsin-Platteville.

FIGURE 10-5 An example of evidence packaging for evidence swabs

Courtesy of Nick Vesper, University of Wisconsin-Platteville.

FIGURE 10-6 Demonstrating how to properly collect a control sample

Courtesy of Nick Vesper, University of Wisconsin-Platteville.

to cut or remove a portion of the stained and unstained area of the item, then collect in the following manner:

- Wear gloves, mask, and eye protection while collecting samples.

- Moisten a sufficient number of cotton swabs to collect the stain. It is better to underestimate the amount of swabs required as additional swabs can always be used.

- Wet the swabs using distilled water, or clean tap water if distilled water is not available (**Figure 10-7**).

- Do not allow the swabs to come into contact with any other object.

- Gently swab the stain with the moistened swabs until the swabs thoroughly absorb the blood and are a dark reddish-brown coloration.

- Continue collecting the stain until it is either completely collected or five swabs have been saturated.

FIGURE 10-7 Demonstrating how to moisten a swab prior to attempting to collect dry blood evidence

Courtesy of Nick Vesper, University of Wisconsin-Platteville.

- Allow the stained swabs to thoroughly air dry either directly on the stained object or on a clean glass microscope slide. To avoid contamination, swabs can be dried by making a small perforation in a pillbox and placing the swab into the perforation. This will allow the swab to dry without contacting any other surfaces.

- Package, label, and seal the air-dried swabs in a paper container (e.g., white slide box, envelope, etc.). Label with a "biohazard" sign.

- Select an unstained area adjacent to the suspected bloodstain and collect a sample from this area as before. This sample will serve as a control. Package, label, and seal this control separately from the stained material.

Evidence Collection

Contamination can take place if someone sneezes or coughs over the evidence or touches his or her hair, nose, or other part of the body and then touches the area containing the sample to be tested. DNA left at a crime scene also is subject to environmental contamination. Exposure to bacteria, heat, light, moisture, and mold can speed up the degradation (or erosion) of DNA. As a result, not all DNA evidence yields usable profiles.

Crime scene personnel should not drink, eat, litter, smoke, or do anything else that might compromise the crime scene. They should remember that valuable DNA evidence may be present even though it is not visible. For example, because evidence could be on a telephone mouth or earpiece, investigators should use their own police radios or cellular phones instead of a telephone located at the crime scene.

To further avoid compromising evidence, any movement or relocation of potential evidence should be avoided. Personnel should move evidence only if it will otherwise be lost or destroyed. Potential evidence can become contaminated when DNA from another source gets mixed with samples gathered for a specific case. In those situations, laboratory analysts have to request samples from all persons with access to the crime scene, including officers and anyone who had physical possession of the evidence while it was being recovered, processed, and examined.

Maintaining a precise chain of custody of all DNA materials collected for testing is critical, as it may at some point become an issue in court. Every action officers take at a crime scene must be fully documented. Improvements in analysis and interpretation of physical evidence recovered from crime scenes continue to develop. Properly documented and preserved DNA evidence will be given increased weight in court, so it is extremely important that an officer's approach to gathering evidence be objective, thorough, and thoughtful.

Contamination and Preservation

DNA evidence can become contaminated when DNA from another source gets mixed with DNA relevant to the case. For this reason, investigators and laboratory personnel should always wear disposable gloves, use clean instruments, and avoid touching other objects, including their own bodies, when handling evidence.

Environmental factors, such as heat and humidity, can accelerate the degradation of DNA. For example, wet or moist evidence that is packaged in plastic will provide a growth environment for bacteria that can destroy DNA evidence. Therefore, biological evidence should be thoroughly air dried, packaged in paper, and properly labeled. Handled in this manner, DNA can be stored for years without risk of extensive degradation, even at room temperature. For long-term storage issues, contact the local crime laboratory.

RIPPED **FROM THE HEADLINES**

Contaminated DNA Swabs Solve the Case of the "Phantom of Heilbronn"

In March of 2009, German police detectives announced that they believed evidence linking 14 murders together, to a supposed serial killer, was in fact a result of contaminated DNA swabs. The killer, referred to as the "Phantom of Heilbronn," had been perplexing German police for almost two years.

The killer was an oddity for a number of reasons. One, she was determined through DNA analysis to be female. Also, DNA had linked her to a total of 40 crimes (including the 14 homicides), ranging from stolen motor vehicles to drug violations. It was not until early in 2009 that police discovered a red flag that signaled that something was amiss. While attempting to establish the identity of a male asylum seeker's charred remains, they found that the fingerprints of the individual contained the killer's female DNA. Perplexed as to how this would be the case, investigators performed the test again, with a separate cotton swab, and no trace of the killer's DNA was discovered.

This led investigators to believe that the DNA connection between all of the supposed serial cases could be connected to a single innocent industry employee, most likely employed in the packaging stage of the swab manufacturing process. This individual, if not adhering to proper protocol could have affected the swabs through sneezing, coughing, etc. Although swabs used for DNA collection are sterilized, and sterilization removes fungi, bacteria, and viruses, it will not destroy DNA.

As a result, Germany's Federal Criminal Police are now investigating at what point in the manufacturing process the contamination occurred. The female donor of the DNA has not been identified, and the 40 criminal cases are now back to stage one.

Information from: Himmelreich, Claudia. (2009). Germany's Phantom Serival Killer: A DNA Blunder. Retrieved on September 15, 2012, from http://www.time.com/time/world/article/0,8599,1888126,00.html.

Other Biological Fluids

In addition to blood at crime scenes there are numerous other biological fluids that may be collected and identified in order to explain what occurred at the scene of the crime. Most will yield the ability to identify DNA from them also. Other fluids that are present at crime scenes,

Safeguard DNA Evidence and Yourself

Biological material may contain hazardous pathogens, such as the Hepatitis A or B virus, which can lead to potentially lethal diseases. At the same time, such material can easily become contaminated. To protect both the integrity of the evidence and the health and safety of law enforcement personnel, crime scene personnel should:

- Wear gloves and change them often.
- Use disposable instruments or clean them thoroughly before and after handling each sample.
- Avoid touching any area where DNA might exist.
- Avoid talking, sneezing, or coughing over evidence.
- Avoid touching one's own nose, mouth, and face when collecting and packaging evidence.
- Air dry evidence thoroughly before packaging.
- Put evidence into new paper bags or envelopes. Do not place evidence in plastic bags or use staples (**Figure 10–8**).

FIGURE 10–8   Proper packaging of blood-stained evidence
Courtesy of Nick Vesper, University of Wisconsin-Platteville.

Information retrieved from National Institute of Justice (NIJ). (July 2003). DNA: What law enforcement officers should know. *NIJ Journal*, 249, 10–15.

DNA Now and in the Future

Broader Implementation of the CODIS Database

States will continue to enact legislation requiring DNA samples from more offenders, resulting in more crimes being solved and increased cooperation among the states. Procedures for making international matches are expected to be developed, especially with Great Britain, which has a well-developed convicted felon database. Increased use of automated laboratory procedures and computerized analyses should improve departmental efficiency and accuracy of handling evidence. Although these timesaving approaches are not expected to replace human judgments in the final review of data, automation of many of the more routine aspects of analysis is expected to result in significant cost savings.

Portable Devices Capable of DNA Analysis

These devices, plus other advances in communications technology, may permit DNA evidence to be analyzed closer to the crime scene.

Remote Links to Databases and Other Criminal Justice Information Sources

Prompt determinations of the DNA profile at the crime scene could speed up identification of a suspect or eliminate innocent persons from being considered suspects. Such forecasts of the future are somewhat uncertain. However, the fact that private laboratories, federal agencies, and universities are aggressively researching these and other new technologies raises expectations that more sophisticated innovations will be developed.

Even with the latest innovations, DNA testing alone cannot provide absolute answers in every case. The prosecutor, defense counsel, judge, and law enforcement should confer on the need for such testing on a case-by-case basis.

Information retrieved from National Institute of Justice (NIJ). (July 2003). DNA: What law enforcement officers should know. *NIJ Journal, 249,* 10–15.

and for which identification is sometimes necessary include but are not limited to semen, saliva, vomitus, perspiration, urine, and fecal matter.

Semen

In 1935, Kutscher and Wolbergs discovered that human semen contains uniquely high levels of seminal acid phosphatase (SAP) compared with other body fluids and plant tissues. SAP is produced by the prostate and is therefore found in both animals and humans. However, it is 20 to 400 times more concentrated within humans than in any other body fluid (Saferstein, 2010). This is the scientific basis for the presumptive ID of semen. Many methods for the presumptive ID of semen have been devised.

One method is utilizing an ALS because seminal fluid contains an acriflavine, which fluoresces bluish-white when exposed to the light from an ALS, with a proper barrier filter. However, this test is not sufficient to presumptively identify semen, as there are numerous other substances that have the same fluorescence. These include: fabric softeners, toothpaste, cosmetics, sweat, and urine. This is a good starting point, however. There are presumptive field test kits to screen for SAP that are more isolating in nature. This test is performed by promoting a color reaction within the sample. In forensic laboratories, alphanaphthyl phosphate is the preferred substrate and Brentamine Fast Blue the color developer. However, Brentamine Fast Blue B is potentially carcinogenic, so liberal applications made directly onto items of clothing or areas of flooring are not recommended.

Confirmatory tests for the presence of semen can only be made at the forensic laboratory. Microscopic identification of spermatozoa is one type of confirmatory test for semen. At the lab, the criminalist will stain the prepared sample using a "Christmas tree" stain test that stains the head of spermatozoa red and their tails (flagella) green. This then provides unambiguous proof that the stain in question contains semen.

Another method to confirm the presence of semen in a sample is for the forensic lab to perform what is known as a *p30 test*. This test is performed when no sperm are found to be present within the sample (e.g., vasectomized male). p30 is a prostate-specific antigen produced in the human male. There have been cases where p30 was detected in samples stored at room temperature for up to 10 years. In fact, sperm can be located within an oral sample for up to 24 hours, and inside of the vagina for up to 72 hours. This provides a finite window of collection opportunities for a crime scene investigator (Saferstein, 2010).

Procedure for the Collection of Seminal Stains

Where a sexual offense has occurred, stains may be found on clothing, bedding, rags, upholstery, or other objects. Seminal stains can be helpful in establishing whether or not an alleged sexual act occurred and can also provide information concerning the man who contributed the semen.

Carefully recover all suspected stained material, including the clothing worn by the victim and the suspect at the time of the offense. Each item of evidence should be packaged separately, labeled, and sealed. Air dry all damp stains in a well-ventilated but draft-free area.

Clean paper should be spread under the item to catch any debris that may be dislodged during the drying process. Package, label, and seal each item along with the paper upon which the item dried. Use only paper containers for packaging (e.g., paper bags). If the suspected seminal stain is on an object that cannot be transported, collect utilizing swabs and distilled water, as with blood evidence.

Standard blood samples are normally used for comparison purposes, rather than collecting semen standards for comparison.

Saliva

Humans produce 1 to 1.3 liters of saliva per day. Its primary purpose is to aid in the initial stages of digestion by lubricating food for ease of swallowing and to begin the process of digestion. However, no test is specific for saliva. Presumptive tests will test for presence of amylase (found in saliva, perspiration, semen, vaginal secretions, and breast milk). However, amylase is found in 50 times higher concentration within saliva. There have been cases where activity has been detected for up to approximately 28 months (Saferstein, 2010).

Saliva stains are not usually evident from a visual examination. However, certain types of evidence frequently contain traces of saliva (e.g., cigarette butts, gummed surfaces of envelopes, stamps, bite marks, areas where oral contact may have occurred, etc.) and sometimes the amount of saliva present is sufficient to determine the DNA type of the individual who is the source of the saliva.

Procedure for the Collection of Evidential Forms of Saliva

Easily transportable objects such as individual cigarette butts and envelopes should be placed in a paper container (e.g., paper bag or envelopes) and the container should be properly labeled and sealed. If transporting the object is not practical, such as in the case of bite marks on the body of sexual assault victims, then the saliva can be collected as follows:

- Moisten a cotton swab with distilled water.
- Shake the swab to eliminate excess water.
- Gently swab the suspected saliva stain. Using a dry swab go over the stained area to absorb any remaining moisture.
- Allow the swabs to thoroughly air dry prior to packaging, labeling, and sealing in a paper envelope. Air drying can be accomplished by making a perforation in the center of a pillbox, inserting the swab into the perforation and allowing the swab to air dry.
- Select an unstained area and collect as before. Package, label, and seal separately from the stained material. This swab will serve as a control.

Standard blood samples are normally used for comparison purposes, rather than collecting saliva standards for comparison.

Other Types of Biological Evidence

Urine

This is a rarely identified biological fluid. The presumptive test for urine by the forensic laboratory tests for the presence of creatinine, which is found in heavy concentrations in urine. It is also found, however, in high concentrations in sweat. There is no confirmatory test that is regularly utilized.

Vomitus

There is no presumptive or confirmatory test for vomitus. However, the material can be tested to determine food content and to compare pH levels.

Vaginal Secretions

In order to meet the elements of sexual assault, often it is necessary to prove that an object was placed within the vagina. In these cases it is necessary for the forensic laboratory to make use of microscopy in order to identify fluids and cells associated with vaginal secretions.

Vaginal secretions in the form of a foreign DNA (DNA that did not originate from the individual swabbed) can sometimes be attributed to another individual when the penis of a suspected sexual perpetrator is swabbed at the time of apprehension. The sample is collected by wetting a cotton swab with distilled water and swabbing the external area of the penis. This type of analysis is most successful when the perpetrator is apprehended shortly after the alleged occurrence of sexual activity, generally within 24 hours and prior to bathing. The outer area of condoms also can yield this type of DNA.

Preservation of Dried Biological Evidence

The ideal way to preserve biological evidence is to freeze it. This can become impractical with large amounts of evidence. Evidence with dried biological stains can be stored in a temperature-controlled room, which is maintained at normal room temperature or colder. Large fluctuations in temperature should be avoided. When biological evidence is returned after processing by the DNA unit of the crime laboratory, it frequently will contain a manila envelope labeled "DNA packet." This packet contains cuttings of stains and extracts of those stains. This packet needs to be frozen. If this packet is included with the evidence, it will be noted on the return release form and the evidence will be labeled "Biological Evidence Enclosed, Please Remove and Freeze."

Sexual Assault

In a rape case, investigators may need to collect and analyze the DNA of every consensual sexual partner the victim had up to four days prior to the assault. Testing can eliminate those partners as potential sources of DNA suspected to be from the rapist. A sample also should be taken from the victim. It is important to approach the victim with extreme sensitivity and to explain fully why the request is being made. A qualified victim advocate or forensic nurse examiner can be a great help.

In sexual assault cases, it is especially important that victims are told why they should not change clothes, shower, or wash any part of their body after an assault. Depending on the nature of the assault, semen may be found on bedding or clothing, or in the anal, oral, or vaginal region. Saliva found on an area where the victim was bitten or licked may contain valuable DNA. If the victim scratched the assailant, skin cells containing the attacker's DNA may sometimes be present under the victim's fingernails. Victims should be referred to a hospital where an exam will be conducted by a physician or sexual assault nurse examiner.

In all cases it is essential to have the victim(s) examined by a medical professional as soon as possible after the assault and before the affected areas (pubic area, vagina, rectum, etc.) or clothing are washed or cleaned.

Evidence on or inside a victim's body should be collected by a physician or sexual assault nurse examiner. A medical examination should be conducted immediately after the assault to treat any injuries, test for sexually transmitted diseases, and collect forensic evidence, such as fingernail scrapings and hair. Typically, the vaginal cavity, mouth, anus, or other parts of the body that may have come into contact with the assailant are examined.

The examiner also should take a reference sample of blood or saliva from the victim to serve as a control standard. Reference samples of the victim's head and pubic hair may be collected if hair analysis is required. A control standard is used to compare known DNA from the victim with that of other DNA evidence found at the crime scene to determine possible suspect(s).

Most forensic laboratories and emergency rooms will have a **<u>sexual assault kit (SAK)</u>** available that can assist the crime scene investigator and attending medical professional in properly collecting the specimens required by the laboratory. This kit can be used to collect appropriate samples from both male and female sexual assault victims and suspects (**Figure 10–9**).

Each kit gives specific collection methods for various types of evidence that must be collected and documented. These include:

- Clothing
- Pubic hair combings
- Vaginal swabs (four) and smear (one)

FIGURE 10–9   An example of a sexual assault kit (SAK)
Courtesy of Nick Vesper, University of Wisconsin-Platteville.

- Cervical swabs (two) and smear (one)
- Rectal swabs (two) and smear (one)
- Oral swabs (two) and smear (one)
- Pubic hair standards
- Penile swab (one)
- Buccal cell standard (cheek or mouthwash)
- Fingernail scraping (if indicated)
- Bite marks (if indicated)
- Toxicology specimens

The clothing of the victim and suspect(s) is the next most important type of evidence. Articles of clothing worn by the victim (and suspect, if possible) should be submitted to the laboratory for examination, as there may be seminal stains, bloodstains, foreign hairs and fibers, or other trace evidence adhering to the clothing. In addition, items at the crime scene may provide important evidence that associates either the victim, the suspect, or both to the scene.

The recommended procedure for the collection and preservation of clothing is as follows:

- Clothing of the victim must be kept separate from that of the suspect at all times.
- Clothing worn at the time of or immediately after the offense must be recovered and preserved. This includes undergarments, handkerchiefs, and sanitary napkins and/or tampons (only if used during or after the offense).
- Garments should be handled as little as possible to avoid the loss of trace evidence.

Additional Considerations for Processing the Scene

Sexual assault crimes involve physical contact between perpetrator and victim. This contact results in the transfer of materials, such as hairs, fibers, and body fluids, particularly seminal fluid and saliva. In many cases, the perpetrator is not known to the victim and the assault occurs in seclusion or with no witnesses. As a result, there are some additional considerations that a crime scene investigator should take in order to ensure the proper documentation and collection of related evidence.

The crime scene investigator should attempt to recover articles such as handkerchiefs, rags, tissues, etc., that may have been used as a wipe after ejaculation. They should also recover and submit any articles that may have become stained during the offense or might have foreign hairs present (bedding, rugs, sofa cushions, etc.).

When condoms are recovered in suspected sexual assault cases, they should be placed in a glass specimen jar and frozen until submitted to the crime laboratory.

WRAP UP

Chapter Summary

The identification, documentation, collection, and preservation of biological evidence are of paramount concern in establishing the facts of a case. It is important that a crime scene investigator realize that there are correct ways to go about such collection efforts, and that there are scientific considerations that pertain to the evidence being properly preserved. If the samples are not properly collected and preserved, subsequent analysis and identification will be nearly impossible.

Review Questions

1. What is TMB and how is it used in relation to biological evidence?

2. _____ is an example of a presumptive search technique that results in chemiluminescence as a result of the chemical reaction occurring between the reagent and the biological stain.

3. Before DNA analysis was used on blood evidence _____ was used to determine the class characteristics of A, B, AB, or O.

4. Who discovered DNA fingerprinting?

5. _____ is the building block for the human body.

6. DNA is a molecule that is formed by linking together a series of repeating units; this is also known as a _____.

7. Complimentary base pairing refers to the fact that _____ always pairs with _____ and _____ always pairs with _____.

8. What is mtDNA?

9. What is CODIS and how is it used?

10. Explain what is meant by a "Christmas tree" stain.

11. What is an SAK and how is it used?

Case Studies

1. Look up the name Anastasia Manahan, who is also known as Anna Anderson. Explain how the use of DNA technology helped to uncover this imposter and set the historical record straight.

2. Look up the name William Gregory and explain how the use of DNA evidence applied to his case and to discovering the truth. Be thorough in your summary.

References

CNN. (2011). *Pakistani doctor faces treason charges after bin Laden raid.* October 6, 2011. Retrieved July 7, 2012, from http://articles.cnn.com/2011-10-06/asia/world_asia_pakistan-bin-laden-investigation_1_senior-pakistani-security-official-bin-osama?_s=PM:ASIA

Doyle, A. C. (1887). *A study in scarlet.* London, United Kingdom: Ward Lock & Co.

Federal Bureau of Investigation (FBI). (2012). *Birth of the FBI's technical laboratory.* Retrieved September 15, 2012 from http://www.fbi.gov/about-us/history/highlights-of-history/articles/laboratory

Golgowski, N. (2011). *DNA tests provide the poop on bad dog owners.* Retrieved June 24, 2012, from http://articles.cnn.com/2011-06-27/us/new.hampshire.dog.dna_1_biopet-vet-lab-pooprints-dna-analysis?_s=PM:US

Himmelreich, C. (March 27, 2009). Germany's phantom serial killer: A DNA blunder. *Time.* Retrieved from http://www.time.com/time/world/article/0,8599,1888126,00.html

National Forensic Science Technology Center (NFSTC). (2012). Confirmatory Tests. Retrieved August 23, 2012, from http://www.nfstc.org/pdi/Subject02/pdi_s02_m02_02_b.htm

National Institute of Justice and Office for Victims of Crime (May, 2001). *Understanding DNA Evidence: A Guide for Victim Service Providers.* Brochure.

National Institute of Justice (NIJ). (July, 2003). DNA: What law enforcement officers should know. *NIJ Journal, 249,* 10–15.

National Institute of Justice (NIJ). (July, 2003). Without a trace? Advances in detecting trace evidence. *NIJ Journal, 249,* 2–3.

Saferstein, R. (2010). *Criminalistics: An introduction to forensic science* (9th ed.). Upper Saddle River, NJ: Pearson Prentice Hall.

Tobe, S. S., Watson, N., & Daéid, N. N. (2007). Evaluation of six presumptive tests for blood, their specificity, sensitivity, and effect on high molecular-weight DNA. *Journal of Forensic Sciences. 52*(1), 102–109.

LEARNING OBJECTIVES

- Explain the forensic significance of bloodstain pattern analysis.
- Understand how the properties of human blood allow bloodshed events to be interpreted.
- Know how impact angle, surface type, and drop height affect a resulting stain and how they are analyzed.
- Differentiate between the primary types of bloodstain patterns found at crime scenes and what can be surmised from their discovery.
- List the correct way to document bloodstain evidence.

Bloodstain Pattern Analysis

> *Art in the blood is liable to take the strangest forms.*
>
> Sherlock Holmes, *The Adventure of the Greek Interpreter, 1893*
> Sir Arthur Conan Doyle (1859–1930)

KEY TERMS

Area of Convergence
Area of Origin
Bloodstain Pattern Analysis
  (BPA)
Cast-off Patterns
Directionality

Expirated Patterns
Passive Bloodstain
Projected Patterns
Skeletonized Stain
Swipe
Terminal Velocity

Transfer Stain
Viscosity
Void Pattern
Wipe

Bloodstain pattern analysis (BPA) is the science of examining and interpreting blood present at a bloodshed event in order to determine what events occurred, in what order, and who possibly left the stains. As with any area of forensic science, this discipline seeks to define the facts surrounding the incident in question. The volume of blood, patterns present, shape characteristics, dispersion, and number of bloodstains present within a scene all play a role in the evaluation and analysis. The training and experience of the crime scene investigator will determine the accuracy of the analysis. BPA is not the answer to all of the questions concerning what happened at the scene of a crime; it is instead a tool within the greater toolbox of crime scene investigation.

History of Bloodstain Pattern Analysis

Much like track impression evidence, the historical origin and skill development of bloodstain analysis most likely dates from the earliest of mankind's hunting efforts. Paleolithic art

---

VIEW FROM AN EXPERT

Alternative Explanations

No competent forensic scientist ever dismisses the possibility that an alternative explanation to his or her own may also explain the physical evidence in any given case. I have observed incompetent "experts" in the discipline of bloodstain pattern interpretation expound on their scenarios and suggest that "these are the undeniable facts and my interpretation is the only possible way in which this pattern could have been produced." Unfortunately, in many instances, these "experts" were proven to be wrong.

One of the most common mistakes the biased "expert" makes is to interpret very finely divided bloodstains as having resulted from a high-velocity impact, specifically from gunshot. The expression that keeps the door open to alternative explanations is "This pattern is similar to, and consistent with, those that result from high-velocity impact such as gunshot." Expirated bloodstains from the nose or mouth can appear identical to those produced from a gunshot wound; even flicking the bristles of a toothbrush that has been dipped into blood will also give identical results. The experienced forensics witness knows the words "never" and "always" should be deleted from his or her vocabulary. "Most unlikely" and "almost always" better demonstrate the objectivity of the witness.

In a significant case in Quebec, a man had been beaten to death in his bedroom. Medium-velocity-impact spatter covered the bed sheets and one of the two suspects had a multitude of small bloodstains on the front of his shirt. The analyst took a look at this shirt and concluded that it was a spatter pattern and placed the accused in the bedroom at the time of the beating. Furthermore, the second burglar told the police that it was the accused who committed the crime and, not surprisingly, the accused said that it was his partner who did the beating. The accused was convicted largely, if not entirely, on the testimony of the bloodspatter "expert" who placed him in the bedroom at the time of the beating.

documents the skill of early human hunters and shows the use of blood tracks to locate prey. Biblical passages relate bloodstains with injury and with mortality. So, it is reasonable to assume that humans have been analyzing bloodstain patterns for well over 4,000 years. Investigators have been attempting to interpret bloodstains for as long as there have been criminal investigations; however, bloodstain analysis as a distinct area of forensic science and crime scene investigation appears to be a more modern occurrence.

The early 1900s saw several prominent scholars and scientists researching and experimenting with blood dynamics and properties of human blood. While numerous individuals recognized the importance of such matters, historically BPA as a forensic discipline is credited to Dr. Paul Leland Kirk of the University of California at Berkeley. In his book *Crime Investigation* (1952, 1974), in the chapter "Blood: Physical Investigation," Kirk explains the benefits of and application of BPA within criminal investigations. Kirk put his teachings into practice when submitting an affidavit of his examination of bloodstain evidence and findings in the case of the *State of Ohio v. Samuel H. Sheppard*, in 1955. In this case,

---

When the accused's shirt was examined by another expert five years later, it was clear that the spatter pattern was not made by blood projected from the beating. Rather, when the innocent burglar entered the bedroom, he was shocked to discover that his partner had killed the victim. He bent down onto the bed and transferred small, fresh bloodstains to the front of his shirt in a mirror image of the pattern on the bed sheet. Had the "expert" who testified for the prosecution taken time to look at the bloodstains on the shirt using a low-power (20x) stereo binocular microscope, he would have seen that all of the blood was on the surface of the fibers with none between the weave pattern—in the "valleys"—as would have occurred with projected blood.

The report of the second expert was so convincing that one of the three judges[1] who heard his testimony during the defense attorney's case wrote that "the nature of the proof, the relevance of the proof, credibility of the expert, and the impact of this proof on the verdict are sufficient to order a new trial in this case." Witnesses are not usually allowed to give evidence in appellate courts. This was the first time a witness ever gave evidence in an appellate court in Quebec, and only the second time in Canada.

When a forensic scientist believes that he or she is right they should not hesitate to give their opinion with conviction, however, when they just think they are right, they should not hesitate to admit there may be an alternative explanation which they have not yet considered, whatever it might be.

Herbert Leon MacDonell, ScD
Director, Laboratory of Forensic Science

---

[1] Judge Michael Prolux, Appellate Court of Quebec, Montreal, February 1, 1994.

Courtesy of Herbert Leon MacDonell, ScD, Director, Laboratory of Forensic Science.

Dr. Kirk testified as to the consideration of drying times for blood and pattern evaluation in an effort to explain the events that had occurred at the Sheppard residence, leading to the death of his wife.

This case and Dr. Kirk's textbook are considered an impetus for the modern forensic study of bloodstain pattern analysis. Afterward, the number of authors postulating on such matters began to increase in a dramatic fashion. One such author was Herbert Leon MacDonell, whose research recreated bloodstains observed at crime scenes. His initial book was *Flight Characteristics of Human Blood and Stain Patterns* (1971). While numerous texts have been published on the topic since, MacDonell is credited for reawakening the discipline and providing the stimulus for professional organizations such as the International Association of Bloodstain Pattern Analysts (IABPA) and International Association of Identification (IAI) to develop and/or begin to offer training and certification in this field. As a result of this professional and academic growth, the discipline as a whole has gained far greater acceptance within courtrooms across the United States.

Properties of Human Blood

A normal healthy adult has approximately 4.5 to 6.0 liters (L) of blood in his or her body. This is important for a crime scene investigator to be aware of, because if there appears to be a volume of blood as large as this, then either the evidence suggests that the injury that resulted in the bloodshed was inconsistent with the sustenance of life or there is blood present from several individuals that has resulted in the volume observed.

Blood will act in a predictable manner when subjected to external forces. The surface tension of blood is slightly less than that of water. Blood falls in a spheroid configuration, not "tear drop" shape as typically drawn and portrayed. The volume of a typical or average drop of blood has been reported to be approximately 0.05 milliliters (ml), with an average diameter of 4.56 mm (while in the air) (Saferstein, 2010). Molecules of blood are mutually attracted to one another, which is called **viscosity**. The more viscous a fluid, the more slowly it flows. Blood is approximately six times more viscous than water and has a specific gravity slightly higher than water.

Bloodstains dry from their perimeter inward toward their center. As the distal margins of the stain dry, they become more resistant to disruption or removal than the stain's still wet interior. As a general guide, a minimum of one minute is required for sufficient drying to create a perimeter stain. Because the drying time of blood is dependent upon the volume of blood deposited, the surface on which the blood is deposited, and the environmental conditions to which it is subjected, this interval may be experimentally determined at the discretion of the blood pattern analysis expert (BPAE).

All of the aforementioned characteristics of blood allow for its subsequent interpretation within the context of crime scene investigation.

Bloodstain Pattern Interpretation

The ability to interpret a bloodshed event should be viewed as a forensic tool that assists the crime scene investigator to better understand what took place and what could not have taken place during a bloodshed event. Information obtained may assist in apprehending a suspect, corroborating a witness' statements, interrogating a suspect, allowing for reconstruction of an event, and possibly exonerating an accused.

Through the careful examination of the physical evidence (bloodstains), the investigator will be able to deduce specific information with regard to the events that occurred during the bloodshed event. The crime scene investigator will observe three primary areas pertaining to the bloodstains in order to assemble his or her findings. The crime scene investigator will look at the size, the shape, and the distribution of the bloodstains. Each of these, separate and in combination, will result in information specific to the event.

Scientific Working Group on Bloodstain Pattern Analysis

Formed in 2002 by the Federal Bureau of Investigation, The Scientific Working Group on Bloodstain Pattern Analysis (SWGSTAIN) was developed "to promote and enhance the development of quality forensic bloodstain pattern analysis (BPA) practices through the collaborative efforts of government forensic laboratories, law enforcement, private industry, and academia" (SWGSTAIN, 2012).

According to the organization's website, SWGSTAIN seeks to:

1. Discuss, share and compare stain pattern analysis methods, protocols, and research for the enhancement of forensic bloodstain pattern analysis (BPA) techniques.

2. Design and encourage the implementation by practitioners of a quality assurance program in bloodstain pattern analysis and to advise the forensic bloodstain pattern analysis community of emerging quality assurance issues.

3. Discuss and share strategies for presenting bloodstain pattern information to meet Frye, Daubert, or other jurisdictional admissibility challenges.

4. Address the development and/or validation of forensic bloodstain pattern analysis methods.

5. Design and encourage the adoption of guidelines to insure the quality of specialized training in the field of bloodstain pattern analysis.

Source: Scientific Working Group on Bloodstain Pattern Analysis. (2012). Home page. Retrieved from http://www.swgstain.org.

Bloodstain Shape

Shape is one of the chief sources of information that a bloodstain possesses. Careful analysis of bloodstain shape will allow the crime scene investigator to determine the direction from which the blood originated. This can be extremely beneficial in helping to understand what occurred at the scene of a crime. In order to determine **directionality** or the direction that blood was traveling, a crime scene investigator need only look at the shape of the bloodstain. The narrow end of an elongated bloodstain will typically point in the direction of travel (**Figure 11–1**). For many stains, particularly those deposited on nonporous surfaces, it may be possible to determine the direction a drop was moving by a comparison of the edge characteristics in the two extreme margins of the stain. That distal margin that displays lesser disruption with respect to its opposing margin was deposited first. The margin that displays the greater disruption was deposited second. In this way, a bloodstain can be said to have a directionality that tracks along the path of its long axis and in the direction that encounters its edge of lesser disruption first and the edge of greater disruption next (**Figure 11–2**).

However, the information derived from a bloodstain's shape does not stop there. When a source of blood is impacted or otherwise subjected to sufficient force, blood droplets will be dispersed, and the resulting blood droplets will be projected upon target surfaces at various impact angles. If the crime scene investigator was to draw an imaginary line through the long axis of each bloodstain in the direction opposite of observed travel they would arrive at a two-dimensional point known as an **area of convergence** (**Figure 11–3**). It is at this point that an event occurred (i.e., impact) that led to the subsequent dispersal of the blood. It must

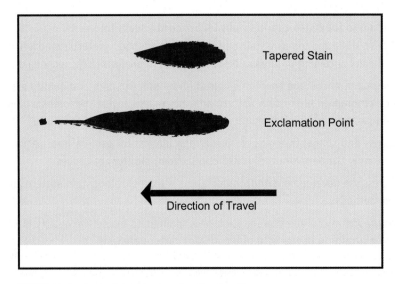

FIGURE 11–1 Determining blood spatter directionality

Courtesy of Erica Milks, University of Wisconsin-Platteville.

FIGURE 11–2   Example of blood spatter directionality

be remembered that this is only a two-dimensional explanation (X and Y axis) and does not determine how far away from the area that the blood event originated; it instead gives an area in which to determine such information. For instance, once the area of convergence within a room has been determined, in order to determine the origin distance from the wall or floor within the area of that room, a third dimension must be considered.

By establishing the impact angles of representative bloodstains and projecting their trajectories back to a common axis (Z) extended at 90 degrees from the intersection of the X and

FIGURE 11–3 Determining area of convergence from blood spatter evidence

Courtesy of Ellie Bruchez, University of Wisconsin-Platteville. Adapted from Bevel, Tom, and Ross M. Gardner (2002),"Bloodstain Pattern Analysis", 2nd Ed.

Y axis, an approximate location of where the blood source was when it was impacted may be established. This area is known as the **area of origin** (**Figure 11–4**).

However, in order to locate this, the examined blood must be analyzed to determine its angle of impact.

Angle of Impact

If blood impacts a target surface at 90 degrees, the resulting bloodstain generally will be circular in shape. Blood droplets that strike a target at an angle less than 90 degrees will create elliptical bloodstains (**Figure 11–5**). This is helpful in understanding the approximate origin of a bloodstain; however, a crime scene investigator is able to gain a much closer approximation when he or she realizes that a mathematical relationship exists between the width and length of a bloodstain, which will allow for the calculation of the angle of impact for the original spherical drop of blood.

To calculate this angle, a crime scene investigator must first measure the width and length of the bloodstain to be analyzed. The width of the bloodstain is then divided by its length. When measuring the length of a bloodstain it is important not to include in this measurement the tail portion of the stain. Inclusion of these trailing edge characteristics in the measurement of length may result in the underestimation of the impact angle of a stain (**Figure 11–6**).

Next, with the help of a scientific calculator, the crime scene investigator should take the resulting answer from the previous computation and utilize the function key, arc sin, sin-1, or inverse sin function, and the corresponding angle of impact will be displayed. A quick test of this will show the earlier summation of a circular bloodstain to be true. For a circular

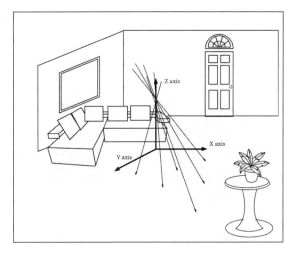

FIGURE 11–4 Determining area of origin for blood spatter

Courtesy of Ellie Bruchez, University of Wisconsin-Platteville. Adapted from Bevel, Tom, and Ross M. Gardner (2002),"Bloodstain Pattern Analysis", 2nd Ed.

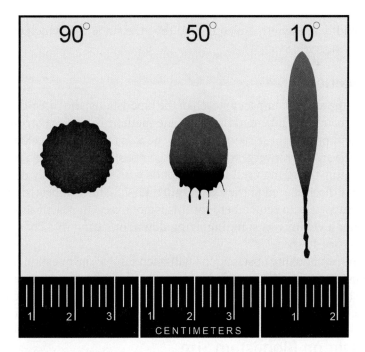

FIGURE 11–5 Determining blood spatter angle of impact (variance between 90 degree and others)

Courtesy of Dana Gavelinger, University of Wisconsin-Platteville.

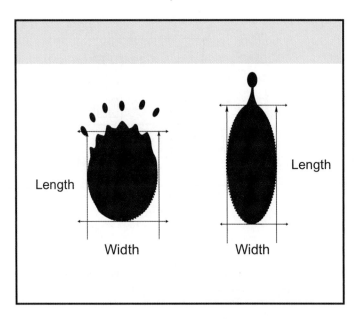

FIGURE 11–6   Measuring bloodstain dimensions to determine angle of impact
Courtesy of Erica Milks, University of Wisconsin-Platteville.

bloodstain, the width and length are equal and thus the sin is 1.0, which corresponds to an impact angle of 90 degrees.

Stringing a Scene

After establishing the angle of impact for each of the bloodstains, the three-dimensional origin of the bloodstain pattern can be determined. One method is to place strings at the base of each bloodstain and project these strings back to the axis that has been extended 90 degrees up or away from the area of convergence. This is accomplished by placing a protractor on each string and then lifting the string until it corresponds with the previously determined impact angle. The string is then secured to the axis (**Figure 11–7**). This is repeated for each analyzed bloodstain. It is important to remember that this is not exact. In practical terms it is used to determine whether a victim was standing, lying down, or sitting in a chair when the blood was spattered (**Figure 11–8**).

Common sense and quality observations will often resolve the question of where someone was when injuries were inflicted. For instance, if no blood spatter appears on a tabletop or chair seat, but spatter associated with a gunshot is found on the underside of the table and chair, the obvious conclusion is that the victim was on or near the floor when shot.

Effect of Height on Bloodstain Size

A blood drop falling through the air will increase its velocity until the force of air resistance that opposes the drop is equal to the force of the downward gravitational pull. At this point

FIGURE 11–7   Determining blood spatter angle of impact (stringing)

Courtesy of Ellie Bruchez, University of Wisconsin-Platteville. Adapted from James, Stuart H., and William G. Eckert, (2003). "Interpretation of Bloodstain Evidence at Crime Scenes."

FIGURE 11–8   Example of stringing a crime scene

FIGURE 11–9   Impact of height on diameter of blood evidence
Courtesy of Erica Milks, University of Wisconsin-Platteville.

the droplet is said to have achieved its **terminal velocity**. Blood therefore falls in a predictable manner and a typical droplet of blood that has a volume of 0.05 ml will then produce bloodstains of increasing diameters when dropped from increasing increments of height onto a smooth, hard surface. The measured diameters will range from 13.0 to 21.5 mm over a dropping range of 6 inches to 7 feet (Saferstein, 2010) (**Figure 11–9**). Drops that fall distances greater than 7 feet, however, will not produce stains with any significant or even perceptible increases in their diameter, as the droplets have reached their terminal velocity and cannot impact the target surface with any greater force.

Types of Bloodstains

All bloodstains left at a crime scene can be grouped into one of four categories: passive, transfer, projected/impact, and miscellaneous (**Table 11–1**). This grouping was first suggested by Jozef Radziki (1960) and is for the large part still in use today.

Passive Bloodstains

Passive bloodstains consist of clots, drips, flows, and blood pools. They are not related to a specific action within the context of the scene with regard to bloodshed violence. Instead, they are the aftermath associated with this violence, as the resulting bloodshed begins to move and cure due to environmental and gravitational forces.

TABLE 11–1 Categories of Bloodstains

Passive	Transfer	Projected/Impact	Miscellaneous
Drips	Pattern	Arterial spurt/gush	Voids
Flow	Wipe	Cast-off	Fly/insect spots
Clot	Swipe	Expiratory	Skeletonized
Pool		Spatter (impact)	

Drip (Blood in Blood)

Drip patterns result from blood dripping into blood. Drip patterns generally display satellite staining that results from the deposition of small droplets that are ejected from the blood pool upon its being struck by a falling drop. Because these ejected blood droplets generally follow arching trajectories, they strike the surface at or near 90 degrees and result in circular to near circular stains. Additionally, because they are generally slow moving, the satellite stains surrounding the central pool of a drip pattern often display an observable thickness because their droplets lack the energy necessary to fully spread themselves over the target surface upon striking it.

The satellite stains in the lateral margins of a drip pattern on a vertical surface often display evidence of gravity effects. Such satellite stains display directionality toward the horizontal surface because the droplets deposited were on the downward flight path of their travel arch. Also, the size of the satellite stains on a vertical surface will generally decrease as the distance from the blood pool that resulted in the drip pattern increases.

Single drops of blood will produce small spatters around the parent stain as a result of striking a rough surface. This is referred to as *secondary* or *satellite* spatter. When multiple free-falling drops of blood are produced from a stationary source onto a horizontal surface, particular drip patterns will result that are large and irregular in shape, with a satellite spatter.

Flow Patterns

Flow patterns are a change in the shape and direction of a bloodstain due to the influence of gravity or movement of the surface and are generally observed in circumstances where a volume of liquid blood moves freely along a downward path.

Flow patterns also may display one or more long, narrow stains that may or may not originate from a distinct bloodstain pattern. Often the terminal end of this narrow stain will show a thickening that represents the residual blood volume whose weight was not sufficient to continue its flow. These narrow stains always will extend in the direction of gravity's influence on the object as it rested at the time of blood flow.

A flow pattern that does not extend downward on the object or surface as observed indicates that the object or surface was moving during blood flow or that it was moved after blood flow had ceased.

Clot

Clotted blood is blood that has undergone the physiological process of fibrin formation that congeals the solid elements of blood into a gelatinous mass. Blood that is shed from the body in sufficient volume to remain liquid for an extended period of time may begin to display clot formation. The minimum time necessary for clot formation to begin generally ranges from 3 to 15 minutes. This time course is dependent on many factors including the volume of blood deposited, the surface on which it is deposited, and the environmental conditions to which it is subjected.

Large blood pools that collect on nonporous surfaces may remain liquid for a sufficient period of time to display clot formation. Blood pools that undergo clot formation generally display large gelatinous masses with serum collections in the peripheral margins of the blood pool.

Individual stains that display clotted material may be produced when already clotted blood is subjected to disruption by a force or action. Such stains may display a central region of dense staining surrounded by a ring of less dense staining. This "bull's eye" or "fried egg" appearance is the result of the deposition of gelatinous clotted material with subsequent radial diffusion of the remaining liquid serum in porous material or continued clot retraction on nonporous surfaces.

Clotted material in the stain(s) of a bloodstain pattern may indicate that the blood that created the pattern was shed and remained undisturbed for a period of time sufficient for clot formation. In this way, the presence of clots within a bloodstain pattern may indicate that some period of time elapsed between the event(s) that resulted in bloodshed and clot formation.

It may not be possible to determine the actual interval of time between the blood's shedding and clot formation, however, unless ancillary information is available concerning the volume of bloodshed and the environmental conditions to which it was subjected. As a result, while the presence of clotted blood within the stains of a bloodstain pattern may indicate a passage of time, care must be taken in any attempt to refine the estimate of such an elapsed interval. At the discretion of the crime scene investigator, this interval may be experimentally determined.

Pooling

This pattern occurs when gravitational forces pull blood to the lowest possible level and there is an accumulation of blood that develops, sometimes referred to as a *blood basin*. This type of pattern allows the crime scene investigator to gauge how much blood could possibly have been lost from the victim, whether or not there was any movement of the victim from the area where the pooling occurred, and a timeframe (due to clotting and drying of the blood within the pool).

Transfer Bloodstains

Transfer stain patterns (sometimes referred to as *contact* patterns) are generally indistinct stains that can be of virtually any size or shape. The physical appearance of such stains is generally mottled with numerous variations in their color and/or density. The shape of a contact/transfer pattern may retain some of the physical characteristics of the object that created it. In this way, the shape of a contact/transfer pattern may suggest the object that created it through the recognizable patent image (**Figure 11–10**).

FIGURE 11–10   Photograph of blood evidence at a crime scene

The direction of motion of a transfer pattern may be determined from the general density distribution of the stain. Generally, a transfer pattern is heaviest in that portion of the stain deposited first, and its density decreases as blood is removed from the object.

Motion Determination from Observation of Transfer Patterns

- Feathered margins may be created as an object gradually comes into or loses contact with a target surface. Generally, feathering displays a gradual decrease in density in the direction of an object's movement. As a result, the trailing edge of a contact/transfer pattern may display lightened staining with respect to the leading edge.

- The presence of distinct front boundaries deposited along the margins of a contact/transfer pattern may allow a direction of movement to be determined. These front boundaries are the result of blood that collects along the leading edge of an object. Because these front boundaries are left where an object loses contact with a surface, they are most numerous in that portion of the stain deposited later.

Swipe

A **swipe** occurs when a bloodied surface rubs across a nonbloodied one. This is beneficial to the crime scene investigator as it will usually give some indication as to movement within the scene. There will be an initial point of impact that leads toward a feathered or disappearing edge. Movement is toward the feathered edge (**Figure 11–11**).

FIGURE 11–11 An example of a swipe pattern

Courtesy of Dana Gevelinger, University of Wisconsin-Platteville.

Wipe

A **wipe** occurs when a nonbloodied surface moves through/across a stationary one. This type of pattern is also able to give the crime scene investigator an idea as to movement at the crime scene, just as with a swipe pattern (**Figure 11–12**).

Pattern Transfer

When an object wet with blood comes into contact with an unstained object or secondary surface, a *blood transfer pattern* occurs. A recognizable image of all, or a portion, of the original surface may be observed in the pattern (e.g., footwear impression, fingerprint).

Projected Bloodstain Patterns

Projected patterns are produced by blood released under pressure such as arterial spurting. These patterns generally result from volumes of blood larger than those that produce passive drop stains or other dynamic patterns (e.g., impact patterns).

If the trajectory of a bloodstream strikes an intervening target, a relatively large central stain is created that is surrounded by numerous spines of varying lengths. The appearance of this peripheral staining may be of value in assessing whether a volume of blood struck an object or surface forcefully. Projected blood streams that do not strike a vertical surface continue along individual parabolic flight paths until they deposit on a horizontal surface.

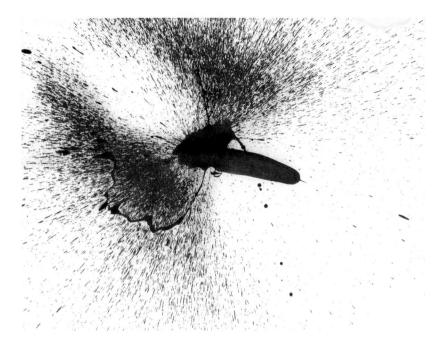

FIGURE 11–12   An example of a wipe pattern (center area which is blurred/smudged), present within impact spatter

Courtesy of Dana Gevelinger, University of Wisconsin-Platteville.

Cast-off

Cast-off patterns are those created when blood is released or thrown from a blood-bearing object in motion (**Figure 11–13**). They can be the result of two basic actions: (1) arc cast-off patterns created when blood is released from an object through the influence of centrifugal acceleration and (2) the instances of cessation, or stop-action, when blood is thrown from an object when the object's motion is abruptly stopped.

Arc Cast-off Patterns. The individual stains of an arc cast-off pattern are generally distributed in a linear configuration and may be suitable for approximating the plane in space through which the blood-bearing object was moved. It may be possible to determine the object's direction of travel based on the shapes of the individual stains within the pattern. The presence of an arc cast-off pattern on a piece of clothing or other evidence item may indicate its association with a blow or other source of cast-off action.

Cessation/Stop-Action Cast-Off Patterns. The individual stains of a cessation cast-off pattern are generally smaller in size than those resulting from passive blood drops and can be a range of shapes. Cessation cast-off patterns generally do not display the linear arrangement of individual stains characteristic of arc cast-off patterns. Because cessation cast-off patterns are created as a blood-bearing object is abruptly stopped, such patterns could be produced by one or more of the impacts received by a blood source. If the blood source receiving the multiple blows is stationary, cessation cast-off patterns may be present within the context of other bloodstain

FIGURE 11–13   Example of a cast-off bloodstain pattern
Courtesy of Dana Gevelinger, University of Wisconsin-Platteville.

pattern types such as impact patterns. In such circumstances, care must be taken in the selection of individual stains for impact site reconstruction to avoid use of stains of cessation cast-off origin.

Determination of Number of Blows

The number of cast-off patterns present may be used to estimate the minimum number of blows received by a given blood source. Because a blow applied to a blood source may not result in the creation of a cast-off pattern, however, it may not be possible to determine with certainty the specific number of blows received.

Handedness Determinations

Handedness determinations may be possible when the locations of the cast-off patterns are limited by the relative positions of the individuals and objects within the scene itself. In the absence of either ancillary information or spatial constraints at the scene, the appearance and location of cast-off patterns are not generally sufficient information on which to base a determination of the handedness of an individual wielding an object.

Not Produced from Initial Impact

Spatter and cast-off patterns are created with subsequent blows to the same general area where a wound has occurred and blood has accumulated. As the object of the injury is swung away and toward the body centrifugal force is generated. If this force is great enough to overcome the adhesive force that holds the blood to the object, blood will be flung from the object and form a cast-off bloodstain pattern. These are typically linear in distribution and frequently are larger in size than impact blood spatters.

Spatter

When a bloodshed event occurs at a crime scene, typically it will result in a spatter pattern. There is no "L" in the word. Those new to the field of bloodstain pattern analysis are constantly reminded that in BPA *spatter* is investigated and documented, not *splatter*. Some of this is semantics, as "splatter" is a verb, and "spatter" can be a verb, noun, and adjective. Truthfully, spatter is a more worthwhile and more descriptive term.

Blood spatter is defined as a random distribution of bloodstains that vary in size and may be produced by a variety of mechanisms. The pattern is created when sufficient force is available to overcome the surface tension of the blood. A crime scene investigator should be aware that a single small stain does not constitute a spatter pattern. Recognition of spatter patterns is important in interpreting the action and events that took place at the scene of the crime. Spatter will vary considerably between gunshot, beating, and stabbing events, and recognition of such may assist the crime scene investigator in determining the mechanism that resulted in the bloodshed. Oftentimes recognition of spatter may allow the determination of an area or location of the origin of the blood source. Recalling Locard's Exchange Principle, if blood spatter is found on a suspect's clothing, it may place them at the scene of a violent altercation.

Impact Patterns

Impact patterns are bloodstain patterns created by a blow or some other force that results in the random distribution of smaller drops of blood. They are therefore technically a subcategory of spatter. Impact patterns may be used to determine the point where the force encountered the blood source (i.e., the impact site).

While an impact pattern may display characteristics indicative of the nature of the blow or force that created it, determinations of the specific object and/or details of the impacting event generally require ancillary information. This information may include investigative information (e.g., crime scene reports, etc.), reconstruction of the point (area) of convergence, point (area) of origin, and/or experimentation. In some circumstances, however, this ancillary information may prove to be insufficient for such determinations.

Low-Velocity Impact Spatter. Stains relating to a low-velocity impact are considered to involve force that is equivalent to the earth's normal gravitational pull, up to a force of 5 feet per second (Bevel & Gardner, 2002). The resulting stain is typically large and has a diameter greater than 4 millimeters (mm). Such bloodstains are usually associated with blood dripping from an injury or weapon (**Figure 11–14**).

Medium-Velocity Impact Spatter. According to Bevel and Gardner (2002), bloodstains associated with this group are typically associated with a pattern and have diameters ranging from 1 to 4 mm; they may be smaller or larger depending on force of impact and quantity of available exposed blood. The force necessary to produce medium-velocity impact spatter is suggested to be between 5 and 25 feet per second (**Figure 11–15**). It must be remembered by the crime scene investigator, however, that the first blow rarely produces spatter. Bloodstains produced from this impact group usually involve those associated with beating and stabbing events. Cast-off stains will sometimes be grouped into this category as well.

FIGURE 11–14   An example of low-velocity impact spatter

Courtesy of Dana Gevelinger, University of Wisconsin-Platteville.

FIGURE 11–15   An example of medium-velocity impact spatter

Courtesy of Dana Gevelinger, University of Wisconsin-Platteville.

High-Velocity Impact Spatter. These stains typically have an associated diameter of less than 1 mm and are associated with a pattern. The force necessary to produce these stains is generally in excess of 100 feet per second (Bevel & Gardner, 2002). Stains associated with this category usually involve those stemming from a gunshot, explosion, or power tool and high-speed machinery injuries.

Stains associated with gunshots may produce minute spatters of blood that may be less than 0.1 mm in diameter. This will create a very distinct "misting" effect that is not seen in beatings, stabbings, or satellite spatter created by blood dripping into blood (**Figure 11–16**). These stains also may exhibit spatter ranging in size from less than 0.1 mm up to several mm. Size range is dependent on the quantity of available blood, the caliber of the weapon, the location and number of shots, and factors such as hair, clothing, etc. When associated with an entrance wound, it is referred to as *back spatter* or *blowback*. This spatter may be found on the weapon and the shooter, especially the hand. When associated with an exit wound, it is referred to as *forward spatter*.

Arterial Spurt

When an artery is breached, blood is projected from it in varying amounts. This pattern can vary in size from large gushing or spurting patterns to very small spray types of patterns.

Projected/impact patterns produced by arterial spurting sometimes may be identified by their forceful appearance as an inverted V-shape pattern. Because the inverted V-shape (if present) is the result of the differential intravascular blood pressure that cycles as the heart contracts and relaxes, it may be possible to identify those portions of the patterns created by less forceful heartbeats (**Figure 11–17**).

Expired

Expired patterns are created when blood is blown out of the nose, mouth, or wound as a result of air pressure and/or airflow and often display numerous, relatively small stain sizes that may vary in shape.

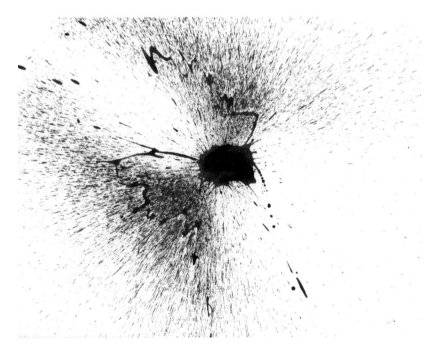

FIGURE 11–16 An example of high-velocity impact spatter (area to the top and lower left of the bloodshed event center)

Courtesy of Dana Gevelinger, University of Wisconsin-Platteville.

FIGURE 11–17 An example of a projected pattern created by an arterial breach

Courtesy of Dana Gevelinger, University of Wisconsin-Platteville.

To differentiate between the individual stains of an expired or impact pattern, serological tests for the presence of amylase may be performed. Additionally, a histological search for squamous epithelial cells may be performed. The presence of bubble rings within the individual stains may also be indicative of an expired pattern.

Identification of expired patterns must be augmented with ancillary information such as photographs, emergency room and autopsy reports, etc. Should such documentation exist and fail to support the existence of a source for an expired pattern, this information may be used to support the conclusion that a specific stain pattern cannot be of expiratory origin.

As a result of trauma, blood will often accumulate in the lungs, sinuses, and airway passages of the victim. In a living victim, this blood will be forcefully expelled from the nose and/or mouth in order to free the airways. These stains may appear diluted due to saliva or nasal secretions, and they may also contain tiny air bubbles.

Miscellaneous Bloodstains

Void

If there is an item or individual between the area of impact and the surrounding surfaces, the object will create a **void pattern** upon the surrounding wall or items. A void is an area that is absent of any projected blood. This void pattern often can be used to determine the size and shape of the interfering object (**Figure 11–18**).

Fly/Insect Spots

This category is included because often the activity of flies within a crime scene can present the crime scene investigator with confusing information about the bloodstain pattern analysis, incorrectly appearing as spatter. Flies may regurgitate, excrete, or track minute amounts of blood around a scene or onto items within the scene, which can appear to be blood spatter but in fact is not a result of the actual bloodshed event.

Skeletonized

When the center of a dried bloodstain flakes away and leaves a visible outer rim, the result is referred to as a **skeletonized stain**. Another type of skeletonized bloodstain occurs when the central area of a partially dry bloodstain is altered by contact or a wiping motion.

Stains are created when a partially dried bloodstain is disrupted by any subsequent action. Such stains retain their outer dried peripheral outlines, but generally the central area will have been partially or completely removed. Because drying time is dependent upon the surface on which blood is deposited and the environmental conditions to which it is then subjected, estimates of drying times must be experimentally determined.

FIGURE 11–18 An example of a void pattern

Courtesy of Dana Gevelinger, University of Wisconsin-Platteville.

Target Surface Considerations

No matter how far a drop of blood falls, it will not break into smaller droplets or spatters unless something disrupts the surface tension and cohesive properties of the droplet. In general, a hard, smooth, nonporous surface such as glass will create little if any spatter. However, in contrast, a rough surface texture such as untreated wood or concrete will create a significant amount of spatter.

Documentation of Bloodstain Evidence

Document the size, shape, and distribution of stains and patterns. Pictures with and without a scale of reference are required in order to accurately re-create the events that occurred to cause the bloodshed. Photographs, sketches, video, and notes all should be done. Overall, mid-range, and close-up photos are suggested in order for the entire event to be understood. If

Certification in Blood Pattern Analysis

In an effort to ensure scientific validity and court acceptance of BPA as a forensic discipline, the IAI has specified specific requirements for those who would seek certification within the field of BPA. According to the organization's web site, they are:

A minimum of forty (40) hours of education in an approved workshop providing theory, study and practice:

- Flight characteristics and stain patterns
- Examination and identification of bloodstain evidence
- Documentation of blood stains and patterns

This forty (40) hour course must include the following:

- Flight characteristics and stain patterns
- Oral and/or visual presentation of physical activity of blood droplets illustrating blood as fluid being acted upon by motion or force. Past research, treatise or other reference materials for the student.
- Laboratory exercises that document bloodstains and standards by previous research.

only close-up photos are taken, the analyst will not have any way to comprehend the overall pattern and distribution of the blood later. Photos and sketches should be completed in such a manner as to allow a third party to utilize the documentation to place the bloodstain patterns and articles of evidence back in their original locations. This process is typically referred to as *reconstruction*. This reconstruction can sometimes involve experimentation as to the timing and manner of bloodstain distribution. In order for this to occur, a crime scene investigator must attempt to re-create every aspect of the crime scene environment in order to determine the age of bloodstains, clots, and patterns. Such re-creation and replication will be necessary in order for associated analytical findings to be admissible within court. For this reason, it is suggested that such experiments be left up to an experienced pattern analyst.

Exercises must include but not be limited to the following:

Falling Blood

- Spot size related to distance fallen and blood volume variations.

Surface Considerations

- Texture: smooth, rough, porous
- Flat or angular surfaces
- Drying time

Impact Angle Determinations

Blood in motion striking a horizontal surface or vertical target. Study of spot size, shape, and spatter characteristics related to:

- Distance fallen
- Speed of travel
- Direction of travel

Increased Blood Volumes

- Stain shape and satellite spatter related to volume and distance
- Radial patterns
- Dripped
- Splashed

Flow Patterns (horizontal/vertical)

- Accumulative/passive
- Secondary, altered

Projected Bloodstains and Patterns

- Static blood affected by impact of object (shoe, hand, etc.)
- Spurted, gushed, expectorated, respirated
- Cast-off: arc of the swing, number of swings or patterns, weapon variations
- Forceful impact spatter patterns

- Blunt force, explosive (gunshot)
- Size, shape, and distribution of spots related to degree of force and distance traveled

Transfer Stains and Impression Patterns

- Secondary targets, intermediate or intervening objects, images and impressions, wipe and swipe patterns (hair, skin, cloth, etc.)

Other Topics Suggested (not required)

- Correlation of stain and patterns to the scene surroundings and/or body trauma
- Serological/DNA considerations
- Chemical and light source absorption and enhancement
- Blood detection/collection techniques
- Stain pattern reconstruction

Courtesy of the International Association of Identification and the Bloodstain Certification Board (2009).

WRAP UP

Chapter Summary

Bloodstain pattern analysis is a contribution to the process of crime scene investigation. It may not necessarily be conclusive by itself. When combined with photographs, sketches, witness statements, and other crime scene evidence, BPA may help to provide for a clearer explanation of the events and ordering of events within a crime scene. When conducted properly, BPA is considered to be a science because the patterns and interpretation of those patterns can be replicated under controlled circumstances.

Review Questions

1. _____ is the science of examining and interpreting blood present at a bloodshed event in order to determine what events occurred, in what order, and who possibly left the stains.

2. What were MacDonell's contributions to BPA?

3. About how much blood is present in a normal, healthy adult body?

4. Identify the three factors whereby an investigator may deduce bloodstain information.

5. The point at which the impact event occurred that led to the subsequent dispersal of the blood is known as the _____.

6. Explain how to calculate the angle of impact of a blood droplet.

7. If the length of a blood droplet is 3.2 cm and the width is 1.8 cm, what was the angle of impact?

8. What angle of impact produces circular blood droplets?
   a. 30°
   b. 45°
   c. 65°
   d. 90°

9. The point at which the force of air resistance that opposes the drop is equal to the force of the downward gravitational pull is known as _____.

10. Single drops of blood will produce small spatters around the parent stain as a result of striking a rough surface. This is referred to as_____.

11. Explain the difference between a swipe and a wipe.

12. A _____ pattern is formed when there is an item or individual between the area of impact and the surrounding surfaces.

Case Studies

Research *State of Ohio v. Samuel H. Sheppard* (1955), and explain how the science of blood pattern analysis aided in the interpretation of crime scene evidence related to this case.

Be specific with regard to impact angle, size, distribution, etc., associated with the homicide case in question.

References

Bevel, T. & Gardner, R. M. (2002). *Bloodstain pattern analysis with an introduction to crime scene reconstruction* (3rd ed.). Boca Raton, FL: CRC Press.

Doyle, A. C. (1892). The adventure of the Greek interpreter. In: The adventures of Sherlock Holmes. *Strand Magazine*.

Kirk, P. L. (1974). *Crime investigation* (2nd ed.). New York: John Wiley & Sons.

International Association of Identification (IAI). (2012). Bloodstain pattern examiner examiner certification requirements. Retrieved August 5, 2009, from http://www.theiai.org

MacDonnell, H. L. (1971). *Flight characteristics of human blood and stain characteristics*. Washington, DC: National Institute of Law Enforcement and Criminal Justice.

Radziki, J. (1960). *Slady Krwi w Praktyce Sledczej (Bloodstain prints in practice of technology)*. Warsaw, Poland: Bibliotecka Kryminalistyczna.

Saferstein, R. (2010). *Criminalistics: An introduction to forensic science* (9th ed.). Upper Saddle River, NJ: Pearson Prentice Hall.

State of Ohio v. Samuel H. Sheppard, 165 Ohio St. 293, 294, 135 N.E.2d 340, 342 (1956).

Scientific Working Group on Bloodstain Pattern Analysis. (2012). Home page. Retrieved June 26, 2012 from http://www.swgstain.org/

© McMac/ShutterStock, Inc.

LEARNING OBJECTIVES

- Understand how impression evidence documentation, collection, and preservation differs from other physical evidence.
- Know what information can be derived from the proper processing of impression-related evidence.
- Differentiate between compression and striated forms of impression evidence.
- Know how to perform SICAR and understand how it can assist with the interpretation of impression evidence.

Impression Evidence

There is no branch of detective science which is so important and so much neglected as the art of tracing footsteps.

Sherlock Holmes, *A Study in Scarlet*, 1887
Sir Arthur Conan Doyle (1859–1930)

KEY TERMS

Compression Evidence
Electrostatic Lifting
    Device (ELD)

Ligature
Negative Impression

Scraping/Striated Evidence
Shoeprint Image Capture and
    Retrieval (SICAR)

What Is Impression Evidence?

Minute imperfections on a large variety of objects such as tools, footwear, tires, and so on produce markings due to their normal (and sometimes unusual) usage. These markings are often characteristic of the type of tool or object used. In many instances, very small and sometimes microscopically unique markings are left that can be traced directly to the object or instrument in question. Two types of marks are made: compression or scraping/striated evidence.

Compression evidence are those marks left when an instrument is in some way pushed or forced into a material capable of picking up an impression of the tool. These would include shoe, tire, bite marks, impressions left by a hammer hitting a piece of wood, breech mark impressions on shell casings, etc.

Scraping or **striated evidence** are those marks produced by a combination of pressure and sliding contact by the tool, which result in microscopic striations imparted to the surface onto which the tool was worked. These include fired bullet striations, or a screwdriver blade dragged over a surface.

Comparative Examination

Comparative examination is the method by which impression-type evidence is studied. Marks left at the crime scene (or castings of the mark) are compared with test markings made by the tool or object in question. Through careful and often tedious examination of the known and questioned evidence, a determination can be made as to whether or not a particular item was responsible for a specific mark. Often the item/items used to strangle or bind a person can be matched through impression evidence comparison.

Types of Impression Evidence

There are numerous types of impressions that are left at crime scenes or upon victims of crimes. Some examples of impressions typically located during crime scene investigation include:

- Footwear
- Tire
- Bite marks
- Tools
- Ligature/binding
- Fabric

Each is important in its own way and has a specific methodology associated with its documentation, collection, and preservation.

Footwear Impression Evidence

The history of using tracks and footwear as a form of identification is far older than that of fingerprints. Since humans first began hunting animals for food the benefit of tracks was obvious. Through keen observation, humans learned to identify their various prey animals and animal behaviors through the patterns made by animals pads and claws/hooves. Being able to discern the direction of travel, the number of animals present, and even whether an animal was injured due to differences in the gait features present increased the success rate of an efficient hunt. However, such knowledge did not simply apply to the gathering of food. Eventually, humans recognized the significance of such information in helping to solve criminal cases as well.

Footwear identification as a criminal justice application has its first recorded application in Scotland in 1786 in a case that involved the murder of a young girl (Hamm, 1989). An astute investigator noticed some footwear impressions that appeared to be boots, and noted from the markings that they appeared newly patched and had a great deal of nails present. The investigator made a crude casting of the impressions. The investigator, understanding that the majority of homicides involve a known person to the victim, compared the cast impression with boots of individuals who attended the victim's funeral. A suspect was found and his footwear was taken for examination. A further comparison of the suspect's footwear to the casting taken on scene led to his conviction for murder.

As was evidenced early in criminal investigative history, footwear impressions provide an important link between the criminal and the place where the crime occurred. Footwear evidence is viewed as proof that an event occurred or a person was present at a given place. Neil Armstrong's footwear impressions on the Moon are some of the most famous prints that are pointed to as evidence that an event occurred. Although footwear impressions are present at many crime scenes, the quantity found is far less than those that are actually present. It goes without question that there are very few crime scenes where the suspect does not walk to or from the scene of the crime. However, although it has been reported that 30% of all crime scenes contain useful shoeprint marks (Alexandre, 1996), very few agencies actually lift footwear evidence, and even fewer submit the gathered evidence for analysis.

Are we missing something? Is valuable evidence being overlooked due to a lack of training and technology with regard to footwear impression collection and analysis? Or is it simply misinformation and uninformed personnel?

The entire footwear recovery process can be time consuming and extremely labor intensive. The number of footwear evidence found at a scene may be so large that the sheer volume makes the entire process of recovery overwhelming and not at all desirable or cost efficient. However, surely this was the case with fingerprints until the age of computerization and a linked database such as the Automated Fingerprint Identification System (AFIS). So, what is the real reason that footwear evidence is not given as much attention as other areas of forensic evidence collection?

It seems that there is a gap between the usefulness and evidentiary value of footwear impressions and gathering that type of impression evidence. If it could be determined that this was because of a lack of training or technology, misinformation, or skewed views relating to footwear evidence, then the positive conclusion of and response to this gap could provide useful information that may lead to an increase in evidence gathering, which in turn might result in successful prosecutions and increased case closures.

Many hold the belief that footwear evidence is purely circumstantial in nature. While a shoeprint does not itself provide the same level of conclusive evidence as a fingerprint, it can act as valuable corroborating evidence. In many cases, footwear impressions can reveal the type, make, model, description, and approximated or precise size of the footwear of the person who wore them. In addition, the location of footwear impressions at the scene can often help in reconstructing the crime. Footwear impressions at crime scenes can be used to corroborate or refute information provided by witnesses of suspects (Bodziak, 2000). Therefore, this evidence should not be neglected or disregarded because it is considered only circumstantial in nature. It can still prove extremely valuable in supporting or refuting the facts of the case.

The average investigator could list many possible reasons why fingerprints would be left at a crime scene and their probable locations. The same investigators are not usually as knowledgeable about footwear impressions, however. Yet with every step that is taken, whether on soil, snow, concrete, a tile floor, carpeting, glass, a wooden window sill, a piece of paper, a bank counter, or on countless other objects and materials, a representation of the characteristics of the shoe sole can be impressed against and retained by that surface, either visible or in latent form that can later be visualized.

"Because of the direct physical contact under the weight of the wearer, there is no doubt that some type of interaction between the shoe and the substrate occurs with each and every step" (Bodziak, 2000, p. 2). An example of this phenomenon can be found in **Figure 12–1**.

FIGURE 12–1 Scaled photograph of a dusty footwear impression left at a crime scene

Where Can Footwear Impressions Be Found?

Footwear marks might not seem like an obvious source of evidence, particularly as they can be difficult to see and may be present along with footwear marks unrelated to the crime. But they can be unique and, if discovered, can provide evidence that a particular shoe was present at the scene of the crime.

Perhaps it would be easier to locate footwear evidence if the individual attempting to collect the impressions understood the basic premise behind footwear. "Three phenomena occur when someone walks across a surface: static charges are created; the surface deforms; and/or there is an exchange of materials between the shoe and the surface" (Bodziak, 2000, pp. 6–8). Footwear marks are hence either two- or three-dimensional depending on the surface.

In soft surfaces, such as mud or snow, a permanent three-dimensional impression is formed (**Figure 12–2**). But on hard surfaces, such as carpet or tiles, any impression is temporary, as the surface will quickly return to its original shape. However, often there will be a two-dimensional residue of marks on hard surfaces due to the transfer of trace materials. Static charges picked up by footwear facilitate this transfer.

It is imperative that crime scene personnel be aware of the full importance of footwear impressions as physical evidence. When securing the crime scene area, they must preserve all forms of evidence, including footwear impressions. Before beginning the crime scene search, careful thought should be given to understanding what occurred at the crime scene, how footwear impression evidence would be relevant and could contribute to the proof of facts, and what areas of the crime scene might be the most logical to check first for footwear impressions.

FIGURE 12–2 Scaled photograph of a footwear impression in dirt

Then a careful and aggressive search for the footwear impressions should begin. "What is not looked for will not be found!" (Bodziak, 2000, p. 2).

Why Is Footwear Impression Evidence Overlooked?

According to Dwane S. Hilderbrand's book, *Footwear, The Missed Evidence* (1999), there are two major reasons why footwear evidence is overlooked. The first is a lack of training and education in the proper search, collection, and preservation methods, and the second is that the evidence is often undervalued or misunderstood. However, with the proper education in footwear evidence, both of these concerns can be overcome. This type of evidence has great evidentiary value when collected and preserved in the correct manner. As mentioned earlier, footwear evidence can reveal the type of shoe, the make, description, and, in some cases, approximate or precise size. When a crime scene is searched and documented in the correct manner, footwear evidence can either provide or assist in determining the number of suspects, their path, their involvement, and the events that occurred during the crime (Hilderbrand, 1999).

William J. Bodziak, retired Federal Bureau of Investigation (FBI) forensic examiner and author of *Footwear Impression Evidence*, believes that there are a number of reasons that finding footwear impressions at a crime scene is often difficult or why the evidence is simply overlooked. These include: (a) not believing that visible and/or latent footwear impressions will be found at the crime scene and not aggressively searching for them; (b) incomplete searches of the scene, possibly due in part to the inability to determine the exact points of entry and exit. Searches may be incomplete because of the lack of proper knowledge of the ways footwear impressions can occur and how they can be found; (c) arrival at the scene after other persons have trampled over the impression evidence and failure to look for footwear impressions in those areas; (d) the combination of shoe and surface characteristics not being conducive to the production of footwear impression evidence; (e) the impressions were intentionally destroyed by the suspect, and; (f) weather destroyed exterior impressions.

The presence of footwear evidence is almost guaranteed at any crime scene involving crimes against person and property. This evidence probably stands a better chance of being present than fingerprints, yet latent footwear evidence is considered to be low on the list of laboratory examinations. Footwear evidence, like fingerprints, only has to be properly searched for and recovered to be of value (Hamm, 1989). If the submission of impression evidence is low in incidence, it is because individuals responsible for the processing of the scenes are not making an effort to obtain this meaningful type of evidence. The reasons for first response officers failing to make an effort to protect scenes and recover footwear evidence can probably be traced to a lack of training in the value of footwear impressions or not being comfortable with the methods of how to properly recover the impression evidence.

Is Footwear Evidence Undervalued or Misunderstood?

Many times, courts have ruled that footwear impression evidence falls under reliable technical or specialized knowledge (such as in *Daubert v. Merrell Dow Pharmaceuticals, 509 U.S. (1993)* and *Kumho Tire Co. v. Carmichael [97–1709], 526 U.S. 137 [1999]*) and is generally admissible expert testimony in a criminal case. However, although footwear impression evidence has been given its credit in our court systems, the subject itself has not been widely publicized.

Another reason that the value of footwear impression identification may be minimized is because it is viewed as only circumstantial in nature. While an item of footwear can be positively identified to a crime scene, who was wearing the shoe at the time the impression was made may be called into question. This same argument could be applied to the science of firearm identification. The bullet can be positively matched to the weapon, but who fired the weapon cannot be discerned from the ballistic analysis. And yet, firearm examination is seen as reliable and there is great emphasis placed on it.

In many instances, footwear impressions can be positively identified as having been made by a specific shoe to the exclusion of all other shoes. This identification is based on a physical match of random individual characteristics the shoe has acquired with those respective features present in the impression. The identification is as strong as that of fingerprints, toolmarks, or typewritten impressions (Bodziak, 2000).

For anyone who has not had the success of locating many footwear impressions at the scene of the crime and is not yet convinced that there are more footwear impressions present than those that are blatantly obvious, two examples are offered. A recent study conducted in several jurisdictions in Switzerland disclosed that footwear impressions were located at approximately 35% of all crime scenes. The crimes investigated in those areas consisted primarily of burglaries (Girod, 1997).

It is important that the value of footwear impression evidence be known to officers in the field and that they know how to recover it. For this reason, it is sometimes necessary to retrain them in the basics. It is necessary to reiterate the importance of effective identification, collection, and maintenance of evidence samples.

Scientific Working Group for Shoeprint and Tire Tread Evidence

The Scientific Working Group for Shoeprint and Tire Tread Evidence (SWGTREAD) was initiated by the FBI "to standardize and advance the forensic analysis of shoeprint and tire tread evidence" (SWGTREAD, 2012), and the first meeting took place in September 2004 in Quantico, VA. According to the organization's web site (http://swgtread.org/), the mission of SWGTREAD is to "provide a professional forum where forensic shoeprint and tire tread examiners can share knowledge, evaluate practices, develop standards, identify research needs and disseminate information" (SWGTREAD, 2012).

Reviewing the Basics

The location of footwear impression evidence, primarily on ground surfaces, makes it sometimes difficult or inconvenient to find, particularly if the impressions are latent or nearly invisible. Specialized lighting techniques are often required along with an aggressive effort to find the impressions (**Figures 12–3** and **12–4**). Many crime scene technicians have had little or no experience in searching for these types of impressions. In other instances, they simply may not have dedicated the time and effort needed to search for this evidence. In addition, the footwear impressions of the subject that may be mixed with those of other persons, such as paramedics and investigators who may have arrived at the scene ahead of the crime scene technician, does not necessarily mean that the suspect's were destroyed, yet many technicians are discouraged by such tracked over areas and mistakenly abandon any efforts to look for impressions.

There are four basic methods of recording footwear impressions at the crime scene: (1) photography, (2) documentation/sketching, (3) casting, and, (4) lifting (Hilderbrand, 1999).

When a footwear mark is found, distance photographs should be taken first to show the position of the mark in relation to its surroundings.

The mark is then photographed close up, with and without a scale. It is important to ensure that the scale is on the same plane as the impression. This is especially important so that the photograph can be enlarged to the actual shoe size. Just as with all crime scenes, the footwear evidence should be thoroughly documented in both the written report and the crime scene sketch.

It is obviously preferable to remove any evidence that has footwear marks on them, and take them into the lab for analysis. However, when this is not possible, an impression of the

FIGURE 12–3 Showing how to utilize oblique lighting to capture the details of a footwear impression

FIGURE 12–4   Footwear impression photographed utilizing oblique lighting

mark must be taken at the scene. Three-dimensional casting is an important part of footwear impression examination. A cast can reveal much more than a photograph, as minor details that may not show up in a photograph have a greater chance of being captured in a cast. Two-dimensional marks are recovered by lifting them onto another surface. This enables greater contrast between the mark and its background, resulting in more detail. Lifting is typically done through the use of gelatin lifters, an electrostatic lifting device, or adhesive lifters.

Gel Lifting of Footwear Evidence

Gel lifters contain a thick, nonaggressive, low-adhesive gelatin layer that permits the lifting of traces from almost every surface, including porous material such as paper or cardboard. Lifted impressions can be taken along for photography or closer examination. Each kind of lifter can be cut to size using scissors and can be marked with the appropriate case information. All lifters are protected by a cover of transparent polyester film. There are several brands and types, but the typical varieties come in black, white, and transparent.

Surfaces from which shoeprints can be lifted using gel lifters include all smooth and hard surfaces such as floor coverings, painted wood, paper, tabletops, etc. They are especially useful in the case of **<u>negative impressions</u>**, when an item of footwear has left its pattern within a dusty area, essentially removing the dust that was present (**Figure 12–5**). Even if the footprints do not show up on initial lighting of the surface and were not visible upon lifting, they may show up under oblique lighting of the lifter surface in a dark room (after removing the polyester cover sheet). Lifters with no apparent prints in normal light can then show a highly detailed image.

FIGURE 12–5 Footwear impression made in dust (a negative impression)

Footwear impressions can be secured using gelatin lifters both before and after applying fingerprint powders. When the use of appropriate lighting reveals latently present impressions, it is not advisable to use powders prior to recovering the impression with a gelatin lifter. When no impressions are found, it is often useful to search or develop footwear impressions using fingerprint powders and then recover the developed impression with a gelatin lifter.

Electrostatic Lifting

Another and more exotic approach to lifting and preserving dust impressions involves the use of a portable **electrostatic lifting device (ELD)**. The principle employed is similar to creating an electrostatic charge on a comb and using the comb to lift small pieces of tissue paper. The device operates by charging a lifting film that has been placed over a surface bearing a dust print impression. During operation, the electrostatically charged lifting film is drawn down to the surface, and the dust particles in the impression are attracted to the lifting film. The construction of the lifting film allows it to store the electrostatic charge, thus retaining the dust particles after the power supply has been disconnected. The impression-bearing film is then viewed with an oblique light source to search for any impressions that may have been recovered. Dust impressions may be enhanced through chemical development also.

The power supply generates either a low-powered electric field of direct voltage, or an impulsive electric field of high voltage. The stronger the electric field, the stronger the device's ability to attract dust impressions to the lifting film. This equipment is designed for lifting of dry dust impressions. It works poorly on wet origin impressions.

Casting Impressions

When shoe marks are impressed into soft earth at a crime scene, their preservation is best accomplished by photography and casting. Class I dental stone, a form of gypsum, is widely recommended for making casts of shoe impressions (Bodziak, 2000). Dental stone, like plaster of Paris, is a form of gypsum, but it provides a superior result. Dental stone is much stronger and therefore does not require reinforcement material to be placed in the cast during pouring. Most importantly, dental stone is more durable and harder than plaster of Paris, which means it can be cleaned in the laboratory with virtually no loss or erosion of forensic detail from the surface.

Casting is conducted to give lifelike reproduction of the original impression. This is of great forensic benefit because it will: (a) back up the scene photograph, (b) provide for tangible three-dimensional evidence, (c) eliminate focus or scale problems, (d) reproduce microscopic characteristics, and, (e) reproduce characteristics of the side of outsoles and midsoles of the shoe that are not usually reproduced or evident in photographs (Hilderbrand, 1999).

The first step of the casting process, after photographs, is that something needs to be placed around the footprint to serve as a dam. Anything that is immersed in the tread impression should not be removed; any loose debris may be removed, but the margins of the shoe impression are fragile and must be avoided. It is suggested that the impression be prepared by spraying a commercial hardener or quick drying lacquer on the surface. (Hair spray typically works for this.) After following the manufacturer's recommended preparation for the dental stone, the material should be poured onto the area to be cast. It is important not to pour the mixture directly onto the impression; it can destroy ridge characteristics of the print. Pouring the mixture onto a spoon held closely to the surface of the impression will prevent damage to the impression. Once the contents have been poured over the impression, all that is left to do is to wait for the casting material to dry (**Figures 12–6** to **12–8**). Once dry, the impression can be removed from the frame and packaged in a paper bag or cardboard box (unused pizza boxes work well for this). Debris should not be removed from the bottom of the casting, as this could potential damage the cast detail. The lab can remove the debris during processing and identification efforts.

Chemical Development of Impressions

A number of chemicals can be used to develop and enhance footwear impressions made with blood. In areas where a bloody footwear impression is very faint or where the subject has tracked through blood and left a trail of bloody impressions, chemical enhancement can visualize latent or nearly invisible blood impressions (Saferstein, 2010). The investigator may adapt any one of several chemical formulas for use in processing footwear evidence. A few examples include luminol, amido black, and leucocrystal violet.

Computerized Footwear Databases

Crime scene footwear classification systems can be utilized to look for possible suspects, to get models and brand names for crime scene impressions, and to link crime scenes together (Mikkonen, Suominen, & Heinonen, 1996). Shoe impression or reference files are not new; they are maintained worldwide by such bodies as the U.S. FBI, the Metropolitan Police Service in London, the National Bureau of Investigation in Finland, and the Bundeskriminalamt in Germany. Without such computerized assistance, time and resources are expended in compiling

FIGURE 12–6 Preparing to cast a footwear impression. Placement of the form/dam

FIGURE 12–7 After pouring

information about a single incident or enquiry that at its conclusion may be discarded (Ashley, 1996).

New computer software may be able to assist the forensic scientist in making shoeprint comparisons. One example is the automated shoeprint identification system developed in England by Foster and Freeman Ltd., called **Shoeprint Image Capture and Retrieval (SICAR)**, which incorporates multiple databases to search known and unknown footwear files for comparison against footwear specimens (Bodziak, 2000). Using this system, an impression from a crime scene can be compared to a reference database to find out what type of shoe caused the imprint. That same impression also can be searched in the suspect and crime databases to reveal if it matches the shoes of a person who has been in custody or the shoeprints left behind at another crime scene. When matches are made during the searching process, the images are displayed side by side on the computer screen (Saferstein, 2010).

In Europe, footwear evidence is the second most collected item of evidence after fingerprints. This high regard for footwear evidence is due, in part, to the fact that police agencies in several countries have created national databases for footwear evidence: United Kingdom, SICAR; Germany, BILDDATEBANK and SCHARS; the Netherlands, REVEZO and TRIS; Switzerland, TDP; and Finland, NBISPDB. SHOE is established in Australia, as well. This capability does not yet exist in the United States (Mankevich, 2002).

Currently, a detective cannot determine if the shoe print under investigation by his or her agency is also appearing at crime scenes in other jurisdictions. The detective also has limited options on how to effectively search for the brand name and manufacturer of the shoe print evidence.

In the past, detectives have resorted to flipping over numerous shoes in shoe stores in the hopes of blindly stumbling upon the correct pair of shoes and matching the crime shoe prints. Flipping through the pages of magazines and catalogs, and surfing online Internet sites are other time-consuming, rarely productive means often used to recognize the brand of shoe prints.

A computerized database of outsole and footwear impression images on a central server would allow case detectives and laboratory analysts the most productive means to search for and recognize footwear's brand and manufacturer without the labor-intensive efforts required in the past.

Footwear impression evidence has repeatedly exhibited its value as a means to provide a criminal investigation with information related to (and often, the actual identification of) the crime perpetrator. One need

© 67photo/Alamy Images.

FIGURE 12–8   Close-up of cast footprint

only recall the preflight activities of the September 11 terrorist group, as they "blended in" and operated for a length of time out of diverse locations such as Florida, Virginia, Massachusetts, Maryland, and Arizona prior to the bombings, to see how associative evidence could help identify and possibly be used to thwart criminal enterprises.

An example of footwear evidence having a direct relation to the Homeland Security issue is Richard Reid's attempt to destroy American Airlines Flight #63 with a bomb that had been inserted in his shoe. On January 25, 2002, an image of the outsole of Reid's shoe was posted on the Wanted Page as Case #2/2002, by the FBI Laboratory, asking if anyone knew the "brand name or manufacturer of the enclosed shoe." Using its SICAR system, Maryland State Police was able to provide the match as "an 'Ashburn' brand of hiking boot" to the FBI Laboratory. The only other law enforcement agency to respond to the request for brand/manufacturer recognition was the National Bureau of Investigation in Vantaa, Finland.

The ability to quickly recognize the brand and manufacturer of footwear impressions is invaluable to detectives during any criminal investigation. Once the brand of shoe prints appearing at a crime scene is known, detectives can focus their investigation upon suspects who conform to the marketing and brand "aura" of the footwear such as age, gender, stature, recreational pursuits, aesthetic, stylistic, and fashion preferences. A recognized footwear brand can be specified during requests for search warrants. It used to be that when there was footwear evidence the detectives would serve a search warrant and take all of the shoes in the house. However, if they were able to know the make, model, and/or brand ahead of time, as specified in the search warrant, they only need to take those shoes that are similar to the outsole pattern identified.

Collection of Footwear Impression Evidence

Footwear impressions may yield information as to the type, make, and approximate size of the shoe or boot. In some cases, conclusive identification can be made, linking a particular shoe to the crime scene impression. The likelihood of conclusive identification is a function of several factors, but it is primarily governed by the amount of wear sustained by the outsole, the ability of the receiving surface to resolve the fine detail of the impression, and the fineness of the material by which the impression is deposited.

A footwear impression may be either positive or negative—that is, the impression may be the result of dust or other material being deposited on a clean surface, or it may be the result of the outsole removing dust or other material from the surface. Either type of impression has the potential of being suitable for comparison and identification. Impressions made in dust, particularly those made on hard, smooth surfaces, are the most likely to yield a conclusive identification. Investigators should be alert to the possibility of such impressions when broken glass is found in an area where the perpetrator could have stepped. Another potential source of such impressions is plastic windows in out-of-the-way areas that are rarely cleaned (such as in gas stations or warehouses). In some cases, the window will be forced out with the foot, or once forced will be stepped on, removing dust from the surface and creating a negative record of the outsole.

Whenever possible, submit the original item on which the impression appears. Lifts made in the field and improperly taken photographs rarely show the fine detail necessary to make a conclusive identification.

The Value of a Footwear Impression

The value of a footprint is determined by the number of class characteristics that match the class characteristics of a suspect item. Agreement in size, shape, or design can only prove that the item in question may have made the impression; a definitive identification cannot be made on the basis of class characteristics alone. It is the presence of the individual characteristics from wear, breaks, or tears that, if numerous, will support an opinion that the cast or recovered impression came from one source and one source only: the suspect item (Saferstein, 2010).

Recovery of Surface or Dust Impressions

(1) Photograph the entire area to show a walking pattern or the relation of impressions to surrounding objects. This means being cognizant of taking proper overall and mid-range photographs. (2) Take a close-up photograph without a scale and then take a properly scaled photograph of each footwear impression. (3) Prepare a proper sketch showing the position of the impression(s) in relation to fixed objects at the scene, utilizing a proper mapping method.

SoleSearcher: FBI Questioned Footwear Examination

SoleSearcher is an innovative investigative tool used by the Questioned Documents Unit (QDU) of the FBI to help determine the brand name or manufacturer of footwear from questioned footwear impressions left behind at crime scenes. Hundreds of these database searches are requested annually by law enforcement agencies in cases that range from burglary to terrorism. The database contains more than 11,000 different shoe outsole designs from more than 370 different footwear manufacturers from around the world. New outsole images are added to the database daily. With so many different manufacturers and a majority of shoes being manufactured overseas, keeping up with all of these shoes is a monumental task.

SoleSearcher was designed using different design icons commonly found on the outsole of shoes. These different design icons are placed on a blank shoe canvas to resemble the questioned footwear impressions. The image is then searched through the database using the specific criteria. If the database produces a shoe outsole that is consistent with the questioned impression, a printout of this shoe outsole is sent back to the contributor. If the contributor has or develops a suspect or a person of interest, the contributor can use this print during a search to obtain the shoes needed to conduct further footwear examinations.

The FBI Laboratory's first footwear reference collection dates back to around 1935. This collection consisted of a series of photographs of shoe soles and heels. These photographs were placed in file cabinets according to manufacturer. The reference file searches were all conducted by hand. Back in the 1930s, this collection was considered complete because all shoes at that time were manufactured in the United States. The shoes were primarily dress shoes and perhaps a small number of casual shoes. Specialty athletic shoes were not introduced until the 1950s and 1960s.

The first computerized footwear database was introduced in the mid-1980s and was housed on a mainframe computer system. In the early 1990s, the footwear database was placed on a personal computer. The manufacturer would send in catalogs, and these outsole images would be scanned into the database. At that time, the database had approximately 2,000 outsole images. Today, the database contains more than 11,000 images. In the future, the Laboratory plans to make SoleSearcher available through a secure network so other law enforcement agencies may electronically contribute and search footwear images in the database.

Source: Federal Bureau of Investigation (FBI). (2007). *FBI Laboratory 2007 Report*. Quantico, Virginia: FBI Laboratory Publication. Retrieved September 15, 2012, from http://www.fbi.gov/about-us/lab/lab-annual-report-2007.

Recovery of Objects and/or Impressions

(1) Recover and preserve the object bearing the impression. (2) If this is impossible, the impressions should be lifted by using an electrostatic lifter, a transparent footwear residue lifter, or a rubber footwear lifter. (3) The object bearing the impression or the lift should then be submitted to the forensics laboratory, along with copies of diagrams, photographs, etc.

Tire Impressions

Just as is the case with footwear impressions, tire tracks are often forgotten or overlooked at crime scenes. This may be due to a lack of knowledge or experience with regards to locating, documenting, and collecting such evidence. However, tire tracks are crucial evidence in proving that a suspect vehicle was present at the crime scene.

Tire impressions reflect the tread design and dimensional features of the individual tires on a vehicle. Tire tread impressions can be compared directly with the tread design and dimension of the tires for a suspect vehicle. If the surface retains sufficient detail, this comparison can result in a positive identification.

Tire tracks are the relation dimensions between two or more tires of a vehicle. By measuring the dimensions of tire tracks at the crime scene, it may be possible to determine or approximate

The Future of Footwear and Tire Impression Evidence Recovery

The day is approaching when it may no longer be necessary to involve oneself in the laborious task of casting a footwear or tire impression. Soon, the technology for digitally documenting and reconstructing a crime scene will be relied upon to assemble a proper facsimile of the impression area. Photographs and "casting" will soon occur in one step. The technology has already been developed and is in the field. All that remains is for personnel to properly mount (90 degrees to the impression) the technology, and for the technology to be competitively priced so as to allow for more users being able to afford and be trained on the technology.

the track width, wheelbase, or turning diameter of the vehicle. Tire tracks can be used to profile the type or size of vehicle used and for other purposes that can help to include or exclude a suspect vehicle.

Tire impressions sometimes permit identification of the type and make of the tire. In some cases, a particular tire may be conclusively identified as the maker of an impression.

Recovery of Tire Evidence

Tire tracks should be documented through photographs, casting, and measurements (**Figure 12–9**), being certain to take overall, mid-range, and close-up photographs. This will show both the orientation of tracks and track detail. Overlap close-up photos and always use a scale so that photos can be blown up 1:1 and spliced to be used for comparison purposes. It is important that the scale be placed on the same plane as the impression. Casting a long tire impression is important and challenging. Any cast of 4 feet or less in length should be cast in its entirety. If the impression is longer than 4 feet, the impression should be cast in manageable sections. Identify each cast with an impression number placard. Be sure to photograph the scene after the casts have been poured, for documentation purposes.

Tire impressions can also be duplicated by inking the suspect tread with fingerprint impression ink and running the inked tire (under load) over paper or clear plastic sheets. These can then be compared to or overlaid onto the cast or scaled photograph of the evidence tread mark. It is suggested that known impression collections include the entire circumference of the tire, not just the suspected location (**Figure 12–10**).

FIGURE 12–9   Scaled photograph of tire impression

FIGURE 12–10 Example of tire track reference evidence

Courtesy of Sirchie Acquisition Company, LLC.

Toolmarks

For the purposes of this chapter, a tool is any instrument or object capable of making a mark on another object. Toolmark identification techniques may be applied to many types of investigations—knife marks on bone, fractured knife blades, homemade explosive devices, crimp marks on detonators, cut marks on wire, fractured radio antennas—including burglary. A close examination of a toolmark may reveal the type of tool, contour of the cutting edge, blade width and color of the tool, or the presence of trace material. Toolmarks may be found at points of entry and exit at victimized premises and upon objects that have been attacked. An impression itself usually renders only class characteristics indicating the type of tool, although it can have unique characteristics that allow it to be matched to a single tool.

A tool retains machined marks from its manufacture, just as firearms do. These marks and striations are changed as the result of nicks and breaks in the tool's working surface that occur as the tool is used and misused. The pattern and shape of these modifications are altered by continued use, further individualizing the imperfections. It is unlikely that any two tools will have manufacturing striations, wear markings, and breaks that are precisely the same. It is these small imperfections that allow the crime laboratory to determine that the impressions at the crime scene were left by a suspect tool.

If a tool edge is scraped against a surface that is softer than the material of the tool, it will leave a series of markings that reflect the pattern of the tool edge. These markings and the imperfections on a suspect tool can be compared in a laboratory with a comparison micro-scope. The comparison may show an association between the marks and the tool. The more individualized the tool edge pattern, the more definitive the comparison.

Recovery of Toolmarks

Whenever possible, toolmarks should be kept in their original condition. This may be done by recovering the whole or part of the object upon which the marks appear. In recovering the mark, it is important that it be protected against dirt, moisture, and scratching during transport. Tissue or other soft paper should be placed over the toolmark in packaging. Casting or other methods of taking impressions of toolmarks should be used only as a last resort.

Suggestions for the Recovery of Toolmarks

- Always submit an object containing the toolmark to the forensic laboratory.
- If not practical to submit the object, remove the section of material containing the toolmark and submit it to the forensic laboratory.
- As a last resort, make a cast of the toolmark.
- Mark, protect, and individually package item(s) containing toolmark(s) and submit them to the forensic laboratory.

Casting of Toolmarks

In the event that, as a last resort, casting the toolmark is necessary, silicone casting materials have been found satisfactory. Indentations can be preserved with a casting compound similar to DUROCAST (manufactured by Sirchie Laboratories; see **Figure 12–11**). The putty-like material enables castings to be made on horizontal or vertical surfaces. The casting material can be molded into a piece long and wide enough to cover the toolmark (**Figure 12–12**). Once pressed gently into the toolmark and allowed to set, the casting material can be removed, and a negative impression of the toolmark will have been transferred to the casting material, which should then be packaged appropriately. Personnel are warned not to use plasticine, plaster of Paris, home repair patch plaster, and related materials, as they have a tendency to shrink and not accurately preserve the impression.

FIGURE 12–11 Durocast impression compound
Courtesy of Sirchie Acquisition Company, LLC.

FIGURE 12–12 Durocast simulated application; in an actual case, gloves should be worn during the application process
Courtesy of Sirchie Acquisition Company, LLC.

Recovery of Tools

Recover all suspect tools and inventory, observing the following precautions, and submit them to the forensic laboratory for examination and comparison with toolmarks:

- Never place a suspect tool in contact with a questioned toolmark or cast.
- Package each tool individually to protect the tool for possible fingerprint, and/or trace material examination.

Bitemark Evidence

Bite marks may occur on the skin of victims of rape or sexual murder, or on a criminal. At times bite marks can be so characteristic that they make the definite identification of a suspect possible. The relative positions of the teeth, their widths, and the distance between them, together with ridges on the edges of the teeth and grooves on the backs or fronts, vary among different individuals and may be clearly evident in the bite mark (**Figure 12–13**).

Bite marks can involve both compression and striated evidence, dependent upon the action occurring at the scene of the crime. These impressions are an outstanding source of physical evidence that can be found on skin, furniture, foodstuffs, chewing gum, and many other objects located at the scene of a crime. There are many criminal incidents that include victims defending themselves by biting their attacker. Sometimes an attacker will bite his or her victim as part of the assault process. As odd as it may seem, there are many times when a criminal will eat at a crime scene and leave behind evidence that may have bite marks present on or in them. All of these instances can be analyzed and the identified impressions documented and compared to a suspect of victim dentition in an effort to corroborate or refute testimonial evidence, and to help place the individual at the scene of the crime.

FIGURE 12–13   Dental impression model

Processing Bitemark Evidence

The potential evidence of a bite mark is not simply the pattern itself but also the saliva and thus the DNA that could be present with the impression. For this reason, the area should be processed as follows:

- Photograph, with and without a scale for reference, utilizing oblique lighting to best distinguish the characteristics of the mark.

- After this has occurred, the area should be swabbed to collect potential DNA evidence.

- If the mark is an evident one, not one that requires "maturing" of the wound, then it is suggested that the crime scene investigator lay a clear piece of acetate over the wound and carefully outline the injury, using a permanent marker on the acetate. This could prove useful for a forensic odontologist to conduct an eventual comparison.

- If the individual is deceased, the medical examiner may elect to excise the portion of the skin baring the impression evidence and preserve it.

- If the area is to be cast, the crime scene investigator should make use of silicon casting material to cast the area and preserve the cast for subsequent analysis.

- Some injuries, if fresh and made to a live person, may require them to "mature" and this will require the crime scene investigator to revisit the injury to take photographs at a later time to provide the best visual evidence.

CASE IN POINT

Bite Marks Bite Back

Perhaps the most famous incident where bitemark evidence was found to have such strong forensic value that it was used to convict was in the case of the notorious serial killer, Ted Bundy. From 1973 to 1978 Bundy was responsible for an undetermined number of murders across the United States. The case that provided the forensic link was when he was finally tied to the murder of Lisa Levy through bite marks that were left on her buttocks during the assault and subsequent murder. An astute officer at the scene of the crime had the forethought to place a ruler next to the marks discovered upon Levy's body and they were then photographed.

Due to a variety of other forensic evidence and investigative leads, Bundy was eventually arrested. Following Bundy's arrest, police obtained a search warrant that allowed them to take a dental impression from Bundy and photograph his front upper and lower teeth and gum areas. During the subsequent trial, the prosecution produced the photographic evidence of the bite marks and the evidence that had been collected of Bundy's teeth. They demonstrated the relationship between the two by placing an acetate overlay of the bite mark on the photo of the teeth. When this was done, it left no reasonable doubt in jurors' minds that it was Ted Bundy's highly irregular teeth pattern that had resulted in the impressions discovered on Levy's body. Based upon this evidence, Ted Bundy was convicted and sentenced to die in the electric chair; he was executed on January 24, 1989.

Information retrieved from http://www.crimeandclues.com/bite_marks.htm.

When crime scene personnel confronted with bitemark evidence do not know the correct way to proceed with the collection efforts, it is important that they consult medical personnel who are knowledgeable on such matters. Many medical personnel have additional training in the recognition of bitemark evidence because they are commonly involved in tending to victims of child and spousal abuse. If this evidence is not properly recognized or processed, critical information may be lost or destroyed.

Ligature/Binding Impressions

Oftentimes, the item that is used to bind, incapacitate, or kill someone will leave an impression within or upon the skin of the victim. These items are referred to as **ligatures**. Ropes, phone cords, and other materials that sometimes are used in strangulation cases will leave behind patterned impression evidence that later can be matched to the item that was used. Depending upon the action that occurred during the criminal event, the ligature or binding impressions can be either striated or compression evidence (**Figure 12–14**).

Processing Ligature Impressions

All ligature or binding impressions should be photographed, typically with the use of oblique lighting in an effort to accentuate the impression through the use of shadows. The area then can be cast making use of a forensic casting silicone material. This should create a scaled replica of the impression that later can be compared to any items believed to have been responsible for the mark.

If the ligature or binding material is still present upon the body of a victim, it is important that the crime scene investigator observe a few key guidelines. Firstly, a body is not to

© Wellcome Trust Library/Custom Medical Stock Photo.

FIGURE 12–14   Example of a ligature/binding impression be touched, moved, or otherwise tampered with without the permission or guidance of the coroner or medical examiner staff (as appropriate). Typically, such items are not removed from the body of a deceased individual until autopsy. If, however, the removal of the item is warranted, and permission is gained, then the ligature should be processed as follows.

The ligature should be photographed in place, prior to removal, both with and without a scale for reference. Next, the item should be carefully removed. If the item is one that includes a knot (e.g., necktie, rope, etc.), the knot should not be untied as this itself is evidence that can give information as to the skill and education of the individual who tied it (e.g., military, Boy Scout, etc.). Instead, the item should be severed at an area not near the knot, which allows the item to be carefully removed. The two fresh ends should then be labeled to differentiate them from any other loose ends of the same material. Some instructors teach that a string should be tied to each fresh end, thus bridging the gap between the new ends, after removal. However, it is the experience of the author that the least amount of touching, damage, and otherwise manipulation of the item of evidence will ensure the preservation of the greatest amount of evidence associated with the event. The item should then be packaged as appropriate, to minimize movement and dislodgement of trace evidence.

Fabric Impressions

Sometimes the movement of an individual at a crime scene can result in fabric impression evidence being left behind. The person may lean up against an object present at the scene of a crime and leave behind the pattern of his or her clothing. If a suspect or victim leans against wet paint, or a dust covered area, sometimes this will result in the pattern of the clothing being left behind, waiting for an astute individual to recognize the evidentiary potential. While clothing itself is not typically individualistic, the way an item of clothing touches or impresses upon another can be individualistic, similar to a jigsaw puzzle piece. Often, if properly documented and collected, the impression can be matched up to an object responsible for leaving the impression. In addition to matching the weave and pattern, the object also may be found to have relating cross-transfer material such as the paint or dust that resulted in the impression (**Figure 12–15**).

Processing Fabric Impressions

As with other impression evidence, proper photographs are paramount. The crime scene investigator also should collect a comparison sample of the dust, paint, or other material in which the impression was left so that it might later be compared against trace materials found on the clothing that left the impression. It may prove useful to cast the impression with the use of silicon casting material.

FIGURE 12–15   Example of a fabric impression made in blood
Courtesy of Dana Gevelinger, University of Wisconsin-Platteville.

WRAP UP.

Chapter Summary

Impression evidence is often uncollected and undocumented due to the laborious nature of the methodology associated with its collection and documentation. Personnel must ensure that they are educated on the forensic potential of impression evidence and how to properly collect and document it. "Commit a crime and the earth is made of glass ... you cannot wipe or cut the foot-track ... so as to leave no inlet or clue, some damning circumstance always transpires" (Emerson, 1841). However, as the information presented within this chapter reveals, and as stated by Professor Locard over 100 years ago, "Only human failure to find it, study and understand it can diminish its value " (Kirk, 1974, p. 2).

Review Questions

1. What are the two types of impression markings?

2. What are the two major reasons foot-wear impression evidence is often overlooked?

3. List three benefits to the investigator casting footwear impressions.

4. What is SICAR and how does it work?

5. Casts of long tire impressions should be kept to what maximum length?

6. What information can be deduced by measuring the dimensions of tire tracks at the crime scene?

7. Why is bitemark evidence sometimes criticized?

8. How was bitemark evidence used in the Ted Bundy case?

9. When presented with a knot on a ligature or binding, how should an investigator proceed with evidence collection and why?

10. A _____ impression may result from a suspect leaning against a surface covered in wet paint or dust.

References

Alexandre, G. (1996). Police Cantonale Neuchateloise, Service d'Identifi-cation Judiciaire. Computerized classification of the shoeprints of burglars' soles. *Forensic Science International, 82*, 59–65.

Ashley, W. (1996). Crime Scene Section, Victoria Science Centre. What shoe was that? The use of computerized image database to assist in identification. *Forensic Science International, 82*, 7–20.

Bodziak, W. J. (2000). *Footwear impression evidence* (2nd ed.). Boca Raton, FL: CRC Press.

Doyle, A. C. (1887). *A study in scarlet*. London, United Kingdom: Ward Lock & Co.

Emerson, R. W. (1841). *Essays, first series*. Compensation. Retrieved September 16, 2009, from http://www.vcu.edu/engweb/transcendentalism/authors/emerson/essays/compensation.html

Federal Bureau of Investigation (FBI). (2007). *FBI Laboratory 2007 Report*. Quantico, Virginia: FBI Laboratory Publication. Retrieved September 15, 2012 from http://www.fbi.gov/about-us/lab/lab-annual-report-2007

Girod, A. (April, 1997). Presentation at the European Meeting for Shoeprint/Toolmark Examiners. The Netherlands.

Hamm, E. D. (1989). Track identification: An historical overview. *Journal of Forensic Identification, 39*, 333–339.

Hilderbrand, D. S. (1999). *Footwear, the missed evidence*. Temecula, CA: Staggs Publishing.

Kirk, P. E. (1974). *Crime investigation* (2nd ed.). New York: John Wiley & Sons.

Mankevich, A. (January, 2002). *SICAR East Coast Network*. Proposal presented to the U.S. Department of Justice, Washington D.C.

Mikkonen, S., Suominen V., & Heinonen P. (1996). Use of footwear impressions in crime scene investigations assisted by computerized footwear collection system. *Forensic Science International, 82*, 67–79.

Saferstein, R. (2010). *Criminalistics, An introduction to forensic science* (7th ed.). Upper Saddle River, NJ: Prentice Hall.

Scientific Working Group for Footwear and Tire Tread Evidence (SWGTREAD). (2012). Mission, history and funding. Retrieved June 26, 2012 from http://swgtread.org/about-us/mission-history-and-funding

Steck-Flynn, K. (2011). *Bite mark analysis*, Retrieved September 15, 2012 from http://www.crimeandclues.com/index.php/forensic-science-a-csi/impression-evidence/17-bite-mark-analysis

© McMac/ShutterStock, Inc.

- Differentiate between ballistics and firearms identification.
- Know what information can be assembled and its potential forensic value resulting from proper processing of a firearms-related crime scene.
- Differentiate between smoothbore and rifled firearms.
- Know how the firing mechanisms of modern firearms and the components of modern ammunition allow for the interpretation and identification of firearms scenes and associated firearms.
- Understand the proper methods associated with documentation, collection, and preservation of firearms-related evidence and why they are used.

Firearms and Ballistic Evidence

> Untutored courage is useless in the face of educated bullets.
>
> General George S. Patton, Jr. (1885–1945)

KEY TERMS

Ballistics
Bore
Caliber
Comparison Microscope
Exterior Ballistics
Firearm
Firing Pin
Gauge
Grooves
Handgun

Integrated Ballistic
  Identification System
  (IBIS)
Interior Ballistics
Lands
National Firearms Act of 1968
National Integrated Ballistic
  Information Network
  (NIBIN)
Primer

Rifle
Rifled Firearm
Rifling
Smoothbore Firearm
Terminal Ballistics
Transitional Ballistics
Zones of Possibility

Introduction to Firearms

Whether because of American heritage or movie exploits, firearms play a large role in American society. Some believe there are too many guns, while others believe that everyone has the right to own a gun for self-defense. Whatever the case, there are millions of them within the United States that help account for the large number of crimes committed daily. According to the United States Department of Justice, the most recent research indicates that:

- In 2008, 303,880 victims of violent crimes stated that they faced an offender with a firearm (National Crime Victimization Survey).

- Incidents involving a firearm represented 7% of the 5.1 million violent crimes of rape and sexual assault, robbery, and aggravated and simple assault in 2008.

- The Federal Bureau of Investigation's (FBI) Crime in the United States estimated that 68% of the 16,929 murders in 2007 were committed with firearms (Bureau of Justice, 2008).

The physical evidence found at a crime scene often includes a firearm or firearm components. It is imperative that personnel tasked with processing and investigating a crime scene understand the forensic potential of such evidence. For the purposes of this text, a **firearm** is any device that expels a projectile or projectiles as a result of an explosive or propellant charge. Crime scene personnel and firearms examiners typically will come into contact with three types of firearms: handguns, rifles, and shotguns. However, it is useful to know that within each category there are several subcategories. This is important because each category and subcategory of firearm operates differently, and each may require different concerns as far as documentation and preservation methods are concerned.

Handguns

A **handgun** is a weapon designed to be held in and fired with one hand. However, anyone familiar with firearms usage will agree that the most accurate way in which to fire a handgun is through the use of two hands, as that position creates a stable shooting platform. There are two primary subcategories of handguns: pistols (semi-automatic and automatic) and revolvers.

Pistols

Most nonrevolver types of handguns are of the semi-automatic variety. A semi-automatic firearm will fire each time that the trigger is depressed and subsequently released for as long as there is ammunition remaining within the firearm. These firearms typically include a spring-loaded magazine, which holds the cartridges and feeds them into the awaiting chamber after the previously spent shell casing has been extracted and ejected as a result of the slide action of the semi-automatic handgun. In some extremely rare cases, a pistol may be of the automatic variety. In this case, the weapon will continue to fire (unless interrupted by a malfunction) as long as the trigger is depressed and there is ammunition within the weapon. In either case (semi-automatic or automatic pistols), expended shell casings will be expelled from the firearm and will remain at the scene unless retrieved by the shooter (**Figure 13–1**).

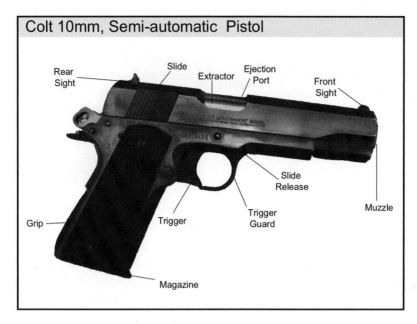

FIGURE 13–1 Characteristics of modern firearms (handgun)
Courtesy of Erica Milks, University of Wisconsin-Platteville.

Revolvers

A revolver is a type of handgun that incorporates a revolving cylinder as the method of containing ammunition and of cycling the ammunition into battery. There are no interchangeable magazines and shell casings of expended ammunition are contained within the cylinder rather than being expelled as in a semi-automatic pistol. At a crime scene involving the use of a firearm, therefore, failure to find expended shell casings might mean that the perpetrator made use of a revolver or he or she picked up the shell casings (**Figure 13–2**).

There are two types of revolvers: single action or double action. A user of a single-action revolver must manually cock it each time before firing. The user of a double-action revolver need only to pull the trigger, which in turn cocks the firearm, and then subsequently fires it.

Rifles

A **rifle** is a weapon designed to be held in two hands when being fired from the shoulder. As with handguns, there are various types. Some rifles are single-shot, slide-action types that will fire one round and then through manipulation of a bolt will extract the spent shell casing and either load another round or the user will have to manually load another. Some are semi-automatic versions, which operate similarly to semi-automatic pistols, firing one round for each depression of the trigger as long as there is ammunition available. Automatic rifles will continue to fire as long as the trigger is depressed and ammunition is available (**Figure 13–3**).

FIGURE 13–2   Characteristics of modern firearms (revolver)
Courtesy of Dana Gevelinger, University of Wisconsin-Platteville.

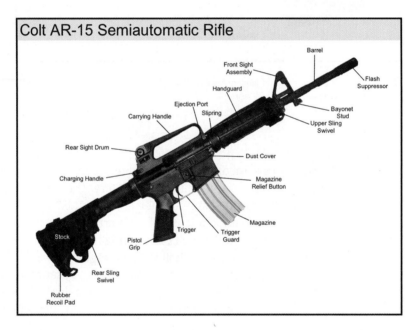

FIGURE 13–3   Characteristics of modern firearms (rifle)
Courtesy of Erica Milks, University of Wisconsin-Platteville.

Rifled Firearms

All of the aforementioned types of firearms are referred to as rifled firearms. A firearm is referred to as either being a smoothbore or rifled depending upon whether or not there is rifling present within the barrel (**Figures 13–4** and **13–5**). Rifled firearms contain **rifling**

The United States: The Most Armed Populace in the World

According to a Reuters news article, written by Laura MacInnis, U.S. citizens own 270 million of the world's 875 million known firearms, according to the Small Arms Survey 2007 by the Geneva-based Graduate Institute of International Studies. About 4.5 million of the 8 million new guns manufactured worldwide each year are purchased in the United States. "There is roughly one firearm for every seven people worldwide. Without the United States, though, this drops to about one firearm per 10 people."

India had the world's second-largest civilian gun arsenal, with an estimated 46 million firearms outside law enforcement and the military, though this represented just four guns per 100 people there. China, ranked third with 40 million privately held guns, had 3 firearms per 100 people.

Germany, France, Pakistan, Mexico, Brazil, and Russia were next in the ranking of country's overall civilian gun arsenals. On a per-capita basis, Yemen had the second most heavily armed citizenry behind the United States, with 61 guns per 100 people, followed by Finland with 56, Switzerland with 46, Iraq with 39 and Serbia with 38.

MacInnis, L. (2007). "U.S. most armed country with 90 guns per 100 people." Thomson Reuters. http://www.reuters.com/article/2007/08/28/us-world-firearms-idusl2834893820070828.

within the **bore** (interior of the firearm barrel). Rifling are the series of spiral grooves that are formed in the bore, which are designed to impart spin upon a projectile as it passes through the barrel to improve its accuracy. The rifling is made up of two components: grooves and lands. The **grooves** are the low-lying portions between the lands within a rifled firearm bore. The **lands** are the raised portion between the grooves within a rifled firearm bore (**Figure 13–6**). During the manufacturing process of a firearm, minute imperfections occur within the barrel that, when combined with the lands and grooves, will impart characteristics upon a bullet passing through the barrel known as striations. These are often unique to a specific barrel, much like a fingerprint is to a finger. The rifling, however, is not intended to be an identifiable "fingerprint." Instead, its design provides ballistics properties for the bullet as it exits the barrel of the firearm. Much like throwing a football, imparting spin upon the projectile gives it stability and provides for a more accurate and predictable trajectory (**Figure 13–7**).

Rifled weapons are classified by their **caliber**, which is the diameter of the bore of a rifled firearm, measured between opposing lands. The caliber is usually expressed in hundredths of an inch or millimeters, for example, .22 caliber and 9 mm (**Figure 13–8**).

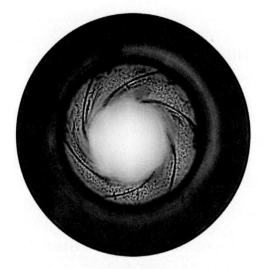

FIGURE 13–4   Photograph of a rifled barrel, showing rifling present within

FIGURE 13–5   Photograph of a smoothbore weapon. Note the absence of rifling within the barrel

LAND

GROOVE

FIGURE 13–6   Bore characteristics of a rifled firearm
Courtesy of Dana Gevelinger, University of Wisconsin-Platteville.

FIGURE 13–7 Photograph of a bullet. Note rifling characteristics and striations

Courtesy of Dana Gevelinger, University of Wisconsin-Platteville.

.45 caliber   9 mm

FIGURE 13–8   Example of how caliber is calculated

Courtesy of Dana Gevelinger, University of Wisconsin-Platteville.

Smoothbore Firearms

As discussed earlier, if there is no rifling present within the firearm bore, then the firearm is referred to as being a **smoothbore firearm**. The most common example of a smoothbore firearm is a shotgun. A *shotgun* is a firearm that, as with a rifle, is designed to be held in two hands and fired from the shoulder (**Figure 13–9**). They are most commonly used to fire pellet loads rather than single projectiles (slugs). While some shotguns are able to interchange and have rifled barrels for firing slugs, the shotgun was originally designed to fire multiple projectiles (shot) that are typically fired through a smoothbore barrel.

FIGURE 13–9   Characteristics of modern firearm (shotgun)

Courtesy of Dana Gevelinger, University of Wisconsin-Platteville.

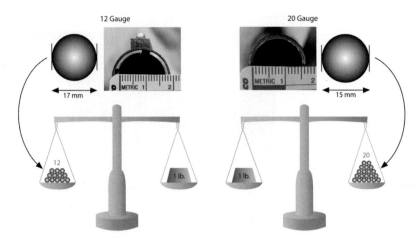

FIGURE 13–10   Explanation of how gauge is determined
Courtesy of Nick Vesper, University of Wisconsin-Platteville.

There are other types of smoothbore weapons that typically include antique black-powder type weapons. However, because not many crime scenes involve such firearms, they are not concentrated on within the confines of this text.

Just as rifled weapons are referred to by their caliber, smoothbore weapons are referred to by their **gauge**. Gauge is the number of spherical lead balls that have the diameter of the interior of the barrel of the firearm that add up to weigh one pound. For example, 12 lead balls having the diameter of the interior of a 12-gauge shotgun barrel (roughly .75 inches) would weigh approximately 1 pound (**Figure 13–10**). An exception to this rule is the .410 gauge, which has an actual bore diameter is .410 inches. This is not meant to confuse the reader, but rather to recognize that referring to "gauge" is not an absolute measure with regards to smoothbore weapons.

Firing Components of Modern Firearms

There are several components within a modern firearm that significantly impact the firing of a round, which result in specific characteristics being passed along to shell casings placed within the chamber. The *breech lock* is a component that supports the base of a cartridge within the chamber. The face of this component, called the breech face, will often leave identifiable marks upon the base of the shell casing. The **firing pin** is the component that strikes the base of the cartridge and causes the initial incendiary event leading to expulsion of the bullet from the barrel. This often leaves marks upon a cartridge case that are identifiable to a particular firearm or brand of firearm (**Figures 13–11** and **13–12**). An *extractor* or *ejector* also may be found within a firearm (nonrevolver) and is responsible for ejecting the spent

FIGURE 13–11   Photograph of the base of a .45 Caliber shell case. Note firing pin mark in center of primer

FIGURE 13–12   Photograph of the base of a 9-mm shell casing. Note distinctive Glock firing pin mark in center of primer

shell casing after it has been fired. This hook-like object is likely to leave a compression or striated mark within the extractor groove at the base of a spent shell casing that is potentially identifiable to a particular firearm. Note that revolvers do not eject spent shell casings and, therefore, revolver ammunition does not contain an extractor groove at its base (**Figure 13–13**).

Characteristics and Components of Modern Ammunition

FIGURE 13–13   Differences between semi-automatic and revolver shell casings (note extractor groove)

A firearm can be a centerfire or rimfire weapon based upon the location of the primer. Centerfire or rimfire refers to the location the firing pin will strike the **primer** on the cartridge to detonate the primer. The primer is a metal cup located within the center of the base of a cartridge that contains a small amount of incendiary compound, which when crushed by the firing pin sets off the initial incendiary event. The primer's explosion sets off the secondary incendiary event: the subsequent lighting of the propellant as a result of the primer flash reaching the propellant through a small hole between the anvil that separates the primer from the smokeless powder propellant. In rimfire weapons (e.g., a .22 caliber), the entire base of the cartridge serves as a primer.

A modern firearm round or cartridge consists of a shell casing, a bullet, propellant, and a primer (**Figure 13–14**). Each of these has its own potential forensic significance, which will be discussed later in the chapter.

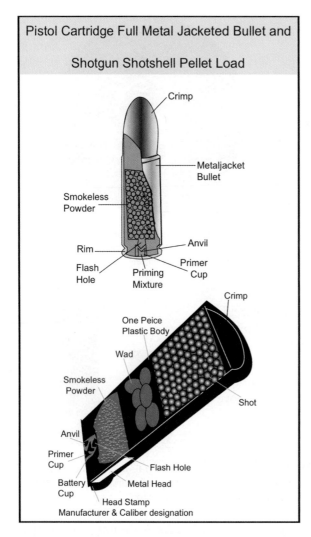

Pistol Cartridge Full Metal Jacketed Bullet and Shotgun Shotshell Pellet Load

Crimp

Metaljacket Bullet

Smokeless Powder

Rim

Anvil

Flash Hole

Priming Mixture

Primer Cup

Crimp

One Peice Plastic Body

Wad

Smokeless Powder

Shot

Anvil

Primer Cup

Flash Hole

Battery Cup

Metal Head

Head Stamp Manufacturer & Caliber designation

FIGURE 13–14   Characteristics of modern ammunition
Courtesy of Erica Milks, University of Wisconsin-Platteville.

Virtually every portion of contemporary ammunition has potential evidentiary value including:

- Propellant
- Elemental makeup of the projectile and primer mixture
- Design characteristics of the bullet
- Wads from shotgun shells (James & Nordby, 2009)

A basic knowledge of these components and their potential evidentiary value is of critical importance for the successful investigation of a shooting incident.

Ballistics

The science of firearms identification is often incorrectly termed "ballistics." In actuality, **ballistics** is the study of a projectile (most likely from a firearm) in motion. There are four distinct areas of ballistics:

- **Interior ballistics** is the study relating to the transition of chemical energy to kinetic energy within the barrel of a firearm and the motion of the projectile(s) as it moves through the barrel.

- **Transitional ballistics** is concerned with the period of time in which the projectile(s) transitions from its movement through the firearm barrel to its flight through the air upon exit from the barrel.

- **Exterior ballistics** is the study of the flight of a projectile beginning at the muzzle end the barrel of a firearm and terminating at the target.

- **Terminal ballistics** deals with the resulting impact and interaction between the projectile and the target matter (Heard, 2008).

Firearms identification, on the other hand, is concerned primarily with the identification of firearms through the examination of fired bullets and cartridges; it is only tangentially related to ballistics.

Firearms Identification

Firearms identification, unlike ballistics, is the discipline of forensic science that is primarily concerned with determining if a bullet, cartridge case, or other ammunition component was fired by a particular firearm. This determination is made by the science of examination and comparison of firearms and ammunition. This identification process typically hinges upon analysis and identification of firearms-related markings. These can include, but are not limited to:

- Striations, land/groove markings on a bullet.
- Cartridge cases will be marked by a number of firearm components:
  - Firing pin marks (rimfire or centerfire).
  - Breechlock marks on primer cap.
  - Extractor/ejector marks on base of cartridge in self-loading or automatic weapons.
- In weapons with magazines, the lips of the magazine may also mark cartridges (Saferstein, 2010).

As a general rule, shotgun barrels do not leave identifiable markings on shot, wads, or shot columns.

Examination of Weapons

As an examination protocol, test firing is not necessarily the first step. There is a possibility that the weapon was last used in a homicide involving a contact wound. If the barrel was in contact with the body upon firing, there may be blood and tissue in the barrel as a result of barrel blowback. The weapon's bore also may have fibers from its owner's pockets. There is also a possibility that the weapon, its components, and its ammunition may retain fingerprints.

Once the firearm has been processed for fingerprints and trace evidence, a complete identification of the weapon should be made. The identification should include the following class characteristics:

- Make or manufacturer
- Type (revolver, pistol, etc.)
- Caliber
- Serial number
- Model
- Number of shots
- Barrel length

The make, manufacturer, and model are determined from names, trademarks, and proof marks placed on various components of the weapon. The caliber of the weapon may be indicated by the name or by trademark information. A weapon may be modified by fitting a different caliber barrel to the weapon's frame.

The **National Firearms Act of 1968** requires retailers to record the serial number of a weapon and the name of its purchaser. Because of the importance of the serial number for tracing a firearm's owner, a criminal may remove the stamped serial number by grinding. If the grinding does not go deep enough into the metal, a stamped serial number may still be recovered by chemical etching, electrochemical etching, or ultrasonic cavitation. Many firearms have parts of the serial number stamped into internal components. Handguns often have the serial number stamped at different locations on the frame.

In a case involving an accidental firing or a firing that occurred during a fight or struggle, the amount of force required to pull the trigger may be important. The trigger pull may be measured by gradually increasing the amount of weight hanging from the weapon's trigger while the weapon is held vertically with the mechanism cocked. The measurement should be made with the actuating force applied to the trigger at the same spot that the finger of a person firing the weapon would be placed.

Examination of Bullets

In the absence of a suspect weapon, a firearms examination is confined to the determination of *class characteristics* of the bullets, such as caliber, direction of twist of the rifling, *degree of twist*, number of lands and grooves, and width of the lands and grooves (**Figure 13–15**). With these data, the firearms examiner may be able to determine the make and model of the firearm that fired the bullets. If there are two or more fired bullets that exhibit the same class characteristics, they are then examined under a **comparison microscope** to determine if the bullets were fired by the same weapon.

FIGURE 13–15   Examples of modern ammunition

Before class characteristics of bullets are determined, the bullets should be examined for the presence of *trace evidence* such as blood, hairs, fibers, wood splinters, glass particles, paint, concrete, or soil particles. A bullet may pick up blood, hairs, and fibers as it passes through a shooting victim. Trace evidence such as wood splinters or glass particles embedded in a bullet indicate that the bullet may have passed through an intermediate object such as a door, wall, or window. Paint, concrete, or soil particles may be found if a bullet ricochets off a hard surface.

Caliber

The caliber of an un-deformed fired bullet may be measured with a micrometer. The diameter of interest is the diameter across the land impressions (which, on the expended bullet, will be indentations made by the barrel lands). Allowance must be made for the fact that firearm calibers are merely nominal indications of the true bore diameters. A group of Colt pistols, all nominally .38-caliber weapons, were found to have bore diameters ranging from 0.348 to 0.395 inch.

The caliber of an intact but badly deformed bullet may be estimated from its weight. The determination of caliber by weight will rarely allow the examiner to specify a particular caliber for the bullet, but certain calibers may be eliminated as possibilities. When the bullet is fragmented, an accurate weight can no longer be obtained. In such a case, the caliber of the bullet may be estimated by measuring the widths of a land impression and an adjacent groove impression (The Diagram Group, 2007).

Number of Lands and Grooves

In bullets recovered intact, the number of lands and grooves can be determined by counting them. In cases where bullets are badly deformed, measurement of the width of the land and groove impressions may be combined with knowledge of the caliber of the bullet to calculate the number of lands and grooves. Because manufacturers use a specific number of grooves in their firearms and this number is generally constant for a given make and model, the number of lands and grooves is an important class characteristic.

Rifling Twists

The direction of twist of the rifling may be determined by inspection of the fired bullet if it is not badly deformed. The rifling may spiral either to the left or to the right. Left-hand twist rifling is often referred to as Colt-type rifling, and right-hand twist rifling is often referred to as Smith-and-Wesson-type rifling.

Land and Groove Width

The width of the land and groove impressions may be measured using a filar micrometer, traveling microscope, or toolmaker's microscope. Measurements are made perpendicular to the axis of the bullet. Observing that the land impressions on a bullet are wider than the groove impressions allows the firearms examiner to eliminate certain makes and models of firearms. Land and groove impressions that are of a markedly different width than the other impressions on the bullet may reflect a defect in manufacture that is extremely rare (The Diagram Group, 2007).

Test Firing for Comparison

Once it has been determined that the class characteristics of the firearm and those of the fired bullets or cartridges are consistent, the weapon must be test-fired to obtain bullets and cartridges for comparative microscopical examination. To obtain test-fired bullets, the firearm is fired into a bullet trap. Most firearms laboratories use some type of water trap to catch fired bullets (**Figures 13–16** and **13–17**).

Bullet Comparisons

Bullet comparisons are made using a comparison microscope. A comparison microscope consists of two compound microscopes, each with its own objectives, stage, and focusing adjustments. The microscopes are joined by a comparison bridge, a system of prism mirrors that brings the images of the two microscopes together so that they can be compared side by side through a single ocular. The images of the two microscopes may be superimposed or they may be viewed side by side, with the field of view divided equally between the two microscopes. The bullets to be compared are attached to short cylindrical bullet holders. The bullet holders slip onto the shafts of the bullet-manipulating mechanisms, which in turn are attached to the microscope stages. The bullet-manipulating mechanisms are provided with universal joints so that the bullets may be oriented at any angle.

Once the bullets are mounted, the examiner begins the search for matching patterns of striations. The limited expansion of jacketed bullets leads to only occasional contact with the bottoms of the grooves, and only the base may be upset sufficiently to seat well in the barrel's rifling. Therefore, the initial examination is most likely to discover a pattern of striations near the base of the bullet. A land impression on a test-fired bullet is compared successively to each

FIGURE 13–16   Portable ballistic trap for the collection of bullet evidence
Courtesy of Savage Range Systems, Inc.

FIGURE 13–17 Portable ballistic trap for the collection of bullet evidence (port view)

land impression on the suspect bullet until a match is obtained or it is determined that no match is possible. Once a match has been made with a pair of land impressions, the bullets are rotated synchronously to see if other matching striation patterns may be observed. If both bullets were fired from the same barrel, numerous matching patterns will be evident. Marks other than land and groove striations may be observed.

Skid marks are caused by the bullet sliding over the beginnings of the lands at the breech end of the barrel. Shaving marks occur when a revolver bullet in the cylinder is not lined up perfectly with the barrel. The bullet will strike the edge of the forcing cone (the flared opening in the revolver's frame in front of the cylinder where the fired bullet enters the barrel), and a portion of the bullet will be shaved off on the side striking the forcing cone. Comparing shaved spots on a bullet may be difficult. Test firing may not always result in a similar shaving, and many shots may have to be fired before a similarly shaved bullet can be obtained.

In an effort to avoid detection, criminals may flatten, bend, or shorten the barrel of a firearm. Flattened barrels may be restored to round, bent barrels may be straightened, or bullets may be forced through the barrels. The marks on bullets fired through the barrel at its original length may not match the marks on bullets fired through a shortened barrel.

The examination of fired bullets may lead to any one of three conclusions:

1. The questioned bullet was fired from the suspect weapon.

2. The questioned bullet was not fired from the suspect weapon.

3. The results of the examinations are insufficient to reach a final determination.

Examination of Cartridge Cases

In examining a fired cartridge case, the examiner using a low-power microscope will note the following:

- Size
- Shape

- Type (rimmed, semi-rimmed, rimless, belted, rimfire, centerfire)
- Size of firing pin impression
- Position of firing pin impression
- Location of extractor marks
- Location of ejector marks
- Any other accidental marks (any mark other than those caused in the manufacturing process)

The shape and location of the firing pin impression on the cartridges of bullets shot from a .22-caliber, single-shot, breech-loading rifle can serve to identify the make and model of the rifle. The relative positions of the extractor and ejector marks on cartridges from self-loading pistols allow the same determination (Girard, 2010). If a suspect firearm is available and if the class characteristics of cartridges from that weapon match those of the questioned cartridge, the examiner fires test shots with the suspect weapon in order to obtain fired cartridges for comparison purposes. The cartridges then are placed inside an iris diaphragm that attaches to the bullet-mounting devices in the comparison microscope. Comparison of the various marks on the fired cartridges begins with the firing pin impressions, firing pin drag marks, and breechblock marks. A match of these marks would show that the same weapon fired both cartridges.

After the examiner evaluates these marks, he or she compares the extractor marks, ejector marks, chambering marks, and magazine (clip) marks. A match of any of these types of marks indicates that the two cartridges have been run through the action of the same weapon but does not establish that they ever passed through the barrel. Cartridge case class characteristics include:

- Caliber (headstamped)
- Manufacturer (headstamped)
- Composition (copper, cupronickel)
- Rim type (rimless, rimmed, semi-rimmed, belted)
- Primer (centerfire, rimfire)

Examination Objectives

Whenever a firearm is discharged in the commission of a crime, physical evidence is likely to be available. Such evidence in the hands of a competent firearms examiner may prove valuable in answering a number of questions. Residue from firing a firearm will remain on surfaces until removed. Barrel blowback will deposit unignited powder, which is expended as a black cloud, on the firearm and the hand and forearm of the individual firing it. Gunshot residue tests can be conducted to determine if residue is present on an assailant's or victim's hand. Although the FBI no longer tests for gunshot residue because of lack of demand and expense, gunshot-residue testing in the field is still an important investigative tool.

Generally speaking the objective of a firearms examination includes:

- Matching/identifying projectiles
- Matching/identifying cartridge cases
- Matching/identifying cartridges
- Matching/identifying extractor marks
- Matching/identifying ejector marks
- Matching/identifying lands and grooves
- Matching/identifying firearms
- Matching firing pin impressions
- Matching machine marks on cartridge case heads
- Matching striations on projectiles
- Assessing trigger pull
- Examining powder residue

Serial Number Restoration

Most modern firearms have a serial number impressed somewhere on the frame, and many have serial numbers located at more than one location. Serial numbers are generally impressed, but some are laser etched or dot matrix punched. The dots are very shallowly punched and are not easily restored once removed. Laser-burned numbers have edges that appear burned. As in the dot matrix impressions, laser-burned numbers are very shallow, easily removed, and difficult to restore (**Figure 13–18**).

CASE IN POINT

St. Valentine's Day Massacre

In 1929, Calvin Goddard was called to Chicago to examine the fired bullets and cartridges recovered in the St. Valentine's Day Massacre. Through careful examination, he was able to determine that the victims of the gangland execution had been killed with two different Thompson submachine guns, one with a 20-round magazine and the other with a 50-round drum magazine (Goddard, 1930). Goddard's impressive performance let to the eventual establishment of a private forensic laboratory in Chicago, under his direction. This laboratory later became the Chicago Police Department Crime Laboratory. Also in 1929, Goddard testified in *Evans v. Commonwelth* (1929), which became the precedent-setting case for the admissibility of comparisons of rifling marks.

Courtesy of Ronald Becker, JD, Professor, Chaminade Institute.

FIGURE 13-18   Example of a serial number
Courtesy of the Austin Police Department, Austin, Texas.

The most commonly applied serial number on firearms is pressure stamped onto the side of the firearm. The numbers are made by using a stamp with a positive impression of the number to be applied. Using great amounts of pressure the number is pressed into the metal creating a negative impression of the serial number. The pressure applied by the stamp causes plastic deformation of the metal, leaving numbers embedded upon the surface of the metal. If one was to look at a metal blank with numbers impressed into it, one might ask where did the metal go that was in the space that is now occupied by the numbers. If they were to turn the blank over he or she might expect the numbers to become a positive extrusion on the back side of the blank but when they examine it the blank is the same width and nothing protrudes from the back. The displaced metal is forced into the molecular space of the metal beneath it, keeping in mind that on the atomic level, everything is made up of empty space although it may appear solid. The strained metal becomes denser as a result of having more of its empty spaces filled with the metal from the impressed numbers. The strained metal is harder and in the same configuration as the numbers above it (Girard, 2010).

The depth of the strained metal depends upon the pressure applied to the stamp and the type of metal. In steel the strained metal is about six times the depth of the impressed numbers. When a serial number is removed for criminal purposes the removal generally stops once the numbers are no longer visible. It is the strained area below the numbers that allows the removed serial numbers to be restored.

In order to restore removed serial numbers the surface must be appropriately prepared. Cleaning the surface allows for examination of the depth of the obliteration. Once cleaned the surface needs to be smoothed by sanding with sand paper of progressively finer grits. Once the surface has been polished the restoration process can begin (**Figure 13–19**).

FIGURE 13-19   Example of restoring a serial number
Courtesy of Sirchie Acquisition Company, LLC.

The two most commonly employed methods of serial number restoration are the magnaflux method and the acid etching method. The magnaflux method is limited in its use to ferrous metals only. In this method the metal containing the serial number is removed from the firearm. A magnet is placed behind the metal at the location of the serial numbers. The area of the obliteration is covered with a mixture of oil and iron shavings. If this method is working properly the metal filings will begin to take the form of the obliterated numbers. The advantage of using the magnaflux method is that it is nondestructive and will allow acid etching as a backup procedure.

FIGURE 13–20 Example of restored serial number after polishing and using acid to etch the metal
Courtesy of Sirchie Acquisition Company, LLC.

Acid etching requires the same preparation of the metal. It should be noted that grinding wheels should not be used on metal that may be subject to serial number restoration. The heat generated from the grinding can adversely affect the underlying surface and the numbers being restored. The advantage of the acid etching method is that it can be used on ferrous and nonferrous metals (most usually aluminum). The acids used can be mixed or purchased pre-packaged to accommodate the metal type. In using a liquid acid solution a dam must be build around the serial number to keep the liquid from flowing away. Clay can be formed into a long tube and used to surround the number on the metal surface. Once the dam is in place the acid can be placed directly onto the metal. To hasten the restoration process an electrical current can be run through the metal. Care must be taken not to etch too much of the metal and once the numbers have been restored an acid neutralizer must be used or the etching process will continue to the destruction of the restored numbers. Documentation of the entire process is vital. The procedure will have to be explained at the time of trial and all supporting documentation will be used to establish that the appropriate protocols have been applied (**Figure 13–20**).

Serial numbers that have not been obliterated but are nonetheless difficult to read may be visualized without using etching acids. Seriously worn serial numbers can sometimes be enhanced with the use of chalk, the type of chalk that carpenters use in their chalk lines. The serial number area must be cleaned and dry, very dry. The powdered chalk should be a contrasting color to the metal of the firearm. Carpenters' chalk comes in a variety of colors, the most common being a cobalt blue and a very visible pink. A fingerprint brush can be used as long as the chalk is applied evenly and thoroughly. Any excess powder can be removed with an alcohol swab. Using alternative or oblique lighting the numbers can be visualized and photographed.

National Integrated Ballistic Information Network

The National Integrated Ballistics Information Network (NIBIN) is a nationally interconnected, computer-assisted ballistics imaging system used by firearms examiners to obtain computerized images of bullets and cartridge cases. The heart of NIBIN is the **Integrated Ballistic Identification System (IBIS)**, comprised of a microscope and a computer unit that captures an image digitally. These images can be compared with images already entered into the system. The system is maintained by the Bureau of Alcohol, Tobacco, Firearms and Explosives (ATF), and the 236 sites are electronically joined to 16 multistate regions (ATF, 2009).

Prior to the creation of NIBIN, the FBI and the ATF established their own computerized ballistics imaging systems. NIBIN was established to incorporate the FBI's Drugfire system and the ATF's Ceasefire system. The NIBIN system uses the ATF's imaging system and the secure, high-speed telecommunications network of the FBI.

Recent bills introduced in Congress would require all manufacturers to supply a spent cartridge and bullet for inclusion in the system before being allowed to sell or import the firearm. This would significantly increase the ability to trace firearms used in crimes. Presently, the participation of federal, state, and local law enforcement agencies in NIBIN is restricted by law to the ballistics imaging of data associated with only those guns used in crimes.

Comparisons of bullet and cartridge case marks were historically accomplished by firearms examiners using comparison microscopes. This process was accurate but slow and labor intensive. In the early 1990s, the ballistics imaging and matching process was computerized. Digital cameras were used to photograph bullets and cartridge cases and scan them into a computer. These images were then analyzed by a software program and stored in a database, making ballistics matching faster. When the computerized system was connected across numerous law enforcement agencies through a telecommunications system, it allowed the rapid comparison of bullets and cartridge cases used in crimes from different jurisdictions. The use of computerized images of bullets and cartridge cases streamlines chains of custody for those bullets and cartridge cases that are to be used in court.

NIBIN is composed of several computer-connected networks, and the goal is for NIBIN data to be shared nationally. The ATF has more than 80 offices around the country that serve as repositories for the deposit and retrieval of ballistic images. Four different types of IBIS make up the NIBIN network:

- *Regional server.* The central data repository for the region, in which all images are stored and bullet/cartridge case correlation requests are executed.

- *Digital acquisition system (DAS) remotes.* An IBIS system composed of a microscope and a computer unit that allows image acquisition or evaluation; these systems are linked to a regional server, where the images are stored and bullet cartridge case comparison or correlation requests are sent.

- *Rapid brass identification (RBI).* A portable cartridge casing system that allows on-site digital capture of fired cartridge cases for transmission to a central IBIS for processing, comparison, and storage.

- *MatchPoint* A desktop computer connected to a DAS remote by a local area network (LAN), allowing bullet cartridge analysis.

IBIS technology is designed to be used without extensive computer training or sophistication. Once entered, a sample that results in a hit (a possible match with a database record) provides demographic information about the crime; images of the correlated cartridge case, which includes the breech face, firing pin, and ejector marks; and images of the correlated bullet, including lands and accidentals.

If the image is captured at a DAS remote, the data is sent to the regional server for comparison. A hit results in the correlation data being returned to the DAS remote. The images are transmitted to the regional server for comparison to the region's database. Again, a hit results in the correlation data being returned to the cooperating DAS, and the RBI user is notified either by email or telephone. Ejected cartridge cases found at a crime scene can be digitized at the scene. The information can be transmitted to a laboratory, where a technician can use the system to conduct a search. If a hit is found, results can be returned to the personnel at the scene while the investigation is still in progress. The IBIS analysis system does not provide matches; as with AFIS, it provides correlations—a short list of possible matches. The final analysis for a match is conducted by a firearms examiner through a comparison microscope (**Figure 13–21**).

Technology has enhanced firearms examination analytical possibilities through the use of three-dimensional (3D) imaging technology. Two-dimensional images are limited in detail and depth. BulletTrax is an example of a 3D IBIS system, which allows for documentation and examination of the entire surface of a cartridge, cartridge case, or projectile (**Figure 13–22**). Three-dimensional software makes a mathematical model of the item viewed and stores the digital model in a database. The technician can then call up a 3D rendering of the object on a high-definition computer monitor (Garrison, 2011).

FIGURE 13–21 Example of an comparison microscope connected to an IBIS station

FIGURE 13–22 Example of a three-dimensional IBIS unit

NIBIN Authority and Effectiveness

FIGURE 13-23   A technician uses an IBIS station to load evidence into NIBIN

NIBIN acquisitions are expressly limited to ballistic information from firearms test fires and fired ammunition components taken into law enforcement custody pursuant to a criminal investigation. Since 1979, ATF's annual appropriations have prohibited the expenditure of funds for consolidating or centralizing federal firearms licensee acquisition and disposition records. Therefore, NIBIN cannot be used to capture or store ballistic information acquired at the point of manufacture, importation, or sale; nor can it be used to capture purchaser or date of manufacture or sale information (**Figure 13-23**).

NIBIN hit process:

- Fired ammunition components are recovered from a shooting scene;
- Imaged onto the network;

Collection and Preservation of Firearms Evidence

Oftentimes it will be necessary for personnel to recover firearms-related evidence from the crime scene. However, bullets may be difficult to recover due to their proclivity of lodging themselves into items and structures (**Figure 13-24**). When it becomes necessary to remove and recover such evidence, only rubber-coated or heavily-taped tools should be used either to probe for bullets or to extract them, so as not to cause damage to, or impart striation evidence upon the recovered evidence. Generally, it is best for the investigator to remove the section of the building structure that contains the bullet so that the forensic firearms examiner can carefully remove the bullet in the laboratory. Care must be taken not to dislodge any trace evidence that may be on the bullet surface. It is recommended to place the bullet or cartridge in a sealed pillbox or plastic vial. The container and its seal are then marked for identification (ID).

The serial numbers of all firearms seized should be recorded by investigators. For safety, loaded weapons should be unloaded before they are transported to the firearms laboratory. Firearms should be securely placed within a container (typically cardboard), with the barrel

- Firearm recovered from a suspect and test-fired;

- NIBIN identifies possible hit and microscopic comparison confirms hit;

- NIBIN partner notifies law enforcement agencies of hit.

NIBIN partner's milestones are:

- ATF has certified more than 1,000 NIBIN users to use the network.

- NIBIN partners have confirmed over 47,000 NIBIN hits.

Most Successful NIBIN Partners:

- New York City Police Department: more than 3,000 hits.

- Illinois State Police-Chicago: more than 2,100 hits.

- Allegheny County (Pa.) Medical Examiner's Office: more than 2,300 hits.

- Newark Police Department: more than 1,200 hits.

- Santa Ana (Calif.) Police Department: more than 1,100 hits.

Federal Bureau of Alcohol, Tobacco, Firearms and Explosives. (ATF, March 2012). "National Integrated Ballistic Information Network (NIBIN) Fact Sheet." http://www.atf.gov/publications/factsheets/factsheet-nibin.html.

end of the firearm noted on the outside of the package. Inside, the firearm should be secured in such a manner that will not allow the firearm to shift or damage the firearm (**Figures 13–25** and **13–26**).

When practical, always render a weapon safe to handle before proceeding with further investigation or examination. When unloading a revolver it must first be ascertained that the weapon is not cocked. Decocking must be done carefully before any further handling. Once decocked the revolver can be opened and the ammunition removed. Each cartridge in the cylinder should be first photographed in place then

FIGURE 13–24 Photograph of a bullet that was removed and cleaned after striking a target

Firearms and Toolmark Examination

Training, education, and desire played a crucial role in my professional development as a forensic scientist in the Firearm and Toolmark Section at the Northeastern Illinois Regional Crime Laboratory (NIRCL) in Vernon Hills, Illinois. My formal education included a Bachelor's of Science degree from the University of Wisconsin–Platteville in Chemistry-Criminalistics with a DNA emphasis. While working on my degree I had the opportunity, though my school, to work as an intern at NIRCL.

Soon, I found myself in the laboratory environment, astonished by the quantity and quality of casework the forensic scientists generated on a daily basis at NIRCL. I was requested to assist in the Firearm and Toolmark Section, where I immediately was captivated by the firearm and toolmark discipline. After my eight-week internship was complete, I was offered a training position in the Firearm and Toolmark Section, which I accepted. As I finished my degree, I eagerly anticipated my return to the laboratory to begin my firearm and toolmark training.

Upon my return to NIRCL, I began my training under a former Association of Firearm and Tool Mark Examiners (AFTE) president. Quickly I discovered the discipline of firearm and tool mark identification was very much an apprenticeship, typically consisting of two years of training, followed by a year of supervised casework. As a trainee, I studied numerous readings, literature, and court rulings accompanied with written and verbal tests, practical examinations, courtroom demeanor training, and supervised casework. Although the training was long and tedious, I found it to be absolutely necessary. I feel the extended instruction was crucial in order to cement the underlying basis of the science: the reproducibility of class and individual characteristics.

Throughout my training I was afforded opportunities to tour several firearm factories, ammunition factories, and tool factories, all of which expanded my appreciation for the discipline. The dedication continued as I became a certified armorer for M-16 rifles, AR-10 rifles, and Glock pistols. I also had the honor of making a television appearance in "Stop the Violence: Conflicts and Resolutions."

removed, taking care to document where each cartridge resided. The method most commonly used for documenting the cartridges is to mark one cylinder opening with a small mark indicating that documentation begins at this spot and that cylinder well is number one. Continuing in a clockwise fashion from the well marked and designated one, each well then becomes the next successive number. The cartridge in each numbered well is then tagged with the corresponding numbered cylinder well (**Figure 13–27**). Working with a semi-automatic pistol

My duties as a firearm and toolmark examiner include the examination of firearms and toolmarks, ammunition components, comparative microscopy, serial number restoration, range proximity of gunshot residue patterns, shot pellet pattern testing, trigger pull analysis, functionality/alteration testing, and examination of evidence for physical fit/fracture matches. Other duties include keeping maintenance logs of instruments, calibration and balance checks, reference collection firearm inventory, and chemical inventory. I also make entries into IBIS, analyze correlations, and provide statistics on IBIS for the ATF.

Throughout my time as a firearm and toolmark examiner, I have come across several firearms and tools that I had not seen previously nor could initially identify. However, firearm and toolmark examiners have many resources at hand to aid in identifying a rare firearm or tool. Some of these resources include colleagues, literature, forensic journals, and AFTE. AFTE is an international professional organization of firearm and toolmark examiners and technical advisors who, through a collaborative effort, hold meetings, publish a scientific journal, and partake in forums to share the knowledge and findings of members across the globe. Due to networking, examiners in this scientific community have an increased ability to assist in many technical issues. Through the networking efforts of these individuals, answers are literally a phone call or email away.

From first stepping into the laboratory environment, to working cases, my passion and dedication to the science of firearm and toolmark identification has only increased. I thoroughly enjoy learning about the rich history of firearm and toolmark identification. I aspire to continue the endeavors of examiners before me. I can attest to the quality and expertise of those before me and those who continue to work diligently in the firearm and toolmark discipline. This is truly a career and profession, not just a job.

Gary M. Lind, B.S.
Forensic Scientist
Firearm & Toolmark ID Section
Northeastern Illinois Regional Crime Laboratory
A Nationally Accredited Laboratory (ASCLD/LAB)

Courtesy of Gary M. Lind, Forensic Scientist, Northeastern Illinois Regional Crime Laboratory.

requires detailed notes and photographs of the weapon and the magazine. The first step is to ensure the weapon is unloaded. This is done by removing the clip/magazine and opening the action. Once the action has been opened the investigator can clear the weapon of any ammunition that may be in the barrel. If possible the slide on the pistol should be left in the open position so that anyone with a need to handle can immediately tell the weapon is unloaded. Many jurisdictions require investigators to mark the weapon in some unique fashion to be able

FIGURE 13–25   Example of packaging a firearm for evidence submittal

FIGURE 13–26   Example of packaging a firearm for evidence submittal

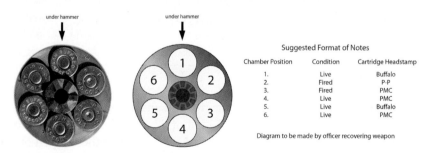

FIGURE 13–27   Example of how to document the position of a revolver cylinder and the location of ammunition

Courtesy of Dana Gevelinger, University of Wisconsin-Platteville.

to identify this weapon to the exclusion of all others. If marking is required it should be done to a place that is not readily removable from the weapon. Most agencies have moved away from engraving an identifying mark on firearms and use serial numbers for identification purposes. Now that fingerprints can be etched into the brass of ammunition, crime laboratories may instruct investigators not to remove cartridges from semi-automatic weapons.

Firearms or other metal objects recovered from water (liquid) should immediately be placed in a container of the same liquid, completely submerged. When in a liquid, the oxidation process is considerably retarded, and during the period necessary to transport the firearm to the crime laboratory only a small amount of change will take place.

Delivery of firearms is best accomplished by transporting the evidence as quickly as possible by the person discovering it. Chain of custody issues can be avoided by keeping the number of people in the chain to an absolute minimum. All firearms should be packaged pursuant to agency protocol, which generally includes boxes, manila envelopes, and paper wrapping. Plastic containers are not good repositories in that they may "sweat" and cause damage to the contents. Firearms recovered in water should be submitted in the same water in a watertight container. However, a firearms examiner must be contacted prior to submission if it is unknown whether the firearm is loaded.

Marking of Ammunition and Components

All firearms and firearms-related items should be handled with the belief they will be fingerprinted. Therefore, only the packaging should be marked. In this manner the possibility of damage, loss, or contamination of trace evidence and destruction of possible fingerprints is greatly diminished. These items should never be packaged in cotton or sealed in plastic. All packages should be properly sealed, with the initials of the collector over the seal, and marked with accompanying information such as the description of the item, source, case number, item number, initials of person collecting, and the date and time collected. In situations where through-and-through penetration of the victim's body has occurred and the bullet is found on the floor, in walls, or other location, bullets or bullet fragments should not be touched with bare fingers. A small piece of clean white paper should be slipped under the bullet, then folded and placed in a rigid container, and finally sealed and identified. This procedure will minimize the possibility that the recovering officer will contaminate traces of blood that may be present on the bullet. The aforementioned recommendations also apply to shotgun pellets and wads.

Many texts suggest that collected ammunition, bullets, or ballistic components should be marked/etched with the collector's initials; however, it is the author's belief and the policy of the majority of ballistic and forensic experts that firearms evidence is no different than any other type of physical evidence. When properly packaged and a proper chain of custody is adhered to, then there is no reason to mark and otherwise contaminate or change any item of evidence.

Visualizing Gunshot Residue

Gunshot residue (GSR) is a type of trace evidence and should be recovered in the same manner (**Figure 13–28**). Firearms examiners may need to use special techniques to visualize GSR patterns on dark or bloodstained clothing, as follows:

- Alternate light sources (ALSs).
- Chemical methods that test for and visualize nitrates present.
- The Griess Test: The chemical reagent reacts with inorganic nitrates in GSR to form an azo dye.
- Maiti Test: The chemical reagent reacts with GSR and appears as blue specks on a yellow background (Saferstein, 2010).

Reconstruction of Shooting-Related Incidents

Oftentimes, it is necessary to reconstruct a shooting-related incident to determine things such as direction of fire, bullet flight path, intermediate targets, zones of potential, and other factors that can have an impact on the outcome of the event. In order to reconstruct an event, it is necessary for the scene to be properly documented and all evidence collected. Once these steps have been taken, then the intrusive actions associated with reconstructive efforts may begin.

FIGURE 13–28 Example of collecting GSR evidence from the hand of a suspected shooter

Bullet Path Determination

Defining a bullet's path at a shooting scene is a useful element of crime scene reconstruction. A shooter's position and final bullet location can both be defined by determining the path of a bullet or bullets through a sequence of materials. Such reconstructions are most accurate when a bullet has created both a bullet hole and a subsequent impact site or two or more bullet holes appear in successive planes of material, for example, in sheet rock on both sides of an interior wall. Inserting rods through the bullet holes (or from bullet hole to impact site) will define a bullet path that can direct the investigator to the shooter's position or to the bullet's likely location. Rods should not be inserted in any bullet hole until documentation and examination of the bullet hole has been completed. Over short distances, string can be attached to the rods to project the bullet path. This technique is especially useful in reconstructing shootings involving vehicles due to their double-panel construction. However, because the projected bullet path increases in distance from the bullet hole, greater imprecision will be introduced into the reconstruction. For bullet path reconstructions over long distances, a combination of spacer cones, rods, and lasers will offer much better precision, especially if meaningful diagramming of the reconstruction is desired (**Figure 13–29**).

Unless a bullet passes through a significant thickness of material, a single bullet hole will usually not allow useful reconstruction of the bullet path. However, bullet direction can be determined from through-and-through bullet holes in many materials. The passage of a bullet through metal will create an indentation on the metal surface facing the bullet origin and metal stretch on the surface in the direction away from bullet origin, clearly defining the direction of the bullet through the metal. Bullets that pass through auto glass, skull, and some plastics will create a crater on the side of the material away from the bullet origin. In other words, the crater opens up in the direction of bullet travel. Even a portion of a bullet hole in a destructively fractured skull can define the direction of the bullet and subsequently establish exit and entrance. The combination of glass cratering and radial glass fracture in a window can even define the sequence of shots through the window, particularly when working with vehicle shootings.

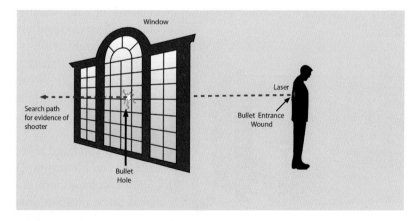

FIGURE 13–29 Determining discharge trajectory and location of shooter

Courtesy of Dana Gevelinger, University of Wisconsin-Platteville.

Evaluating and Documenting Zones of Possibility

While observing and documenting the crime scene, personnel begin to develop theories of possibilities and potential areas from which the shooting event could have originated. It is important to narrow down areas of possibility and areas of impossibility regarding the event, so as to reduce the suspect pool, tighten the story, and come as close as possible to the truthful events that transpired. While determining a trajectory may not definitively place an individual in a specific position or location, it can serve to eliminate individuals or locations, and exclusions are just as important to investigative efforts as inclusions. What is essential to determine in such a case would be what is referred to as **zones of possibility**. These zones of possibility are documented to establish limits as to what is likely, what is possible, and what is impossible, based upon the evidence presented (Moran, 2001). The zones are commonly identified as follows.

Zone 1

Probable: The area of greatest probability. The location of this zone is typically at a point along the identified trajectory that is at or lower than the likely shooter's shoulder height, and which is considered most comfortable and most logical, given the context of the scene being evaluated. This zone is further established and narrowed through inclusion of other scene-related shooting incident evidence such as muzzle-to-target data evaluation (**Figure 13–30**).

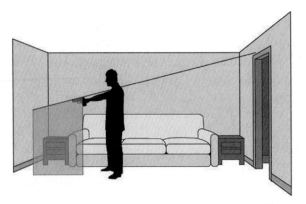

FIGURE 13–30   Zone 1: Probable
Courtesy of Gabbie Mears, University of Wisconsin-Platteville.

Zone 2

Possible: This zone includes possible locations where a shooter could have been when the shot was fired, but which would include an awkward stance or position. This typically involves any position along the identified trajectory path that is higher than the likely shooter's shoulders but which could still be reached by the shooter. For instance, it may be possible for a shooter to reach his or her arms up to the ceiling and bend his or her wrist so as to place the firearm on the trajectory, but such a position would not likely be a logical firing position unless there was an obstruction, a struggle, or some event that necessitated the awkward angle and positioning (**Figure 13–31**).

FIGURE 13–31   Zone 2: Possible
Courtesy of Gabbie Mears, University of Wisconsin-Platteville.

Zone 3

Impossible: This zone includes the areas within the identified shooting area that would be impossible for the shooter to have stood and fired the shot. In this area, the shooter would be physically incapable of aligning the firearm along the identified trajectory. Such impossibilities could be as a result of height, obstructions, or other factors (**Figure 13–32**).

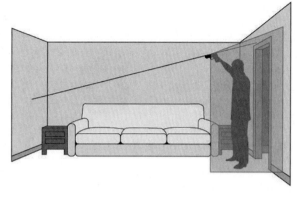

FIGURE 13–32 Zone 3: Impossible
Courtesy of Gabbie Mears, University of Wisconsin-Platteville.

Not all shooting-related incidents will have all three zones of possibility present. For instance, in an event involving level flight, no higher than a possible shooter's shoulders, there would only be two zones present. Zone 1 would include the probable area and Zone 3 would include the area outside of the room or vicinity from which the shot could not have originated. There would be no Zone 2.

Range-of-Fire Estimation from Powder and Pellet Patterns

In the reconstruction of shooting incidents the range and direction of fire are of paramount importance. Gunshot residue is typically used to measure these patterns. Gunshot residue consists of particles from the gun barrel, particles from the bullet surface, particles originating from the propellant, and particles originating from the primer. This residue is projected in a roughly conical cloud in the direction of the target (**Figure 13–33**).

Additionally, examiners using GreissTest, DTO (dithiooximide), and sodium rhodizonate for range determination for muzzle to target distance. These color tests help visualize patterns of nitrate/nitrite, copper, and lead residues, respectively. Firearms examiners also can estimate ranges of fire from shotgun pellet patterns. A widely used rule-of-thumb is that the pellets spread one inch for each yard down range. The sizes of shotgun pellet patterns are affected by the choke of the shotgun barrel. Sawing off the barrel of a shotgun may increase the size of the pellet patterns it will fire.

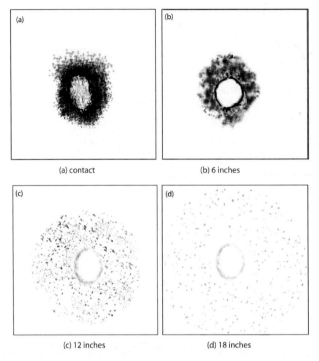

(a) contact

(b) 6 inches

(c) 12 inches

(d) 18 inches

FIGURE 13–33 Determining proximity of firearm at the time of discharge

Courtesy of Ellie Bruchez, University of Wisconsin-Platteville.

Range-of-Fire Estimation

Forensic pathologists usually place the range from which a GSW was inflicted into one of several categories:

1. **Distant:** No detectable GSR reaches the skin or clothing of the victim. GSWs consist of a circular or elliptical defect in the skin, which is surrounded by a "marginal abrasion ring" where the skin has been stretched and torn by the bullet entry.

2. **Close Range/Intermediate Range:** GSR reaches the skin/clothing of victim and stippling/tattooing is present.

3. **Near Contact/Contact:** Often produces a *stellate defect*, which is an irregular, blown-out entrance wound. This type of wound is caused by the propellant gases separating the soft tissue from the bone and creating a temporary pocket of hot gas between the bone and the muzzle of the weapon. Blood and other tissue may be blown back into the muzzle of the weapon and onto the hand and forearm of the shooter.

WRAP UP

Chapter Summary

Gunshot wounds are the most common homicidal injury within the United States as this country has more firearms per capita than any other nation on the earth. As such, the documentation, collection, and subsequent analysis of firearms-related evidence is often of paramount importance in an investigation involving a firearm. It is imperative that a crime scene investigator know the proper methods to collect firearms evidence that will result in the best evidentiary value. In order to achieve this end, the crime scene investigator must know the precise potential forensic value of the various components. Sometimes firearms evidence will yield only class characteristic information, but often, when properly documented and collected, firearms evidence can result in individual characteristics that are capable of being traced back to a single source.

Review Questions

1. A _____ is any device that fires a projectile or projectiles as a result of an explosive or propellant charge.

2. _____ is the discipline of forensic science with the primary concern of determining if a bullet, cartridge case, or other ammunition component was fired by a particular firearm.

3. _____ is the study of a projectile (most likely from a firearm) in motion.

4. Sawing off the barrel of a shotgun may _____ the size of the pellet patterns it will fire.

5. The diameter of the bore of a rifled firearm is known as its _____.

6. _____ is the number of spherical lead balls having the diameter of the interior of the barrel that weigh one pound.

7. Rifled firearms either have a twist to the _____ as in a Colt, or to the _____ as in a Smith and Wesson.

8. Which chemical test for the presence of GSR forms blue specks on a yellow background?

9. Explain what NIBIN is and how it is used in regards to ballistics evidence.

10. The heart of NIBIN is _____, comprised of a microscope and a computer unit that captures an image digitally.

Case Studies

Research the names John Allen Muhammad and Lee Boyne Malvo as they relate to a series of firearm-related cases. Summarize how the documentation, collection, preservation, and subsequent analysis of firearms-related evidence resulted in their convictions.

References

Bureau of Alcohol, Tobacco, Firearms and Explosives (ATF). (July 11, 2009). *Illinois state police mark 1000th 'hit' using ATF's ballistic imaging.* Retrieved September 15, 2012, from http://www.nibin.gov/press/il-state-pd-mark-1000th-hit-using-atf-ballistic-imaging.pdf

Bureau of Justice. (2008). Firearms and crime statistics. Retrieved August 23, 2012, from http://bjs.ojp.usdoj.gov/content/guns.cfm

The Diagram Group. (2007). *The new weapons of the world encyclopedia.* New York: St. Martins.

Garrison, D. (2011). Recent Advances in Forensic Ballistics. *Evidence Technology Magazine.* Wordsmith Publishing. Kearney, MO.

Girard, J. E. (2010). *Criminalistics: Forensic science, crime and terrorism.* Sudbury, MA: Jones and Bartlett.

Goddard, C. H. (1930). St. Valentine's Day massacre: A study in ammunition tracing. *American Journal of Police Science* 1, 60–78.

Heard, B. J. (2008). *Handbook of firearms and ballistics: Examining and interpreting forensic evidence.* Hoboken, NJ: Frank Willey.

James, S. H., & Nordby, J. J. (2009). *Forensic science* (3rd ed.). Boca Raton, FL: CRC Press.

Moran, B. (2001). *Shooting incident reconstruction,* presentation to the Association of Crime Scene Reconstruction, Las Vegas, NV, October 2001.

Patton, G. S. (1885–1945). "P" is for personal courage. Retrieved August 23, 2012, from http://permanent.access.gpo.gov/lps1786/vign7.html

Saferstein, R. (2010). *Criminalistics: An introduction to forensic science* (9th ed.). Upper Saddle River, NJ: Pearson Prentice Hall.

© McMac/ShutterStock, Inc.

Drug Evidence

Half of the modern drugs could well be thrown out of the window, except that the birds might eat them.

Dr. Martin Henry Fischer (1879–1962)
Professor Emeritus in Physiology, University of Cincinnati

KEY TERMS

Clandestine Laboratories
Controlled Substance
Controlled Substances
   Act (CSA)
Depressant
Dillie-Koppanyi
Drug

Duquenois-Levine
Gas Chromatography
Hallucinogen
Marquis Test
Mass Spectrometry
Microcrystalline Test
Narcotic

Schedules
Scott Test
Screening Test
Stimulant
Van Urk

Drug-Related Evidence in Crime Scene Investigation

While illegal drug use within the United States appears to have leveled off, and in some cases even declined, it is by no means absent from society or crime scenes. It is important for the crime scene investigator to have a good foundation as to what substances are considered to be "drugs" and how they should properly document, collect, package, and preserve such substances. Typically, when one talks of "drugs" one is in fact referring to "controlled substances." However, it is important to differentiate between the two, because the distinctions between the two terms relate to the investigative importance and criminal wrongdoing associated with each.

A **drug** is any chemical substance, other than food, that is intended for use in the diagnosis, treatment, cure, mitigation, or prevention of disease or symptoms. These can be dispensed and used either by prescription or over-the-counter (OTC). Possession of an OTC drug does not require a prescription and is not illegal (except in bulk as is associated with the manufacture of methamphetamine, which will be discussed later in this chapter).

Controlled substances, on the other hand, are those substances (typically drugs) whose possession or use is regulated by the government (**Table 14–1**). Title 21 of the United States Code (21 USC) defines these substances (United States Department of Justice [USDOJ], 1990).

The Controlled Substances Act

The **Controlled Substances Act (CSA)**, Title II and Title III of the Comprehensive Drug Abuse Prevention and Control Act of 1970, are the legal foundation of the U.S. government's fight against the abuse of drugs and other substances. This law is actually a consolidation of numerous laws regulating the manufacture and distribution of narcotics, stimulants, depressants, hallucinogens, anabolic steroids, and chemicals that are used in the illicit production of controlled substances.

Drug Scheduling

The CSA places all substances that were in some manner regulated under existing federal law into one of five **schedules**. This placement is based upon the substance's medical use, potential for abuse, and safety or liability for psychological and/or physical dependence.

Proceedings to add, delete, or change the schedule of a drug or other substance may be initiated by the Drug Enforcement Administration (DEA), the Department of Health and Human Services (DHHS), or by petition from any interested person. The scheduling is conducted through the cooperation between DHHS and the DEA, with both the legal and scientific/medical communities weighing in on the process.

TABLE 14–1   Types of Controlled Substances

Types of Controlled Substances	Examples	Legitimate Uses
Stimulants	cocaine, amphetamines, methamphetamine	Legitimate uses include increased alertness, reduced fatigue, weight control, and topical analgesic (pain-killing) action.
Depressants	barbiturates, sedatives, and tranquilizers	Legitimately used to obtain release from anxiety, for the treatment of psychological problems, and as mood elevators.
Narcotics	opium, morphine, heroin, methadone, codeine, Dilaudid	Legitimately used for pain relief, antidiarrheal action, and cough suppression.
Anabolic steroids	nandrolene, oxandrolene, oxymetholone, and stanoxolol	Used legitimately for weight gain; for treatment of arthritis, anemia, and cancer treatments.
Inhalants	nitrous oxide, super glue, gasoline, chloroform, freon, and toluene	Legitimately used for a variety of purposes, but very few of them related to inhalation.
Cannabis	marijuana, hashish, cannabis plants, sinsemilla, and hashish oil (all of which are collectively referred to as marijuana)	No legitimate use according to federal law.
Hallucinogens	lysergic acid diethylamide (LSD); phencyclidine (PCP); peyote; mescaline; psilocybin; 3,4methylene-dioxyamphetamine (MDA); methylenedioxy-methamphetamine (MDMA)	No legitimate use according to federal law.

Introduction to Drug Classes

The CSA regulates five classes of drugs: narcotics, depressants, stimulants, hallucinogens, and anabolic steroids. Each class has distinguishing properties, and drugs within each class often produce similar effects. However, all controlled substances, regardless of class, share a number of common features. The purpose of this chapter is to familiarize the reader with some of these shared features and to give definition to terms frequently associated with these drugs.

Scheduling of Controlled Substances

According to the 2005 edition of the DEA publication, *Drugs of Abuse*, the five schedules into which substances may be placed are as follows:

Schedule I

- The drug or other substance has a high potential for abuse.
- The drug or other substance has no currently accepted medical use in treatment in the United States.
- There is a lack of accepted safety for use of the drug or other substance under medical supervision.
- Examples: heroin, LSD, marijuana, and MDMA.

Schedule II

- The drug or other substance has a high potential for abuse.
- The drug or other substance has a currently accepted medical use in treatment in the United States or a currently accepted medical use with severe restrictions.
- Abuse of the drug or other substance may lead to severe psychological or physical dependence.
- Examples: morphine, PCP, cocaine, methadone, and methamphetamine.

Schedule III

- The drug or other substance has less potential for abuse than the drugs or other substances in schedules I and II.

All controlled substances have abuse potential or are immediate precursors to substances with abuse potential. With the exception of anabolic steroids, controlled substances are abused to alter mood, thought, and feeling through their actions on the central nervous system (brain and spinal cord). Some of these drugs alleviate pain, anxiety, or depression. Some induce sleep and others energize. Though therapeutically useful, the "feel good" effects of these drugs contribute to their abuse. The extent to which a substance is reliably capable of producing euphoria increases the likelihood of that substance being abused.

- The drug or other substance has a currently accepted medical use in treatment in the United States.

- Abuse of the drug or other substance may lead to moderate or low physical dependence or high psychological dependence.

- Examples: Anabolic steroids, codeine and hydrocodone with aspirin or Tylenol, and some barbiturates.

Schedule IV

- The drug or other substance has a low potential for abuse relative to the drugs or other substances in Schedule III.

- The drug or other substance has a currently accepted medical use in treatment in the United States.

- Abuse of the drug or other substance may lead to limited physical dependence or psychological dependence relative to the drugs or other substances in Schedule III.

- Examples: Valium and Xanax.

Schedule V

- The drug or other substance has a low potential for abuse relative to the drugs or other substances in Schedule IV.

- The drug or other substance has a currently accepted medical use in treatment in the United States.

- Abuse of the drug or other substances may lead to limited physical dependence or psychological dependence relative to the drugs or other substances in Schedule IV.

- Examples: cough medicines with codeine.

U.S. Drug Enforcement Administration (DEA). (2005). Drugs of abuse. Retrieved September 29, 2012, from http://naabt.org/documents/Drugs%20of%20abuse%20DEA.pdf.

In legal terms, the nonsanctioned use of substances controlled in Schedules I through V of the CSA is considered drug abuse. While legal pharmaceuticals placed under control in the CSA are prescribed and used by patients for medical treatment, the use of these same pharmaceuticals outside the scope of sound medical practice is also drug abuse.

Individuals who abuse drugs often have a preferred drug that they use, but may substitute other drugs that produce similar effects (often these are found in the same drug class) when they have difficulty obtaining their drug of choice. Drugs within a class are often compared with each other with terms like potency and efficacy. Potency refers to the amount of a drug that must be taken to produce a certain effect, while efficacy refers to whether or not a drug is capable of producing a given effect regardless of dose. Both the strength and the ability of a substance to produce certain effects play a role in whether that drug is selected by the drug abuser.

It is important to keep in mind that the effects produced by any drug can vary significantly and are largely dependent on the dose and route of administration. Concurrent use of other drugs can enhance or block an effect, and substance abusers often take more than one drug to boost the desired effects or counter unwanted side effects. The risks associated with drug abuse cannot be accurately predicted because each user has his or her unique sensitivity to a drug. There are a number of theories that attempt to explain these differences, and it is clear that a genetic component may predispose an individual to certain toxicities or even addictive behavior.

In the sections that follow, each of the five classes of drugs is reviewed and various drugs within each class are profiled. Although marijuana is classified in the CSA as a hallucinogen, a separate section is dedicated to that topic. There are also a number of substances that are abused but not regulated under the CSA. Alcohol and tobacco, for example, are specifically exempt from control by the CSA. In addition, a whole group of substances called inhalants are commonly available and widely abused by children. Control of these substances under the CSA would not only impede legitimate commerce, but would likely have little effect on the abuse of these substances by youngsters. An energetic campaign aimed at educating both adults and youth about inhalants is more likely to prevent their abuse. To that end, a section is dedicated to providing information on inhalants.

Narcotics

The term **narcotic**, derived from the Greek word for stupor, originally referred to a variety of substances that dulled the senses and relieved pain. Today, the term refers to opium, opium derivatives, and their semisynthetic substitutes. For the purposes of this text, the term narcotic refers to drugs that produce morphine-like effects.

Narcotics are used therapeutically to treat pain, suppress cough, alleviate diarrhea, and induce anesthesia. Narcotics are administered in a variety of ways. Some are taken orally, transdermally (skin patches), intra-nasally, or injected. As drugs of abuse, they are often smoked, sniffed, or injected. Drug effects depend heavily on the dose, route of administration, and previous exposure to the drug. Aside from their medical use, narcotics produce a general sense of well-being by reducing tension, anxiety, and aggression. These effects are helpful in a therapeutic setting but contribute to their abuse.

The poppy plant, *Papaver somniferum*, is the source for nonsynthetic narcotics (**Figure 14–1**). It was grown in the Mediterranean region as early as 5000 BC, and has since been cultivated in a number of countries throughout the world. The milky fluid that seeps from incisions in the unripe seed pod of this poppy, since ancient times, has been scraped by hand and air-dried to produce what is known as opium. A more modern method of harvesting is by the industrial poppy straw process of extracting alkaloids from the mature dried plant. The extract may be in

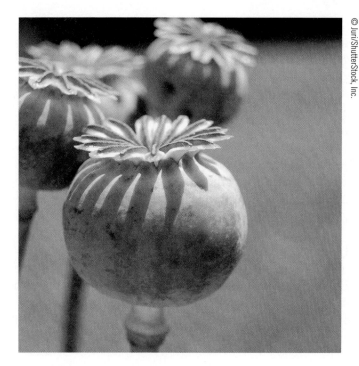

© Juri/ShutterStock, Inc.

FIGURE 14–1   Photo of poppy plant

liquid, solid, or powder form, although most poppy straw concentrate available commercially is a fine brownish powder. More than 500 tons of opium or equivalents in poppy straw concentrate are legally imported into the United States annually for legitimate medical use (United Nations, 2010).

Opium

There were no legal restrictions on the import or use of opium until the early 1900s. In the United States, the unrestricted availability of opium, the influx of opium-smoking immigrants from East Asia, and the invention of the hypodermic needle contributed to the more severe variety of compulsive drug abuse seen at the turn of the 20th century. In those days, medicines often contained opium without any warning label. Today, state, federal, and international laws govern the production and distribution of narcotic substances.

Morphine

Morphine is the principal constituent of opium and ranges in concentration from 4% to 21%. Commercial opium is standardized to contain 10% morphine. In the United States, a small percentage of the morphine obtained from opium is used directly (about 20 tons); the remaining is converted to codeine and other derivatives (about 110 tons). Morphine is one of the most effective drugs known for the relief of severe pain and remains the standard against which new analgesics are measured. Like most narcotics, the use of morphine has increased significantly in recent years. Since 1998, there has been about a twofold increase in the use of morphine products in the United States (United Nations, 2010).

Traditionally, morphine was almost exclusively used by injection. Today, morphine is marketed in a variety of forms, including oral solutions, immediate and sustained-release tablets and capsules, suppositories, and injectable preparations.

Codeine

Codeine is the most widely used, naturally occurring narcotic in medical treatment in the world. However, most codeine used in the United States is produced from morphine. Codeine is medically prescribed for the relief of moderate pain and cough suppression.

Heroin

First synthesized from morphine in 1874, heroin was not extensively used in medicine until the early 1900s. Commercial production of the new pain remedy was first started in 1898 (United Nations, 2010). It initially received widespread acceptance from the medical profession, and physicians remained unaware of its addiction potential for years. The first comprehensive control of heroin occurred with the Harrison Narcotic Act of 1914. Today, heroin is an illicit substance having no medical utility in the United States. It is in Schedule I of the CSA (**Figure 14–2**).

Four foreign source areas produce the heroin available in the United States: South America (Colombia), Mexico, Southeast Asia (principally Burma), and Southwest Asia (principally Afghanistan). South America and Mexico supply most of the illicit heroin marketed in the United States. South American heroin is a high-purity powder primarily distributed to metropolitan areas on the East Coast. Heroin powder may vary in color from white to dark brown because of impurities left from the manufacturing process or the presence of additives. Mexican heroin, known as black tar, is primarily available in the western United States. The color

FIGURE 14–2   Varieties of heroin
Courtesy of the DEA.

and consistency of black tar heroin result from the crude processing methods used to illicitly manufacture heroin in Mexico. Black tar heroin may be sticky like roofing tar or hard like coal, and its color may vary from dark brown to black (**Figure 14–3**).

In the past, heroin in the United States was almost always injected, because this is the most practical and efficient way to administer low-purity heroin. However, the recent availability of higher purity heroin at relatively low cost has meant that a larger percentage of today's users are either snorting or smoking heroin, instead of injecting it (**Figure 14–4**). This trend was first captured in the 1999 National Household Survey on Drug Abuse, which revealed that

FIGURE 14–3   Black tar heroin
Courtesy of the Austin Police Department, Austin, Texas.

FIGURE 14–4   Heroin volcanoes

60% to 70% of people who used heroin for the first time from 1996 to 1998 never injected it (Substance Abuse and Mental Health Services Administration [SAMHSA], 1999). This trend has continued. Snorting or smoking heroin is more appealing to new users because it eliminates both the fear of acquiring syringe-borne diseases, such as HIV and hepatitis, as well as eliminating the social stigma attached to intravenous heroin use. Many new users of heroin mistakenly believe that smoking or snorting heroin is a safe technique for avoiding addiction. However, both the smoking and the snorting of heroin are directly linked to high incidences of dependence and addiction.

Oxycodone

Oxycodone is synthesized from thebaine. Like morphine and hydromorphone, oxycodone is used as an analgesic. Historically, oxycodone products have been popular drugs of abuse among the narcotic abusing population. In recent years, concern has grown among federal, state, and local officials about the dramatic increase in the illicit availability and abuse of Oxycontin products. These products contain large amounts of oxycodone (10 to 160 mg) in a formulation intended for slow release over about a 12-hour period.

Abusers have learned that this slow-release mechanism can be easily circumvented by crushing the tablet and swallowing, snorting, or injecting the drug product for a more rapid and intense high. The criminal activity associated with illicitly obtaining and distributing this drug as well as serious consequences of illicit use, including addiction and fatal overdose deaths, are of epidemic proportions in some areas of the United States.

Hydrocodone

Hydrocodone is an effective cough suppressant and analgesic. All products currently marketed in the United States are either Schedule III combination products primarily intended for pain management or Schedule V antitussive medications often marketed in liquid formulations. The Schedule III products are currently under review at the federal level to determine if an increase in regulatory control is warranted.

Hydrocodone products are the most frequently prescribed pharmaceutical opiates in the United States with over 111 million prescriptions dispensed in 2003 (United Nations, 2010). Despite their obvious utility in medical practice, hydrocodone products are among the most popular pharmaceutical drugs associated with drug diversion, trafficking, abuse, and addiction. In every geographical area in the country, the DEA has listed this drug as one of the most commonly diverted. Hydrocodone is the most frequently encountered opiate pharmaceutical in submissions of drug evidence to federal, state, and local forensic laboratories. Law enforcement has documented the diversion of millions of dosage units of hydrocodone by theft, doctor shopping, fraudulent prescriptions, bogus "call-in" prescriptions, and diversion by registrants and Internet fraud.

Hydrocodone products are associated with significant drug abuse. Hydrocodone was ranked sixth among all controlled substances in the 2006 Drug Abuse Warning Network (DAWN) emergency department (ED) data (SAMHSA, 2008). Poison control data, DAWN medical examiner (ME) data, and other ME data indicate that hydrocodone deaths are numerous, widespread, and increasing in number. In addition, the hydrocodone acetaminophen combinations (accounting for about 80% of all hydrocodone prescriptions) carry significant public health risk when taken in excess.

Fentanyl

First synthesized in Belgium in the late 1950s, fentanyl, with an analgesic potency of about 80 times that of morphine, was introduced into medical practice in the 1960s as an intravenous anesthetic. Illicit use of pharmaceutical fentanyls first appeared in the mid-1970s in the medical community and continues to be a problem in the United States. To date, over 12 different analogues of fentanyl have been produced clandestinely and identified in the U.S. drug traffic. The biological effects of the fentanyls are indistinguishable from those of heroin, with the exception that the fentanyls may be hundreds of times more potent. Fentanyls are most commonly used by intravenous administration, but like heroin, they may also be smoked or snorted.

Methadone

German scientists synthesized methadone during World War II because of a shortage of morphine. Although chemically unlike morphine or heroin, methadone produces many of the same effects. It was introduced into the United States in 1947 as an analgesic (Dolophine). Today, methadone is primarily used for the treatment of narcotic addiction, although a growing number of prescriptions are being written for chronic pain management. It is available in oral solutions, tablets, and injectable Schedule II formulations.

Methadone's effects can last up to 24 hours, thereby permitting once-a-day oral administration in heroin detoxification and maintenance programs. High-dose methadone can block the effects of heroin, thereby discouraging the continued use of heroin by addicts in treatment. Chronic administration of methadone results in the development of tolerance and dependence. The withdrawal syndrome develops more slowly and is less severe, but more prolonged than that associated with heroin withdrawal. Ironically, methadone used to control narcotic addiction is encountered on the illicit market. Recent increases in the use of methadone for pain management have been associated with increasing numbers of overdose deaths.

Stimulants

Stimulants, sometimes referred to as uppers, reverse the effects of fatigue on both mental and physical tasks. Two commonly used stimulants are nicotine, which is found in tobacco products, and caffeine, an active ingredient in coffee, tea, some soft drinks, and many nonprescription medicines. Used in moderation, these substances tend to increase alertness. Although the use of these products has been an accepted part of U.S. culture, the recognition of their adverse effects has resulted in a proliferation of caffeine-free products and efforts to discourage cigarette smoking.

A number of stimulants, however, are under the regulatory control of the CSA. Some of these controlled substances are available by prescription for legitimate medical use in the treatment of obesity, narcolepsy, and attention deficit disorders. As drugs of abuse, stimulants are frequently taken to produce a sense of exhilaration, enhance self-esteem, improve mental and physical performance, increase activity, reduce appetite, produce prolonged wakefulness, and to "get high." They are among the most potent agents of reward and reinforcement that underlie the problem of dependence.

Stimulants are diverted from legitimate channels and clandestinely manufactured exclusively for the illicit market. They are taken orally, sniffed, smoked, and injected. Smoking, snorting, or injecting stimulants produce a sudden sensation known as a rush or a flash. Abuse is often associated with a pattern of binge use: sporadically consuming large doses of stimulants over a short period of time. Heavy users may inject themselves every few hours, continuing until they have depleted their drug supply or reached a point of delirium, psychosis, and physical exhaustion. During this period of heavy use, all other interests become secondary to re-creating the initial euphoric rush. Tolerance can develop rapidly, and both physical and psychological dependence occur. Abrupt cessation, even after a brief two- or three-day binge, is commonly followed by depression, anxiety, drug craving, and extreme fatigue known as a crash.

Therapeutic levels of stimulants can produce exhilaration, extended wakefulness, and loss of appetite. These effects are greatly intensified when large doses of stimulants are taken. Physical side effects, including dizziness, tremor, headache, flushed skin, chest pain with palpitations, excessive sweating, vomiting, and abdominal cramps, may occur as a result of taking too large a dose at one time or taking large doses over an extended period of time. Psychological effects include agitation, hostility, panic, aggression, and suicidal or homicidal tendencies. Paranoia, sometimes accompanied by both auditory and visual hallucinations, may occur also. Overdose is often associated with high fever, convulsions, and cardiovascular collapse. Because accidental death is partially due to the effects of stimulants on the body's cardiovascular and temperature-regulating systems, physical exertion increases the hazards of stimulant use.

Cocaine

Cocaine, the most potent stimulant of natural origin, is extracted from the leaves of the coca plant (*Erythroxylum coca*), which is indigenous to the Andean highlands of South America. Natives in this region chew or brew coca leaves into a tea for refreshment and to relieve fatigue, similar to the customs of chewing tobacco and drinking tea or coffee.

Pure cocaine was first isolated in the 1880s and used as a local anesthetic in eye surgery. It was particularly useful in surgery of the nose and throat because of its ability to provide anesthesia as well as to constrict blood vessels and limit bleeding. Many of its therapeutic applications are now obsolete due to the development of safer drugs.

Illicit cocaine is usually distributed as a white crystalline powder or as an off-white chunky material. The powder, usually cocaine hydrochloride, is often diluted with a variety of substances, the most common being sugars such as lactose, inositol, and mannitol, and local anesthetics such as lidocaine. The adulteration increases the volume and thus multiplies profits. Cocaine hydrochloride is generally snorted or dissolved in water and injected (**Figure 14–5**).

Crack, the chunk or "rock" form of cocaine, is a ready-to-use freebase (**Figure 14–6**). On the illicit market, it is sold in small, inexpensive dosage units that are smoked. Smoking delivers

© Gary Paul Lewis/ShutterStock, Inc.

FIGURE 14–5   Example of cocaine and related paraphernalia

FIGURE 14–6   (A) Crack cocaine; (B) Crack cocaine cookie (crack in the shape of the container in which it was formed)
Courtesy of the Austin Police Department, Austin, Texas.

large quantities of cocaine to the lungs, producing effects comparable to intravenous injection. Drug effects are felt almost immediately, are very intense, and are quickly over. Once introduced in the mid-1980s, crack abuse spread rapidly and made the cocaine experience available to a wide range of people and socioeconomic backgrounds. It is noteworthy that the emergence of crack was accompanied by a dramatic increase in drug abuse problems and drug-related violence within the United States.

Cocaine is the third most commonly used illicit drug (following marijuana and psychotherapeutics) in the United States. According to the 2008 National Survey on Drug Use and Health, 1.9 million Americans, age 12 or older, have used cocaine in the past month (DHHS, 2008).

Amphetamines

Amphetamine—dextroamphetamine, methamphetamine, and their various salts—are collectively referred to as amphetamines. In fact, their chemical properties and actions are so similar that even experienced users have difficulty knowing which drug they have taken (**Figure 14–7**).

Amphetamine was first marketed in the 1930s as Benzedrine in an OTC inhaler to treat nasal congestion. By 1937, amphetamine was available by prescription in tablet form and was used in the treatment of the sleeping disorder, narcolepsy, and the behavioral syndrome called minimal brain dysfunction, which today is called attention deficit hyperactivity disorder (ADHD). During World War II, amphetamine was widely used to keep the fighting men going.

As use of amphetamines spread, so did their abuse. In the 1960s, amphetamines became a perceived remedy for helping truckers to complete their long routes without falling asleep,

FIGURE 14–7   Varieties of methamphetamine

for weight control, for helping athletes to perform better and train longer, and for treating mild depression. Intravenous amphetamines, primarily methamphetamine, were abused by a subculture known as speed freaks. With experience, it became evident that the dangers of abuse of these drugs outweighed most of their therapeutic uses.

Increased control measures were initiated in 1965 with amendments to the federal food and drug laws to curb the black market in amphetamines. Many pharmaceutical amphetamine products were removed from the market, including all injectable formulations, and doctors prescribed those that remained less freely. Recent increases in medical use of these drugs can be attributed to their use in the treatment of ADHD. Amphetamines are all controlled in Schedule II of the CSA.

To meet the ever increasing black market demand for amphetamines, clandestine laboratory production has mushroomed. Today, most amphetamines distributed to the black market are produced in **clandestine laboratories** (**Figure 14–8**). The investigation of clandestine laboratories is one of the most challenging efforts of law enforcement. No other law enforcement activity relies on forensic science as heavily. It is important in these situations that personnel take proper precautions while attempting to maximize physical evidence recovery efforts.

Methamphetamine laboratories are, by far, the most frequently encountered clandestine laboratories in the United States. The ease of clandestine synthesis, combined with tremendous profits, has resulted in significant availability of illicit methamphetamine. Methamphetamine produced in home labs is becoming increasingly more common due to the availability and legality of the common ingredients used to manufacture the drug. One of the primary ingredients of methamphetamine is pseudoephedrine, a common OTC drug that has become increasingly controlled by vendors due to this epidemic, although it is still not technically a controlled drug. However, due to legislation in a great many of states, possession of large amounts of pseudoephedrine tablets, or other precursor ingredients of methamphetamine, can subject the possessor to criminal charges for taking a substantial step toward, or possessing items used in, the manufacture of a controlled substance. While there has been a significant increase in "Mom and Pop" type home laboratories, there are large amounts of methamphetamine that are also illicitly smuggled into the United States from Mexico and Southeast Asia.

Amphetamines are generally taken orally or injected. However, the addition of ice, the slang name for crystallized methamphetamine hydrochloride, has promoted smoking as another mode of administration. Just as "crack" is smokable cocaine, "ice" is smokable methamphetamine. Methamphetamine in any form is highly addictive and toxic.

The effects of amphetamines, especially methamphetamine, are similar to cocaine, but their onset is slower and their duration is longer. In contrast to cocaine, which is quickly removed from the brain and is

© NBC Universal, Inc./AP Photos.

FIGURE 14–8   A clandestine methamphetamine laboratory

almost completely metabolized, methamphetamine remains in the central nervous system longer, and a larger percentage of the drug remains unchanged in the body, producing prolonged stimulant effects. Chronic abuse produces a psychosis that resembles schizophrenia and is characterized by paranoia, picking at the skin, preoccupation with one's own thoughts, and auditory and visual hallucinations. These psychotic symptoms can persist for months and even years after use of these drugs has ceased and may be related to their neurotoxic effects. Violent and erratic behavior is frequently seen among chronic abusers of amphetamines, especially methamphetamine.

Depressants

Historically, people of almost every culture have used chemical agents to induce sleep, relieve stress, and allay anxiety. While alcohol is one of the oldest and most universal agents used for these purposes, hundreds of substances have been developed that produce central nervous system depression. These drugs are called **depressants** and have also been referred to as downers, sedatives, hypnotics, minor tranquilizers, and anti-anxiety medications. Unlike most other classes of drugs of abuse, depressants are rarely produced in clandestine laboratories. Generally, legitimate pharmaceutical products are diverted to the illicit market. A notable exception to this is a relatively recent drug of abuse, gamma hydroxybutyric acid (GHB).

Barbiturates were very popular in the first half of the 20th century. In moderate amounts, these drugs produce a state of intoxication that is remarkably similar to alcohol intoxication. Symptoms include slurred speech, loss of motor coordination, and impaired judgment. Depending on the dose, frequency, and duration of use, one can rapidly develop tolerance, and physical and psychological dependence on barbiturates. With the development of tolerance, the margin of safety between the effective dose and the lethal dose becomes very narrow. That is, in order to obtain the same level of intoxication, the tolerant abuser may raise his or her dose to a level that may result in coma or death. Although many individuals have taken barbiturates therapeutically without harm, concern about the addiction potential of barbiturates and the ever increasing number of fatalities associated with them led to the development of alternative medications. Today, less than 10% of all depressant prescriptions in the United States are for barbiturates.

Benzodiazepines were first marketed in the 1960s. Touted as much safer depressants with far less addiction potential than barbiturates, today these drugs account for about one out of every five prescriptions for controlled substances. Although benzodiazepines produce significantly less respiratory depression than barbiturates, it is now recognized that benzodiazepines share many of the undesirable side effects of the barbiturates. A number of toxic central nervous system effects are seen with chronic high-dose benzodiazepine therapy, including headaches, irritability, confusion, memory impairment, and depression. The risk of developing oversedation, dizziness, and confusion increases substantially with higher doses of benzodiazepines. Prolonged use can lead to physical dependence even at doses recommended for medical treatment. Unlike barbiturates, large doses of benzodiazepines are rarely fatal unless combined with other drugs or alcohol. Although primary abuse of benzodiazepines is well documented, abuse of these drugs usually occurs as part of a pattern of multiple drug abuse. For example, heroin or cocaine abusers will use benzodiazepines and other depressants to augment their "high" or alter the side effects associated with overstimulation or narcotic withdrawal.

There are marked similarities among the withdrawal symptoms seen with most drugs classified as depressants. In the mildest form, the withdrawal syndrome may produce insomnia and anxiety, usually the same symptoms that initiated the drug use. With a greater level of dependence, tremors and weakness are also present, and in its most severe form, the withdrawal syndrome can cause seizures and delirium. Unlike the withdrawal syndrome seen with most other drugs of abuse, withdrawal from depressants can be life threatening.

Barbiturates

Barbiturates were first introduced for medical use in the early 1900s. More than 2,500 barbiturates have been synthesized, and at the height of their popularity, about 50 were marketed for human use. Today, about a dozen are in medical use. Barbiturates produce a wide spectrum of central nervous system depression, from mild sedation to coma, and have been used as sedatives, hypnotics, anesthetics, and anticonvulsants. The primary differences among many of these products are how fast they produce an effect and how long those effects last. There is a variation in scheduling (Schedule III to Schedule IV) within this group of controlled substances. Those scheduled as IV have effects that are realized in about one hour and last for about 12 hours, and are used primarily for daytime sedation and the treatment of seizure disorders. Those scheduled as III exhibit onset of action from 15 to 40 minutes, and the effects last up to six hours. These drugs are primarily used for insomnia and preoperative sedation. Veterinarians also will make use of them for anesthesia and euthanasia.

Benzodiazepines

The benzodiazepine family of depressants is used therapeutically to produce sedation, induce sleep, relieve anxiety and muscle spasms, and to prevent seizures. Of the drugs marketed in the United States that affect central nervous system function, benzodiazepines are among the most widely prescribed medications. Fifteen members of this group are presently marketed in the United States, and about 20 additional benzodiazepines are marketed in other countries. Benzodiazepines are controlled in Schedule IV of the CSA.

Benzodiazepines are classified in the CSA as depressants. Repeated use of large doses or, in some cases, daily use of therapeutic doses of benzodiazepines is associated with amnesia, hostility, irritability, and vivid or disturbing dreams as well as tolerance and physical dependence. The withdrawal syndrome is similar to that of alcohol and may require hospitalization. Abrupt cessation of benzodiazepines is not recommended and tapering down the dose eliminates many of the unpleasant symptoms.

Given the millions of prescriptions written for benzodiazepines, relatively few individuals increase their dose on their own initiative or engage in drug-seeking behavior. Those individuals who do abuse benzodiazepines often maintain their drug supply by getting prescriptions from several doctors, forging prescriptions, or buying diverted pharmaceutical products on the illicit market. Abuse is frequently associated with adolescents and young adults who take benzodiazepines to obtain a "high." This intoxicated state results in reduced inhibition and impaired judgment. Concurrent use of alcohol or other depressants with benzodiazepines can be life threatening. Abuse of benzodiazepines is particularly high among heroin and cocaine abusers. A large percentage of people entering treatment for narcotic or cocaine addiction also report abusing benzodiazepines. Alprazolam and diazepam are the two most frequently encountered benzodiazepines on the illicit market.

Flunitrazepam

Flunitrazepam (Rohypnol) is a benzodiazepine that is not manufactured or legally marketed in the United States, but is smuggled in by traffickers. In the mid-1990s, flunitrazepam was extensively trafficked in Florida and Texas. Known as roofies and roach, flunitrazepam gained popularity among younger individuals as a "party" drug. It has also been utilized as a "date rape" drug. In this context, flunitrazepam is placed in the alcoholic drink of an unsuspecting victim to incapacitate them and prevent resistance from sexual assault. The victim is frequently unaware of what has happened to them and often does not report the incident to authorities. A number of actions by the manufacturer of this drug and by government agencies have resulted in reducing the availability and abuse of flunitrazepam in the United States.

Gamma hydroxybutyric acid (GHB)

In recent years, gamma hydroxybutyric acid (GHB) has emerged as a significant drug of abuse throughout the United States. Abusers of this drug fall into three major groups: (1) users who take GHB for its intoxicant or euphoriant effects; (2) bodybuilders who abuse GHB for its alleged utility as an anabolic agent or as a sleep aid; and (3) individuals who use GHB as a weapon for sexual assault. These categories are not mutually exclusive and an abuser may use the drug illicitly to produce several effects. GHB is frequently taken with alcohol or other drugs that heighten its effects and is often found at bars, nightclubs, rave parties, and gyms. Teenagers and young adults who frequent these establishments are the primary users. Like flunitrazepam, GHB is often referred to as a "date-rape" drug. GHB involvement in rape cases is likely to be unreported or unsubstantiated because GHB is quickly eliminated from the body, making detection in body fluids unlikely. Its fast onset of depressant effects may render the victim with little memory of the details of the attack.

GHB produces a wide range of central nervous system effects, including dose-dependent drowsiness, dizziness, nausea, amnesia, visual hallucinations, hypotension, bradycardia, severe respiratory depression, and coma. The use of alcohol in combination with GHB greatly enhances its depressant effects. Overdose frequently requires emergency room care, and many GHB-related fatalities have been reported.

The abuse of GHB began to seriously escalate in the mid-1990s. For example, in 1994, there were 55 emergency department episodes involving GHB reported in the DAWN system. By 2006, there were 3,330 emergency room episodes. DAWN data also indicated that most users were male, less than 25 years of age, and taking the drug orally for recreational use. GHB was placed in Schedule I of the CSA in March 2000 (SAMHSA, 2008).

Cannabis

Cannabis sativa L., the cannabis plant, grows wild throughout most of the tropic and temperate regions of the world. Prior to the advent of synthetic fibers, the cannabis plant was cultivated for the tough fiber of its stem. In the United States, cannabis is legitimately grown only for scientific research.

Cannabis contains chemicals called cannabinoids that are unique to the cannabis plant. One of these, delta-9-tetrahydrocannabinol (THC), is believed to be responsible for most of the characteristic psychoactive effects of cannabis.

Cannabis products are usually smoked. Their effects are felt within minutes, reach their peak in 10 to 30 minutes, and may linger for two or three hours. The effects experienced often depend upon the experience and expectations of the individual user as well as the activity of the drug itself. Low doses tend to induce a sense of well-being and a dreamy state of relaxation, which may be accompanied by a more vivid sense of sight, smell, taste, and hearing, as well as by subtle alterations in thought formation and expression. High doses may result in image distortion, a loss of personal identity, fantasies, and hallucinations.

Three drugs that come from cannabis—marijuana, hashish, and hashish oil—are distributed on the U.S. illicit market. Having no federally accepted medical use in treatment in the United States, they remain under Schedule I of the CSA. Today, cannabis is illicitly cultivated, both indoors and out, to maximize its THC content, thereby producing the greatest possible psychoactive effect.

Marijuana

Marijuana is the most frequently encountered illicit drug worldwide (**Figure 14–9**). In the United States, according to the 2003 Monitoring the Future study, 57% of adults aged 19 to 28 reported having used marijuana in their lifetime (Johnston, O'Malley, & Bachman, 2003). Among younger Americans, 17.5% of 8th graders and 46.1% of 12th graders had used marijuana in their lifetime (United Nations, 2010). The term marijuana, as commonly used, refers to the leaves and flowering tops of the cannabis plant that are dried to produce a tobacco-like substance. Marijuana varies significantly in its potency, depending on the source and selection

GHB Usage as a Predatory Drug

GHB is a clear, odorless liquid, slightly thicker than water. Its only detection is that it has a salty taste. It is virtually undetectable by victims, users and yes . . . even the cops! Its effects are not felt for two to four hours, and users commonly do not remember what happened during that time. GHB can easily be slipped into any drink (most commonly alcoholic beverages). GHB causes the body's functions to slow dramatically. Breathing can decrease to six times per minute. Heart rate can slow to 25 beats per minute.

FIGURE 14–9 Marijuana

of plant materials used. The form of marijuana known as sinsemilla (from Spanish, *sin semilla*: without seed), derived from the unpollinated female cannabis plant, is preferred for its high THC content. Marijuana is usually smoked in the form of loosely rolled cigarettes called joints, bongs, or hollowed out commercial cigars called blunts. Joints and blunts may be laced with a number of adulterants including phencyclidine (PCP), substantially altering the effects and toxicity of these products. Street names for marijuana include pot, grass, weed, Mary Jane, and reefer. Although marijuana grown in the United States was once considered inferior because of a low concentration of THC, advancements in plant selection and cultivation have resulted in higher THC-containing domestic marijuana (**Figures 14–10** and **14–11**).

Marijuana contains known toxins and cancer-causing chemicals. Marijuana users experience the same health problems as tobacco smokers, such as bronchitis, emphysema, and bronchial asthma. Some of the effects of marijuana use also include increased heart rate, dryness of the mouth, reddening of the eyes, impaired motor skills and concentration, and hunger with an increased desire for sweets. Extended use increases risk to the lungs and reproductive system as well as suppression of the immune system. Occasionally, hallucinations, fantasies, and paranoia are reported. Long-term chronic marijuana use is characterized by apathy; impairment of judgment, memory, and concentration; and loss of interest in personal appearance and pursuit of goals.

Hashish

Hashish consists of the THC-rich resinous material of the cannabis plant, which is collected, dried, and then compressed into a variety of forms, such as balls, cakes, or cookie-like sheets. Pieces are then broken off, placed in pipes, and smoked. The Middle East, North Africa, and Pakistan/Afghanistan are the main sources of hashish (DEA, 2005).

Hashish Oil

The term hash oil is used by illicit drug users and dealers, but is a misnomer in suggesting any resemblance to hashish. Hash oil is produced by extracting the cannabinoids from plant material with a solvent. The color and odor of the resulting extract will vary, depending on the type of solvent used. In terms of its psychoactive effect, a drop or two of this liquid on a cigarette is equal to a single "joint" of marijuana (DEA, 2005).

FIGURE 14–10　A marijuana grow

FIGURE 14–11　Large scale trafficking in marijuana (processing evidence of)

Hallucinogens

Hallucinogens are among the oldest known group of drugs used for their ability to alter human perception and mood. For centuries, many of the naturally occurring hallucinogens found in plants and fungi have been used for a variety of shamanistic practices. In more recent years, a number of synthetic hallucinogens have been produced, some of which are much more potent than their naturally occurring counterparts.

The biochemical, pharmacological, and physiological basis for hallucinogenic activity is not well understood. Even the name for this class of drugs is not ideal, because hallucinogens do not always produce hallucinations.

RIPPED FROM THE HEADLINES

DEA Moves Quickly to Control Synthetic Pot

In 2010, a blend of household herbs, laced with synthetic marijuana, became wildly popular. The herbal blend, known as "K2" or "Spice," was openly sold in head shops as well as over the Internet. As with most recreational drugs, little is known about the long-term impacts of the substances, but people who smoked it were often seen at hospitals with symptoms ranging from racing heart rates to paranoia to sometimes near death experiences. According to a press release from the DEA, in March of 2011, "the United States Drug Enforcement Administration (DEA) exercised its emergency scheduling authority to control five chemicals (JWH-018, JWH-073, JWH-200, CP-47,497, and cannabicyclohexanol) used to make so-called 'fake pot' products. Except as authorized by law, this action makes possessing and selling these chemicals or the products that contain them illegal in the United States. This emergency action was necessary to prevent an imminent threat to public health and safety."

They are designated as Schedule I substances, the most restrictive category under the Controlled Substances Act. Schedule I substances are reserved for those substances with a high potential for abuse, no accepted medical use for treatment in the United States, and a lack of accepted safety for use of the drug under medical supervision.

"Young people are being harmed when they smoke these dangerous 'fake pot' products and wrongly equate the products' 'legal' retail availability with being 'safe,'" said DEA Administrator Michele M. Leonhart. "Parents and community leaders look to us to help them protect their kids, and we have not let them down. Today's action, while temporary, will reduce the number of young people being seen in hospital emergency rooms after ingesting these synthetic chemicals to get high."

Information from U.S. Drug Enforcement Administration (DEA). (March, 2011). Retrieved July 7, 2012, from http://www.justice.gov/dea/pubs/pressrel/pr030111p.html.

Taken in nontoxic dosages, these substances produce changes in perception, thought, and mood. Physiological effects include elevated heart rate, increased blood pressure, and dilated pupils. Sensory effects include perceptual distortions that vary with dose, setting, and mood. Psychic effects include disorders of thought associated with time and space. Time may appear to stand still and forms and colors seem to change and take on new significance. This experience may be either pleasurable or extremely frightening. It needs to be stressed that the effects of hallucinogens are unpredictable each time they are used.

Weeks or even months after some hallucinogens have been taken, the user may experience flashbacks, which are fragmentary recurrences of certain aspects of the drug experience in the absence of actually taking the drug. The occurrence of a flashback is unpredictable but is more likely to occur during times of stress and seems to occur more frequently in younger individuals. With time, these episodes diminish and become less intense.

RIPPED FROM THE HEADLINES

Bath Salts

Beginning in 2010, hallucinogens that were legally sold as "bath salts" for homeopathic remedies began taking the U.S. populace by storm and had law and drug enforcement officials scrambling for a response. The substances were available at area convenience stores and via the Internet, selling for approximately $20, and packaged as bath salts or plant food, but almost always marked "not for human consumption." "It's a derivative that's very similar to amphetamines, and its side effects are largely the same side effects we see with amphetamines in large dose," said Jeffrey Baldwin, Professor and Vice Chair of Pharmacy Practice and Pediatrics at the University of Nebraska Medical Center in Omaha. The drugs are typically snorted, smoked or injected; however, some are even mixing them in beverages. "If you take the very worst of some of the other drugs—LSD and MDMA with their hallucinogenic-delusional–type properties; PCP with extreme agitation, superhuman strength and combativeness; as well as the stimulant properties of cocaine and meth—if you take all the worst of those and put them together this is what you get. It's ugly," added Mark Ryan, director of the Louisiana Poison Control Center.

"On Friday, October 21, 2011, DEA published a final order in the Federal Register exercising its emergency scheduling authority to control three synthetic stimulants that are used to make bath salts, including: Mephedrone, 3,4 Methylenedioxypyrovalerone (MDPV), and Methylone. Except as authorized by law, this action makes possessing and selling these chemicals, or the products that contain them, illegal in the United States. This emergency action was necessary to prevent an imminent threat to the public safety. As a result of this order, these synthetic stimulants are designated as Schedule I substances under the Controlled Substances Act."

Information from: Gardner, A. (2011). Hallucinogens Legally Sold as "Bath Salts" a New Threat. Retrieved August 25, 2012, from http://www.womenshealth.gov/news/headlines/649596.cfm.

The abuse of hallucinogens in the United States received much public attention in the 1960s and 1970s. A subsequent decline in their use in the 1980s may be attributed to real or perceived hazards associated with taking these drugs.

However, a resurgence of the use of hallucinogens is cause for concern. Fortunately, the 2008 National Survey on Drug Use and Health reports that the prevalence of hallucinogen use has remained relatively constant, from 0.5 percent in 2002 to 0.4 percent in 2003, 2004, 2005, 2006, 2007, and 2008 (SAMHSA, 2008). Hallucinogenic mushrooms, LSD, and MDMA are popular among junior and senior high school students who use hallucinogens.

Lysergic Acid Diethylamide (LSD)

Lysergic acid diethylamide (LSD) is the most potent hallucinogen known to science as well as the most highly studied. LSD was originally synthesized in 1938 by Dr. Albert Hoffman. However, its hallucinogenic effects were unknown until 1943 when Hoffman accidentally consumed some LSD. It was later found that an oral dose of as little as 0.000025 grams (25 micrograms, which is equal in weight to a couple grains of salt) is capable of producing rich and vivid hallucinations. Because of its structural similarity to a chemical present in the brain and its similarity in effects to certain aspects of psychosis, LSD was used as a research tool to study mental illness (United Nations, 2010). LSD abuse was popularized in the 1960s by individuals like Dr. Timothy Leary, who encouraged American students to "turn on, tune in, and drop out." LSD use has varied over the years, but it still remains a significant drug of abuse. In 2003, lifetime prevalence of LSD use for 8th and 12th graders was 2.1 and 5.9%, respectively.

The average effective oral dose is from 20 to 80 micrograms with the effects of higher doses lasting for 10 to 12 hours. LSD is usually sold in the form of impregnated paper (blotter acid), typically imprinted with colorful graphic designs (**Figure 14–12**). It has also been encountered in tablets (microdots), thin squares of gelatin (window panes), in sugar cubes (**Figure 14–13**) and, rarely, in liquid form.

FIGURE 14–12   LSD paper designs
Courtesy of the Austin Police Department, Austin, Texas.

Physical reactions may include dilated pupils, lowered body temperature, nausea, cutis anserine ("goose bumps"), profuse perspiration, increased blood sugar, and rapid heart rate. During the first hour after ingestion, the user may experience visual changes with extreme changes in mood. In the hallucinatory state, (often referred to as a "trip" because it is often described as though the person is experiencing a hallucinogenic trip outside of their body), the LSD user may suffer impaired depth and time perception, accompanied by distorted perception of the size and shape of objects, movements, color, sound, touch, and the user's own body image. During this period,

FIGURE 14–13 Sugar cube acid

the ability to perceive objects through the senses is distorted: a user may describe "hearing colors" and "seeing sounds." The ability to make sensible judgments and see common dangers is impaired, making the user susceptible to personal injury. After an LSD "trip," the user may suffer acute anxiety or depression for a variable period of time. Flashbacks have been reported days or even months after taking the last dose.

Psilocybin and Psilocyn

A number of Schedule I hallucinogenic substances are found in nature. Psilocybin and psilocyn are obtained from certain mushrooms indigenous to tropical and subtropical regions of South America, Mexico, and the United States (**Figure 14–14**). As pure chemicals at doses of 10 to 20 mg, these hallucinogens produce muscle relaxation, dilation of pupils, vivid visual and auditory distortions, and emotional disturbances. However, the effects produced by consuming preparations of dried or brewed mushrooms are far less predictable and largely depend on the particular mushrooms used and the age and preservation of the extract. There are many species of so-called "magic" mushrooms that contain varying amounts of these tryptamines, as well as uncertain amounts of other chemicals. As a consequence, the hallucinogenic activity as well as the extent of toxicity produced by various plant samples are often unknown.

Peyote and Mescaline

Peyote is a small, spineless cactus, *Lophophora williamsii*, whose principal active ingredient is the hallucinogen mescaline (3, 4, 5-trimethoxyphenethylamine). From earliest recorded time, peyote has been used by natives in northern Mexico and the southwestern United States as a part of their religious rites.

FIGURE 14–14 Psilocybin mushrooms

The top of the cactus above ground—also referred to as the crown—consists of disc-shaped buttons that are cut from the roots and dried. These buttons are generally chewed or soaked in water to produce an intoxicating liquid. The hallucinogenic dose of mescaline is about 0.3 to 0.5 grams and lasts about 12 hours. While peyote produced rich visual hallucinations that were important to the Native American peyote users, the full spectrum of effects served as a chemically induced model of mental illness. Mescaline can be extracted from peyote or produced synthetically. Both peyote and mescaline are listed in the CSA as Schedule I hallucinogens.

Methylenedioxymethamphetamine (MDMA, Ecstasy)

3,4-Methylenedioxymethamphetamine (MDMA, Ecstasy) was first synthesized in 1912 but remained in relative obscurity for many years. In the 1980s, MDMA gained popularity as a drug of abuse resulting in its final placement in Schedule I of the CSA. Today, MDMA is extremely popular. In 2005, it was estimated that two million tablets were smuggled into the United States every week (United Nations, 2010).

MDMA produces both amphetamine-like stimulation and mild mescaline-like hallucinations. It is touted as a "feel good" drug with an undeserved reputation of safety. MDMA produces euphoria, increased energy, increased sensual arousal, and enhanced tactile sensations. However, it also produces nerve cell damage that can result in psychiatric disturbances and long-term cognitive impairments. The user will often experience increased muscle tension, tremors, blurred vision, and hyperthermia. The increased body temperature can result in organ failure and death.

MDMA is usually distributed in tablet form and taken orally at doses ranging from 50 to 200 mg. Individual tablets are often imprinted with graphic designs or commercial logos, and typically contain 80 to 100 mg of MDMA (**Figure 14–15**). After oral administration, effects are

FIGURE 14–15   Examples of MDMA tablets
Courtesy of DEA.

felt within 30 to 45 minutes, peak at 60 to 90 minutes, and last for 4 to 6 hours. Analysis of seized MDMA tablets indicates that about 80% of all samples actually contain MDMA, while the other 20% contain amphetamine, methamphetamine, or both.

Some of these differ from one another in potency, speed of onset, duration of action, and capacity to modify mood, with or without producing overt hallucinations. The drugs are usually taken orally, sometimes snorted, and rarely injected. Because they are produced in clandestine laboratories, they are seldom pure and the amount in a capsule or tablet is likely to vary considerably.

According to the National Survey on Drug Use and Health, initiation of MDMA use has increased from 1993 until 2001, when it peaked at 1.8 million new users. In 2002 the number declined to 1.1 million. Two-thirds (66%) of new MDMA users in 2002 were 18 or older, and 50% were male (SAMHSA, 2011).

Phencyclidine and Related Drugs

In the 1950s, phencyclidine (PCP) was investigated as an anesthetic but, due to the side effects of confusion and delirium, its development for human use was discontinued. It became commercially available for use as a veterinary anesthetic in the 1960s under the trade name of Sernylan and was placed in Schedule III of the CSA. In 1978, due to considerable abuse, phencyclidine was transferred to Schedule II of the CSA and manufacturing of Sernylan was discontinued. Today, virtually all of the phencyclidine encountered on the illicit market in the United States is produced in clandestine laboratories.

PCP is illicitly marketed under a number of other names, including angel dust, supergrass, killer weed, embalming fluid, and rocket fuel, reflecting the range of its bizarre and volatile effects. In its pure form, it is a white crystalline powder that readily dissolves in water. However, most PCP on the illicit market contains a number of contaminants as a result of makeshift manufacturing, causing the color to range from tan to brown, and the consistency from powder to a gummy mass. Although sold in tablets and capsules as well as in powder and liquid form, it is commonly applied to a leafy material, such as parsley, mint, oregano, or marijuana, and smoked (**Figure 14–16**).

The drug's effects are as varied as its appearance. A moderate amount of PCP often causes the user to feel detached, distant, and estranged from his surroundings. Numbness, slurred speech, and loss of coordination may be accompanied by a sense of strength and invulnerability. A blank stare, rapid and involuntary eye movements, and an exaggerated gait are among the more observable effects. Auditory hallucinations, image distortion, severe mood disorders, and amnesia may also occur. In some users, PCP may cause acute anxiety and a feeling of impending doom; in others, paranoia and violent hostility; and in some, it may produce a psychosis indistinguishable from schizophrenia. PCP use is associated with a number of risks, and many believe it to be one of the most dangerous drugs of abuse.

Ketamine

Ketamine is a rapid-acting general anesthetic. Its pharmacological profile is essentially the same as phencyclidine. Like PCP, ketamine is referred to as a dissociative anesthetic because patients feel detached or disconnected from their pain and environment when anesthetized

FIGURE 14–16   Marijuana cigarettes soaked in PCP
Courtesy of Austin Police Department, Austin, Texas.

with this drug. Unlike most anesthetics, ketamine produces only mild respiratory depression and appears to stimulate, not depress, the cardiovascular system. In addition, ketamine has both analgesic and amnesic properties and is associated with less confusion, irrationality, and violent behavior than PCP. Use of ketamine as a general anesthetic for humans has been limited due to adverse effects including delirium and hallucinations. Today, it is primarily used in veterinary medicine, but has some utility for emergency surgery in humans.

Although ketamine has been marketed in the United States for many years, it was only recently associated with significant diversion and abuse and placed in Schedule III of the CSA in 1999. Known in the drug culture as Special K or Super K, ketamine has become a staple at dance parties or "raves." Ketamine is supplied to the illicit market by the diversion of legitimate pharmaceuticals (Ketaset, Ketalar). It is usually distributed as a powder obtained by removing the liquid from the pharmaceutical products. As a drug of abuse, ketamine can be administered orally, snorted, or injected. It is also sprinkled on marijuana or tobacco and smoked. After oral or intranasal administration, effects are evident in about 10 to 15 minutes and are over in about an hour.

After intravenous use, effects begin almost immediately and reach peak effects within minutes. Ketamine can act as a depressant or a psychedelic. Low doses produce vertigo, ataxia, slurred speech, slow reaction time, and euphoria. Intermediate doses produce disorganized thinking, altered body image, and a feeling of unreality with vivid visual hallucinations. High doses produce analgesia, amnesia, and coma.

Inhalants

Inhalants are a diverse group of substances that include volatile solvents, gases, and nitrites that are sniffed, snorted, huffed, or bagged to produce intoxicating effects similar to alcohol. These substances are found in common household products like glues, lighter fluid, cleaning fluids, and paint products (**Figure 14–17**). Inhalant abuse is the deliberate inhaling or sniffing of these substances to get high, and it is estimated that about 1,000 substances are misused in this manner. The easy accessibility, low cost, legal status, and ease of transport and conceal-ment often lead to inhalants being one of the first substances abused by children.

For example, volatile solvents are found in a number of everyday products. Some of these products include nail polish remover, lighter fluid, gasoline, paint and paint thinner, rubber glue, waxes, and varnishes. The gas used as a propellant in canned whipped cream and in small lavender metallic containers called whippets (used to make whipped cream) is nitrous oxide or laughing gas (the same gas used by dentists for anesthesia). Butyl nitrite, sold as tape head cleaner and referred to as rush, locker room, or climax, is often sniffed or huffed to get high.

Inhalants may be sniffed directly from an open container or huffed from a rag soaked in the substance and held to the face. Alternatively, the open container or soaked rag can be placed in a bag where the vapors can concentrate before being inhaled. Some chemicals are painted on the hands or fingernails or placed on shirt sleeves or wrist bands to enable an abuser to continually inhale the fumes without being detected by a teacher or other adult.

Inhalants depress the central nervous system, producing decreased respiration and blood pressure. Users report distortion in perceptions of time and space. Many users experi-ence headaches, nausea, slurred speech, and loss of motor coordination. Mental effects may include fear, anxiety, or depression. A rash around the nose and mouth may be seen, and the abuser may start wheezing. An odor of paint or organic solvents on clothes, skin, and breath is sometimes a sign of inhalant abuse. Other indicators of inhalant abuse include slurred speech or staggering gait, red, glassy, watery eyes, and excitability or unpredictable behavior.

For more information regarding inhalants, contact the National Inhalant Prevention Coalition by telephone (1-800-269-4237) or on the Internet (http://www.inhalants.org).

Steroids

When athletes gather, the issue of per-formance-enhancing drugs, especially anabolic steroids, once again gains interna-tional attention. These drugs are used by high school, college, professional, and elite

© spirit of america/ShutterStock, Inc.

FIGURE 14–17   Examples of inhalants

amateur athletes in a variety of sports (e.g., weight lifting, track and field, swimming, cycling, and others) to obtain a competitive advantage. Body builders and fitness buffs take anabolic steroids to improve their physical appearance, and individuals in occupations requiring enhanced physical strength (e.g., body guards, night club bouncers, construction workers) are also known to use these drugs.

Concerns over a growing illicit market, abuse by teenagers, and the uncertainty of possible harmful long-term effects of steroid use led Congress in 1991 to place anabolic steroids as a class of drugs into Schedule III of the CSA. The CSA defines anabolic steroids as any drug or hormonal substance chemically and pharmacologically related to testosterone (other than estrogens, progestins, and corticosteroids) that promotes muscle growth.

Once viewed as a problem associated only with professional and elite amateur athletes, various reports indicate that anabolic steroid abuse has increased significantly among adolescents. According to the 2003 Monitoring the Future Study, 2.5% of 8th graders, 3.0% of 10th graders, and 3.5% of 12th graders reported using steroids at least once in their lifetime (United Nations, 2010).

Most illicit anabolic steroids are sold at gyms, competitions, and through mail-order operations. For the most part, these substances are smuggled into the United States from many countries. The illicit market includes various preparations intended for human and veterinary use as well as bogus and counterfeit products. The most commonly encountered anabolic steroids on the illicit market include testosterone, nandrolone, methenolone, stanozolol, and methandrostenolone.

A limited number of anabolic steroids have been approved for medical and veterinary use. The primary legitimate use of these drugs in humans is for the replacement of inadequate levels of testosterone resulting from a reduction or absence of functioning testes. Other indications include anemia and breast cancer. Experimentally, anabolic steroids have been used to treat a number of disorders including AIDS wasting, erectile dysfunction, and osteoporosis. In veterinary practice, anabolic steroids are used to promote feed efficiency and to improve weight gain, vigor, and hair coat. They are also used in veterinary practice to treat anemia and counteract tissue breakdown during illness and trauma.

When used in combination with exercise training and a high protein diet, anabolic steroids can promote increased size and strength of muscles, improve endurance, and decrease recovery time between workouts. They are taken orally or by intramuscular injection. Users concerned about drug tolerance often take steroids on a schedule called a cycle. A cycle is a period of between 6 and 14 weeks of steroid use, followed by a period of abstinence or reduction in use. Additionally, users tend to stack the drugs, using multiple drugs concurrently. Although the benefits of these practices are unsubstantiated, most users feel that cycling and stacking enhance the efficiency of the drugs and limit their side effects.

Another mode of steroid use is called pyramiding. With this method users slowly escalate steroid use (increasing the number of drugs used at one time and/or the dose and frequency of one or more steroids), reach a peak amount at mid-cycle, and gradually taper the dose toward the end of the cycle. The escalation of steroid use can vary with different types of training. Body builders and weight lifters tend to escalate their dose to a much higher level than do long distance runners or swimmers.

The long-term adverse health effects of anabolic steroid use are not definitely known. There is, however, increasing concern of possible serious health problems associated with the abuse of these agents, including cardiovascular damage, cerebrovascular toxicity, and liver damage.

Physical side effects include elevated blood pressure and cholesterol levels, severe acne, premature balding, reduced sexual function, and testicular atrophy. In males, abnormal breast development can occur. In females, anabolic steroids have a masculinizing effect, resulting in more body hair, a deeper voice, smaller breasts, and fewer menstrual cycles. Several of these effects are irreversible. In adolescents, abuse of these agents may prematurely stop the lengthening of bones, resulting in stunted growth. For some individuals, the use of anabolic steroids may be associated with psychotic reactions, manic episodes, feelings of anger or hostility, aggression, and violent behavior.

Over the last few years, a number of precursors to testosterone have been marketed as dietary supplements in the United States. New legislation has been introduced in Congress to add several steroids to the CSA and to alter the CSA requirements needed to place new steroids under control in the CSA.

Current and Future Drug Trends

According to the United Nations Office on Drugs and Crime's *World Drug Report 2010*, there are encouraging signs about drug use declining around the world. The first encouraging sign is that coca cultivation in the Andean countries continues to fall, driven by significant declines in Colombia. Global demand for cocaine has also stabilized, although the decline in the United States is offset by alarming increases in some European countries. Secondly, the production and consumption of amphetamine-type stimulants (ATS) has leveled off, with a clear downward trend in North America and, to a lesser degree, Europe. Thirdly, the health warnings on higher potency cannabis, delivered in past *World Drug Reports*, appear to be getting through. For the first time in years, there is not an upward trend in the global production and consumption of cannabis. Fourthly, opium production, while significant, is now highly concentrated in Afghanistan's southern provinces. Indeed, the Helmand province is on the verge of becoming the world's biggest drug supplier, with the dubious distinction of cultivating more drugs than entire countries such as Myanmar, Morocco, or even Colombia. Curing Helmand of its drug and insurgency cancer will rid the world of the most dangerous source of its most dangerous narcotic, and go a long way to bringing security to the region.

Another source of good news is that drug law enforcement has improved: almost half of all cocaine produced is now being intercepted (up from 24% in 1999) and more than a quarter of all heroin (against 15% in 1999) (United Nations, 2010).

Evolution of the World Drug Problem

The world's drug problem is being contained. In 2005–2006, the global markets for the main illicit drugs—the opiates, cocaine, cannabis, and ATS—remained largely stable (United Nations, 2010). Particularly notable is the stabilization seen in the cannabis market, which had been expanding rapidly for some time. In line with a long-term trend, the share of total drug production that is seized by law enforcement has also increased: some 42% of global cocaine production and 26% of global heroin production never made it to consumers. Of course, within this aggregated picture there remains considerable variation. Most notably, heroin production continued to expand in the conflict-ridden provinces of southern Afghanistan. While global heroin consumption does not appear to be growing, the impact of this surge in supply needs to be monitored carefully.

How Is Drug Production Changing?

Most of the world's drug markets start with the farmer. Unlike other crops, however, the cultivation of opium poppy, coca leaf, and cannabis take place under threat of eradication, and so the location and the number of hectares tilled vary substantially from year to year. Around 92% of the world's heroin comes from poppies grown in Afghanistan. Despite a massive increase in opium poppy cultivation in Afghanistan in 2006, the global area under poppy was actually 10% lower than in 2000. This decline was mainly due to sustained success in reducing cultivation in Southeast Asia. Poppy cultivation in the Golden Triangle has fallen by some 80% since 2000 (United Nations, 2010).

Most of the world's cocaine comes from coca leaf cultivated in Colombia, Peru, and Bolivia. The global area under coca cultivation fell by 29% to some 156,900 hectares between 2000 and 2006, largely due to reductions of coca cultivation in Colombia. The areas under coca cultivation in Peru and Bolivia increased over this period but remained significantly below the levels reported a decade earlier (United Nations, 2010).

It is impossible to accurately estimate the location and total number of hectares under cannabis, because it is grown in at least 172 countries, often in small plots by the users themselves. There is an important distinction between the extent of drug crop cultivation and the extent of drug production, however. Crop yields can be affected by weather conditions and changes in production technology, among other things. As a result, long-term declines in cultivated area do not necessarily translate into declines in total production. Opium production in Afghanistan rose almost 50% in 2006, bringing global heroin production to a new record high of 606 metric tons (mt) in 2006, exceeding the previous high (576 mt in 1999) by 5%. Similarly, the success in the reduction of coca cultivation from 2000 to 2006 has not led to a commensurate decline in cocaine production, apparently due to improvements in coca cultivation and cocaine production technology. Cocaine production has remained largely stable over the last few years, estimated at 984 mt in 2006 (United Nations, 2010).

ATS are manufactured illicitly using legally produced precursors, and thus global production can only be estimated indirectly. This production appears to be stable, however, at about 480 mt in 2005. At the same time, seizures of ATS labs and precursors declined dramatically, likely a result of improved precursor control and significant reductions in domestic production operations in key markets such as the United States.

Crime Scene Search

In a contraband drug investigation, the crime scene investigator is typically looking for evidence that has been hidden on the person, in a dwelling, or in a vehicle. When doing so, it is important to remember the rules of evidence and the requirements for establishing a chain of evidence. As with all aspects of evidence collection it is imperative that the crime scene investigator be aware of current laws regulating search and seizure activities (Fisher, 2004).

Collection and Preservation of Drug Evidence

All illicit substances should be photographed as they were found. All drugs should be accurately weighed. The gross weight of the package, including the drug and packaging materials, should be determined and recorded. Individual pills, tablets, packets, balloons, etc., should be counted and the number written on the outer package and within the written report.

Some departments/jurisdictions require that a presumptive field test be conducted on a substance that is believed to be a controlled substance, prior to its preservation and prior to charging the person in possession. This is typically performed through the use of a NARC ID kit or NARCOPouch, which is a portable chemical-color test for the presumptive analysis of a substance. This will then be followed up by a secondary presumptive test and confirmatory analysis at the forensic laboratory.

Forensic Analysis of Controlled Substances

Once at the forensic laboratory, the identification (ID) of controlled substances is divided into botanical and chemical examinations. Botanical exams identify physical characteristics specific to plants that are considered controlled substances. Chemical exams use wet chemical or instrumental techniques to identify specific substances that are controlled by statute. For each examination a series of tests is administered to the sample. Each test is more specific than the last. At the end of the sequence, the examiner is able to determine if there is a controlled substance in the sample and identify it.

VIEW **FROM AN EXPERT**

Everything Old Is New Again

Controlled substance crime labs tend to experience a "cyclic" nature in terms of drug submissions. Of course, there are always the routine drugs that remain popular such as cocaine, marijuana, etc., as well as some newly synthesized drugs arising on the scene, but some drugs seem to be very popular, fade into oblivion, and then make a resurgence for a new generation to experiment with. Some of the typical drugs that follow this pattern are PCP (1-phenycyclohexyl piperidine or phencyclidine), LSD (lysergic acid diethylamine), and even methaqualone (commonly referred to as quaaludes or "ludes") to name a few. In the 60s and 70s these drugs were commonly associated and very popular with the hippie movement and rock concerts. LSD in fact was discovered by accident in 1938 and was heavily promoted by Timothy Leary in the 1960s for its ability to "expand consciousness." PCP was developed in the 1950s as a surgical anesthesia before becoming a popular hallucinogen. These drugs faded from popularity in the 70s until outlaw motorcycle gangs (OMG), like the Hell's Angels and the Pagan's, made PCP and methamphetamine ("speed" or "crank") their main sources of income. After a tough crackdown on PCP, many of the OMG members were arrested and sent to prison. With the advent of mandatory minimum sentencing guidelines under federal law statutes, many convicted OMG members were sent away for 20 years. PCP then disappeared from many areas of the country until around the year 2000, when many of the former OMG members were released from prison. This was also a time when the Internet became widely popular and chemical synthesis routes were now readily accessible rather than doing research at a library or having a former PCP "cook" walk someone through their process or recipe.

LSD was also a very popular hallucinogenic drug of the 60s and 70s and while one could argue that it never really quite had the comeback as, say, PCP, it still remains a drug encountered by crime labs. LSD is used in microgram quantities and typically is sprayed on perforated cardboard or paper commonly referred to as blotter tabs. It was thought that at one time there were only two to three LSD chemists in the United States, as the typical production is somewhat difficult and potentially dangerous (because a very small amount is considered a normal dose, one could easily "dose" themselves unintentionally during the production process). It was not surprising when a large LSD lab was discovered by local authorities in Europe. Investigators replaced all the lighting with black (long wave UV) lighting, because LSD will fluoresce in this kind of light. This was the only way to ensure where LSD was or what it came into contact with during the production process.

Methamphetamine is one of the more popular drugs of previous generations that never really seemed to fade away, but became more popular as new synthesis routes improved its purity level. One of the more popular forms of methamphetamine today is typically referred to as "ice" as it has the appearance of ice crystals or broken glass and can achieve purity levels greater than 98%.

Heroin is also a widely popular drug from the 60s that was typically associated with inner-city poor people or linked to deaths of rock stars from overdose. Heroin was typically of low purity (2–3%) and required "free basing" to allow for the user to inject the drug. One popular comedian, Richard Pryor, even set himself on fire trying to do this. However, with the emergence of the HIV virus commonly linked to needle sharing, heroin remained a back alley "dirty" drug. But as heroin purity levels increased, the ability to inhale or "snort" the drug, similar to cocaine, made heroin widely popular in many affluent communities. It also snared a new generation of young people who became addicted to the drug. Although heroin seems to remain widely popular in the north central and northeast sections of the United States, it also has become the drug of choice for some users who typically abuse prescription drugs.

Currently, prescription drug abuse is a growing problem. One of the most widely abused drugs is oxycodone. As the demand for this drug increases so does the price. Ironically, this is a contributor to a new generation of heroin users. People previously addicted to the painkiller oxycodone turned to heroin because its cost was cheaper in some areas of the northeast. Crime lab analysts frequently encounter the reemergence of these "well-established" illegal drugs. However, due to the advent of the Internet, old synthesis routes and new "designer" drugs are emerging based on scientific papers published long ago that are now readily accessible with the click of a mouse. One example of this is an infamous case that resulted from a clandestine lab response in 2004 where ATF agents served a warrant for weapons in central Pennsylvania. When they entered the house they discovered glassware and a number of chemicals. They notified the DEA who, in turn, called the lab to inquire about the possible uses for the list of chemicals. Upon hearing the list of chemicals it was determined that a possible fentanyl lab was in production. The responding agents were then cautioned to get out and await chemist response. The lab determined that the deadly drug fentanyl was being synthesized via a new synthesis route from notes found at the scene. This led to an Internet search where the "recipe" for this was readily available. The historic route (the Jaansen method) for this deadly drug required a sophisticated laboratory and glassware, as well as a highly experienced chemist. The new Internet recipe called for rudimentary equipment and could be performed by anyone with a minimal chemistry background. The new Internet synthesis version (the Siegfried method) was reproduced in the crime lab with a high yield and could be readily purified. The immediate concern became the ease in which it could be synthesized, as fentanyl is typically used during anesthesia and for terminal cancer patients for the control of extreme pain. A lethal dose of fentanyl is about 10 micrograms (or about 3 grains of salt) and is readily absorbed through the skin. The consequences of the ease of this synthesis became apparent in early 2000 when a series of overdose (OD) deaths occurred in and around the Harrisburg, PA area. Initially, these were linked to heroin ODs, but were later determined to be fentanyl ODs as the street drug dealers began selling heroin laced with fentanyl. This put crime labs on high alert because the handling of these cases required a heightened sense of safety and needed to be prioritized due to the many deaths that were occurring in some areas of the country. In some cases, the users were found dead with hypodermic needles still in their arms, and parents were finding high school children unresponsive in their beds after experimenting with the drug. In almost all cases, it was their first and last experimentation with the fentanyl-laced heroin. Due to extensive media reports and a disruption to the main source of supply, this fentanyl situation was ultimately averted. However, well over 100 deaths were attributed to this drug, and it still remains an easy, but deadly synthesis route few should undertake.

Today, designer drug problems are commonly associated with synthetic marijuana-type compounds. The compounds commonly referred to as K2, Spice, etc., are readily sold at head shops and local convenience stores and are typically labeled as incense or "not for human consumption" to forego regulation laws. Due to a number of deaths associated with these emerging products, many states have banned their sale and distribution. Again, unfortunately many of these products were synthesized by the chemist, J. W. Hoffman, in the 1990s as a thesis project. Many of the compounds he and his team synthesized to mimic tetrahydrocannibonol (THC, the active ingredient in marijuana) he named after himself with names such as JWH-018, JWH-222, etc. This research was readily available on the Internet and was utilized by some Asian companies to illegally produce these "Spice" and "K2" products. As the state and federal governments move to regulate the chemicals in these products, many new chemicals are popping up as a way to circumvent established laws and regulations. This has always been a source of concern for law enforcement and crime laboratories. As laws are passed for certain chemicals, producers begin to synthesize new compounds in the hopes that the new synthesized compounds will have the same desired effect as the banned compound. Historically, this has been the case for drugs such as ecstasy that mimic methamphetamine, but it has also backfired when the recreational drug known as MPTP was produced and ultimately caused Parkinson's disease in users. The challenges that crime labs will likely see in the near future are these new designer drugs. Almost as soon as they are identified and methodology is developed to identify them, laws are passed that prohibit or regulate their ingredients. As soon as this happens, newly created compounds or other ingredients are utilized to produce the products. It is a constant struggle for crime labs and the law enforcement community to stay ahead of the curve with these compounds because synthesis of many of them can be difficult or expensive.

Thomas Blackwell, Laboratory Director

DEA Northeast Laboratory, NYC

"These views expressed are mine alone and do not necessarily represent the views of DEA, the U.S. Department of Justice or an officer or entity of the United States."

Courtesy of Thomas Blackwell, Forensic Chemist.

Botanical Analysis

These are the most common examinations performed in the controlled substance section of a forensics lab. Examinations are typically associated with such substances as marijuana, peyote, mushrooms, and opium. Marijuana examinations typically exceed 50% of the forensic laboratory's caseload. As a rule, by education and training, the examiner is a chemist, not a biologist or a botanist. He or she has been trained in the ID of whether plant material is or is not marijuana, etc. Beyond that the examiner should not render an opinion as to the identity of the substance.

Marijuana Analysis

The analysis of marijuana is a two-step process. The first step establishes the plant or plant material as marijuana through its physical characteristics (microscopic exam). The second step is to establish the presence of the plant resin that contains the psychoactive components. A chemical color test is then used to confirm the presence of cannabinoids, specifically Delta 9 tetrahydrocannabinol (THC), which is the primary psychoactive compound.

This chemical-color test is known as the Duquenois-Levine test. Additional confirmatory chemical and instrumental tests for marijuana resin include chromatographic exam, thin layer chromatography (TLC), and gas chromatography (GC) (Saferstein, 2007).

Chemical Analysis

The balance of the samples encountered by the controlled substance section requires the ID of specific compounds within a mixture. The composition of the samples may vary, but the procedure remains the same. Each sample requires a screening step, an extraction or sample preparation stem, and a confirmatory step. Tests can be further subdivided into wet chemical and instrumental procedures. Wet chemical procedures are used as a screening method or for sample preparation. Instrumental procedures are used for screening or as a confirmation tool.

Screening Tests

In a **screening test**, a specimen is subjected to a series of reagents that yield characteristic colors for commonly encountered drugs. Screening tests are used both in the lab and in the field. Ease of application makes color testing an efficient field-based method for achieving a tentative, presumptive identification of a drug. Color reactions are useful for screening purposes but do not result in a conclusive identification.

Five color test reagents are commonly used:

1. **Duquenois-Levine** is a test for marijuana (see Figure 14–29). When applied to marijuana, the reagent turns violet (Figure 14–30). The reagent is composed of three solutions: Solution A consists of 2% vanilla and 1% acetaldehyde in ethyl alcohol, solution B is concentrated hydrochloric acid, and solution C is chloroform.

2. The **Marquis test**, which screens for heroin, morphine, and opium derivatives, turns purple in their presence. The reagent can also be used for amphetamines and meth-amphetamines; in their presence, the mixture turns orange-brown. This reagent is composed of 2% formaldehyde in sulfuric acid.

3. **Van Urk** reagent, in the presence of LSD, turns blue-purple.

4. **Dillie-Koppanyi** is a test for barbiturates, in whose presence the reagent turns violet-blue.

5. The **Scott test** is a screen for cocaine. It renders a blue color upon application of solution A to a specimen containing cocaine. The blue transforms into pink upon application of solution B, and the blue color reappears in the chloroform layer upon addition of solution C.

Most labs and some field tests are completed using an open system with sealed bottles of solvents and reagents. The solvent dissolves and the reagent, an acid, causes a reaction. The color of that reaction has been recorded and can be expected of the appropriate solvent and reagent when placed on the questioned substance. The specimen to be tested is placed on a porcelain dish or in a Petri dish. The appropriate amount of solvent is placed on the specimen and allowed a few minutes to do its work. Once the suspect material has been dissolved, the appropriate reagent is then dropped onto the specimen. If the solution turns a particular color and that color is consistent with the drug being tested, the test is positive. The test is recorded and the record retained for further investigation and trial. The open containers of acid are broken or spilled easily, making the system hazardous; the Occupational Safety and Health Administration recognizes the procedure as highly hazardous.

A safer way to conduct field tests is to use commercial products that have solvent and reagent ampoules embedded into the package; the ampoules are broken in a particular sequence (**Figure 14–18**). This reaction takes place inside a sealed container, so the possibility of spills is eliminated from the testing equation. Each ampoule causes a reaction that is color coded to the drug for which the test is being conducted. The ampoules contain reagents that are acids and that when improperly broken may cause stains, burns, and damage to clothes, so care must be taken when conducting the tests. Disposable rubber gloves are fundamental to drug testing (Nitrile gloves are designed specifically for handling these types of substances).

Each drug testing kit provides the drug pouch or disposable chemical applicator; tubette; and a small, sterile, toothpick-sized drug scoop. When preparing the pouches or tubettes, it is important to use only a sterile device for picking up the suspect drug and placing it into the package. Often investigators will use a knife or pen that is not sterile, thereby contaminating any test results. It is also important not to overload the pouch or tubette with the suspect drug; a very small quantity will produce the reaction. Whichever is being used, pouch or tubette, once the first ampoule is broken, after the test material has been added it must be agitated for a minimum of 30 seconds to one minute. This agitation allows the solvent to dissolve the drug and the reagent to react with the dissolved drug. After each ampoule is broken it must be agitated to facilitate the desired reaction.

FIGURE 14–18 Duquenois-Levine reagent and Scott reagent presumptive field test kits

Once the test is complete, it is important to document each step of the testing process. The tests themselves are only determinative of probable cause and will dissipate over time. They will not be available for trial, because once the test is complete and recorded, the specimen is disposed of or destroyed. The only thing left reflecting the test will be the record made in writing at the time of the field test.

Color reactions differ based on the testing medium and method. The official definition of color reactions is a measurement and analysis of color by comparison with a standard, and typically the colors are on the front of the pouch. In tubes, the standard is the color of the printing on the box or the color of the printing on the caps. We are seeking a match to the family of colors only, not the exact color shown.

There are three factors that affect the color reaction:

- Quality
- Quantity
- Agitation

The quality of the substance used for the test will affect the color intensity. A more pure substance may display darker colors and weaker substances lighter colors. The amount of the substance used will affect the intensity of the color reaction to varying degrees. It is necessary to agitate the sample vigorously to allow the chemistry to react properly with the substance itself. Depending on the agitation, color may increase or decrease.

Various cutting agents may create immediate heat and expansion within the test. If this reaction occurs, the clip on pouches can be canted 45 degrees, thereby allowing any generated heat or expansion to escape the pouch. Venting the pouch should dissipate most of the expansion and heat without destroying or contaminating the sample being tested. Once the pressure and heat have been reduced, the pouch can be re-closed and the clamp pushed back into position, allowing the reaction to develop fully and color analysis to continue.

Preparing Materials for Field Testing

All substances must be prepared properly prior to testing to facilitate the best reaction. The investigator must wear rubber gloves whenever testing or preparing to test, both for protection and to avoid allegations of cross-contamination. It is important to remember that the purity of what is being tested is always in question. If what is found is pure and in powder or liquid form, the unclad hand may absorb the drug or the hands may transfer what has been picked up by the hands to the face and eyes. Once absorbed, there is no way to anticipate the drug reaction, which may be from mild to lethal. That is why the protocol always includes rubber gloves and field testing rather than barehanded handling of drugs and tasting them as a field test. Only an actor pretending to be an investigator would be so foolish as to taste something the purity and identity of which has yet to be determined.

If the substance to be tested is in capsules, the capsule can be separated by twisting the two parts of the capsule in opposite directions, allowing the contents to pour onto paper or a sterile surface. Sometimes the material in the capsule becomes caked and does not pour or comes out in chunks. Generally rolling the capsule half between forefinger and thumb will dislodge the contents; the powder can be crushed with a gloved finger and then lifted and placed inside the testing package.

Tablets must be reduced to powder or small fragments prior to testing. This can be done by crushing with the thumb or the heel of the hands. The powder will disperse beyond the hands, so it is important to have paper in place to capture as much of the powder as possible. Should it be necessary to use something harder than a hand or fingers to crush the tablet, shroud the tool in an unused rubber glove before applying pressure to the tablet. Using something to crush the tablet that is not sterile will lead to allegations of cross-contamination. Powders often arrive or are distributed in large chunks. Reduce chunks to powder for testing. Break off a piece from the large chunk to obtain a sample that can be crushed in the same manner as tablets.

Liquids are the most dangerous controlled substances that may require field testing. The liquid may be highly volatile, or it may interact with water or other substances to cause an explosive reaction. The best rule to follow when dealing with liquids is to take them to the lab to be tested. Should it be necessary to field test liquids, do it carefully and use very small amounts. Moisten a sterile cotton swab with the liquid and then allow it to dry. Once dried, the swab portion can be cut off and deposited into the testing medium.

Remember that any positive reaction is for probable cause purposes only. Any evidence pertaining to the test at the time of trial will be based on the information recorded from the testing process.

Confirmatory Tests

Each screening test is insufficient by itself to prove a drug's identity, but the proper protocol will generate a combination of test results characteristic of only one chemical substance. Drug identification protocols generally rely upon a combination of test types to confirm a drug's identity, possibly including color tests, microcrystalline tests, chromatography, spectrophotometry, and mass spectrometry.

Microcrystalline Tests

Microcrystalline tests are more specific than tests based on color responses to chemical reagents. In a **microcrystalline test**, a small quantity of the substance is placed on a microscopic slide, and a drop of chemical reagent is added. The chemical reagent causes a precipitate reaction, creating crystals of a size and shape characteristic of a particular drug. The connection between types of crystals and types of drugs has become well established, and the results of microcrystalline tests are admissible at the time of trial. These tests can be conducted in the presence of diluents. Although the crystal structure and size may be altered by the diluents, experienced examiners can make the identification despite the alterations. When the appropriate color tests and microcrystalline tests are conducted in accordance with a standard protocol, the results point to only one drug (Smith, 2004).

Chromatography

Both gas and thin-layer chromatography can be used to separate out diluents and identify the drug that remains. Chromatography involves a comparison of a known substance with an unknown substance. It is necessary to have some idea what the suspected substance is before drug analysis chromatography can be conducted. Generally, color and microcrystalline tests precede chromatography.

Gas Chromatography. Chromatography theory is based on the fact that chemical substances have a tendency to partially escape into their surroundings when dissolved in a liquid or when absorbed on a solid surface. In a beaker of water covered with a bell jar and kept at a constant temperature, the water in the beaker is in a liquid phase and the air above the beaker is in a gas phase. The molecules of oxygen and hydrogen escaping from the water through evaporation are in their gas phase, and those remaining in the water are in their liquid phase. As the gas molecules continue to escape, they will begin to accumulate above the water. The random movement of the molecules will carry some back into the water. A point will be reached at which the number of molecules escaping the water is equal to the number of molecules returning to the water. At this point the liquid phase and the gas phase are in equilibrium (Smith, 2004).

The distribution of a gas between its liquid and gas phases is dependent upon the solubility of the gas: the higher the solubility, the greater the tendency to remain in the liquid phase. During a chromatographic process, one phase is kept in continuous motion in a fixed direction. If two or more gases are dissolved in water, chromatography will occur when the air is forced to move continuously in one direction over the water. The gas with less solubility will have a greater number of molecules escaping into the gas phase than the other gas, and these molecules will travel faster than the molecules of the more soluble gas. After a period of time, the molecules of the two gases will become completely separated. The process can be viewed as a race. At first, the participating substances are mixed together at the starting line. As the race progresses, the substance that is more movable (moving phase) will charge ahead of the substance that prefers solubility (stationary phase) (Smith, 2004).

In **gas chromatography**, called the moving phase, the carrier gas flows through a column constructed of glass. The stationary phase is a thin film of liquid contained within the column. As the carrier gas flows through the column, it carries along with it the components of a mixture that has been injected into the column. Those components having a greater affinity for the moving gas phase will travel through the column at a faster rate than those having a greater affinity for the stationary liquid phase. Eventually, after the mixture has traversed the length of the column, it will emerge separated into its component parts (Saferstein, 2007).

As the constituent components emerge from the column, they pass through a detector that creates a written record as a function of time. This written record of the separation is called a chromatogram. A typical chromatogram will show a series of peaks, each corresponding to a component of the mixture. The time required for a component to emerge from the column is known as the retention time. This serves as an identifying characteristic of a material. Two or more substances may have comparable retention times under similar chromatographic conditions; thus, the results of gas chromatography can only be considered presumptive and must be confirmed by other procedures.

An advantage of gas chromatography is that it can yield quantitative results. The amount of a substance passing through the detector is proportional to the peak recorded. By chromatographing a known concentration of a material and comparing the result with that of the sample, the concentration of the sample may be determined.

Thin-layer Chromatography. This type of chromatography incorporates a solid stationary phase and a moving liquid phase to separate the constituents of a mixture. An absorbent plate is coated with a thin film of silica gel or aluminum oxide and is held in place with plaster of Paris. If the specimen to be examined is a solid, it must first be dissolved in a solvent. A few microliters of the solution is spotted onto the lower edge of the plate, which is then placed upright in a closed chamber that contains a selected liquid to which fluorescent dye has been added. The placement is made so that only the bottom edge of the plate is resting in the liquid (test spots may not touch the liquid). The liquid will slowly rise up the plate (by capillary action). As the liquid moves past the test spots, the components of the sample will become distributed between the plate and the rising liquid. Those components that are the least soluble will travel up the plate faster than those components that are more soluble. When the liquid has traveled 10 cm past the test spots, the development is complete, and the plate is removed, dried, and examined (Smith, 2004).

The plates are placed under ultraviolet light, revealing those materials that fluoresce as bright spots on a dark background. Another method of visualization involves the use of a reagent spray that causes the separated spots to color. The unknown sample must be developed alongside a standardized sample on the same thin-layer chromatographic plate. If the standard and the test materials travel the same distances up the plate, they can tentatively be identified as being the same. The identification is not conclusive and requires confirmation (Smith, 2004).

The distance a spot has traveled up a thin-layer plate can be assigned a numerical value known as the Rf value. This value is defined as the distance traveled by the component divided by the distance traveled by the moving liquid phase. Because the liquid phase is allowed to travel 10 cm, the Rf value will be in tenths of a centimeter (e.g., if the spot moved 8 cm, the Rf value would be 0.8). Years of research and testing have produced much published data relating to the proper selection of thin-layer chromatography conditions for separating and identifying specific classes of substances, including drugs (Smith, 2004).

Mass Spectrometry

The ability of gas chromatography to separate a complex mixture into its constituent parts, although reliable, predictable, and replicable, is still only presumptive. An expert cannot base his or her opinion solely on chromatographic retention time, but by coupling gas chromatography and **mass spectrometry**, a definitive identification can be made. After the mixture has been separated by the gas chromatograph, a direct connection of the chromatograph columns and the mass spectrometer allows each component to flow into the spectrometer as it leaves the chromatograph. The material enters a high-vacuum chamber in which a beam of high-energy electrons is aimed at the sample molecules. The electrons collide with the molecules, causing them to lose electrons and to acquire a positive charge (i.e., to become ions). The ions are unstable and almost instantaneously decompose into numerous smaller fragments. The fragments are passed through an electric field, where they are separated according to their masses. Under carefully controlled conditions, no two substances produce the same fragmentation pattern. The fragmentation patterns are distinctive enough to be considered fingerprints (Yinon & Zitrin, 1977) (**Figure 14–19**).

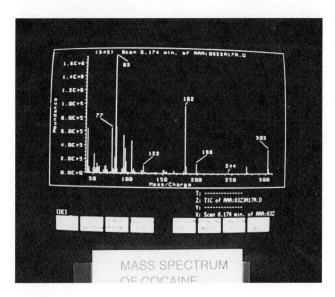

FIGURE 14–19   Analysis of crack cocaine sample by mass spectrometer
Courtesy of Austin Police Department, Austin, Texas.

This technique can conclusively identify a chemical substance even in minute concentrations. The combination of gas chromatograph and mass spectrometer is further enhanced when linked to a computer system (**Figure 14–20**). Accuracy, speed, and sensitivity are added to the procedure, along with the capability to record and store data. The system is able to detect and identify substances present in one millionth of a gram. Computer comparisons can be run of unknown substances, avoiding the necessity of a control specimen.

FIGURE 14–20   Gas chromatograph/mass spectrometer linked to a computer

WRAP UP

Chapter Summary

Drug-related evidence is quite prevalent at modern crime scenes. It is wise for a crime scene investigator to have a thorough understanding of the various types of drugs and controlled substances, paraphernalia associated with each, indicators of use, and effects of their use. This information will greatly assist crime scene personnel with the correct manner in which on-scene documentation, collection, and preservation methods should progress. Because possession or use of the substance is the criminal offense, it is imperative that proper methods be followed to ensure the admissibility of evidence.

Review Questions

1. List the five classifications of drugs formed by the DEA and DHHS and provide an example of each.

2. Explain what is meant by cycling, stacking, and pyramiding as they relate to steroid use.

3. _____ are those substances (typically drugs) whose possession or use is regulated by the government.

4. Drug scheduling is conducted through a cooperative effort of the _____ and the _____.

5. All controlled substances, with the exception of _____, are abused to alter mood, thought, and feeling through their actions on the central nervous system.

6. What does the acronym DAWN stand for and how does it affect drug evidence?

7. Which narcotic is also used in the treatment of narcotic addiction?

8. Rophies, roofies, and roach are all common names for which controlled substance?

9. What does the acronym GHB stand for and what are its effects?

10. The most frequently encountered illicit drug worldwide is _____.

11. 3,4-Methylenedioxymethamphet-amine is also known as _____.

References

Fischer, M. H. (1879–1962). Quotations by author. Retrieved September 11, 2009, from http://www.quotationspage.com/quotes/Dr._Martin_Henry_Fischer/

Fisher, B. A. J. (2004). *Techniques of crime scene investigation* (7th ed.). Boca Raton, FL: CRC Press.

Gardner, A. (2011) *Hallucinogens legally sold as "bath salts" a new threat.* Retrieved August 25, 2012, from http://www.womenshealth.gov/news/headlines/649596.cfm

Johnston, L. D., O'Malley, P. M., & Bachman, J. G. (2003). *Monitoring the future national survey results on drug use, 1975–2002* (p. 520). Volume I: Secondary school students (NIH Publication No. 03-5375). Bethesda, MD: National Institute on Drug Abuse.

Saferstein, R. (2007). *Criminalistics: An introduction to forensic science* (9th ed.). Upper Saddle River, NJ: Pearson Prentice Hall.

Smith, F., & Siegel, J. (2004). *Handbook of forensic drug analysis.* Totowa, NJ: Humana Press.

Substance Abuse and Mental Health Services Administration (SAMHSA). (1999). *National Household Survey on Drug Abuse.* National Clearinghouse for Alcohol and Drug Information (NCADI). Retrieved September 29, 2012, from http://store.samhsa.gov/product/National-Household-Survey-on-Drug-Abuse-NHSDA-1999/BKD376

Substance Abuse and Mental Health Services Administration (SAMHSA). (2008). *Drug abuse warning network, 2008: National estimates of drug-related emergency department visits.* Rockville, MD: U.S. Department of Health and Human Services. Retrieved on September 29, 2012 from http://www.samhsa.gov/data/2k11/DAWN/ED/DAWN2k8ED.htm

Substance Abuse and Mental Health Services Administration (SAMHSA). (2011). *2010 National Survey on Drug Use and Health: Summary of National Findings,* NSDUH Series H-41, HHS Publication No. (SMA) 11-4658. Rockville, MD: Substance Abuse and Mental Health Services Administration.

United Nations. (2010). *World Drug Report 2010.* United Nations Office on Drugs and Crime. Retrieved July 4, 2012, from http://www.unodc.org

U.S. Department of Health and Human Services (DHHS), Office of Applied Studies. (2008). *National Survey on Drug Use and Health.* Retrieved September 29, 2012, from http://oas.samhsa.gov/nsduh/2k8nsduh/2k8Results.pdf

U.S. Drug Enforcement Administration (DEA). (2005). *Drugs of abuse.* Retrieved September 29, 2012, from http://naabt.org/documents/Drugs%20of%20abuse%20DEA.pdf

U.S. Drug Enforcement Administration (DEA). (2011). *Chemicals used in "Spice" and "K2" type products now under federal control and regulation.* Retrieved July 7, 2012, from http://www.justice.gov/dea/pubs/pressrel/pr030111p.html

U.S. Department of Justice. (November 29, 1990). Title 21 United States Code (USC) *Controlled Substances Act.* Retrieved September 29, 2012, from http://www.deadiversion.usdoj.gov/21cfr/21usc/index.html

Yinon, J., & Zitrin, S. (1977). Processing and interpreting mass special data in forensic identification of drugs and explosives. *Journal of Forensic Sciences, 224,* 742–747.

© McMac/ShutterStock, Inc.

LEARNING OBJECTIVES

- Understand the forensic potential of digital evidence.
- Know how to properly document, collect, and preserve digital evidence.
- Understand how GPS technology can aid law enforcement with conducting investigations.

Digital Evidence

Computers can figure out all kinds of problems, except the things in the world that just don't add up.

Isaac Asimov (1920–1992)

KEY TERMS

Computer Network
Contraband

Digital Evidence
Handheld Devices

Instrumentality
Peripheral Devices

Introduction to Digital Evidence

More and more frequently computers and other digital devices are being used as a component of criminal activity, and when such devices are found at a crime scene they should be regarded as a possible source of evidence. While the majority of agencies and departments cannot afford to train or equip personnel to specialize in the processing and analysis of digital evidence, it is important for a crime scene investigator to have a basic knowledge of the forensic potential of digital evidence, and how to proceed when confronted with such evidence. However, if at any point the investigator is unsure of the correct steps to take, a knowledgeable professional should be contacted.

Computers are being used to store records of drug transactions, money laundering, child pornography, prostitution, and many other criminal activities. The information presented in this chapter refers specifically to standalone digital components and computers. If the crime scene investigator suspects that a network, mainframe, or some other type of system may be involved, then a computer specialist should be consulted prior to disturbing or seizing any of the components. Computer technology is constantly changing, and seizure methods may change in the future. Therefore, if the crime scene investigator has any questions, he or she should contact the forensic laboratory for technical assistance.

Criminal Use of Digital Equipment

The United States Department of Justice (USDOJ) categorizes computers that are used in a criminal manner in one of three ways: contraband, instrumentality, or "mere" evidence (NIJ, 2008). If a digital device is found to be illegally possessed or for some legal reasons is illegal to possess, it is considered **contraband**. If a device, system, or its associated hardware played a significant role in the commission of a crime, then it is considered an item of **instrumentality**. Any system or device that is termed "mere" evidence is oftentimes not seized, but instead the goal is acquiring the data that is of evidentiary value from the device, while adhering to computer forensic principles. However, before this is done, it is important to first examine the manner in which crime scene investigators and first responders should treat digital evidence.

What follows is information assembled by the USDOJ's National Institute of Justice (NIJ) in a special report called *Electronic Crime Scene Investigation: A Guide for First Responders, Second Edition* (2008).

Digital Evidence

Digital evidence is information and data of value to an investigation that is stored on, received, or transmitted by an electronic device. This evidence is acquired when data or electronic devices are seized and secured for examination.

Digital Evidence

- Is latent, like fingerprints or DNA evidence
- Crosses jurisdictional borders quickly and easily
- Is easily altered, damaged, or destroyed
- Can be time sensitive

National Institute of Justice (NIJ). (April, 2008). Electronic crime scene investigation: A guide for first responders (2nd ed.). Retrieved October 2, 2012, from http://www.nij.gov/pubs-sum/219941.htm.

When dealing with digital evidence, general forensic and procedural principles should be applied:

- The process of collecting, securing, and transporting digital evidence should not change the evidence.
- Digital evidence should be examined only by those trained specifically for that purpose.
- Everything done during the seizure, transportation, and storage of digital evidence should be fully documented, preserved, and available for review.

First responders must use caution when they seize electronic devices. Improperly accessing data stored on electronic devices may violate federal laws, including the Electronic Communications Privacy Act of 1986 and the Privacy Protection Act of 1980. First responders may need to obtain additional legal authority before they proceed. They should consult the prosecuting attorney for the appropriate jurisdiction to ensure that they have proper legal authority to seize the digital evidence at the scene.

In addition to the legal ramifications of improperly accessing data that are stored on a computer, first responders must understand that computer data and other digital evidence are fragile. Only properly trained personnel should attempt to examine and analyze digital evidence.

Handling Digital Evidence at the Scene

Precautions should be taken in the collection, preservation, and transportation of digital evidence. First responders may follow the steps listed below to guide their handling of digital evidence at an electronic crime scene:

- Recognize, identify, seize, and secure all digital evidence at the scene.
- Document the entire scene and the specific location of the evidence found.
- Collect, label, and preserve the digital evidence.
- Package and transport digital evidence in a secure manner.

Golden Rules of Crime Scenes Involving Digital Evidence

There are questions to ask and general principles to follow when responding to any crime scene in which computers and electronic technology may be involved. Several of those are as follows:

- Officer safety—secure the scene and make it safe.

- If you reasonably believe that the computer is involved in the crime you are investigating, take immediate steps to preserve the evidence.

- Do you have a legal basis to seize this computer (plain view, search warrant, consent, etc.)?

- Do not access any computer files. If the computer is off, leave it off. If it is on, do not start searching through the computer.

- If you reasonably believe that the computer is destroying evidence, immediately shut down the computer by pulling the power cord from the back of the computer.

- If a camera is available, and the computer is on, take pictures of the computer screen. If the computer is off, take pictures of the computer, the location of the computer, and any electronic media attached.

- Do special legal considerations apply (doctor, attorney, clergy, psychiatrist, newspapers, publishers, etc.)?

United States Secret Service. (2007). *Best practices for seizing electronic evidence: A pocket guide for first responders*, Volume 3. U.S. Department of Homeland Security.

Electronic Devices: Types, Description, and Potential Evidence

Internally attached computer hard drives, external drives, and other electronic devices at a crime scene may contain information that can be useful as evidence in a criminal investigation or prosecution. The devices themselves and the information they contain may be used as digital evidence. In this chapter, such devices are identified, along with general information about their evidential value.

Some devices require internal or external power to maintain stored information. For these devices, the power must be maintained to preserve the information stored. For additional information about maintaining power to these devices, refer to the device manufacturer's web-site or other reliable sources of information.

Computer Systems

A computer system consists of hardware and software that process data and is likely to include:

- A case that contains circuit boards, microprocessors, hard drive, memory, and interface connections
- A monitor or video display device
- A keyboard
- A mouse
- Peripheral or externally connected drives, devices, and components

Computer systems can take many forms, such as laptops, desktops, tower computers, rack-mounted systems, minicomputers, and mainframe computers. Additional components and peripheral devices include modems, routers, printers, scanners, and docking stations. Many of these are discussed further in this chapter.

A computer system and its components can be valuable evidence in an investigation. The hardware, software, documents, photos, image files, email and attachments, databases, financial information, Internet browsing history, chat logs, buddy lists, event logs, data stored on external devices, and identifying information associated with the computer system and components are all potential evidence.

Storage Devices

Storage devices vary in size and the manner in which they store and retain data. First responders must understand that, regardless of their size or type, these devices may contain information that is valuable to an investigation or prosecution. The following storage devices may be digital evidence.

Hard Drives

Hard drives are data storage devices that consist of an external circuit board; external data and power connections; and internal magnetically charged glass, ceramic, or metal platters that store data. First responders also may find hard drives at the scene that are not connected to or installed on a computer. These loose hard drives may still contain valuable evidence.

External Hard Drives

Hard drives can be installed in an external drive case. External hard drives increase the computer's data storage capacity and provide the user with portable data. Generally, external hard drives require a power supply and a universal serial bus (USB), FireWire, Ethernet, or wireless connection to a computer system.

Removable Media

Removable media are cartridges and disk-based data storage devices. They are typically used to store, archive, transfer, and transport data and other information. These devices help users share data, information, applications, and utilities among different computers and other devices (**Figure 15–1**).

Thumb Drives

Thumb drives are small, lightweight, removable data storage devices with USB connections. These devices, also referred to as flash drives, are easy to conceal and transport. They can be found as part of, or disguised as, a wristwatch, a pocket-size multi-tool such as a Swiss Army knife, a keychain fob, or any number of common and unique devices (**Figure 15–2**).

Memory Cards

Memory cards are small data storage devices commonly used with digital cameras, computers, mobile phones, digital music players, personal digital assistants (PDAs), video game consoles, and handheld and other electronic devices.

Storage devices such as hard drives, external hard drives, removable media, thumb drives, and memory cards may contain information such as email messages, Internet browsing history, Internet chat logs and buddy lists, photographs, image files, databases, financial records, and event logs that can be valuable evidence in an investigation or prosecution.

Handheld Devices

Handheld devices are portable data storage devices that provide communications, digital photography, navigation systems, entertainment, data storage, and personal information management.

Handheld devices such as mobile phones, smart phones, PDAs, digital multimedia (audio and video) devices, pagers, digital cameras, and global positioning system (GPS) receivers

FIGURE 15–1   An example of an external storage device

FIGURE 15–2   An example of media cards

Storage Media

Storage media is used to store data from electronic devices. As a result, these items also should be considered evidence when processing a crime scene involving digital evidence. These items may vary in memory quantity, depending upon size and recentness of the technology.

Proper Storage Media Collection

- Collect instruction manuals, documentation, and notes.
- Document all steps involved in seizure of storage media.
- Keep away from magnets, radio transmitters, and other potentially damaging devices.

United States Secret Service. (2007). *Best practices for seizing electronic evidence: A pocket guide for first responders,* Volume 3. U.S. Department of Homeland Security.

---

may contain software applications, data, and information such as documents, email messages, Internet browsing history, Internet chat logs and buddy lists, photographs, image files, databases, and financial records that are valuable evidence in an investigation or prosecution (**Figure 15–3**).

Peripheral Devices

Peripheral devices are equipment that can be connected to a computer or computer system to enhance user access and expand the computer's functions. The devices themselves and the functions they perform or facilitate are all potential evidence. Information stored on the device regarding its use also is evidence, such as incoming and outgoing phone and fax numbers; recently scanned, faxed, or printed documents; and information about the purpose for or use of the device. In addition, these devices can be sources of fingerprints, DNA, and other identifiers.

© CLIPAREA I Custom media/ShutterStock, Inc.

FIGURE 15–3 Examples of handheld digital devices (camera, GPS, smart phone)

PDAs, Cell Phones, and Digital Cameras

Personal digital assistants, cell phones, and digital cameras may store data directly to internal memory or may contain removable media. The following details the proper seizure and preservation of these devices and associated removable media:

- If the device is "off," do not turn it "on."
- With PDAs or cell phones, if a device is on, leave it on. Powering down the device could enable the password, thus preventing access to evidence.
- Photograph device and screen display (if available).
- Label and collect all cables (to include power supply) and transport with device.
- Keep device charged.
- If device cannot be kept charged, analysis by a specialist must be completed prior to battery discharge or data may be lost.
- Seize additional storage media (memory sticks, compact flash, etc.).
- Document all steps involved in seizure of device and components.

United States Secret Service. (2007). *Best practices for seizing electronic evidence: A pocket guide for first responders*, Volume 3. U.S. Department of Homeland Security.

RIPPED FROM THE HEADLINES

iPhone Yields Forensic Evidence in Trial of Dr. Conrad Murray

In the trial of Dr. Conrad Murray, Michael Jackson's attending physician at the time of his death, prosecutors called upon Drug Enforcement Agency (DEA) computer forensic expert Stephen Marx to examine and analyze data contained within Murray's cell phone to find potential evidence to explain the pop icon's death. Marx was able to extract information from the doctor's iPhone, including a recording of Jackson speaking in a slow and slurred manner. There were also digital medical charts, emails, and documentation of extended non-urgent phone calls placed prior to and after Jackson's death, which all contributed to Murray eventually being found guilty of manslaughter in the wrongful death of Michael Jackson

Information from Gardner, David. (2011). Jury shown photos of child-sized porcelain doll found in bed with Michael Jackson when he died. Retrieved on October 2, 2012, from http://www.dailymail.co.uk/news/article-2045737/Conrad-Murray-trial-Michael-Jacsons-doll-drug-stash-shown-jurors.html.

Computer Networks

A **computer network** consists of two or more computers linked by data cables or by wireless connections that share or are capable of sharing resources and data. A computer network often includes printers, other peripheral devices, and data-routing devices such as hubs, switches, and routers. The networked computers and connected devices themselves may be evidence that is useful to an investigation or prosecution. The data they contain may be valuable evidence and may include software, documents, photos, image files, email messages and attachments, databases, financial information, Internet browsing history, log files, event and chat logs, buddy lists, and data stored on external devices. The device functions, capabilities, and any identifying information associated with the computer system; components and connections, including Internet protocol (IP) and local area network (LAN) addresses associated with the computers and devices; broadcast settings; and media access card (MAC) or network interface card (NIC) addresses may all be useful as evidence.

Other Potential Sources of Digital Evidence

First responders should be aware of and consider as potential evidence other elements of the crime scene that are related to digital information, such as electronic devices, equipment, software, hardware, or other technology that can function independently, in conjunction with, or attached to computer systems. These items may be used to enhance the user's access to and expand the functionality of the computer system, the device itself, or other equipment.

The device or item itself, its intended or actual use, its functions or capabilities, and any settings or other information it may contain are potential evidence.

Investigative Tools and Equipment

In most cases, items or devices containing digital evidence can be collected using standard seizure tools and materials. First responders must use caution when collecting, packaging, or storing digital devices to avoid altering, damaging, or destroying the digital evidence. Avoid using any tools or materials that may produce or emit static electricity or a magnetic field as these may damage or destroy the evidence.

Should the complexity of an electronic crime scene exceed the expertise of a first responder, the first responder should request assistance from personnel with advanced equipment and training in digital evidence collection. The technical resource list at the Electronic Crime Partner Initiative (2008) website provides additional information for these situations.

Tools and Materials for Collecting Digital Evidence

In addition to tools for processing crime scenes in general, first responders should have the following items in their digital evidence collection toolkit:

- Cameras (photo and video)
- Cardboard boxes

- Notepads
- Gloves
- Evidence inventory logs
- Evidence tape
- Paper evidence bags
- Evidence stickers, labels, or tags
- Crime scene tape
- Antistatic bags
- Permanent markers
- Nonmagnetic tools

First responders also should have radio frequency–shielding material such as faraday isolation bags or aluminum foil to wrap cell phones, smart phones, and other mobile communication devices after they have been seized. Wrapping the phones in radio frequency–shielding material prevents the phones from receiving a call, text message, or other communications signal that may alter the evidence.

Securing and Evaluating the Scene

The first responder's primary consideration should be officer safety and the safety of everyone at the crime scene. All actions and activities carried out at the scene should be in compliance with departmental policy as well as federal, state, and local laws.

After securing the scene and all persons at the scene, the first responder should visually identify all potential evidence and ensure that the integrity of both the digital and traditional evidence is preserved. Digital evidence on computers and other electronic devices can be easily altered, deleted, or destroyed. First responders should document, photograph, and secure digital evidence as soon as possible at the scene.

When securing and evaluating the scene, the first responder should:

- Follow departmental policy for securing crime scenes.
- Immediately secure all electronic devices, including personal or portable devices.
- Ensure that no unauthorized person has access to any electronic devices at the crime scene.
- Refuse offers of help or technical assistance from any unauthorized persons.
- Remove all persons from the crime scene or the immediate area from which evidence is to be collected.
- Ensure that the condition of any electronic device is not altered.
- Leave a computer or electronic device off if it is already turned off.

Components such as keyboard, mouse, removable storage media, and other items may hold latent evidence such as fingerprints, DNA, or other physical evidence that should be preserved. First responders should take the appropriate steps to ensure that physical evidence is not compromised during documentation.

Evidence Collection

The first responder must have proper authority—such as plain view observation, consent, or a court order—to search for and collect evidence at an electronic crime scene (**Figure 15–4**). The first responder must be able to identify the authority under which he or she may seize evidence and should follow agency guidelines, consult a superior, or contact a prosecutor if a question of appropriate authority arises.

The following is a general reference guideline for consent forms pertaining to computers and electronic media. Consult your District Attorney or Assistant U.S. Attorney regarding consent language applicable to your jurisdiction.

CONSENT TO SEARCH ELECTRONIC MEDIA

I, _____, hereby authorize _____, who has identified himself/herself as a law enforcement officer, and any other person(s), including but not limited to a computer forensic examiner, he/she may designate to assist him/her, to remove, take possession of and/or conduct a complete search of the following: computer systems, electronic data storage devices, computer data storage diskettes, CD-ROMs, or any other electronic equipment capable of storing, retrieving, processing and/or accessing data.

The aforementioned equipment will be subject to data duplication/imaging and a forensic analysis for any data pertinent to the incident/criminal investigation.

I give this consent to search freely and voluntarily without fear, threat, coercion or promises of any kind and with full knowledge of my constitutional right to refuse to give my consent for the removal and/or search of the aforementioned equipment/data, which I hereby waive. I am also aware that if I wish to exercise this right of refusal at any time during the seizure and or search of the equipment/data, it will be respected.

This consent to search is given by me this _____ day of, _____ 20_____, at _____ am/pm.

Location items taken from: _____

Consenter Signature: _____

Witness Signature: _____

Witness Signature: _____

FIGURE 15–4 Example of a consent to search form (USSS)

United States Secret Services. (2007). Best practices for seizing electronic evidence: A pocket guide for first responders, Volume 3. U.S. Department of Homeland Security.

Evidence Collection and Chain of Custody: Things to Remember

Cybercrime and the investigation and prosecution of cybercriminals have always fascinated me. As an investigator and academician in the study of computer forensics, I was able to merge my favorite subjects in one field: law, criminal justice, psychology, and computer and information science. My work experience as an investigator has taught me many important lessons about criminal behavior and appropriate investigative techniques. One important lesson that I learned concerning computer forensics is that it is imperative for an investigator to look for evidence of a cybercrime beyond computers, mobile phones, and other electronic devices such as printers, scanners, copiers, CDs, DVDs, Blue-Ray disks, external hard drives, universal serial bus (USB), flash drives, magnetic tape data storage devices (e.g., linear tape-open or LTO), cameras, fixed telephony, faxes, pagers, personal data assistants (PDAs), portable media players (e.g., Apple's iPod), iPads, and gaming consoles (e.g., Microsoft's Xbox, Sony PlayStation 3, and Nintendo Wii). Nondigital evidence often plays a vital role in the investigation.

An investigator should photograph and collect books and other relevant evidence to his or her investigation. Often, individuals keep password and/or decryption keys within their view. As such, notes, papers, post-its, and other such items that are on a desk, table, bookcase, computer, and/or related devices and or on walls or boards close to the computer may hold such information and thus should be collected. Concerning the search for evidence, an investigator should look under desks, tables, and in areas of concealment

---

Digital evidence must be handled carefully to preserve the integrity of the physical device as well as the data it contains. Some digital evidence requires special collection, packaging, and transportation techniques. Data can be damaged or altered by electromagnetic fields such as those generated by static electricity, magnets, radio transmitters, and other devices. Communication devices such as mobile phones, smart phones, PDAs, and pagers should be secured and prevented from receiving or transmitting data once they are identified and collected as evidence.

Safeguarding Data

If information stored within a computer is incriminating, users can devise methods to destroy the data if an unauthorized person attempts to use the system. For this reason, it is essential that precautions be taken to safeguard the evidence when a computer is seized. When crime scene personnel discover a computer, they should immediately remove everyone near the computer, and inside manuals and books. Any trash bins should also be checked for potential evidence. Basically, investigators should look everywhere they are authorized to by law. Furthermore, the physical evidence (e.g., trace and impression, such as fiber, hair, dust, and fingerprints) that might be on or near the computer, keyboard, mouse, and other related electronic devices must not be overlooked.

However, evidence collection is only one part of the job. A computer forensics investigator must ensure that evidence is properly recorded (e.g., through notes, sketches, photographs, and video), labeled, packaged, collected, transported, analyzed, and stored. The procedures for the handling and preservation of evidence must be thoroughly documented. If I had to choose the most important part of an investigation—one that an investigator and those involved in the investigation should pay the most attention to—I would have to say that it is the chain of custody. A chain of custody log helps uphold the integrity and ensure the admissibility of the evidence that is collected. The chain of custody will include information about the person who collected the evidence, where and how the evidence was collected, which individuals took possession of the evidence, and when they took possession of it. The preservation of a chain of custody is critical; without it, important evidence to the case will be inadmissible in court. Accordingly, it is important to remember that the chain of custody must be maintained at all times.

Marie-Helen Maras, PhD
Assistant Professor of Criminal Justice at SUNY and Adjunct Professor at NYU
Former Command Investigator and Law Enforcement Specialist, U.S. Navy

Courtesy of Marie-Helen Maras, PhD, Assistant Professor, State University of New York-Farmingdale.

from the area and not allow any further contact with the computer system, because a single keystroke can execute a program that erases information. Take a photograph of the screen to document any information that is displayed and then immediately unplug the computer. Unplug the computer from the back of the central processing unit (CPU or main box), not from a wall receptacle. Uninterruptible power supplies (UPS) are common and can be programmed to execute destructive processes upon loss of power from a wall receptacle. Do not use the power switch, because it can be rigged to damage the hard drive or other components.

Do not execute any commands on the computer prior to pulling the plug. Commands, such as DIR and PARK, can be altered to execute destructive processes. If there is a modem connected, unplug the modem cable from the wall. Leave the connections on the back of the computer undisturbed until they can be documented. Photograph the cable connections at the rear of the computer. Mark all cables with evidence tape or tags and mark the corresponding ports on the computer in an identical manner. Photograph and document peripherals and the marked connections on the back of the computer system prior to disconnection. This will facilitate the reassembly of the computer system and the peripherals in the office, courtroom, or at the laboratory. It is recommended that all computer hardware, software, disks, and manuals be seized. It is a reasonable and common practice to retain business records on computer media, in addition to the traditional (paper) method used to maintain and store business records and documents.

All Computer Hardware Should Be Seized

Conducting a search of a computer system, documenting the search, and making evidentiary and discovery copies is a lengthy process. It is necessary to determine that no security devices are in place that could cause the destruction of evidence during the search, and in some cases, it is impossible even to conduct the search without expert technical assistance. Because it would be extremely difficult to secure the system on the premises during the entire period of the search, and computer evidence is extremely vulnerable, removal of the system from the premises will assist in retrieving the records authorized to be seized, while avoiding accidental destruction or deliberate alteration of the records. All peripherals should be seized, because some software programs are designed to work with specific hardware. Without all the components connected, it may be difficult, if not impossible, to recover and print the files of interest.

All Computer Software and Disks Should Be Seized

Specific software programs may be needed to view files stored on the system. Also, it would be impossible, without examination, to determine that disks purporting to contain standard, commercially available software have not been altered or used to store records instead. It is also possible that disks may contain information other than what is labeled, and unlabeled disks may contain files.

All Manuals and Pieces of Paper Found Near the Computer Should Be Seized

The analyst may have to refer to the manual and handwritten notes to operate the system and to recover the records authorized to be seized. Many programs can be password protected, and it is common for users to write passwords and other information in manuals and on scraps of paper.

Computers, Components, and Devices

To prevent the alteration of digital evidence during collection, first responders should first:

- Document any activity on the computer, components, or devices.
- Confirm the power state of the computer. Check for flashing lights, running fans, and other sounds that indicate the computer or electronic device is powered on. If the power

state cannot be determined from these indicators, observe the monitor to determine if it is on, off, or in sleep mode.

Packaging, Transportation, and Storage of Digital Evidence

Digital evidence, and the computers and electronic devices on which it is stored, is fragile and sensitive to extreme temperatures, humidity, physical shock, static electricity, and magnetic fields.

The first responder should take precautions when documenting, photographing, packaging, transporting, and storing digital evidence to avoid altering, damaging, or destroying the data.

Packaging Procedures

All actions related to the identification, collection, packaging, transportation, and storage of digital evidence should be thoroughly documented. When packing digital evidence for transportation, the first responder should:

- Ensure that all digital evidence collected is properly documented, labeled, marked, photographed, video recorded or sketched, and inventoried before it is packaged. All connections and connected devices should be labeled for easy reconfiguration of the system later.

- Remember that digital evidence may also contain latent, trace, or biological evidence and take the appropriate steps to preserve it. Digital evidence imaging should be done before latent, trace, or biological evidence processes are conducted on the evidence.

- Pack all digital evidence in anti-static packaging. Only paper bags and envelopes, cardboard boxes, and anti-static containers should be used for packaging digital evidence. Plastic materials should not be used when collecting digital evidence because plastic can produce or convey static electricity and allow humidity and condensation to develop, which may damage or destroy the evidence. (*There are some specific bags that appear to be plastic but which are known as electrostatic discharge [ESD] or "anti-static" bags. These are static shielding bags that are safe for packaging electronic and digital components. They are also known as "metal-in shielding bags" because the protective metal shield is sandwiched between two plastic layers.*) (**Figure 15–5**)

- Ensure that all digital evidence is packaged in a manner that will prevent it from being bent, scratched, or otherwise deformed.

- Label all containers used to package and store digital evidence clearly and properly.

- Leave cellular, mobile, or smart phone(s) in the power state (on or off) in which they were found.

Standalone Home Personal Computer

For proper evidence preservation, follow these procedures in order:

- Do not use computer or attempt to search for evidence.
- Photograph computer front and back as well as cords and connected devices, as found. Photograph surrounding area prior to moving any evidence.
- If computer is "off," do not it turn "on."
- If computer is "on" and something is displayed on the monitor, photograph the screen.
- If computer is "on" and the screen is blank, move mouse or press spacebar (this will display the active image on the screen). After image appears, photograph the screen.
- Unplug power cord from back of tower.
- If the laptop does not shut down when the power cord is removed, locate and remove the battery pack. The battery is commonly placed on the bottom, and there is usually a button or switch that allows for the removal of the battery. Once the battery is removed, do not return it to or store it in the laptop. Removing the battery will prevent accidental start-up of the laptop.
- Diagram and label cords to later identify connected devices.
- Disconnect all cords and devices from tower.
- Package components and transport/store components as fragile cargo.
- Seize additional storage media.
- Keep all media, including tower, away from magnets, radio transmitters, and other potentially damaging elements.
- Collect instruction manuals, documentation, and notes.
- Document all steps involved in the seizure of a computer and components.

- Package mobile or smart phone(s) in signal-blocking material such as faraday isolation bags, radio frequency–shielding material, or aluminum foil to prevent data messages from being sent or received by the devices. (First responders should be aware that if inappropriately packaged or removed from shielded packaging, the device may be able to send and receive data messages if in range of a communication signal.)
- Collect all power supplies and adapters for all electronic devices seized.

Networked Home Personal Computer

For proper evidence preservation, follow these procedures in order:

- Unplug power to router or modem.
- Do not use computer or attempt to search for evidence.
- Photograph computer front and back as well as cords and connected devices, as found. Photograph surrounding area prior to moving any evidence.
- If computer is "off," do not turn it "on."
- If computer is "on" and something is displayed on the monitor, photograph the screen.
- If computer is "on" and the screen is blank, move mouse or press spacebar (this will display the active image on the screen). After image appears, photograph the screen.
- Unplug power cord from back of tower.
- Diagram and label cords to later identify connected devices.
- Disconnect all cords and devices from tower.
- Package components (including router and modem) and transport/store components as fragile cargo.
- Seize additional storage media.
- Keep all media, including tower, away from magnets, radio transmitters, and other potentially damaging elements.
- Collect instruction manuals, documentation, and notes.
- Document all steps involved in the seizure of a computer and components.

United States Secret Service. (2007). Best practices for seizing electronic evidence: A pocket guide for first responders, Volume 3. U.S. Department of Homeland Security.

Transporting the Evidence

Computers are delicate electronic instruments that are sensitive to temperature, physical shock, static electricity, and magnetic fields. When transported, care should be taken to ensure that computer components are well cushioned and protected. The original box and packaging material, if it can be located, is a good container for storing and transporting the computer. Magnetic media, such as computer hard drives, floppy disks, magnetic tapes, etc., are very sensitive to magnetic fields. When placing computer evidence in a car, remember that police

FIGURE 15–5 Computer hardrive packaged in an ESD bag

radio transmitters are strong sources of magnetic fields. Do not place computer evidence in the trunk of a car if the trunk contains a police radio.

Cell Phones and Global Positioning Systems

There is yet another area of digital evidence that proves useful from an investigatory side, in a processing manner, and as a public service as well. Global positioning system (GPS) devices are available as handheld devices and are even included in most phones and PDAs. GPS technology can be utilized to document crime scenes; however, with the improvement of and increased access to GPS technology, law enforcement also has the resources to track individuals, corroborate information, and from a crime scene aspect, map and sketch large scenes.

Cell phone technology has become important in criminal investigations as people are relying more upon their phones for conducting business and personal activities, whether legal or illegal.

GPS built into cell phones allows authorities to track criminals and people in need of help. Every time that a cell phone is turned on it sends a registration message, including the serial and phone numbers, to the closest cellular tower. A tower receives signals from cell phones on all sides of it. The tower then divides the area around it into three equal sectors. A GPS locator pinpoints the sector where the phone is calling. There are over 200,000 cellular towers placed across the United States.

Due to this technology, dispatchers can often deploy searchers within 100 feet of the caller's location, even if the caller is unable to ascertain his or her current position. If a caller makes use of an older phone without GPS, searchers can narrow down the caller's location by using three towers to triangulate a phone's last known spot by measuring the time that it takes signals to reach the towers. Law enforcement has three options for locating a person through his or her cell phone, depending upon the scenario:

1. Single cell tower search
2. GPS tracking
3. Cell tower triangulation

Most phones and digital devices allow the user to manually turn off the GPS feature; however, the device will automatically activate the GPS when a call is placed to 911.

Some ways that law enforcement currently makes use of GPS technology are as follows:

- Stolen cars that are equipped with GPS can be tracked and recovered. Instead of being involved in a police pursuit, which can create a greater risk to the public, a stolen vehicle can be located by law enforcement through the use of GPS technology. Once the stolen vehicle has reached a destination where law enforcement deems it is safe, those in the vehicle can be apprehended in a safer manner.

- Many jurisdictions have begun to use GPS bracelets on parolees as a way of monitoring their whereabouts. This technology also can be used to investigate and to enforce restraining orders through a similar method of having offenders fitted with a GPS bracelet.

- In recent times, law enforcement has made use of GPS-equipped vehicles and other items as bait in law enforcement sting operations, particularly with regard to investigating stolen vehicle crime rings, and also construction site equipment thefts.

Tracking Technology

A quick search of the Internet will yield hundreds of sites and devices that can enable someone to track a person or object through the use of GPS technology. Some of these devices are small enough to fit within purses, vehicles, or even small electronic items. Some have the purpose of legitimately tracking shipments, items, vehicles, or persons. Others, however, can be used for criminal purposes, including stalking.

The courts are somewhat split on whether or not such planting of GPS equipment is an invasion of the 4th Amendment right to privacy. A 2009 ruling in the state of Wisconsin stated that GPS technology was simply another method of documenting a movement of a vehicle on a public roadway, rather than use personal observation, which would have otherwise been legal, and therefore a search warrant was not a requirement (Foley, 2009). During the same year, a court in the state of New York ruled that law enforcement must obtain a search warrant before such GPS tracking can occur (Chan, 2009). Hence, the district attorney of the jurisdiction in question should be contacted prior to implementing the use of GPS technology for investigatory purposes, such as tracking movement.

There is also the possibility of utilizing geographic information systems (GIS) to map criminal movement and activities. Most wireless phones have GIS technology embedded, which further adds to the ease of tracking movements. Again, it is suggested that prior to using such evidence, the district attorney be notified to see if a search warrant is a requirement or not.

RIPPED FROM THE HEADLINES

Man Charged with Stalking Using GPS

The *Wisconsin State Journal* ran an article on February 15, 2008 reporting that the husband of a Madison, Wisconsin police officer had been charged with four felonies after he had secretly placed a GPS tracker in his wife's car and had used her name and password to access the police department's computer system.

The case involved the husband tracking the movements of his police wife as she was involved with an extramarital affair with another officer with whom she worked. At one point she told her lover that she believed that she was being followed by her husband and he suggested that perhaps her husband had placed a GPS tracking device within her car. The two searched her car and located such a device.

The use of digital technology to track his wife's whereabouts went deeper yet. After the stalking behavior was reported to law enforcement, police searched the husband's home computer and his computer at his place of employment. The home computer was found to contain key-tracking software that allowed the husband to identify his wife's login identity and password, and for him to then access the Madison Police Department's scheduling system that contained work and vacation schedules. On his work computer, police found evidence that the husband had accessed his wife's personal emails and printed off communication between she and her law enforcement lover.

The husband was eventually found guilty of three felony counts of stalking and identity theft. As a side note, infidelity is a moral offense in the state of Wisconsin, with no criminal penalty.

Information retrieved from Singletary, K. (2008, February 15). Man is charged with stalking. He's accused of putting a GPS device in the car of his estranged wife. *Wisconsin State Journal.*

WRAP UP

Chapter Summary

We live in a digital world. Nearly all of our daily activities are captured, scheduled, or recorded on a digital device. This technology has enabled society to work more efficiently and has significantly reduced its reliance upon paper products and resources, thus proving more environmentally friendly. There are, however, drawbacks to this digital phenomenon. As with all aspects of life, criminals use this technology to further their activities, requiring that law enforcement stay abreast of the latest methods of digital evidence documentation, retrieval, and preservation. Failure to stay current on such matters will result in cases being lost. However, the very same technology that is a scourge also aids law enforcement and crime scene personnel through the production of new technology that expedites and makes more efficient the processing methodologies used while processing a modern crime scene.

Review Questions

1. If a device, system, or its associated hardware played a significant role in the commission of a crime, then it is considered an item of _____.

2. _____ is information and data of value to an investigation that is stored on, received, or transmitted by an electronic device.

3. A crime scene investigator needs to remember that digital evidence on computers and other electronic devices can be easily _____, _____, or _____.

4. If an electronic device is discovered to be "on," what should be done before the item is unplugged?

5. Through the use of GPS technology, law enforcement is able to _____, _____, and _____.

6. What are the three ways that law enforcement might use a cell phone to locate an individual?

Case Studies

1. Look up the following case, stemming out of Beaver Dam, WI, involving child pornography on the student companion Web site at go.jblearning.com/CrimeSceneInvestigation2. Explain how investigators used digital evidence from Michigan and Illinois to track down suspects.

2. Access the following story regarding the use of cell phone technology on the student companion Web site at go.jblearning.com/CrimeScene-Investigation2. Explain how digital technology was used during the investigative process and how absent this technology, the suspect may not have been convicted.

3. Research the name Tanya Rider, of Seattle, on the student companion Web site at go.jblearning.com/CrimeSceneInvestigation2 and explain how cell phone technology is credited with saving her life and changing the focus of her missing persons investigation.

References

Chan, S. (May 12, 2009). Police used GPS illegally, court rules. *New York Times*. Retrieved August 19, 2009, from http://www.nytimes.com/2009/05/13/nyregion/13gps.html

Electronic Crime Partner Initiative. (April, 2008). *Technical resources* (2nd ed.). Retrieved October 2, 2012, from http://www.ecpi-us.org/files/219941.pdf

Foley, R. J. (2009, May 7). Wisconsin court upholds GPS tracking by police. *Chicago Tribune*. Retrieved October 2, 2012, from http://geodatapolicy.word press.com/2009/05/15/

Gardiner, D. Jury shown photos of child-sized porcelain doll found in bed with Michael Jackson when he died. *The Daily Mail Online*. Retrieved from http://www.dailymail.co.uk/news/article-2045737/Conrad-Murray-trial-Michael-Jacksons-doll-drug-stash-shown-jurors.html

Maras, M. H. (2012) *Computer forensics: Cybercriminals, laws and evidence*. Sudbury, MA: Jones and Bartlett Learning.

National Institute of Justice (NIJ). (April, 2008). *Electronic crime scene investigation: A guide for first responders* (2nd ed.). Retrieved October 2, 2012, from http://www.nij.gov/pubs-sum/219941.htm

Singletary, K. (2008, February 15). Man is charged with stalking. He's accused of putting a GPS device in the car of his estranged wife. *Wisconsin State Journal*. Retrieved October 2, 2012 from: http://host.madison.com/news/local/article_abf0e2e6-15ba-5813-8bb6-b775b8d53257.html

United States Secret Service. (2007). *Best practices for seizing electronic evidence: A pocket guide for first responders*, volume 3. U.S. Department of Homeland Security.

Specialized Investigations

© McMac/ShutterStock, Inc.

- Describe the various types of homicides.
- Gain a foundation in forensic pathology and differentiate between cause and manner of death.
- Recognize the various contributors to the determination of a postmortem interval.
- Understand the various types of trauma and how each is identified and investigated.
- Know the correct methods of evidence documentation, collection, and preservation associated with a death scene.

Death Investigation

You can take him to the mortuary now.

Sherlock Holmes, *A Study in Scarlet* (1887)
Sir Arthur Conan Doyle (1859–1930)

KEY TERMS

Adipocere	Exsanguination	Perimortem
Algor Mortis	Homicide	Postmortem
Antemortem	Hyperthermia	Postmortem Interval (PMI)
Asphyxia	Hypothermia	Putrefaction
Autopsy	Incision	Rigor Mortis
Biological Profile	Justifiable Homicide	Stippling
Cadaveric Spasm	Laceration	Tache Noire
Cause of Death	Livor Mortis	Taphonomy
Cone of Foam	Manner of Death	Tardieu Spots
Death	Mummification	Vitreous Draw
Decomposition	Penetrating Gunshot Wound	
Excusable Homicide	Perforating Gunshot Wound	

Introduction to Death Investigation

For the purposes of this text, and most criminal investigations, **death** is the irreversible cessation of circulatory and respiratory functions. No crime scene and subsequent investigation will require as much from crime scene personnel as will a death investigation. Personnel will be called upon to use all aspects of their training and education in an effort to determine whether or not the death was natural or unnatural. However, not every death scene is a homicide, and not every homicide is a murder. It is important to understand the differences between the various classifications of deaths.

Challenges in the Investigation

Death investigations have added difficulty due to a number of challenges that exist in comparison to other types of investigations. One of the largest is pressure by the media and the public. The public has a desire and a right to feel safe. It is up to the police to ensure that the community is safe and that the reason for the death is determined in an effort to alleviate community concerns for future safety.

Sometimes this is not as easy as it would appear, however. Although there might be a death, there also might be difficulty establishing that the death is unnatural or that a crime has been committed. If the death involves advanced decomposition of remains or is particularly gruesome, then it may be difficult to identify the victim. Lastly, as will be discussed further within this text, establishing the cause, manner, and time of death is not always as simplistic as is shown in modern forensic television and movie dramas, and in many cases is particularly difficult.

Homicide

Homicide is the killing of one person by another. A basic requirement in a homicide investigation is to establish whether death was caused by a criminal action. Murder and homicide are not synonymous. All murders are homicides (and criminal); however, not all homicides are murders (or criminal). Although the term homicide is usually associated with crime, not all homicides are crimes.

Excusable homicide is the unintentional, truly accidental killing of another person. It is the result of an act that under normal conditions would not cause death, or from an act committed with due caution that, because of negligence on the part of the victim, results in death (e.g., running in front of a car).

Justifiable homicide is the killing of a person under authority of the law. This includes killing in self-defense or in the defense of another person if the victim's actions and capability present imminent danger of serious injury or death. It also includes killing an enemy during wartime, capital punishment, and deaths caused by police officers while attempting to prevent a dangerous felon's escape or to recapture a dangerous felon who has escaped or is resisting arrest.

Suicide versus Homicide

More Americans die by suicide than by homicide. Research studies have shown that 85% of suicides are premeditated and that 90% of those who take their lives communicate their intentions to someone they know (Bennett & Hess, 2001). Three basic considerations to establish if a death might be a suicide include:

1. The presence of the weapon or means of death at the scene.
2. Injuries or wounds that are obviously self-inflicted or that could have been inflicted by the deceased.
3. The existence of a motive or intent on the part of the victim to take his or her own life.

All death investigations should be treated as homicide investigations, regardless of the initial reporting or theory that the death is a suicide. This ensures that the investigation does not become narrowly focused or only documents evidence that supports the theory of suicide.

Preliminary Investigation

Regardless of what is reported, at any scene the first priority is to give emergency aid to the victim if he or she is still alive or to determine that death has occurred. Signs of death include lack of breathing, lack of heartbeat, lack of flushing of the fingernail bed when pressure is applied to the nail and then released, and failure of the eyelids to close after being gently lifted. Another quite obvious sign of death is advanced decomposition and related insect activity. Often, if there are remains with insects coming and going from the body, it does not require one to be a physician to determine that the person is in fact dead.

In cases of sudden, unexpected, suspicious or unnatural death (homicide, accident, or suicide), the coroner/medical examiner (ME) must be notified and her or his representative will be responsible for the body remains and the subsequent death investigation. The crime leading to the death, and the investigation concerned with such, remains the responsibility of law enforcement. It is imperative that the agencies work together in an effort to ensure the proper investigatory outcome. It is the responsibility of the coroner/ME to establish the cause and manner of death. It is in these instances when forensic pathology becomes a part of the investigative process. It should be noted that there is a difference between a "coroner" and a "medical examiner." A coroner is an elected official, second to the sheriff, within a jurisdiction. This is typically a sworn law enforcement position. The position of coroner does not necessarily require that a person be a physician, whereas a medical examiner is a physician

TABLE 16–1   U.S. State Medico-Legal Investigation by Type

Type	Number	State
Medical Examiner System	**22**	
State Medical Examiners	19	Alaska, Connecticut, Delaware, District of Columbia, Iowa, Maryland, Massachusetts, New Hampshire, New Jersey, New Mexico, Oklahoma, Oregon, Rhode Island, Tennessee, Utah, Vermont, West Virginia
District Medical Examiners	1	Florida
County Medical Examiners	2	Arizona, Michigan
Mixed Medical Examiner and Coroner System	**18**	
State Medical Examiner and County Coroners/Medical Examiners	7	Alabama, Arkansas, Georgia, Kentucky, Mississippi, Montana, North Carolina
County Medical Examiners/ Coroners	11	California, Hawaii, Illinois, Minnesota, Missouri, New York, Ohio, Pennsylvania, Texas, Washington, Wisconsin
Coroner System	**11**	
District Coroners	2	Kansas, Nevada
County Coroners	9	Colorado, Idaho, Indiana, Louisiana, Nebraska, Nevada, North Dakota, South Carolina, South Dakota, Wyoming

Data from Hanzlick, R. (2006). Death investigation: Systems and procedures. Boca Raton, FL: CRC Press.

and is not elected. Sometimes the position and person are one and the same; however, the terms mean different things and have different requirements. **Table 16–1** shows the state-by-state breakdown of medico-legal investigation type within the United States.

Forensic Pathology

Forensic pathology is the branch of medicine that applies the fundamentals and knowledge of the medical sciences to the problems in the field of law and those that relate to public health and safety. It involves the investigation of sudden, unnatural, unexplained, or violent deaths.

In their role as coroners and MEs, forensic pathologists are responsible for answering the following questions:

- Who is the victim?
- What injuries are present?
- When did the injuries occur?
- Why and how were the injuries produced?

The primary role of the ME is to determine the manner of death and cause of death.

Manner of Death

The **manner of death** refers to the circumstances under which the cause of death occurred. The manner of death may be classified as natural or unnatural. A death is classified as natural when it is caused by disease. Other deaths are classified as unnatural and are given the following categories: homicide, suicide, accident, or undetermined, based on the circumstances surrounding the incident causing death.

Cause of Death

The **cause of death** is the injury or disease responsible for the pathological and physiological disturbances that resulted in death. In other words, it is the medical reason for death. If a cause cannot be found through observation, an autopsy is normally performed to establish the cause of death.

The Forensic Autopsy

An **autopsy** is the medical dissection and examination of a body in order to determine the cause of death. Sometimes there will be religious implications of such a dissection that must be addressed by investigative personnel. Some religions believe that desecration of the body is improper and unacceptable from a faith standpoint. However, although perhaps strongly believed, religion does not trump a criminal investigation regarding the collection and preservation of evidence. This can be extremely difficult to address, and must be handled in a professional manner, explaining the necessity of a thorough investigation.

A forensic autopsy entails the removal of internal organs through incisions made in the chest, abdomen, and head. It is customary for a forensic pathologist to prepare a written report of each autopsy examination. It is considered a gross exam if it deals with what is seen by the unaided eye.

An exam is microscopic if it involves the examination of tissue under a microscope. Most reports of a gross autopsy consist of discussions of external examination, medical treatment, evidence on the body, evidence of injuries, dissection technique, diagnoses, and toxicology reports.

Time of Death Determination

No problem in forensic medicine has been investigated as thoroughly as that of determining the time of death on the basis of postmortem findings. An effort to find the moment of death for a person dates back to as early as 1247 AD with the first known forensic handbook written by Sung Tz'u (Sachs, 2001). In his book, *The Washing Away of Wrongs*, Tz'u noted that decomposition rates change between seasons, even stating that winter decomposition rates will be five times slower than that of summer, and occur at a different rate in heavier people.

Repeated experience teaches the investigator to be wary of relying on any single observation for estimating the time of death. Factors that help in estimating the time of death include:

- Hypostasis/postmortem lividity/livor mortis
- Rigor mortis
- Algor mortis
- Vitreous draw
- Appearance of the eyes
- Stomach contents
- Stage of decomposition
- Evidence suggesting a change in the victim's normal routine

Many methods remain in use today to help investigators estimate the time of death, which is usually referred to as the **postmortem interval (PMI)** of a victim. PMI is the time that has elapsed since a person has died. While only an estimate, it assists in narrowing the interval between death and discovery, providing a timeline for investigators to begin the search for the suspect. The PMI is estimated through various scientific observations of the changes that occur in a body after death. The scientific observations are based on the biological processes of the body when it is both living and dead. The heart circulates oxygen-rich blood throughout the body but also has the important role of removing bacteria and waste from the body. With death, the heart stops pumping, gravity causes blood to settle, and the bacteria remain in the body. Although their host is deceased, bacteria continue to thrive. These physiological events all contribute to the beginning of the decomposition process.

Hypostasis/Postmortem Lividity/Livor Mortis

Livor mortis is another aid in PMI estimations when combined with both algor mortis and rigor mortis. Also known as postmortem lividity, **livor mortis** is the visible color change that occurs from the pooling of blood once the heart stops pumping (**Figure 16–1**). The onset of lividity begins within a half an hour after death. Until the point at which lividity is set, blanching may occur, and the lividity may shift if the victim's body position is changed. Blanching can be noticed when applying pressure to an area where lividity is present; if the lividity temporarily disappears upon the application of pressure, lividity is not yet set. It becomes set once the blood clots. The timeframe in which lividity sets varies but typically occurs between 8 and 12 hours. After 8 to 12 hours, the blood will congeal within the capillaries or diffuse into the surrounding tissues, both of which will result in a lack of blanching being present and the inability for displacement of blood.

FIGURE 16–1 Figure showing livor mortis/postmortem lividity

In some cases of advanced stages of lividity, the capillaries may burst and cause what appear to be small, pinpoint hemorrhages, which are termed **Tardieu spots**. This is especially common in the lower extremities in situations involving hanging.

Lividity appears purple in color, which is caused by the dying, deoxygenated blood. The color of lividity presents several problems. In some instances, lividity may be mistaken for bruising or injuries that occurred prior to death, and in other instances it may be undetectable due to the color of a victim's skin or blood loss. Once again, because of the disparity in the timeframe and the difficulty in detecting it, lividity is simply another tool to be used in combination with algor mortis and rigor mortis to estimate a timeframe for death. Together, these three methods can be used to help investigators estimate the time of death, but these at the most are only present for up to 60 hours (Bennett & Hess, 2001).

Hypostasis/Postmortem Lividity/Livor Mortis

- The medical condition that occurs after death and results in the settling of blood in areas of the body closest to the ground.
- The skin will appear as a dark blue or purple color in these areas.
- Onset is immediate and continues for up to 12 hours after death.
- The skin will not appear discolored in areas where the body is restricted by either clothing or an object pressing against the body, but will instead lack coloring due to blanching.
- Can be useful in determining if the victim's position was changed after death occurred.

Rigor Mortis

FIGURE 16-2   Figure showing rigor mortis

Rigor mortis, or the stiffening of the body, is another factor considered when estimating the PMI. Rigor mortis begins one to four hours after death. Ultimately, rigor mortis is the contraction of body muscles; it begins in the smaller muscle groups and progresses to the larger groups, and may be found first in the jaw and neck. It is the direct result of chemical changes that occur within the body upon death. Adenosine 59-triphosphate (ATP) nucleotide in cells is the chemical "energy" that allows muscles to contract and relax. Following death, the body's supply of ATP is depleted and lactic acid is produced, which results in the contraction of muscles. This chemical reaction is responsible for the fixation of a body in its position of rigor (stiffened muscles) (**Figure 16-2**).

Because ATP is affected by muscle movement, there is no standard for the amount present in the body. Strenuous exercise, excitement, or a struggle before death will affect the amount of ATP present, which in turn directly affects the onset of rigor mortis. This is because muscles that were used extensively just prior to death will contain more lactic acid, which expedites the rigor process.

In temperate climes, rigor mortis becomes completely set by approximately 12 hours after death. It will then remain in place for approximately 12 hours, at which time it will begin to dissipate, disappearing after approximately another 12 hours. Rigor mortis has many other factors that affect the time of onset and duration in a cadaver, including temperature and body size. Warmer temperatures may accelerate the progression of rigor mortis, while colder temperatures may significantly slow down the progression; rigor mortis may never develop in obese

Rigor Mortis

- The medical condition occurs after death and results in the shortening of muscle tissue and the stiffening of body parts in the position they were in when death occurred.
- Appears within the first 24 hours and disappears within 36 hours.
- It can be useful in determining if the victim's position was changed after death occurred.

people, but it may be expedited in lean people. These disparities clearly demonstrate that PMI estimations must be combined with other means in order to find a more accurate timeframe.

Cadaveric Spasm

In some instances of death, there is evidence of immediate rigor known as **cadaveric spasm**. This characteristic is present with no prior period of flaccidity and no extended onset. It typically involves the victim's hands clenched around an object, such as a weapon, debris from a lake floor, clothing, or another object. Cadaveric spasm is sometimes associated with events such as drowning or homicide events that involved considerable excitement or tension preceding death.

Algor Mortis

The temperature of the body as well as the environment combined with other environmental and biological factors affect the rate of decomposition. Temperature has been a tool for determining the PMI since the early studies of the Greeks and the Egyptians more than 2,000 years ago (Sachs, 2001). In 1868, Dr. Harry Rainy from the University of Glasgow conducted many studies on the change of body temperature after death. While his research was rudimentary, he did monitor the temperatures of the dying and dead in the hospital and morgue until family members claimed the body, and through careful analysis devised a mathematical formula for the rate of temperature loss that is still used today (Sachs, 2001).

The body's loss of heat, or **algor mortis**, is based upon simple physics: heat loss will occur until the body reaches the temperature of the surrounding environment (ambient temperature). Numerous environmental factors can significantly alter the rate of heat loss. Humidity, wind, ambient temperature, body temperature at the time of death, surface the body is on, body position, body size and composition (fat acts as an insulator), and clothing all can affect the rate of heat loss of a body. It has even been suggested that the amount of blood that has been lost from a body may drastically affect this rate, because essentially the blood will be at the same temperature as the body and the less blood remaining in the body is one less source of heat (Sachs, 2001).

Forensic studies conducted by Rainy incorporated Newton's Law of Cooling, which says that heat loss is directly proportionate to the difference from the environment. Rainy concluded that the body will lose approximately one-tenth of its remaining heat each hour, using his equation derived from analyses of rectal temperatures. His study results showed that temperature differed drastically depending on the location from where it was taken, and that a deep rectal temperature, close to the organs, was less likely to be affected by environmental conditions such as wind and humidity (Sachs, 2001). He then calculated that the time of death could be determined by the difference between the rectal temperature at the time of death and the environmental temperature (D), the rectal temperature after one hour (tI), and the rate of change between the initial rectal temperature and tI (R). Rainey's equation is:

$$\frac{\log D - \log tI}{\log R} = X \text{ (time since death)}$$

Algor Mortis

- Postmortem changes cause a body to lose heat. The process in which the body temperature continually cools after death until it reaches the ambient or room temperature is algor mortis.

- It is influenced by factors such as the location and size of the body, the victim's clothing, and weather conditions.

- As a general rule, beginning an hour after death, the body will lose heat at a rate of approximately 1° to 1.5°F per hour until reaching ambient temperature. However, this is only an estimate!

Much like Sung Tz'u, Rainy stated that this time could not be exact but should be within a range of four hours (Sachs, 2001). He found that sometimes the body would not lose heat for up to four hours, and in some cases the body would actually show a rise in temperature. This may be attributed to the enzymes within the body still breaking down sugars, starches, and fats before ultimately self-destructing and converting into lactic acid. This process causes biochemical heat that ultimately may increase the body's temperature. This action in addition to bacteria remaining within the body suddenly thriving could account for the increase in postmortem body temperature (Sachs, 2001).

Although there are what seem to be endless amounts of variables that affect the body temperature, algor mortis is still widely used throughout the United States as a beginning estimation of time of death. Algor mortis is best used as a predictor within the first 10 hours after death, where the heat is lost at approximately 1.5°F per hour. This is based on the assumption that the body was at the normal internal temperature of 98.6°F and that the environmental temperature is between 70°F and 75°F. However, with so many varying climates throughout the United States, a touch test is often used as a predictor. If the body is warm, death is within a few hours; if a body is cold and clammy, death occurred between 18 and 24 hours ago (Geberth, 1996). This method also may be combined with rigor mortis to give a closer timeframe: if the body is warm and flexible, death is within a few hours; if warm and stiff, death is within a few hours and half a day; cold and stiff, death is within half a day to two days; and finally, if the body is cold and not stiff, death occurred more than two days prior (Sachs, 2001).

Vitreous Draw

A relatively recent method of assisting with determination of PMI is to use a syringe to take a sample of ocular fluid (vitreous humor) from the eye to determine potassium levels. This is referred to as a **vitreous draw**. Studies have shown that following death, cells within the inner surface of the eyeball will begin to release potassium into the ocular fluid. Through the collection and analysis of the amount of potassium present at various intervals after death, the forensic pathologist can determine the rate at which potassium is released into the vitreous humor. This allows the time of death to be approximated.

Appearance of the Eyes

The eyes are often the first part of the body to exhibit the earliest signs of postmortem change. This can include corneal clouding due to the eyes remaining open following death. A thin film can often be observed within minutes of death, converting to complete cornea clouding being observed within two to three hours, postmortem. If, however, the individual's eyes are closed, the corneal film development may be delayed by several hours, and corneal cloudiness may not be present for over 24 hours.

If the individual dies in an arid environment, and his or her eyes are open at the time of death, the exposed area of the eyeball (sclera) may develop a brownish-black line known as **tache noire** (black spot).

Eyeball collapse, resulting from absence of intraocular fluid within the eyeball, typically will occur after 24 hours; however, it may take as long as four or five days following death.

Stomach Contents

The theme of variance continues when examining stomach contents. Stomach contents have been examined in a hope to determine the PMI. This may even include the contents throughout the gastrointestinal tract. Like the heart, digestion halts after death occurs and, therefore, the amount of food in the stomach combined with the knowledge of when the victim's last meal was eaten should be able to present a narrow timeframe for death. Digestion occurs as a process and the presence of food or digested materials in the stomach and small intestines can give a timeframe for death. Digestion rates may have extreme variance from victim to victim, however, due to metabolism, activity prior to death, or narcotics.

Decomposition

The postmortem breakdown of body tissues is referred to as **decomposition**. During this process, the components that make up the tissues of the body will begin to leak and break down. The bacteria and other microorganisms present within the body (mouth, digestive tract, etc.) thrive on the newly unprotected organic components of the body, resulting in **putrefaction** (postmortem changes produced as a result of actions by bacteria and microorganisms).

Putrefaction

These decompositional changes are entirely dependent upon environmental conditions and the health of the victim prior to death. From an environmental standpoint, changes that occur within temperate climates in a matter of days may be evident in a warm environment within only hours. Additional considerations such as the victim's proximity to a heat source also may exacerbate putrefaction, while exposure to cold will significantly retard the process. Proximity to a heat source is not the only concern with regard to positioning and location of a victim. The rate of putrefaction is also dependent upon whether or not the victim is exposed to air, buried, or in water. In general, putrefaction is more rapid in air than in water, and in water is more rapid than in soil. Approximately one week in air is the equivalent of two weeks in water and approximately seven to eight weeks in a soil environment (Becker, 2005). Putrefaction is more accelerated in obese victims and significantly slower in infants and thin individuals.

Under normal conditions, decomposition will initially be visually present within 24 to 30 hours. Early forms will manifest themselves as bluish-green discoloration of the abdomen region, due to the thriving bacteria present within the colon and digestive tract. The area of greatest discoloration is typically the lower right area of the abdomen.

The next phase of putrefactive changes to the body is gaseous bloating. As bacteria proceed to break down body tissues and organic material within the body, methane is produced, which causes certain areas of the body to swell and bloat. This is especially true of the abdominal area but often is found in the breasts and scrotum as well.

Next, dark purple and green discoloration of the face is common, along with purging of decomposition fluids from the orifices of the body. The discoloration of the face typically will spread to the chest and extremities within 36 to 48 hours after death. This period is character-ized by venous marbling, a breakdown of the walls of the veins and arteries of the body with the seepage of blood into the surrounding tissues (**Figure 16–3**).

Decomposition will continue to progress with the separation of the epidermal and dermal skin layers, resulting in what is commonly referred to as gloving (on the hands) or stocking slippage (on the legs or feet) (**Figure 16–4**). This is especially true for bodies that have been immersed in water for a considerable amount of time or were involved in second-degree burns.

Insect Activity

Insects are a foreign contributor to the process of decomposition, and yet their contribution is an increasingly effective manner of estimating the PMI of a victim. Forensic entomology is the study of insects and other arthropods as they relate to a criminal investigation. Forensic entomology is a relatively new area of study in determining the PMI that has been evolving since the 1980s. Entomology may prove useful in identifying previous locations of a body, but most importantly, how long a body has been dead. Through progression of insect eggs and their presence on a body or even insect bite marks left postmortem, a PMI may start to be established. As a body continues to decompose, different odors attract different insects. Although the specific type of the insect may vary, insects within the same family tend to

FIGURE 16–3 Decomposition (bloating, veinous marbling, and abdominal discoloration)

FIGURE 16–4 Decomposition (slippage, epidermis separation)

appear on a carcass at the same stage. The stages of decomposition harbor conditions that are good for different families of insects, which make the order of their appearance, regardless of the region, fairly predictable.

Insects found on a body are characterized into the following categories: (a) scavengers of the body, (b) predators and parasites of the scavengers and the body, (c) predators and parasites of only the scavengers, and (d) insects that use the body as a shelter. The first insects typically present on a body are flies, which will show up soon after death occurs and inhabit the body until the advanced decay stage. Soon after they arrive, the flies lay eggs on the body, typically in the corners of the eyes, mouth, and other mucous membrane areas, as well as in open wounds. A minimum time of death can be established once the eggs develop into maggots. The maggots will proceed to rapidly consume the soft tissues of the body and will concentrate on body openings and wounds or perforations to the body. Therefore, if a decomposing body is found with a high concentration of maggot activity in a certain area, it sometimes can be deduced that the area was most likely the site of a wound to the individual (defensive wounds on hands, gunshot wound [GSW] in chest, etc.). In cases of contact or close-range firearms injuries it is common for the maggots to consume the surrounding flesh but leave soot-covered flesh or bone untouched.

The succession of insects continues as beetles and other predators, such as wasps, arrive to prey on the maggots. This continues in a predictable manner, allowing forensic entomologists to determine the time of death of the victim by determining the insect present on the carcass and the current stage of development of the insect (**Figure 16–5**).

FIGURE 16–5   Insect larvae activity

Many insect inhabitants occupy the carcass in overlapping periods with other insects, making the PMI estimation much easier. Although this method of PMI estimation has many benefits, insects are very sensitive to environmental changes as well as the manner of death. As with other areas of PMI estimation, temperature and humidity both affect the activity of insects on a body: while warmer temperatures accelerate insect activity, cooler temperatures retard insect activity, with activity even ceasing during periods of extreme cold.

Mummification

Mummification is the dehydration of soft tissues as a result of high temperatures, low humidity, and wind or other form of ventilation. The skin will appear brown, leather-like, and tight. The mummification process begins at the tips of the fingers and toes and progresses toward the hands and feet, face, and other extremities. Fingers found in a mummified state cannot be inked and fingerprinted. The fingers first must be soaked in warm water so that the tissues will rehydrate, which allows them to be more pliable and closer to their original texture so that the ridge detail can be documented correctly.

In cases where mummification is allowed to become fully developed, a body will be preserved for a relatively long period of time. The rate at which mummification develops is a factor of environmental elements and conditions in the vicinity of the body, but often will require a postmortem interval of longer than three months to develop fully. This of course can be exacerbated by extreme heat and low humidity, for example, being present indoors during the winter months, with the furnace on, or if present in an arid, desert climate.

Adipocere

When a body is exposed to conditions of high humidity and high temperatures, it will often exhibit signs of **adipocere**. Adipocere is the hydration and dehydrogenation of the body's fat, which results in an off-white, waxy, clay-like substance that in many cases preserves the body and retards the decomposition process. It is especially common in the subcutaneous tissues of body extremities, the face, buttocks, breasts, and in individuals with a high percentage of body fat.

Evidence Suggesting a Change in the Victim's Normal Routine

Yet another indicator of postmortem interval involves evidence within a victim's home, place of business, car, etc., that suggests an interruption or break in behavior, or aids in isolating specific dates. Examples include:

- Dated items in a fridge
- Newspapers or mail
- Answering machine/voicemail messages

Forensic Entomology

Forensic entomology, once considered an esoteric science, has gained popularity in recent history. This is due, in part, to the success of crime drama television shows, such as *CSI: Crime Scene Investigation* on CBS, and other popular shows, such as *Dirty Jobs* on the Discovery Channel. High-profile cases, with televised courtroom proceedings and consistent media attention, have also brought this unique forensic application into the layperson's household. For example, forensic entomology experts figured prominently in both *California v. David Alan Westerfield* and *Florida v. Casey Anthony*. Television is just one outlet that has brought this science to the attention of the general public. There are many other avenues that have contributed to the increased attention to forensic entomology, as the reader can most likely attest.

Not only is the general public more aware of the benefits of forensic entomology, so are professionals in related forensic fields. Crime scene investigators and pathologists, for example, are more aware of the potential uses of insect evidence and take the time to recognize, collect, and preserve such specimens. In addition, forensic professionals are also more open to collaboration with forensic entomologists. Thus, increased attention on forensic entomology has benefitted law enforcement, overall.

Naturally, increased popularity and attention goes hand in hand with increased scrutiny and criticism. The shortcomings and weaknesses of forensic entomology, which exist in any discipline, have been exposed in courts of law, in the media, and even by forensic entomologists themselves. Observers of criminal trial coverage may notice that different forensic experts, after analyzing the same evidence, arrive at different conclusions. It is not unusual for experts to disagree, hence the calling of different witnesses by the prosecution and defense in a criminal trial. However, when the difference in postmortem interval estimation differs dramatically, eyebrows are raised. Such variations are due, in part, to the lack of consistent analytical protocols. Each practitioner has their own methods and preferred analytical schemes. There is now a concerted effort within the forensic entomology community to standardize analytical methods. In fact, many forensic disciplines are reevaluating their current practices in response to the recent report, "Strengthening Forensic Science in the United States: A Path Forward" (National Research Council, 2009). Congress instructed the authors of this report to evaluate the status of forensic science in the United States and offer suggestions for improvements and future directions. The report presents recommendations regarding standardization, validation, accreditation, certification, research, etc.

With respect to forensic entomology research, one limitation is the difficulty in obtaining specimens for decomposition research. Because forensic entomology primarily focuses on issues related to human injury and death, it would be ideal to use human cadavers as research subjects. However, human cadavers for use in research are relatively difficult, although not impossible, to obtain. As a substitute for human samples, the domesticated pig has become the specimen of choice for decomposition research. Schoenly et al. (2007) found that similar insect species are attracted to both pig and human remains. Although pig cadavers are easier to obtain, their expense can limit the number of samples used in a particular research project. Ultimately, this leads to a limited sample size and, as a result, a less-than-robust statistical analysis. Michaud et al. (2012) discuss the lack of replication (i.e., the limited number of pig subjects) as well as the misunderstandings between replicates and samples (i.e., pseudoreplication). Researchers are addressing issues related to experimental design and statistical analyses via journal articles, professional presentations, conference workshops, etc. Organizations such as the North American Forensic Entomology Association (NAFEA) and the European Association for Forensic Entomology (EAFE) are ideal settings for such discussions.

Challenges such as these will shape the future of forensic entomology and, undoubtedly, improve the strength and rigor of the science. This is the natural progression when the forces of both scientific peer review and the adversarial judicial system are at work. Not only is this healthy for the science of forensic entomology itself, but it also benefits the field of criminal investigation. Practitioners and the general public, alike, will reap the benefits of constructive criticism and healthy discourse.

Diana G. Johnson, M.S.
Assistant Professor
Criminal Justice Department
University of Wisconsin – Platteville
Platteville, WI 53818

References

Michaud, J. P., Schoenly, K. G., & Moreau, G. (2012). Sampling flies or sampling flaws? Experimental design and inference strength in forensic entomology. *Journal of Medical Entomology, 49*(1), 1–10.

National Research Council. (2009). *Strengthening forensic science in the United States: A path forward.* Washington, DC: The National Academies Press.

Schoenly, K. G., Haskell, N. H., Hall, R. D., & Gbur J. R. (2007). Comparative performance and complementarity of four sampling methods and arthropod preference tests from human and porcine remains at the Forensic Anthropology Center in Knoxville, Tennessee. *Journal of Medical Entomology, 44*(5), 881–894.

- Computer activity (email)
- Receipts
- Calendars/date books

Taphonomy

In order to study human remains, knowledge about the human physical form and function must be combined with scientific input regarding postmortem changes. The combined information is essentially the postmortem history of the body, which is referred to as **taphonomy**. Examples of postmortem changes could include partial decomposition, alteration and scattering by scavengers, movement and modification by flowing water, freezing, or mummification.

The study of taphonomy requires input from forensic experts in a variety of fields. Essentially, all of the biological and geological sciences overlap in the study of taphonomy. Anthropologists, entomologists, botanists, biologists, geologists, archeologists, pathologists, and many others often are called to contribute to telling the story or giving the history of a body following death. Assembling a taphonomic history of a body involves accounting for information relating to the circumstances of the death event itself as well as the interval of time between death and discovery and collection of the body. This includes any modifications to the hard and soft tissues of a body by environment, activity, event, and scavengers. It has already been discussed that it is a difficult process to collect accurate data and determine PMI, and this difficulty is significantly compounded through the activities of weather, insects, rodents, and other animals. Small gnaw marks on bone by rodents sometimes can be mistaken for tool or weapon marks by an untrained eye. Cockroaches, ants, and other insects will sometimes leave postmortem bite marks on a body that will be mistaken for defensive wounds or other perimortem-related trauma. This natural scavenging activity can add a greater degree of difficulty to the investigative process when the involved scavenger removes a bone, limb, or other portion of a body and drags it away to its burrow or den. Often these components will go undiscovered even after a thorough search.

One of the largest parts of a taphonomic history involves the interpretation of traumatic injuries to the body. It must be determined whether the injuries were made before death and were beginning the healing process, if they occurred at or near the time of death, or if they were injuries to the body after death.

Antemortem Trauma

Antemortem injuries are those sustained prior to death and that have healed or begun to heal. These can include injuries such as broken bones that have been cast or set, cuts that have been stitched or begun healing on their own, or other injury activities where evidence of healing is shown.

Postmortem Trauma

A body may be subjected to modification by an assortment of taphonomic methods after death. These injuries are referred to as occurring **postmortem**. These types of injuries can include carnivores, freezing and thawing, transport by flowing water, and many other events that may damage bone or soft tissue. Such postmortem damage is not related to the cause of death and must be differentiated from perimortem trauma. This is accomplished by noting the patterns of bone breakage and identifying modifications made by scavengers, plants, or other weather-related or geological processes.

Perimortem Trauma

Perimortem injuries are those that show evidence of having occurred at or near the time of death. These show no signs of healing, but do show signs that the body was still alive at the time of injury (as evidenced by hemorrhaging, subcutaneous blood, etc.). This type of injury can occur with hard tissues (bones) as well. However, unlike soft tissue, bone will not exhibit vital reaction and requires several days of healing time in order to see evidence of healing. Therefore, bone damage that shows no signs of healing and for which no postmortem explanation exists often is considered to be related to perimortem causes. There are several classifications of perimortem-related injuries. These include mechanical trauma (sharp force injuries and blunt force injuries), thermal trauma, chemical trauma, and electrical trauma.

Sharp-Force Injuries

A sharp-force injury is a subcategory of mechanical trauma that refers to injuries received from sharp implements, such as knives, machetes, saws, and axes. The amount of mechanical force required for a sharpened instrument to exceed the tensile strength of tissue is significantly less than the force required with a blunt object. Sharp objects produce incised wounds, known as **incisions** (**Figures 16–6** and **16–7**). In deaths resulting from sharp trauma, the cause is typically due to **exsanguination**, death due to loss of blood/bleeding out.

Defensive Wounds

In cases involving sharp-force injuries, it may be necessary to determine whether or not the person sustained defensive wounds during the altercation resulting in death. Persons who are beaten or stabbed to death typically will have defense wounds on the little finger side of the forearm and palm of the hand, sometimes resulting in the severing of fingers in sharp force injury instances. However, the absence of such injuries does not necessarily mean that the victim did not see his or her attacker or was suicidal. If the victim is restrained by physical or chemical means, then no defensive wounds will be present. One of the most common methods of chemical restraint is alcohol.

FIGURE 16–6   Example of an incision made from a stabbing incident involving a knife

FIGURE 16–7   Scaled photograph of the same incision

Blunt-Force Injury

Another subcategory of mechanical trauma is blunt-force injury. Blunt objects produce **lacerations**. Blunt traumas are further subdivided into nonfirearm and firearm groups. Typically, deaths due to blunt trauma are the result of significant damage to the brain or from laceration to the heart or aorta, which then leads to exsanguination.

Firearms Injuries

Injuries by firearm are the most common suicidal and homicidal wounds that are seen in the United States. They may be classified as close/near contact, intermediate range, or long range. Firearm injuries can be further classified as penetrating or perforating. A **penetrating gunshot wound** has an entrance wound but no exit and, therefore, a projectile should be recovered at autopsy for every penetrating GSW. A **perforating gunshot wound** has an entrance wound and an exit wound. This means that generally no projectile will be recovered by a pathologist at autopsy. This is important information to relay back to those responsible for processing the crime scene, as a projectile should be recovered on scene for each identified exit wound.

Suicide versus Homicide Sharp Injuries

Suicide indicators

- Hesitation wounds
- Wounds under clothing
- Weapon present, especially if tightly clutched
- Usually wounds at throat, wrists, or ankles
- Seldom disfigurement
- Body not moved

Homicide indicators

- Defense wounds
- Wounds through clothing
- No weapon present
- Usually injuries to vital organs
- Disfigurement
- Body moved

Contact/Near Contact Injury. Firearms injuries that are made at contact or near contact range (less than 0.5 centimeters from the target) will exhibit signs of blackening and charring of the skin. Depending upon the body location of the injury, the skin also may show stellate (star-like) lacerations that originate at and radiate away from the point of impact (**Figure 16–8**). These lacerations form because the gas blown into the wound results in the skin being torn apart. The gases associated with a firearm discharge also will cause red discoloration of the underlying tissue and hemoglobin present within a wound. This cherry red discoloration is similar to that found within the skin and organs in carbon monoxide–related deaths.

Intermediate Range Injury. As the distance increases between the barrel of a firearm and its target, the effect of the gas and associated unburned powder accompanying the event diminishes. Intermediate range injuries are considered to be those occurring at a distance of between 0.5 centimeters and approximately 1 to 1.5 meters. At this distance, unburned powder

FIGURE 16–8   Contact wound to the head
Courtesy of Steven Hanson, former chief investigator, Bexar County MEO.

that penetrates the skin produces a defect injury known as **stippling** (**Figure 16–9**). This injury occurs as the result of impact of burned and unburned particulates associated with the discharge of a firearm. They surround the bullet impact wound in a roughly circular pattern due to the fact that gunpowder is discharged in a conical pattern as it exits a firearm. This pattern is seen to enlarge as the muzzle-to-target distance is increased. Such stippling patterns are not typically observed at a range greater than 1 to 1.5 meters because the speed of the powder slows sufficiently so that it cannot penetrate the skin.

Distant Range Injury. A GSW that occurs at a muzzle-to-target distance greater than 1 to 1.5 meters will lack the characteristics exhibited by close contact and intermediate range injuries (i.e., soot damage and stippling). It is typical for a distant wound to exhibit a circular skin defect known as a marginal abrasion ring around the entrance wound edges. This is due to the stretching of the skin relating to the blunt-force trauma.

Entrance and Exit Wounds. Conventional wisdom is that GSW exits are larger than entrance wounds; however, this is not always true. In most cases it is advisable to not make assumptions as to entrance or exit wounds at the scene of a crime or within a report. The autopsy process will determine which wounds are associated with an entrance or an exit of a projectile (**Figure 16–10**).

Other Blunt-Force Trauma Injuries

Another type of blunt-force trauma injury encountered in crime scene investigations is that of a bumper fracture (**Figure 16–11**). These types of blunt-force injury are typically seen in motor vehicle versus pedestrian types of accidents, where the bumper of the automobile strikes the victim and causes lacerations and broken bones at the height of the vehicle.

FIGURE 16–9 Example of stippling

Courtesy of Steven Hanson, former chief investigator Bexar County MEO.

FIGURE 16–10 Gunshot entrance wound

FIGURE 16–11 Example of "bumper fractures"

If the suspect car is found and the height of the bumper is measured off of the ground, it may be found to match the corresponding height of the injuries on the victim. If the measurement is less than the para height of the bumper-to-ground distance, then that may be evidence that the vehicle was in the act of breaking upon striking the victim (and there should then be corresponding skid marks to corroborate that assumption). If the height of the injuries is longer than the height, then the vehicle may have been accelerating at

Suicide versus Homicide Gunshot Wounds

Suicide indicators

- Gun held against skin
- Wound in mouth or in right temple if victim is right-handed and left temple if left-handed

Homicide indicators

- Gun fired from more than a few inches away
- Angle or location that rules out self-infliction
- Shot through clothing
- No weapon present

the time of impact. There is typically other evidence on scene to corroborate this, and it is simply one way in which forensic pathology and investigation of injuries can aid the investigatory process.

Chemical Trauma Injuries

In approximately 50% of deaths, ethyl alcohol is a contributing factor to the death (James & Nordby, 2003). In most cases of alcohol-related deaths, it is alcohol-induced comas that result in the cessation of respiratory functions, resulting in death. However, another common chemical injury is that of carbon monoxide–related poisoning, resulting in death. Carbon monoxide–related deaths are characterized by the victim's cherry red skin.

Thermal Trauma Injuries

If an individual is exposed to excessive heat or cold the result can be death. **Hypothermia**, the lowering of the body's core temperature, results from exposure to excessive cold. **Hyperthermia**, a rising of the body's core temperature, is the result of exposure to excessive heat. People who die at the scenes of fires most commonly succumb from the inhalation of carbon monoxide and/or other products of combustion rather than thermal-related injuries.

Electrical Trauma Injuries

Electrical-related deaths are quite rare, resulting in approximately 1,000 fatalities a year within the United States (Spitz, 1993). High voltage–related deaths are quite evident and present little difficulty for the examining pathologist. High-voltage burns can result in poration, the flow of a current through tissues that creates holes in the membranes of the cells. This often leads to loss of limbs. High voltage burns are characterized by ferning marks on the body (**Figure 16–12**).

FIGURE 16–12   Figure showing "ferning" from an electrocution

Whereas the passage of low voltage electricity through a person may cause cardiovascular-related difficulties, death can be due to the heart experiencing ventricular fibrillation that can lead to non-resuscitability within minutes. Low voltage may or may not produce electrical burns and will rarely exhibit signs of ferning.

Asphyxia-Related Deaths

Asphyxia is the interruption of oxygenation of the brain. There are a number of ways for this interruption to occur. These include, but are not limited to, drowning and strangulation.

Drowning

Drowning is death by asphyxiation from immersion in water or other liquid. There are several forensic ways to determine whether or not a body recovered from water died as a result of drowning or was dead prior to entering the water. At autopsy, the forensic pathologist can conduct a lung "float test." If a person died due to drowning, his or her lungs will be heavier and will sink when exposed to this test. There is also the possibility of conducting microscopic examination and analysis of bone marrow collected from the victim to look for the presence of microorganisms known as diatoms, which are present within water and if ingested by the victim will find their way into the marrow. This can also prove or disprove drowning.

Manual Strangulation and Hanging

Asphyxial deaths associated with strangulation will often necessitate determining whether or not the event was self-induced or homicidal in nature. To determine this, the hyoid bone of the neck is typically examined at autopsy to see if fracture has occurred. Fracturing of the hyoid typically will be found only in cases of manual strangulation. Manual strangulation constricts the airway by compressing the neck or crushing the airway. Ligature strangulation, whether

FIGURE 16-13 Photo showing ligature marks

from hanging or garroting, characteristically does not involve fracture of the hyoid. In addition to the lack of fracturing of the hyoid bone, there are ligature differences between hanging and strangulation-related deaths. Typically, the ligature marks made by hanging will be vertical, making a U-shape that extends under the victim's chin and around the back of the ears, whereas homicidal strangulation ligature marks typically will be horizontal marks extending from front to back, and may include an area near the back of the victim's neck where the ligature material was crossed, tied, or pressed against the victim to ensure the constriction of airflow (**Figure 16-13**). Hanging-related deaths typically involve the victim dying as a result of cutting off the blood supply (and relaying oxygen) to the brain through pressure placed on the carotid arteries, versus strangulation, which compacts or crushes the trachea, thus depleting the intake of oxygen and thereby causing death.

Homicide, Suicide, or Accidental?

In attempting to determine whether or not an asphyxial death was suicidal, accidental, or homicidal, the following suggestions are offered. It must be remembered, however, that all deaths should be investigated as homicides until such point as the evidence determines otherwise.

- Most cases of choking, drowning, and smothering are accidental.
- Most cases of hanging are suicides.
- Most cases of strangulation are murder.

Deaths Due to Drug Overdose

In some cases of drug overdose and drowning, the victim will exhibit signs of froth emanating from the mouth and nostrils. This froth is sometimes referred to as a **cone of foam**. It is a result of severe pulmonary edema and may appear initially off-white but will advance to pinkish in color as the decomposition process advances.

Public Assistance in Death Investigations

Death investigations are complex and oftentimes confusing undertakings. In some cases, it may be necessary to seek the assistance of the public in attempting to gain information that can assist in determining the activities associated with a death or the identity of a recovered victim. In these cases, a **biological profile** is developed that is distributed to the media through law enforcement channels. A biological profile is assembled by studying the remains and noting characteristics of shape and size, which may allow an estimation of height, build, age, sex, ancestry, and any individual features such as tattoos, jewelry, medical apparatus, and clothing. Stature is estimated by measuring total body (or skeletal) length. Unique antemortem characteristics such as a healed bone fracture or an unusual dental configuration are also included. The goal of developing a profile is to describe the individual in such a way that law enforcement or acquaintances can narrow the range of possible identities.

This process is used extensively where prisoners of war (POWs) and missing in action (MIA) service members are concerned. Hickam Air Force Base, Hawaii, is home to the Joint POW/MIA Accounting Command (JPAC). According to the JPAC Website, the "mission of the Joint POW/MIA Accounting Command (JPAC) is to achieve the fullest possible accounting of all Americans missing as a result of the nation's past conflicts. The highest priority of the organization is the return of any living Americans that remain prisoners of war." This mission dates back to World War II. While most countries throughout the world bury their war dead where they fall or are found, the United States vows that it will do everything in its power to bring service members remains home (JPAC, 2009).

This promise results in joint-service teams traveling to burial and crash sites around the world. Once teams have recovered remains and they are repatriated within the United States, the command's forensic laboratory attempts to identify them. The laboratory portion of JPAC, referred to as the Central Identification Laboratory (CIL), is the largest forensic anthropology laboratory in the world. The lab consists of state-of-the-art instrumental and analytical techniques to determine identity from the remains. DNA sampling and other cutting edge forensic equipment is advancing JPAC experts ability to make positive identifications that were once impossible.

According to JPAC, since its inception, on average, JPAC identifies about six MIAs each month. To date, the U.S. government has identified over 1,300 individuals. At any given time, there are more than 1,000 active case files under investigation (JPAC, 2009).

Reality Television Meets Real-World CSI

In August of 2009, a man was searching through a rubbish bin in Buena Park, Orange County, California, looking for recyclables. What he instead discovered was a young female's remains packed into a suitcase. This find would eventually launch an international investigation involving a reality television star and crime scenes in both the United States and Canada.

On August 14, the body of Jasmine Fiore, an aspiring actress and swimsuit model, was found within a suitcase. At the time, investigators were unaware of the identity of the remains. The remains were badly mutilated and it was discovered that the female's fingers and teeth had been removed, most likely to prevent identification. Identification was made by investigators through the serial numbers on the victim's breast implants, positively identifying the victim as Jasmine Fiore.

Ms. Fiore, 28, had married Ryan Jenkins, 32, a U.S. reality television star, in a Las Vegas wedding ceremony earlier the same year. The investigation revealed that the couple checked into a San Diego hotel on August 13, and that Mr. Jenkins checked out alone the next morning. Mr. Jenkins immediately became a person of interest to the investigation. Authorities were initially unable to locate Mr. Jenkins, although his boat was found in a marina not far from the U.S.–Canada border, just south of Vancouver. The body of Ryan Jenkins was eventually discovered in a motel room in British Columbia on August 23, where he had killed himself.

Martinez, E. (August 24, 2009). Wanted for bikini model murder, reality star Ryan Jenkins commits suicide. *CBS News.* Retrieved October 2, 2012, from http://www.cbsnews.com/8301-504083_162-5257356-504083.html.

WRAP UP

Chapter Summary

Postmortem interval estimations are extremely important in death investigations. A timeframe can be established in order to aid investigators with their search for the suspect. Numerous methods are used to narrow down the PMI and all are affected by environmental changes as well as many other variables. The PMI cannot currently be determined by the use of any one method, but a more accurate range may be determined through a combination of all the methods and consideration of environmental conditions.

PMI is not the only consideration when investigating a death. One must also consider the cause and associated manner of the death. This can include analysis of the circumstances surrounding the death as well as the injuries associated with the death. In looking at the history of the body after death, and the history of the person preceding his or her death, one will be able to best determine whether or not the death was natural or unnatural.

Review Questions

1. The irreversible cessation of circulatory and respiratory functions is known as _____.

2. Explain the differences between excusable homicide and justifiable homicide.

3. Explain the differences between cause of death and manner of death.

4. What is blanching and how is it relevant to death investigations?

5. The postmortem breakdown of body tissues is referred to as _____.

6. Explain the differences between antemortem, perimortem, and postmortem injuries.

7. Knowledge about the human physical form and function combined with scientific knowledge about postmortem changes as applied to the study of human remains is known as _____.

8. Death due to a loss of blood is known as _____.

9. _____ is the interruption of oxygenation of the brain.

10. What is PMI and how is it calculated?

11. Which chemical is looked for in a vitreous draw?

References

Becker, R. F. (2005). *Criminal investigation* (2nd ed.). Sudbury, MA: Jones and Bartlett Publishers.

Bennett, W. W., & Hess, K. M. (2001). *Criminal investigation* (6th ed.). Belmont, CA: Wadsworth.

Doyle, A. C. (1887). *A study in scarlet*. London, United Kingdom: Ward Lock & Co.

Geberth, V. J. (1996). *Practical homicide investigation: Tactics, procedures, and forensic techniques* (3rd ed.). Boca Raton, FL: CRC Press.

James, S. H., & Nordby J. J. (2003). *Forensic science*. Boca Raton, FL: CRC Press.

Joint POW/MIA Accounting Command (JPAC), United States Department of Defense. (2009). *Mission overview*. Retrieved October 2, 2012, from http://www.jpac.pacom.mil/index.php?page=mission_overview

Sachs, J. S. (2001). *Corpse: Nature, forensics, and the struggle to pinpoint time of death*. Cambridge, MA: Perseus Publishing.

Spitz, W. U. (1993). *Medicolegal investigation of death* (3rd ed.). Springfield, IL: Charles C. Thomas Publishing.

© McMac/ShutterStock, Inc.

- Recognize what constitutes arson.
- Distinguish some of the motives for committing arson.
- Describe the types of evidence to be sought at an arson crime scene.
- Identify the types of evidence to be sought at an explosion crime scene.

Arson and Explosive Investigation

You will admit, Watson, that these facts are very suggestive. In each case there is evidence of a poisonous atmosphere. In each case, also, there is combustion going on in the room—in the one case a fire, in the other a lamp. The fire was needed, but the lamp was lit—as a comparison of the oil consumed will show—long after it was broad daylight. Why? Surely because there is some connection between three things—the burning, the stuffy atmosphere, and, finally, the madness or death of those unfortunate people. That is clear, is it not?

Sherlock Holmes, *The Adventure of the Devil's Foot* (1910)
Sir Arthur Conan Doyle, (1859–1930)

KEY TERMS

Accelerant
Arson
Delay Device
Detonation Point
Direct Evidence
Flammable Range

Flash Point
High-Order Explosive
Incendiary Evidence
Low-Order Explosive
Masking Fire
Microtaggants

Point of Origin
Pyrolysis
Pyromaniac
Secondary Device
Spontaneous Combustion

Investigating Arson

Arson is usually divided into two categories: arson and aggravated arson. The latter involves risk of human injury, whereas the former does not. Many states have recognized a number of different types of arson and have provided specific statutory prohibitions and sanctions for them. States having hot, dry summers have passed arson laws pertaining to fires that get out of hand and cause extensive property damage; although not technically arson (because of the absence of intent), they are nonetheless prohibited and may be cause for the application of legal sanctions.

In 2009 the Federal Bureau of Investigation (FBI) provided data from 14,957 law enforcement agencies that reported 58,871 arsons. Arsons involving structures made up 44.5% of the total number of arsons reported. Mobile property comprised 28.4% of the reported arsons. "Other" types of property accounted for 27.1 % of reported arsons. The average dollar loss was $17,411. The number of arsons reported in 2009 was a 10.8% decrease over arsons committed in 2008 (FBI, 2009).

Who Is Responsible for Investigation of Arson?

Traditionally, the responsibility for investigating fires fell to firefighters. Just as they had equipment to conduct water rescues and were therefore given the responsibility for recovering drowning victims, they had expertise in fighting fires and were therefore given the responsibility for investigating them. Time has shown that specialized skill, experience, and equipment are required to conduct an effective arson investigation, prompting many fire departments to do one of two things: (1) report suspected arson to the police for investigation, or (2) train firefighters as arson investigators.

The role of firefighters is generally to fight fires and in the process report anything suspicious that might indicate arson. They are not usually trained or equipped to investigate arson. Unfortunately, neither are most police investigators. The law enforcement community rarely pays much attention to deliberately set fires unless they are started to conceal a more serious offense such as homicide or burglary. The thinking generally is that the insurance industry will handle the investigation and there is no sense in duplicating efforts. Although the insurance carrier's adjuster or investigator may investigate a fire, he or she will arrive on the scene long after the fire has been extinguished and long after prospective witnesses have disappeared and prospective evidence has been destroyed or removed.

Fires and explosions provide little information upon which an investigation can proceed. Information that is available is generally circumstantial. Arson and bombings are committed with some degree of planning, and the arsonist or bomber is usually far from the scene when the crime is discovered and investigators respond. The extensive destruction at the scene renders most evidence unidentifiable or unusable. Oftentimes, arsonists will make use of an **accelerant** to start or maintain a fire. An accelerant is something used to start or increase a fire's potential to burn. It is typically an ignitable liquid. The laboratory can provide only limited assistance in identifying ignitable liquids that may have been deployed or in reconstructing igniting or detonating devices. Although forensic scientists may be able to identify minute amounts of an ignitable liquid in the materials provided for examination, there is no scientific test that will determine whether a particular arsonist used the ignitable liquid, unless a suspect is taken into custody with evidence of the ignitable liquid on clothing or in a container.

The cause of a fire may be readily apparent or may require extensive examination. Fires may be caused by accident or intent. One way of proving intent is by ruling out accidental causes of the fire. A final determination must take into consideration numerous factors and deserves a complete and meticulous investigation. Only properly trained and experienced investigators can conduct that type of investigation. Normally, an ordinary match will ignite fuels. However, other ignitors must be considered; electrical discharges, sparks, and chemicals may provide temperatures in excess of the ignition temperature of most fuels.

A fuel will interact with oxygen to produce a flame only when the fuel is in a gaseous state. This is true even if the fuel feeding the flame is wood, paper, cloth, plastic, or gasoline. In the case of a liquid fuel, the temperature must be high enough to vaporize the fuel. The vapor that forms burns when it mixes with oxygen. The **flash point** is the lowest temperature at which a liquid gives off sufficient vapor to form a mixture with air that will support combustion. Once the flash point is reached, the fuel can be ignited by some outside source of high temperature. The ignition temperature is always higher than the flash point. With a solid fuel, the process of generating vapor is more complex. Solid fuel will burn only when it is exposed to heat that is great enough to break down the solid into a gaseous product. The chemical decomposition is called **pyrolysis**. Gaseous fuel and air will only burn if their composition (the fuel–air mix) lies within certain limits. If the proportion of fuel to air is too low or too high (as in a flooded auto carburetor), combustion will not occur. The range in which air and fuel will support combustion is called the **flammable range** (Chandler, 2009).

There are instances in which a fuel can burn without a flame. A burning cigarette or red-hot charcoal is an example of glowing combustion or smoldering. Combustion is taking place on the surface of a solid fuel in the absence of heat high enough to break down the fuel into a gaseous product (pyrolyze the fuel). This same phenomenon can be seen in wood fires once all the gases have been expended; the wood continues to smolder until all the carbonaceous residue has been consumed (Saferstein, 2010).

Tabloids and tabloid television shows have convinced the public that fire may begin as the result of **spontaneous combustion**. Some have gone so far as to insist that humans can combust spontaneously. Regardless of what scriptwriters suggest, there is no documented case of a human spontaneously combusting. Spontaneous combustion of non human materials is a product of a natural heat-producing process. This process is caused and maintained by poor ventilation. Hay, for example, stored in hot unventilated areas is a conducive medium for the growth of bacteria that generate heat. If left unventilated at elevated temperatures long enough, the hay may be ignited by the activity of the bacteria. Paint, oily rags, and various chemicals left in a hot unventilated area also may ignite. Spontaneous combustion is seldom the cause of a fire but often is invoked as the cause.

The focus of every arson investigation is the fire's **point of origin**. The investigation must begin as soon as possible after the fire has been reported, preferably while it is still burning. The fire itself may provide information about its nature and origin. The direction the fire travels will be helpful in determining where it began (**Figures 17–1, 17–2A,** and **17–2B**).

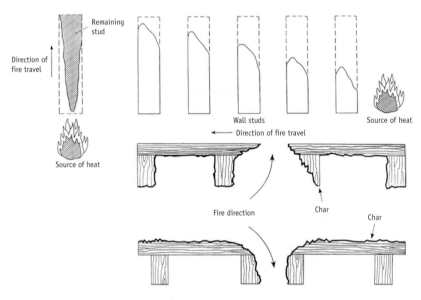

FIGURE 17–1 Determining fire travel direction

FIGURE 17–2A Direction of fire travel (couch burning)
Courtesy of Nick Vesper, University of Wisconsin-Platteville.

FIGURE 17–2B   Direction of fire travel (couch moved)
Courtesy of Nick Vesper, University of Wisconsin-Platteville.

If there are numerous fires spread out over a burning structure, arson should be presumed. Ignitable liquids that may have been used to start the fire have detectable odors and smoke coloring. The inability of firefighters to gain access to the building suggests that the fire began accidentally or that someone with a key started the fire. In addition to what the fire can tell, witnesses on the scene may be helpful in gathering information about the fire. Investigators will want to note the following:

- When the fire was first discovered
- The size of the fire upon discovery
- Who discovered the fire
- Who reported the fire
- Unusual activity around the premises before the fire
- Unusual or unidentified persons in the area (Chandler, 2009)

Often a **pyromaniac** will return to the scene to enjoy the fruits of his or her labor. It is important to begin the investigation by taking pictures of those watching the fire to identify any known fire starters or persons who neither work nor live in the area. Professional arsonists may linger to determine if the fire set will be sufficient to destroy the building and the evidence of arson.

Once the fire has been extinguished, entry should be made as soon as it is safe. Recording the scene photographically is the first priority. A thorough search of the premises is required, for subsequent entries may have to be based on probable cause and a search warrant. Time is working against the investigator. Most fires are started or accelerated with petroleum-based hydrocarbons. Any remaining residue can evaporate in a matter of hours. Salvage operations may begin quickly, or a search of the premises for survivors or bodies may be conducted. It is imperative that the examination of the crime scene begin before it has been disturbed if possible; if it is not possible, the evidentiary value of the photographs will increase.

Arson Evidence

Two types of evidence are available to the arson investigator:

1. **Direct evidence** that links the arsonist to the fire, such as eyewitness identification or motive.
2. **Incendiary evidence**, which includes crime scene debris, observed burning characteristics, and an absence of accidental causation (Saferstein, 2010).

Motives for Arson

The motive for arson may be general (e.g., vandalism) or specific (e.g., commercial arson to collect insurance). Common motives include profit, vandalism, revenge, crime concealment, and thrill seeking (pyromania).

Fires for profit are common and are generally started as an alternative to financial failure or partner disenchantment. The target of the fire may not be the building alone. A thorough investigation of the paper trail associated with the business may not reveal anything confirming the fire. An absence of expanded or new insurance coverage might suggest that no profit motive exists. The relevant insurance, however, may cover the goods stored rather than the business itself. It is not unusual for fires to be set to rid the owner of a cumbersome or outdated inventory. There is usually some evidence to support the hypothesis that the fire was set to destroy the inventory. Valuable items that the owner does not wish to "liquidate" may be removed from the premises or replaced with outdated items insured at new-merchandise prices.

Automobile owners plagued with mechanical difficulties or monthly payments that they can no longer maintain may burn their cars for the insurance coverage and the relief of getting rid of a lemon. The vehicle will be reported stolen after the fire is set so that the owner avoids being stopped in a reportedly stolen vehicle. The time at which the vehicle was torched and the time it was reported stolen may be useful in investigating the auto arson. Additionally, items of commercial or sentimental value may have been removed from the vehicle prior to the burning. It is much more common for a stolen vehicle to be abandoned in a watery depository than for the thieves to burn it. If a vehicle is reported stolen and is subsequently discovered burned, there is a very good possibility that it was an owner arson. The only practical reason fire would be used to destroy a stolen vehicle would be to cover up a more serious offense (e.g., a homicide, a robbery, or a hit and run).

Fires started by vandals cause untold property loss each year. The intent is generally to start a fire of a particular thing in a specific area for the "fun of it" or because "nobody was using it anyway." Schools and school-related buildings may be set on fire by disgruntled students (which would make the fire one of revenge rather than pure mischief). Field or forest fires started

Convicted Arsonist Commits Suicide in Court

On June 28, 2012, as the jury foreman of a Phoenix jury uttered the word "guilty" regarding defendant Michael Marin's trial for arson, the defendant placed his head in his hands and appeared to place something into his mouth and then retrieved a bottle of liquid from his briefcase and took a drink. Moments later, Marin collapsed, face first onto the courtroom floor. Attempts to revive him in the courtroom, by the same investigator who built the case against him, were unsuccessful and Marin was pronounced dead shortly after at an area hospital. Marin likely swallowed a poison pill as the verdict was read and he was found guilty of setting fire to his $3.5 million Phoenix mansion and faced from 10 to 21 years in prison. The subsequent arson investigation found Marin to have only $50 in his bank account, after having nearly $900,000 the year prior, and he faced a looming balloon payment on the property of $2.3 million within a matter of days. On July 5, 2009, Marin escaped an inferno at the 10,000 square-foot home using a rope ladder, while wearing a scuba mask and scuba tank to avoid inhaling smoke, which he just happened to have handy in his bedroom at the time of the blaze. Investigators eventually determined that there were several places within the residence where intentional fires were set and Marin was subsequently arrested for felony arson.

Information from AP. (2012, June 28). Myers, Amanda L. "Suicide by poison suspected in courtroom death." http://www.kmov.com/news/national/Suicide-by-poison-suspected-in-courtroom-death-160971445.html.

as a prank often grow into major fires that destroy thousands of acres. The investigation of a vandalistic fire begins at the point of origin, and the investigators attempt to locate witnesses who have seen young people playing in the area. Most of these types of fires are set by juveniles without much planning, using a match or lighter as an igniter (sophisticated ignition systems are not going to be found at this crime scene). Most vandal arsonists remain uncaught (Kolko, 2002).

Occasionally a firefighter will set a fire that appears to be vandalism for the purpose of being part of the team called in to put out the fire. This type of arson, because of motive, falls in a category by itself. The ultimate objective may be for profit (fires keep firefighters employed) or self-aggrandizement (the firefighter has an opportunity to do something heroic). Obviously, a firefighter arsonist is the most difficult type to catch, because he or she has extensive knowledge of fires and their investigation.

Fires for revenge are cowardly but nonetheless lethal. The cast of potential characters ranges from spurned suitors to disgruntled employees, and the motives range from racism to anger caused by a neighborly dispute. Once revenge has been selected as a possible motive, the list of suspects should be short and illuminating. These fires may be the product of long-range planning or may be fairly spontaneous. The modus operandi, which can range from igniting drapery in a hotel to setting ignition devices around the perimeter of a building, will vary, but the motive will steer the investigation.

Masking fires set to mask the commission of other crimes (e.g., homicides) are the major focus of arson investigations conducted by police agencies. The investigator must not only conduct a thorough arson investigation but also must observe the rudiments of, say, a homicide investigation at the same time. The main question confronting an investigator in arson with human victims is whether the fire was set to effect the death of the victims or whether the deaths were unintended consequences of the arson.

People love fire. It is hypnotic and simultaneously warming and comforting, not to mention romantic. People will turn the air conditioner on to be able to have a fire in the fireplace to create an intimate environment. Folks gathered around a campfire share not only its warmth but also each other's. Our love affair with fire has brought us to the pinnacle of technological refinement, but fire is also the source of a morbid fascination because of the havoc it can wreak when released. There are those among us who long to "release the beast" those who set fires out of a sexual obsession and who will continue to set fires until stopped. Pyromaniacs (serial fire starters) are generally compulsive, and their fires are unplanned. Many believe this type of fire starting is one of a trilogy of behaviors that together are characteristic of serial killers (the other two are bedwetting and animal torture).

Incendiary Evidence

Fires tend to move upward, and therefore the point of origin is often the lowest point that shows intense burn characteristics. In addition, the arsonist may have used *trailers, streamers,* or *plants* to spread the fire (**Figure 17–3**). Gasoline-soaked rags, paper trails, or other devices used to ensure that fire starts and spreads may have not completely burned. Gasoline residue soaked into unburned furnishings or cracks in the flooring material may be retrievable, indicate the origin of the fire, and serve as evidence of arson (Chandler, 2009).

Igniter containers may be left at or near the scene. Most arson fires (except for those set by vandals) are started with the use of an igniter other than a simple match. An ignition device allows the arsonist to exit the building safely or provides for ample time to secure an alibi for the time the fire was set. Igniters can be very complex or deceptively simple. The more complex the igniting device, the more likely unburned remains will exist.

Collecting Evidence

The containers of choice for holding evidence in an arson investigation are unused paint cans (**Figure 17–4**). Once evidence of arson has been discovered, the material should be placed in an airtight container, leaving one-third of the volume in the container empty. In order for the laboratory to run tests, three things are necessary:

1. An uncontaminated sample
2. A sufficient sample
3. A background sample (control)

FIGURE 17–3   Straw streamers (A), burning streamers (B and C), and burned streamer (D)
Courtesy of Ronald Becker, JD, Professor, Chaminade Institute.

FIGURE 17–4   Unused paint can used for storing arson evidence
Courtesy of Sirchie Acquisition Company, LLC.

Contamination is a byproduct of fire and the extinguishing of the fire. Additional contamination resulting from mishandling is what must be avoided. Containers made of plastic or polyethylene will react with hydrocarbons and may result in the destruction of hydrocarbon vapors. When gathering material for collection, the investigator should try to preserve sizable specimens. The point of origin should produce a gallon of porous material, soot, and debris and any other substances thought to contain accelerant residue. It is important that all materials suspected of containing volatile liquids be accompanied by a thorough sampling of similar but relatively clean control specimens from an area of the fire in which accelerants are thought to have been absent. The laboratory scientists will check the control materials to ensure they are free from flammable residues, thereby removing cleaning solvents or other household hydrocarbons as possible sources of contamination.

Nothing should be touched or moved before measurements and photographs have been taken and sketches made. The presence of hydrocarbon containers should be noted. In most arsons, an incendiary or detonation device of some type is employed to allow the arsonist to depart the scene or to establish an alibi. Such devices may be as complex as a remote control detonator or as simple as a candle embedded in gasoline. Remnants of **delay devices** may be discovered near the point of origin.

Investigating Explosions

At times an investigator will respond to the scene of an explosion. Just as all fires are not criminal in nature, not all explosions are criminal. Construction accidents, defective home-heating devices, or a tanker truck hauling a volatile chemical all could cause an explosion. However, there are explosions that do occur for criminal or terrorist reasons. Those that do occur for criminal or terrorist reasons typically make use of an explosive.

The steps employed in the investigation of an explosion are generally the same as for arson, but there are several additional considerations. The chances of finding a large amount of trace evidence are remote. Like fire, an explosion is the product of combustion accompanied by the creation of gases and heat. It is the sudden buildup of expanding gas pressure at the point of detonation that produces the disruption of the explosion. Chemical explosions can be classified on the basis of the velocity of energy waves transmitted upon detonation.

Categories of Explosives

According to the Department of Homeland Security (2008) *Incident Response to Terrorist Bombings*, explosives can be divided into three categories: pyrotechnics, propellants (both of which are called low explosives), and high explosives. These categorizations depend, in part, on the manner of use of the materials

Low-order explosives involve a relatively slow rate of conversion to a gaseous state. The energy wave generated travels at a speed of less than 1,000 meters per second. The most widely used explosives in the low-order group are black powder and smokeless powder. Low-order explosives can be ignited by heat and are usually ignited with a lighted fuse.

High-order explosives change rapidly to a gaseous state upon ignition. The energy wave created travels at a rate between 1,000 and 9,000 meters per second. Dynamite is the most common high-order explosive, although composition C-4 (made of RDX, the most popular and powerful of the military explosives) is also used. Unlike low-order explosives, high-order explosives must be detonated by an initiating device. The most common initiator is a blasting cap. However, a simple ignition switch can be used to provide the spark necessary to detonate high-order explosives. Sometimes a cell phone is used to "call" a device and provide the detonation. The Bali bombings (October 12, 2002), Madrid bombings (March 11, 2004), London bombings (July 7, 2005), and the bombing of a Saudi palace (August 28, 2009) have all recently been attributed to mobile phone detonation (Maras, 2012).

Explosive Investigation

While the majority of explosive investigations are typically handled by military and federal authorities, in today's world of increasing domestic terrorism activities, more often local authorities are being placed in the position of being first responders to critical incidents relating to explosions. There are two types of bombing incidents: predetonation and postdetonation. Predetonation incidents include bomb threats, suspicious item incidents, and situations involving suspected suicide bombers. Postdetonation incidents on the other hand include situations where explosives have already been detonated.

Predetonation

Although the nightly news typically teems with stories of suicide bombers and suspicious incidents, bomb threats are the most common type of predetonation incident. Most of these are hoaxes and are reported simply as a prank. Sometimes there are ulterior motives such as cancelling school, work, a controversial community event, etc. However, many agencies and school districts now impose significant penalties on individuals who communicate bomb threats. Statutes covering these situations have been upgraded in many jurisdictions and callers now face large fines and even imprisonment.

The initial first responder at a suspicious item incident is typically a law enforcement officer. He or she should immediately evacuate persons from around the suspected item or areas where devices could be located. In no case should anyone other than a certified bomb technician attempt to handle or render safe any suspected explosive device. The Department of Homeland Security recommends the actions of first responders at a predetonation incident not be observed or recorded by personnel who do not have a legitimate requirement to document such actions. Written summaries, audio or video recordings, or police responses can be used by bombers in planning subsequent attacks.

Postdetonation

As with the response to all scenes, the first priority of the initial response to a postdetonation incident is the safety of the public and the first responders. Every effort must be made to avoid additional casualties. All responders should be alert for any item that could be a secondary device or any location where a secondary device can be concealed. A **secondary device** is a second bomb placed at a scene to detonate after the original explosion. Secondary devices are typically placed to target emergency responders and investigators at the scene of a bombing. Law enforcement officers, firefighters, medical personnel, and other emergency response personnel should continually observe their operational areas for any signs of secondary devices. If a suspected secondary device is observed, the incident commander should be notified and recall procedures implemented immediately. The search for secondary devices should also include staging areas, command posts, rest and rehab areas, and triage areas.

Scene Search

The search should focus on locating the site of the device and identifying the type of explosive used. The point of detonation will often leave a gaping hole surrounded by scorching. The type of explosive used may be determined by inspecting the residue at the scene. Wood, metal, and fiberglass samples surrounding the **detonation point** should have sufficient residue to allow identification of the explosive. The entire area must be searched systematically to recover any

Responses to Predetonation Situations

- Do not touch an item that could contain explosive material.

- Always move people away from a suspicious item—never try to move the item away from people.

- Never use a radio, cellular telephone, or other transmitter within a minimum of 300 feet of a location where there is a suspected or actual explosive device.

- Pay close attention to appropriate evacuation distances.

- Be aware of the potential for secondary devices.

Adapted from Department of Homeland Security. (2008). *Incident response to terrorist bombings*. Washington, DC: US Government Printing Office.

trace of a detonating mechanism. Particles of explosives will be embedded in the pipe cap or threads of a pipe bomb. All materials gathered from the site of an explosion must be packaged in separate containers and labeled with all pertinent information (International Association of Arson Investigators, 2012).

Many manufacturers of dynamite include magnetic **microtaggants** in each stick. These fluorescent, color-coded, multilayered particles identify the residue as dynamite and indicate the source of manufacture. The color should make the taggants visible to ultraviolet light, and their magnetism should make them susceptible to a magnet. Electric shunts from blasting caps, clock mechanisms, batteries, and pieces of wrapper may survive the explosion and concomitant fire. In those instances where humans have been the victims of a vessel fire, their remains should be bagged. Their clothing should not be removed (Girard, 2010).

Zones and Perimeters

Multilevel containment is often suggested as a scene preservation and containment method to ensure the integrity of evidence and safety of personnel. The investigation and processing of a postdetonation incident is one that certainly calls for such a methodology to be employed. In such an instance, there will be the establishment of three specific zones within what will be considered the crime scene. These are broken down into hot, warm, and cold zones (**Figure 17–5**).

Hot Zone

The hot zone includes the area that encompasses significant structural collapse or damage and extends to the point where a person would be relatively safe from blast, fragmentation, or shrapnel from secondary devices, if they should prove to be present in the same location

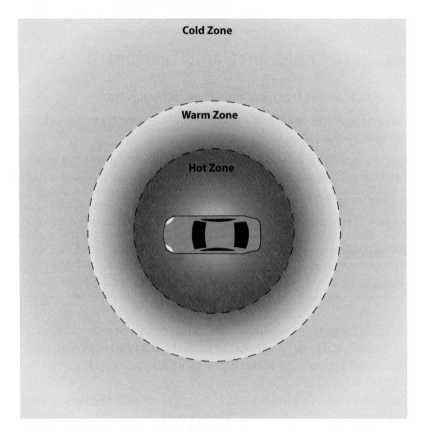

FIGURE 17–5   Example of multizone containment used in explosive investigations
Courtesy of Nick Vesper, University of Wisconsin-Platteville.

as the original device. This area can differ significantly in size and will shrink as the threat of secondary devices diminishes. The only personnel authorized in the area are first responders who have been trained and equipped to operate in the high-hazard environment and have a legitimate need to be in the area. This group includes firefighters and emergency medical personnel conducting rescue operations, bomb technicians, and specially trained law enforcement officers.

Warm Zone

The diameter (Y) of the warm zone is determined by identifying the distance from the seat of the explosion (or ground zero) to the farthest point where evidence can be visually identified (X), then adding half that distance (50% of X).

The formula is X + .50X = Y (**Figure 17–6**).

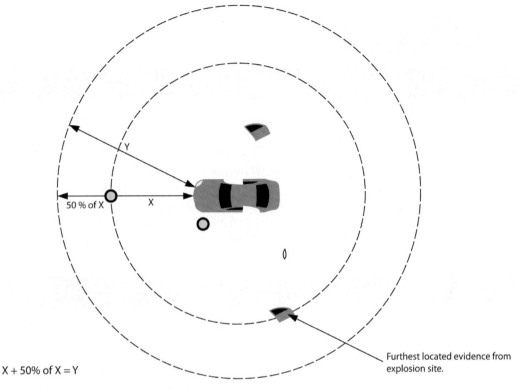

X + 50% of X = Y

FIGURE 17–6   Example of how to calculate warm zone diameter
Courtesy of Nick Vesper, University of Wisconsin-Platteville.

Cold Zone

The cold zone encompasses the area required for the command post, staging areas, temporary morgue, and a designated area for victims' families. This special area for victims' families is typically used to discourage family members from trying to approach the target to assist in rescue operations or attempt to obtain information concerning their loved ones.

Evidence Collection

Much like fire debris, postblast evidence should not be placed into paper or plastic bags. The use of nylon arson bags or empty metal cans is recommended. For some objects that are not practical to collect, such as a building, the surface needs to be swabbed with a cotton swatch to test for residue. The swabs should then be placed into a glass jar or vial.

WRAP UP

Chapter Summary

To properly investigate a fire, the investigation needs to begin during firefighting operations. First responders' observations of people in the area of the fire and what the fire looked like can help in an investigation and are of vital importance. The investigator does not need to be a firefighter; however, a basic understanding of firefighting techniques will aid investigators in the interpretation of a fire scene. Fire and explosive scenes must be approached in the same, methodical manner as all other crime scenes. The crime scene investigator should approach the fire scene or scene of an explosion as though it were a criminal event and allow the physical evidence found to point them in the direction of classifying the fire or explosion as intentional, accident, or an act of God.

Review Questions

1. What distinguishes simple arson from aggravated arson?

2. How are igniters and delay devices used in arsons?

3. What makes something burn?

4. What is the value of smoke color and odor to the arson investigator?

5. How does spontaneous combustion occur?

6. What kinds of evidence are available to the arson investigator?

7. How does an arsonist's motive assist in an arson investigation?

8. What are the most common motives for arson?

9. What is a masking fire?

10. What is a pyromaniac, and what is the serial killer trilogy?

11. What are streamers used for?

12. Where does the arson investigation begin?

13. What is the significance of the point of origin of the fire?

14. Why is it necessary to provide the laboratory with a background sample from the fire?

15. Why do fire departments investigate boat arsons?

16. What is the difference between a high-order and low-order explosive?

17. What is the detonation point?

18. What are microtaggants?

References

Chandler, R. K. (2009). *Fire investigation*. Clifton Park New York: Delmar.

Department of Homeland Security. (2008). *Incident response to terrorist bombings*. Washington, DC: U.S. Government Printing Office.

Department of Homeland Security. (2002). *Arson detection for the first responder: ADFR-student manual*. Washington, DC: U.S. Government Printing Office.

Federal Bureau of Investigation (FBI). (2009). *Uniform crime report*. Washington, DC: Department of Justice.

Girard, J. E. (2010). Criminalistics: *Forensic science, crime and terrorism*. Sudbury: Jones and Bartlett.

International Association of Arson Investigators. (2012) *Fire investigator: Principles and practice to NFPA 921 and 1033*. Sudbury, MA: Jones and Bartlett.

Kolko, D. J. (2002). *Handbook on firesetting in children and youth*. San Diego: Academic Press.

Magnuson, E. (1990, April 9). "The devil made him do it." *Time*, 38.

Maras, M. (2011). *Computer Forensics: Cybercriminals, Laws and Evidence*. Burlington, MA: Jones & Bartlett Learning.

Myers, A. L. (2012). Suicide by poison suspected in courtroom death. *Associated Press*. Retrieved July 6, 2012, from http://www.kmov.com/news/national/Suicide-by-poison-suspected-in-courtroom-death--160971445.html

O'Connor, J., & Redsicker, D. (1997). *Piratical fire and arson investigation* (2nd ed.). Boca Raton, FL: CRC Press.

Saferstein, R. (2010). *Criminalistics: An introduction to forensic science* (10th ed.). Englewood Cliffs, NJ: Prentice Hall.

© McMac/ShutterStock, Inc.

- Understand the safety concerns that apply when processing an underwater crime scene.
- Understand the environmental concerns and challenges when documenting and processing an underwater crime scene.
- Describe black water diving including its dangers and what causes it.
- Know the proper documentation, collection, and preservation methods associated with underwater evidence and underwater crime scenes.
- Describe the duties of a DMORT and know why and when one is utilized.
- Know the proper documentation, collection, and preservation methods associated with both buried and scattered human remains.

Special Scene Considerations

Law enforcement agencies must encourage their officers to see the benefits of exploring new methods of investigating underwater crime scenes and not rely solely on past policies and procedures.

Ronald F. Becker (2000)

KEY TERMS

Black Water Diving
Buoyancy Control Device
(BCD)
Cadaver Dogs

Disaster Mortuary
Operational Response
Team (DMORT)
Probing

Underwater Search and
Evidence Response Team
(USERT)

Underwater Crime Scene Response

When an investigation leads to an underwater environment, it becomes an underwater criminal investigation. Its process should be as forensically thorough and systematic as any crime scene process conducted out of water. However, unlike the separation of duties often found in land-based investigations, underwater scenes typically call for the investigator to become the crime scene photographer, fingerprint specialist, and evidence recovery specialist. They also call for the investigator to be a skilled diver. This is an extremely specialized position requiring specific training and equipment.

Underwater Investigative Teams

The first documented dive team dedicated to investigative purposes was the Miami-Dade County Underwater Recovery Unit, which was established in 1960. The Miami-Dade team was assembled due to the increasing number of water-related crime scenes occurring within the water-laden area of Miami-Dade County (Becker, 2005). Federal agencies also found reason for training and equipping such teams as a result of national and world situations. The Federal Bureau of Investigations (FBI) established its first **Underwater Search and Evidence Response Team (USERT)** in 1982 (FBI, 2009). There are currently four such teams in the United States, and they are located in New York, Washington, Miami, and Los Angeles. The teams are managed from the FBI Laboratory in Quantico, Virginia. Each team is composed of 12 members; however, divers respond and fill in on other teams as necessary. The USERTs have been used in a number of newsworthy events that include searching for evidence and remains in the explosion of TWA Flight 800; preventative diving to search for explosives under the spectator stands for the 1996 Atlanta Olympic Games; and also overseas in such terrorist attacks as that on the 2000 bombing of the USS Cole (Becker, 2005).

While the FBI maintains several well-trained and extremely well-equipped dive teams, many municipal, county, and state agencies across the country also have realized the necessity and benefit of implementing diver operational teams.

Why Is an Investigative Dive Team Necessary?

A common misconception is that evidence that has been submerged lacks the forensic value of evidence found top-side (**Figure 18–1**). There are numerous cases where submerged items have yielded identifiable blood evidence, fingerprints, hair and fiber evidence, and many other types of trace evidence that have aided in identifying the perpetrator of the criminal act. Some people would question why a body would have to be handled any differently in water than out of water. However, bodies should be placed in body bags when found underwater because correctly processing and packaging them it can result in a variety of forensic evidence being saved. Bagging a body underwater minimizes damage and postmortem injuries to the body, maintains hair and fiber evidence, and keeps clothing intact.

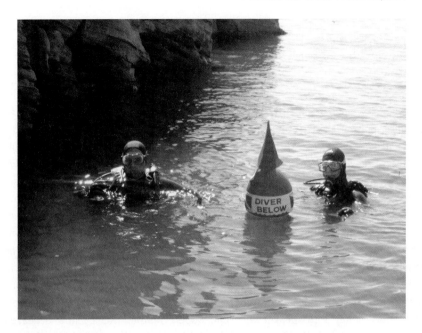

FIGURE 18–1   Forensic divers prepare to deploy to recover crime scene evidence

Investigators must understand the value and necessity of properly collecting, marking, and recording the location of items recovered from a dive site. Often investigators, administrators, crime lab personnel, and prosecutors lack knowledge and training about the underwater investigative process. Because of this deficit, they are unfamiliar with the forensic value and scientific methodology involved with underwater crime scene processing. For instance, if only a diver is aware of the evidentiary value of collecting control samples from the water and bottom material, then investigators may not understand or request the steps to be done. Collection of proper control and elimination samples for exclusion of background and marine debris is as important below the water as it is above. Because the ultimate goal of any underwater crime scene is not merely the salvaging and recovery of submerged items, but discovery of the truth and conviction of the perpetrators, dive teams must adapt to accomplish such tasks.

Where Is Investigative Diving Used?

The working environment for the underwater investigator is much different than those shown on television or in movies. A typical work environment could consist of diving in a quarry, dirty river, raw sewage facility, or any of a host of other less than hospitable environments. Investigative diving can occur in any environment, at any time of the day, and in any area involving a body of water. In the vast majority of these cases, the visibility confronting the forensic diver will be less than three to four feet. In some instances, the visibility will be so drastically reduced that a diver's gauges will not be readable or even visible. This is referred to as **black water diving**. Unlike in a land-based criminal investigation where one or two persons

VIEW **FROM AN EXPERT**

Public Safety Diving

When I spoke to the participants in the International Police Divers Symposium in 1999 I bemoaned the present state of forensic science as it applied to submerged evidence. All public safety diving equipment, at the time, was being manufactured by recreational scuba diving manufacturers and was either black or dark blue. I recall getting a laugh when I said that were I entangled while submerged in black water I would rather have a flashing neon dry suit than a black one. I talked about how ineffective black plastic body bags were for bagging bodies in the water and how a tight mesh bag would allow excess water to drain out. Both have become realities. I spoke of the legal prerequisite for geographically locating evidence, maintaining chains of custody, and the packaging and handling of submerged evidence. I described a method of measurement that could be used in water with zero visibility. I talked about measuring to the water course's bottom rather than to buoys and described trilateration. Trilateration has become the default for the geographical location of evidence and the concomitant sketch produced.

I remember being a co-speaker with Cpl. Robert Teather (RCMP) now deceased, at the U.S. Department of Justice Regional Public Safety Diver's Seminar in 1999 and airing our differences over the handling of recovered firearms. He believed it best to preserve the serial numbers and rifling by recovering the weapon and sealing it in a container filled with oil. Bob was a good friend, but I always believed that other types of information could be found on a submerged firearm and advocated the marine archaeological approach to the recovery of artifacts—bag in water, in the water. My method has become the default and two significant propositions made it so. First, in the Sept.–Oct. 2011 issue of *Evidence Technology Magazine*, FBI Physical Scientist/Forensic Examiner Mary Kathryn Book discovered that firearms submerged in fresh or saltwater could retain recoverable fingerprints. Then Dr. John Bond, forensic scientist

could effectively work some scenes, in a black water diving environment, the underwater investigator relies upon the coordinated efforts of the dive team to ensure both survival and success. This dive team includes both the surface personnel and fellow underwater investigators (**Figure 18–2**).

Who Should Comprise the Team?

Depending upon the location, there are volunteer teams, teams of fire and rescue personnel, law enforcement teams, and in some cases a collaboration of all of these. All types are involved in attempting to fill the niche of "underwater investigator." The problem is that when dealing with a potential crime scene, the question shouldn't be "Who can help?" Rather, the question at Northhamptonshire Police, discovered that fingers secrete salt and that salt can etch a fingerprint into the soft surface of a brass shell casing. That fingerprint can be visualized even though the cartridge has been fired. Conventional surface fingerprints are destroyed by the high temperatures achieved during ignition so it is significant that these etched fingerprints survive firing and submersion.

Second, in the 2011 airing of a CSI episode "Tell Tale Heart" a murder had been committed and the firearm was believed to have been deposited in a golf course pond. A brief scene shows the firearm submerged in water in a Tupperware container being handed to one of the CSI team members. You know that when you see it on CSI it must be true.

In 1995, in a book called *The Underwater Crime Scene,* and again in 2006, I wrote that the future of underwater evidence recovery would include a day when the commercial training of police divers would become obsolete. That police agencies would shoulder the responsibility to train "police divers" and that fire departments would get out of the underwater evidence recovery business. I believed then and I believe now that there should be two standards: one for fire departments conducting rescues and one for police agencies processing underwater crime scenes. For in the final analysis it makes no more sense to have police fight fires than it does for firefighters to process underwater crime scenes. I recognize the tremendous contribution firefighters have made to the underwater recovery process, but it is past time to recognize that it makes no difference who recovers submerged evidence—it is a police function. As such, all entities involved in the recovery of submerged evidence should be trained to understand the forensic and legal ramifications of the underwater recovery process.

Ronald Becker, JD
Professor, Chaminade University
(Co-author of *Criminal Investigation*, 4th Edition, [2013], Jones & Bartlett Learning)

Courtesy of Ronald Becker, JD, Professor, Chaminade Institute.

should be, "Who *should* help?" Except in very few instances (e.g., an arson investigation), fire departments do not investigate or become involved with criminal investigations on land. Therefore, why should they participate or why are they qualified to investigate crime scenes when the environment has changed to underwater? Law enforcement does not allow fire or rescue personnel to investigate a homicide occurring within a residence. So why then allow them to investigate a crime scene underwater?

It must be realized that in some instances, if fire departments do not train their personnel to respond to underwater scenes then nobody will. However, if a need has been documented and recognized, then law enforcement agencies should not ignore the responsibility and defer to fire or rescue personnel. The responsibility for investigating crime scenes belongs with the criminal justice community.

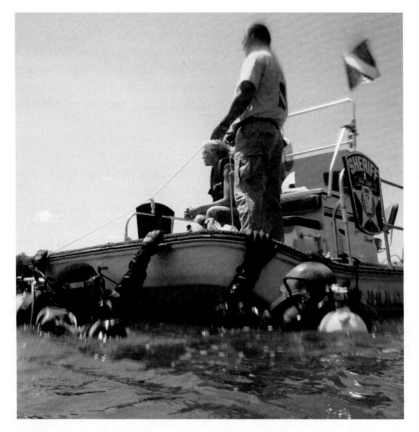

FIGURE 18–2 Dive team members processing an underwater crime scene

Team Design

There are many different theories and operational plans for the makeup of an underwater investigation team. However, at the bare minimum, the following personnel are required.

Team Leader/Commander

As in any operational response performed by law enforcement, it is crucial to have an incident commander for each scene. This duty falls to the Team Leader/Commander. This individual is not in the water and is responsible for supervising the diving process and ensuring that the individuals involved are conducting their tasks in a safe and proper manner. This individual is also responsible for ensuring that the members acquire the equipment and training necessary to conduct their jobs, as well as documenting all training, medical, and other personnel issues.

Line Tenders

Due to environments of low visibility, fast moving water, and other hazardous situations, divers are typically tethered to a line that is tended by someone above the water. These individuals are the eyes and ears for the forensic diver. It is preferable to have a tender be a current or former diver so that he or she is familiar with the underwater environment. In some jurisdictions, underwater communication gear has been implemented that is similar to that worn by tactical teams. However, even in these cases, and certainly in those where such communication gear is not possessed, communication between the tender and a diver occurs through a process of predetermined line tugs. This communication can involve such matters as changes of direction, status checks, ascents, and emergencies. Line communication varies by team, but training must take place, and communication must be understood by all team members.

Divers

There is no set number of divers for an operational dive team, but it is recommended that at the very minimum there be two divers for any dive situation. The primary diver is the person who is in the water and actively searching or investigating the scene. The safety diver (sometimes referred to as a 100% diver) is either in the water or out of the water and fully geared up with the ability to enter the water to provide emergency backup or aid to the primary diver. In some situations, a backup diver (90% diver) may be used as the backup to the primary diver and as a safety diver should the safety diver find him or herself deployed.

The team set up is similar to the arrangement law enforcement and fire agencies typically utilize in dismantling clandestine laboratories. This is the case due to the similarities between the two environments. In both cases personnel are confronted with hazardous and inhospitable environments that require the use of respiratory and exposure equipment. Both situations are physically taxing on an individual and require that there be constant monitoring and documentation to avoid overexertion or other potentially fatal situations. It is for this reason that both situations involve the use of safety or standby personnel (**Figure 18-3**).

FIGURE 18-3   Members of a dive team conduct a search for a missing person

Assembling, Equipping, and Training the Team

It is suggested that all members of an agency dive team be full-time, trained members of that agency for liability, training, and policy and procedure purposes. However, some smaller agencies with limited resources require volunteers to supplement their dive recovery operations. Other departments sometimes share equipment and members. This is often pointed to as being "cost effective"; however, it can prove problematic when divers from one location fail to respond, or when the necessary equipment is in another location other than where it is needed. Some locations have solved these problems by establishing specialized regional dive teams. One team (perhaps fire department personnel) is trained in and specializes in rescue diving while another team (law enforcement) specializes in evidence search, recovery, and collection. This minimizes evidence handling and ensures that the necessary equipment is operationally available.

There must be minimum entry requirements established for team membership. Many times this minimum certification is a recreational certification such as the Professional Association of Dive Instructors (PADI), National Association of Underwater Instructors (NAUI), Scuba Schools International (SSI), and/or other recognized organizations. Often teams will write their own standard operational guidelines (SOGs) that list the minimum entry requirements and establish training and equipment requirements. As a point of caution in this world of lightning litigation, all established requirements for a dive team must be job related. If the requirements are not shown to be specifically related to the job applied for or involved in, they could be challenged as being discriminatory based on age, race, gender, or disability.

In addition to being (at a minimum) recreationally certified, all applicants should be required to pass a thorough and appropriate medical physical to verify their ability to perform tasks and to set a baseline for future medical exams. After joining the team, all team members should undergo annual dive physicals. Dive physicals should be administered also following any dive-related injury, major injury or illness, or any medical procedures that could interfere with the performance of duty.

The merits and benefits of fielding an underwater investigation team are many; however, with this comes the equally involved and elaborate budget and steps necessary to do so. This should not dissuade law enforcement from the assembly of such resources to ensure that each scene is processed in its entirety to the best of the agency's ability. All too often underwater crime scenes—and the evidence contained therein—are not properly documented or processed. This failure can result in a loss, contamination, or inadmissibility of the evidence. Proper underwater crime scene processing and documentation methods will ensure that the evidence is located, properly documented, preserved, and able to be used in subsequent litigation. It is important that the underwater investigation team be properly trained as well as take part in ongoing training specifically relating to matters of crime scene documentation and processing methods involving the underwater environment.

Today's crime scene investigator is well versed in the methodology and logistics associated with crime scene processing and documentation. However, what if the crime scene in question was located underwater? Would the same practices and methodologies apply? Would the same equipment and personnel be appropriate?

Oftentimes, the standard operating procedures (SOPs) associated with processing crime scenes are forgotten or ignored when encountering an underwater crime scene. There are many reasons this occurs, some of which include equipment, manpower, and/or environmental issues. More often it is a result of improperly trained or equipped personnel or a case of rushing and thinking that, "it won't really matter as long as we get the stuff." However, the underwater scene and its contents are equally important and subject to the same scrutiny and legal considerations as a land-based scene, so it should be processed in an equally thorough and competent manner.

Personnel Requirements and Training

The first obvious hurdle is that typically an underwater scene will require the investigator to submerge him or herself in order to document the scene. This usually requires that the investigator be a certified diver in order to effectively document an in-water event. With an exception being very shallow water photography that can be accomplished by either wading or taking photographs from a boat or other floating object, the individual tasked with the duty must be a competent swimmer and underwater diver as well as a skilled photographer.

Whenever a person enters an environment for which his or her body was not meant to live within, there are hazards, risks, and restrictions involved. The individual assigned the duty of underwater photography must be both physically and mentally capable of venturing into and working within the underwater environment.

Several organizations can certify an individual as a diver. Some are dedicated to recreational divers and a more civilian concentrated population (PADI, NAUI, SSI), and others are specifically related to public safety professionals (Dive Rescue International, Miami-Dade). Each has a purpose and a niche; however, the important matter is that an underwater investigator be certified, comfortable, and competent so that he or she can effectively perform the assigned duties.

Processing and Documenting an Underwater Scene

When encountered with an underwater crime scene, the investigation team must take into account that there are multiple scenes and levels that must be accounted for. Just as in an above-water scene, multiple methods of documentation must occur. These remain the same as for land-based operations. They are typically still photography, videography, sketching/mapping, and the written report.

Documenting the Surface Crime Scene

When documenting the scene through these four methods, the investigation team must remember that there are two types of scenes that must be documented. The first is the surface scene. This includes any water access points such as piers, shorelines, or waterfronts, as well as the surface of the water. All of the aforementioned must be thoroughly searched, photographed, and located items of evidence noted on a sketch.

Documenting the Underwater Crime Scene

The other type of scene is the submerged scene. The submerged scene has the added difficulty of depth as well as the aforementioned environmental issues and visibility issues that compound the problem. This is why it is imperative that only those individuals who have received proper training and certification in such matters be utilized to conduct underwater search and recovery operations. The submerged scene includes the objects located at depth as well the level at which they were found. It is a three-dimensional scene, often with very little in the way of fixed markers or items to aid in reference. Just as with the surface scene, this area must be thoroughly searched. Items of evidence must be photographed, marked, and their positions and depths noted on a sketch. They must then be collected and preserved.

Searching for and Marking Evidence

In addition to proper personnel, underwater investigative teams also must possess the necessary equipment to conduct proper underwater crime scene processing. One item of value where searches are concerned is sonar. It can help to locate items of evidence, as well as identify potential hazards.

A number of different search techniques are utilized for underwater investigation, dependent upon the item being searched for, condition of the water, and location of the body of water. Briefly, some of these methods are described.

Once an item of evidence is located, it is suggested that the position of the item be marked. This is especially important in areas of low visibility. The are several suggested methods for doing this, but the most common method is to "float" a marker buoy, which consists of an inflated buoy attached to a line affixed to the item of evidence or to a tie down in close proximity to the item. This will serve several purposes. First, it allows the investigator to follow the line down directly to the item. Second, it allows surface personnel to visually gauge the evidence location and assist in crime scene sketching. It is important to remember not to mark too many items of evidence in an area with marker buoys while divers are in the water, as it becomes increasingly possible that divers will become entangled. The scene will have to be processed in sections. Global positioning system (GPS) devices are also available that can be used to more easily and safely mark items of evidence. In either case, it is important that the underwater investigator take note of the depth at which the item was discovered. It is suggested that the diver or dive team assemble a diver's slate (i.e., underwater note pad) made specifically for the purpose of annotating underwater scene information (**Figure 18–4**).

Photographing in the Underwater Environment

It is not enough to be a skilled top-side photographer and think that one will be equally as successful employing that knowledge and technique sublevel. Several issues must be addressed in order to effectively and accurately capture the underwater crime scene.

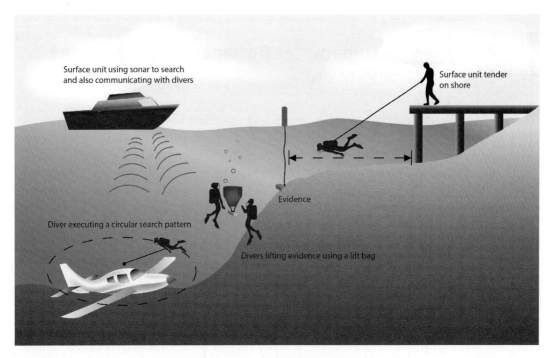

FIGURE 18–4   Example of the multiple facets of underwater crime scene investigation
Courtesy of Dana Gevelinger, University of Wisconsin-Platteville.

Underwater Equipment

The first obstacle is equipment. A photographer is not typically able to employ the same photographic equipment that he or she uses for land-based crime scenes. Special marine or underwater cameras must be used or underwater housings utilized to encapsulate the equipment. This requires the photographer to have a working knowledge of the use and maintenance of such equipment. However, having the correct equipment is not enough. The photographer must next overcome the difficult environmental issues involved with underwater photography.

Environmental Issues

The first major environmental issue encountered by the underwater photographer is distortion. Water refracts light rays differently underwater. Unlike above the water, underwater light refraction causes objects to be magnified. For this reason images and distances are distorted. In fact, objects underwater will appear approximately 33% larger. Thus, it is extremely important to include a scaled object for reference. Although the scale will also be magnified, it will be magnified in direct relation to the object in question, thereby enabling a viewer to interpret the true size and dimension of the subject matter.

CASE IN POINT

Underwater Documentation of a Bank Robbery

Two men allegedly held up a local branch bank with a semiautomatic assault rifle and a handgun, fired one shot, doing no harm, and made off with approximately $110,000. The suspects, both wearing ski masks, were seen leaving the bank by an off-duty firefighter who called dispatch on his cell phone to report the violation. The firefighter followed the two men in his vehicle as they left the bank premises in a vehicle. Due to the firefighter's descriptions and real-time updates, police officers were able to intercept the vehicle prior to it leaving the area. The suspects became involved in a high-speed pursuit, covering approximately 13 miles, and in which three law enforcement agencies participated.

At one point, while driving over a highway viaduct that passed over an area lake, several objects were seen thrown out of the passenger window of the suspect vehicle. The suspects were observed splitting up in the area of a subdivision, when the passenger exited the vehicle, while the vehicle was moving. The driver continued on, and the passenger was pursued by police while he broke into and ran through several houses in an attempt to elude them. The passenger was seen to be carrying a semiautomatic rifle during the foot pursuit. The suspect on foot managed to evade officers and was not found until several hours later, after calling his girlfriend from a payphone to come pick him up. The suspect did not have a firearm in his possession at the time of his arrest. The vehicle pursuit finally terminated when the suspect vehicle disregarded a traffic control device and collided with another passenger vehicle, resulting in the occupant's death and the incapacitation of the suspect driver.

Upon investigation of the incident, crime scene investigators found one spent 40-caliber shell casing in the lobby of the bank. One firearm, an AR-15 assault rifle, was located in the living room of a home in which the passenger was seen entering. There was no additional firearm located in the vicinity of the foot pursuit, nor in the vehicle of the suspect driver. The assault rifle that was located was missing the magazine. The bag containing the money was found within the vehicle.

The money found in the possession of the driver was what would be considered a "smoking gun" in most cases. However, because the possession of semiautomatic weapons and their use in a federal offense carried additional repercussions, it was imperative that the firearm evidence be located.

The firearm located on the living room floor was photographed and collected for evidence. Pursuing officers recalled that the passenger had possibly thrown something out of his window while the vehicle traversed the viaduct crossing over the lake. Investigators were sent to the location to determine if there had been an attempt to destroy or ditch evidence. When investigators arrived, they soon recognized that it would not be possible to conduct a thorough investigation without divers. The dive team was mobilized and responded to the location. The dive team included a crime scene technician whose duty was the documentation of the scene and the collection of any discovered evidence.

The crime scene technician was tasked with documenting both the submerged and surface scene. He photographed the suspected entry area of the unknown objects from numerous angles, including from the position of the viaduct from which they were believed to have been thrown. The technician also photographed the presence of the dive team while conducting the search and all equipment associated with the effort.

The dive team entered the water and subsequently found one high capacity magazine for a .223 rifle, the same caliber as the assault rifle that had been located in the living room (**FIGURE 18–5**). The team also discovered a magazine for a 40-caliber semiautomatic handgun, the same caliber as the expended cartridge found in the bank. Nothing else was located that was believed to be associated with the alleged crime. The magazines were photographed *in situ* by the crime scene technician, utilizing the underwater system assigned to him.

FIGURE 18–5 Photograph of a rifle magazine located in water. Note the distortion of the item caused by light refraction

Visibility in the dive area was less than two feet. Photographs were difficult. An extreme amount of environmental debris had been disturbed as a result of the search performed. This resulted in severe turbidity and added to photographic backscatter. The photographer elected to shoot the scene using available light, thereby avoiding backscatter. A fast shutter speed was used due to movement of both the diver and the water surrounding the subject matter. The items were photographed both with and without a scale of reference. Coloration was yellow/green due to the severe algae growth in the marine environment. A color correction filter was not used. Underwater video was also taken utilizing the same underwater photographic equipment.

The underwater photographs were a large part of this investigation and showed an attempt to disguise evidence associated with criminal activity. It also helped tie the expended round in the bank to the individuals, because the round did not match the firearm located in the living room. The round, however, did match one of the magazines found and photographed in the lake, although the related handgun was never located.

Despite the assistance of the public and numerous police searchers, the semiautomatic handgun was never located. There were several points within the vehicle pursuit when the vehicle was lost from law enforcements' line of sight, and the firearm was possibly discarded during one of those moments. The evidence located, however, was sufficient to convict both men of federal charges for bank robbery, possession of illegal firearms, use of a firearm to commit a felony, and also first-degree murder for the killing of the driver of the passenger vehicle.

Coloration and Lighting

Another major problem is subject coloration (**Figure 18–6**). As depth increases, light rays of red, orange, and yellow are filtered out by the water. Eventually, the diver is left with only blue and green rays. Even in the clearest of waters, only blue and green wave lengths typically penetrate at a depth of over 30 feet. This depth is significantly reduced if the water is polluted or murky. One way in which the photographer can overcome this loss of color is to shoot the photograph facing upward toward the surface, thereby utilizing the most natural light penetration available.

Because natural light is quickly absorbed or scattered by water, artificial light is often essential. The addition of a strobe, thereby adding electronic flash lighting to the scene, is useful for two reasons: to illuminate the subject matter, and to obtain the true color of underwater objects and surroundings. However, water is significantly more dense than air and an electronic flash typically will not penetrate or light objects further away than 6 to 8 feet, depending on the strength of the strobe employed.

Color correction filters can be attached to the lens in instances where overall photos are being taken and a strobe will not illuminate the subject matter; however, a strobe must not be used for this purpose and it must be reflected on a diver's photo log. Remember, the important thing about crime scene photography is that it is a true and accurate portrayal of the scene as it was when the photograph was taken. Technically, the scene was viewed by the photographer in unnatural colors of shades of green and blue, not in the "true" colors compensated for by the filter. However, the filter does make the photo more realistic as to what the subject matter would or should look like were it not for the environmental abnormalities associated with being underwater.

In addition to distortion, coloration, and lighting issues, often the environment itself will create difficulty for the underwater photographer. Silt, sediment, algae, and pollution can create

FIGURE 18–6 Photograph of a cartridge casing located at an underwater crime scene

black water diving conditions. In these conditions visibility can be less than 1 or 2 feet. It is especially important for the photographer to have good diving skills to ensure proper buoyancy so as not to disturb the environment and affect photo quality.

Suggestions for Adapting to Underwater Environmental Issues

To overcome the difficulties encountered when photographing an underwater scene, a few basic methods can be employed, as follows:

- *If possible, stay shallow.* This will reduce the color loss from light reaching the subject matter. However, if the crime scene is deep and photographs must be taken at a greater depth, the use of a strobe or color correction filter must be employed.

- *Whenever possible, use a strobe (electronic flash).* This will replace the light that is lost underwater.

- *Stay close to your subject.* Because of underwater distortion, coloration issues, and environmental haze, it is wise to keep the distance between the subject and camera as close as possible.

- *Maintain proper buoyancy.* If a diver-photographer is able to maintain his or her proper positioning (referred to as "attitude"), it will reduce or eliminate distortion and obliteration caused by stirring up environmental elements.

Evidence Recovery

Items of evidence recovered from water will require special handling and packaging. Just as in a surface level investigation, the ultimate success of an underwater investigation is determined by the proper location, preservation, and documentation of the evidence. In addition to the obvious underwater hazards and inconveniences that affect search and documentation efforts, bottom suction is another factor that affects evidence recovery.

This phenomenon typically occurs in areas containing silty or soft mud bottoms. Because of the laws of physics, raising an object that is in suction contact with the bottom requires greater lifting force than on land. However, an attempt to exert too much pressure on the item to gain its release can result in a runaway item that could injure the investigator or be lost to the current. For this reason, heavy lift bags are typically used to lift objects underwater. A lift bag is slowly inflated with one of the diver's underwater air sources, and when inflated, will help to raise the object safely. Most of these lift bags contain overpressurization valves that release air from the lift bag as the bag ascends and aids in controlling the item's ascent to the surface (**Figure 18–7**).

Depending upon the item, sometimes it is suggested to package the item underwater, thereby ensuring the collection of any trace material adhering to the item. Often it is suggested that the item be packaged in the water in which it was found to slow environmental deterioration possibly caused by removing the item from water. It is extremely important that an individual familiar with the collection and preservation of underwater evidence be utilized for such matters.

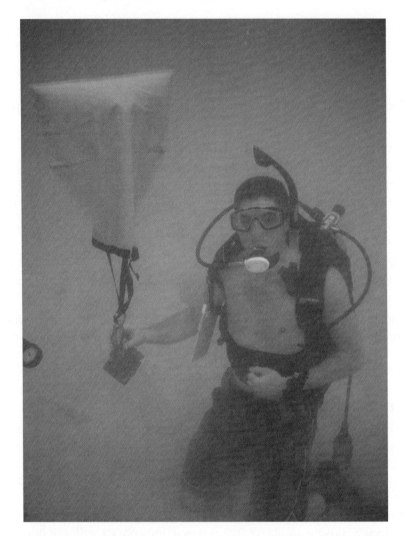

FIGURE 18–7   A diver demonstrates the use of a lift bag to recover underwater evidence

Not Everything Is Submerged

Many of those involved with investigating an underwater crime scene will lose sight of the fact that not all evidence associated with the event is submerged. In fact, a great deal of the time investigative personnel will encounter black water or other environmental conditions that make underwater photography useless. However, even if the environmental conditions do not allow for photographs to be taken, there is plenty of surface level material that should still be documented. The recommended items to remember to photograph include:

- Object or subject entry point or route
- Object or subject exit point or route

- Overall photographs of geographical area adjacent to the water
- Photographs of personnel and equipment utilized in the operation (for liability reasons)
- Photographs of staged equipment and personnel not utilized in the operation (for liability reasons)

Underwater Investigation Safety

Obviously, the goal of any criminal investigation—to include the photographic documentation of such an event—is to determine whether or not a crime has been committed, and if so, to document and collect evidence to identify and prosecute the guilty party. However, during this process the safety of all personnel involved in the process is paramount (**Figure 18–8**). Underwater photography is no exception to this rule. The underwater environment is inherently dangerous. It is foreign to humans and hard on equipment. The additional weight and bulk of the required equipment result in fatigue, entanglement, and other safety issues. The photographer should ensure that all of his or her equipment is connected properly and does not present an entanglement threat. A neck strap should never be used. Instead, equipment should be affixed to the wrist, dry suit, or **buoyancy control device (BCD)**, which is the jacket-like piece of equipment used to keep the diver neutrally buoyant. It is extremely important to learn dive-related skills from a certified professional and to participate in ongoing education and training related to the underwater environment to ensure both the safety and competency of the underwater investigator.

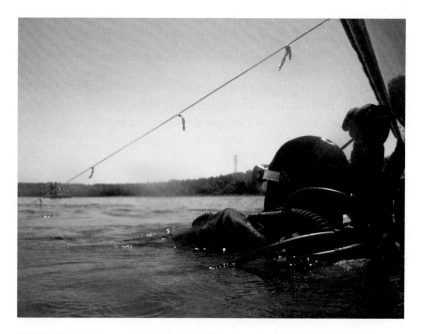

FIGURE 18–8 A diver makes use of a safety line to search a scene

Buried Remains

Although buried remains account for relatively few domestic forensic cases, proper scene processing methodology of such bears mention in light of recent world and domestic events. There are many agencies and individuals within the United States who are donating their time and talents both domestically (Hurricane Katrina; September 11, 2001 terror attacks) and internationally (Thailand's tsunami, mass graves of Kosovo) to assist with the processing of mass disasters and mass gravesites. Typically, these individuals are part of what is referred to as a **Disaster Mortuary Operational Response Team (DMORT)**. DMORT is a program of the U.S. Department of Health and Human Services that responds only when requested by local law enforcement agencies. The goal of DMORT is to assist local authorities during a mass fatality incident that is beyond the scope of local agency resources and abilities. Sometimes these instances will involve buried remains associated with human rights abuses, war crimes, and genocide. In any event, whether a mass event or an isolated case, buried remains present the problem of being difficult to locate.

Locating Buried Remains

There are a variety of techniques available to assist law enforcement with locating the buried remains of an individual or individuals. Witness statements typically form a starting point, and more sophisticated methods of probing, trenching, photography, **cadaver dogs** (trained to seek out the scent of decomposition), instrumental sensing, and ocular clues help to define a more specific area. Often a clandestine gravesite area will exhibit signs such as the discoloration of vegetation, primary and secondary areas of depression, and cracked soil that are clues to the investigation team of potential buried remains at the location (Ramey Burns, 2006) (**Figure 18–9**).

The preferred strategy is to progress from nonintrusive methods toward more destructive activities. Nonintrusive methods include remote sensing technologies such as airborne near infrared imaging. Intrusive methods include any activities that disturb a site. Examples include digging, probing, disrupting vegetation, and compacting the soil.

Turning to Specialized Organizations

As a rule, buried remains should be recovered by individuals familiar with archeological techniques. One such agency is NecroSearch International, located in Fort Collins, Colorado. NecroSearch is a private, volunteer organization whose mission is to both train and assist law enforcement agencies in the search for and/or recovery of human remains and evidence. Due to the fact that NecroSearch International is a private organization, it can only respond to assist at a crime scene when asked to do so by the law enforcement agency in charge of a case, so that the scene and related evidence will not be compromised. (For more information on NecroSearch International, visit http://www.necrosearch.org/.)

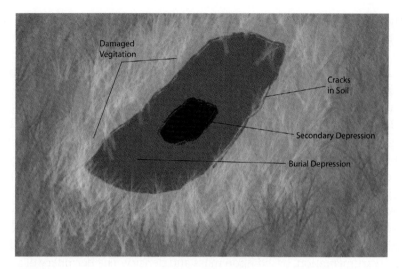

FIGURE 18–9   Characteristics of a clandestine gravesight
Courtesy of Erica Milks, University of Wisconsin-Platteville.

Effect of Burial Depth

Research has shown that buried bodies typically decompose at a slower rate than bodies that are discovered on the surface. Of course, this is mostly dependent upon the amount of time that a body lay exposed prior to burial. If insects are given a chance to lay their eggs, insect propagation and development can continue along with the subsequent decomposition and degradation of a body after burial.

Depth of burial has an effect on both decomposition and discovery. Temperatures within deeper graves (deeper than 2–3 feet) remain relatively stable, whereas shallower graves are more susceptible to the fluctuations of related surface temperatures. The soil density of a gravesite also has a bearing on the decomposition process, to include the tampering of the remains by scavengers. Except for extremely shallow graves or those in noncompacted soil, burial of remains offers protection of the remains from scavenging.

Processing Locations Involving Buried Remains

The area should be properly photographed before any work is begun at the site. Then the area to be searched and excavated should be organized into a grid in order to best preserve the information present within it. If available, a metal detector may be employed for surface investigation. If metallic objects are located they should be marked with flags. The area should also be examined for insect and larvae activity that may be associated with the body. If located, these should be collected and preserved.

A location should be set aside for a "screening area" in which surface materials and material eventually removed from the gravesite can be systematically searched through to locate small items (broken bones, fibers, insects, bullets, shell casings, etc.) sometimes missed in the excavation process. This should be located in an area that has already been searched and is in close proximity to the grave.

The next step in the process is to set up a staging area for equipment and the grave excavation process. This area should extend several yards, in all directions, surrounding the suspected gravesite. Vegetation and debris not associated with the burial should then be cut down and removed and screened. It may be advisable to once again make use of a metal detector after the vegetation and debris have been removed. Any discovered items should be documented and preserved.

In many instances relating to buried remains, it is helpful to have an idea as to the position of the body prior to beginning the excavation process. This can sometimes be determined through visual cues such as secondary depressions, and also from the use of ground-penetrating radar or other instrumentation, based upon mass and density. The periphery of a gravesite can be determined through the use of the same instrumentation, in a nonpenetrating manner, or through **probing**, which is much more invasive and risks damaging potential evidence, but is very easy, inexpensive, and efficient. Probing involves pushing a metal rod into the ground and marking where the rod enters more easily than its surroundings. This is measuring for soil density, and can also give some idea as to grave depth. Once the periphery has been determined, it is identified through the use of evidence flags or driving stakes into the ground (**Figure 18–10**). After the outer perimeter of the likely site is established, it is suggested that there be a grid developed to assist with documentation efforts. In order for the grid to be established, it is necessary to identify a reference point and then set about developing a grid system containing right angles. As items of evidence are discovered, they are mapped to the nearest corner points of their grid zone (**Figure 18–11**).

FIGURE 18–10 Evidence flags denote the periphery of a suspected clandestine gravesite (note top-side vegetation already removed)

FIGURE 18–11 Example of establishing a grid over a clandestine gravesite

Once the excavation process has begun, it should proceed slowly, deliberately, and systematically. The work should involve small instruments, rather than taking a shovel or backhoe approach. Small trowels and brushes are the tools of choice for this undertaking, in order to minimize the loss or destruction of evidence.

In cases where the body is relatively fresh or still in the soft-tissue decomposition process, it will be necessary to minimize damage to the body. In these cases, the exposed skin, especially the hands, feet, and head, should be bagged and/or covered in order to minimize environmental exposure and best preserve trace evidence.

All material removed from the grave area should be screened in an effort to discover additional evidence that might have eluded investigators upon the initial excavation and removal process. For this step, the material is sifted through screens of various widths, in order to systematically process and discover evidence of various sizes (**Figure 18–12**). If the material removed is mud, then water can be used to wash the material through the screen grates. Those individuals responsible for screening material should be experienced in the identification of small bones and other forensically significant material. The bones of small children, teeth, and broken hyoid bones for instance are quite small and often go undetected by the untrained eye.

Throughout the excavation process, at regular intervals and when encountering items of importance, photographs and/or video should be taken. This will ensure proper documentation of the event as well as serve as a record for the measures undertaken in an effort to properly process the evidence associated with the case (**Figure 18–13**).

When the remains have been completely exposed, they should be removed to a body bag for transportation and examination to the medical examiner's office. Personnel must also remember to inspect the surface areas of the original grave excavation for the presence of toolmarks or footwear impressions that could help in identifying a suspect. After the body has been removed, the floor of the grave should be excavated and screened down several additional inches in order to ensure that any artifacts that may have settled (teeth, bullets, etc.) are recovered.

FIGURE 18–12 Crime scene personnel process material associated with a clandestine gravesite

FIGURE 18–13 Crime scene personnel document a clandestine gravesite

Sketching and Mapping the Scene

There are a number of methods to choose from when sketching and mapping the scene of a clandestine gravesite. The important thing to remember is that with a burial, a minimum of two sketches will be necessary. The documentation process should include an overhead view and an elevation view at the very minimum (**Figure 18–14**).

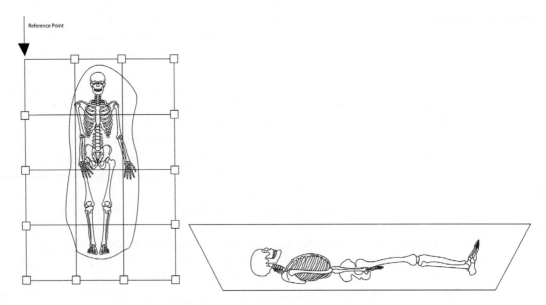

FIGURE 18–14   Mapping and sketching a clandestine gravesight
Courtesy of Ellie Bruchez, University of Wisconsin-Platteville.

WRAP UP

Chapter Summary

While each investigation and each crime scene presents its own challenges there are some that call upon a crime scene investigator to utilize very specialized training. Two of the most challenging crime scenes encountered by crime scene personnel are those involving underwater crime scenes and the investigation of buried remains. Each requires additional skills above and beyond the "routine" crime scene processing methodology. These situations present additional difficulties and hazards to crime scene personnel. The work is hard and logistically cumbersome. However, when employed, the proper processing of these difficult scenes can be the turning point in a case.

All too often, underwater crime scenes and scenes involving buried remains are not properly documented or processed. This failure can result in a loss, contamination, or inadmissibility of the evidence. Proper scene processing and documentation methods will ensure that the evidence is located, properly documented, preserved, and able to be used in subsequent litigation. It is important that the investigation team be properly trained and take part in ongoing training that is specifically related to matters of crime scene documentation and processing methods involving the underwater environment and clandestine gravesites. What is not looked for will not be found. What is not found cannot be analyzed to uncover the truth.

Review Questions

1. What are the two benefits of using floating marker buoys?

2. DMORT is the acronym for _____.

3. Which federal agency established USERTs and how are they used?

4. A common misconception is that submerged evidence lacks the _____ of evidence found top-side.

5. Another name for the safety diver is the _____.

6. The two types of scenes that need to be processed in an underwater investigation are _____ and _____.

7. Approximately how much larger than actual size will objects underwater appear?

8. Silt, sediment, algae, and pollution can create what are called _____ conditions.

9. The jacket-like piece of equipment used to keep the diver neutrally buoyant is called a _____.

10. Pushing a metal rod into the ground and marking where the rod enters more easily than its surroundings in order to determine the location of burial is known as _____.

References

Becker, R. F. (2000). Myths of underwater recovery operations. *The FBI Law Enforcement Bulletin, 69*, 1–5.

Becker, R. F. (2005). *Underwater forensic investigation.* Upper Saddle River, NJ: Prentice Hall.

Federal Bureau of Investigation (FBI). (2009). Retrieved October 2, 2012 from: http://www.fbi.gov/news/stories/2009/august/diveteam_082109

Ramey Burns, K. R. (2006). *Forensic anthropology training manual* (2nd ed.). Upper Saddle River, NJ: Prentice Hall.

Appendix A

Crime Scene Investigation Historical Timeline

Date	Historically Significant Event
	Ancient
Prehistoric	Evidence of fingerprints in early paintings and rock carvings found throughout the human-populated world.
	1000s
c. 1000	An attorney within the Roman courts proved that bloody palm prints were intended to frame a blind man in his mother's murder.
	1100s
1100s	Establishment of the *Crowners* (First Coroner's Office) in England.
	1200s
1248	The Chinese book entitled, *Xi Yuan Ji Lu* (*Collected Cases of Injustice Rectified*) described how to distinguish drowning due to strangulation. This was the first known record of medical knowledge being applied to crime solution.
	1500s
1543	Andreas Vesalius publishes *De Humani Corporis Fabrica*, a seven-volume book on the structure of the human body. This essentially defined the science of anatomy.
1554	Ambrose Paré's research relating to gunshot wounds (GSWs) published. His official autopsy studies were an effort to describe how GSWs were inflicted and to prove that they were not themselves poisonous.
	1700s
1784	In England, John Toms was convicted of the crime of murder based upon the first documented use of physical matching evidence. In the case, a torn edge of newspaper was found within a firearm that in turn matched a remaining piece discovered within his pocket.

Date	Historically Significant Event Period
	1800s
1813	In France, Mathiew Orfila was credited with the development of the science of toxicology and with the first recorded use of a microscope to analyze blood and semen stains.
1835	Henry Goddard was the first credited with the analysis of ballistic evidence to catch a murderer. His analysis involved visible flaw comparison in a bullet that was then traced back to the mold that produced it.
1845	The New York Police Department was established.
1849	In Chicago, Allen Pinkerton was appointed as the city's first detective. This was noteworthy because it was the first known separation of investigations and police patrol.
1857	The New York Police Department established an investigative division and developed a photo gallery of criminals.
1858	In India, British civil servant William James Herschel used thumbprints to identify Indian workers who signed official contracts. This was the first official use of the observed unique patterns of an individual's fingerprint.
1865	The United States Secret Service was created in response to an increase in finding counterfeit currency.
1870	The United States Department of Justice was created.
1879	In France, Alphonse Bertillon developed the first scientific method of identification, known as anthropometry.
1880	In Tokyo, Scottish physician Henry Faulds published a paper in the peer-reviewed scientific journal, *Nature*, suggesting that fingerprints at a crime scene could be used to identify a criminal. In one of the first recorded cases involving fingerprints, Faulds used his theory to eliminate suspicion of an innocent man and identify the criminal in a burglary in Tokyo.
1887	The first Sherlock Holmes detective story, *A Study in Scarlet*, was written by Sir Arthur Conan Doyle. Doyle referred to the not yet developed science of serology within the text.

Date	Historically Significant Event Period
1893	In Germany, Hans Gross published *Handbuch fur Unter-suchungsrichter als System der Kriminalistik (Criminal Investigation)*, the first known treatise on criminal investigation. This text provided the first descriptions of the importance of reconstructing a crime scene and the use of physical evidence in crime solving. Gross is often credited with creation of the term criminalistics.
	1900s
1901	Austrian biologist and physician, Dr. Karl Landsteiner discovered human blood grouping relating to whole blood.
1903	At Leavenworth Federal Penitentiary, Kansas, Will and William West were indistinguishable by visual and anthropometric measurements. This showed the weakness of the system of anthropometry and strengthened the science of fingerprints after the men were later (1905) easily differentiated by examining their fingerprints.
1907	Chief of Police August Vollmer, in Berkley, CA, instituted a formal procedure for the handling of physical evidence after a failure to indict a suspect.
1910	Edmond Locard established the first police crime laboratory in Lyon, France.
1915	In Italy, Dr. Leon Lattes developed a method to determine blood grouping of a dried bloodstain.
1920	In France, Locard published *L'enquete Criminelle et les Methods Scientifique*, in which he presented his cross transfer exchange principle, stating "every contact leaves a trace."
1923	August Vollmer established the first forensic laboratory in the United States at the Los Angeles Police Department.
1929	In Chicago, the "Scientific Crime Laboratory of Chicago" was established by Colonel Calvin Goddard, its first director, at the Law School of Northwestern University, after his work on the St. Valentine's Day Massacre.
1932	The Federal Bureau of Investigation (FBI) established its crime laboratory.
1937	Dr. Paul Leland Kirk established the first university criminalistics program at the University of California-Berkeley.
1950	The American Academy of Forensic Sciences (AAFS) was formed, and began publication of the *Journal of Forensic Sciences* (JFS).

Date	Historically Significant Event Period
1953	Dr. Kirk published *Crime Investigation: Physical Evidence and the Police Laboratory*, which brought increased scientific rigor into criminal investigations nationwide.
1966	The Supreme Court ruled in *Miranda v. Arizona* that the accused has the right to remain silent and that statements made by defendants while in law enforcement custody may not be used against them unless the police have advised them of this right. This case had a significant impact on the value of physical evidence.
1980's	Automated Fingerprint Identification System (AFIS) was established. This helped to dramatically increase fingerprint comparison rates.
1987	DNA profiling was introduced for the first time in a United States criminal court to convict Tommy Lee Andrews of a series of sexual assaults in Orlando, Florida.
1999	The FBI upgraded and integrated its computerized AFIS system, dubbing it the Integrated Automated Fingerprint Identification System. This system allowed for paperless submission, storage, and search capabilities.
1999	The ATF and FBI combine to organize the National Integrated Ballistics Information Network (NIBIN). This system allowed for the paperless comparison, submission, storage, and search of firearms and ballistic evidence.
2002	FBI forms scientific working groups to explore and define functional guidelines for various subdisciplines of forensic science.
2005	Forensic Technology Incorporated (FTI) announced the development of a three-dimensional bullet imaging system, IBIS-TRAX 3D, which uses confocal microscopy to simulate a three-dimensional image of fired bullets and cartridge cases.

Sources

Block, E. B. (1979). *Science vs. crime: The evolution of the police lab*. San Francisco, CA: Cragmont Publications.

Dillon, D. (1977). *A history of criminalistics in the United States 1850–1950*. Doctoral Thesis. Berkeley, CA: University of California, Berkeley.

Else, W. M., & Garrow, J. M. (1934). The detection of crime. *The Police Journal*, xiv–xv.

Gaensslen, R. E. (1983). *Sourcebook in forensic serology*. Washington, DC: U.S. Government Printing Office.

Gerber, S. M., Saferstein, R. (1997). *More chemistry and crime: From Marsh arsenic test to DNA profile*. Washington, DC: American Chemical Society.

German, E. (1999). *Cyanoacrylate (Superglue) Discovery Timeline*. Retrieved August 23, 2009, from http://onin.com/fp/cyanoho.html

German, E. (1999). *The History of Fingerprints*. Retrieved August 23, 2009, from http://onin.com/fp/fphistory.html

Kind, S., & Overman, M. (1972). *Science against crime*. New York: Aldus Book Limited, Doubleday.

Morland, N. (1950). *An outline of scientific criminology*. New York: Philosophical Library.

National Institute of Justice. *Firearm Examiner Training: History*. U.S. Department of Justice. Retrieved on July 6, 2012 from http://www.nij.gov/training/firearms-training/module02/fir_m02_t19.htm

Olsen, R. D., Sr. (2008). A fingerprint fable: The Will and William West case. (Initially published in: [1987]. *Identification News,* which became *Journal of Forensic Identification*, 37, 11.) Retrieved August 23, 2009, from http://www.gaston.k12.nc.us/schools/northgaston/Marr%20Class%20Webpage/Forensic%20Science/PDF/Will%20and%20William%20West.pdf

Thorwald, J. (1966). *Crime and science*. Translation, Winston R & Winston C. New York: Harcourt, Brace & World, Inc.

Appendix B

Forensic Databases

Integrated Ballistic Identification System (IBIS)

Maintained by the U.S. Bureau of Alcohol, Tobacco, Firearms and Explosives' National Integrated Ballistic Information Network, this forensic database contains bullet and cartridge casings that have been retrieved from crime scenes and test-fires of guns found at a crime scene or on a suspect. A limitation of this database is that there must be a suspected gun in order to make a comparison. Because the database contains information on bullets and casings—and not on specific guns—a test-fire bullet from a gun must be compared to a bullet found at a crime scene, for example, to determine whether a bullet came from a specific gun. A comparison microscope is used to perform a manual examination. For more information, see http://www.atf.gov.

Paint Data Query (PDQ)

Maintained by the Royal Canadian Mounted Police (RCMP), PDQ contains the chemical compositions of paint from most domestic and foreign car manufacturers and the majority of vehicles marketed in North America after 1973. The PDQ software is free to agencies that supply a minimum of 60 paint samples per year. The database information comes from the street (more than 60% from body shops and junkyards) and from manufacturers. In 1998, the RCMP entered into agreements with the German Forensic Institute and the Japanese National Police Agency, which resulted in 1,500 samples being added to the database each year. Due to proprietary reasons, not all manufacturers, however, are willing to divulge the chemical composition of paint used on their vehicles. If a particular sample has not been entered into the database from the street, it is not possible to obtain a match.

Each paint layer is examined to determine the spectra and chemical composition. The chemical components and proportions are coded into the database. These known samples are compared against a paint sample from a crime scene or a suspect's vehicle to search the make, model, and year of manufacture of a vehicle involved in a hit-and-run or other criminal activity. For more information, see http://www.rcmp-grc.gc.ca.

TreadMark

The number of shoe prints at a crime scene can be so large that the process of impression recovery becomes very time consuming. TreadMark is a commercial product that uses four parameters—pattern, size, damage, and wear—to identify individual outsole impressions. These are then compared with shoe print data from two sources: suspects in custody and crime scenes. A match could yield the name, date of birth, criminal record number, places of interest, and similar offenses for possible suspects.

Impressions from a crime scene are obtained using the current recovery methods of photograph, gel lift, dust lift, and adhesive lift. These are input directly into the analytical system by high-resolution digital imaging. The same procedure is used with an impression of a suspect's shoe print: It is photographed using a high-resolution digital camera, and these impressions (along with the offender's details) are input into the analytical system, where the operator can measure, analyze, and compare crime scene and suspect images. Both image sources can be searched within themselves and against each other, allowing such images to be transmitted to other users. For more information, see http://www.csiequipment.com/systems.aspx.

SoleMate

This commercial database contains information—manufacturer, date of market release, an image or offset print of the sole, and pictorial images of the uppers—for more than 12,000 sports, work, and casual shoes. Sold on DVD, the product is updated and distributed to subscribers every 3 months. One limitation is that different manufacturers often use the same sole unit and, therefore, it may be difficult to determine the exact make and model of a shoe. The software links such records, however, so that all footwear that might match a crime scene print can be considered.

The pattern of an unidentified shoe print is assigned a set of codes to isolate basic features, such as circles, diamonds, zigzags, curves, and blocks. Options, with variations, are presented pictorially, which allows an investigator to code features that best match the shoe print. These codes form the database search, with results presented in descending order of pattern correlation. For more information, contact Foster & Freeman USA Inc., at 888-445-5048 or http://www.fosterfreeman.com.

TreadMate

The pattern of an unidentified tire mark is assigned a set of codes for pattern features, such as waves, lines, diamonds, zigzags, curves, and blocks, which then form the basis of the database search. Results are presented in descending order of correlation. For more information, contact Foster & Freeman USA Inc., at 888-445-5048 or http://www.fosterfreeman.com.

Forensic Information System for Handwriting (FISH)

Maintained by the U.S. Secret Service, this database enables document examiners to scan and digitize text writings such as threatening correspondence. A document examiner scans and digitizes an extended body of handwriting, which is then plotted as arithmetic and geometric values. Searches are made on images in the database, producing a list of probable "hits." The questioned writings, along with the closest hits, are then submitted to the Document Examination Section for confirmation. For more information, see http://www.secretservice.gov/forensics.shtml.

International Ink Library

The collection—maintained jointly by the U.S. Secret Service and the Internal Revenue Service—includes more than 9,500 inks, dating from the 1920s. Every year, pen and ink manufacturers are asked to submit their new ink formulations, which are chemically tested and added to the reference collection. Open-market purchases of pens and inks ensure that the library is as comprehensive as possible.

Samples are chemically analyzed and compared with library specimens. This may identify the type and brand of writing instrument, which can be used to determine the earliest possible date that a document could have been produced. If the sample matches an ink on file, a notation is made in the database. The U.S. Secret Service generally provides assistance to law enforcement on a case-by-case basis. For more information, contact 202-406-5708.

Ident-a-Drug

The Therapeutic Research Center, a private company, publishes a computer program and book to help identify drugs in tablet or capsule form. To make an identification, sufficient information about the unknown drug must be available. Data used for comparison purposes contain codes that are imprinted on tablets and capsules, information on color and shape, the national drug code (NDC #), and drug class. Schedule information is shown if the drug is a narcotic or in one of the U.S. Drug Enforcement Administration schedules. For more information, see http://www. therapeuticresearch.com.

Ignitable Liquids Reference Collection (ILRC)

Maintained by the National Center for Forensic Science, this database and associated liquid repository allows a laboratory to isolate an ignitable liquid of interest for inclusion in an in-house reference collection. Designed for screening purposes only, it parallels—but does not replace— American Standard Testing Materials requirements for an in-house reference collection. A laboratory does not need to adopt the ILRC classification system to use this database.

Users enter the name of the liquid into the searchable database. The database can also be organized by classification of the liquid for quick reference. Users can then purchase samples of the liquid. Commercial samples are obtained directly from manufacturers and distributors. The products are then repackaged for distribution using the product name and sent to forensic science laboratories. For more information, see http://ilrc.ucf.edu.

Integrated Automated Fingerprint Identification System (IAFIS)

This FBI-maintained database contains:

- Fingerprints acquired after arrest at the city, county, state, and federal levels.
- Fingerprints acquired through background checks for employment, licensing, and other noncriminal justice purposes (if authorized by state or federal law).
- Latent prints found at crime scenes.

Although IAFIS offers electronic search and storage capabilities, it has some limitations. The database contains the fingerprints of only a small percentage of the population. Moreover, to make a comparison, the latent print must be of sufficient quality to identify certain individual characteristics. For example, the cores and deltas must be present in the print to determine the orientation of the print.

The database receives data electronically, in hard copy, or in a machine-readable data format. IAFIS accepts, stores, and distributes photographs, including the results of remote 10-print and latent searches. These are returned electronically to the requesting agencies with a list of potential matching candidates and their corresponding fingerprints for comparison and identification. For more information, see http://www.fbi.gov/hq/cjisd/iafis.htm or contact the FBI's Criminal Justice Information Services Division at 304-625-2000.

Combined DNA Index System (CODIS)

This FBI-run database blends forensic science and computer technology into a tool for solving violent crimes. CODIS enables federal, state, and local crime labs to exchange and compare DNA profiles electronically, thereby linking crimes to each other and to convicted offenders. CODIS uses two indexes: (1) the Convicted Offender Index, which contains profiles of convicted offenders, and (2) the Forensic Index, which contains profiles from crime scene evidence.

Searches are performed to find a match between a sample of biologic evidence and an offender profile. Matches made between the Forensic and Offender Indexes provide investigators with the identity of a suspect. DNA analysts in the laboratories share matching profiles, then contact each other. See http://www.fbi.gov/hq/lab/html/codis1.htm.

Appendix C

Crime Scene Equipment

TABLE C–1 Equipment Needed by the Initial Responding Officer(s)

Essential*	Optional
Consent/search forms	Audiotape recorder
Crime scene barricade tape	Camera with flash and extra film
First-aid kit	Chalk
Flares	Directional marker/compass
Flashlight and extra batteries	Disinfectant
Paper bags	Maps
Personal protective equipment (PPE)	Plastic bags
Reflective vest	
Tape measure	
Tarps to protect evidence from the weather	
Traffic cones	
Waterless hand wash (towelette with germicide)	
Wireless phone	

* Essential items should be in police vehicles or readily available to the initial responding officer(s).

The National Institute of Justice. (2004, June). *Crime Scene Investigation: A Reference for Law Enforcement Training*, U.S. DOJ, Office of Justice Programs. NCJ200160.

TABLE C–2 Equipment Needed by the Crime Scene Investigator/ Evidence Technician

Essential*	Optional
Bindle paper	Audiotape recorder
Biohazard bags	Bloodstain pattern examination kit
Body fluid collection kit	Business cards
Camera (35 mm) with flash/film tripod	Chalk
Casting materials	Chemical enhancement supplies
Consent/search forms	Entomology (insect) collection kit
Crime scene barricade tape	Extension cords

Essential*	Optional
Cutting instruments (knives, box cutter, scalpel, scissors)	Flares
Directional marker/compass	Forensic light source (alternate light source, ultraviolet (UV) lamp/laser, goggles)
Disinfectant	Generator
Evidence collection containers	Gunshot residue kit
Evidence identifiers	Laser trajectory kit
Evidence seals/tape	Maps
First-aid kit	Marking paint/snow wax
Flashlight and extra batteries	Metal detector
High-intensity lights	Mirror
Latent print kit	Phone listing (important numbers)
Magnifying glass	Privacy screens
Measuring devices	Protrusion rod set
Permanent markers	Reflective vest
Personal protective equipment (PPE)	Refrigeration or cooling unit
Photographic scale (ruler)	Respirators with filters
Presumptive blood test supplies	Roll of string
Sketch paper	Rubber bands
Tool kit	Sexual assault evidence collection kit (victim and suspect)
Tweezers/forceps	Shoe print lifting equipment
	Templates (scene and human)
	Thermometer
	Traffic cones
	Trajectory rods
	Video recorder
	Wireless phone

* Essential items should be in police vehicles or readily available to the crime scene investigator/evidence technician.

The National Institute of Justice. (2004, June). *Crime Scene Investigation: A Reference for Law Enforcement Training*, U.S. DOJ, Office of Justice Programs. NCJ200161.

Appendix D

Examples of Evidence Collection Kits

Blood Collection

Bindle
Coin envelopes
Disposable scalpels
Distilled water
Ethanol
Evidence identifiers
Latex gloves
Photographic ruler (ABFO scales)
Presumptive chemicals
Sterile gauze
Sterile swabs
Test tubes/test tube rack

Bloodstain Pattern Documentation

ABFO scales
Calculator
Laser pointer
Permanent markers
Protractor
String
Tape

Excavation

Cones/markers
Evidence identifiers

Metal detectors
Paint brushes
Shovels/trowels
Sifting screens
String
Weights
Wooden/metal stakes

Fingerprint

Black and white film
Brushes
Chemical enhancement supplies
Cyanoacrylate (superglue) wand packets
Flashlight
Forensic light source
Lift cards
Lift tape
Measurement scales
Powders

Impression

Bowls/mixing containers
Boxes
Dental stone
Evidence identifiers
Measurement scales
Permanent markers
Snow print wax
Water

Pattern Print Lifter

Chemical enhancement supplies
Electrostatic dust lifter
Gel lifter
Wide format lift tape

Toolmarks

Casting materials

Trace Evidence Collection

Acetate sheet protectors
Bindle paper
Clear tape/adhesive lift

Flashlight (oblique lighting)
Forceps/tweezers
Glass vials
Slides and slide mailers
Trace evidence vacuum with disposable
    collection filters

Trajectory

Calculator
Canned smoke
Mannequin
Laser
Mirror
Protractor
String
Trajectory rods

Source: National Institute of Justice. (June, 2004). *Crime Scene Investigation: A Reference for Law Enforcement Training*, U.S. Department of Justice, Office of Justice Programs. NCJ200160.

Appendix E

Processing the Scene of Mass Fatality Incidents

Initial Considerations

The complete and accurate identification of remains and evidentiary processing begins at the scene of the mass fatality incident. In most circumstances, the medical examiner/coroner has the ultimate responsibility for the recovery and identification of the deceased. The remains/evidence processing teams have to assume that any mass fatality scene could be a crime scene. They are expected to carefully document every piece of physical evidence recovered from the scene. The scene should be large enough to ensure its protection from public access until all agencies have agreed to release the scene. Although teams can discard information later, scene processing always involves the physical destruction of the actual scene, and additional information may not be recoverable after the scene has been processed and released. Efficient information recovery proceeds from the least intrusive to the more intrusive (e.g., taking photographs is allowed only after teams locate, flag, and sequentially number the remains). Although protocols may change in the middle of an event depending on the scope and extent of the incident, documenting every aspect of the remains and the evidence processing operation will ensure the preservation of information.

Before processing the scene, the incident command, in consultation with the medical examiner/coroner, is expected to:

A. Identify team leaders responsible for remains/evidence processing.

B. Determine the size and composition of the remains/evidence processing teams (usually a function of the team leaders), which may include:

    1. Medical examiner/coroner

    2. Forensic anthropologist

    3. Odontologist

    4. Police crime scene investigator

    5. Forensic photographer

    6. Evidence technician

    7. Scribe/notetaker

C. Integrate the remains/evidence-processing teams according to existing interagency jurisdiction and chain of command. The scope and extent of the mass fatality incident determines the number of agencies involved.

D. Establish and/or verify control over access to the scene.

E. Establish communication among transport vehicles, the incident command, and the morgue.

F. Establish an on-scene remains-processing station.

G. Consider the recovery of remains and personal effects as evidence and preserve the chain of custody throughout the recovery operation.

Effective organization and composition of the remains/evidence-processing teams ensures the proper collection and preservation of remains, personal effects, and evidence.

Establish a Chain of Custody

Establishing and maintaining a chain of custody verifies the integrity of the evidence. The remains/evidence-processing teams are expected to maintain the chain of custody throughout the recovery process. Throughout the investigation, those responsible for preserving the chain of custody are expected to:

A. Document the time of arrival and departure of other personnel at the scene.

B. Establish a standard numbering system at the scene that relates back to the location of the remains/evidence. Ensure that the numbering system is:

    1. Internally consistent and cross-referenced with other agencies

    2. Expandable

    3. Simple to interpret

    4. Capable of indicating where the remains, personal effects, and evidence were recovered

    5. Capable of tracking remains, personal effects, and evidence throughout the investigation

    6. Related to subsequent individual results without error

    7. Integrated into all protocols and reports

C. Document the collection of evidence by recording its location at the scene and time of collection.

D. Document all transfers of custody (including the name of the recipient and the date and manner of transfer).

Maintaining the chain of custody by properly documenting, collecting, and preserving the evidence ensures its integrity throughout the investigation.

Scene Imaging and Mapping Principle

The remains/evidence-processing teams can use a grid system to divide the scene into manageable units to show the location and context of items (i.e., their positions relative to other items) at the scene. A grid system may need to be three-dimensional.

The remains/evidence-processing teams are expected to:

A. Record overall views of the scene (e.g., wide-angle, aerial, 360-degree) with a designated photographer to relate items spatially within the scene and relative to the surrounding area. A combination of still photography, videotaping, and other techniques is most effective. Remember to:

    1. Consider muting the audio portion of any video recording unless there is narration.

    2. Minimize the presence of scene personnel in photographs/videos.

    3. Maintain photo and video logs.

B. Identify boundaries and fixed landmarks (e.g., a utility pole, building corners, or global positioning system [GPS]–located points).

C. Establish a primary point of reference for the scene.

D. Divide the scene into identifiable sectors and create a checkerboard.

E. Use accurate measuring devices.

The remains/evidence-processing teams are responsible for establishing an accurate, logical mapping system for the scene.

Document the Location of Remains, Personal Effects, and Evidence

The remains/evidence-processing teams are expected to include documentation in the permanent record of the scene. Photographic documentation creates a permanent record of the scene that supplements the written incident reports. The teams are expected to complete this documentation, including location information, before the removal or disturbance of any items. Videotaping may serve as an additional record but not as a replacement for still photography.

The remains/evidence-processing teams are expected to:

A. Photograph individual items (midrange and close) with an identifier (e.g., a grid identifier and/or individual item number) and scale. Consider including a directional compass arrow that points north.

B. Attach identifying numbers and flag all remains, personal effects, and evidence in the grid:

    1. Use a waterproof ink marker.

    2. Ensure that numbers on the flags correspond with those on the remains and are also clearly discernible in the photograph.

C. Ensure that the systematic on-scene documentation of all remains, personal effects, and evidence includes:

    1. The sequential numbering system at the scene

    2. Recovery location information

    3. Notes that may help with personal identification or scene reconstruction (e.g., generic descriptors, such as a foot or shoe)

    4. Documentation of the evidence collector (e.g., the collector's unique identifier and the date and time of recovery)

D. Conduct the systematic removal of remains, personal effects, and evidence:

    1. Using a permanent marker, mark the outside of the primary bag or container and tag with the identifying number, the collector's unique identifier, and the date and time of collection.

    2. Place the same identifying number on the inside of the body bag or other bag or container.

    3. Do not remove any personal effects on or with the remains. Transport all personal effects on or with the remains to the morgue.

    4. When necessary, wrap the head before moving it to protect cranial/facial fragments and teeth.

E. After removing the remains, photograph the areas from which evidence was recovered to document whether anything was under the remains.

F. After the remains/evidence-processing teams have cleared the area and before releasing the scene for public access, conduct a final shoulder-to-shoulder sweep search to locate any additional items.

The remains/evidence-processing teams must properly document the collection of all remains, personal effects, and evidence before removing them from the scene.

On-Scene Staging Area

The remains/evidence processing teams should use the on-scene staging area for checking documentation, maintaining the chain of custody, and conducting potential triage functions. At this area, the remains/evidence-processing teams can add notes to aid personal identification at the morgue (e.g., comments about tattoos, marks, and scars) and identify contents of body bags (e.g., watches, body parts). The remains/evidence-processing teams are responsible for closing and locking body bags at this point.

The remains/evidence-processing teams are expected to:

A. Establish a staging area proximate to the incident scene that provides maximum security from public and media scrutiny and access (including a no-fly zone over the site).

B. Remand evidence that is not required to accompany the remains to the mortuary to the custody of the appropriate agency.

C. Maintain the chain of custody of body bags:

    1. Maintain a log of the body bags that are transported from the staging area to the morgue.

    2. Record drivers' names and the license numbers of vehicles.

    3. Record dates and times that all vehicles leave for the morgue.

D. Maintain equipment and supplies at the staging area. Inventory resources may include:

    1. A large tent

    2. Body/storage bags

    3. Litters, gurneys, and stretchers for remains transport

    4. Refrigeration vehicles

    5. Emergency lighting

    6. Sawhorses with plywood boards for makeshift examination tables

    7. Tarpaulins or other screening materials to create visual barriers

    8. Decontamination control

    9. Inventory control system

    10. Equipment storage

    11. Personal protective equipment

E. Notify the morgue when transport of remains will begin.

The remains/evidence-processing teams are expected to maintain a secure triage area for initial examination of remains and other evidence and to ensure secure transport to the morgue. Strongly consider placing forensic identification specialists at the staging area, as the initial evaluations at this point will dictate the efficiency of subsequent morgue operations.

Source: National Institute of Justice (NIJ). (2005, June). *Mass Fatality Incidents: A Guide for Human Forensic Identification*. Retrieved August 23, 2009, from http://www.ncjrs.gov/pdffiles1/nij/199758.pdf.

Appendix F

Professional Organizations Pertaining to Crime Scene Investigation

American Academy of Forensic Science
http://www.aafs.org/

American Board of Criminalistics
http://www.criminalistics.com/

American Board of Forensic Document Examiners
http://www.abfde.org/

American Board of Medicolegal Death Investigators
http://www.slu.edu/organizations/abmdi/

American College of Forensic Examiners
http://www.acfei.com/

Association for Crime Scene Reconstruction
http://www.acsr.org/

Association of Firearm and Tool Mark Examiners
http://www.afte.org/

Association of Forensic Document Examiners
http://www.afde.org/

Evidence Photographers International Council
http://www.epic-photo.org/

International Association of Arson Investigators
http://www.firearson.com/

International Association of Bloodstain Pattern Analysis
http://www.iabpa.org/

International Association of Computer Investigative Specialists
http://www.iacis.com/

International Association of Forensic Nurses
http://www.forensicnurse.org/

International Association of Identification
http://www.theiai.org/

International Crime Scene Investigators Association
http://www.icsia.org/

National Association of Document Examiners
http://documentexaminers.org/

Glossary

Accelerant: Any substance used to accelerate (and sometimes direct) the spread of a fire.

Accreditation: An endorsement of a forensic laboratory's policies and procedures by law enforcement professional organizations or industry; a necessary component of establishing credibility within the court system. To qualify for accreditation, a crime laboratory must meet minimum requirements set forth by the certifying authority.

ACE-V: Acronym for Analysis, Comparison, Evaluation, and Verification. A method devised for the scientific comparison of prints to either identify a print (via individualization, as having originated from the same source) or exclude impressions as having no common origin.

Adipocere: The hydration and dehydrogenation of the body's fat, which results in an off-white, waxy, clay-like substance that in many cases preserves the body, and retards the decomposition process; commonly found in the subcutaneous tissues of body extremities, the face, buttocks, breasts, and in individuals with a high percentage of body fat.

Agglutination: The process that creates a network of linked cells from the antibodies that attach themselves to the cells.

Algor Mortis: Postmortem cooling of the body. Heat loss will occur until the body reaches the temperature of the surrounding environment (ambient temperature).

Alternate Light Source (ALS): Light-emitting devices supplied with colored filters that filter the source light so that the potential evidence can be viewed with light of a narrow wavelength range, rather than at the usual "white light" viewing range.

American Academy of Forensic Sciences (AAFS): A multidisciplinary professional organization that provides leadership to advance science and its application to the legal system. The objectives of the Academy are to promote education, foster research, improve practice, and encourage collaboration in the forensic sciences.

Antemortem: Prior to death.

Anthropometry: A series of 11 body measurements of the bony parts of the body, and an in-depth description of marks (scars, moles, warts, tattoos, etc.) on the surface of the body; developed by Alphonse Bertillon.

Antibody: A substance in the body that reacts with another substance called an antigen.

Antigens: A substance, such as bacterium, virus, or protein, that, when coming into contact with an appropriate tissue in an animal body, stimulates that tissue to produce a state of resistance or sensitivity to infection by the organism (bacterium or virus) or to a toxic substance (such as dust).

Area of Convergence: A two-dimensional point, derived from analyzing bloodstain directionality. It is used to ascertain the point from where an event occurred (i.e., impact) that led to the subsequent dispersal of the blood. This is only a two-dimensional explanation (X and Y axis) and does not determine how far away from the area that the blood event originated; instead it provides an area in which to determine such information.

Area of Origin: (1) Fire. The large track of space or area where a fire would have started. It can be located where the fire was able to grow and develop. (2) Blood Pattern Analysis. By establishing the impact angles of representative bloodstains and projecting their trajectories back to a common axis (Z), extended at 90 degrees from the area of convergence, an approximate location of where the blood source was when it was impacted may be established.

Arson: The willful and malicious burning of a person's property.

Asphyxia: The interruption of oxygenation of the brain (e.g., drowning, strangulation, etc.).

Associative Evidence: Evidence that can be attributed to, or associated with, a particular person, place, or thing, thus establishing inferred connectivity.

Automated Fingerprint Identification System (AFIS): An automatic pattern recognition system, for the identification of fingerprints that consists of three fundamental stages: data acquisition, feature extraction, and decision-making.

Autopsy: The medical dissection and examination of a body in order to determine the cause of death; entails the removal of internal organs through incisions made in the chest, abdomen, and head.

Backlogged: A case where the analysis has not been completed within 30 days of the item being submitted to the lab.

Ballistics: The study of a projectile (most likely from a firearm) in motion.

Barrier Protection: Involves creating a barrier between the personnel and their surroundings to ensure that they are not contaminated by the scene and that they themselves do not contaminate the scene and evidence therein.

Bayesian Statistics: A statistical method based on Bayes's theorem (a theorem in probability theory named for Thomas Bayes) used in clinical decision analysis and in the evaluation of diagnostic tests, disease progression, case control studies, and certain types of clinical trials.

Biological Profile: A description of an individual in such a way that law enforcement or acquaintances can narrow the range of possible identities. The profile is assembled by studying the remains of an individual, and noting characteristics of shape and size, which may allow an estimation of height, build, age, sex, ancestry, and any individualistic features such as tattoos, jewelry, medical apparatus, and clothing.

Black Water Diving: Conditions where silt, sediment, algae, and pollution create underwater visibility that is typically less than one foot.

Bloodborne Pathogen: Microorganisms found within the blood that can cause infection and disease, and may be transported in other biological fluids.

Bloodstain Pattern Analysis (BPA): The science of examining and interpreting blood present at a bloodshed event in order to determine what events occurred, in what order, and who possibly left the stains.

Blood Type: Determined by the kind of antigen on the surface of each red blood cell.

Bore: Interior of a firearm barrel.

Buoyancy Control Device (BCD): The jacket-like piece of equipment used to keep a diver neutrally buoyant.

Cadaver Dogs: Canines that are trained to seek out the scent of decomposition; used in area searches for a victim(s) or for clandestine gravesites.

Cadaveric Spasm: Immediate stiffening of a dead body, with no prior period of flaccidity and no extended onset. It will typically involve the victim's hands clenched around an object, such as a weapon, debris from a lake floor, clothing, or another object, and sometimes is associated with events (i.e., drowning or homicide) that involved considerable excitement or tension preceding death.

Caliber: Diameter of the bore of a rifled firearm, measured between opposing lands; usually expressed in hundredths of an inch or millimeters.

Cast-off Patterns: Bloodstain patterns created when blood is released from an object through the influence of centrifugal acceleration, cessation, or stop-action.

Cause of Death: The injury or disease responsible for the pathological and physiological disturbances that resulted in death; the medical reason for death.

Certification: A voluntary process of peer review by which a practitioner is recognized as having attained the professional qualifications necessary to practice in one or more disciplines of criminalistics.

Chain of Custody: A log or other record of who collected and subsequently handled evidence of a crime. Accurate accounting strengthens the court case; if evidence is found to be illegally collected, whether intentionally or unintentionally, then it will be found to be inadmissible in court.

Circumstantial Evidence: A series of facts that, although not the fact at issue, through inference tends to prove a fact at issue.

Clandestine Laboratories: Where the production of illicit compounds are done whether or not the laboratories are true laboratories.

Classification: A formula given to a complete set of 10 fingers as they appear on a fingerprint card generally based on pattern type, ridge count, or ridge tracing. The FBI National Crime Information Center—Fingerprint Classification (NCIC-FPC) and Henry System are used to classify prints.

Close-Up Photographs: A type of image that allows the viewer to see all evident detail on a particular item of evidence. This frame is filled with the evidence itself; photos are taken with and without a scale; and can be called comparison, examination, or macro photographs.

Code of Ethics: A contract signed by an employee who agrees to function by the terms of employment or membership. This code lists what the department or organization believes are acceptable behaviors, professional expectations, and values to which employees should adhere. Failure to comply with the code can result in job dismissal or removal of membership and certification.

Combined DNA Index System (CODIS): An electronic database of DNA profiles administered through the Federal Bureau of Investigation (FBI), where federal, state, and local crime labs can share and compare DNA profiles to match DNA from crime scenes with convicted offenders and other crime scenes.

Command Post: Established to coordinate on-scene activities and efforts; also called incident command under the incident command and control structure. From this location, all supervisory decisions are made and the crime scene is managed.

Comparison Microscope: Two compound microscopes connected by an optical bridge; allows two specimens to be viewed side-by-side.

Complimentary Base Pairing: The unique way that the two strands of the DNA double-helix formation are bonded together. Bases in the necleotides (adenine [A], cytosine [C], guanine [G], and thymine [T]) on each strand align in specific paired combinations, where G always pairs with C, and A always pairs with T (see *Deoxyribonucleic Acid*).

Compression Evidence: Marks left when an instrument is in some way pushed or forced into a material capable of picking up an impression of the tool.

Computer Network: Two or more computers linked by data cables or by wireless connections that share or are capable of sharing resources and data.

Concentric Fractures: Cracks or breaks that appear to make a typically broken series of concentric circles around an impact point.

Conchoidal Fractures: Stress marks in glass that are shaped like arches, located perpendicularly to one side of the glass surface, and curved nearly parallel to the opposite glass surface.

Cone of Foam: In some cases of drug overdose and drowning, the victim will exhibit exudates in the form of froth emanating from the mouth and nostrils; a result of severe pulmonary edema; may appear initially off-white but will advance to pinkish in color as the decomposition process advances.

Contraband: An item that is found to be illegally possessed or for some legal reasons is illegal to possess.

Controlled Substance: A substance (typically a drug) whose possession or use is regulated by the government; Title 21 of the United States Code (21 USC) defines the substances.

Controlled Substances Act (CSA): Title II and Title III of the Comprehensive Drug Abuse Prevention and Control Act of 1970 regulate the manufacture and distribution of drugs and other substances placed by the Drug Enforcement Agency (DEA) or the Department of Health and Human Services (DHHS) into five schedules based upon medical use, potential for abuse, and safety or potential for dependence.

Cortex: The region of hair between the medulla and cuticle in the hair shaft, which contains the pigment cells responsible for imparting hair color characteristics.

Credentials: A certificate, letter, experience, or anything that provides authentication for a claim or that qualifies somebody to do something. In the context of forensic and crime scene–related work, credentials as an expert will be established by the court through questioning pertaining to the witness' education, training, and experience.

Crime: An act or the commission of an act that is forbidden by a public law and that makes the offender liable to punishment by that law.

Crime Scene: Anywhere that evidence may be located that will help explain the events that occurred.

Crime Scene Investigation (CSI): The systematic process of documenting, collecting, preserving, and interpreting physical evidence associated with an alleged crime scene, in an effort to determine the truth relating to the event in question.

Crime Scene Sketch: A permanent mapped record of the size and distance relationships of the crime scene and the physical evidence within it; serves to clarify the special information present within the photographs and video documentation, because it allows the viewer to easily gauge distances and dimensions.

Criminalistics: The application of science through the analysis of physical evidence within the enforcement of law.

Cross-Contamination: The movement or transfer of material between two objects during the investigative processing efforts; should be avoided when possible.

CSI Effect: A phenomenon whereby forensic drama television has created unreasonable expectations in the public, thereby increasing the prosecution's burden of proof, while presenting an air of infallibility with regards to forensic science; also has educated the public and increased the overall interest in the area of forensic science and crime scene work.

Cuticle: The outermost layer of hair; contains the scaly protective layer that covers the shaft of the hair. Each species has identifiable cuticle characteristics.

Cyanoacrylate Ester Fuming: A technique that stabilizes latent prints using super glue. Super glue is induced to fume and the fumes interact with latent fingerprint residue by polymerizing them, yielding a stable friction ridge impression off-white in color (see *Latent Prints*).

Daubert Standard: From the case *Daubert v. Merrell Dow Pharmaceuticals*, 509 U.S. 579 (1993), the court held that federal trial judges are the gatekeepers of scientific evidence. Under this standard, trial judges must evaluate whether testimony is both relevant and reliable, resulting in a two-pronged test of admissibility.

Death: The irreversible cessation of circulatory and respiratory functions.

Decomposition: Postmortem breakdown of body tissues.

Delay Device: An incendiary or detonation device of some type that is employed to allow the arsonist to depart the scene or establish an alibi.

Deoxyribonucleic Acid (DNA): The nucleic acid that contains the genetic instructions used for the growth, development, and programmed death for cells of all organisms and some viruses; is a double-helix structure.

Depressant: Type of psychoactive drugs that temporarily reduce or incapacitate a specific area of the body or mind; also referred to as downers and sedatives.

Detonation Point: The location point where the device was detonated.

Digital Evidence: Information and data of value to an investigation that is stored on, received, or transmitted by an electronic device.

Dillie-Koppanyi: A test for barbiturates, in whose presence the reagent turns violet-blue.

Direct Evidence: A type of evidence that proves a fact without the necessity of an inference or a presumption.

Directionality: In a crime scene, the direction that blood traveled that is determined by the bloodstains' shape.

Disaster Mortuary Operational Response Team (DMORT): A program of the U.S. Department of Health and Human Services that responds only when requested by local law enforcement agencies. Its goal is to assist local authorities during a mass fatality incident that is beyond the scope and abilities of local agencies.

Drug: Any chemical substance, other than food, which is intended for use in the diagnosis, treatment, cure, mitigation, or prevention of disease or symptoms.

Duquenois-Levine: A chemical color test that is used to confirm the presence of cannabinoids which is the primary psychoactive compound.

Electrostatic Lifting Device (ELD): A type of machine that operates by electrically charging a lifting film that has been placed over a surface bearing a dust print impression. During operation, the electrostatically charged film is drawn down to the surface, and the dust particles in the impression are attracted to the lifting film. The construction of the lifting film allows it to store the electrostatic charge and thus retain the dust particles after the power supply has been disconnected. The impression-bearing film is then viewed with an oblique light source to search for any impressions that may have been recovered.

Ethics: The study of moral standards and how they affect conduct.

Evidence: Anything that can help to prove or disprove that a crime was or was not committed, and by whom.

Excusable Homicide: Unintentional, truly accidental killing of another person; the result of an act that under normal conditions would not cause death, or from an act committed with due caution that, because of negligence on the part of the victim, results in death.

Expert Witness: A person who is called to answer questions on the stand in a court of law in order to provide specialized information relevant to the case being tried.

Expired patterns: Images created when blood is blown out of the nose, mouth, or wound as a result of air pressure and/or airflow; often numerous, relatively small stain sizes are displayed that may vary in shape.

Exsanguination: Death due to loss of blood or bleeding out.

Exterior Ballistics: The study of the flight of a projectile beginning at the muzzle end of the barrel of a firearm and terminating at the target.

Extractor: A component found within the chamber area of a firearm (nonrevolver) that is responsible for ejecting the spent shell casing after it has been fired. This hook-like object will often leave a compression or striated mark within the ejector groove at the base of a spent shell casing that is potentially identifiable to a particular firearm (also called an extractor).

FBI National Criminal Identification Center—Fingerprint Classification (NCIC-FPC): A system of fingerprint classification developed by the FBI that assigns a 20 character string of letters and numbers to a person's fingerprints. The database is used to compare existing prints with those from unsolved crimes.

Federal Rules of Evidence (FRE): Adopted in 1975, these rules govern the introduction of evidence within proceedings, both civil and criminal, in U.S. Federal Courts. While they did not specifically apply to suits brought within state courts, the rules of many states have been closely modeled upon the provisions found within the FRE.

Final Sketch: A finished rendition of the rough sketch usually prepared for courtroom presentation; often will not show all of the measurements and distances originally recorded on the rough sketch but only significant items and structures. It may be either inked or a computer model, in a manner that is not able to be modified. The sketch is clutter-free and should accurately depict all pertinent items of evidence, typically through the use of an accompanying legend (see *Rough Sketch*).

Firearm: Any device that can fire a projectile or projectiles as a result of an explosive or propellant charge.

Firing Pin: The component in a firearm that strikes the base of the cartridge and causes the initial incendiary event leading to expulsion of the bullet from the barrel. These may leave marks upon a cartridge casing that may be identifiable to a particular firearm or brand of firearm.

First Responder: The police officer, fire fighters, and/or emergency medical personnel who is dispatched or arrives at the potential crime scene first.

Flammable Range: The mixture of fuel vapors and oxygen, expressed as a concentration (percentage) of fuel vapors in air, which will result in flammability.

Flash Point: The lowest temperature at which a solid or liquid material produces sufficient vapors to burn under laboratory conditions.

Forensic Crime Laboratory: A scientific laboratory (with at least one full-time natural scientist) where physical evidence in criminal matters is examined; staff provides reports and opinion testimony with respect to such physical evidence in courts of law. These laboratories provide services for all levels of government.

Forensic Science Educational Program Accreditation Committee (FEPAC): A professional working group established by the American Academy of Forensic Science (AAFS) to maintain and enhance the quality of forensic science education through a formal evaluation and accreditation of college-level academic programs.

Fruit of the Poisonous Tree Doctrine: If evidence is found to be illegally collected (whether intentionally or unintentionally), the evidence will be found to be inadmissible in court.

Frye Test: The Federal Court of Appeals ruling (*Frye v. U.S.* 293 F. 1013 [D.C. Cir. 1923)]; held that evidence could be admitted in court only if "the thing from which the deduction is made" is "sufficiently established to have gained general acceptance in the particular field in which it belongs."

Gas Chromatography: The carrier gas flows through a column constructed of glass (also called the moving phase).

Gauge: The number of spherical lead balls that have the diameter of the interior of the barrel of the firearm that add up to weigh one pound.

Grooves: The low-lying portions between the lands within a rifled firearm bore.

Hallucinogen: A type of drug or substance that, taken in nontoxic dosages, produce changes in perception, thought, and mood.

Handgun: A type of weapon designed to be held in and fired with one hand; two primary subcategories are pistols (semi-automatic and automatic) and revolvers.

Handheld Devices: Portable data storage devices that provide communications, digital photography, navigation systems, entertainment, data storage, and personal information management.

Hearsay: Unfounded information that is heard from other people. It must be corroborated by other sources to be admissible in court.

Henry System: Developed by Sir Edward Henry, a system of print classification used for well over a century. The system was built around the individual's whorl patterns in a fingerprint (primary classification) that were subdivided into five categories depending upon the type and size of the patterns.

High-Order Explosive: A type of material designed to detonate and yield a near instantaneous release of energy; chemically detonates at a speed greater than 3,300 feet per second.

Homicide: The killing of one person by another.

Hyperthermia: Rising of the body's core temperature.

Hypothermia: Lowering of the body's core temperature.

IDLH Environment: Level A of the PPE levels, contains the greatest risk for exposure to potentially life-threatening biological hazards. IDLH stands for immediately dangerous to life or health.

Incendiary Evidence: Includes crime scene debris.

Incision: A type of wound caused by sharp force trauma.

In Situ: When items have not been moved, altered, or otherwise molested, and can be documented in their originally discovered location and condition.

Instrumentality: A device, system, or its associated hardware that has a significant role in the commission of a crime.

Integrated Ballistic Identification System (IBIS): A national imaging system developed by the FBI and ATF that digitally records images from fired bullets and cartridge cases used in crime scenes and test fires from recovered firearms for comparison with those used in unsolved crimes.

Interior Ballistics: The study relating to the transition of chemical energy within the barrel of a firearm and the motion of the projectile(s) as it moves through the barrel.

Investigate: To make a systematic examination, or to conduct an official inquiry.

Iterative Process: Where the investigator continually re-checks and re-analyzes the crime scene to assure that processing is done properly; continues until the results are negative, meaning that nothing further is required, and nothing has been overlooked.

Justifiable Homicide: The killing of a person under authority of the law. Includes killing in self-defense, killing an enemy during wartime, capital punishment, and deaths caused by police officers while attempting to prevent a dangerous felon's escape or to recapture a dangerous felon who has escaped or is resisting arrest.

Known Evidence: Any type of evidence that originates from a known, acknowledged, or accounted for source that is to be compared to an unknown or questioned material.

Laceration: A type of wound caused by blunt force trauma; subdivided into firearm and non-firearm types.

Lands: The raised portion between the grooves within a rifled firearm bore.

Latent Prints: Finger, hand, or other body part prints that require additional processing to be rendered visible and suitable for comparison.

Legend: A note of explanation inserted outside of the sketch area that relates to a specific item, symbol, or information contained within the graphical representation of a sketch (see *Rough Sketch*).

Ligature: An item used to bind, incapacitate, or kill; often leaves patterned impression evidence that can be matched later to the item that was used; the ligature or binding impressions may be either striated or compressed.

Livor Mortis: The visible color change that occurs from the pooling of blood once the heart stops pumping; also called hypostasis or postmortem lividity.

Locard's Exchange Principle: Whenever two objects come in contact with one another, a cross-transfer of evidence occurs.

Low-Order Explosive: A type of material that burns or detonates at a speed lower than 3,300 feet per second; they typically involve pyrotechnics that create smoke, light, heat, and sound.

Luminol: A type of presumptive search technique for blood that results in chemiluminescence as a result of the chemical reaction occurring between the reagent and the biological stain. It is fast acting and must be documented in darkness, with photography in an expeditious manner.

Manner of Death: Circumstances under which the cause of death occurred; is classified as natural or unnatural. A death is classified as natural when it is caused by disease. Other deaths are classified as unnatural, including: homicide, suicide, accident, or undetermined, based on the circumstances surrounding the incident causing death.

Mapping: Measurements and drawings associated with a crime scene. The basic methods utilized for crime scene sketching and mapping are: (1) baseline, (2) rectangular coordinates, (3) triangulation, and (4) polar/grid coordinates (see *Rough Sketch*).

Marquis Test: Tests for heroin, morphine, and opium derivatives.

Masking Fire: Fire set to mask the commission of other crimes.

Mass Spectrometry: After the mixture has been separated by the gas chromatograph, a direct connection of the chromatograph columns and the mass spectrometer allows each component to flow into the spectrometer as it leaves the chromatograph.

Mechanical Loss: When, through the efforts of saving a life, evidence is lost. This is an accepted loss of physical evidence, and is easily articulated in the court.

Medulla: The innermost region of hair in the hair shaft. In humans it is amorphous and lacks visible cellular material, whereas the medulla of other species is often seen as cellular in nature, with some displaying characteristics similar to a bead of pearls.

Microcrystalline Test: A small quantity of the substance is placed on a microscopic slide, and a drop of chemical reagent is added. The chemical reagent causes a precipitate reaction, creating crystals of a size and shape characteristic of a particular drug.

Microtaggants: These fluorescent, color-coded, multilayered particles identify the residue as dynamite and indicate the source of manufacture.

Mid-range Photographs: Their purpose is to frame the item of evidence with an easily recognized landmark, which visually establishes the position of the evidence in the scene in relationship to the item's surroundings.

Minutia: Tiny variations and irregularities within fingerprint ridges that are identifiable; also known as ridge characteristics.

Miranda Ruling: From the 1966 case of *Miranda v. Arizona*, mandated greater emphasis on the collection, preservation, and analysis of physical evidence. Established the Constitutional rights of an accused individual to be advised they can have legal counsel and can remain silent. Eliminated confessions by suspects and placed the emphasis on physical evidence relating to the crime in question.

Mitochondrial DNA (mtDNA): Found outside of the cell nucleus and is inherited solely from the mother. Each cell contains one nucleus and hundreds to thousands of mitochondria. Therefore, there are hundreds to thousands of mtDNA copies in a human cell compared to just one set of nuclear DNA in that same cell.

Morals: Although similar to values, morals are more widely reaching, socially accepted rules of conduct. A person is judged by others by societal definitions of immorality/morality.

Multi-level Containment: A crime scene preservation method utilizing several tiers of perimeters; the most effective for ensuring evidence integrity while also allowing a workable scene structure.

Mummification: The dehydration of soft tissues as a result of high temperatures, low humidity, and wind or other form of ventilation. Skin will appear brown, leather-like, and tight. The mummification process begins at the tips of the fingers and toes and progresses towards the hands and feet, face, and other extremities.

Narcotic: Derived from the Greek word for stupor, originally referred to a variety of substances that dulled the senses and relieved pain. Currently refers to opium, opium derivatives, and their semisynthetic substitutes; here the term refers to drugs that produce morphine-like effects.

National Firearms Act of 1968: Requires retailers to record the serial number of a weapon and the name of its purchaser.

National Integrated Ballistic Information Network (NIBIN): A networked computer database of fired cartridge casing and bullet images used by crime laboratories; developed to solve open cases by allowing firearms examiners to compare existing evidence with fired bullets, cartridge casings, shotgun casings, and firearms recovered in other jurisdictions.

Negative Impression: A type of pattern that an item, such as footwear, has left in a dusty area, essentially removing the dust that was present.

Ninhydrin: A chemical used to detect ammonia or amino acids within print residue. It reacts with these amino acids and forms a bluish-purple color; most useful on porous surfaces (e.g., paper and raw wood) and is primarily used in document processing efforts.

Nucleotide Polymer: It is a molecule that is formed by linking together a series of repeating units known as nucleotides.

Overall Photographs: Taken with a wide angle lens or in a fashion that allows the viewer to see a large area in the scene. This documents the condition and layout of the scene as found and helps to eliminate issues of subsequent contamination (e.g., tracked blood, movement of items). Typically they are shot from the four corners of a crime scene looking inward.

Passive Bloodstain: A type of blood evidence that is not related to a specific violent action within the context of the scene. They are the aftermath associated with this violence, as the resulting bloodshed begins to move and cure due to environmental and gravitational forces.

Patent Prints: Finger or other body prints that require no processing to be recognizable and may be suitable for comparison.

Penetrating Gunshot Wound: A type of firearm projectile injury with an entrance but no exit, thus allowing a projectile be recovered at autopsy.

Perforating Gunshot Wound: A type of firearm projectile injury with an entrance wound and an exit wound. Generally no projectile will be recovered by a pathologist at autopsy; those responsible

for processing the crime scene should try to recover a projectile for each identified exit wound.

Perimeter: The outer confines of a crime scene; involves some sort of delineation (e.g., plastic tape, rope, etc.) or physical boundary as to what area is considered inside of the supposed crime scene, and what is external to the area of investigation.

Perimortem: At or near the time of death.

Peripheral Devices: Equipment that can be connected to a computer or computer system to enhance user access and expand the computer's functions.

Perjury: A lie told within a court of law by someone who has taken an oath to tell the truth.

Personal Protective Equipment (PPE): A type of barrier protection that typically consists of gloves, Tyvek suits, shoe covers, eye protection, and respiratory equipment; designed to protect crime scene personnel from the hazards inherent at the scene.

Photo Log: A permanent written record of all information pertaining to photodocumentation. Department policy often dictates what is included in a photo log; however, the following information should be included: date, time, case number, agency name, photo equipment used, numerical ordering of each photo taken, brief description of photo taken, direction facing for each photo taken, approximate distance from subject matter in each photo taken, and shutter speed, aperture setting, and ISO if taken on film (digital cameras automatically record such photo information).

Photo Placard: A handwritten or agency-developed sheet or board that lists pertinent case information for the photographs to follow. Taking a shot of the placard as the first photo on a roll of film or digital card ensures that personnel know which photographs pertain to a particular case and identifies the photographer.

Physical Evidence: Any type of evidence that has an objective existence; anything with size, shape, and dimension. Examples are gases, fingerprints, glass, paint, hair, blood, soil, and drugs. Also called real evidence.

Plant: A pool of flammable liquids or pile of combustibles (newspapers, rags, etc.) that is used to heat up a fire at a select location; designed to produce hot heat in the specific area the arsonist wishes to cause great damage; also called a booster.

Plastic Prints: A type of finger or other body print having a distinct three-dimensional appearance; these often do not require further processing.

Point of Origin: The location where a fire actually started; the place where it began.

Points of Comparison: Matching ridge characteristics between two compared prints. In the United States, prints should match at 12 points of comparison before an identification can be considered as positive. Current training in fingerprint comparison stresses that the quality of the print and the quality of the comparison are more important than placing emphasis on a numerical match.

Postmortem: After death.

Postmortem Interval (PMI): Time elapsed since a person died; estimated through various scientific observations of the biochemical changes that occur to a body after death.

Preliminary Scene Survey: An overview of the entire crime scene to identify any threats to the scene's integrity and ensure protection of physical evidence. The primary purpose is to carefully assess the scene for logistical and safety considerations.

Primary Packaging: The trace evidence is placed onto a clean sheet of paper and the paper is then folded into thirds and then into thirds again, with one end of the paper tucked back into itself so as to safely encapsulate the trace material.

Primary Scene: The first encountered location where evidence was located, which often is the location where dispatch sends the officer, or from which a witness called in a complaint.

Primary Transfer: Occurs when a fiber from a fabric is transferred directly onto a victim's clothing.

Primer: In a firearm, the metal cup located within the center of the base of a cartridge that contains a small amount of incendiary compound that, when crushed by the firing pin, sets off the initial incendiary event. In rimfire weapons (e.g., a .22 caliber), the entire base of the cartridge serves as a primer.

Probability: Frequency with which an event will occur; also known as the odds of occurrence.

Probing: An invasive search technique that attempts to locate a gravesite periphery through pushing a metal rod into the ground and marking where the rod enters more easily than its surroundings; soil density is measured and this also gives some idea as to grave depth.

Product Rule: When the frequency of independently occurring variables is multiplied together to obtain an overall frequency of occurrence for the event or item.

Proficiency Testing: A measure for determining whether lab workers as individuals and the lab as a whole are operating at an industry established standard.

Projected Pattern: Images produced by blood released under pressure (i.e., arterial spurting). These patterns generally result from volumes of blood larger than those that produce passive drop stains or other dynamic patterns (i.e., impact patterns).

Protocols: The steps and processes that are undertaken by the laboratory to ensure that the correct tests are performed accurately.

Putrefaction: Postmortem changes produced as a result of biochemical actions by bacteria and microorganisms.

Pyrolysis: Transformation of a compound into one or more other substances by heat alone.

Pyromaniac: Serial fire starters.

Quality Assurance (QA): A method to ensure and verify quality control. A laboratory's QA assessment measures are necessary to oversee, verify, and document the performance of the laboratory.

Quality Control: Measures to ensure that analysis results meet a specified standard of quality.

Questioned Evidence: Any type of evidence or material of an unknown, unacknowledged, or unaccounted for source.

Radial Fractures: Breaks or cracks originating from the point of impact and moving away from that point, in a radiating pattern.

Rifle: A type of weapon designed to be held in two hands while being fired from the shoulder.

Rifled Firearm: A type of weapon that contains rifling within the bore of the firearm's barrel.

Rifling: The spiral grooves that are formed in the bore of a firearm that is designed to impart spin upon a projectile as it passes through the barrel. The rifling is made up of grooves and lands; a spinning projectile improves its accuracy to impact its target.

Rigor Mortis: Stiffening of the body postmortem. It involves the contraction of body muscles, beginning in the smaller muscle groups and progressing to the larger groups and is a result of chemical changes that occur within the body upon death.

Rough Sketch: A hand-drawn image developed while on-scene, typically during the crime scene assessment/ preliminary scene evaluation phase, to assist with development of a strategic plan for processing. The sketch is not done to scale, can be drawn with any implement (crayon, chalk, pencil, pen, etc.), and is crude in its artistry. As work progresses at the crime scene, the sketch will include not only the crude crime scene layout, but also be used to record measurements of items and structures, and distances between items.

Schedules: Placement of drugs or substances into one of five schedules according to the Controlled Substances Act. This is based upon the substance's medical use, potential for abuse, and safety or liability for psychological and/or physical dependence.

Scientific Investigation Method: An iterative process incorporating the fundamental principles behind the scientific method, which guides the investigator in ensuring a thorough and systematic investigatory methodology.

Scientific Method: Utilizes principles and procedures in the systematic pursuit of knowledge involving the recognition and formulation of a problem, the collection of data through observation and experiment, and the formulation and testing of a defined hypothesis.

Scientific Working Group on Friction Ridge Analysis, Study and Technology (SWGFAST): A working group established in 1997 in response to a number of inconsistencies and controversies relating to fingerprint identification and technological advancement; operates through Federal Bureau of Investigation sponsorship with a mission to assist the latent print community in providing the best service and product to the criminal justice system.

Scott Test: Screen test for cocaine.

Scraping/Striation Evidence: Marks produced by a combination of pressure and sliding contact by a tool that result in microscopic patterns imparted to the surface onto which the tool was worked.

Screening Test: A specimen is subjected to a series of reagents that yield characteristic colors for commonly encountered drugs.

Secondary Device: A second explosive bomb placed at a scene to detonate after the original explosion. Secondary devices are typically targeted at emergency responders and investigators who respond to a bombing.

Secondary Packaging: Serves to protect the primary packaging from damage and ensures that no trace material will be added to nor lost from the initial evidence that was collected.

Secondary Scene: Other crime scenes that are later identified as being associated with a primary scene.

Secondary Transfer: Occurs when already transferred fibers on the clothing of a suspect transfer to the clothing of a victim.

Sexual Assault Kit (SAK): Tools and instructions to assist the crime scene investigator and attending medical professional to properly collect and document the specimens required by the laboratory; can be used to collect appropriate samples from both male and female sexual assault victims and suspects.

Shoeprint Image Capture and Retrieval (SICAR): An automated shoeprint identification system, developed in England by Foster and Freeman Ltd., which incorporates multiple databases to search known and unknown footwear files for comparison against footwear specimens found in crime scenes.

Skeletonized Stain: The center of a dried bloodstain flakes away and leaves a visible outer rim.

Small Particle Reagent (SPR): A suspension of molybdenum sulfide grains in water and a detergent solution. The grains adhere to the fatty components of a latent print deposit, and assist with the visualization of latent print evidence.

Smoothbore Firearm: Type of firearm weapon with no rifling present within the bore.

Spatter: A random distribution of bloodstains that vary in size and may be produced by a variety of mechanisms. The pattern is created when sufficient force is available to overcome the surface tension of the blood.

Spoliation: The intentional or negligent altering of evidence.

Spontaneous Combustion: A product of a natural heat-producing process.

Stellate Defect: An irregular, blown-out entrance wound associated with a gunshot. This type of wound is caused by the propellant gases separating the soft tissue from the bone and creating a temporary pocket of hot gas between the bone and the muzzle of the weapon.

Stimulant: A type of drug or substance (also called uppers) that can reverse the mental and physical effects of fatigue.

Stippling: Type of injury resulting from an impact of burned and unburned particulates associated with the discharge of a firearm. They surround the bullet impact wound in a roughly circular pattern due to the fact that gunpowder is discharged in a conical pattern as it exits a firearm.

Swath: The effective area a searcher can cover while conducting a search.

Swipe: Occurs when a bloodied surface rubs across a nonbloodied surface.

Tache Noire: If an individual dies in an arid environment and his or her eyes are open at the time of death, the exposed area of the eyeball (sclera) may develop a brownish-black line.

Taphonomy: The study of postmortem changes to the body. Examples include: normal decomposition; alteration and scattering by scavengers; and movement and modification by flowing water, freezing, or mummification.

Tardieu Spots: In some cases of advanced stages of lividity, the capillaries may burst and cause what appear to be small, pinpoint hemorrhages.

Terminal Ballistics: Deals with the resulting impact and interaction between the projectile and the target matter.

Terminal Velocity: An object falling through the air will increase its speed of descent until the force of air resistance that opposes the item is equal to the force of the downward gravitational pull.

Testimonial Evidence: Vocal statements most commonly made while the speaker is under oath, typically in response to questioning; also may be made by witnesses, victims, or suspects during the course of the investigation, while not under oath.

3R Rule: Radial fractures form a *Right* angle at the *Reverse* side to which force was applied.

Trace Evidence: Any evidence that is small in size, such as hairs, fibers, paint, glass, and soil, which would require microscopic analysis in order to identify it.

Trailers: Arrangement of a combustible or flammable material (solids, liquids, or combinations of both) to ensure a fire is carried from one location to another. A trailer is regularly placed from a point of exit to the area the arsonist wants to be the area of origin; also used to connect multiple plants within a structure.

Transfer Evidence: A type of evidence that is passed from one item to another, typically as a result of contact or action. Careful analysis of this evidence can associate the questioned evidence with a known source.

Transfer Stain: Generally indistinct stains that can be of virtually any size or shape. The shape of a transfer pattern may retain some of the physical characteristics of the object that created it. In this way, the shape of a transfer pattern suggests the object that created it through the recognizable patent image.

Transient Evidence: Physical evidence present at the crime scene that is either fragile or at great risk for loss, alteration, or destruction if not properly identified, documented, collected, and preserved as soon as possible.

Transitional Ballistics: Concerned with the period of time in which the projectile(s) transition from its movement through the firearm barrel to its flight through the air upon exit from the barrel.

Trier of Fact: A judge or magistrate in a trial by the court, or a jury of one's peers in a trial by jury, whose duty it is to weigh the evidence presented and determine guilt or innocence.

Underwater Search and Evidence Response Team (USERT): First formed in 1982, four USERT teams of 12 members each (located in New York, Washington, Miami, and Los Angeles) are managed by the FBI in Quantico, Virginia. USERTs can perform surface and underwater crime scene investigations in a variety of wet environments nationwide; also provide guidance, advice, and training to the public service community.

Universal Precautions: These are typical good hygiene habits: handwashing and use of barriers and aseptic techniques, and appropriate handling of cutting or puncturing objects like needles, syringes, and razor blades (called sharps).

Values: Beliefs of an individual or group, for or against something in which they have some emotional investment; rules by which an individual makes decisions as to what is right or wrong.

Van Urk: Test for the presence of LSD.

Viscosity: Mutually attracted to one another; in this text, pertains to the properties of blood. The more viscous a fluid, the more slowly it flows; blood is approximately six times more viscous than water.

Vitreous Draw: A method of assisting with determination of the time of death in a postmortem investigation, in which a syringe is used to take a sample of ocular fluid (vitreous humor) from the eye to determine potassium levels.

Void Pattern: Created when blood is blown out of the nose, mouth, or wound as a result of air pressure and/or airflow; often displays numerous, relatively small stain sizes that may vary in shape. Also, the blank space against a surface inside of a spatter or smear (in a bloodstain) or char (in fire) where an object or person has been removed after the event occurred.

Voir Dire: Preliminary examination of a witness or juror to determine his or her competency to give or hear evidence.

Walk-Thru: Once the scene is secure, investigative personnel should conduct a preliminary scene survey.

Wipe: Occurs when a non-bloodied surface moves through or across a stationary one.

Zones of Possibility: Used to establish limits as to what is likely, what is possible, and what is possible based upon the evidence presented.

Index

Numbers